IN MY TIME OF DYING

In My Time of Dying

A HISTORY OF DEATH AND THE DEAD IN WEST AFRICA

JOHN PARKER

PRINCETON UNIVERSITY PRESS
PRINCETON & OXFORD

Copyright © 2021 by Princeton University Press

Princeton University Press is committed to the protection of copyright and the intellectual property our authors entrust to us. Copyright promotes the progress and integrity of knowledge created by humans. Thank you for supporting free speech and the global exchange of ideas by purchasing an authorized edition of this book. If you wish to reproduce or distribute any part of it in any form, please obtain permission.

Requests for permission to reproduce material from this work should be sent to permissions@press.princeton.edu

Published by Princeton University Press
41 William Street, Princeton, New Jersey 08540
99 Banbury Road, Oxford OX2 6JX

press.princeton.edu

All Rights Reserved

First paperback printing, 2025
Paperback ISBN 9780691271354

The Library of Congress has cataloged the cloth edition as follows:

Names: Parker, John, 1960– author.
Title: In my time of dying : a history of death and the dead in West Africa / John Parker.
Description: Princeton : Princeton University Press, 2021. | Includes bibliographical references and index.
Identifiers: LCCN 2020034619 (print) | LCCN 2020034620 (ebook) | ISBN 9780691193151 (hardcover) | ISBN 9780691214900 (ebook)
Subjects: LCSH: Death—Africa, West—History. | Death—Africa, West—Religious aspects. | Funeral rites and ceremonies—Africa, West. | Africa, West—Social life and customs.
Classification: LCC GT3289.A358 P37 2021 (print) | LCC GT3289.A358 (ebook) | DDC 306.90966—dc23
LC record available at https://lccn.loc.gov/2020034619
LC ebook record available at https://lccn.loc.gov/2020034620

British Library Cataloging-in-Publication Data is available

Editorial: Ben Tate and Josh Drake
Production Editorial: Ellen Foos
Production: Danielle Amatucci
Publicity: Alyssa Sanford and Amy Stewart
Copyeditor: Ben Wilson

Jacket/Cover image: Terracotta funerary sculpture, Ghana, 19th century.
© The Trustees of the British Museum

This book has been composed in Arno

CONTENTS

List of Illustrations vii
Acknowledgements ix

Introduction ... 1
1 Cultural Encounter ... 9
2 Body, Soul and Person ... 26
3 Speaking of Death ... 42
4 Grief and Mourning ... 58
5 Gold, Wealth and Burial ... 76
6 Faces of the Dead ... 92
7 The Severed Head ... 107
8 Slaves ... 124
9 Human Sacrifice ... 139
10 Poison ... 155
11 Christian Encounters ... 172
12 From House Burial to Cemeteries ... 191
13 Ghosts and Vile Bodies ... 210
14 Writing and Reading about Death ... 228

15	The Colony of Medicine	245
16	Wills and Dying Wishes	259
17	Northern Frontiers	277
18	Reordering the Royal Dead	291
19	Making Modern Deathways	308
	Conclusion	326

Glossary 331
Notes 335
Index 381

ILLUSTRATIONS

Figures

1.1.	The *ntumpan*, or 'talking' drums	19
2.1.	*Nkonnwa tuntum*, or blackened ancestral stools	29
3.1.	Keeping death in abeyance during wartime	56
4.1.	A funeral, from de Marees (1602)	62
4.2.	Musketry at a funeral	64
4.3.	*Akunafo*, or widows	65
4.4.	Women *werempefo*, or 'official mourners'	68
6.1.	Terracotta funerary sculpture	94
6.2.	*Asensie*, or 'the place of pots'	99
7.1.	'The chief's orchestra'	114
7.2.	Gold trophy head	121
9.1.	A brass gold-weight, or *abramo*, representing an *obrafo* and his victim	144
9.2.	An elderly *obrafo* holding the *sepow* in his mouth	147
13.1.	A *begyina ba*, or 'come-and-stay child'	217
18.1.	The *baamu*, or royal mausoleum, at Bantama	297
19.1.	A modern funerary sculpture of Christiana A. Ansa	318

Maps

1.	The precolonial Akan world	x
2.	The colonial-era Gold Coast	xi

ACKNOWLEDGEMENTS

THIS BOOK was mostly written during a research fellowship in 2016–18 that was generously funded by the Leverhulme Trust. I would like to thank Robert Whiteing for guiding me through the fellowship application, Florence Bernault and Louis Brenner for writing in support of it, and Rosalind Coffey and David Bannister for teaching my undergraduate history courses at SOAS University of London while I was on leave. Ella Jeffreys helped with archival research at the Accra headquarters of the Public Records and Archives Administration Department, previously the National Archives of Ghana. Over many years I have been kindly and efficiently looked after by the staff at the archives in Accra, Kumasi, Tamale, Koforidua and Cape Coast, as well as by those at the Manhyia Records Office in Kumasi. Special thanks goes to Ben Tate, my commissioning editor at Princeton University Press, who took a chance on a book somewhat beyond his established remit. Derek Mancini-Lander read and provided insightful suggestions on a number of draft chapters. Finally, I would like to acknowledge six friends from whom I have learned a great deal over the years about Ghanaian history and culture: Jean Allman, Tom McCaskie, Richard Rathbone, the late Kwame Arhin, the late Eric Twum Barimah and Emily Asiedu.

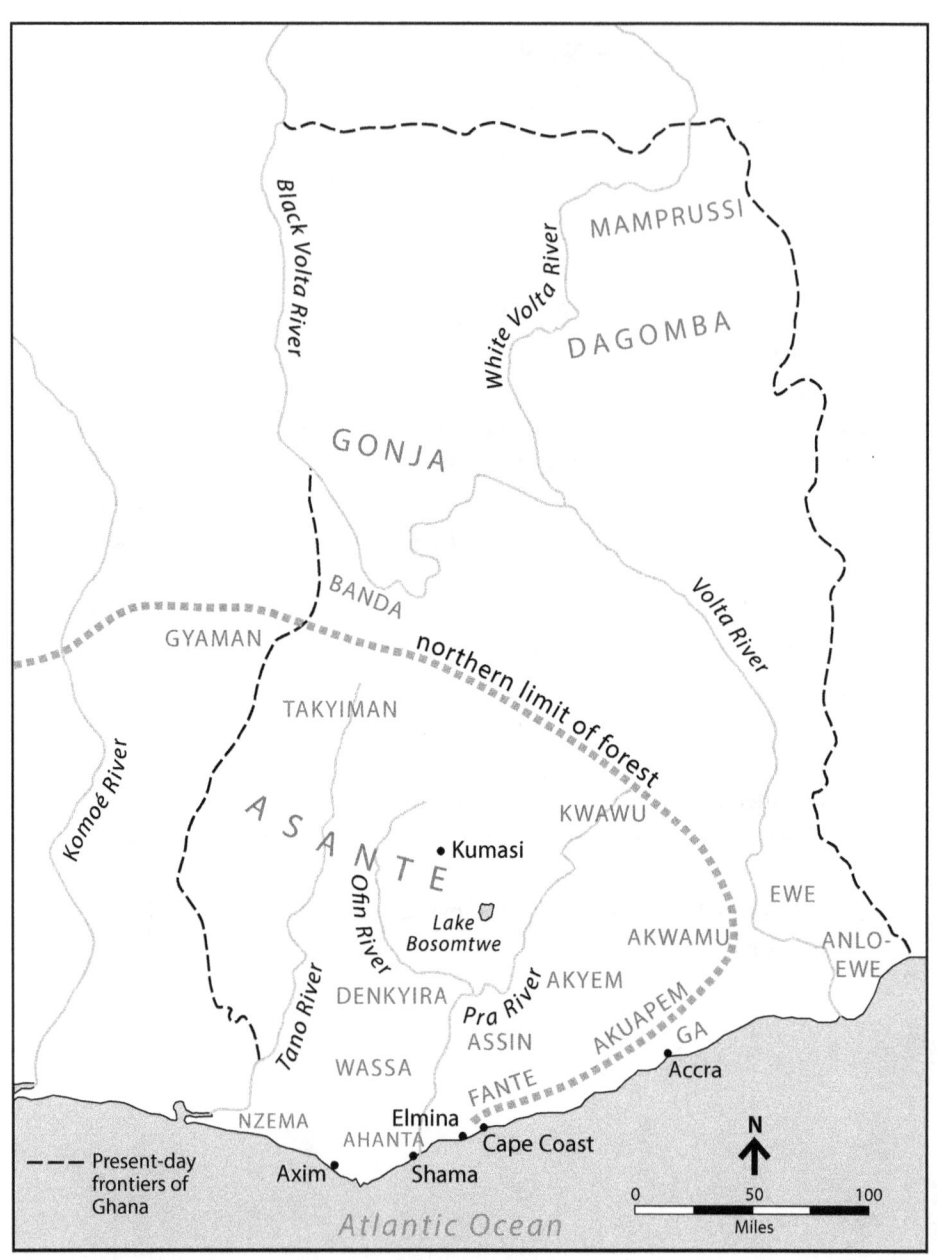

MAP 1. The precolonial Akan world.

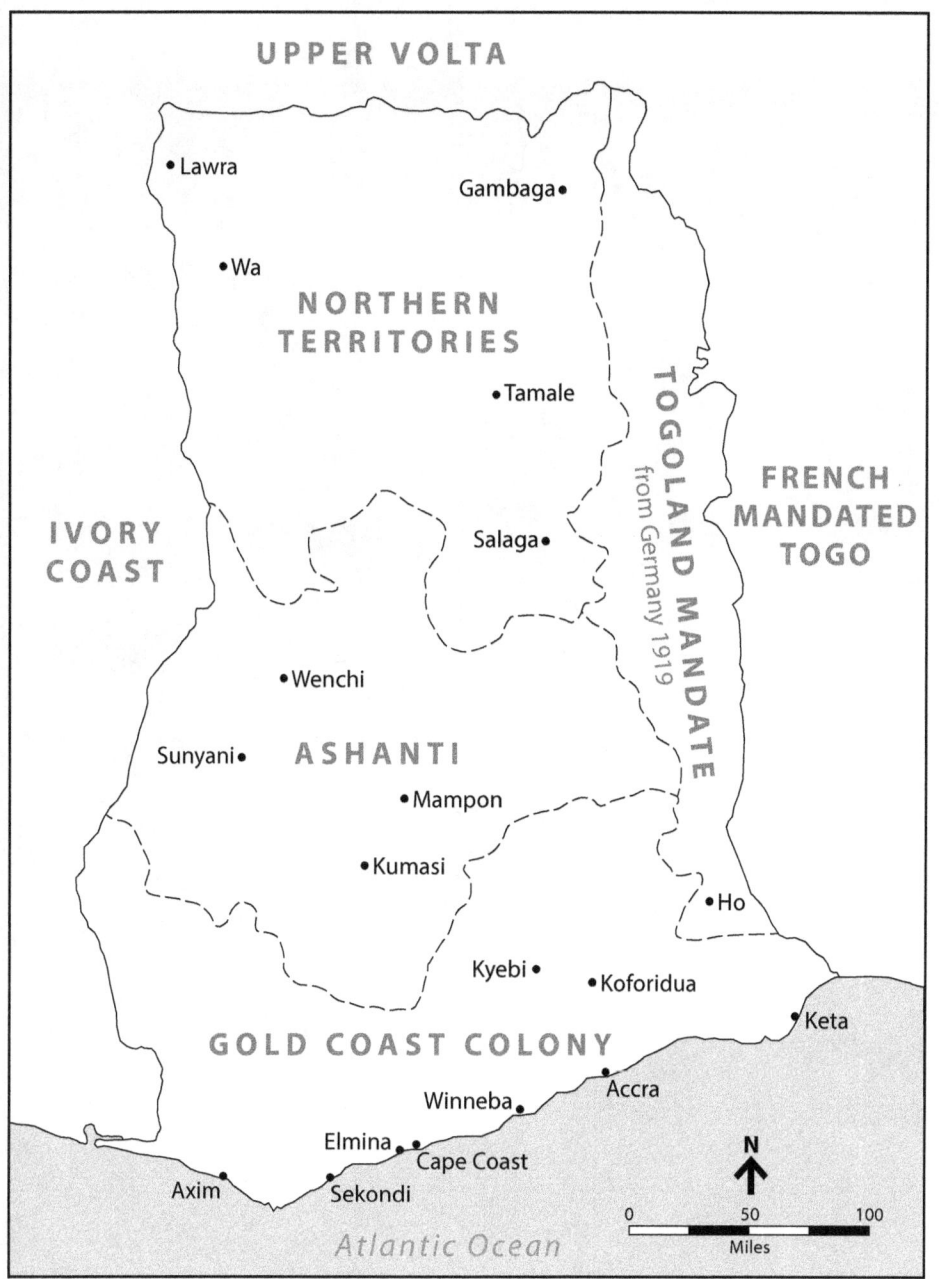

MAP 2. The colonial-era Gold Coast.

IN MY TIME OF DYING

Introduction

THIS BOOK IS about death, dying and the dead in Africa. Its focus is one region of the continent, encompassed by the present-day nation of Ghana, but through this case study seeks to contribute to an understanding of the history of death more broadly. If the book's geographical frame is restricted, its chronological reach is generous, extending over some four centuries, from around 1600 to the 1950s. Indeed, the use of Ghana as a case study was in part determined by a desire to think about changing perceptions, experiences and cultures of mortality in Africa over as long a period as possible. While the dearth of sources for much of the continent south of the Sahara presents formidable challenges to the writing of this sort of cultural history, the region first encountered by European mariners in the 1470s and dubbed by them the Gold Coast offers at least a possibility to do so. A two-hundred-mile stretch of West Africa's Atlantic littoral, the Gold Coast and its tropical forest hinterland was dominated by a people who would emerge as one of the most prominent of the continent's diverse state-builders: the Akan. Responding to global demand first for gold and then for slaves, the Akan and their neighbours mobilized commercial wealth to create a sequence of centralized kingdoms and a sophisticated political culture. These processes culminated in the rise at the start of the eighteenth century of the great forest kingdom of Asante, which dominated the region until its eclipse by British imperialism in the 1890s. This long history of encounter and creativity is fundamental to the project of writing about death across the divide between the precolonial and colonial eras of African history. Not only did it shape one of the continent's most vibrant mortuary cultures; it gave rise to a rich array of oral and written sources which enables something of that culture to be reconstructed.

My interest in death and in the relationship between the living and the dead in West Africa was fashioned by a variety of factors. I had encountered death as a force shaping culture and social change in the course of previous research on the history of Ghana: in the nation's capital city, Accra, where the British colonial regime had first intervened into established practices of burying the dead, and, on a broader canvas, in the emergence over the first half of the twentieth century of popular healing movements which responded to a perceived crisis in mortality by combating the malign forces threatening wellbeing and social cohesion.[1] Yet it was stories of the dead, the dying and the bereaved in creative writing and in music from beyond Ghana which inspired me to consider if such accounts might be excavated from records of the African past. I am thinking here of novels such as William Faulkner's *As I Lay Dying* (1930), in which episodes in the death and burial of Addie Bundren are recounted by various members of her family as they cart her body to Jefferson, Mississippi, so that it might be interred among her own people. My title, *In My Time of Dying*, has a similar cadence but is taken from an old gospel-blues refrain sung in a range of versions by African American musicians, none more famously than that recorded in 1927 by the gravel-voiced Texan Blind Willie Johnson as 'Jesus Make Up My Dying Bed'.[2] That and scores of other such recordings from the 78 rpm era also triggered my curiosity about the ways in which ordinary folk over time and across cultures have struggled (and as often as not, I suspect, failed) to make sense of their own and others' mortality. Did traces of a particular West African attitude towards the ends of life—an apparent ability to stare death squarely in the face—somehow survive the horrors of the Middle Passage and enslavement to resurface in these haunting blues songs? Perhaps—although a similar steely-eyed vision can be heard in other genres of folk music, such as the Appalachian murder ballad (also drenched in death, but rooted in the ancient bardic traditions of the British Isles).[3] Be that as it may, these scratchy old recordings in which the spectre of death seems ever present drew me to similarly introspective meditations on mortality from West Africa: to the funeral dirges and instrumental mourning music of the Akan and their neighbours and, through that haunting soundscape, to the dead themselves.[4]

A second inspiration was the sheer ubiquity in contemporary Ghana of the funeral as a dazzling and very public celebration of the dead. If historically in West Africa mortuary rituals were often the most important of all rites of passage, then this remains the case today: over much of Ghana, Saturday is funeral day.[5] From the congested centres of the country's modern cities to isolated rural communities, the bereaved, immediately discernible by their distinctive funeral cloth and by the noisy entanglement of grief and celebration, are everywhere visible. Walls of buildings are typically plastered with obituary notices, bearing portraits of the deceased and headlined with statements reflecting abiding ideas about the distinction between a good and bad death: 'Call to Glory' or 'Celebration of Life' for those who died at an advanced age, for example; 'Gone Too Soon' or 'What a Shock!' for those who did not. The exuberance of Africa's modern funerary cultures is perhaps nowhere more emblematic than in the famous designer coffins of the Ga people of Accra: the brilliantly conceived and brightly painted animal-, vegetable-, fish-, automobile-, tool-, Bible-, pen- and even beer-bottle-shaped receptacles for the dead, which first appeared in the 1950s and now grace art galleries and museums in the West. In Ghana today, as in Africa more broadly, funerals are important and the dead are all around. Whether taking the form of mortal remains, of hallowed ancestors, of spectral revenants or of memories, they continue to cohabit intimately with the living. If what Robert Pogue Harrison terms the 'dominion of the dead' has been of supreme historical importance to Western civilization, then so too has it been to that of Africa.[6] To borrow a concept from another insightful recent book, Thomas W. Laqueur's *The Work of the Dead*, the African dead continue to have much cultural work to do.[7] What that work is and how it has developed over the centuries lies at the heart of this book.

Long a concern of theological, philosophical and, from the nineteenth century, sociological and anthropological inquiry, death was not given sustained historical treatment until the 1960s, when French scholars of the Annales school began to consider how attitudes to mortality might serve as indicators of broader social change in early modern Europe.[8] The best known of these scholars in the anglophone world was Philippe Ariès, whose *Western Attitudes toward Death* (1974) and subsequent *The Hour of Our Death* (1981) set out a grand narrative in which death's long-established intimacy with the living shifted to its being rejected, sequestered and denied in the modern world.[9] Much subsequent scholarship has taken as a starting point Ariès's thesis on what he considered to be the unhealthy 'denial of death' in post-Enlightenment Europe. In an era increasingly suspicious of grand narratives, this thesis has been widely critiqued by historians seeking to emphasize more nuanced patterns of continuity and change in the care of the dead.[10] Others looking beyond modern Europe, however, have been less critical, including Jan Assmann, whose analysis of the conceptual world of ancient Egyptian mortuary culture stands as perhaps the finest historical study of death in Africa:

> When it comes to the importance of death, [Egypt] is admittedly an extreme example. But this has largely to do with the fact that that we view ancient Egypt from the standpoint of a culture that is equally extreme, but in the opposite direction. From the point of view of comparative anthropology, it is we, not the ancient Egyptians, who are the exception. Few cultures in this world exclude death and the dead from their reality as radically as we do. Living with the dead and with death is one of the most normal manifestations of human culture, and it presumably lies at the heart of the stuff of human existence.[11]

That said, if the recent boom in the study and portrayal of death is anything to go by, it is perhaps less of a taboo in the contemporary world than previously thought. Suddenly, from scholarly writing and museum exhibitions to artistic production and popular culture, reflection on death and the ends of life seems to be everywhere.[12] Journals such as *Death Studies*, *Omega* and *Mortality* publish a range of transdisciplinary research, while popular histories and ethnographies cater to a general readership interested, as one contribution puts it, in 'how humans invented death'.[13] Meanwhile, a burgeoning academic literature seeks to extend our understanding of the history of death beyond its initial focus on a somewhat normative 'Western culture'—which has often meant France and Britain. From China and Japan to the world of early Islam, from Russia to Mexico, death is emerging at the cutting-edge of historical research.[14] In recent years this work has encompassed the early modern Atlantic world, and it is here, in the zone of cross-cultural encounter forged by the violence of conquest and the slave trade, that the ranks of the nameless West African dead have begun to come into focus.[15]

In Africa itself, death is also emerging as a topic of scholarly concern. Prompted in part by the existential threat of the HIV/AIDS pandemic, by the shifting worldviews associated with the expansion of new forms of Christianity and by the striking prominence of mortuary cultures, this literature has begun to explore the continent's contemporary 'deathways' and 'necrogeographies'. The funeral as a site both of sociability and of contest has emerged as one key area of interest. So too have the impact of biomedicine on registers of morbidity and mortality; the shifting terrain of grief, loss and mourning; and, to borrow Katherine Verdery's term, the political life of dead bodies.[16] If Verdery's widely cited book on southeastern Europe examines the meaning of mortal remains in a context of post-socialist change, then much of this recent work on Africa is similarly located in a specific political context: that of the postcolony, or, even more specifically, that of neo-liberal Africa in its contemporary 'post-postcolonial' moment.[17] It is, that is to say, mostly anthropological rather than historical, with only a limited sense that apparent transformations in contemporary cultures of death might be part of deeper patterns stretching to the colonial era and beyond, to the precolonial past.[18]

Mortuary rites and the veneration of ancestors became, of course, stock-in-trade concerns of colonial-era anthropology in Africa. Research on the societies of the northern savanna frontiers of the British-ruled Gold Coast is prominent in these fields, notably that by Meyer Fortes and by Jack Goody, whose *Death, Property and the Ancestors* (1962) would influence the pioneering generation of historians of death in Europe.[19] In present-day Ghana, mortuary practices continue to attract the gaze of anthropologists, resulting in an extensive body of work on the cultures, the politics and, above all, the economics of the contemporary funeral.[20] As in the rest of the continent, however, there has been little in the way of sustained historical thinking about the dominion of the dead.[21] It is this gap in our historical understanding that *In My Time of Dying* seeks to address.

As in the West, contemporary creative arts in Ghana have also begun to engage with death, dying and the dead. In 2014, while I was conducting archival research for this book, Accra's annual Chale Wote street-art festival took as its theme 'Death: An Eternal Dream into Limitless Rebirth'. 'Why death?' the festival programme asked. 'It surrounds us in Ghana. Funerals every weekend are important social affairs. Obituary portraits hang on buildings, walls, and gates across the country. In fact, ethnic groups across Ghana possess a wealth of stories about death that are passed privately from generation to generation through family accounts.'[22] The written historical record too has much to say on the matter, yet the stories it tells are often discordant and unsettling. While the ubiquity of the dead suggests that the region has charted a different trajectory than that of the 'death-denying' twentieth-century West, this history is not simply one of some indomitable spirit in the face of mortality. Rather than hallowed ancestors being simply benevolent guardians of community wellbeing, there is every indication that their presence—like the generations of the dead famously described by Karl Marx at the opening of *The Eighteenth Brumaire of Louis Bonaparte*—weighed heavily upon the mind of the living.[23]

None of this is to argue that death, in Africa or beyond, necessarily has what can be recognized as a coherent historical narrative. Writing a cultural history of death, I have found, is a bit like writing a history of 'life': like the dead, it is everywhere but nowhere—the invisible, looming antimatter of human existence. 'Our awareness of death and the dead stands at the edge of culture', Laqueur has cautioned. 'As such they may not have a history in the usual sense but only more and more iterations, endless and infinitely varied, that we shape into an engagement with the past and the future.'[24] This illusiveness is compounded by the difficulties in extracting thought, belief or, to use the Annales term, *mentalité* from historical sources, whether texts, oral traditions, embodied practices or material remains. Dead bodies and the beings that have vacated them evoke awe, uncertainty and fear, Verdery argues, but she does not regard 'these cosmic conceptions strictly as "ideas", in the cognitive realm alone. Rather, they are inseparable from action in the world—they are beliefs and ideas materialized as action.'[25] These ideas may not have a linear history 'in the usual sense'—but they are, I hope to show, historical. That said, the profound nature of such conceptions, Peter Brown has pointed out, contribute too to the fact that burial customs 'are among the most notoriously stable aspects of human culture.'[26] Moreover, Brown writes of Roman North Africa in a more recent work, 'the dead were everywhere, but only very few are now visible to us. Nothing reveals more harshly the stratified nature of ancient societies than the utter silence of the vast majority of the dead'.[27] Perhaps, when push comes to shove, it is fictional writing and the lapidary statements of our old bluesmen and women which are better placed than historical analysis to confront the silence and the void.[28]

It is with these challenges in mind that I have chosen to structure *In My Time of Dying* in nineteen short chapters, encompassing a diverse range of themes in the study of death and the dead. The sequence of topics has a broad chronological thrust, from the era of the Atlantic slave trade in the seventeenth and eighteenth centuries to that of so-called legitimate commerce and creeping British imperial expansion on the Gold Coast in the nineteenth century and on to the period of colonial rule in the first half of the twentieth century. At that point my material dovetails into the corpus of anthropological work on Ghana's postcolonial deathways. This shifting economic and political frame certainly impacted upon the dominion of the dead. Yet I have sought to keep it in the background, in an attempt to escape the tendency, still apparent in much scholarly writing on Africa, to privilege the continent's encounter with Europe as the principal dynamic of its modern history. Like the recent book by Kwasi Konadu on one part of the diverse Akan world—a work which, tellingly, opens with an account of the funeral of its protagonist—the emphasis is on how African historical actors themselves sought to manage death, in 'our own way, in this part of the world'.[29] The result is therefore not a linear narrative: a number of chapters focus on a discrete episode—on Verdery's 'beliefs and ideas materialized as action'—but then slip their temporal moorings in order to consider how that particular aspect of mortuary culture may have unfolded over time.

Neither is it an account of all the unpleasant ways that people died in the past—although one chapter is about human sacrifice, another is about poison, while another considers changes in epidemiology in the twentieth century. Other themes include the abiding symbolic power of mortal remains, the remembrance of the dead who were hallowed and the problem of dealing with those whose who were not. A crucial historical thread emerging from the mid-nineteenth century is the effort to manage African death by an unstable coalition of the British colonial state, Christian missions, reformist local elites and the regime of biomedicine. These self-appointed representatives of modernity together mounted an assault on established forms of mortuary practice deemed outdated or unacceptable: ritual immolation; house burial; and the profane treatment of the corpses of witches, slaves and those, such as women who died in childbirth, deemed to have died a bad death. Despite the silences noted above, the documentary residue of this bureaucratic project—'the colonial archive'—combined with a precocious African-owned press, provides a relatively rich range of sources. Entangled with these processes were shifting perceptions of the afterlife and the meaning of death associated with the eschatology of Christian missions. For many Ghanaians, by the era of regained sovereignty in the 1950s—and increasingly so today—it was indeed Jesus who would make up their dying bed.

Many of these historical processes are explored with a particular emphasis on the dominant Akan culture of present-day southern Ghana. Others are not, looking instead to the Ga and other non-Akan-speaking peoples of the country's southeast, to the Gur-speaking peoples of the northern savanna region or to the polyglot urban cultures of the trading towns of the Gold Coast. The distinction is often due to the availability of historical evidence. Yet the absence of quotation marks around 'Akan' or any of these identities should not be taken to imply, despite the comments in the Chale Wote festival programme, that they form clearly defined, unitary 'ethnic groups' bound together by language, territory, kinship norms or religious belief and practice.[30] Within the extensive domains of Asante, in particular, considerable regional diversity is apparent, and on or beyond Asante's frontiers lay other Akan and Bono kingdoms whose identity was in part shaped by resistance to its imperial ambitions. Neither does it suggest that these linguistic or political communities today are necessarily the linear inheritors of the mortuary cultures which can be glimpsed in oral histories and the documentary record of the opening era of Atlantic encounter. Rather, the argument is that mortuary cultures were themselves key elements in the historical fashioning of identity—including that of the Akan world and its diverse political entities. The cultural work of the dead, that is to say, was directed towards the creation and the maintenance of the world of the living.

1

Cultural Encounter

WILLEM BOSMAN WAS 16 years old when he arrived on the Gold Coast as an employee of the Dutch West India Company in 1688. After serving there for fourteen years and rising to the position of chief factor at the company's headquarters at Elmina, Bosman returned to Holland, where in 1704 he published an account of his experiences in West Africa. Translations into other European languages followed and the book soon became recognized as a valuable source of knowledge on the Guinea coast. Of concern to us are Bosman's observations about death and dying and, more broadly, about the worldview and imaginaries of the Akan-speaking peoples among whom he lived. These matters certainly attracted his attention; he devoted one chapter of his book to 'the religion and idolatry of the Negroes' and another to disease, medicine and 'their notions and superstitious customs relating to death and funerals'.[1] It is the existence of such European accounts that allows us to reconstruct something of the quotidian experiences of life and death on the coast of West Africa in the opening centuries of Atlantic commerce. Yet the titles of Bosman's chapters, with their language of idolatry and superstition, indicate the interpretive challenges which these textual sources present. As recent scholarship on frontiers of cultural encounter in the early modern era has made clear, written sources, far from being disinterested repositories of knowledge, are themselves the product of the unstable, contested transactions which they seek to record. Both the encounter itself and its documentation, that is, can be seen to have been shaped by 'implicit ethnographies' held by all participants—of the self as well as of the other.[2] Their leitmotif, in West Africa as elsewhere, 'is a tangled knot of realities and representations'.[3]

This opening chapter begins to set out the landscape of that encounter as it unfolded on the Gold Coast from the late fifteenth century. It does not seek to provide a comprehensive social, political or cultural background for what will follow; these factors will emerge when and where they are relevant to the history of death and the dead. Rather, its focus is a set of fundamental metaphysical questions that, in the broadest sense, framed understandings of life and death among the Akan and their neighbours: where did mankind come from? how did death come into the world? where do people go when they die? By beginning our story with Willem Bosman the intention is not to recapitulate older ideas of the coast of Guinea as a 'white man's grave'. Rather, it is to suggest that the reality and representation of the African encounter with mortality became entangled with the encounter with European others.

Bosman opens his discussion of African belief with the first of these questions. He observes that almost all 'the Coast Negroes believe in one True God, to whom they attribute the Creation of the World and all things in it', yet insists that this perception is derived not from 'the Tradition of their Ancestors . . . but to their daily Conversation with the Europeans, who from time to time have continually endeavoured to emplant [sic] this Notion in them'. Bosman offers two pieces of evidence for this. 'First, that they never make any Offerings to God, nor call upon him in time of need; but in all their Difficulties, they apply themselves to their Fetiche.'

> The Second is, the different Opinions which some of them have kept concerning the Creation; for up to this day quite a few among them believe that Man was made by Anansie, that is, a great Spider: the rest attribute the Creation of Man to God, which they assert to have happened in the following manner: They tell us, that in the beginning God created Black as well as White Men to people the world together; thereby not only hinting but endeavouring to prove that their race was as soon in the World as ours; and to bestow a yet greater Honour on themselves, they tell us that God having created these two sorts of Men, offered two sorts of Gifts, *viz.* Gold, and the Knowledge or arts of Reading and Writing, giving the Blacks the first Election, who chose Gold, and left the Knowledge of Letters to the White. God granted their Request, but being incensed at their Avarice, resolved that the Whites should for ever be their Masters, and they obliged to wait on them as their Slaves.[4]

Bosman was not the first European on the Gold Coast to reflect on African beliefs or to speculate about the assimilation of Christian motifs into local traditions.[5] He was, however, the first to set down this particular creation myth, which would continue to be recorded, with subtle variations, over the coming centuries. We begin with Bosman, too, because of the weight of theoretical interpretation that has been placed upon his work. Owing to its wide dissemination, degree of insight and originality (many accounts of the era plagiarized earlier works), his *Description of the Coast of Guinea* has long been recognized as an essential source for the history of seventeenth-century West Africa. In a recent sequence of essays, moreover, William Pietz identified Bosman as the key mediator of what he called 'the Enlightenment theory of fetishism'. Derived from the medieval Portuguese *feitiço* (magical charm; *feitiçaria*: sorcery), the word 'fetish' (Bosman's 'Fetiche') came to be used by both Africans and Europeans, from Senegal in the north via the lower Guinea coast to Kongo and Angola in the south, to refer to ritual objects, deities and spiritual forces and to religious practice itself. Fetish, Pietz argues, 'as an idea and a problem, and as a novel object not proper to any prior discrete society, originated in the cross-cultural spaces on the coast of West Africa during the sixteenth and seventeenth centuries'.[6] From there it was carried into the broader Atlantic world and, ultimately, into the notion of 'fetishism' as the index of a Western theory of value.

Pietz's idea that certain forms and representations of religious belief and practice emerged from the crucible of cultural encounter provides a useful tool for thinking about the Gold Coast in the era of Atlantic commerce. That the creation myth is the product of a cross-cultural space is readily apparent: not only does it seek to explain the coexistence of Africans and Europeans; it reflects upon the transactional nature of their relationship on the Gold Coast. It is certainly possible to regard the myth as a reflection of Bosman's own sense of cultural superiority, 'a corroboration of his idea that Africans were ignorant people led simply by greed and interest'.[7] I would argue, however, that it is more interesting than that. In an essay developing Pietz's thesis, Roger Sansi-Roca too readily dismisses this view of a people alienated from their creator and beholden to 'fetishes' as a representation shaped by a hard-headed Protestant sensibility. Neither is it enough, as Christiane Owusu-Sarpong does in a recent analysis of Akan funerary texts, simply to wave away a subsequent account of the myth as 'ethnocentric'.[8] Far from being a jaundiced or aberrant misreading, the myth accords with a range of other sources which share its rather pessimistic and troubled worldview. These include traditions of how death followed mankind into the world. We will return to Bosman and this other evidence below. First, it is important to establish the context in which these sources emerged: the opening phase of the encounter between Africans and Europeans on the Gold Coast.

The reconfiguration of the relationship between West Africa and Europe in the course of the fifteenth century was a central dynamic in the forging of the early modern world. The maritime frontiersmen of this process were the Portuguese, who, fired by a combination of crusading zeal and a desire to break into the trans-Saharan trade in gold, edged their way south around the Atlantic coast of Africa in a sequence of exploratory voyages. By the 1440s, Portuguese mariners had reached the Senegal River, where they gleaned more information about the organization of Saharan commerce in the domains of the empire of Mali. By 1460 they had reached Sierra Leone and in 1471 pushed on to a stretch of coast where, at the settlement of Shama, near the mouth of the Pra River, they were able finally to purchase quantities of gold. The Portuguese were rarely permitted to enter the hinterland behind what they would dub the Costa da Mina (Coast of the Mine), but the Pra formed one arm of a river system draining a densely forested, auriferous basin populated by another set of hardy frontiersmen. These forest dwellers called themselves Akan, a term which in their language, Twi, carried connotations of original settlement and cultural propriety. After ten years of itinerant coastal trade, the Portuguese secured permission from a local Akan ruler twenty miles to the east of Shama to establish a permanent fortress, and in January 1482 began the construction of what would be the first European building in the tropics, the fortress of São Jorge da Mina (known later as Elmina). From there they forged lucrative commercial relationships with the Akan and their fellow Twi-speaking Bono (or Bron) neighbours, who populated the forest–savanna fringe to the north, along with members of the far-flung Mande-speaking trading diaspora originally from the domains of Mali. The Portuguese eventually diverted perhaps half of the trans-Saharan gold trade to Lisbon, boosting crown revenues and thereby funding further seaborne expansion into the Indian Ocean and to Brazil. The old Mediterranean-centred world had begun to be supplanted by a new Atlantic economy, in which the gold-producing Akan and their neighbours on the Costa da Mina were to play a pivotal role.

All of this is well known.[9] While the initial exploration of Atlantic Africa in the fifteenth century is fairly well documented, however, the subsequent century and a half of Portuguese trade and settlement on the Mina coast is less so. In contrast to Upper Guinea, no synoptic Portuguese account of the region was written, leaving historians reliant on scraps of fugitive information to shed light on the nature of local societies.[10] One episode that has been recorded in some detail is the establishment of São Jorge da Mina in 1482. This foundational moment in Afro-European relations is preserved in two chronicles: that by the royal chronicler Rui de Pina, writing circa 1500–1510s, and that by João de Barros, who had served at the fort in the 1520s and whose account was published in his *Decadas da India* in 1552. With the exception of fleeting onshore encounters noted by the Flemish sailor Eustache de la Fosse two years earlier, it includes the first recorded conversation between an African and a European on the Gold Coast. This dialogue, between the commander of the Portuguese expedition Diogo de Azambuja and the local Akan ruler, whose name is given as Caramansa, is of interest because it concerned, among other things, matters of death and the afterlife. Some explanation of these sources, drawing on the textual analysis by P.E.H. Hair, is in order here.[11]

Neither of our chroniclers witnessed the events they describe, but it is likely that the account by Rui de Pina—and quite possibly that by João de Barros—was based on a firsthand report, which has not survived, by Azambuja. That much of the incidental detail accords with subsequent ethnographic observation suggests the accuracy of the source material. The problem is that the tenor of the conversation between Azambuja and Caramansa in the two versions is quite different: while Pina explains Portuguese motives as purely commercial and secular, Barros lays emphasis on a desire for religious conversion—giving rise to a discussion of Christian eschatology. While there can be no doubt that Barros drew on the account by Pina, what remains unclear is whether Barros included material left out by Pina or simply embroidered his narrative in order to give it a more godly spin. Hair suggests that the latter is more likely, although he concedes that Azambuja's approach may not have been 'quite as devoid of specific reference to religious conversion as Pina's account would seem to indicate'.[12] Either way, this ur-encounter, as both event and representation, is saturated with the sort of 'implicit understandings' that would come to characterize the history of the cross-cultural coastal space in the centuries that followed.

Disembarking on 19 January 1482 at the settlement described two years earlier as a 'village of two parts', Azambuja and his crew said mass and sent a message requesting an audience with the local ruler, Caramansa. Caramansa's precise identity remains a matter of speculation: de la Fosse had noted the existence of two rulers—the *manse* and the *caramanse, le roi et vice-roi*, respectively—which suggests that the latter may have been the coastal representative of an Akan kingdom based further inland, possibly Eguafo to the west or Fetu to the east.[13] The meeting took place the following day, when Caramansa, surrounded by court dignitaries and warriors, received the Portuguese in full state. 'These noblemen wore rings and golden jewels on their heads and beards', Azambuja was recorded by Barros as having observed with interest. 'Their king, Caramança, came in their midst, his legs and arms covered with golden bracelets and rings, a collar around his neck, from which hung some small bells, and in his plaited beard golden bars.' In Barros's account, Azambuja, thanking the king for his hospitality, explained that the king of Portugal wished to repay him with love, a love

> which would be more advantageous than his, for it was love for the salvation of his soul, the most precious thing that man had, because it gave life, knowledge, and reason, which distinguished man from beasts. And he who wished to know it, must first know of the Lord who made it, that is God, the maker of sky, sun, moon, earth, and all upon it—He who made the day and night, rain, thunder, and lightening, and created the crops which nourished man . . . to whom their souls would go after death, to give account of the good and evil they had done during this life . . . and the bad He thrust into an abyss of the earth called Hell, the dwelling of devils who tormented their souls. . . . King João had sent to ask Caramança to recognize this God as Creator and to worship Him, to promise to live and die in this Faith.[14]

There is nothing especially surprising about Azambuja's eschatological gambit, which was typical of such opening encounters in the age of Iberian discovery and the church militant. Caramansa's response is of greater interest. 'Though Caramança was a savage man', Barros writes, 'he was of good understanding, both by nature and by his intercourse with the crew of trading ships, and possessed clear judgement'. Having listened carefully, 'he fixed his eyes on the ground for a space, and then replied: he received as a mark of graciousness from the King . . . the desire shown both for the salvation of his soul and for the matters touching his honour'—but suggested that existing trade visits might be better for relations than a permanent Portuguese settlement. It was only when Azambuja explained that he was bound to follow his king's commands, 'fearing to disobey him more than death itself', that Caramansa relented. 'These words, and the obedience they signified, so amazed Caramança that he clapped his hands, and the negroes also did this as a sign of agreement.'[15] Work began on the fortress the following day.

Analysis of this scene has focused more on its commercial than its cosmological implications. One exception is an essay by the doyen of Akan history, Ivor Wilks, in which he examines a sequence of indigenous oral sources for the origins of mankind, of human culture and of death.[16] These are called, in the Twi plural, *adomankomasem*—that is, tales concerning Odomankoma, the byname or aspect of the Akan supreme deity Onyame associated specifically with creation. These traditions of origin have been preserved in a variety of contexts, but most prominently in the rhythmic and tonal language of the *ntumpan*, or famous 'talking' drums.[17] Wilks argues that Azambuja's emphasis on God as creator meant that the translator—almost certainly a local African who had learned some Portuguese from the previous decade of trading contact—would have rendered His name as Odomankoma. We will return to Odomankoma, creation and death. If Caramansa offered his views on the creator deity in return, however, they were not recorded. Yet one intriguing aspect of the meeting as preserved by Barros is something that was *not* spoken: the pause when 'he fixed his eyes on the ground for a space' before responding to Azambuja. What might have been running through Caramansa's mind as he collected his thoughts at that moment? Hair speculates that his hesitation might be explained by a combination of wise reflection and established oratorical practice—'but may also have been due to some puzzlement, possibly arising from the interpreter's reshaping of Azambuja's words to meet his own understanding and translating capacity, as well as his own discretion in presenting outlandish concepts to an African of superior status and power.'[18] This might be taken further. If we extrapolate later Akan decorum relating to *awude*, 'things pertaining to death', to 1482, then it is likely that Caramansa, and his surrounding dignitaries, would indeed have been taken aback, if not made aghast, by the explicit reference to his own demise. To speak of a ruler's death—especially to his face and in the performative space of a courtly gathering—was an offence of the utmost gravity. Given the complex transmission of these events, it is perhaps best not to read too much into this—although Caramansa's reflective pause is no less likely to have happened than any of the actual dialogue and, in its precision, somehow rings true.

What manner of people were these, who would tempt fate by brazenly pronouncing on a ruler's death and the posthumous fate of his 'soul', or, in the likely Twi translation, *kra*? Caramansa responded to his visitor's request graciously, albeit in the first instance negatively. In another intriguing detail provided by Barros, Caramansa gestured towards the waves breaking over the rocky shore, in order to support his argument that proximate neighbours, like the land and the sea, are inevitably drawn into conflict:

> For friends who met from time to time treated each other with greater affection than if they were neighbours. And this was the heart of man at work, just as the waves of the sea beat against that reef of rocks which lies there,

because of its neighbourly contact with the reef and because the latter stops it from extending itself at will over the land, on contact the sea beats so violently that from wildness and pride it flings its waves to the sky, this fury causing two losses, one to itself as it rages, the other to its contact which it damages.[19]

It was only when Azambuja responded by emphasizing his subordination in matters of life and death to his own monarch—thereby restoring a degree of hierarchical decorum that his interlocutor could recognize—that Caramansa relented.

From the outset, Caramansa's rhetorical device reminds us, cultural encounter on the Gold Coast was situated on the seashore, where, in the centuries that followed, it would largely remain. Africans and Europeans met, transacted their business and observed each other across beaches, and it was to those littoral spaces that local rulers sought to limit the presence of 'their' strangers.[20] This narrow performative space was given added symbolic weight by the fact that the shoreline (Twi: *nsuano*) was perceived as a ritually charged liminal zone separating outposts of human culture in the seaside towns from the untamed, dangerous realm of nature that was the sea. This ritual landscape may contain a clue to the identity of Caramansa as the coastal 'viceroy' of an inland-based kingdom: a seventeenth-century English source indicates that the king of Fetu—the state which might have exercised authority over Elmina—was on accession prohibited from ever setting eyes on the sea, necessitating the appointment of a captain to manage Atlantic commerce.[21] Indeed, that ritual power became only too apparent to the Portuguese within a matter of days, when a violent dispute arose after their masons began to break rocks on the shoreline with which to construct the fort. 'The negroes could not bear such an offence against that spirit which they worshipped as their God', Barros wrote. 'Kindled with fury, which the devil fanned so that they could die before baptism—which some of them received later—they seized their arms, and on impulse briskly attacked the men at work.'[22] Azambuja was forced to restore good relations by distributing gifts, although whether Caramansa remained on hand is unclear. The enigmatic viceroy, 'after a brief and forceful appearance on the historic stage', thereafter disappears from the documentary record.[23]

Despite Azambuja's declaration of faith, proselytization under Portuguese patronage would make little headway into the societies of the Mina coast. Any impulse to implant Christianity was constrained by the limited reach of the royal trading operation, which at its height in the mid-1500s maintained the fortress of São Jorge and three coastal outposts at Shama, Axim and Accra, the last in the Ga ethnic region to the east of the Akan. São Jorge had a resident priest who attended to the spiritual needs of the Portuguese, living and dead: his principal duty was to offer a weekly mass for the repose of the soul of Prince Henry the Navigator, as stipulated in the prince's will.[24] Until the advent of a short-lived mission by Augustinian friars in the 1570s, there was little attempt at outreach beyond Elmina; neither was there any development of an indigenous clergy, as in the kingdom of Kongo in present-day Angola. One partial exception was the state of Fetu, where in 1503 the king and some of his subjects received baptism; ten years later, the same king (or possibly a successor) expressed a wish 'that all his land should become Christian'.[25] This was not to be, although a residual interest in Christianity among Fetu's ruling elite is apparent: again in 1576, the king, six of his sons and three nephews were baptized by the Augustinians.[26] Fetu aside, the Christian community largely comprised resident Portuguese, their African mistresses and Euro-African progeny, and their retainers and associates in the settlement that grew up around the walls of São Jorge. Portuguese efforts remained focused on the bartering of gold in exchange for copperware, cloth and, in the early sixteenth century, slaves, purchased from further down the Guinea coast to the east.

Societies on the Gold Coast underwent significant transformation owing to their engagement with the nascent Atlantic economy. Indeed, Wilks has argued that the impact of maritime trade extended deep into the forest hinterland, where the exchange of gold for hard metal and for slave labour facilitated the carving out of settled agricultural societies and Akan state-building. As revisionist critiques of that thesis indicate, the difficulty is to achieve an appropriate balance between continuity in indigenous political, economic and cultural forms, on the one hand, and change generated by external forces, on the other.[27] This challenge is particularly pronounced when considering the largely incommensurable realms of epistemological and religious belief. Outright 'conversion' may have been negligible during the opening phase of maritime trade—and would remain so once the Portuguese were supplanted by northern European rivals in the mid-seventeenth century—but how far did the broader cultural encounter of which Christian doctrine was a part refashion local worldviews?

In order to consider this question, we must return to the demiurgic figure of Odomankoma. In response to critics who have argued for a much longer time frame for the transition from a hunter-gatherer society to one based on sedentary agriculture in the Akan forest, Wilks reiterated his 'big bang' thesis by mobilizing additional evidence from the *adomankomasem*. Among both the northern (Bron) and the southern (Akan) branches of the Twi-speaking peoples, he argued, what these tales describe is not the actual creation of mankind but the forging of settled society based on agriculture, gold production and the creation of matrilineages, clans and then kingdoms. 'Odomankoma and the "big bang"', he concludes, 'are two ways of conceptualizing one and the same thing'.[28] The debate over the periodization of these processes is important, but it need not divert us from our focus on the metaphysics of creation and of death. In this respect, two key aspects of the *adomankomasem* can be emphasized. First, the original people created by Odomankoma, the *tetefo*, or those of ancient, 'forgotten' times, were invariably perceived to have either emerged from holes in the ground or descended from the sky; the fact that they came from nowhere else served to underpin their status as autochthones, masters of the land. Second, *tetefo* may have founded communities, but they were not remembered and revered as *nananom* (ancestors). Why? Because they existed in a time before death. The precise content of traditions of origin are specific to particular communities, but the most famous aspect of Odomankoma was his final, fatal act of creation, encapsulated in the maxim *odomankoma boo wuo maa wuo kum no*: 'Odomankoma created death (*wuo*, or *owuo*) only for death to kill him'.[29]

The 'death' of Odomankoma has been interpreted in a variety of ways. For the pioneering nationalist scholar J. B. Danquah, writing in the 1930s–40s in an attempt to assimilate Akan belief to Christian ethics, 'there is something very brilliant and hopeful and comforting about the Akan doctrine of divinity: it promises immortality to man. If the living God can die and still be alive, cannot His children also enjoy the like immunity?'.[30] As T. C. McCaskie has argued with regard to the Akan forest kingdom of Asante, however, such comforting communalist ethics are deeply ahistorical, ignoring both the imprint of political power on the realm of belief and the myriad 'pessimistic readings of historical reality, of situational positioning in the world, of felt limitations to experience, and of brittleness in the edifice of human moral order'.[31] Such pessimistic readings of the human experience emerge in a variety of ways throughout the historical record, fundamentally shaping attitudes towards death and the ends of life.

One manifestation of this gloomy outlook is the notion of the withdrawal of Odamankoma from human affairs owing to the frailty, folly or duplicity of

FIGURE 1.1. The *ntumpan*, or 'talking' drums, which recount the *adomankomasem* and the names and deeds of the hallowed dead. Photograph taken by R. S. Rattray of the *okyerema* (drummer) Osei Kwadwo demonstrating how on 7 January 1922 he recorded the history of the Mampon kingdom of Asante, which opened with the stanza 'Odomankoma 'Kyerema se / Oko babi a / Wa ma ne-he mene so / akoko bon anopa': 'The divine drummer announces that / Had he gone elsewhere (in sleep) / He has now made himself to arise / As the fowl crowed in the early dawn'. See Rattray, *Ashanti*, 278. This and other drum recordings are preserved in the R. S. Rattray Cylinder Collection in the British Library. Pitt Rivers Museum, University of Oxford, 1998.312.379.1.

mankind—or, it was often said, of womankind: driven to distraction by the incessant hammering of women's pestles as they pounded the staple forest crop, yam, into *fufu*, Odomankoma turned his back on the world, leaving it in the charge of a teeming array of lesser deities or, as Bosman would have it, 'fetishes', called *abosom*. It was only then that he created death, dispatching a goat to inform mankind but to reassure them that 'even if you die, you will not be completely lost; you will come to me in the sky'.[32] In an example of the stereotypical myth of the 'message which failed', the goat dallied and was overtaken by a second, fearsome message carried by a sheep: that death, instead, 'would be the end of all things'. In a version told to the missionary Edmond Perregaux in Asante at the turn of the twentieth century, shortly afterwards 'the first case of death took place, and God taught men to bury their dead. He also told them that as a foil to death they should be given the capacity to multiply'.[33] Here we see a key element of Akan metaphysical thought: the linking of birth with death, the bookends of an individual existence which gives meaning to life. Another version, recorded in the 1880s, puts the matter succinctly: 'without man's death, he does not give birth'.[34]

Bosman's creation myth can be seen to have been modified from the older *adomankomasem* to take account of the arrival of Europeans and intriguing technologies. Such anxieties about human limitations in an insecure world were in no way exclusive to the Akan. An aloof, 'withdrawn' creator god; a spiritual realm dominated by capricious and often vindictive lesser deities; a threatening, irruptive nature that threatened constantly to overwhelm the fragile realm of culture—all were standard cosmological elements in many parts of the African continent. So too was the notion that death, once created, was allowed into the world by a dreadful mistake or by the trope of the 'wrong choice' evident in the myth reported to Bosman. Compare J.D.Y. Peel's comments on the Yoruba peoples some two hundred miles to the east: 'The Yoruba, like other populations of precolonial Africa, existed in a state of chronic cognitive deficit, forever aware that their stock of knowledge, although extensive, was liable to fail to meet their survival needs or to quell their anxieties'.[35] Neither were the *odomankomasem* the only narrative vehicles for the origins of life and death. As Bosman observed, 'quite a few among them believe that Man was made by Anansie', the trickster spider whose adventures formed a parallel cycle of mythic tales, the *anansesem*, and whose identity was sometimes conflated with that of Onyame.[36]

By the 1590s, when Dutch trading voyages began to undermine Portuguese dominance of trade and to produce a wider range of written sources, there is clear evidence for the emergence of the cross-cultural space from which Pietz's hybridized notion of the 'fetish' arose. The outstanding record produced by the advent of Dutch activity is that of Pieter de Marees, who visited the Gold Coast on a number of occasions in the 1590s. The three fundamental components of the Akan cosmological scheme are recognizable from de Marees's account: the withdrawn creator god, named as 'Iuan goemain' (i.e., Nyankonpon, like Odomankoma, one of the bynames of Onyame); an array of deities or '*fetisso*' (i.e., *abosom*; sing. *obosom*) to whom everyday worship was directed;

and 'ordinary articles of Sorcery, which they use to exorcise something and to ensure that the *Fetisso* may leave the dead in peace' (i.e., *asuman*; sing. *suman*: lesser ritual powers often manifested in physical amulets). While de Marees did not consider these beliefs and attendant ritual practices to be in essence satanic, it is clear that the attempt by his interlocutors to explain the volatile nature of ritual power, in particular that of the *abosom*, led him to suspect that 'they have dealings with the Devil'. 'We once sat down with them and talked, asking them about their religion and their opinion concerning such things . . . when asked about their God, they say he is black as they are and is not good, but causes them much harm and grief . . . they regard their *Fetisso* as good and bad.'[37] Those he spoke with were intrigued to hear of the very different, unambiguous nature of the Europeans' god:

> We answered that our God is white as we are, is good and gives us many blessings; that he came down to earth to bring us salvation and was shamefully killed by another people for our benefit; that when we die, we go will go and live with him in Heaven, and will not have to trouble ourselves there about eating and drinking. This much surprised them and they were pleased to hear us talking about it. They concluded that we were God's children and that he told us everything. This made them complain, asking why our God did not tell and give everything to them as he does to us, and why he did not give them Linen, Cloth, Iron, Basins, and all sorts of Goods as he does to us.[38]

When de Marees reassured his interlocutors that God too provided for them—'although they do not know him, he has given them gold, Palm wine, *Millie* and Maize, Chickens and Oxen, Sheep, *Bannanas*, Yams and other Fruits'—they dismissed this, observing that gold and food crops were quite patently a gift of the earth and fish a gift of the sea, while other fruits had been first brought by the Portuguese.

The vague outlines of the creation myth recorded by Bosman a century later are discernible here: a beneficent god who has favoured Europeans with an array of desirable manufactures (or the knowledge to make them), leaving Africans to struggle with a capricious, unstable metaphysical world and with material goods limited to gold and foodstuffs.[39] The local perception that Europeans had the upper hand in the exchange of hard metal for soft metal was not yet apparent in an earlier Portuguese report, which noted that Africans 'value Portugal less than their own [kingdoms] since they have gold in these, which they know to be much finer a metal than that used for bracelets—just as we here equally hold Portugal is better than Guinea'.[40] In light of the dichotomy between gold and literate knowledge at the heart of Bosman's creation myth, however, it is interesting to note that the same Portuguese author reports seeing 'many blacks, youths and boys, going about carrying papers and books in their hands'.[41] De Marees, in contrast, picks up on the note of pessimism that runs through much subsequently reported metaphysical reflection, most obviously with respect to the testy *abosom* and in the belief (although this is missed by the Dutchman) that human foible led Odomankoma to withdraw from direct intercourse with the world he had made.

What of the afterlife? A crewman on a Dutch ship in 1603–4 recorded a striking perception: 'When their king dies, all his nobles who sit with him in council must die too, as must his slaves. They chop them all into small pieces, which they throw here and there over the open country, professing that when their people die, they come to the country of the Whites, and there too the king must have people to wait on him. That is why so many must die with him, and for that reason they make all their dead quite white before burying them'.[42] Of note here is the understanding that the dead might either go to the afterworld of Europeans or actually become white. This may well be a misreading of funerary culture: the faces of corpses, mourners and of sacrificial victims were indeed often smeared with white clay, or *hyire*—but this colour symbolism had ritual connotations above and beyond mimicry of European phenotypes. Consider, however, an account by Michael Hemmersam of his arrival at Elmina in 1639, two years after the Portuguese fortress finally fell to the Dutch. Walking towards the castle, an African woman 'sprang up to me, offering me her hand and wanted to talk to me'. 'This greatly startled me', Hemmersam writes, 'and I asked those who . . . understood the language what this meant . . . They said that when one of them died, they supposed that he travelled to another place. Now since this Mooress's husband had died a short time before, she said it was me, and I was her deceased husband, who had become white through death'.[43] 'When a person's end is at hand', Hemmersam would later learn, 'they ask him why he wants to leave them and die; whether he lacks food and drink, wives and children . . . and where he wishes to go—to which country, among Christians or heathens'.[44] Again, this does not quite accord with later ethnographic observation: these questions were actually posed posthumously, to the deceased's corpse. Yet the notion that a choice of afterlife was now on offer was noted too by Bosman, who was told that some people at least 'are persuaded that after Death, they are transported to the Land of the Blanks or Whites, and changed into white Men'.[45]

The identification of Europeans as some kind of revenant was a not uncommon trope in zones of encounter in the early modern world. The incident involving Hemmersam happened at Elmina, the focus of Euro-African engagement on the coast to that point and where by the 1630s an estimated half of the total population of some eight hundred were reported to be Catholics. Unsurprisingly, the faith of these converts was suspected of being less than absolute. 'I have found some who could tell a lot about the birth of Christ, the Last Supper, his bitter passion, death and resurrection', de Marees noted; the vicar of São Jorge, however, writing in 1632 to the Vatican, reported that the ostensibly Christian town was thoroughly corrupted with 'superstitious and magical rites'.[46] Yet notions of posthumous racial fluidity and magical transformation were not monopolized by Africans. That same year, the last Portuguese governor of São Jorge, Pedro Mascarenhas, sailed from Lisbon with three wooden statues, of the Virgin Mary, St Francis of Assisi and St Antony of Padua, with which to adorn the castle's church. As his ship approached the coast, it was discovered that the face and hands of the figure of St Francis had turned from white to black. 'This change of colour', an astonished Mascarenhas wrote, 'is a most certain sign from St Francis of Assisi that he wants to be the Negroes' patron Saint. Having become a Negro to the Negroes that he might win them to heaven, he hereby gives promise that through his spiritual sons, the Franciscan priests, the Negroes shall receive the gift of the Catholic faith'.[47]

The sign from St Francis turned out to be a false prophecy. The worldwide Dutch assault on the possessions of the unified crowns of Portugal and Spain saw the fall of Elmina in 1637, followed by that of their last outpost at Axim five years later. This was to usher in a new era of maritime commerce on the Gold Coast, dominated by chartered companies of rival northern European trading nations—principally Holland, England and Denmark, with more ephemeral participation from Sweden, Brandenburg Germany and France. The expansion of slave plantations in the Americas, moreover, caused an export trade that hitherto had been dominated by gold to be replaced by one in which the proportion of African slaves increased steadily. Access to European firearms facilitated the rise of militarized state-building projects in the forest hinterland: by the mid-seventeenth century, two interior Akan kingdoms, Denkyira and Akwamu, dominated, respectively, the central Pra–Ofin river basin and the eastern Gold Coast. Around 1700, Denkyira was in turn overthrown by a newly forged military alliance, which would soon emerge as the most expansive and powerful of Akan kingdoms and the apotheosis of indigenous statecraft: Asante.

In contrast with the peoples of the Atlantic seaboard, those of the forest kingdom of Asante had little direct intercourse with Europeans and their ideas until the nineteenth century. It is striking, therefore, that T. E. Bowdich, a member of the first British diplomatic mission to visit the Asante capital, Kumasi, in 1817, was given an account of creation which explained the difference between Africans and Europeans in the same terms as that recounted to Bosman:

> In the beginning of the world, God created three white men and three black men, with same number of women; he resolved, that they might not afterwards complain, to give them the choice of good and evil. A large box or calabash was set on the ground, with a piece of paper, sealed up, on one side of it. God gave the black men the first choice, who took the box, expecting it contained every thing, but, on opening it, there appeared only a piece of gold, a piece of iron, and several other metals, of which they did not know the use. The white men opening the paper, it told them every thing. God left the blacks in the bush, but conducted the whites to the water side (for this happened in Africa) communicated with them every night, and taught them to build a small ship which carried them to another country, whence they returned after a long period, with various merchandise to barter with the blacks, who might have been the superior people.[48]

Bowdich speculated on how notions of the afterlife were shaped by this sense of alienation from the creator. 'With this imaginary alienation from the God of the universe, not a shade of despondency is associated; they consider that it diminishes their comforts and their endowments on earth, but that futurity is a dull and torpid state to the majority of mankind.'[49] For a minority, however, the afterlife offered more than just torpidity:

> The kings, caboceers, and the higher class, are believed to dwell with the superior Deity after Death, enjoying an eternal renewal of the state and luxury they possessed on earth. It is with this impression, that they kill a certain number of both sexes at the funeral customs, to accompany the deceased, to announce his distinction, and to administer to his pleasures. The spirits of the inferior classes are believed to inhabit the house of the fetish, in a state of torpic indolence, which recompenses them for the drudgery of their lives, and which is truly congenial to the feelings of the

Negro. Those of superior wisdom and experience, are said to be endued with foresight after death, and to be appointed to observe the lives, and advise the good of those mortals who acknowledge the fetish.[50]

Here Bowdich refers to a further key element in the Akan cosmological spectrum: *nananom*, the ancestors. If lucky enough to have experienced a fulfilling life culminating in a good death, the dead followed in the footsteps of Odomankoma by continuing to live in the afterlife. They remained in intimate intercourse with the living, 'appointed to observe their lives'. It is to these ideas we turn to next.

2

Body, Soul and Person

TO THINK HISTORICALLY ABOUT DEATH, we need too to think about being alive. Just as the living know that one day their bodily existence will come to an end and they will join the ranks of the dead, so the dead—whether they are aware of the fact or not—were once living people. Ideas about what constitutes a person, about the relationship between the person and the physical body, and about what remains of that personhood once the body itself is dead and buried are therefore fundamental to how any society approaches matters of mortality. In the opening words of his analysis of these understandings in Enlightenment-era Britain, Roy Porter put the matter quite simply: 'Who are we?'[1] Porter's answer, in a nutshell, was that notions of who, or what, humans are changed significantly in the eighteenth century, when 'individuals reformulated the problems of existence and made sense of the self, with a changing, and waning, reference to the soul'.[2] As new scientific and philosophical thought mounted a challenge to the assumed existence of the disembodied soul, it led also to a reappraisal of the human body; 'the two', Porter argues, 'have been symbiotic in the refiguring of the self'.[3] Bodies, souls and the self, in other words, cannot simply be taken for granted: definitions of their nature have varied widely across and within cultures and have been subject to contest, debate and transformation over time.

How did the African peoples of the Gold Coast and its hinterland conceive the body, the soul and the person? What was seen to constitute a human being and what happened to those elements after death? These questions have been of considerable interest to scholars of many parts of Africa and elsewhere in the non-Western world: first to colonial-era ethnographers and sociologists wishing to establish typologies of so-called primitive thought, and more recently to those concerned to interrogate and destabilize these typologies.[4] In the last two decades, the body—including the colonized body—has emerged as a focus of historical as well as anthropological inquiry.[5] Crucial to this development has been the influence of postmodernist thinkers such as Roland Barthes, Jacques Derrida and Michel Foucault, whose iconoclastic theories, as Porter points out, have served to challenge the very narrative of the triumph of the autonomous modern self; for Foucault in particular, the Enlightenment was more about imposing control over the body through a bureaucratic regime of 'biopower' than about the championing of the individual.[6] Foucauldian theory has in turn been critiqued for being overly deterministic in its view of the social construction of the body at the expense of individual human agency and 'embodied' experience.[7] It is in the context of these debates that ontological thought in the non-Western world is of comparative importance, as the European-dominated Enlightenment narrative is one of progressive disenchantment and of the freeing of the individual from the meshes of kinship and community. If, as is widely understood, African ontologies (i.e., theories of being) defined the person less as an autonomous, bounded individual than as part of broader communal, political and spiritual identities, then to what extent can this be equated, in the Enlightenment narrative, with a 'primitive' past or, in the Foucauldian counter-narrative, with a negation of selfhood that would simply be reinforced by the regime of modern biopower?

Considering these issues historically in sub-Saharan Africa presents formidable challenges. Written sources which touch on matters of bodies, souls and the self date back on the Gold Coast to the seventeenth century, although, as we have begun to see, these may tell us as much about the perceptions of their European authors as they do about the African societies they were observing. It would not be until the emergence of a local print culture in the late nineteenth century that Africans themselves began to produce the sort of reflections on the nature of the self that Porter uses for eighteenth-century Britain—by which time, many members of the literate Gold Coast intelligentsia had absorbed a humanist view of personhood in some ways distinct from established understandings (see chapter 14). At the same time, others began to record the laws, customs and worldviews of local societies—and, as we have seen with J. B. Danquah, in some cases to attempt to reconcile these with Western thought. Important evidence is provided by the work of colonial-era ethnographers, in particular that of R. S. Rattray and, subsequently, Meyer Fortes, both of whom were concerned to record the beliefs and customs of the Akan and the savanna peoples to their north before they were irreparably eroded by social change. Christian conversion is a further complicating factor: whereas the Enlightenment narrative posits the progressive displacement of church-sanctioned eschatology by scientific secularism, the spread of mission Christianity on the Gold Coast from the mid-nineteenth century can be seen to represent not a disenchantment but a re-enchantment of older notions of body and soul. The historical picture, then, is poorly documented and complex. The aim in this chapter is to sketch a set of normative logics, drawing on some key seventeenth- and eighteenth-century sources, together with later ethnographic works and secondary scholarship. The task will then be to insert these logics into history.

———

From the outset of the cultural encounter on the Gold Coast, it is apparent that Europeans were fascinated—sometimes mesmerized—by African bodies. Both chronicles of the ur-encounter of 20 January 1482 convey a powerful sense of the Portuguese gaze being drawn to the appearance of the assembled Africans: their colour, comportment, anointment, decoration and clothing, and what these might reveal about the nature of local society. One thing that Azambuja did recognize with approval was the embodiment of order and hierarchy—and, promisingly, that that hierarchy was already reflected in the display of European commodities. 'Their dress was their own flesh', João de Barros wrote of Caramansa's warriors, 'anointed and very shining, which made their skins still blacker, a custom which they effected as an elegancy. Their privy parts only were covered with the skins of monkeys or woven palm leaves—the chiefs' with patterned cloth, which they had from our ships'.[8] Hierarchy and power were also observed to be projected by bodily comportment: Caramansa, 'to impress his dignity . . . walked with very slow and light steps, never turning his face to either side'. This was a component of what the Akan called *akyea*, 'gait', one element of an elaborate register of cultural codes embodied in the person of office-holders.[9] It was observed again in 1555 by the English trader William Towerson. Landing at Shama, Towerson and his crew were met by 'the captaine of the towne, being a grave man . . . we saluted him and put off our caps, and bowed ourselves, and hee, like one that thought well of himself, did not move his cap, nor scant bowed his body, and sate him down very solemnly upon his stoole'.[10] This passage is also notable in that it represents an early record of the use by the Akan of wooden stools (Twi: *nkonnwa*; sing. *akonnwa*) as royal regalia. Aside from being a synecdoche for the state, the stool as material object was the most potent mnemonic for the royal dead: if their owners died a good death, they would be ritually 'blackened' and

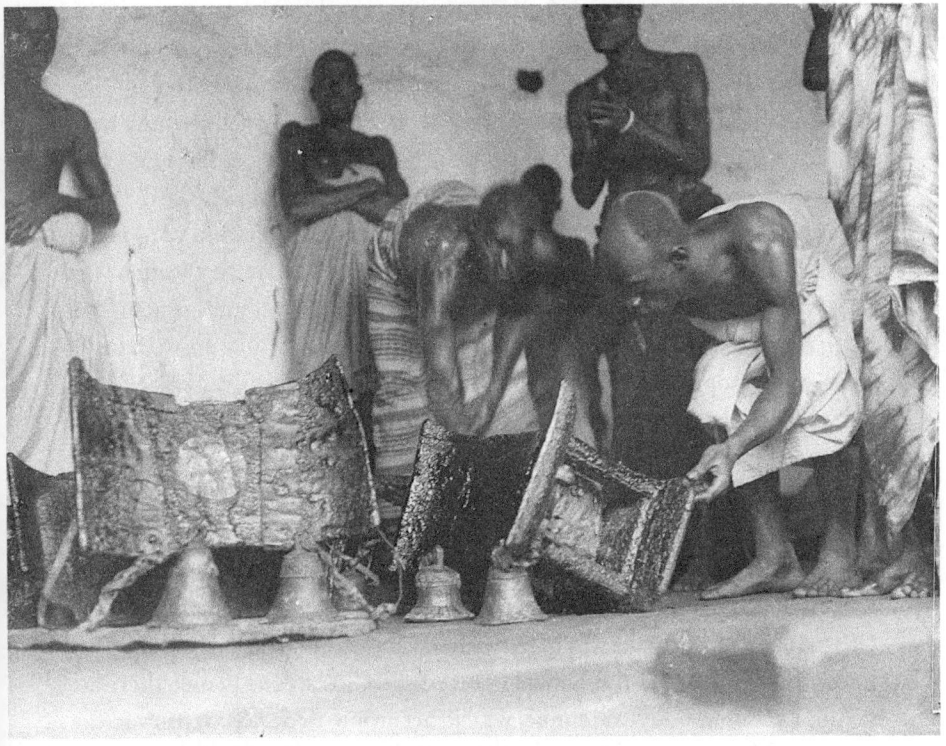

FIGURE 2.1. *Nkonnwa tuntum*, or blackened ancestral stools. Photograph taken by R. S. Rattray on 21 December 1921 at Mampon, in Asante, at a *wukuadae*, or Wednesday *adae* ceremony, when the departed spirits of royal ancestors are called back onto their stools to receive the adulation of the living. Here, the stools, resting upon the bells which summon the dead, are smeared with the blood of sacrificed sheep by the *akonnwasoafohene*, or head stool-carrier, distinguished by his specially patterned hair. Pitt Rivers Museum, University of Oxford, 1998.312.603.1; published as figure 32 of *Ashanti*, facing 113.

retained as hallowed *nkonnwa tuntum*, serving as a vessel for the spirit of the deceased ancestor.

Such observations of the African body would recur in the centuries which followed. Pieter de Marees devoted four full chapters of his 1602 account to the physique, comportment and bodily decoration of the men and women of the Gold Coast. Much of this description was complimentary, reflective perhaps of the humanist revival which, according to Porter, saw the macabre medieval perception of the vile body being supplanted by 'the body noble, beautiful, orderly, ideal, the dignity of human nature'.[11] 'The men of this country are of fine stature', de Marees wrote, 'with beautiful limbs, long legs and well chiselled bodies, which one can observe easily enough, as they go around with most of their body naked'.[12] They are, he thought, 'all that a fine, upright Man should be. They are good workers and have bodies as strong as Trees'.[13] The women too met with de Marees's approval, despite some qualms about their relaxed attitudes to sexuality: 'they have firm bodies and beautiful loins, outdoing the womenfolk of our Lands in strength and devotion' and, like the men, 'are also very conscious of the way they walk and of their clothes'.[14] He too stressed the ways in which *akyea* projected status: 'When they walk in the streets, they look straight ahead and will not raise their eyes until someone of higher rank addresses them. To him they will speak and give answer; but if spoken to by someone of lower standing, they will not answer, but will address him in an unfriendly way and show him an angry face'.[15] 'They have a very high opinion of themselves', Danish pastor Johannes Rask put it a century later, 'and walk with very proud gait and in a Spanish manner'.[16]

Rask served as chaplain at the headquarters of the West India and Guinea Company at Christiansborg from 1708 to 1712, the first of a sequence of keen and often sympathetic Danish observers of Ga society on the eastern Gold Coast. Like de Marees, he was taken with the impressive physique, cleanliness, health and refined bodily manners of his African hosts: 'The people there are without a flaw in body and limbs, which, according to our conviction in the necessity of swaddling babies, must seem almost unbelievable; but I can not remember ever seeing anyone who was deformed or with crooked limbs, such as are found in great numbers among us'. Rask could only conclude that 'parents make an end of, and dispose of, those children who had some flaw or anything lacking in body and limbs, and only raise those who are flawless'.[17] There is certainly evidence that newborns with the most alarming physical deformities were disposed of; the more general point, however, is that both the Akan and their Ga neighbours placed an enormous weight on the perfection and wholeness of the body.[18] As to the Ga's apparent longevity and robust physical health, Rask offered this assessment: 'They are sound and healthy and live long, although their food is truly poor, but what I think prolongs their lives is that they are always in good spirits and laughing, never in despair or ever worried about anything; and thus they preserve their spirit, and their bodies are not overworked either, since they take both their sorrow and their work in the easiest way possible, this remarkable folk'.[19]

The sinister underbelly to such commentary was that by the early eighteenth century, the prosperity and wellbeing of the principal Gold Coast towns was based increasingly on the slave trade. As the value of slave exports surpassed that of gold, commerce became based on the so-called *pieza* system, the mechanism of Atlantic exchange calculated by the normative value in trade goods of an enslaved human body (Spanish *pieza* or Portuguese *peça*: 'piece').[20] The refined manners, material consumption and perhaps even the growing sense of autonomous self of those freeborn elites able to harness the forces of Atlantic commerce, that is to say, were based to a considerable extent on the subjugation and commoditization of other bodies—the bodies of those whom, it can safely be supposed, were far from being 'always in good spirits and laughing, never in despair'. Enslavement was achieved by an extreme form of involuntary individuation: the removal of a person from the protective networks of kin and community that, as elsewhere in Africa, defined at a fundamental level the concepts of both personhood and 'freedom'. Whether destined for delivery into the dungeons of the European forts to await shipment to the Americas or into the slave retinues of local elites, the victims of this process were subjugated by actual or threatened physical violence. Such violence was enacted at Osu, the Ga seaside town surrounding the Dane's Christiansborg Castle, during the yearly 'slave-custom', which, according to Ray Kea, served to distribute 'terror and death among the servile population' by the ritual dismemberment of an enslaved captive. During the custom, Kea explains, 'the victim was decapitated amidst the drinking, dancing, and shouting of the *odehe* participants'. His or her jawbone was then carried through the town in what was 'a collective celebration of the *nyonji*'s . . . defeat and subordination' and the triumph of the slave-owning elite's 'achievements, realizations, acquisitions, and accumulations'.[21]

We will return to this and other forms of corporeal violence in the chapters which follow. It can simply be noted here that if a heightened sense of physical wholeness underpinned the role of the human body as a vehicle for a range of powerful mystical elements which transcended it in both space and time, then so too did it retain a degree of sacred power after death and dismemberment.[22] Porter's comments on modern Europe, moreover, apply equally to Atlantic West Africa in the same period: 'refined bodily manners would be elevated above coarse flesh via the "civilizing process"; vile bodies would be firmly consigned to their place; and their subjugation would be reinforced through the pains and penalties of the law (corporal and capital punishment), through training and work discipline (the curse of labour), and through more stringent control of leisure and sexuality'.[23]

If written accounts provide some sense of embodied practices on the Gold Coast in the opening centuries of Atlantic commerce, they have less to say about how the human body was understood to be constituted. It was only from the late nineteenth century that sources begin to identify the full repertoire of ontological categories, fragments of which had been encountered by puzzled observers in previous centuries. With the exception of the Talensi and Dagara peoples of present-day northern Ghana, whose notions of personhood of both the living and the ancestral dead were subjected in the mid-twentieth century to sustained analysis by the social anthropologists Meyer Fortes and Jack Goody, most of this scholarship has focused on the Akan.[24] Yet even here problems of interpretation remain. In 1927 Rattray could write that the Akan 'use a number of names which have been roughly translated into English by the words "soul" or "spirit" or "ghost", without any clear attempt to find out if these words to an Ashanti are synonymous terms, or refer to different kinds of soul or spirit, or to a series of multiple souls, or particular spirits, with different functions during life and with a varying destination after death'; by the 1980s, two eminent Ghanaian philosophers, both native Twi-speakers trained in metaphysics, were still unable to agree on those definitions and relationships.[25] Thus, after over a century of inquiry, McCaskie was forced to acknowledge 'the elusive resistance of *all* aspects of this subject to formal analysis . . . for the lacunae inhere directly in those blanknesses where Asante interrogation of being itself breaks down in mystery'.[26]

Aside from the awesome mysteries of being which confounded even those societies with faiths based on written doctrine, it should be reiterated that for the Akan and their neighbours, speaking openly about matters of life and death was appropriate only in certain circumstances and only when approached with the necessary gravity and lexical circumlocution. Early European observers often misread the ensuing reticence as pagan embarrassment when confronted by a superior, revealed faith. 'If you ask them anything about their faith', the French trader Villault observed in 1666, 'they lower their eyes to the ground and say nothing, although one of them said that the whites have a God who is very good to give them another life'.[27] Eight decades later, the Danish trader Rømer, who lived at Christiansborg for ten years and counted a number of Ga ritual experts as close friends, knew better: 'They do not like to hear any mention of death, which, according to their beliefs, is the greatest evil they experience'. Rømer illustrated this point with an anecdote about how he once gravely offended his friend Adoui, a local broker. Adoui had been feeling unwell and came to the fort for a glass of brandy. 'While my servant was away fetching it', Rømer recounted, 'I asked him who would be the successor in his service when he died. He became quite upset at this, stood up and answered, "God has sent me into the world with many years on my head. Do you think I am like the Whites, who come and go? But since you wish to know, don't you know my brother Atte?" He did not wait for his brandy, but went away'.[28]

Let us begin with a reflection on de Marees's comment that the Africans had 'bodies as strong as trees'. A linguistic coincidence, perhaps, but his turn of phrase neatly captures a fundamental Akan perception of the body, or *onipadua*, as a 'human tree' (*onipa*, person + *dua*, tree). This association is unsurprising in a society carved from a forest environment in which towering tropical hardwoods were the most prominent natural feature. Indeed, Akan culture was full of symbolic references to trees and to the wood they yielded: if the human body was seen to be like a tree, then trees in turn shared certain attributes with humans and needed to be treated accordingly. Not only might they serve as shrines harbouring a deity; certain trees were themselves seen as sentient beings which required propitiation if they were to be cut down and transformed into the stuff of material culture. Rattray in the 1920s observed how a carver of *ntumpane*, or talking drums, would approach the *tweneboa* tree with a prayer: 'I am coming to cut you down and carve you, receive this egg and eat . . . do not let the iron cut me; do not let me suffer in health'; after the tree was felled and the drum carved, 'the wandering spirit whose habitation or body has been destroyed is . . . enticed to enter once again the material substance where it dwelt when the tree was alive'.[29] Thus, the spirit of the tree itself spoke through the verbalized rhythms of the *ntumpane*.

The tree with the most powerful 'spirit' was the *gyadua*, or great shade tree, which as a rule grew at the centre of every Akan forest settlement. Consecrated by the burial of powerful medicine at its base—including, according to some sources, the body of a human sacrifice—the *gyadua* served ritually to protect the community, the shade offered by its foliage symbolically associated with the enveloping embrace of Akan kingship. In times of war, this sacred tree was defended to the last; an Asante army, Rattray was informed by the elders of the kingdom (*oman*) of Kokofu, 'on capturing a town, always cut down the *gyadua*'—a calamity which they themselves had experienced during the civil war of the 1880s. If the tree is uprooted in a storm or otherwise falls down, a Kokofu informant reported, 'its funeral custom will be held, mourning clothes will be put on, and *ntwuma* (red funeral clay), and the drums will beat *damarifa*'.[30] So too was the death of a king, or *omanhene*, never spoken of directly but referred to by the circumlocution *odupon kese atutu*, 'a great tree has fallen'. 'When pointing to a grave', Eva Meyerowitz noted, 'it is the rule to say "*me kura dua mu*", "I cling to a tree"'.³¹

If Akan culture remained ontologically entangled with the forest environment from which it emerged, however, it was also conceived as quite distinct from it. Hostile, implacable and teeming with physical and spiritual danger, the forest, as McCaskie has written, 'stood ever ready to subvert and to annihilate the niche of cultural space'.³² Coastal peoples such as the Ga looked on the sea with a similar wary ambivalence. Humankind belonged in the realm of culture first forged by primordial ancestors, who heroically constructed its foundational ideological edifice: kinship. And it was structures of kinship—the matrilineage for the Akan and the patrilineage for the Ga, Ewe and peoples of the savanna north—within which personhood was firmly embedded. People lived, and died, as members of these collectives, the unmarked graves of the dead lying in the humus of the forest floor or under the pounded earth floors of houses a reminder of the degree to which the individual was subsumed by family and community. Unity between the living and the massed ranks of ancestors was particularly pronounced at the level of kingship: the Akan *omanhene* was the living embodiment of the deeds and virtues of his predecessors, speaking of their past achievements as if they were his own.

The tension between individual personhood and collective identity was reflected in the multiple elements understood to comprise a human being. Let us consider the nature and posthumous destination of each in turn, focusing on the better-known Akan example but bearing in mind that neighbouring peoples possessed similar, if slightly variant, conceptual schema.³³ The *kra* (or *okra*), sources agree, is that which most closely resembles the notion of a soul. It was seen to exist before and after the earthly life of an individual, being given to each person by the supreme god Onyame and returning to Onyame on his or her death, and to be the bearer of that person's *nkrabea* (fate or destiny). 'God has sent me into the world with many years on my head': here Adoui is referring to the 'destiny' borne by his (in the Ga cognate) *kla*. The *kra* was within but at the same time somehow distinct from a person, like a shadowing guardian which dispensed advice of varying worth; thus, in times of prosperity or success, it was said that *me kra di m'akyi*, 'my *kra* protects me', but in times of adversity it was castigated as *okrabiri*, a 'black' or evil *kra*, requiring propitiation. The *kra* was also seen to activate the *honhom*, or breath; when a person died, it was said that *ne honhom ko*, 'his breath is gone', which was caused by the *kra* having departed the body. The departure of the *kra* from the body was often arduous, as it had to labour up a steep hill before finally climbing a ladder on its journey back to Onyame—this was the proverbial 'ladder of death', often depicted as a symbol on *adinkra* mourning cloth, funerary pots and brass goldweights. The journey could readily be seen in the *opere*, the gasps or agonies of the dying person; if the person rallied and lived on, then the *kra* was seen to have been called back. Forty days after death, the *kra* was required to give an account of itself before a tribunal of predeceased elders; if found wanting, it was sent back to earth to be reincarnated in a yet-to-be-born child, who, while still in the womb, is 'given a command (*hyebea*) by Nyame—some say by the deceased, who becomes the child's spiritual parent—to complete or to perfect the *kra* by doing good deeds'.[34]

Like the *kra*, the *sunsum* was perceived as a sort of spiritual shadow, from which it derived its name (*sunsuma*: shade or shadow). In contrast to the fixed nature of the former, however, the *sunsum* was both ephemeral and mutable: not being a gift of Onyame, it was not venerated, existed on earth for only as long as its solitary human vehicle, and could actively be modified in order to become more 'heavy' (*duru*) and thus afford greater spiritual protection. This notion that the *sunsum* had a weight gave it a close association with an individual's personality; thus, someone with a strong personality would be described as having a 'heavy' *sunsum*, while a gentle or timid person would have a 'light' *sunsum*. Unlike the *kra*, it could also temporarily leave the body— which was what was perceived to occur during dreams. Such volatility also made the *sunsum* susceptible to attack from disease or from *bayi*, 'witchcraft', especially during its nocturnal roaming: 'it may encounter other *sunsum* and get knocked about, when you will feel unwell, or killed, when you will sicken and die', one of Rattray's informants said.[35] 'The frailty of the *sunsum*', according to Meyerowitz, 'can be seen from a line in a very ancient song called Owuo Papa, the Death Fan: "With no more force than the wind stirred by a fan, Death can at any time blow the *sunsum* into the other world"'.[36] It was the *sunsum*, Meyerowitz was told, which after death—if the death, that is, was a 'good' one—became a *saman*, an ancestral spirit which resided in *asamando*, the afterworld. If the death was 'bad', then the *sunsum* became a restless ghost, often seen at night sitting at crossroads 'looking as if they were forever seeking something, or trying to find their way back to life in order to put things right'— this despite the fact that their *kra* may have returned to Onyame and been reincarnated. Entire communities or states were also seen to possess a collective *sunsum*; the most famous historical example was that of the Asante kingdom, manifested in the *sika dwa kofi*, the Golden Stool.

If the *kra* and the *sunsum* were 'divine' elements, then *mogya* and *ntoro* were human in origin, transmitted by an individual's mother and father, respectively. *Mogya* is 'blood', both physiologically and metaphorically, so was the element which determined membership of an *abusua*, a matrilineage, and as such defined the Akan system of kinship and jural citizenship. As in many cultures, blood was regarded with ambivalence: symbolic of life but also of death, cleansing but also potentially polluting, it had profound implications for the gendered dynamics of the social order. At the most fundamental level, *mogya* defined Akan exogamy: no two members of the same *abusua* could marry or have children. As for the destination of the essence of the *mogya* after death, the evidence is contradictory. In contrast with Meyerowitz, Rattray understood that it was the *mogya*, 'the blood and body soul', rather than the *sunsum*, which became a *saman* and went 'to live in the spirit world to await a chance of reincarnation'.[37] 'It seems to be accompanied to the spirit world by the *kra*', Rattray continued, 'but this is not quite clear'. One thing, however, was clear: 'A woman of a particular clan (blood) only gives rebirth to a "ghost" of her clan. *Obi now obi saman* (one does not give birth to some one else's ghost) is a saying which has all the force of a legal axiom'.[38]

Finally, a person's *ntoro* comes from the father. If *mogya* in its physical form was blood, then *ntoro* was identified with semen; the two combined in the womb to mould the human embryo. There, Rattray notes, they are met by the *kra:* '"the *kra* is the stranger", say the Ashanti, "for it found the *mogya* (blood soul) and the *ntoro* actually in possession of the infant, they having been in the child since conception took place"'.[39] With regard to the construction of the body, the *mogya* was often seen to form the flesh and blood and the *ntoro* the bones. In terms of kinship, the *ntoro* served to define a person's patrilineal affiliation to one of up to a dozen cultic groups (the precise number varies), which, like the *sunsum*, were also seen to influence individual character. The relationship in Akan society between the dominant *abusua* and the subordinate *ntoro* groups—as well as that between any individual's matrilineal and patrilineal identity—was of great sociological importance: how it defined personhood was a central concern of Fortes's anthropological work on Asante from the 1940s. It also had profound historical implications, particularly at the level of dynastic politics, which can be seen often to have been driven by the tension between these competing identities. Rattray was led to understand that the *ntoro* 'does not accompany the *saman* to the spirit world, but is separated from it . . . joins the group *ntoro* god (*obosom*) or spirit, and is reincarnated again through any male of the same *ntoro*'.[40] An ideal procreative union, therefore, was a 'cross-cousin marriage' (or in Twi, *mogya awadie*, 'blood marriage'), which would ensure the inheritance of desired ancestral traits from both the mother's and father's lines. Northern savanna peoples shared this bifurcated view of the body and its dissolution: for them, it was the subordinate matrilineal person—the soft body—which died, but the dominant patrilineal person 'lived on', symbolized in the survival of the hard bones.

All four of these components of the body and person were acknowledged, addressed and reflected upon in a myriad of ways, from everyday discourse and ritual performance to that associated with the great state events such as the yearly Odwira festival and, of course, with the celebration of mortuary customs. Their precise nature and posthumous destination were certainly open to speculation, but such issues, far from being a matter of esoteric knowledge, were part of lived experience. As late as the 1940s, Meyerowitz was able to observe that 'to-day all *rites de passage*—conception, birth, marriage and death—are governed largely by *ntoro* in most parts of Asante and the southern Akan states'.[41] Historically, both the *kra* and the *ntoro* were regularly and solemnly 'washed' (*dware*), a ritual undertaken on a weekly basis and with a high degree of elaboration for kings, or *amanhene*, whose soul, broadly defined, was identified with that of the entire kingdom. A visible manifestation of the *kra* was the existence of *akrafo*. First reported on the coast in the eighteenth century and distinguished by their wearing of a large gold pectoral disc, *akrafo* (sing. *okra*) were young men and women who acted as the spiritual guardian of the *kra* of an *omanhene* or other royal and were responsible for its washing. Reportedly well looked after, highly respected and exempt from the obligations of ordinary subjects, they were, however, destined to be immolated upon the death of their master.[42] Whether this was because of their role as an embodied manifestation of the royal *kra* or for the more instrumental reason that, as intimate palace attendants, it was in their interest to preserve the life of their master, is a matter of interpretation. What is clear is that the logic of human sacrifice was propelled by a belief that the *asamando* existed as a shadowy replication of the known world, or *wiase* (lit. 'under the sun'). It was, that is, a realm in which kings would remain as kings and slaves as slaves, and where the former would continue to require the services of the latter. Carefully strangled to prevent the shedding of any blood, Basel Mission pastor Theophilus Opoku reported from the Akan kingdom of Akuapem in 1906, the executed *akrafo* had in the past been interred in the royal grave in order to show that they remained 'in the hands of their royal Superior or Master for life and for death'.[43] This was perhaps the most explicit example of the impress of political power upon conceptions of body and soul.

One further embodied element must also be noted: *sasa* (variously, *sesa* or *sisa*), defined by Rattray as 'the invisible spiritual power of a person or animal, which disturbs the mind of the living, or works a spell or mischief upon them'.[44] How *sasa* relates to the four-way conceptual design of personhood is far from clear, as a number of early sources appear mistakenly to conflate it with one or the other of those elements. Wilhelm Müller, who served as chaplain at the Danish fort in the Fetu region in the 1660s, was led to believe that *sasa* was the 'immortal soul' of the deceased, although in his accompanying Twi vocabulary defined it with more accuracy as 'an evil spirit'.[45] Likewise, A. B. Ellis, some two centuries later, thought that 'when a man dies his *kra* becomes a *sisa*', although, again, was closer to the mark when explaining that, after a death, 'the *sisa* can remain in the house with the corpse it lately tenanted as a *kra*, and can annoy and living and cause sickness'.[46] One crucial characteristic of *sasa*, as identified by Rattray, was that it was the one spiritual element that was unambiguously shared by humans with other living things, including trees.[47] It is therefore likely to be *sasa* that is being referred to in seventeenth-century accounts of the metempsychosis of souls; Ellis, too, was led to understand that it could 'sometimes enter the bodies of ferocious or mischievous animals for the purpose of gratifying revenge, and injuring those who have in former days injured the human bodies in which they lived'.[48] As the mystical element released by death which posed the greatest immediate danger to the living, it was *sasa*, therefore, which needed carefully to be neutralized by mortuary ritual. Such ritual extended to the conducting of funeral rites for spiritually powerful animals (*sasa mmoa*) and, as we have seen, for certain trees. 'Persons who are always taking life have to be particularly careful to guard against *sasa* influence', Rattray noted, 'and it is among them that its action is mainly seen, e.g. among executioners, hunters, butchers, and ... sawyers—who cut down the great forest trees'.[49]

That these mystical components of being were understood to go off in different directions after death raises an important question: To what extent did the posthumous 'soul' retain a sense of personhood? 'We asked where they go and where their body journeys when they have passed away and are dead', de Marees wrote. 'They answered that it is quite dead and they do not know of any resurrection on the Last Day, as we do. They do know that they go to another world when they die (although they do not know where) and in that respect their condition is different from that of Animals; but they are unable to explain to you the place where they go, whether it be under the ground or up in Heaven.'[50] Müller was also confronted by this uncertainty: 'Regarding the article of the resurrection of the dead, they believe that man's soul, which they call *essessan* [i.e., *sasa*?], is immortal, but they can give no information about the condition of souls after this life'. The general opinion, he noted, was that 'after casting off their mortal coil they come to a wonderful country, especially if someone has led a good life here and committed no sin or evil... but if someone has led an evil life and thus left behind no good name, their pagan opinion is that he can nowhere rest or have a permanent abode, but must wander from one place to another as a ghost'. Some, however, 'hold that the soul of the deceased, after the opinion of Pythagoras, enters a dumb beast, a lion, tiger, dog, cat or ape'—Müller citing an episode when a *caboceer*, observing the behaviour of a baboon on board an English ship, 'was quite convinced that the soul of an old woman who had recently died at Fetu had entered the animal'.[51] For the French mariner Jean Barbot, 'some believe that the soul perishes together with the body, as in the case of animals, some say that they do not know where it goes; and others that people's souls are incorporated into animals without their essence being changed'.[52] For Bosman, as we have seen, transmigration was not between humans and animals but between different kinds of humans: 'others are persuaded that after Death, they are transported to the Land of the Blacks or Whites, and changed into white Men: this is somewhat like the *Metempsychosis* of *Pythagoras*, and serves to hint how much more honourable they account the white Man beyond themselves.'[53]

By the standards of emerging Enlightenment thought, the hesitation of Africans to pronounce definitively on the posthumous fate of the soul can only be described as sensible. As a contemporary writer, Sir Thomas Browne, ruefully observed, 'a Dialogue between two Infants in the womb concerning the state of this world, might handsomely illustrate our ignorance of the next'.[54] Or, as an Akan proverb puts it, *asaman, wonko nsan mma*, 'the afterworld is not a place one can visit and return from again'.[55] For the Akan, as for the Ga, Ewe and others, the fundamental thing about the dominion of the dead was its striking similarity to that of the living. '*Srahmanadzi* is like the world', Ellis was told by his Fante-Twi speaking informants, 'with towns, villages, forests, mountains, rivers, etc. It is believed to be beneath the earth, and to be less bright than the world of the living'.[56] If the *kra* was understood to ascend via the ladder of death skyward to Onyame, however, it is far from clear that the *sunsum* descended to a gloomy netherworld. In contrast to Ellis, earlier accounts suggest that *asamando* was thought to be located neither above nor below the world of the living but laterally to it. When Müller inquired in Fetu where the land of the dead was, most people 'answer that there is a distant path behind Accania'—that is, beyond the Akan kingdoms of the forest to the north.[57] This was confirmed by Bosman, who wrote that 'the Deceased are immediately conveyed to a famous River, situate in the Inland Country, called *Bosmanque*'. That is, to the sacred Lake Bosomtwi in Asante, a watery manifestation of the *obosom* Twe, or Twe Akowuakra: 'Twe, to whom all those departing this life must say farewell'.[58] There, 'their God enquires what sort of Life they have lived'; if virtuous, 'they are gently wafted over the River', but if not, 'his God plunges him into the River, where he is Drowned and Buried in Eternal Oblivion'.[59] For the Ga, too, the passage to the afterlife was understood to be a lateral movement across a body of water, sometimes perceived to be in the interior to the north and sometimes to be the River Volta to the east.[60]

A vernacular text published and translated by the pioneering missionary linguist J. G. Christaller in his 1881 Twi dictionary under the entry for *asaman* brings a number of these issues together, and raises some new ones:

> It is said: In the realm of the dead there are kings as well as subjects (slaves). If you were sick in this world for a long time, you will be restored to health there after three years; but one who died in battle or by accident will be well again . . . in a month or so. It is said: the realm of the dead is below (in the earth) [*fam*]; some say: it is above (in heaven) [*soro*]; about this there is no surety. Where one is taken to, when one dies, there his spirit [*saman*] is; when you die and they take you to the spirits' grove [*asamanpow*], then your spirit is in the grove. The town (or country) of the spirits [*nsamanfo no kurom*] is not in the grove, but in the earth; it is a large town (city) a long way off, and in going there a mountain has to be ascended. The way of one who died a common death [*owu wu-pa*] is dark in heaven; but if one who died in battle or by accident takes that way, some of the white clay, with which he is rubbed, drops down, therefore his way (the milky way) appears white. In the spirits' grove the departed spirits do not stay always; only on certain single days they come and assemble there for drinking or eating or playing.[61]

'In Akan conceptions', the Ghanaian philosopher Kwame Gyekye argues, 'what exists is primarily spiritual. There is a firm belief in the world of spirits (*asamando*), where all the dead live a kind of life patterned on the earthly one'.... Thus, the Akan belief in disembodied survival in the form of a spirit or soul presupposes a nonmaterial conception of a human being. The ontological pull of the Akan language towards materialism is consequently enfeebled'.[62] Gyekye's analysis requires qualification. Not *all* the dead did continue to live on as *nananom asamanfo*, hallowed ancestors. Both Bosman and Christaller point to the fact that reaching the afterworld was far from easy: the former to a degree of eschatological 'judgement', which often turned on the manner of death; the latter to the existence of the *asamanpow*, the 'accursed grove' on the edge of every settlement where the corpses of those deemed unfit for ancestral status were unceremoniously dumped and which continued to be haunted by eerie revenants. Like the world of the living, the dominion of the dead was shaped by kinship—but it was one where hierarchy and inequality too lived on.

3

Speaking of Death

THE SECOND HALF OF the seventeenth century was a time of profound change in the political landscape of the Akan forest. By the 1660s, two states, Denkyira in the central Ofin-Pra river basin and Akwamu in the hinterland of the eastern Gold Coast, had risen to a position of dominance in each region. Both were important suppliers of commodities to the European outposts on the coast, principally gold and slaves, respectively, and both in exchange imported firearms in order to expand their military capacity and strengthen centralized political power. The era of the gradual settlement of the forest and the consolidation of localized 'estates' by agricultural and gold-mining entrepreneurs was being supplanted by one characterized by the forging of kingdoms and an increasingly elaborated political culture. By the dawn of the eighteenth century, the fortunes of Akwamu and Denkyira had diverged: whereas the former had exercised its new-found military prowess by conquering the neighbouring Ga kingdom and extending its reach to the Atlantic seaboard, the former had been overwhelmed by a military alliance led by one of its own tributaries, the upstart estate of Kumasi, in the region of Kwaman. That alliance came to be known as Asante, whose subsequent imperial expansion would represent the apotheosis of Akan state-building. The violence on the eastern Gold Coast, where by 1730 Akwamu power would, in turn, be overthrown, we will return to in a subsequent chapter. Here our concern is the rise of the Asante forest kingdom and what oral histories of that epochal event have to say about death, dying and the dead. The focus will be on an aspect of Akan mortuary culture touched on in the previous chapters: the ways in which death was spoken about or, as was often the case, *not* spoken about.

Asante tradition records that the kingdom was forged by the combined genius of two men: Osei Tutu, the *omanhene* of Kumasi and then the first Asantehene, and Komfo Anokye, the ritual specialist or 'priest' (*okomfo*)

Anokye; these two were ably assisted by a third figure, the military commander Amankwatia. Theirs is a history that was familiar throughout Asante across the centuries, one endlessly recounted at firesides alongside the mythic cycles of *odamankomasem* and *anansesem* and the traditions of settlement of families, clans and stools. It was also one of interest to the European trading companies on the Gold Coast, which were eager to forge commercial links with the new power in the interior and whose written records permit a chronological frame to be placed on events. Yet it is a history that is characterized too by silences, contradictions and interpretive complexities, nowhere more so than with respect to the death of Osei Tutu during a military campaign against the neighbouring Akyem kingdoms in 1717. For the Asante, that was a calamity of such magnitude that it could never openly be spoken of and was alluded to only by way of elaborate circumlocution. Such was the horror and silence surrounding the event that for many years modern historians were uncertain about its exact date and, even if an Asantehene did perish on the Pra River in 1717, whether that Asantehene was in fact Osei Tutu. Unsurprisingly, the death of Osei Tutu continues readily to be told by the descendants of his Akyem enemies, for whom it was a great victory: I have myself heard it recounted with gusto on a number of occasions. The Akyem, in turn, employ the same hushed tones and lexical avoidance to refer to the calamitous death of their own kings, whose decapitated heads joined that of the defeated Denkyirahene Ntim Gyakari in the ossuary of the royal mausoleum in Kumasi as treasured mnemonics for the implacable nature of Asante imperial power.[1]

Speaking openly about death in many cultures has historically been fraught with a certain mystical danger. This was most pronounced with regard to the death of kings, whose role as the embodiment of the state served to heighten that danger to an unparalleled degree and called for intricate and sustained mortuary ritual in order to control and neutralize it. Akan orality, in common with that of many non-literate societies, was profoundly shaped by a recognition of the ambivalent nature of the spoken word. For the Akan, the word held power, but also, when used inappropriately, grave peril. The Twi language was hedged by a complex array of verbal taboos: the two principal categories were *ammodin* (unmentionable words) and *ntam* (oaths), but a range of other linguistic features such as *kwatisem* (avoidance terms), *kasakoa* (metaphor), *akutia* (innuendo) and *ebe* (proverb) all served to contain the potency of the word. For the Fante, for example, *ammodin* included words for such everyday (but symbolically potent) objects as *womma* (pestle), *waduro* (mortar) and *prae* (broom). It was in the political realm, however, that the strictures on orality were most apparent. The rigorous enforcement of laws governing appropriate language is well attested throughout the historical record, particularly with respect to one topic: *owu*—death. It was in the matter of the mortality of the powerful that lexical avoidance was at its most elaborated. No great chief or royal, as already noted, was ever said to have 'died' (*wawu*); rather, their passing was reported metaphorically as *odupon kese atutu*, 'a great tree has fallen', *nana ko akuraa*, '*nana* has gone to the village' or, adding a further layer of circumlocution, *okyeame ho dodo no*, 'the *okyeame* (the chief's linguist) is indisposed'.[2] Even ordinary folk did not 'die'; *yereto ne mme*, it was said: 'palm trees [for use at the funeral] are being felled'.

It was the loathsome spectre of death which was evoked by the swearing of an oath. *Ntam* took a variety of forms. Perhaps the most common was that known as *nsedie*, by which the uttering of the name of a particular *obosom* served to bring the deadly wrath of the deity down on either the speaker or the person against whom the oath was spoken, if a stated covenant was broken or a declaration was untrue. As the verbal oath was often underpinned by the ingestion of some sanctified substance, this was known by Europeans in the era of the slave trade and beyond as 'eating fetish'. From as early as the sixteenth century, sources point to the gravity with which eating fetish was regarded, whether as a result of a mundane dispute or as a tool of statecraft. As reported by de Marees in 1602, if a husband suspected a wife of being unfaithful, 'he confronts her with it and makes her eat salt on it, with some other conjuration of her Idol or Fetissos. The woman will gladly take the oath if she knows she is not to blame . . . but if she knows that she is not innocent, she will not dare to take the oath, fearing that her Fetisso will kill her for taking a false oath; in that manner she betrays herself and it all leads to a separation from her Husband'.[3] That same dread was observed in 1753 by British governor Thomas Melvil, as he struggled to forge a treaty with Fante notables: 'They are a faithless and rapacious people. A consciousness of this appeared when they drank the Fettish, no sooner did the Braffoe's Son and Curranteers see the Fettish water, than their countenances altered, a sudden tremor seized 'em, and such a languor that they had scarcely spirits to pronounce the words of the Oath, and put their hands to the paper'.[4] That Europeans readily conformed to the local culture of oathing in order to oil the wheels of merchant capitalism serves to underline its importance; indeed, the oath can be seen as a central dynamic of the cross-cultural coastal space in which, as Pietz argues, the hybrid notion of the 'fetish' itself emerged.

Ntam also took the form of oaths associated with particular corporate groups, whether a family, clan, chiefly office (stool) or entire *oman*, or kingdom. Rather than directly invoking a named deity, such oaths evoked a remembered—but never openly spoken of—calamity of the past. As in medieval and early modern Europe, where 'God's bones' or 'God's wounds' ('zounds!') were the most powerful profanities, *ntam* often referred to particular body parts.[5] These may have alluded to a remembered injury to a revered ancestor, but more broadly reflected a perception of the sacredness of the human body and a sensitivity towards talking aloud about it. At the level of the state, however, the *ntam* was invariably a euphemistic allusion to a catastrophic military defeat, typically in the form of the location of that calamity coupled with the day of the week on which it occurred. Each kingdom had its 'great oath' or *ntam kese*, and the most famous of all was that of Asante, which alluded to the death of Osei Tutu. Such was its gravity that the actual formulation was rarely, if ever, uttered—the euphemism having its own circumlocutions. Joseph Dupuis, a British envoy who visited Kumasi in 1820, witnessed a pronouncement of the *ntam kese*, and his account remains unsurpassed in the historical record in capturing the power of the word for the Akan:

> The words, as recorded, are deemed too profane to utter, unless in a whisper between friends; and this redoubtable oath is most commonly taken by inference only, as, the dreadful day, the days of God's chastisement, etc. The effect of these expressions only, as I have witnessed at the court, clouds every brow with woe, from the king to the slave who stands behind his chair. Many fly from the presence,—such, for instance, who are not men of influence . . . Others cover their faces with both hands, uttering at the time a charm or invocation to the patron Gods to shield them from the ominous import of those words, and the effects of the king's wrath or sorrow.[6]

Such was its power that the *ntam kese* had its own personified identity; as one early twentieth-century Akan observer wrote, 'it is worshipped like a god'.[7]

All of this stood in contrast to speaking of the ancestral dead themselves, whose names reverberated endlessly through formalized public pronouncement and everyday discourse. Key vehicles for the former were royal praise poems (in Asante, *apaee*) and funeral dirges, both of which featured the 'strong names' and heroic deeds of the hallowed dead.[8] It was quotidian conversation with the dead, however, which perhaps best underlined the profound belief that, as for the ancient Egyptians, 'one lives after death if the name is mentioned'.⁹ This reflexive referencing of the dead is noted throughout the historical record, but evocatively captured by Thomas Kyei in his memoir of a childhood in early colonial Asante. Recalling his great-grandmother's 'unbounded pride' in her *abusua*, or matrilineage, Kyei wrote that 'whenever she mentioned the name of some of her departed relatives, the old woman raised herself slightly up [from] her wooden stool and said, "*Asomasi, mete ne soa, masoore!*" ("So-and-so, I rise in his/her honour!")'.¹⁰ For the Akan, real horror lay in the opposite: for one's name to be neglected, forgotten or intentionally obliterated from the historical record. The result was posthumous isolation—to be 'lost'.

———

In January 1896, Asantehene Agyeman Prempeh was arrested by a British expeditionary force and exiled to the Gold Coast, where he and other members of the royal court were detained as political prisoners for a year before being relocated to Sierra Leone and then, in 1900, to the Seychelles. It was there, in 1907, that the deposed Asantehene began to compile the *atetesem*, the historical traditions, of the ruling Oyoko dynasty of the forest kingdom. Based in large part on the encyclopaedic knowledge of his mother, the Asantehemaa (or 'Queen Mother') Yaa Kyaa, 'The History of Ashanti Kings and the Whole Country Itself' is the earliest authoritative recension of Asante origins and perhaps the first example of history writing in English by any African ruler.¹¹ Its opening cycles, Wilks has noted, 'display a remarkable awareness of the transformation of society from one dominated by hunters to one dominated by cultivators'.¹² At the beginning of the world—when 'the thing to do is hunting'—a hunter went into the forest and encountered a ratel, or honeybadger, which informed him that people would soon be arriving on the earth. Sure enough, a gold chain descended from the sky, down which climbed a herald, a women bearing a stool and then Ankyewa Nyame, the apical ancestress of the Oyoko lineage or *abusua*. Ankyewa Nyame settled at Asantemanso in the Adanse region, where other people appeared from holes in the ground to join her: 'the first came, and she was nearly bear a child [*sic*] and at that time people can go to heaven, and return afterwards'. This was a time, that is, of the advent of human reproduction—but before that of death. It is notable that the pregnant woman was already in possession of a medicine called *damtua* and two *asuman*, sacred powers manifested as protective amulets, one of which, named

Kwabena, would continue to be worn exclusively by royal wives during pregnancy to ensure a successful birth.[13]

Subsequent cycles continue the narrative of incremental human increase among the Oyoko and the elaboration of the broader Akan social order. Ankyewa Nyame gave birth to a daughter, Birempomaa Piese, who in turn had ten children; meanwhile, other settlers were drawn into the Oyoko ambit. By now, however, death was beginning to make its presence felt: Ankyewa Nyame and Birempomaa Piese both died at Asantemanso, as did the latter's three sons, who succeeded in turn to the headship of the family. It was a son of one of these, named Kwabia Anwanfi, who determined that the Oyoko must disperse from Asantemanso in order to find new living space. Overcrowded and threatened by rising death rates ('for all their families finished dieing' there, Prempeh recorded), the Oyoko moved first to nearby Kokofu and then, under Kwabia Anwanfi's successor Oti Akenten, to Kwaman.[14] There, they used gold to purchase a tract of land from its original owner and founded the settlement of Kumasi, 'under (*ase*) the *kum* tree'. 'The protohistoric period', Wilks writes, 'is giving way to the historic; Oti Akenten was succeeded by Obiri Yeboa, and Obiri Yeboa by Osei Tutu, first Asantehene, whose death in 1717 is reported in contemporary European sources'.[15] The Oyoko tradition of origin is consistent with those of the other great exogamous matriclans, whose ancestresses are also remembered to have either descended from the sky or emerged from the ground in the same region. The vertical axis underpinned their rights as first peoples, just as the inhumation of the dead served further to humanize and lay claim to the land. So too can all these apical ancestresses be traced back four or five generations from historically identifiable figures in the late seventeenth or early eighteenth centuries, a correspondence which, according to Wilks, strongly suggests that the Akan social order coalesced in the forest heartland in the course of the sixteenth century.[16]

It was as part of its account of the reign of Oti Akenten that *The History of Ashanti Kings* introduces the figure of Osei Tutu. Osei Tutu was the son of one of Birempona Piese's granddaughters, Manu, and generally regarded as a nephew of Oti Akenten and his successor Obiri Yeboa. The ancestress of all subsequent Asantehenes, Manu is notable too for being the first Asante royal about whose funeral custom anything is recorded: 'When Manu the mother of the great King Ossai Tutu died, the body was put at Ajusuo so that those people will have a look on the body'.[17] The context for this tradition suggests that it sought to assert the subordinate status of the Anyinase branch of the

Oyoko settled at Kokofu Adweso ('Ajusuo'), who 'were not the real Yukus, but they were as a nurse to the real Yukus'; whatever that precise relationship was, the laying out of Manu's body at Adweso points to the importance of the right to look upon a corpse as a mark of kinship and belonging. It is in the context of Oti Akenten's purchase of the land at Kwaman, too, that 'The History of Ashanti Kings' first mentions the existence of the kingdom of Denkyira, whose kings, we know from Dutch sources, dominated the region from their capital Abankeseso, some forty miles to the southwest, by the late 1650s. After the Oyoko's move to Kwaman, Denkyirahene Boamponsem demanded that Oti Akenten pay an annual tribute in palm oil as well as send one of his family as a hostage in order to guarantee his tributary status. That hostage was Osei Tutu, who was accompanied to Abankeseso by seven servants, among them Amankwatia as his 'chair bearer' (i.e., *akonnwasoafo*, stool carrier). Their fate, from the outset, would be entangled with that of Denkyira.[18]

The relationship between Boamponsem and Osei Tutu was initially cordial but in time deteriorated. As is so often the case in Akan oral histories, the catalyst for political breakdown was remembered as sexual transgression: either Boamponsem seduced Osei Tutu's wife or, according to the pioneering Ga historian Carl Reindorf, Osei Tutu seduced Boamponsem's sister.[19] Either way, Osei Tutu and his servants fled back to Kumasi before seeking refuge in Akwamu to the east. It is around this point in the narrative, as Oti Akenten's successor Obiri Yeboa was preparing to make war against the neighbouring estate of Domaa, that Komfo Anokye enters the picture. Reindorf has Komfo Anokye, 'the far-famed fetish priest . . . who was full of magical powers', being invited to Denkyira by Boamponsem in order to cure his only sister's barrenness and thereby to produce an heir; 'The History of Ashanti Kings' first has him prophesizing that Obiri Yeboa's planned campaign against Domaa would end in defeat and therefore escorting Osei Tutu to safety in Akwamu.[20] Despite the difference in detail, both accounts emphasize his role in mobilizing ritual power in support of Osei Tutu's successful military campaigns against his immediate neighbours and, ultimately, in the epochal Asante victory over their Denkyira overlords.

The broad thrust of events as detailed in the oral histories is confirmed by the written records of Europeans on the Gold Coast, whose imports of munitions were keenly sought by the competing forces in the forest interior. Denkyirahene Boamponsem was well known to the Dutch: Bosman reported on the circumstances of his death in 1694 (on which more below), as well as having heard a version of his confrontation with Osei Tutu over their respective sexual prerogatives.[21] Dutch sources also name Osei Tutu and Amankwatia as the leading figures of the emerging Asante military coalition. In the east, Akwamu too was known by the European companies as a lucrative market for firearms and a pioneer in their use, and it is notable, as Reindorf observed, that Osei Tutu's sojourns there and in Denkyira provided him with 'the opportunity of acquiring the politics of the two principal powers then existing'.[22]

There is, however, no explicit mention of Komfo Anokye either in contemporary European records or in any subsequent written source until the end of the nineteenth century; indeed, the earliest mention of the 'far-famed fetish priest' by name was in Reindorf's *History*, published in 1895. Given the subsequent acknowledgement of Komfo Anokye's pivotal role in the emergence of Asante, this absence has given pause to the forest kingdom's leading historians.[23] Did Komfo Anokye actually exist? Or, as McCaskie has argued, is his existence less important than his cognitive role throughout Asante history 'as a matrix or force field within which the sanctioned definitions of ordered society can be located and fixed'?[24] Wilks dismissed such hermeneutical inquiry as 'highly obscure and unrewarding'.[25] Yet it is of importance to our interests here, precisely because it is around the figure of Komfo Anokye that a range of concerns about the management of death in an increasingly ordered society begin to emerge.

Neither were these concerns limited to the subsequent reification of Komfo Anokye in Asante as demiurgic lawgiver and ur-*okomfo*. For it seems likely that by the late 1690s, rumour of the famed priest's magical prowess had reached the Gold Coast. In his chapter on African religion and as part of his explanation of 'Notions of a Future State', Bosman included the following passage:

> The Inland Negroes make those Blacks who live amongst us believe, that a great Feticheer or Priest lives in a very fine House with them; of which they relate nothing but Miracles: They affirm, that he commands the Weather, that he can make it come down soft or hard at his Pleasure and drive it out again; that though his House is without any Roof, yet it is always sheltered from Rain; that he not only knows all things past, but can as accurately foretell all future Events as if they were present before his Eyes, and Cures all sorts of Distempers . . . It is before this Negroe, his Country-Men assert, that those who die thereabouts have to appear to be examined by him; upon which if they are found to have led a good Life, he sends them away in Peace to a happy Place: but if on the contrary, he kills them a second time with a Club made on purpose for that use, and placed before his dwelling

Place, that it always be ready at Hand. From hence you may easily inferr, whether this Negroe is not incredibly Reverenced and Esteemed by his Country-men; and indeed they look upon him as a sort of Demi-God: So slyly hath this Rogue insinuated this great Opinion of himself into the Minds of his Neighbours that (this being no old Story, the Priest at present living) they every Day relate fresh Miracles of him.[26]

Is this a reference to Komfo Anokye? Is impossible to be certain, but there is every indication that it is. The figure described here certainly accords with later Asante traditions of Anokye as a miracle-working *okomfo* with a unique combination of prophetic insight, curative powers, the ability to exert control over nature, and judicial authority. In light of Anokye's role as the author of Asante's legal code—his famous '77 laws'—the last is especially notable. The judicial power of the 'great Feticheer', however, serves to complicate the matter, as it is that of a living figure pronouncing on the fate of the dead. The passage served to illustrate Bosman's discussion of the various perceptions of the posthumous fate of the soul: that is, while most Africans believed that they go to another world to live again 'in the same Character as here', some believed that they would be conveyed to Lake Bosomtwi, where they will be judged and either gently wafted to 'a Land abounding in all kinds of Happiness' or plunged into the water and eternal oblivion. As we have seen, others, still, believed that they might go either to 'the Land of the Blacks or Whites'. Wilks and McCaskie deal with this problem in different ways. For Wilks, the explanation lies in the likelihood that 'Bosman's informants, employees of the Dutch, had been made well aware that Christian morality rested upon the notion of a Day of Judgement and . . . obligingly introduced the idea into their reports about the interior.'[27] This cannot be discounted, although the understanding that the 'soul' underwent interrogation before being permitted to proceed to *asamando* was not necessarily derived from Christian eschatology, even on the Gold Coast. Such a notion of 'exclusion' had long existed also in the forest interior, well beyond the reach of Christian ideas, and has been identified elsewhere in Africa as well.[28] McCaskie makes that point, noting too the parallels between Bosman's account and the custom of post-mortem trial, 'whereby an accused corpse might be (*a*) cleared, and sent to the ancestors in *asaman* or (*b*) found guilty, and thrown headless into *asamanpow*, "the abode of ghosts"'.[29]

Neither of these readings is entirely satisfactory—but the interpretive problem is intractable. It may be that Bosman's local interlocutors conflated cosmological notions of the afterlife with rumours of a miracle-working prophet: that the *okomfo*'s roofless house was mysteriously 'always sheltered from Rain', it might be noted, accords with the perceived nature of deceased ancestors' dwellings in *asamando*. Whether that reported individual was the demiurgic Komfo Anokye or not, what can be said with certainty is that *akomfo*, charged with mediating the relationship between the social order and the invisible realm of spiritual power, were intimately concerned with life and death, with the boundary between corporeal existence and physical dissolution.[30] Such matters adhere repeatedly to the figure of Komfo Anokye in the corpus of traditions which trace his miraculous feats from his encounter with Osei Tutu in Akwamu to their return to Kumasi, the early military campaigns against the rival estates surrounding Kwaman and on to the victory over Denkyira and his mediating role in the appearance of the *sika dwa kofi*, 'the Golden Stool', as the vessel of the *sunsum* or soul of the emergent Asante nation.

It is notable too that the final breakdown in the relationship between Kwaman and Denkyira is remembered as arising from the circumstances surrounding the death of Boamponsem. As recorded in 'The History of Ashanti Kings', another tributary, the *oman* of Assin to the south, was required to send to Denkyira a yearly tribute of a barrel of imported European liquor. The tribute that year was delivered by one Oduro to Boamponsem, but when 'the servants opened the barrel and as the king was presenting his glass to be filled, a big fly came out and flew away. His servants said "Do not drink this liquor master", but the King disobeyed and drank some. When the King drunk, he got fever, [from] which he afterwards died'.[31] This event can be dated to circa 1694, as it was cited by Bosman in support of his discussion of the importance of post-mortem inquiry into the cause of death among the coastal Akan. 'For though 'tis probable and apparent that he dyed a Natural Death, occasioned either by sickness, extreme old Age, Wounds, or some Mortal Distemper', Bosman explained, 'this will not satisfy them in the least; it must certainly proceed from some other Cause, according to the Proverb, *Death is never without a Cause*; which is no where in the world better believed than here'.[32] Such was the case in 1694, when, with both Dutch and Brandenburger trade emissaries present at the Denkyira court, Boamponsem died, an event which 'exposed their Lives to the utmost danger; for the Relations of the Deceased, ridiculously supposing they had occasioned his Death, seized and bound them; after which they made enquiry by their Priests whether the Present they brought were not poisoned or conjured'.[33] The *akomfo* pronounced them innocent—presumably because, according to Oyoko tradition, it was Oduro of Assin who was found to have killed Boamponsem with the poisoned liquor. Oduro escaped and fled to Kumasi, where Osei Tutu refused to surrender him or to pay a fine imposed as punishment by the new Denkyirahene, Ntim Gyakari. Both sides prepared for the inevitable war.

It is unnecessary to rehearse a blow-by-blow account of the preparation for war, the conflict itself or its aftermath. The unfolding of events between 1699 and 1701 was monitored from the Gold Coast by the Dutch, who were keen to supply muskets to the warring parties and to ensure an ongoing commercial relationship with whoever should prevail.[34] Yet Oyoko traditions place less emphasis on gunpowder technology than on the prowess of Komfo Anokye's magical arsenal in overcoming the superior military capacity of the Denkyira enemy. 'The History of Ashanti Kings' details 'the principal wonders done by prophet Annochi' in aid of the war effort: these include turning himself into a woman and making love with Ntim Gyakari in order to sap his manly strength, secreting a medicine in the enemy camp and, perhaps most emblematically, demonstrating mastery over the forest environment once the battle had commenced by wondrously increasing the size of trees in order to absorb the Denkyira fusillades.[35]

Such deeds are common to traditional histories of apparently heaven-sent victories in many parts of the world, their miraculous nature employed to explain not only the turn of events but, with the benefit of hindsight, their inevitability.[36] Yet they are also devices which can be seen to encapsulate, albeit fantastically, documented historical processes. One is of particular relevance to us here, as it addresses the issue of the emerging sovereignty on the part of Akan leaders over life and death: the 'miracle' by which Komfo Anokye sought to alleviate the numerical preponderance of Denkyira's forces by attracting dissident elements within the kingdom to the Kwaman cause. The matter concerns certain groups subjugated by Denkyira during its rise to regional dominance which were retained as *akyere*, that is, captives destined for sacrifice at royal funerals or at key moments in the ritual calendar. These captives, Reindorf records, were called 'red clay people' or 'Bontwumafo' (i.e., 'Bo[amponsem's] *ntwoma fo*'—*ntwoma* being the ochre-coloured clay used to decorate the face and bodies of the bereaved at funerals and of *akyere* destined for ritual immolation) and their treatment, according to some of his Asante informants, was a crucial factor in the defeat of Denkyira.[37] Ntim Gyakari, Reindorf recounts, took a wife from the servile Bontwumafo, and when his mother fell mortally ill, the wife warned her kinfolk of their impending immolation at her funeral custom. 'The whole tribe now fled for protection to the Asantes', who 'on that account stayed away from the funeral'—both actions tantamount to an act of open rebellion.[38] Asante stool histories attest that other groups followed the lead of the Bontwumafo in fleeing the despotism of Ntim Gyakari to join Osei Tutu's emerging coalition. These demographic movements proved crucial as the final battle was joined at Feyiase in 1701. In November of that year, news reached the Dutch that 'the Assjanteese'—the first appearance of the term in the historical record—'had a complete victory over the Dinquirase'.[39] The Dutch dispatched a European officer to the Asante camp, where, according to Bosman, the victors amassed an enormous plunder, with 'Zay's [i.e., Osei Tutu's] Booty alone amounting to several thousand Marks of Gold'. 'Thus you see the towering Pride of *Dinkera* in Ashes, they being forced to fly before those, whom they not long before thought no better than their Slaves, and themselves now being sold for Slaves.'[40] "The King of Denkira brought 200,000 men and the Ashantis 20,000', 'The History of Ashanti Kings' records, 'but through the genius of Annochi the Ashantis defeated the people and became the leading nation over all the largest countries about it'.[41]

In contrast to the dense body of oral traditions celebrating the triumph of Osei Tutu and the forging of the Asante kingdom, the death of the first Asantehene is hedged about with circumlocution and awkward silence. 'The History of Ashanti Kings' concludes only with a vague allusion to his demise, ending *in medias res* with a discussion of the rise to prominence of the two contenders for the succession, Boa Kwatia and Opoku Ware, and signalling that the latter was the more suitable candidate. While it was certainly well understood that Osei Tutu died in the course of a military campaign against the Akyem kingdoms to the southeast, the precise circumstances were, from the very outset, rarely if ever openly spoken of and therefore of enduring dispute. His death, the Basel Mission pastor N. V. Asare reported in the early twentieth century, was 'shrouded ... in absolute secrecy. But because the war was prolonged and the people no longer saw the king, they guessed (what had happened)'.[42] Nevertheless, the early nineteenth-century British envoys Bowdich and Dupuis were both discreetly informed that Osei Tutu was shot and killed in his hammock when his rearguard was annihilated in an Akyem ambush.[43] Dupuis alone was also told—quite possibly by his interlocutors in Kumasi's resident Muslim community—that that body of the king was never recovered.

Reindorf, who consulted both authors, insisted that 'this account of the king's death is refuted by the Asantes'. 'They say', he wrote, 'the king was infirm and not in good health when forced to take the field against the rebellious Akems, and although the army was proceeding successfully in its mission, the king very unfortunately died a natural death. Opoku Ware, not informing the nobles and generals of what had taken place, coffined the remains of the monarch, and ordered it to be carried in the rear of the army'.[44] This received version of events was also conveyed to Reindorf's fellow native pastor, Rev. Asare. At the time of the Akyem war, Asare was told,

> Osei Tutu was very old; it was at this battle front that 'the great tree was uprooted', and his nephew Opoku Ware was enstooled in his stead. Osei Tutu's body was embalmed and put in a coffin. The body was then carried behind the Asante soldiers wherever they went, as if it was the force motivating the army to fight. Once, they engaged the Akyem in a very tough battle. That day the Akyem forced the Asante to retreat and in the process they nearly lost Osei Tutu's coffin. It was with great difficulty that *Kotoko* were able to escape and hide the coffin. Immediately the king venerated that day, and commemorated [it] by making an oath in memory of the great and brave king's death. This has earned Osei Tutu the appellation: '*Adaka gyeaboo; ono na wawu na n'amu di ako*' (The coffin that receives bullets; he is the dead one whose corpse still fights).[45]

A second authoritative corpus of traditions prepared by Prempeh's successor as Asantehene reiterated this account, emphasizing too the role of Komfo Anokye, who foresaw that the aged king was nearing death. 'If the king died in Asante', Anokye prophesized, 'all what he had done . . . to establish the Asante Kingdom on a firm and sure basis would be undone, and the string that bound the kingdom would break, and the kingdom would be shattered'.[46] Osei Tutu therefore agreed to take the field, possibly breaking an older custom barring rulers themselves from coming into proximity with and 'seeing' death.[47]

These studied circumlocutions and retrospective narratives led to an initial degree of confusion among modern historians of Asante. In an early paper, Wilks and co-author Margaret Priestley used European records to date the above events to 1717, but, mislead by a report—almost certainly mistaken—reaching Cape Coast of the death of the Asante king in 1712, speculated that the individual who died in 1717 was likely not to have been Osei Tutu but a successor whose brief reign was expunged from historical memory.[48] For Priestley and Wilks, the second crucial piece of evidence was Dupuis's statement that Osei Tutu's body was never recovered. That it fell into the hands of the Akyem, they argued rightly, would have constituted a disaster of the utmost gravity, 'for no relic was more highly prized, for magico-ritual purposes, than the skull of an enemy's king'. The very name of that king, therefore, 'would become a *kunorokosem*, something known but not to be mentioned, its utterance strongly tabooed (*akyiwadie*)'.[49] This thesis was critiqued and refuted by subsequent historians and, unsurprisingly, by Asantehene Osei Agyeman Prempeh II (1931–70) himself, who, Wilks later acknowledged, considered it gravely but 'assured me that we were wrong. I am now convinced that we were'.[50] Osei Agyeman Prempeh gave no consideration at all, however, to another matter raised by Wilks: a Dutch report from 1706 which appeared to suggest that an elderly Osei Tutu had abdicated power to his general, Bantamahene Amankwatia. 'He was incensed', Wilks reported, the Asantehene sternly reminding him of Amankwatia's slave origins as a humble stool bearer. '"Where did he come from? Nobody knows. Amankwatia Panin was no-one at all. It is an insult to say that Amankwatia Panin was made regent. Don't tell any Asante man that. It is bad talk."'[51]

The date and circumstances of Osei Tutu's death and the fate of his mortal remains as historical events are of less concern to us than their enshrined ideological meanings—the slightest deviation from which was deemed, as Osei Agyeman Prempeh II phrased it, 'bad talk'. As far as the Asante were concerned, their first king's smoked body was returned to Kumasi and after its dissolution his rearticulated skeleton safely installed in the royal mausoleum at Bantama—despite claims by the Akyem that they in fact possessed it.[52] His death was thereafter enveloped in the *ntam kese*, the 'great oath', the uttering of which, as witnessed by Dupuis, clouded 'every brow with woe'. 'As even the natural death of an Asante monarch is a great national calamity, that in camp is a thousand times worse', Reindorf explained. 'Hence, when any of the warriors was asked as to the rumours of the king's death, his reply was, "Mekoroe na mante" [or *mekoee dee nanso mante*] i.e. I joined the campaign, but never heard of it. This became the oath "Koromante", the most binding and dreadful of Asante oaths, which still embalms the memory of the most powerful and victorious king Osei Tutu'.[53] Other sources make a connection between the utterance *koromante* and a place name, either a nearby village or, alternatively, the coastal town of Kormantse, where a catastrophic sequence of royal deaths was said to have occurred during Asantehene Osei Tutu Kwame's military campaign against the Fante in 1807.[54] Be that as it may, the 'embalming' of Osei Tutu's death in the *ntam kese* became the most emblematic and ideologically

FIGURE 3.1. Keeping death in abeyance during wartime. Bantamahene Osei Bonsu (1901–16; later Mamponhene 1916–30) photographed by R. S. Rattray wearing a *batakari*, or battle smock, studded with protective *asuman* and Muslim amulets. Pitt Rivers Museum, University of Oxford, 1998.312.556.1; published as figure 16 of *Religion and Art in Ashanti*, facing 20.

powerful of an extensive range of verbal avoidances surrounding the topic of death and mortality. It might be suggested that the creation of highly elaborated royal funerary cultures among the Akan was a way of negotiating a matter of such gravity that it simply could not be spoken of.

By 1718, Osei Tutu's loyal stool carrier turned military commander Amankwatia too was dead. His demise was, in turn, embalmed by the oath of the Bantama stool, *Amankwatia Kwasiada*, 'Amankwatia Sunday'. For his successors as Bantamahene, the word *ntwoma*—the red clay that Amankwatia was plastered with when at one desperate moment in the conflict he offered himself up for ritual immolation—became *ammodin*, unmentionable.[55] Komfo Anokye, the oral histories recount, lived for some time into the reign of Opoku Ware, repairing as a revered figure to his home village of Agona Akyempim. It was from there that he set out to work his final miracle, one so audacious that, had he succeeded, it would have surpassed even those associated with the defeat of Denkyira: the conquest of mortality itself.[56]

Leaving Agona in charge of his nephew Kwame Siaw, Komfo Anokye announced that he would seclude himself—his corporeal body—within his house, from where his spirit would 'set out in quest of a medicine against death'. He would be absent, he warned, for seven years and seventy-seven days, 'and that during all that time no one must weep or fire a gun, or mourn for him, although he appeared to be dead'.[57] After seven years and seventy days, Rattray was told in the 1920s, Kwame Siaw declared his uncle really was dead and ordered his funeral custom to begin; the 'History of Ashanti' elaborates on Kwame Siaw's motives, insisting that he wished to possess Komfo Anokye's gold and to succeed him as Agonahene. As the funeral got underway, a passing traveller encountered a man approaching Agona, who enquired why the sounds of firing and wailing were coming from the town. On being informed that the people were celebrating the funeral of Komfo Anokye, the man said that he was Anokye and was returning having secured the secret of immortality. Komfo Anokye pointed out a small *otwe* antelope (Maxwell's duiker) and directed the traveller to kill it and bring him the hide, from which he fashioned a *nkontwima*, the strip of leather used by *akomfo* to resolve intractable issues; if people wanted to look into the future, he said, then from now on they should use the *nkontwima*. He then asked the traveller to inform the people that he had been successful in his quest to secure the secret of immortality, but because of the disobedience of Kwame Siaw and the Agona, 'he would go away for ever, and the Ashanti would never find the medicine against death, whose great taboo was the holding of a funeral custom'.[58] Komfo Anokye then disappeared from the earth, the location of the encounter coming to be called *owuoso*, 'the place of death'. Once again, folly, disobedience and greed combined to ensure that humankind remained beholden to *owu*'s all-conquering sway.

4

Grief and Mourning

CHARLES BANNERMAN WAS the Gold Coast's first African newspaperman. Born in 1828, he was the eldest son of James Bannerman, Accra's leading merchant in the first half of the nineteenth century, and Yaa Hom, a daughter of Asantehene Osei Yaw Akoto. In 1857, Charles founded the *Accra Herald* (later the *West African Herald*), where in 1859 he published an autobiographical account of his childhood education in England and of a visit home, aged 13, in 1841. What made this visit so memorable was that he was greeted on arrival by the sad news that one of his aunts had just died. 'According to the custom of this country you must see her before she is buried', his father told him. 'Go, then, with this girl and see the body.'

> I was taken through the town to a large stone house. On entering the court of this dwelling, I observed appearances of great activity. Great number of females of all ages were going to and fro, some carrying little stools, some with flasks of liquor, others carrying cases with decanters in them. They were smoking, many of them, some were half tipsy, and all were in very high spirits. The scene upstairs was very different. I passed through a long gallery and a large hall into a handsomely fitted up bedroom. This hall and gallery were crowded with native women, on the countenances of whom sat unmistakable signs of grief. The bedroom was filled also with females. On a large bed lay the figure of a mulatto lady calmly reposing in death. She was covered with valuable gold ornaments. Rings glittered on her cold fingers, beautiful bracelets shone on her wrists; splendid chains round her neck, and a doubloon had been tied over each eye. The body was dressed in the gayest raiment. The moment I entered the room, low moans broke out from several ladies present, and many of the attendants bust out crying. I was led up to the side of the bed and made to put my hand on the hand of my dead

aunt. . . . That day she was buried, and the noise, and bustle and excitement of an African funeral were for the first time . . . presented to my notice. All that day, all that night, and for a week after, there was continual drumming, and shouting and firing of muskets and drinking of rum, and visiting and after an interval of 3 weeks, all this drumming, firing, drinking, and shouting, began again, and was renewed again and again at intervals during nearly a year.[1]

This chapter considers the most striking aspect of the scene that greeted the young Charles Bannerman as he entered his late aunt's house: the dominant role of women in managing the newly dead and in exuberant expressions of grief and rituals of mourning. Entangled with the gendered dynamics of grief and mourning is a second theme: the sensory spectacle of funeral celebrations. That the deceased was in this instance a woman—and an elite Euro-African woman from Accra, at that—does not make it a peculiar case; the prominence of women in the management of death was quite typical throughout the Gold Coast, the Akan forest and into the savanna beyond.[2] So too was the startling juxtaposition of grief and gaiety in funeral celebrations, the combination of 'very high spirits' and 'unmistakable signs of grief', that struck Bannerman. Neither of these features was unique to local funerary cultures: distinctions in gender roles with regard to the expression of grief and to scripted mourning rituals have been noted across time in many parts of the world, while revelry has been observed as a characteristic of African American funerals in the slave and post-emancipation societies of the New World.[3] Less attention, however, has been paid to these aspects of bereavement in West Africa itself. In what ways did gender roles inform grief and mourning among the Akan and their neighbours? What explains the widely reported combination of intense lamentation and explosive revelry in funeral celebrations?

Any attempt to consider these matters from a historical perspective must be framed by the rich comparative literature in anthropology and sociology. An abiding concern with mortuary ritual can be traced to the emergence of social anthropology in the mid-nineteenth century, but it took definitive shape with the publication in 1907 of Robert Hertz's essay on the 'collective representation of death'.[4] A student of Émile Durkheim, Hertz used data on the Dayak of Indonesia to demonstrate how a complex sequence of obsequies served to detach the deceased from the living and then to close the resulting tear in the fabric of society. The three central actors in this drama were the corpse, the detached soul and the bereaved, whose expressions of grief, he argued, were shaped as much by culture as by reflex emotion. Hertz's seminal analysis established the agenda for much subsequent inquiry. Thus, in a major treatment of mortuary customs first published in 1979, Peter Metcalf and Richard Huntingdon returned to Hertz's central concerns with secondary burial and with the relationship between emotion and ritual.[5] Three years later, Maurice Bloch and Jonathan Parry edited a volume which focused on symbols of fertility, sexuality and rebirth in funerary rituals, criticizing Metcalf and Huntingdon for ignoring Hertz's thesis of the social construction of emotion.[6] In the second edition of their book, Metcalf and Huntingdon responded that Bloch and Parry misleadingly privileged the role of ritual as a device of social regulation and control; 'the relationship between ritual and emotion', they concluded, 'is not causally determinative in either direction' but 'mutually communicative'.[7]

These approaches offer critical insight into grief and mourning in the Akan world. The Hertzian model of the primary and secondary funeral separated by an unstable and emotionally fraught liminal period was precisely that of *amanhene* and, with a lesser degree of complexity, of most freeborn individuals not cursed with a 'bad' death. Bloch and Parry's emphasis on the link between mortuary ritual and ideas of fertility and rebirth is also prominent in Akan understandings of life and death. Underpinning the central role of women in managing the dead, it took its most elaborated form during Odwira and equivalent yearly festivals such as the Ga Homowo, when society in its entirety entered a period of intense communication with the ancestral dead. Care is needed, however, with anthropological theory, especially with regard to what McCaskie considers its 'tendency constantly to reduce *action* to *ritual*'. The action referred to here is the imprint of Asante political power and its ability to 'rupture, transgress and rewrite the cultural charter'.[8] The same might be said for more mundane forms of action exercised by ordinary people as a part of everyday lived experience. Others have made the same point, stressing the imperative to distinguish between established cultural norms, on the one hand, and the individual emotional subjectivity of loss, rage, confusion, anxiety and agony, on the other.[9] Methodological problems remain: although bringing emotion into the frame was a central goal of Ariès and other pioneering historians of death, it is not easy to gauge how people in the past really felt or how much those individual feelings can tell us about societies at large. We need to be aware, Richard J. Evans cautions, 'of the gains that can be made for historical knowledge through a focus on the history of the emotions, but also of its pitfalls'.[10]

Accounts of funeral customs on the Gold Coast dating back to the seventeenth century provide evidence for the fundamental repertoire of action and ritual triggered by the arrival of death. They tend, however, to be limited to what unfolded in the public realm, so need to be considered in combination with more recent sources in order to reconstruct the complex unfolding of the mortuary drama. If any feature of that drama can be said to be at all 'typical', it is the striking visibility of women in the display of grief and in subsequent rituals of mourning. Female domination of public space was apparent from the moment a death was announced by a sudden outburst of wailing and the ensuing eruption of women into the streets of a town or village. 'As soon as the sick Person is expired', Bosman wrote, 'they set up such a dismal Crying, Lamentation and Squeaking, that the whole Town is filled with it; by which 'tis soon published that some Body is lately dead: besides which, the youth of the Deceased's Acquaintance generally pay their last Duty of Respect to him, by firing several Musquet-Shot'.[11] Here we see the 'scenes of furious despair which take place when death sets in' noted by Hertz. 'It seems that the entire community feels itself lost, or at least directly threatened by antagonistic forces'.[12]

That was indeed the case. Yet subsequent sources suggest that far from this explosion of grief happening 'as soon as the sick person is expired', it appears to have been unleashed only once the body had carefully been prepared behind closed doors and the authorities of the town formally informed of the death. Before that, the 'funeral wail' could not happen and emotions had to be held firmly in check.[13] Within the house, elderly women of the deceased's lineage had already taken charge of the ritual washing and initial preparation of the corpse. 'The women of the *abusua*, under directions of the senior old lady, came and washed the body', M. J. Field observed of a death in Akyem Kotoku in 1938, '"for his body is theirs"'.[14]

Once the corpse was ready and the doors of the deceased's residence thrown open, the initial imperative in terms of the public performance of grief was for sheer noise, generated by the female voice and, with the acquisition of European firearms from the sixteenth century, gunfire. De Marees too emphasized the 'great clamour, wailing and crying'; Rask, 'a horrible screeching and howling'.[15] 'Adumissa's death was ... announced by a discharge of musketry', Sara Bowdich wrote of a dramatically staged public suicide in early nineteenth-century Cape Coast. 'The slaves [of the house] rushed out, screaming and tearing their hair and clothes.'[16] 'The sting of a serpent, or the application of

FIGURE 4.1. A funeral. Plate 17 from de Marees, *Description* (1602). De Marees's caption reads: 'In this picture you may see what Ceremonies they perform when they bury the dead. *A*. is the Grave in which the deceased will be buried, with all the things which they bury with the deceased and place upon the grave. *B*. shows their way of mourning and the People who take the deceased for burial. The ones in front prance along, playing Cymbals; the others follow the Corpse and do nothing but wail and make a great clamour. *C*. when the deceased has been buried in the Grave, the Women crawl back and forth over the Grave and make a great clamour. *D*. when they have finished crawling over the Grave, they go to the water in order to wash their body in the Sea, and then they go home to have a good time together'.

some horrible instrument of torture, could not produce more excruciating distortions than we behold them suffering, while writhing under the first stroke of their bereavement', Brodie Cruickshank observed of the Fante region in the nineteenth century.[17] Reporting from Accra in the same period, by which time gun ownership had expanded considerably, Monrad suggests that the firing of muskets now dominated the human voice, at least for deceased of high status: 'As soon as a Negro of importance is dead a number of musket shots are fired outside the house and also around the town . . . Thus the death is made generally known. . . . the Negroes load their guns so heavily that you think you are hearing a cannon shot when they are fired. . . . Without noise the Negro is not in his element'.[18]

That may have been so, but the sonic explosion had a more specific explanation: the dead, especially in the liminal period before the closure of the initial round of rites eight days after death, were believed to be hovering nearby and to retain some degree of sensory perception. One common understanding was that they needed audibly to be alerted that family and community were attending with due seriousness to their departure. Rattray was told in the 1920s, however, that gunpowder was essential both '"to fire a farewell to the body", and to prevent the *saman* (ghost) hearing all that was said: "the noise makes the ghost deaf"'.[19] Yet another explanation is that the 'sound barrage' created by both musketry and subsequent music formed a protective sonic barrier which allowed the ancestors safely to enter the space of the funeral and to carry the deceased away with them to *asamando*.[20]

Musketry was generally performed by men, but women soon regained centre stage. 'A number of women of nearly all ages now betake themselves to the house of mourning', Monrad continues. 'During proficient drinking of brandy . . . they set up a howling and weeping, the like of which you can hardly conceive if you have not yourself been witness to it. Both truths and untruths are called out to the honour of the deceased. They beat themselves dreadfully, especially on the breast, clap their hands, and tears roll, literally, over the entire bodies of the raving matrons'.[21] Such lamentation typically extended to an insistent interrogation of the corpse, the grieving women demanding to know why they had been so cruelly abandoned and pleading with the deceased to return; 'talking to him and asking him why he died', de Marees observed in 1602, 'with a lot of childplay similar to that which the Jews often practice'.[22] Meanwhile, special food (Twi: *kra aduane*) was prepared for the journey of the deceased and placed around the corpse, which, Rattray noted in the 1920s,

FIGURE 4.2. Musketry at a funeral. Photograph taken by Rudolf Fisch at the town of Koforidua between 1885 and 1911. Basel Mission Archives QD-32.008.0272.

'has been laid on its left side purposely to leave the right arm and hand free for eating'.[23]

If the deceased was married, bereaved spouses (*akunafo*) were kept well apart from this process. As in many cultures, the imperative was to separate the spouse from the dangerous spirit of the deceased and from the wider community. Both sexes went through this process of separation, although it was more pronounced and elaborated for widows, who were draped with garlands of pungent *emme* leaves, rough fibres and dirty old snail shells in order to ward off the sexually ravenous ghost of their deceased husband. 'If the Deceased be a Man, his Wives immediately shave their Heads very close, and smear their

FIGURE 4.3. *Akunafo*, or widows, photographed by R. S. Rattray in the early 1920s. The three women each wear a variety of accoutrements designed to symbolize their widowhood and to ward off the *sasa* of their deceased husband: wreaths of the creeper *asuani* ('tears'); russet brown *kuntunkuni* cloth; tied above their elbow, strands of *edowa* palm fibre which float behind them as they dance ('Had we wings we would fly to him'); and packets of pungent *emme* and *nunum* seeds. Pitt Rivers Museum, University of Oxford, 1998.312.477.1, published as figure 67 of *Religion and Art in Ashanti*, facing 172.

Bodies with white Earth, and put on an old worn-out Garment', Bosman wrote; 'thus adjusted they run about [the] Street like mad Women (or rather like She-Devils or Hell-Furies) with frightful cries and clamour, throughout the Town, continually repeating the Name of the Dead, and reciting the great Actions of his past Life'.[24] As de Marees first recorded, the spouse was expected to sit at the side of the corpse, 'holding in his hand a bunch of straws or tree-bark, with which he strokes the face of the deceased, weeping all the time and saying from time to time to the deceased "Anzy"'.[25]

Once the corpse and food were laid out and mourners had gathered, the formal 'wake' (*apese*) began, with the initial hysterical lamentation now replaced with a rolling sonic barrage, as observed by Bannerman, of firing, drumming, singing and shouted exhortation. 'Every one becomes very drunk', Rattray noted in the 1920s, adding to centuries of commentary on the prominent role of alcohol in lubricating the process of mourning. 'But we should not pass a very severe judgement on this account', he cautioned. 'Grief and sorrow are very real where the clan (blood) relations are concerned, for the tears demanded by social custom are none the less a token of genuine grief. For others, not clansmen and women, such occasions are perhaps not too tragic, and on this account these rites seem to the uninstructed to be somewhat heartless shows, as mirth and jollity are not altogether absent.'[26]

In light of debates over the extent to which emotion is socially constructed, it is notable that the apparent ability of grieving women to turn these anguished displays on and off at will drew considerable comment from European and, by the late nineteenth century, elite African male observers. We will return to demands in the era of colonial rule for the elimination of 'excessive' funeral customs, but it can be noted here that across time many observers expressed doubts as to just how genuine these expressions of grief were. Royal African Company officer Henry Meredith, for example, also viewed the Gold Coast funeral as 'a conjunction of condoling and carousing':

> until the body is deposited in the ground, it is a continual scene of dancing, singing (or rather shouting), firing volleys of guns, and, at intervals, lamentable exclamations, that do not betoken much *real* anguish or sorrow. It is necessary to remark, that all this is a customary action that must be followed, and the actors are principally persons employed for the occasion, who have no inward feeling of grief, excepting what sympathy will create. After the interment, and when calmness, we may say, is restored, we then behold real sorrow and affliction, and the habitation of the departed may be appropriately termed the house of mourning.[27]

As Meredith indicates, care is needed to distinguish between private grief and performative mourning, between the period of immediate loss and subsequent obsequies, and to take account of the range of relationships the bereaved had with the deceased. The last of these variables is crucial, given the imperative for all members of a family, of the wider community and of representatives of communities beyond to attend funerals.

Bosman is useful on this point: 'While the Women . . . are thus showing off outside, the nearest Relatives sit with the Corpse inside the house; they lament loudly too and wash and cleanse the body, preparing it for burial. Other Friends who had some relationship with the Deceased also assemble from all

Places, to be present at the Mourning Rites; he that is negligent herein being sure to bleed very freely if he cannot urge lawful Reasons for his absence.'[28] Monrad provides further insight from early nineteenth-century Accra: 'the closest female relatives are close to the body, dressed poorly, and awash in tears, which, in fact, are often sincere. This, however, is by no means the case with the rest of the howling swarm. A Negress can cry at will, and when asked about this, she answers honestly and naively enough, "For what else have I my tears?" A Negro male considers it unmanly to cry, and he does so only in very extreme circumstances'.[29] Much of the commotion, however, was considered not to be generated by real grief. 'I have many times seen women prepare to cry before entering the city', Perregaux reported from Kumasi in the 1890s. 'Often after having shed tears in the house of death, they go out laughing and chatting with friends.'[30] As the Euro-African emissary Vroom said of the obsequies of the princess Akua Bedua in Kumasi in 1894, 'The wild dances of the king and his Chiefs; the sobs and groaning of the women which suddenly gave way to singing and dancing gave this public procession an appearance of ghastly confusion of mourning and mirth'.[31]

The replacement of frenzied bodily abasement with dance and of wailing with musical dirges would come later in proceedings. Sung exclusively by women, these dirges were the 'truths and untruths called out to the honour of the deceased' noted by Monrad, improvised with a fluid combination of established references to ancestors and praise of the qualities and achievements of the deceased individual. 'There is often much beauty and simplicity of feeling expressed in these unpremeditated songs', wrote Cruickshank, who had a good understanding of the agile improvisation on display.[32] Ghanaian musicologist J. H. Nketia has subjected a collection of these texts to sophisticated analysis, serving to establish the Akan funeral dirge as an important genre of African oral literature. Of concern here is what their performance tells us about the tension between culture and emotion in the display of grief. As Nketia makes clear, the expectation was that women should skilfully—and, to some extent, competitively—perform their emotion: 'grief and sorrow may be personal and private, nevertheless Akan society expects that on the occasion of a funeral they should be expressed publicly through the singing of the dirge'. Those less sorrowful faced a different challenge: 'pretence is condemned and mock-sadness is discouraged. A tear should fall, lest you are branded a witch and a callous person. If a tear is physiologically difficult to shed, you must induce it by some means'.[33] The performance of dirges, moreover, encapsulated a further key element in funerary culture: that lamentation was not necessarily limited to grief for the recently deceased. 'From among the

FIGURE 4.4. Women *werempefo*, or 'official mourners', whose tasks on the death of a king traditionally included seizing the stool of the deceased and performing the frenzy of grief by 'turning over the market' (*dwabum*) and making immediate human sacrifices. Photograph taken by R. S. Rattray at Nsoko in the Bron region at the funeral celebration of one Ame Yao and the queen mother Akua Ata, who had died 27 and 26 years earlier, respectively. Pitt Rivers Museum, University of Oxford, 1998.312.480.1; published as figure 79 of *Religion and Art in Ashanti*, facing 181.

confused noises will be heard the voice of many a women mourner singing a dirge in pulsating tones in honour of the dead or ancestors or some other person whose loss she is reminded of by the present death', Nketia writes. '"One mourns one's relation during the funeral of another person" (*Obi ayie ase yesu yen ni*), says the Akan maxim.'[34]

A spectrum of other factors conditioned the emotional intensity of bereavement as well as the appropriate degree of mourning ritual. Perhaps the most fundamental was the age of the deceased. Death at one of the two extremes of the human lifecycle was regarded as a special case. Infants did not become fully human until eight days after birth; those who failed to survive to that point were seen to be sprites who, having sniffed the air of the known world and not liking the look of it, slipped back into the continuum of pre-life and afterlife. They were neither mourned—publicly, at least—nor properly interred: their corpses were usually deposited on the middens at the edge of settlements in the liminal zone between culture and nature. So too were the corpses of women who died in childbirth, an event regarded as a horrific conflation of the two carefully mediated passages between biological and otherworldly existence. At the other extreme, very old people were certainly mourned, but often without the intense anguish of a person perceived to be cut down before their time. Social status also shaped grief and mortuary ritual: again, at one end of the spectrum, slaves often died unmourned and their corpses disposed of casually in the bush. The death of the wealthy and the powerful, in contrast, was followed by highly elaborated obsequies which often included the immolation of human sacrifices. Then there is the whole spectrum of 'bad deaths', those perceived to have been caused either by supernatural forces or by malign human intervention in the form of 'witchcraft' or 'poison'. In such cases, grief often became entangled with anger and suspicion about possible living perpetrators or with apprehension about the lingering hostility and desire for vengeance on the part of the deceased. The pleading questioning of the deceased by the bereaved therefore led on to a more formal, judicial interrogation of the corpse in order to determine the cause of death, known in Twi as *afunsoa*, 'carrying the corpse'.

One further variable can be noted: the presence or absence of a body. This, too, has featured in cross-cultural studies of bereavement, particularly in light of recent psychological understandings of the concept of emotional 'closure'. It was of considerable importance among the Akan and their neighbours, for whom interment in home soil was seen to be critical for the posthumous peace of mind of the deceased. Monrad also reflected on this issue, in a description of a group of women he witnessed grieving on the Accra seafront for a downed relative: 'They filled the air with their screams, threw themselves down in the sand, which they scratched up with their nails, demanding the return from the ocean of the deceased from passers by, from the fetishes, and from the ocean which had swallowed him. They tore their clothes to shreds and injured their bodies. Their pain was evidently intensified by the fact that they could not show the remains of their beloved the final honours'.[35] The dreadful grief observed here was certainly exacerbated by the fact that drowning, whether the body was recovered or not, was considered to be a particularly bad death, invariably caused by spiritual malevolence.

The situation which most commonly resulted in the absence of a corpse was, however, that of warfare. Here, as in the death of rulers, personal grief intersected with a broader communal despair, nowhere more powerfully documented than by the two missionary hostages Ramseyer and Kühne who witnessed the scenes in Kumasi which greeted news of the decimation of an Asante army by British forces in late 1873. On 18 December, Asantehene Kofi Kakari publicly received news from the front of the number of fallen, including many leading chiefs. 'Suddenly a cry of distress arose which rolled like a wave through the whole town, and people ran into the street painted red, crying and howling till I was cut to the heart. The sacrifices were then freed from their chains, and after being pierced through the cheeks, beheaded amidst the beating of drums.' Even at this moment of political calamity, the fundamental gender distinction in the culture of mourning is apparent: 'Dumb and depressed the king returned home; and the queen mother is said to have mourned in the street with her court ladies, her hands folded over her head; for the loss is dreadful.'[36] Three days later, what mortal remains that could be retrieved from the battlefield were brought into Kumasi: 'whole rows of boxes were carried past wrapped in precious materials, followed by their (supposed) mourning wives, and their attendants painted red. . . . Very few could be seen in the crowd who were painted white, the majority of the people were wailing in the red ornaments of mourning.'[37]

If grief and mourning had a powerful sonic element, then it also had a distinctive visual register, marked most emphatically by colour. In common with many African cultures, the Akan and their neighbours possessed a symbolic scheme based on the tripartite black/white/red spectrum—although a range of other colours such as yellow (gold), green (the forest) and blue (love and sexuality) also conveyed particular meanings. The fundamental cognitive distinction was that between white (Twi: *fufu*), symbolizing harmony, consensus and 'coolness'; red (*kokoo*), which conveyed dissonance, disorder, rupture and 'hotness'; and black (*tuntum*), imagined, renowned artist Kofi Antubam explains, 'in terms of night, vice, deepened feelings of melancholy, and such vicious spiritual bodies as the devil and death.'[38] Black also signified the 'heaviness' of old age, ancestordom and history—most emblematically in the *nkonnwa tuntum* or hallowed blackened stools of the dead.

As the scenes witnessed in Kumasi in 1873 indicate, the most visible vehicle for these signifying colours was the female body and the principal media were red clay (*ntwoma*), white clay (*hyire*) and, increasingly over time, cloth. The bodies of the dead, of both genders, were also often chalked with *ntwoma* and *hyire*, as were those of the living whose life was about to be extinguished by ritual sacrifice or judicial execution. Despite the basic red/white/black semiotic code, however, the precise circumstances governing which of the colours were used are not entirely clear. De Marees in 1602 says that a corpse, on being laid out, is sprinkled with 'Ashes and the dust of Tree Bark' (suggesting a combination of white and red colouring, the latter from *odame*, red bark powder); three hundred years later, Rattray observed in Asante that the head of corpses were sometimes shaved and marked with alternate red, white and black stripes. 'This, I am informed, is done that the dead person may be readily recognized if he or she walks as a *saman* (ghost).'[39] Bosman says that grieving widows covered themselves with 'white earth'—clearly *hyire*. There are indications that hierarchy and the nature of the death determined the predominant colour scheme: the use of *ntwoma* to redden female mourners appears to have been associated with the death of royals or others of high status and is particularly well documented in Asante, where, as Bowdich observed, 'on the death of a respectable man ... all the females of the family daub their faces and breasts with red earth of which they build their houses, parade the town (distinct from the men) lamenting and beating themselves, assume mean attire, abstain from all nourishment but palm wine, and sleep in the street until the corpse is buried.'[40]

The symbolic meanings conveyed by clays and powders were replicated in the evolution of mourning cloth (Twi: *ayitam*). Establishing the history of this development is difficult, as from their first appearance in the historical records *ayitam* appear to have varied according to region, the gender and status of both deceased and mourner, and the sort of death—with different styles also worn at successive stages of a funeral custom. The most notable Akan cloths were the vermilion *kobene* and the russet brown and black patterned *kuntunkuni*, although among the Ga and Ewe on the eastern Gold Coast, white and blue appears to have been the dominant colour of mourning.[41] The Akan also had an indigo blue cloth, *birisii*, worn, most commonly by women, between the time a corpse was wrapped or coffined for burial and for the subsequent forty days. At that point, it was often replaced with *adinkra*, a lighter coloured cloth stamped with a range of symbolic motifs often reflecting on the nature of mortality such as the 'ladder of death'.[42] Early sources also recorded the dressing of corpses in richly patterned cloth, de Marees noting the use of a woollen fabric 'specially made for the purpose; it is manufactured in the Interior and is red, blue, black and white'.[43]

The normative calendar for the resumption of celebrations was the fifteenth, fortieth and eightieth day after death, followed by its anniversary. At all of these events, demonstrative mourning by women was essential in order to continue to reassure the deceased of the ongoing goodwill of the living. Gender roles in the forty-day ceremony were reported by Meyerowitz to have taken a very particular form: a time 'of great happiness and joy, because it is believed that by now the *kra* has reached heaven', it culminated for deceased royals in a rite in which young women dressed as male warriors and engaged in mock battles. 'To-day . . . they content themselves with swaggering about in men's cloths and smoking cigarettes', she observed in the 1940s—although the unusual sight of women smoking was pointed out by Bannerman in 1841 and can still be seen in Ghana today.[44] Circumstances such as the loss of a body in warfare, however, sometimes meant that funerals might be delayed for years, which prolonged the liminal phase and obliged wives to remain in mourning and largely isolated from normal society. 'A long time after, perhaps ten or twelve Years', Bosman was astounded to observe, 'as Opportunity offers, the Funeral Ceremonies of such a person are held with the same Pomp and Splendour as if they had died a few Days past: after which the said Wives cleanse themselves; lay off their mourning-clothes and dress themselves again like the others'.[45]

Various lines of interpretation arise from the foregoing descriptions. First, we must consider why it was that women commanded the centre stage of the Akan mortuary drama. Beyond vague references to the ur-role of women as nurturers or their greater capacity to express heightened emotion, this question has been neglected in the literature. At a fundamental level, there is certainly evidence for an ontological equivalence between birth and death and for the imperative for women to preside over both. A suggestive starting point are the reflections of J. B. Danquah, who, following on from his analysis of Odomankoma and death, lays emphasis on the lexical affinity between the Twi *awo*, birth, and *owu*, death. Death tends to be juxtaposed with life, Danquah argues, but for the Akan 'the true contrast of death is birth, not life'.[46] He sees this affinity as reflecting and in turn shaping attitudes towards mortality: 'to the Akan, therefore, death is . . . not life's contradiction or negation but an instrument of higher consummation, a planting or fruition of it'.[47] That consummation was a matter to be celebrated, the real tragedy being if an individual died without contributing to the increase of the community, 'in which case his death is more than calamitous, it is a vacuum'.[48] Just as women manage the drama of birth, so too must they mediate that of death. The referencing of the *awo/owu* tension at a critical moment of the Asante Odwira festival, McCaskie notes, served to render the polarity of birth and death 'in starkly explicit expression'.[49] Death, that is to say, was seen to give birth to the ancestral dead. 'Perhaps this is one reason why women have traditionally played such crucial roles in ritualized mourning and lamentations in general', Robert Pogue Harrison suggests. 'For dying in the full human sense is a kind of birth, while the afterlife—understood phenomenologically and not necessarily religiously or doctrinally—is the new and altered condition the dead are born into.'[50] If the exact location of that afterworld was a matter of speculation, then there was no doubt about the destination of the corporeal body: it went down into the ground, the domain of the earth goddess Asaase. Asaase took two forms: Asaase Afua, goddess of procreation, and Asaase Yaa, 'the mother of the dead who lie buried in her "pocket" (*kotoku*)'.[51]

A second issue leads on from Danquah's insights into death as a consummation rather than a negation of life, which go some way in explaining the ambivalence of funeral celebrations. Put simply, death unleashed a gamut of conflicting and volatile emotions, manifested in the widely reported mixture of grief and gaiety, mourning and mirth. There is no doubt that death generated considerable anxiety among the bereaved, for whom any oversight or neglect in the repertoire of funerary rituals might spell vengeful intervention from the angry spirit of the deceased. This ambivalence comes across in the writing of the Danish pastor Monrad, who was particularly attuned to the entanglement of celebration and apprehension among the Ga of Accra in the early nineteenth century. 'The natives' tender love for their dead, mixed with fear of doing them harm' was most apparent, Monrad noted, during the actual burial, when 'much is made of the casting on of earth' in order to 'prevent the deceased from rising from the dead and doing harm to the survivors'. 'When the coffin was set into the grave', he observed in one instance, 'a number of women came running with the daily clothing of the deceased, and his household articles, and [threw] them all into the grave, all the while making frantic gestures and screams, as if to say, "Take your things and leave us in peace!"'[52] At the same time, a death served to open up a direct line of communication with the invisible realm, as Field recognized in the 1930s: women's wailing, 'if noted carefully, are found to be more than mere noisy lamentations. They are nearly all requests to the dead person to greet So-and-so, who died last year, to ask So-and-so not to forget the old home but to send a blessing, to ask the old people to send back a dead child or send a child to some hitherto barren woman. Above all, the dead man is begged to return again, reborn, before long.'[53]

Finally, there is the divergence between the formalized, communal articulation of grief and mourning, on the one hand, and the personal agony of loss, on the other. In terms of the 'psychological work' that, from a cross-cultural perspective, mortuary customs are seen to do, the former can be said to be designed to alleviate the latter. They are, moreover, often regarded by scholars as succeeding in that aim; thus, Osei-Mensah Aborampah comes to the comforting conclusion that 'Akan culture provides members of the society with a highly adaptive means of mourning the dead', which in turn ensures a 'systematic and positive adjustment to human loss'.[54] The problem, however, is that while the exuberant sequence of mortuary action appears to point to its utility in this respect, the historical record contains only fragmentary glimpses of the acute and sometimes prolonged emotional dissonance that could result from bereavement. We simply do not know enough about private grief—about the sorrow and affliction inside what Meredith called 'the house of mourning'—to come to any definitive conclusion on the matter. How did men grieve? What those few glimpses into the house of mourning do indicate is that prolonged and sometimes debilitating torment seems to be especially associated with the loss of near and dear through what was deemed to be a 'bad' death. Not only was loss compounded and complicated by the burden of shame brought upon the surviving family, it meant that rather than being properly laid to rest, the spirit of the deceased was left in torment—and therefore more likely in turn to torment the living.

One category of the tormented dead and their traumatic psychological impact on the living will be considered in chapter 7: those whose decapitated heads had fallen into the hands of their enemies. But we can conclude with a discrete example of a different sort of violent death, a murder, which is suggestive of the complex entanglement of culture and emotion in the fashioning of grief. The murder occurred in August 1813 and the victim was a woman named as Acquishebah, a slave belonging to the British fort at Sekondi on the western Gold Coast. Acquishebah disappeared after she had been sent to nearby Dixcove to purchase some fowls, and when her bound and horrifically mutilated body was discovered it was apparent that she had been subjected to dreadful sexual violence.[55] Five days later, the body of a small child who accompanied her was also found nearby, with similar marks of violence. 'I am sorry to say

Effuah, Company Slave, sister to Acquishebah is seriously ill', the officer in charge of Sekondi fort reported a week later. Given the nature of her sister's death, this is not surprising. But Afua's own explanation of her trauma is revealing. Her collapse, Bayley wrote, is 'proceeding partly from her sorrow, partly from an Idea, that the Fetish wants her to die to accompany her sister'.[56] Three days later, the suspected murderer, a slave belonging to the neighbouring Dutch fort, was apprehended, but Bayley reported that 'I am much afraid of having to inform you of the death of the Company's slave girl Effuah 'ere long. I have procured a very clever black doctor a Company's slave belonging to Taccoradie Fort . . . ; it was the only chance I had of saving her'.[57] At this point the sequence of letters ends, so whether the African doctor was able to save Afua is unknown. Neither do we know of the extent to which company slaves were able to manage their own mortuary rites. The loss of will to go on living and express desire to join a loved one in death is, of course, a widely recognized aspect of extreme grief. Afua's fear that 'the fetish' wanted her dead, in contrast, is a culturally specific interpretation of her situation. Just as a death served to reopen the wounds incurred by the previously dead, so too does it point to one's own inevitable demise, a fear encapsulated in the Akan saying often heard at funerals: *mesu me wu da mu*, 'I am weeping over the day I will die'.[58]

5

Gold, Wealth and Burial

GOLD LIES AT the heart of the history of Ghana. It was the production of gold that drew the Twi-speaking Bono and Akan peoples into trade networks spanning the Sahara desert, that from the 1470s brought them into commercial contact with Europeans on the Atlantic seaboard, and that underpinned the consolidation of settled agriculture and statecraft in the tropical forest. If for Europeans that part of West Africa was intrinsically associated with the supply of the precious metal—first as the Costa da Mina, then as the 'Gold Kingdom of Guinea' and finally as the Gold Coast—then for its inhabitants, gold (*sika*) was 'located conceptually and materially at the very core of the historical experience of their society and culture'.[1] *Sika sene, biribi ansen bio* runs one of a host of Akan proverbs attesting to the importance of monetary wealth: 'Gold (or money) is beyond everything, nothing is beyond that'.[2] The material role of gold, as a commodity, a currency and a substance of artistic transformation, is voluminously documented and has been the subject of extensive historical inquiry. Much of that inquiry has been focused on Asante, the emergence of which as the apotheosis of Akan state-building was predicated upon the exchange of gold for unfree labour and the accumulation of wealth and authority by an emergent ruling elite of entrepreneurial 'big men', or *abirempon*. This exchange value amplified the conceptualization of gold as a potent demiurgic substance—symbolized, for the Asante, in the Golden Stool as the vehicle for the *sunsum*, or 'soul' of the nation.[3]

This chapter considers the material and conceptual roles of gold in matters of death and burial on the Gold Coast and in the Akan forest in the era of Atlantic commerce. Death and the ends of life, it argues, were intimately bound up with ideologies concerning gold, wealth, accumulation and increase. One aspect of this role has been identified by historians as crucial to an understanding of the changing contract between Asante state and society:

inheritance and death duties.[4] Another has been touched on only in passing: the interment—and the periodic disinterment—of gold in graves. Both, in essence, were about exchange: exchange between generations, and between the living and the dead. 'Funeral obsequies in Ashanti', Rattray wrote in the 1920s, 'are inseparably associated with the rights of inheritance'.[5] Death represented an ultimate accounting, and the passing on of wealth 'the final item in the ledger that indicated the relative degree of the individual's success in contributing beyond his own gratification to the maintenance, enlargement and continuity of the realm of culture'.[6]

It was in Asante, too, that the symbolic power of gold reached dizzying heights of complexity. An account of Asantehene Opoku Ware which reached the Gold Coast in the 1740s captures this as well as any, conjuring an image of a latter-day El Dorado, 'the gilded one' of Spanish American legend:

> Oppoccu holds audience outside his house under a large tree with many branches and leaves on it, a tree [entirely] made of gold. His throne is a lump of gold with rope bound around it and poles through the rope, requiring the use of eight men to carry it in and out. Together with the throne they bring out a gold basin into which he places his feet. His servants anoint his body twice a day with tallow, and then strew fine gold dust on it, as well as in his hair, and in this guise he holds audience. If a copper engraver were to draw Oppoccu's portrait he would have to portray Oppoccu on his throne with his Big Men around him, his whole body shining with the gold dust sticking to his tallow-smeared skin.[7]

In death as in life, the bodies of the rich and powerful were gilded in the same fashion, extending the symbolic power of gold into the grave and the afterlife beyond. 'Various methods of preserving the king's body after death came into use', oral traditions of the earliest Akan states record, 'and in all cases gold, symbol of light and life, was used to ensure his immortality'.[8]

Elaborating on Wilks's analysis of wealth in Asante, McCaskie argues that from the emergence of the kingdom in the late seventeenth century through to the mid-nineteenth century, the matrix of ideas concerning gold, accumulation and the fiscal appropriation of self-acquired wealth can be characterized by continuity and gradual amplification. Individuals were encouraged to generate and accumulate wealth in the form of gold dust (*sika futuro*), but at the end of their life it would pass to the state as death duties; gold unearthed by mining operations in the form of nuggets (*sika mpokowa*), in contrast, was claimed by the Asantehene from the outset. From the late nineteenth century and into the era of British colonial rule in the twentieth century, that hegemonic ideology first faltered and then broke down. As Wilks demonstrated, the ideology of wealth was encapsulated in the dualism of two hallowed objects: the Golden Stool (*sika dwa kofi*), symbolizing 'the highest level that political power was exercised (*tumi*)', and the Golden Elephant Tail (*sika mena*), symbolizing 'the highest level at which wealth was appropriated (*gye*)'.[9] There was only one Golden Stool; but successive Asantehenes, down to Asantehene Kwaku Dua Panin (1834–67), each consecrated their own Golden Elephant Tail. The right to use an elephant-tail switch, moreover, was conferred by the Asantehene on an individual *sikani* ('man of money'; pl. *sikafo*) who had demonstrated outstanding success in wealth creation. These individuals were thereafter known as *obirempon*, and the honour was a rare and exalted one: in the entire nineteenth century, only three men are recorded as having undergone the complex—and, for them, enormously expensive—ceremony.[10] Such public acclamation pointed to the economic contract between state and society: that wealth creation was seen to be a process of social rather than individual increase, undertaken, in McCaskie's words, 'in conscious discharge of duties towards the achievement of the ancestors and of responsibilities towards the "historic" future represented by the unborn'.[11] The cycle of life and death, in other words, was entangled with notions of wealth, achievement and the enlargement of human culture. As the guardian of culture, the Asantehene was also the ultimate recipient of wealth, which flowed into the state's coffers through a variety of mechanisms. The principal fiscal instrument was death duties.

Given the importance of death duties for the Asante state, it is surprising how little is known about them. Part of this is because the system began to falter in the mid-nineteenth century, when the regime of Kwaku Dua Panin broke the established social compact by imposing exploitative levels of fiscal extraction as expanding private trade with the European entrepôts on the Gold Coast enlarged the ranks of *sikafo* and gave them an alternative commercial model based on free-market individualism. Thus, the Golden Elephant Tail as the ur-symbol of appropriation can be seen to have 'withered away' in the last quarter of the century, as the fiscal system imploded in the era of state contraction, civil war and, ultimately, British colonial conquest. Unlike the Golden Stool, little appears to have been known about the *sika mena* in the twentieth century, with the result that historians have struggled to provide a convincing reading of its symbolism. Wilks posits that as the mightiest of forest beasts, the elephant 'despite the handicap of a short tail ... is still able to sweep (*pra*) flies away'—a locution which accords with the term *ahoprafo* (lit. 'sweepers'), the bearers who carried the elephant-tail switch of the *abirempon*. 'The *mena* or *mmara*, then, may signify not so much wealth as such but achievement: that is, the ability to overcome—to sweep aside—problems.'[12] Perhaps. McCaskie points to an additional physical attribute, offering that 'in the structural sense the elephant's tail "presides" over the discharge or production of excrement' and therefore references a cognitive connection between gold (and wealth, more broadly) and shit.[13] Again, there is little evidence to support this connection. Yet its location within a set of ideas about the transformation of matter is certainly suggestive of the coming together in the grave of gold and another unclean substance: decomposing human flesh.

The dynamics of the system of death duties are also somewhat opaque. There were two categories of levy, *awunnyadie* and *ayibuadie*, although the distinction between them remains a matter of debate. Both were said by mid-twentieth-century informants to be 'ancient', while Reindorf recorded the system as being instituted during the era of state expansion under Opoku Ware (1720–50).[14] *Awunnyadie* (lit. 'things left behind after death') appears to have been imposed on all self-acquired movable property, while *ayibuadie* ('something for the funeral') was an additional discretionary impost on the successor of a deceased office-holder.[15] The issue was addressed by two of the most knowledgeable chiefs in early colonial Kumasi, Adontenhene Kwame Frimpon and Akyeamehene Kwasi Nuama, when it emerged as a bone of contention during an enquiry in 1924–25 into the constitution of the Adonten stool. Nuama put the matter succinctly: 'There is a difference between *awunyadie* and *ayibuadie*. The latter is an amount which the King took from the successor to a chief. The former is the share which he took from the deceased's estate.'[16] The system was described in 1817 by Bowdich, who placed the 'gold dust of all deceased and disgraced subjects' at the head of a list of revenues accruing to the Asante state.

> The King is heir to the gold of every subject, from the highest to the lowest; the fetish gold and the cloths are generally presented by him to the successor to the stool, from which the slaves and other property of the deceased are inseparable. The King contributes to the funeral custom to validate his claim, and usually bestows ten periguins [i.e., *mperedwan*] of the gold dust

on the successor, (if of a rich man,) who is in all cases liable for the debts of the deceased, though the amount is generally made good to him sooner or later, if he has influence with those about the King, or recommends himself to his notice personally. This law is sometimes anticipated, by a father presenting his children with large sums of gold just before his death. Boiteëm, the father of Otee, one of the King's linguists, is known to have done so, but the son discovers his wealth very deliberately.[17]

Debate has also turned on the magnitude and socio-economic impact of this appropriation. In line with the prevailing ideology of the *okinaba*, the good citizen, as one who 'by the exercise of his, or her, own skills and industry made money and therefore at death became ... a benefactor of the nation', Wilks stresses the hegemonic nature of the system. Wealthy subjects 'enjoyed in life the prestige and respect that was in fact to be paid for at death, when officials of the treasury would value their property and take the death duties'.[18] McCaskie too focuses on the impact of *awunnyadie* upon the wealthiest echelon of Asante society, characterizing it at its operational height between the 1760s and 1860s as a tightly regulated system which prevented the emergence of a class of hereditary property owners and allowed the state an effective 'monopoly over access to wealth and its redistribution'.[19] Despite the instance cited by Bowdich (on which more below), evasion was seen as scandalously antisocial and punished severely, so it was correspondingly rare. The capacity of the state to exercise this monopoly, however, has been qualified by the economic historian Gareth Austin. While acknowledging that gold was taxed heavily, Austin takes issue with the first sentence of Bowdich's explanation: that 'the King is heir to the gold of every subject, from the highest to the lowest'. Considering evidence for the nineteenth century, Austin pointed to the system's reciprocal nature also noted by Bowdich, concluding that 'the treasury taxed the estates of commoners rather than seizing them' and that 'death duties do not seem to have been a barrier to modest self-improvement amongst the mass of the population'.[20]

How was this appropriation entangled with the broader drama of death and funeral celebration? Precolonial sources are few, but in the 1920s both Kwame Frimpon and Rattray stressed the essential reciprocity of the transaction. 'The law was that whenever a person dies the family reported to the immediate

Chief', Frimpon stated when asked to explain *awunnyadie* to the 1925 Adonten enquiry. 'He must then inform the Head Chief. The Head Chief sends gold dust, pillows, mat and about 4 cloths and rum—sometimes a sheep (this depends on the importance of the deceased) to the family . . . for the celebration of the funeral custom.'[21] This repertoire of items composed the *nsa*, the 'funeral contributions', and their ostensible purpose was to be interred with the corpse in order to be used by the deceased in the afterworld. As Bowdich grasped, they also validated the claim to *awunnyadie*; elsewhere he added that 'the body is washed; greased, and wrapped in cotton cloths; these cloths the king is obliged to furnish, to vindicate his claim as heir (for the use of the state) to all the gold dust of the deceased'.[22] For the deceased, 'it is of paramount importance that his body is covered with the Omanhene's present', Danquah explained with reference to the kingdom of Akyem Abuakwa. 'It has to be taken to, and shown to the people (Kings, Chiefs and people) in Asaman (Hades) as a mark of evidence to them of his importance on this earth.'[23] European merchants on the Gold Coast well understood the key role of cloth in the contribution and were careful to make lavish gifts in order to maintain commercial relationships.[24]

Adontenhene Frimpon also pointed to the imperative that all deaths must promptly be reported to the appropriate authorities, by them to their immediate superiors, and so on. This swift transmission of the tidings of death is well documented and continued into the twentieth century after the collapse of *awunnyadie*. When the system was in force, the reception of tidings and delivery of the *nsa* was followed by the 'locking down' of the deceased's movable assets—including the physical securing of his or her private chest—in order, once the funeral was over, to weigh the gold dust and to enumerate slaves, cloths and, in the case of men, wives, who were also an inheritable item. According to Frimpon, one half of such assets would typically be retained by the state, with the other half 'returned' to the surviving family.

The Adontenhene then went on to explain the functioning of the rather more complex custom of *ayibuadie*. *Ayibuadie*, he stated, was synonymous with *amuhuma*—that is, a piece of cloth belonging to the deceased that was torn up and bound around the chests of mourners in order to express grief.[25] It was levied on an office-holder's successor when, as in the case of an Adonten *obirempon*, 'his personal effects are not examined by the King's Messenger' and 'the King took nothing out of his effects'. *Ayibuadie* or *amuhuma* was also paid, at least within the Adonten division, to fellow stool-holders, Frimpon explaining that 'when the elder dies the younger fall upon [i.e., makes financial demands of] his successor. It is because the younger stools being brothers incur expenses in attending my funeral customs, and must be requited by my successor.... They had each to send a subject for execution during the funeral custom, and I had to do the same when one of them died'.[26] 'Instead of a Chief coming down upon the estate of a dead subject, i.e. sending his *Sana Hene* (Treasurer) to lock up his rooms and boxes until the value of an estate had been assessed', Rattray confirmed, 'he might leave the amount to be paid in death duties to the discretion of the relatives of the deceased. The levy then assumed more the appearance of a voluntary contribution on their part, "to bind the breast of the Chief", "whose heart was sore" owing to the loss of his subject and friend'.[27] Yet even for Rattray, whose inclination was always to stress the genius of Asante statecraft in the creation of a 'constitutional' system of consensual checks and balances, that appearance was a legal fiction: a chief—and, ultimately, the Asantehene—'would take care to see that the balance struck between what came in from *ayibuadie* or *muhoma* and what went out in funeral contributions (*nsa* or *nsawa*) was in his favour'.[28] The performative nature of the custom was well captured by the detained missionaries Ramseyer and Kühne in July 1872, when they were summoned to the palace in Kumasi to witness such an exchange between Yaw Boakye, a son of the late Asantehene Kwaku Dua Panin who was belatedly celebrating the funeral of his mother and brother, and the current Asantehene Kofi Kakari. After receiving a procession bearing gifts from Yaw Boakye, Kofi Kakari in turn 'gave his presents consisting of gold, various ornaments, clothing, etc, carried in three divisions. At the head of each marched a royal messenger, loudly proclaiming to all the chiefs what the king gave for the funeral celebration, in money, jewels, dresses, sheep and finally in human sacrifices'.[29] *Awunnyadie*, in contrast, was not disguised by the niceties of reciprocity. 'It is different', stated Frimpon bluntly. 'The awunyadie shows the power which the overlord has over the subordinate.'[30]

The exercise of this power can be considered by looking at the career of one of the most famous of Asante *abirempon*. Born around 1730, the son of an immigrant from Denkyira, Yamoa Ponko made his fortune by trading with the savanna kingdom of Gonja, to the north of Asante.[31] By the 1760s, he began to invest in land and subjects, and in recognition of his success was appointed to occupy the Ankaase stool. Shortly after that, a new opportunity for advance presented itself: the newly enstooled Asantehene Osei Kwadwo (1764–77) imposed a military tax, *apeatoo*, on all office-holders; when the Hiahene, head of the Kyidom division, of which the Ankaase stool was a part, was unable to pay, Yamoa Ponko assumed the debt, settled it and was thereby awarded the office of Kyidomhene. As Kyidomhene, Yamoa Ponko further consolidated his wealth and influence under Asantehene Osei Kwame (1777–1803). At some point in the 1780s, he attained the accolade of *obirempon*, displaying his wealth in a ceremony of such opulence that in the mid-twentieth century it was still remembered in oral traditions. Traditions also preserved a further, highly unusual, feature of Yamoa Ponko's elevation to the ranks of *abirempon*: he agreed to hand the entirety of his property to over Osei Kwame on the condition that the Asantehene personally preside over his funeral. Such a request was quite contrary to custom: as a rule, the Asantehene—indeed, any Akan *omanhene*—did not personally attend funerals, where the taint of death might endanger their sacred role as guardians of the cultural order. Had not Yemoa Ponko been utterly secure in his personal relationship with Osei Kwame—he had acted as the latter's childhood guardian for three years—it is hard to imagine the request even being made, let alone agreed to. Yet the Asantehene acquiesced, and on Yemoa Ponko's death (around 1785) is remembered as acting as the principal mourner at a grand funeral custom. If, as Wilks argues, 'lavish funerals were made for the wealthy, in recognition of their contribution to the national well-being—*rites de passage* into the land of the ancestors where they would continue to enjoy their high status', then that for Yamoa Ponko became the template for achievement.[32] His name was remembered as a byword for success in accumulation and its recognition.

The traditions on which this account is based have less to say about the actual transaction of the death duties. There is no record of the amount of gold dust left by Yamoa Ponko, although there is every indication that throughout his career he had been careful to transfer privately acquired land, subjects and gold—in the form of ornaments and jewellery, the so-called fetish gold mentioned by Bowdich—into stool property, thus rendering them not subject to *awunnyadie*. Such a strategy was part of a spectrum of tax avoidance rather than outright evasion by the burial of gold, which was a capital offence. Another method was recorded by Bowdich: the attempt by the wealthy trader and *okyeame* Boakye Yam, 'Boiteëm', to circumvent the law by transferring part of his gold to family members before his death in around 1814. The fact that this transfer was well known suggests that it may not have been entirely successful. Bowdich does not say whether the Asantehene's exchequer recovered the amount, although elsewhere he notes that Boakye Yam left five four-gallon jars and two flasks of gold dust: a total of twenty-two gallons, 22,000 *mperedwan* or approximately 49,500 troy ounces of gold, worth the equivalent of

£176,000 at the nineteenth-century conversion rate of £8 to one *peredwan*.[33] This sort of fortune was exceptional, but provides an indication of the magnitude of wealth creation by individual entrepreneurs and of the financial resources available to the Asante state. Cruder attempts at evasion, if detected, could result in calamity for those concerned. A notable case is recorded from the reign of Asantehene Osei Yaw Akoto (1823–34), which appears to have involved an effort to emulate the special mortuary treatment accorded to Yamoa Ponko two generations before. Akuropenhene Kwadwo Gyamfi reportedly made the same offer to the Asantehene as had Yamoa Ponko; Osei Yaw Akoto accordingly presided over his funeral—but when his pots of gold dust were opened, they were found to be adulterated with brass filings. Kwadwo Gyamfi's corpse was promptly disinterred, tried and beheaded.[34]

Despite the severity of such punishments, avoiding death duties became more common as Asante underwent a series of profound crises in the final quarter of the nineteenth century. The fiscal system may have begun to be called into question during the reign of Kwaku Dua Panin, whose draconian methods of appropriation threatened the new-found wealth of the growing ranks of private traders. A sign of the times occurred in 1862, when an elderly *sikani* named Kwasi Gyani was accused of hoarding gold nuggets; summoned to court in Kumasi, he fled to the British-protected territories on the Gold Coast, where he explained 'that the King desires only to entrap him, take his head, and afterwards possession of his property'.[35] It was during the weak and divisive reigns of Kofi Kakari (1867–74) and his brother Mensa Bonsu (1874–83) and the rudderless years of civil war that followed, however, that the historic contract appears to have broken down. 'It is [an] abominable and nefarious law because it kept back the improvement of Ashanti countries, sowed seed of discontent, agitation, general unrest, and disturbances', a group of businessmen protesting against the threatened reintroduction of *awunnyadie* wrote to the colonial administration in 1930. 'Before the advent of the British Government into Ashanti, Ashanti man from fear of properties being ransacked by the Ohene could not openly declared [*sic*] his wealth but would hide his treasures in the earth and this accounts for the general retrogression in the olden days.'[36] This admission provides a point of entry into the second of our themes: the burial of 'treasures in the earth' not just as a means of tax evasion but by the interment of gold in graves. If the ostentatious display of golden regalia was a key mechanism in asserting the ideology of accumulation and affirming state power, then the concealment of gold in the ground from whence it came amplified its demiurgic power.

It is likely that gold in the form of nuggets, dust and worked artefacts was used by the Akan and their neighbours to adorn the human body, both dead and alive, before becoming commoditized as a result of international trade. 'Our ancestors were not selling the gold-dust until the white man came', the elders of the Fante state of Eguafo stated in the 1970s. 'They were using it for personal adornment and also for burials.'[37] The former was recorded in 1482 by Azambuja, who was struck by how Caramansa and his nobles were laden with golden ornaments and nuggets. The latter was preserved in traditions in the Bono region, where, Meyerowitz was told, the corpses of ancient kings were laid 'in a coffin placed in a recess of the grave; his head, hand and feet rested in bowls filled with gold dust, and gold dust was used to dust his face and to fill the seven openings of his body—eyes, ears, nostrils and mouth'.[38] It was through these early Bono kingdoms straddling the forest–savanna fringe that gold exports flowed north across the Sahara, exchanged for a range of commodities which in turn flowed south from the Mediterranean world. These included fine brass bowls from Mamluk Egypt, which appear to have provided the model for the locally cast ritual vessels (*kuduo*) used to deposit gold in graves.[39] On the Atlantic littoral, however, 'it is difficult to know what knowledge they had of Gold long ago', de Marees wrote in 1602. 'According to what the Negroes say about it themselves, they knew only a little about it and it was not much valued among them.' Yet after a century of Portuguese demand, 'it is as much esteemed among them as among our people, indeed even more; for they are more parsimonious and keener on it than any people of our nation . . . and therefore they say Gold is our God'.[40]

Beyond these oral traditions, there is no firm documentary or archaeological evidence from the coast for gold adorning dead bodies before the mid-seventeenth century. De Marees was intensely concerned with gold as well as being interested in local mortuary customs, but neither he nor subsequent early seventeenth-century observers mention gold as part of the repertoire of grave goods. In the 1660s, however, Dapper noted that 'persons of quality are laid in a chest, others bound in a mat with their best garments, and some ornaments of gold, but they take them away as soon as the corpse is laid in the ground'.[41] By the end of the century, it is clear that the corpses of the wealthy were not only richly adorned with gold when on public display during mortuary customs, but that gold was also being interred in the grave. Evidence comes from accounts of grave robberies as well as of funerals. 'A Negro's Funeral, if he was of some consequence, is very costly', Bosman wrote. 'Distinguished persons are richly cloathed when put into the Coffin; besides which several fine Cloaths, Gold *Fetiches*, high-prized Corals, . . . *Conte di Terra* [i.e., precious trade beads], and several other valuable Things are put into the Coffin to him, for his use in the other Life, they not doubting that he may have occasion for them.'[42] An attempt to loot such goods was reported in 1686: when a man who had entered the English fort at Sekondi at night was shot and wounded, he admitted that a great *caboceer* was buried there and he wished to steal the gold from the grave.[43]

The robbing of graves for gold—and perhaps simply for their desecration—was also reported as an instrument of warfare during the upsurge of military violence from the late seventeenth century. Johannes Rask arrived at the Danish headquarters in Accra in 1708, shortly after a ferocious Akwamu campaign on the eastern Gold Coast:

> When an Akra [i.e., Ga] dies, the deceased, according to his fortune, is given some gold to take with him in his grave, nor do his friends neglect to give him a *pankis* [cloth] . . . so that whenever he rises again he will not arise naked or poor. This is because they think that he either rises among the Whites in our country—and they have noticed that nakedness is held to be shameful among us—or at any other place on the Coast. The Aqvambues knew about this habit among the Akras during the war that had been waged just before I arrived there, and knew how to make use of it. Therefore they dug up and rummaged around in all the houses where they knew some *kabuseers* had lived a long time ago, to see if they could find any treasure, since the most prominent among them were usually buried in their own houses.[44]

The despoiling of graves was also reported from the Akan interior in 1718, when an Aowin army descended upon a defenceless Kumasi—Asante forces being engaged in Akyem in the campaign in which Osei Tutu lost his life—from where it was said that they had returned 'with a considerable booty, including 20,000 women and children, that they found no resistance, and that they have exhumed the dead Assiantyins. It is said that they have found much gold and *konte de terra* . . . and that they would come shortly to trade.'[45]

Rask's account points to a divergence between the mortuary customs of the coastal towns and interior Akan kingdoms: whereas the former came to be characterized by intramural sepulture, or house burial, the latter tended to inter their dead in family or clan burial grounds in the forest, beyond the space of culture. It is unclear when either option first emerged, although written and archaeological evidence suggests an ongoing variety of burial practices across the region.[46] Like the adornment of corpses with gold, house burial on the coast begins to appear in sources by the late seventeenth century: a passing mention is made by Bosman, who notes, after a description of what might be taken as a 'normal' burial, that 'others interr their Dead secretly in their own houses, though they give out that they preserve the Corps in the former manner'.[47] In what might be interpreted as a reflection of an increasingly commercialized society characterized by individual accumulation, the custom became the norm in coastal towns over the course of the eighteenth century, particularly among the Ga. 'The corpse is normally buried in the house where the person has lived, but no one, except for the closest friends, knows the [exact] place', Rømer observed in Accra in the 1740s; four decades later, Isert stressed that 'every single Black is buried in the room in his house where he died'.[48] After a residence in Accra in 1805–9, the Danish pastor Monrad reflected on why the custom might have arisen:

> At times, when a very prominent man dies it happens that they bury his coffin in one place and his body in another, out of fear that it could be dug up and mishandled. This is especially feared when he leaves behind him debt or powerful enemies in the vicinity. There is a strong belief that the deceased can be tortured by the maltreatment of his body. In war, therefore, graves are often vandalized and sometimes, in times of peace, they are attacked by greedy hands, although this happens only rarely. The Negroes' corpses are so beloved by their survivors that they bury them, most often, in the house where they actually lived, about 2 *alen* deep in the earth.[49]

In Asante, where house burial did not become the norm, iron bars were placed above the corpse to warn of the presence below of a treasure trove, which was guarded by the supernatural sanction that for a stranger to unearth and look upon it would result in death.[50]

By the eighteenth century, then, the mortal remains of the wealthy and powerful were as a matter of course accompanied into the afterworld with gold and other precious artefacts. In the coastal town of Elmina, the archaeological record reveals, these grave assemblages included 'Chinese porcelain plates, Rhenish *Krüge*, creamware and whiteware mugs, and whiteware ointment jars, as well as pewter tankards, European clay pipes, jewelry, and a wide variety of glass beads'.[51] The gold took two forms: so-called fetish gold, or intricately worked jewellery, trinkets and regalia, and gold dust, *sika futuro*. The latter might be deposited in brass pots (*kuduo*) or imported flasks and jars, placed in pouches attached to the corpse, or sprinkled over the body and adhered to it—as we have seen with Asantehene Opoku Ware in life—by a coating of tallow or of shea butter from the northern savanna.[52] As with the living, the greater the degree of wealth and power of the individual, the richer the adornment of the deceased. Particular attention was given to the corpses of Akan *ahemmaa*, or 'queen mothers', who were seen in important ways to preside over the cycle of life and death. Whereas it was generally regarded as taboo to place silver in a grave, the corpses of *ahemmaa* often wore silver, which was regarded as cool, calming and peaceful—the ideal attributes of a queen mother—in contrast to the 'heat' of yellow gold. According to Meyerowitz, the seven openings of the face and the vagina were filled with silver dust—a further symbolic link, perhaps, between birth and death.[53] 'The gold buried with members of the royal family, and afterwards deposited with their bones in the fetish house at Bantama, is sacred', Bowdich explained of Asante. This gold cannot thereafter be used, he goes on, except 'to redeem the capital from the hands of an enemy, or in extreme national distress; and even then, the king must avoid the sight of it, if he would avoid the fatal vengeance of the fetish or deity'.[54]

As these restrictions on the use of the gold in the Asante royal mausoleum at Bantama indicate, grave gold was generally regarded as a reserve of wealth to be drawn upon in times of need.[55] For a family to open the grave of an ancestor and disinter the deposit of gold was therefore not necessarily seen as an act of desecration—although the circumstances under which such a removal was considered appropriate and who had the right to do so could be matters of some dispute. In 1738, a controversy is recorded at Cape Coast concerning the opening of the grave of the late African wife of the English trader James Phipps, prompted by a belief that a considerable amount of gold which should have been left as part of her legacy had been buried by her servants with the object of subsequently removing it.[56] Reports from the Gold Coast suggest that by the early nineteenth century, graves were regularly opened by the families of the deceased in order to remove the gold, an action which in some cases caused consternation but in others was considered a matter of course; according to one observer, 'the dead are buried with their ornaments, but at the end of a year exhumed, the body turned on its side to make it more comfortable, and then the ornaments removed from it'.[57] 'These buried treasures often form stores of wealth', one visitor reported in the late nineteenth century; 'I have heard a native of Accra state that he has lived for years upon his ancestors!'.[58]

Let us end by returning to the nexus of ideas surrounding gold, power and death via one infamous case of alleged grave robbery, at the pinnacle of the Asante social order. When Kwaku Dua Panin died after thirty-three years on the Golden Stool in 1867, the *adaka kese*, or 'great chest', which contained the kingdom's reserves of gold dust was reputed to be full. Yet his successor Kofi Kakari was a notorious spendthrift, rapidly frittering away the store of wealth accumulated by his uncle. A key source for Kofi Kakari's profligacy is the history written by Basel Mission pastor N. V. Asare in the early twentieth century: 'when he was taken inside the palace upon his enstoolment, Kakari was overwhelmed at the sight of so much gold in various receptacles. His immediate reaction was: "There is this much gold while people suffer amidst hunger and poverty". He began doling it out. He threw out handfuls of gold dust to the performers who pleased him. Thus, he earned the nickname *osape*'.[59] Kofi Kakari also departed from Kwaku Dua's policy of favouring mercantilism over military adventure: 'on the day he was sworn into office', Asare records, 'he held a flint lock in his mouth to indicate to the people that they should be prepared because his objective was war'.[60] Kofi Kakari's profligacy and militarism both ended in disaster. By the early 1870s, there was rising alarm within the court over the squandering of state wealth: a leading office-holder was reportedly executed for suggesting that the Asantehene rein in his spending, and the rescheduling of the 1871 Odwira may have been due to concerns about giving the Asantehene access to the reserves of sacred gold stored at the Bantama mausoleum and necessary to hold the festival.[61] The following year, Kofi Kakari's mother, Asantehemaa Afua Kobi, appears reluctantly to have transferred control over further state funds to her son—but these too were soon spent.[62] Then, in 1873, the decision to launch a military campaign into the British Gold Coast Protectorate backfired spectacularly. On the cusp of a new and more assertive European imperial age in Africa, the government in London responded by dispatching an expeditionary force to confront the Asante advance; by early 1874, Kofi Kakari's army had been defeated and British forces had advanced into Asante and briefly occupied Kumasi itself.

It was at this nadir of his career that Kofi Kakari allegedly fell upon the royal mausoleum in order to obtain further funds. Arranged before each of the coffins containing the rearticulated skeletons of those Asantehenes who had died in office were *kuduo* filled with gold dust. Distinct from that stored in the *adaka kese*, this gold was owned by the *asamanfo*, or ancestral spirits, of the departed Asantehenes and reserved, as Bowdich explained, for use at times of 'extreme national distress'. An amount was also 'borrowed' by the reigning Asantehene from his deceased forebears each year in order to finance Odwira; in both cases, the understanding was that the gold used must be replaced. No full account of the destoolment proceedings against Kofi Kakari in October 1874 exists, although we do know that he rejected the charges concerning the Bantama gold, quite possibly on the grounds that the dire situation he found himself in did indeed equate with one of national distress.[63] Yet the charges went beyond misuse of the *sika futuro* stored in the *kuduo*: according to an account given to a British envoy by Kumasi office-holders in 1883, Kofi Kakari instructed the guardians of the mausoleum 'to dig up the bodies' of his grandmother Asantehemaa Afua Sarpon and of his great-uncle Asantehene Osei Yaw Akoto. 'They did so as directed by him and took from the coffins all the gold dust, gold trinkets, gold chains, agri beads, and handed them all over to Kalkali.'[64] In line with his past behaviour, he gifted many items of jewellery to his various wives, and it was thus that Asantehemaa Afua Kobi was shocked to recognize certain pieces 'as having been worn years before by those who were then lying buried in the Bantamah'—that is, by her own mother, Afua Sarpon. Afua Kobi duly reported the matter to the Kumasi chiefs. Declaring that his own mother had disgraced him, Kofi Kakari threatened to destroy himself and the Golden Stool by gunpowder explosion, before backing down and agreeing to abdicate. The Asantehene himself, we might conclude, had violated the solemn exchange contract with his own ancestors and paid the heaviest of prices, one, that is, which would taint his reputation in the afterlife. He was a failed king; his mortal remains would never lie alongside those of his hallowed predecessors in the mausoleum he had desecrated.

'Fundamentally', Allan Kellehear writes, 'the good death as a rite of passage must pay its dues to the prevailing responsibilities of social reciprocity, economic exchanges and moral expectations of the community.'[65] At the core of this notion in the Akan world was the effort to forge bonds of mutual obligation between the living and the ancestral dead. Underpinning the enlargement of state power was a further elaboration of the ideology of the good death, which saw self-acquired wealth in the form of gold pass not just to the afterworld but to the state—the guarantor on earth of the cosmic order. Duty to the dead thus came to incorporate the fiscal instrument of 'death duties', both taking an increasingly monetized form in the age of Atlantic commerce and then breaking down in the face of political and social disruption from the late nineteenth century. Yet the good death, as Kellehear acknowledges, was a contested space, as we will see with the emergence from the mid-nineteenth century of written wills and testaments. The surreptitious hoarding of wealth and the desecration of graves make only too clear that prevailing responsibilities and moral expectations, moreover, might at any point be disrupted by cupidity, self-interest, vanity and ambition.

6

Faces of the Dead

MORTAL REMAINS, tombs and interred grave goods have for many centuries provided scholars with a tangible entry into how people in the past thought about death.[1] So too have artistic representations of death, dying and the dead themselves. This chapter considers the most visible material manifestation of funerary culture on the Gold Coast and in its forest hinterland before the twentieth century: commemorative terracotta sculptures of the dead. The Akan and their neighbours may have privileged the funeral over all other rites of passage and devoted much attention to maintaining a cordial relationship with their ancestors, but they were parsimonious when it came to artistic engagement with the dead. Unlike in many societies, from ancient Egypt to medieval Christian Europe and on to modern Mexico, death in Ghana has not left a powerful visual residue. Even within West Africa, the Akan region is notable for the absence of art that served to mediate with ancestors and the spirit world: in contrast to cultural zones to the west, north and east, it had, for example, no masking tradition.[2] The existence of funerary sculpture is therefore of considerable importance and the terracottas have attracted the attention of both archaeologists and art historians, assuming a place alongside metalwork, textiles and wood-carving in the spectrum of Akan achievement in the plastic arts. At least one historian has also made a thought-provoking intervention into this literature, arguing that what he calls the 'figurine cults' may have originated in mimicry of religious statues introduced into the Gold Coast by the Catholic Portuguese.[3] Less has been written, however, about the role of the terracottas within the wider Akan funerary complex. The focus here is on these evocative sculptures, but the aim, in the spirit of Sir Thomas Browne's reflections on ancient British burial urns, is that they illuminate something of that broader history of death.

The display of memorial sculptures on or near graves on the Gold Coast was noted by a number of observers over the centuries, beginning with de Marees in 1602. The figures themselves began to attract some scholarly attention in the early colonial period but were not excavated and analysed by archaeologists until the 1950s, by which time their use was becoming a thing of the past.[4] Identification of sites has been facilitated by the fact that sculptures (known by a variety of Twi terms: *nsanie*, 'things of clay'; *nsodea*, 'things of ashes'; *abodie*, 'things of stone'; *mma*, 'children'; or simply *ntiri*, 'heads') tend to be concentrated in locations known to local communities as *asensie*, 'the place of pots'. The first major excavation of an *asensie*, at Ahinsan, in the Adanse region in southern Asante, yielded some 150 terracotta heads, while a second, at Twifo Heman, near the Pra River in today's Central Region, yielded another thirty. Only three other sites have been properly excavated (with stratigraphic control and radiocarbon dating), all in the early 1990s and all in southern Asante near Ahinsan. Countless thousands of heads, however, have been collected in an ad hoc manner from a broad swathe of southern Ghana, from the Accra plains in the east to the present-day frontier with Côte d'Ivoire in the west—many by antique dealers who have sold them into the international market in African art. The sculptural tradition also extends into the Akan-speaking corner of southeastern Côte d'Ivoire, notably among the Sanwi and Anyi peoples around the Krinjabo lagoon. The Ahinsan and Twifo Heman finds have been dated to between the mid-seventeenth and early eighteenth centuries, while the more recently excavated sites range from a fifteenth-century *floruit* (Adansemanso) to one post-1650 and another post-1800.[5]

Funerary sculptures were sometimes complete human effigies made of either terracotta or wood, but the vast majority of surviving examples are ceramic heads—either created in that form or broken off from their torsos or the pot lids to which they were attached. The heads range in size from two or three inches in height (these often with long, tapered necks, enabling them to be planted in the ground) to life-size, and in style from abstracted to naturalistic. Across these spectrums of size and degree of naturalism, two basic forms can be identified: one in which the head is fashioned as a solid, flattened disc and the other, invariably hollow, shaped as a three-dimensional human head. Facial features tend to be quite simply moulded and accepted notions of beauty and status, such as a high forehead and fatty 'neck-rolls', accentuated. Yet close attention is often paid to distinctive features such as scarification patterns, hairstyles and, in some examples, jewellery. Many seem originally to have been

FIGURE 6.1. Terracotta funerary sculpture. One of two heads given by Adansehene Kwabena Fori to R. P. Wild, Gold Coast inspector of mines, in the early 1930s. Kwabena Fori informed Wild that he remembers such heads being crafted by an old woman when he was a boy (in the 1850s–60s), but that they had not been made for many years. They were placed directly on the graves of chiefs, queen mothers and elders rather than in an *asensie*, he recalled, and human hair was inserted into the attached cylinder: see Wild, 'Baked Clay Heads'. Height: 27 cm. Courtesy of the Trustees of the British Museum.

painted, while others have a highly burnished black patina or are covered with a red slip. These stylistic details, combined with evidence from written sources and from more recent ethnographic accounts, point to a key characteristic: that the sculptures were designed to be portraits of particular individuals. There is evidence too that they tended to be made by women and were fashioned either as that individual approached death or soon after their demise, to be used at key moments of the funeral ceremonies.⁶ Other heads were portraits of living servants or office-holders, placed in courtly ensembles around those representing the royal dead. Either way, *nsanie*, 'things of clay', are the faces of the dead, emerging from the humus of the forest floor to look silently back at us from across time.

———

The most informative early written sources for the sculptural tradition on the Gold Coast littoral describe highly elaborated and large-scale ensembles of figurines displayed on the grave or mausoleum of individuals of high status. In distinguishing between obsequies for ordinary folk and for people of wealth and status, de Marees identifies two distinctive features of the latter, aside from the fact that 'much more mourning and sadness is shown about it': human sacrifice and the display of funerary sculptures. Ordinary people and chiefs alike were interred with a wide range of personal items: 'clothes, weapons, Pots, Pans, Stools, Spades and similar chattels which he has used during his lifetime are brought to the Grave, buried with him and put around the Grave, so as to serve him in the other World in the same way as they did during his life on this earth'.⁷ 'But as a King needs more services than an ordinary person, many people also have to journey with him, accompany him on the way and serve him in the other World', de Marees explains. The bodies of those killed—slaves offered up by retainers, as well as the deceased's own wives—were interred with the body; the slaves' decapitated heads were arranged on the grave 'as a great ornament in honour of the King', alongside quantities of food and drink to sustain the retainers on their journey. Finally, 'all his Nobles, who used to serve him are modelled from life in earth, painted and put in a row all around the Grave, side by side. Thus their Sepulchres are like a House and furnished as if they were still alive; and this Sepulchre of the King is kept in high esteem and carefully guarded'.⁸ Slaves, that is to say, accompanied the deceased to the *asamando* in the flesh, while noble retainers got to go along as clay simulacra.

Unlike de Marees, French mariner Jean Barbot does not seem to have witnessed an actual funeral but does provide a valuable description of funerary sculpture at Elmina in 1682. Close to the castle, Barbot saw 'several tombs or little monuments, with abundance of puppets and antick ridiculous figures, which, as I was told, are of some kings, and other notable persons buried there, all adorn'd with imagery and other baubles'.⁹ He also alludes to a crucial aspect of royal mortuary practice not mentioned by de Marees or other seventeenth-century observers: that the remains of kings might be interred twice, first at 'a place in the forest', along with all the 'victuals, clothing and gold, but also . . . many slaves of both sexes', and subsequently, after decomposition and the re-articulation of the skeleton, in a mausoleum. 'They are accustomed to decorate these [mausoleums] with a large number of clay busts representing men and women', he explained. 'These busts are painted in various colours and garnished all over with coral and fetishes. At Mina . . . I saw several such mausoleums, for *brafos* and officers, including one for a relative of the king of Fetu, which had between 35 and 40 of these busts, displayed on posts and in a semi-circle in the midst of fetishes. All around them were several pots of palm wine and meat, together with leaves and branches from fetish trees.'[10] Müller and Bosman noted the display of funerary terracottas only in passing, although neither associated them particularly with deceased of high status. 'They are supposed to represent the deceased', the former wrote, while Bosman added that the figures were ceremonially washed on the occasion of the funeral celebration one year after the first.[11]

Two further descriptions from the mid-nineteenth century add detail to the nature of the assemblages seen by de Marees and Barbot. 'Upon the death of a great man', the Cape Coast–based merchant Brodie Cruickshank wrote in 1853, 'they make representations of him, sitting in state, with his wives and attendants seated around him'.

> Beneath a large tree in Adjumacon, we once saw one of these groups, which had a very natural appearance. The images were, some jet black, some tawny-red, and others of all shades of colours between black and red, according to the complexion of the originals, whom they were meant to represent. They were nearly as large as life, and the proportions between the men and women, and boys and girls, were well maintained. Even the soft and feminine expressions of the female countenance were clearly brought out. The cabboceer and his principal men were represented smoking their long pipes, and some boys upon their knees were covering the fire in the bowls, to give them a proper light. There is no apotheosis of the dead intended by these representations: they are simply monuments to their memory like the statues of our great men. No care is paid to their preservation after they have been set out for exhibition, but there they remain until they crumble to pieces. It is chiefly women who are employed in making these figures.[12]

In 1840, the Methodist missionary Robert Brooking witnessed the construction of such an ensemble towards the end of the cycle of funeral rites of a powerful Ga office-holder of Accra who had died some months before. A mile beyond the town limits, a hundred images were arranged under roofed structures forming three sides of a square, the fourth side acting as an entrance to 'this town in miniature'. 'In these sheds they were all placed in a seating position, with tables before them on which were placed food of various kinds, decanters, and bottles of rum, with dram glasses and tumblers and jugs of water. Some of these figures were neatly dressed . . . , strings of valuable beads ornamented their persons and one even had a gold chain about his neck, some had large tobacco pipes in their mouths, and were waited on by boys of the same materials.'[13] It is unclear whether either of these assemblages was associated with an actual grave site. The likelihood is that they were not, especially with respect to that at Accra, where the bodies of both office-holders and ordinary townspeople tended to be interred within their houses. What they may have been were the beginnings of an *asensie*, a concentrated deposit of funerary heads and other ritual ceramics often adjacent to but distinct from burial grounds themselves. Kwabena Wiredu, James Bellis's informant at Twifo Heman, reported that as late as the First World War he had observed the people of one town in the kingdom of Wassa going into the bush to pour libation to the 'ancestral images' contained in such a ceramic royal court.[14] The prominence of the smoking pipes—tobacco having been introduced into West Africa as part of the Columbian exchange—is striking. Noted as a feature of funerary sculpture in other parts of the continent, such as the lower Congo, it might be read not just as a favoured pastime of the deceased but as an indication of the reflective and authoritative disposition that he was expected to carry into the afterlife.[15]

An indigenous oral tradition reflecting on the placement of *nsanie* can also be noted. It comes from Reindorf's pioneering history and concerns an early eighteenth-century ruler of the southeastern Akan kingdom of Agona, Nyako Kwaku.[16] Nyako was remembered as a tyrannical and cruel figure, who was overthrown in an invasion by neighbouring kingdoms and, having fled into the bush, murdered by the family of one of his victims. The tradition that, for Reindorf, best encapsulated Nyako's erratic behaviour involved the funeral of his mother. Noting that it was customary 'to make figures or statues of the deceased, either of clay or wood, which are placed under a shed outside the town, and honoured by daily meat offerings', Reindorf recounts how Nyako objected to these offerings being eaten by wild animals. 'He said, "Spirits are like winds, and therefore the spirit of my mother can enjoy the meal anywhere else than on the roads". He accordingly ordered that the statue and offerings be placed at the top of a large silk-cotton tree, guarded by a sentry who would 'cry to travellers passing by, "Wouldn't you look at the statue of Nyako Ako's mother?" Hence, when children are cross and trouble their mothers by crying, the mothers usually tell them, "Mayest thou weep on and die, even if thou could do me once the honour of placing my statue and meal on a silk-cotton-tree!"'.[17]

———

More recent ethnographic evidence throws further light on the function of the funerary images and the *asensie*, the 'place of pots'. In 1927, Rattray set out in some detail the successive stages of the obsequies of an ordinary Asante.[18] On the day of burial, usually the third after death, the party bearing the body to the clan burial ground, or *asamanpow* (the thicket of ghosts), is led by the deceased's spouse, who carries on his or her head a pot containing three stones and known as the *kuna kukuo*, 'the widow's or widower's pot'. At the point where the general mourners turn back to leave the family to proceed to the graveside, the spouse—for he or she is not 'family'—turns; allows the pot to fall to the ground and shatter, to release the stones; and then runs into town without looking back. The symbolic role of ceramics continues three days later, on *sora da*, 'the day of rising', six days after death, when ritual action is focused on a temporary roofed structure containing a mortar and pestle, a strainer, three hearthstones (*bukyia*), a newly made pot, and a spoon. Food is cooked using the utensils and a pot called the *abusua kuruwa*, the 'family' or lineage pot, is produced, which generally has a lid topped by the sculpture representing the deceased. ('The Dutch writer Bosman mentions these', Rattray notes.) The heads of family members are now shaved and the hair is placed in the pot. At dusk the pot, the utensils and the cooked food are all carried to the *asamanpow*, the family again being very careful never to look behind, and are all deposited not on the grave but in the *asensie*. The association of the terracotta figurines with this wider funerary assemblage is confirmed by Bellis's excavation of the *asensie* at Twifo Heman, which revealed numerous *bukyia* composed of three upturned hearth pots. That spherical portrait heads commonly have a hole in the back also suggests that they themselves may have acted as receptacles for the hair of the deceased or of mourners in lieu of an *abusua kuruwa*.[19] Further rites normally follow on the eighth, fifteenth,

FIGURE 6.2. *Asensie*, or 'the place of pots'. Photograph taken by Friedrich Ramseyer between 1888 and 1908 and captioned 'Place where the pots of the deceased are kept'. Basel Mission Archives D-30.23.022.

fortieth and eightieth day after death, as well as on the first anniversary—but it is on the *sora da*, Rattray writes, that 'the ghost departs to the land of spirits'.

A decade later, in 1938, Rattray's successor as Gold Coast government anthropologist, M. J. Field, gained further information on the manufacture and use of funerary terracottas when she attended the week-long 'farewell celebration' for the late *omanhene* of the Akan state of Akyem Kotoku, who had died some months before.[20] On the climactic day of the celebration, the *abusua kuruwa* of the *omanhene*, together with those of more recently departed chiefs and members of the royal family, were paraded through the kingdom's capital, Oda. 'All these dead people', Field wrote, 'were believed to be "travelling together"'. The glazed black terracottas atop the pots had been made by an elderly woman from nearby Nyakrom, 'one of the few remaining good exponents of her craft'. Field called on this woman during the production process, but she would allow neither her 'nor anyone else to see the images being made lest the likeness of the personality of the spectator rather than that of the dead person should accidentally get into the image'. The figurines, dressed in rich clothes, were placed under palm-leaf awnings in Oda's main square, where 'their living friends came and saluted them and bade them farewell'. They were then carried to the *barim*, or royal mausoleum, while 'the crowd waved and shouted Good-bye with much emotion'. The following day, as specially appointed royal officials 'sat in the square and counted out the money—rice-bags full of it—that had been contributed towards the expenses', the late *omanhene*'s successor took Field to the *barim*, where, 'after due prayers and libations', he allowed her to photograph the terracotta images. Field admitted that she missed much of the complex ceremonial, but two things she did not miss: 'the solidarity of the *oman* and the solidarity between the living and the dead'.[21]

Similar scenes were recorded six years later at the final obsequies of Nana Sir Ofori Atta, the *omanhene* of the neighbouring kingdom of Akyem Abuakwa. On the evening of the sixth day of the celebrations, Sunday 27 February 1944, after a memorial service at St Mark's Anglican Church, the *abusua kuruwa* of the late ruler, topped by an effigy 'wearing a gold crown and royal robes adorned with costly jewels, carrying a gold sword of state ... and canopied by two state umbrellas', was paraded in a palanquin through the streets of the capital, Kyebi.[22] In front of the sculpture in the palanquin and wearing the late *omanhene*'s battle smock sat the so-called *awusu*—that is, one of the king's *akrafo*, young boys who embodied his *kra* or 'soul' and who in the past would have been destined for ritual immolation. 'The *atumpan* drums rolled, horns bellowed, guns volleyed, and women and girls shrieked and wailed at this moving sight', wrote one observer, Kwame Frimpong. 'The *abusuakuruwa* looked in every respect like the late Okyenhene.' Earlier in the week, before the appearance of the terracotta sculpture, a different and innovative medium of portraiture was also put on display: a photograph of the late Ofori Atta. The image seems to have been treated with some reverence—'behind this photograph stood two musketeers', Frimpong noted, 'their faces painted one red and one black'—an early sign of the way in which photography would supplant the terracottas as the primary medium for displaying the faces of the dead.

What Frimpong did not record—and what was only fully to emerge in the course of a criminal trial eight months later—was that at the same moment as the terracotta effigy of the late king was passing through the streets of the capital, eight of his kinsmen lured one Akyea Mensah, the *odikro*, or headman, of the town of Apedwa, into the royal palace and decapitated him. It was last proven instance of an alleged 'human sacrifice' associated with the funeral of an Akan royal in the colonial Gold Coast—all eight men were convicted of murder and sentenced to death, three of whom, after a prolonged legal process, were hanged in 1947.[23]

Field was privileged to have been allowed entry to the precincts of the Akyem Kotoku royal mausoleum to view, let alone to photograph, the *nsanie* in 1938. Much of the ceremony surrounding the sequence of funeral rites for Akan *amanhene* and other royals was secretive and the sacred sites were strictly off-limits to the general public. 'What is about to be recorded', Rattray wrote, in a typically revelatory tone, of his description of the funeral of kings, 'is still known only to a very few Ashanti themselves, who are connected with the royal mausoleums at Bantama and at the *Barim Kese*'—that is, the 'great *barim*' or *asonyeso*, 'the place of drippings', where for eighty days the royal corpse was first laid to allow the flesh to fall from its bones.[24] Even if he had been able to witness the funeral of an Asantehene—the last full funeral had been for Kwaku Dua Panin in 1867 and the next, with significant modifications, would be for Agyeman Prempeh in 1931—it is unlikely that he would have been able to add a great deal to the rather sketchy account recorded in 1927. One source, however, does address the matter of terracotta portraiture as it relates to Asante royalty, and it comes from the highest echelon of political power: *The History of Ashanti Kings*. Associated with Agyeman Prempeh's account are a number of preliminary manuscripts, one of which is titled 'Bodies of Men of Regiments Organized by King Otti Akenten'—the late seventeenth-century *omanhene* who first established Kumasi as a seat of power. Inserted into an explanation of one of those bodies of men, the *asoamfo*, or royal hammock-bearers, is a unique account of the *sora* of an Asantehene, which resonates with that described for an ordinary Asante subject by Rattray and with the 'farewell celebrations' described for the two Akyem rulers.[25]

The *sora* ('S-oulah') of an Asantehene, it is revealed, took place on the eighth day of the *afehyia* ('Yer-tua ayier'), the great anniversary celebration of the king's death. The day began with the Kontihene and the Akomhene, two of the ranking Kumasi military commanders, mobilizing warriors to accompany the Golden Stool to the forest of Fafrahamoo, to the southwest of the city. Meanwhile, the current Asantehene and leading representatives of the ruling Oyoko clan gather at the ward of Sanyaase, while the Akyempenhene directs the ritual clearing of the path leading to the Kumasi ward of Daaboase— 'at that place is found the statues or earthen busts of Ashanti Kings'. An arch of tree branches cut during the path-clearing is then constructed outside the Asantehene's palace, under which a new terracotta of the late king is placed 'in an earthen pot . . . on a special stool . . . and all the decorations and Jewelleries of the Ashanti King is placed around the bust according to its proper situations'. The bust, it is noted, is 'sculpted by a society of women' from Abuakwa, the pottery-making centre to the northwest of Kumasi. The Kontihene and Akomhene then bring the Golden Stool back from the forest and hand it over to the Asantehene. In the afternoon a chosen Oyoko woman carries the pot containing the bust to Daaboase, 'and there a great procession of princes, princesses, royal families and chiefs follow with all the decorations of the King behind and before, in order just as when a living King is in full uniform'. From the arch to Daaboase, the account concludes,

> a man servant is taken from each Department of the royal house and placed right and left along the road with an executioner behind each man . . . and when the procession has reached Darboasy, three big stones are chosen and are placed in triangular form as a cooking tripod and these chosen servants are killed and [their] legs broken [i.e., severed] and the broken legs are placed on the three sides of the tripod just as fire woods are placed between tripods for cooking and the pot with the statue is placed on the tripod. . . . This is to prove that the ceremony of the deceased sovereign is completely ended.[26]

'We know of no comparable account of funerary practices for an Asantehene', the editors of the critical edition of *The History of Ashanti Kings* note. 'Rattray describes certain rites, but made no reference to the sculpting of a bust of a dead king by the women of Abuakwa.'[27] In fact, one other source does describe this process: the account of Agyeman Prempeh's own *afehyia* in 1932—an event modified in the era of colonial rule by the absence of the killing of the royal servants on the path to Daaboase.[28] We will return to this event, and to the question of human sacrifice, in later chapters. Here, attention can simply to drawn to the dramatic elaboration of the symbolic role of the *bukyia*, the three hearthstones, against which, Agyeman Prempeh revealed, were stacked dismembered limbs 'just as fire woods are placed between tripods for cooking'.

Together with issues of form and function, archaeological and art historical literature on Akan funerary sculpture has been concerned with the issue of origins. Early suggestions about where the terracotta tradition may have 'come from' were characterized, in the absence of anything approaching firm evidence, with typically speculative notions of diffusion from the Sudanic zone or from the region of Nigeria. Rejecting these theories, Timothy F. Garrard advanced an alternative hypothesis: that the tradition was inspired by Catholic statuary in the churches of the Portuguese trading stations on the Mina coast. Garrard bases this argument on three main lines of evidence: that neither scientific dating nor written sources indicate the existence of terracottas before the sixteenth century; that most have been found in the southern reaches of the Akan forest, with few coming from the Asante heartland and none from the Bono region, to the north; and that written accounts of the parading of figures, such as those quoted above by Field and Frimpong, evoke the carrying of statues of saints and the Virgin Mary in the Latin world. Inspired by events such as the miraculous transformation of the statue of St Francis in 1632 and by the residual presence in Elmina of an indigenous *irmandade* (a Portuguese Catholic brotherhood) venerating an image of St Anthony, local peoples, Garrard suggests, carried the 'cult' along trading routes 'to all those inland states which, through the gold trade, had close and immediate contact with Europeans on the coast'. 'In view of the parallels in appearance, function and associated ritual', he argues, 'it is difficult to resist the conclusion that Akan terracotta figurines took their inspiration from the same source'—that is, from Elmina's sixteenth-century *irmandade*.[29]

I would argue that it is not at all difficult to resist this conclusion. Garrard's hypothesis is carefully constructed and, in light of the apparent influence of Christian concepts on the Gold Coast already discussed, not beyond the realm of possibility. Yet the evidence is, at best, circumstantial and, at worst, based on the sort of morphological similarities that once characterized now outdated theories of cultural diffusion. The role of terracottas in recoverable histories of death and burial, not their putative origins, is our concern here, so the issue need not detain us further. It can be noted, however, that the absence of excavated terracotta sites north of Adanse does not necessarily mean—as is clear from both Rattray's account and Prempeh's *History of Ashanti Kings*—that they did not exist in what would later become the Asante heartland. The most recent radiocarbon dates from Adansemanso, moreover, serve to disrupt Garrard's diffusionist chronology, and it is perhaps telling that neither Doran Ross nor Herbert M. Cole, the leading art historians of Ghana—nor indeed Garrard himself—choose to advance the thesis in recent surveys of Akan art.[30]

What, then, can be concluded about these evocative terracotta portraits? First, the fact that they were created by women potters underlines the crucial gender dynamics of funerary culture. Garrard makes much of the apparent absence of terracottas in the Bono region on the forest–savanna fringe, although a tradition was recorded there in the 1940s that Kyereme Mansa (one of the ancient *ahemaa*, or 'queen mothers', of the Bono-Takyiman kingdom) 'is remembered as an excellent potter and patroness of potters, to whom she gave permission to use the human figure in ceramics'.[31] Agyeman Prempeh and Field both point to women as the creators of *nsanie*; so too does the pioneering collector of the colonial period R. P. Wild, whose informants in Agona Swedru told him of a famous potter named Sekyiwa, who died around 1928 and 'was supposed to have supernatural powers'. 'She used to take some water in a brass pan and invoke the spirit of the deceased, which appeared in the water.'[32] Among the Akan and their neighbours on the Gold Coast, as in many parts of Africa, women were generally responsible for all pottery-making—but this does not detract from their role in fashioning objects of such powerful symbolic importance. Again, we see women 'giving birth' to the ancestral dead.

Second, we must consider the symbolic function of the terracottas. Wild's account of the potter Sekyiwa and Field's of the elderly woman at Nyakrom both point to a ritual process by which the 'spirit' or the 'likeness of the personality' of the deceased was drawn into the figurine. So too does the testimony of Kwabena Wiredu, who told Bellis that when living in Wassa in the 1910s he witnessed people posing for portraits, as well as potters gazing into a pan filled with palm oil and set on a fire in order to catch a glimpse of the already dead. Whether this spirit was seen to be the *kra* or the *sunsum* (or a fragmented element of either) is unclear—although evidence does suggest that the role of the image as a venerated receptacle of personhood was ephemeral. Cruickshank's observation that 'no care is paid to their preservation after they have been set out for exhibition' appears to be accurate; from an art historical perspective, the artist and scholar Kofi Antubam decried the fact that such lovely sculptures were 'thrown away into the cemetery and left to the mercy of the seasons and forest growth.'[33] There is also no doubt that the terracottas, like much Akan artistic production, bore the imprint of political power. Most written sources associate them with the ruling elite, either as the large-scale simulacra of royal courts described by de Marees in 1602 and by others in the nineteenth century, or as effigies deployed in the funeral celebrations of *amanhene* reported by Agyeman Prempeh, Field and Frimpong. As such, they can be seen to have served visually to reinforce the continuation of the hierarchy of the known world into the *asamando*: the notion that kings would remain as kings and their *nkoa*, or subjects, as *nkoa*. In this respect, the connections between the tradition of terracotta display and that of mortuary slaying—so graphically portrayed by Prempeh—is revealing. Here, again, we glimpse the entangled realms of power, religion and art.[34]

In this respect, we can return to one puzzling morphological feature of funerary heads: that a great many bear carefully fashioned scarification marks. These include large, finely wrought examples which otherwise seem to be portraits of elite individuals. Yet the Akan, in contrast to the peoples of the savanna region to the north, did not practice facial scarification; indeed, for the former it served to identify so-called *nnonkofo* as culturally inferior and enslaveable. What might this tell us about their function? Bellis offers an intriguing, and plausible, hypothesis, based in part on the interpretation of Kwabena Wiredu and other informants at Twifo Heman: that where such scarification marks do appear, they may represent an attempt to deceive harmful spiritual forces by disguising the true identity of the deceased. As we will see, such a subterfuge was commonly mounted when a newborn child was perceived as being in danger of being snatched back by death: the parents pretended to neglect the child, who was often given a 'horrible name' and, in time, *nnonkofo*-style scarification marks.[35] If *nsanie* represented both the elite dead and those who continued to serve them, then the boundary between the two was in some cases perhaps deliberately obfuscated.

Finally, there is the issue of historical change. The key question here is the extent to which funerary portraiture shifted from being a prerogative of ruling elites to one employed across a broader spectrum of society. Opinions on this vary: while some scholars stress an underlying continuity of form and function, others stress transformation. On the basis of the most recent archaeological evidence, Brian Vivian shows that over time *asensie* became less elaborated, with increasingly less complex assemblages and representational forms less defined by the formal canon of beauty and status. This appears to suggest a broadening of the tradition from the ruling elite to a least some 'commoners'— perhaps generated by an increasing diffusion of wealth through society as a result of the expanding exchange economy.[36] Nii Otokunor Quarcoopome also argues for dynamism, concluding that while 'terracotta art might have begun as a royal prerogative, it transformed from a grave decoration to an elaborate, recurrent public ritual, organized not only for chiefs but for the wealthy in general'.[37] Perhaps—although the absence of accounts of the parading of images in the early documentary sources does not mean that such rituals did not happen, while as early as 1682 Barbot saw sculptural displays for kings 'and other notable persons'. New archaeological finds may provide additional evidence. One thing is certain: across the centuries, these haunting terracotta faces continue to evoke the spirit of the dead. Ritually, they may have played a key role in removing this spirit both from its corrupting body and from the world of the living. Yet artistically, as Roland Barthes wrote of the medium that ultimately would supplant the terracottas, they recall 'that rather terrible thing which is there in every photograph: the return of the dead'.[38]

7

The Severed Head

JOHN KONNY WAS one of a new class of wealthy brokers that emerged on the western Gold Coast in the late seventeenth century. Born around 1670 in the Ahanta region, he rose to prominence as an agent of the short-lived Brandenburg African Company, founded in 1682 and which the following year built a fort on Cape Three Points in an attempt to break into the expanding export trade in slaves.[1] Like his contemporaries Edward Barter (d. 1704) and John Kabes (d. 1722), Konny sought to parlay his role as a middleman for European trade into independent commercial clout and political authority. The world of Atlantic commerce he insinuated himself into, however, was a violent and capricious one. When in 1718 the Brandenburgers abandoned the coast and sold up to their erstwhile Dutch rivals, the latter moved to eject Konny from his position on Cape Three Points. A force of 120 soldiers was sent to retake the fort, but as Dutch records note, 'as soon as these men set foot on shore they were met with a heavy fire, and in a few minutes most of them were dead'.[2]

Three years later, Konny remained entrenched in his stronghold, extracting a lucrative duty of one ounce of gold from every ship stopping to take on water. It was then, in June 1721, that he was visited by two Royal Navy men-of-war, whose surgeon, John Atkins, left a record of the encounter. An initial failure to pay Konny's duty resulted in a display of the pugnacious qualities that had seen off the Dutch threat: he promptly imprisoned a dozen sailors, whose officer, 'endeavouring to distinguish to John the Difference of a King's Ship from others, got his Head broke: John (who understands English enough to swear) saying, by G—me King here'.[3] Accepting six ounces and an anchor of brandy in recompense, Konny extended his hospitality to the ships' officers. Regaling them with an account of his defeat of the Dutch, he explained how his forces ambushed the landing party, 'outnumbered and cut them in pieces' and how he set about 'paving the entrance of his Palace soon after, with their Skulls'.[4]

Intrigued, Atkins pursued the topic on a subsequent visit to John's well-appointed stone residence:

> Finding our Landlord cheerful and familiar, I ventured to ask him what was become of the Dutchmen's Skulls that lately paved the entrance of his House. He told me very frankly, that about a Month before our Ship's Arrival, he had put them all into a Chest with some Brandy, Pipes, and Tobacco, and buried them; for, says he, it is time that all Malice should depart, and the putting up a few Necessaries with the Corps, such as they loved, is our way of respecting the deceased. Among themselves, I learned it was customary with the Rich, to sacrifice a Slave or two also at their funerals. The under Jawbones of these Dutchmen he shewed me strung, and hanging on a Tree in the Courtyard.[5]

John Konny's triumphant display became the stuff of local legend: in 1893, the colonial officer A. B. Ellis noted that 'the tradition of these doings, considerably exaggerated, still lingers on in the neighbourhood'.[6] Kwame Daaku, a historian of a later, nationalist generation, however, lamented that it 'is an unfortunate memorial for a man who not long after his victory over the Dutch decently "interred" his trophies in accordance with the custom of his country'.[7] Yet Daaku's judgement that Konny's cranial pavement, together with the tradition that he reserved one skull, lined with silver, for use as a drinking vessel, was 'unfortunate', in contrast to his 'decent' burial of his trophies, imposes the sensibilities of a 1960s present onto the past. Far from representing some indecent aberration, the preservation and aesthetic display of the mortal remains of vanquished foes as mnemonics of military prowess and embodiments of ritual power was as ubiquitous a 'custom of the country' as the proper interment of one's own near and dear. Underlying such display was a range of what Julia Kristeva has called 'capital visions'—that is, understandings of the severed human head as a metaphor for the sacred, as an encapsulation of horror and as an ideological artefact saturated with meaning.[8] If across cultures dead bodies have been understood to hold some great if often indeterminate potency, then that potency was encapsulated in the head. The startling transfiguration effected by its removal from the torso can be seen as the apotheosis of corporeal violence and appropriation.[9]

Accounts of the curation of enemies' skulls (Twi: *ntikoraa*, sing. *tikoraa*, from *ti* or *tiri*, 'head') on the Gold Coast date back to the late sixteenth century. De

Marees counted up to fifty of them placed around the grave of a king of Eguafo near Komenda; these, he was informed, belonged to Portuguese soldiers killed in a war in the 1570s.[10] In 1633, the French Capuchin Father Colombin observed at Komenda that if the body of a successful warrior was being buried, 'then all his trophies, human skulls, would be displayed on the grave as a sign of his prowess. Such enemy skulls were esteemed so highly that they were guarded in private homes like a treasure. In some places the skulls were even used as goblets'.[11] Colombin then made a point that would be confirmed by numerous accounts over the centuries: that the acquisition of enemy heads was a key element of local warfare. 'The sex, age, or condition of the victim', he believed, made 'no difference whatsoever'—although on that score he was misinformed: the identity of the skull, as we shall see, did indeed make a difference, with those of powerful chiefs carrying great significance.

In the immediate aftermath of battle, the severed head itself served as the focus of triumphal celebration. Writing of the Fetu region in the 1660s, Müller observed that victorious warriors adorned themselves splendidly in full military regalia and paraded around the countryside with musicians, family and retainers, who carried the heads of the vanquished. 'If they come to any place, be it the public market, an important man's courtyard or even one of the forts . . . they throw the heads of their enemies which they have obtained down on the ground; and everyone—young and old, men and women—runs up in excitement and treads on them with his feet.'[12] After these processions, the heads and other body parts were boiled in pots—not as an indication of cannibalism, as de Marees had supposed, but in order cleanly to extract the skull and bones. While the warrior retained the skulls, he freely distributed the jaws to his slaves, who 'tie the jawbones to sticks and dance with them day and night, until they can no longer speak'.[13] Aside from being treasured at home and then placed on the grave of their owners, relics were also attached to battle-dress, to the handles of swords, and, most notably, to the side of drums and to elephant tusk trumpets. 'At Accra', Barbot wrote, 'I saw one [warrior] who had 21 of these dry skulls and jaw-bones attached to his cap and his drum.'[14]

These observations tend to be made matter-of-factly rather than in any obviously lurid or racially censorious manner. In an age when Europeans might regularly witness extreme physical punishment involving the grisly dismemberment of bodies and their subsequent public display, there was nothing particularly exoticized about their descriptions of the use of crania on the Gold Coast. Indeed, after visiting John Konny in 1721, Atkins proceeded to Cape Coast, where he acted as recorder for the trial of a party of captured pirates, whose bodies after execution were directed to be hung in chains around the town until the flesh fell from the bones.¹⁵ Neither were such customs peculiar to the Gold Coast: the acquisition and symbolic display of the human head in the Dahomey kingdom on the Slave Coast to the east, for example, was of a magnitude and elaboration which went beyond that of the Akan region.¹⁶ By the eighteenth century, moreover, sources begin to yield insight into the psychology, the cosmology and the ideology shaping the treatment of severed heads. For this we turn from the western to the eastern reaches of the Gold Coast and to the memoirs of Ludewig Rømer, who from 1739 to 1749 was factor at the Danish West India and Guinea Company's headquarters of Christiansborg Castle at the Ga town of Osu.

Rømer was a slave trader but also a keen observer of Ga culture whose considerable insight into the spiritual realm was acquired from his close friend Okpoti, a *caboceer* of the neighbouring seaside town of Labadi and a priest, or *wulomo*, of its famous oracle shrine of Lakpa. He introduces a chapter on Ga religion with a reflection on local sensitivities surrounding that realm. 'We have to be a long time on the Coast before a Black will give any answer to our questions about his religion. Furthermore, we must, in fact, have been there for several years without anyone seeing us laugh at their ceremonies, or, when they answered our questions, without a European ridiculing them'. To illustrate this, Rømer recounts a typical conversation with Okpoti (Putti):

> I can recall that, one afternoon, Caboceer Putti came to see me, bringing greetings from the fetish (the oracle) . . . and he added a request for a bottle of brandy. However, since it had not been long before that I had given him some brandy, I objected, adding the challenge that his fetish, while not as great and powerful as the fetish of the Fante, was more thirsty for brandy than that one was. If, I said to Putti, your fetish can lift an ox or cow up into the air, as the Fante fetish can, I would be willing to wager our old ox to see it happen. Putti answered that the Labode fetish was unable to do this. I asked why not, and received an answer that the ancestors of the Fantes were all with God, but our own (the Labodes') had died in war. Thereupon, when I asked if those who died in war did not also go to God, he fell silent, and sent away on an errand an old Negro who was with him. Then, when we were alone, he answered my question thus: 'Don't you know, master, that the Blacks cut each other's heads off in war, and do you think that God receives people without heads? Can he not get enough people who die in their homes and are buried with their heads on?' I had to be satisfied with the answer.¹⁷

Okpoti's discreet explanation for the greater ritual efficacy of the Fante *obosom* Nananom Mpow relative to that of the *jemawon* Lakpa points to a fear, shared by both Akan and Ga, that entry of the deceased into the community of the afterworld was prevented by decapitation. Whether this fear can be considered a doctrinal 'belief', however, is debatable—as perhaps indicated by the rhetorical nature of Okpoti's suggestion. It was not so much the separation of head and body per se but the removal of the former into alien hands without proper interment that caused the greatest anxiety. Bosman had observed how 'the Negroes are strangely fond of being buried in their own Country', but if anybody died at too great a distance to carry home the entire corpse and 'if he have any Friends or Acquaintance there, they cut off his Head, one Arm, and one Leg, which they cleanse, boil, and carry to his own Country, where they are interred with fresh Solemnity'.[18] This accords with the reported practice of warriors cutting off and removing the heads of their own fallen comrades on the battlefield in order that they not fall into the hands of their enemies.[19] As we have seen with the corpse of Osei Tutu, remains might also be smoked in order to preserve them while being carried home. The horror of one's head being acquired by an enemy also explains the propensity for warriors, when facing inevitable defeat, to commit suicide by gunpowder explosion or musket shot to the head—thereby destroying the cranium in the process.

The issue of decapitation and expectations of the afterlife extended into the enslaved Gold Coast diaspora of the wider Atlantic world. The hope of a posthumous return home to Africa was widely reported from the Americas, as was the belief among slave-owners that decapitation represented the ultimate punitive sanction against rebellion.[20] Such eschatological violence began in the slave-owning communities of the seaside towns themselves, as well as on board ships before or during the Middle Passage. Commenting on the posthumous beheading of the body of a leader of an attempted shipboard rebellion on the Gold Coast in 1721, the slave trader William Snelgrave explained that 'many of the Blacks believe, that if they are put to death and not dismembered, they shall return again to their own Country'. He notes, however, a degree of scepticism among his particularly tough-minded Gold Coast captives: 'But neither the Person that was executed, nor his Countrymen of Cormantee (as I understood afterwards) were so weak as to believe any such thing; tho' many I had on board from other Countries had that opinion'.[21] That may have been so, but it is difficult when examining punitive violence against enslaved peoples to separate out eschatological anxiety from the sheer visceral horror that such theatrical displays were designed to instil.

The political context on the eastern Gold Coast is also important for an understanding of Okpoti's reflections. The war he refers to was the calamitous rupture of 1677–81, when the centralized Ga state was conquered and destroyed by the Akan kingdom of Akwamu. Sporadic resistance continued, until finally suppressed by the Akwamu at great loss of life in 1702. Akwamu rule was imposed on the eastern coast until 1730, a decade before Rømer's arrival, when it was overthrown by a rebellion of the Ga and their Akyem allies. The half-century of subjugation to the Akwamu may have been over, but the humiliations and depredations of the period left the Dane's Ga interlocutors with a profoundly melancholy outlook tinged by nostalgic memories of a lost 'golden age'. The custom of accumulating the severed heads of enemies was held by Okpoti to be a recent innovation pioneered by the brutally militarized Akwamu, whose decapitation of so many Labadis had denuded the tutelary deity Lakpa of 'followers' and thereby sapped its oracular and protective powers.

Rømer went on to elaborate on the motivations for decapitation, which he admits were entangled with a broader escalation of violence associated with the European demand for slaves.

> Should the Aqvamboes [Akwamus] capture any of their traditional enemies, the Akron and Agona Negroes, and among the prisoners is an old man, or a member of one of the prominent families, they do not sell him but torture him dreadfully, finally cutting off his head, and boiling the flesh in a pot so that the bones or skull are bare. Then the entire nation gathers in the Residence. Their king and prominent people make sport of the head, wipe their feet on the jawbone . . . , pound on the skull, spit on it, etc. The Agona and Akron Negroes do the same to any prominent Aqvamboes whom they take as prisoners. Finally, they tie the skulls to their drums, so that they may have a great many heads hanging on the town's drum. They believe that the spirit or soul of the murdered Black experiences very great pain from the sound and noise of the drum, and they are not satisfied with having tortured him in life but also want to torment him after death.[22]

As in many cultures, the placing of the feet on the head was rooted in a bodily register which held the head to be the seat of intellect and personhood and the foot to be the foundation of physical and, by extension, political strength. A person's *kra* was seen to reside in the head. As Bowdich would later note of Asante military culture, the 'heads of the slain are hurried into the rear, to be pressed by the foot of the reclining general, who, in his affected contempt of the enemy, has his draft-board before him'.²³ The preservation of the dry relics, Bowdich was told in confidence, stemmed from an anxiety to keep the dead man's vengeful *sasa* at bay: 'if they did not, their vigour and courage would be secretly wasted by the haunting spirit of the deceased'.²⁴

The curation of relics on musical instruments appears to have been motivated by the same reason. Attaching crania to the side of the great *fontomfrom* state drums and jawbones (*mmodwe*; sing. *abodwe*) to ivory trumpets transferred the spiritual power of the dead to the instrument: the trumpets were known by the Asante as *mmodwe-mmodwe*, and it is tempting to suggest that their speech-like calls were understood to be enhanced by the body part associated with verbal communication.²⁵ The torment effected on an enemy's hollow cranium by the booming of the *fontomfrom* must further be explained by the notion that the deceased retain some degree of sensory perception. Oral traditions record that another drum ensemble, the *apirede*, employed crania as the actual instruments, the sound of the wooden drumsticks on the skulls simulating the sparse, dry sounds of the dead. Even when this instrumentation was discontinued in the twentieth century, Nketia noted, the *apirede* retained a fearful reputation, tradition maintaining that 'it was first heard by someone at a burial grove where he found "ghosts" playing and dancing to it'.²⁶

Torments, of course, were designed to be directed not just at the dead but at their living kin. 'No misery among Christians', Rømer continues, 'is comparable to the agony and pain that a Black experiences when the heads of his forefathers are in the hands of the enemy'.

> It rankles and offends him as long as he exists on earth; and he bequeaths that rankling and pain to his descendants, who, in turn, during their lifetimes plot how they can retrieve the head and wreak revenge on the descendants of their ancestor's enemies.... On the few occasions I have engaged in confidential conversations with such Blacks, I started by assuring them that the deceased felt not the slightest pain, no matter how much his enemies mistreated the dead body or bones ... One of them asked me to say no more, and assured me that meeting one of his friends or acquaintances, he did not dare to look at him. He felt that he could read in everyone's eyes that they were saying, 'Fetch back the head of your king, your ancestors, your friends!'²⁷

That same agony was also captured by Rask, who served at Christiansborg Castle during the period of Akwamu overrule. Noticing one morning a woman

FIGURE 7.1. 'The chief's orchestra'. Photograph taken by Friedrich Ramseyer in 1888–9 in Abetifi, in the Akan kingdom of Kwawu. Behind the *ntumpan* stands a *fontomfrom* drum hung with human crania; leaning on it is an *obrafo* or executioner wearing his knives in a scabbard on his shoulder. To his right stand two *akrafo* wearing their *akrakonmu*, or gold pectoral discs; at either end of the group two men hold elephant-tusk trumpets decorated with *mmodwe*, or jawbones. Basel Mission Archives QD-30.043.0056.

standing behind the fort's smithy crying and talking softly to herself, he was told that she was 'making her weekly sacrifice at the spot where the Aqvambus, in the last war, had decapitated her sister. I was informed . . . that it was the custom among the Akras to offer such sacrifices weekly, on the day of the friend's death, with some beer or brandy'.[28] If such a horrific loss could provoke an unquenchable rage and thirst for vengeance among men, then this touching scene points to a quieter if equally painful grief perhaps more associated with women.[29]

Such rage and grief could indeed flow down the generations. Whereas living war captives were often ransomed back to their families at exorbitant cost, cranial war trophies were only very rarely surrendered. Müller offers an account of an incident in 1666–7, when the refusal of the Fetu to return the head of the son of an *omanhene* of Akyem brought them to the brink of ruin. The powerful Akyem withdrew their merchants, cut off trade to the coast and threatened to invade Fetu with overwhelmingly superior forces. 'In the end the Accanish king accepted a large sum of gold', Müller writes—but the Fetu kept their head: it is likely that it was one of the crania that Villault saw displayed on 16 April 1667, when they defiantly celebrated the anniversary of their victory.[30] Rømer cites one memorable incident, however, when the oracular deity Nananom Mpow insisted that the Fante return the crania of their vanquished foes, 'who were just as dear to him (the fetish) as was the Fante nation'. Creating a ferocious storm in his sacred grove, the great *obosom* refused to be placated with the sacrifice of slaves and would not be calmed until 'the heads of the Akron and Agona caboceers were delivered back to their surviving relatives, and the Fantes themselves had to pay for them to be given an honourable funeral. They even had to be present at the funeral and bury them'.[31] Even referring to the abuse of an ancestor's head was regarded with horror: among the most graphic Twi profanities were the curses *wo samanfo mfa ye ti new*, 'may your ancestral spirits chew their own heads', and *wo samanfo mfa nankasa*, 'may your ancestral spirits take their bones (and eat them)'.[32]

Rømer condemns Europeans for condoning and indeed taking part in such treatment of mortal remains. The jawbones of vanquished enemies, he notes, were regularly sent to the forts, where the factors were required to place their foot on them before any captives would be delivered up.[33] He reserved special criticism for the English, who, in an interesting parallel with the case of John Konny, retained the heads of thirty enemy warriors in an iron chest in Cape Coast Castle until their descendants paid for the cost of the conflict. What he does not mention is that the Danes themselves had gone one stage further when in 1723 they had wilfully destroyed the head of Dutch Accra chief Ama Tsuma by shooting it from a cannon—an act of desecration which continued to have damaging political ramifications twenty-five years later.[34] By the early nineteenth century, European sensibilities about the display and circulation of corporeal remains would begin to shift—something that their African interlocutors took heed of. When in 1823 Ajumakuhene Apea entered British governor Sir Charles McCarthy's war camp at Anomabo, his state drums were observed to be carefully 'covered with tartan plaid, to hide the skulls and jawbones of his conquered enemies, . . . he being fearful, from the character he had heard of his excellency, that they might give offence'.[35]

The severing of a head and the retention, display and tormenting of the skull was therefore a method of maintaining domination over one's enemies—the deceased himself and his anguished living relatives. Yet because the head was so loaded with ritual power, it was also potentially dangerous. Victorious warriors may have delighted in tormenting their dead rivals, yet that delight may have been tempered by an anxiety that the disembodied spirits, like their living relatives, also thirsted for revenge.[36] Let us consider another anecdote from the alert Rømer. It concerns one Kwate, an inhabitant of Dutch Accra, who was in conflict with a local priest, or *wulomo*. When the *wulomo* disappeared, the deity over which he presided was asked what had become of him—answering that he had been murdered by Kwate. The townsfolk searched Kwate's house, discovering not only the head of the *wulomo* but those of thirty other people, 'all of whom had been his enemies'. 'This devilish Qvaté had diverted himself every night with these skulls', Rømer reported. 'He had a large hole or cellar dug and had covered it with boards upon which he laid his mat, or bed, and there he slept. You might say he brooded over these heads. He picked them up at night, pounded on the skulls with an iron stick, and derided them in other ways. The only punishment he received was that his eldest son had to shoot him to death, and each of the families of the dead was able to retrieve the head belonging to that family.'[37] What we seem to have here is not the sanctioned acquisition of crania in warfare but evidence of a psychopathic serial killer, whose furtive obsession with the remains of his victims is recognizable from well-documented modern-day examples. Like the victorious warrior gloating over his battlefield trophies, Kwate desired to exert mastery over his enemies; in his case, however, it was his enemies' mortal remains that appeared to have exerted a morbid and destabilizing power over him.

Was it an anxiety to avoid the vengeful *sasa* of the decapitated Dutchmen which prompted John Konny to take up his trophy pathway and inter their skulls out of harm's way? Or was the decision prompted by political expediency, a magnanimous gesture which would help secure a deal with his European rivals? Atkins had no more to say on the matter, although the careful interment of the relics with brandy, pipes and tobacco suggests that the spirits of the deceased were being equipped for a belated entry into the afterworld. Yet if those lost spirits required their heads to be decently interred for this journey, they seemingly did not require the same of their jawbones—which in 1721, it will be recalled, remained strung on a tree in Konny's courtyard. Konny's change of heart had its limits: he may have desired that 'all malice should depart', but was not willing completely to give up the relics that signified his hard-fought struggle for local power.

Speculating on the historical development of the custom of displaying enemy skulls, Rømer observes that while it was believed by his Ga informants to have originated with the militaristic Akwamu, it was under the Asante that it reached its greatest expression. After the first Asante military clash with the Akyem, he was told, there were 'on display no heads of the Akim kings or Big Men killed', but as a result of the campaign of 1742, which extended Asante authority over Accra and the eastern Gold Coast, 'the Assiantes have more than 4,000 Akim heads ... in order to make themselves more fearful and visit on their enemies more disdain, shame and humiliation'.[38] Here we see an early glimpse of the ideological mobilization of mortal remains that would emerge as a striking element in Asante imperial statecraft. Nowhere is the potent symbolic role of the severed head more profound than in the historical traditions of the death of Gyamanhene Kwadwo Adinkra.

The war waged by Asantehene Osei Tutu Kwame (1804–23) against the Gyaman kingdom in 1818–19 became one of the best-remembered episodes in the Asante past. Like his earlier campaign against the Fante, which in 1807 culminated in the Asantehene plunging a sword into the sea and thereby earning his byname of Bonsu, The Whale, the hard-won victory against Gyaman is prominent in the oral histories of various Asante stools and in the *apaee*, the praise poems celebrating his reign. Falling between the visits of Bowdich and Dupuis to Kumasi, it also attracted the attention of both—not least, for Dupuis, because the huge number of enslaved war captives emerged as a topic of discussion in the context of British abolitionism. If military conflict ending in defeat or disaster was only ever spoken of by the Akan in the most circumspect tones, then that culminating in victory, the plunder of riches and the death of an implacable enemy was lauded as an achievement of the highest order. For the Asante in 1818, that enemy was the rebellious Kwadwo Adinkra, whose skull would join those of other defeated *amanhene* in the Bantama mausoleum and whose name continues to be recalled in the patterned *adinkra* funerary cloth.

A great deal is known about the politics on the northwestern frontier of the empire which led to Adinkra's rebellion against Kumasi overrule, about the war itself and about its aftermath.[39] Our concern here, however, is with the treatment of Adinkra's mortal remains, accounts of which are far richer than those of Asante's other great military adversaries. The precise manner of the Gyamanhene's death is unclear, although the weight of evidence suggests that after the defeat of his forces in the decisive battle in mid-1818, he committed suicide by taking poison. Typically, accounts stress that his defeat was supernaturally presaged and that he was all too aware of his impending doom. According to Reindorf, he consulted an oracle via an intermediary Muslim cleric, who directed that two rams, one representing Adinkra and the other Osei Bonsu, be set to fight. When the ram representing him was beaten and 'knowing now what would be the result of the impending invasion, Adinkra spent a whole week in drinking, dancing, and singing, in anticipation of his own funeral'.[40] A tradition from the neighbouring Takyiman kingdom holds that owing to the support of the great Bono *obosom* Taa Kora, which, its mediums reported, had already shot Adinkra's soul with a golden bullet, the Asantehene too was secure in his knowledge of the outcome.[41] Yet it is the treatment of Adinkra's dead body that is the key issue. Historical traditions agree that Adinkra's son Apaw, in a desperate effort to prevent his father's cranium from falling into the hands of the Asante, severed the head from the corpse and sewed it into the belly either of a dead and disembowelled Gyaman warrior or, in most versions, of a pregnant woman, concealing the body under a pile of others killed on the battlefield.[42] Captured by the Asantes, Apaw refused to reveal the location of his father's body, declaring that it would never be found. Yet the Asantes persisted, and, variously, either Apaw capitulated or the aggrieved mother of the woman in whose belly the head was concealed led them to the body. Nearby lay a headless corpse identified as that of Adinkra. 'Delirious with joy' and to 'thunderous rejoicings', the Asante forces took possession of the head and trunk of their adversary.

The recovery of both is crucial to the accounts of what came next. In line with customary procedure for cases of treason and other serious crimes, Osei Bonsu ordered that Adinkra be posthumously tried. 'The Asantes then sowed [*sic*] the dead king's head on his body', Reindorf writes, 'dressed and seated him, and held a court in which the king brought his charges against Adinkra. The elders went into a consultation and brought a verdict of guilty. Adinkra was then, according to Asante custom, beheaded by the executioner'.[43] Osei Bonsu, as ventriloquized in his *apaee*, was thereby able to declare on his triumphant re-entry into Kumasi that 'when Adinkra, the king of Gyaman, struggled against me, I fought with him, killed him and cut off his head'.[44] As his successor Kwaku Dua Panin explained to visiting missionary T. B. Freeman in 1842, 'the King, as he said he would . . . gave his body to the beasts, and the eagles ate out his eyes'.[45] Adinkra's attempt to escape retribution by taking his own life failed, as did Apaw's effort to avoid the ultimate shame of his father's head being secured as a trophy of war. From the Asante perspective, justice was done and imperial power prevailed. The securing of Adinkra's head continued, however, to be a close-run thing: on the return to Kumasi the precious trophy was dropped—or perhaps propelled itself—into the Tain or, in some versions, the Tano River, where it was lost until, after the pouring of libation to the great *obosom* Tano, it was given back up by the waters.[46] A century later, on 5 May 1922, Rattray witnessed a ceremony at the Taa Kora shrine at Tano Oboase, near the source of the river whose spiritual manifestation was lauded for having killed Adinkra: *Obosom a ofiri bomu, Wo na wokum Adinkira*, the officiating *okomfo* called upon the deity; 'God who comes from within the rock, You who slew Adinkira'.[47]

In the spectrum of Kristeva's 'capital visions', the memory of the severed head of a king being inserted into the corpse of a pregnant woman—replacing the eviscerated foetus—is powerful and extreme. What meanings might have adhered to it? The first point to make is that despite the horrifically inventive method devised by Apaw to conceal his father's head, the imperative to do so was driven by a fundamental cultural logic: the dread that one's own head, or the head of a close relative, might fall into the hands of an enemy. Here lay the real horror—the converse of the 'delirious joy' reportedly displayed by the triumphant Asante. Second, while the episode is extraordinary, it may not have been unprecedented. In 1817—the year before the death of Adinkra—Bowdich was informed of a strikingly similar incident during an Asante campaign in the late eighteenth century against Banda (or Banna), a kingdom which bordered Gyaman on the northwestern frontier of the empire. Facing defeat, the Bannahene ('Odrasee') 'to prevent his head being found, which circumstance he knew would sorely disquiet the enemy, and solace his own people, ordered, just before he killed himself, a woman to be sacrificed, and the abdomen being ripped, his head to be sewn up within it, and her body afterwards to be buried in the heap of the slain. It was discovered by bribes, and is now on one of the King's great drums'.[48]

The sources here appear contradictory. Bowdich dates the war to the reign of Asantehene Osei Kwame (1777–1803) but is corrected on this score by Dupuis, who insists that no such campaign took place and that the story of the king's head 'has no foundation whatsoever, according to the testimony of Moslems and idolaters'.[49] As Wilks recognized, the matter appears to have been complicated by Asante strictures on speaking openly of the dynastic past when that past clashed with current political sensibilities. In the 1818–19 Gyaman war, that is to say, the incumbent Bannahene was a valued ally, whose forces turned the tide at a critical moment in the Asante's favour. The following year the Bannahene was present in Kumasi to be rewarded for his signal contribution to the victory, receiving a reported 4,700 enslaved Gyaman captives and delivering a declamatory oration lauding Osei Bonsu's ferocious military prowess.[50] In such circumstances, the fact that his predecessor's head had been acquired in such a bizarre manner and that the skull was preserved as a trophy was deemed unmentionable. 'The censors had been active', Wilks writes. 'What was in fact historically accurate had become, nevertheless, actionable gossip—*konnurokusem*.'[51] Indeed, there can be no doubt that Bowdich's 'Odrasee' was Bannahene Worosa, the acquisition of whose head, actually by Osei Kwadwo (1764–77), is recorded by Reindorf and features in many Asante stool histories. A Dutch document confirms that such a war took place in 1773–4. While none of the traditions mention the story of the concealing of the head, all agree that Worosa, aside from being a fierce military adversary, was a strikingly handsome man with a fine beard and noble, flat forehead— features which were depicted in the gold replica of the head which was attached to one of the great royal swords, called Worosa-ti, 'Worosa's head'.[52]

What the various sources suggest, therefore, is that the story of a rebellious king defeated on the northwestern frontier of the empire whose severed head was recovered from inside the belly of a pregnant woman was first associated with Bannahene Worosa and subsequently with Gyamanhene Adinkra. After being reported by Bowdich in 1817, the episode disappears from traditions of the defeat of Worosa; by the time the well-informed Reindorf was compiling Asante historical material from the mid-nineteenth century, it was unambiguously associated with Adinkra. Perhaps unsurprisingly, Banda oral histories throw little light on the matter, confirming only that Worosa was defeated and his head removed to Kumasi.[53] Political expediency may indeed have led Osei Bonsu to forbid on pain of death that it ever be spoken of again. Leaving aside the possibility that such a bizarre event occurred in the same region twice, why, then, did the narrative thereafter adhere to accounts of Adinkra? A partial answer may lie in the unsettling nature of the story itself, in the way that its gruesome juxtaposition of birth and death, of male and female, and of head and womb was seen by the Asante to encapsulate the character of their adversary.

That Adinkra's head was sewn into a woman's womb was only the most unsettling of a range of allusions throughout the oral traditions to gender reversal and sexual ambiguity. These allusions had a structural underpinning, in that from the incorporation of Gyaman into the ambit of Asante power in the

FIGURE 7.2. Gold trophy head, representing a slain adversary of Asante, possibly Bannahene Worosa. One of the largest solid-gold figures known to have been produced in Africa, this head was taken by the British during their one-day occupation of Kumasi in February 1874. The projections at the corners of the mouth represent the *kra* departing the body. Wallace Collection/Bridgeman Images, London. Height: 20 cm.

early eighteenth century, the Asantehene referred to the Gyamanhene as *me ye*, 'my wife'. Such a lexical transfer of the relations of domestic power to the political realm was not unusual but took on a particular resonance in the context of the deteriorating relationship between the two kingdoms from around 1811. In short, Asante traditions stress that Adinkra was a weak and effeminate character who was dominated by an aggressively assertive, 'masculine' sister or wife, or both. It was this defiant female figure who, in the face of his initial meek acquiescence, bullied him into resisting Asante demands and who ordered the manufacture of a golden stool in imitation of the *sika dwa kofi*—the act which served as the final catalyst for war. Thus, Bowdich records that Adinkra's sister Tamia (or Tawia), 'of masculine spirit and talent', informed Asante envoys, 'with more force than delicacy, that her brother and she must change sexes, for she was most proper for a King, and would fight to the last'.[54] In Asare's version, it is Adinkra's wife, Soko Abenaa, who insists 'that he should exchange his manhood for her womanhood'.[55] References to this gender reversal and to the concealment of Adinkra's head, are also woven through Osei Bonsu's *apaee*: in one version, the episode is alluded to by the phrase *ama yede Adinkra ahye nwoma mu*, 'and they hid Adinkra in a sack of hide'.[56] In another, 'it is said that Kwadwo Adinkra fell pregnant and gave birth to Ama Tawia'.[57]

The feminized image of Adinkra in Asante historical traditions stands in sharp contrast to that of Worosa, remembered as the most worthy and stubborn of adversaries rather than for the ignoble fate recounted by Bowdich. Yet in the end, both would be subject to the same posthumous indignity: their skulls preserved in the ossuary of the Bantama mausoleum and the gold effigies of their heads part of the paraphernalia of the Golden Stool. The collection of crania of vanquished *amanhene* began in the 1690s with those of Osei Tutu's earliest adversaries, the kings of Domaa and Hwereso, followed by that of Denkyirahene Ntim Gyakari in 1701, and was enlarged throughout the eighteenth century with those of three Akyem kings, a Takyimanhene and an earlier Gyamanhene. After the addition of the skulls of Worosa and Adinkra, only one more of significance was added in the nineteenth century: that of Sir Charles McCarthy, the governor of the British settlements on the Gold Coast, whose rash attempt to confront the Asante military presence in Fante country ended badly in 1824. The crania were arranged in the mausoleum before the coffin of the Asantehene responsible for their defeat; were tended by the priestly guardian assigned to the relics of that Asantehene; and, each year at Odwira, were given over to the presiding *adumfo* (executioners) to placate the lingering animosity of the individuals to whom in life they had belonged. 'On this occasion', Rattray was told, 'the skulls were smeared with bands of red clay interspersed with white' and decorated with sprigs of *emme* and other leaves, 'the smell of which was supposed to drive away *sasa* (evil revengeful spirits)'. 'As the king sat among his chiefs, each skull was placed on the ground before him, and upon each in turn he placed his foot, saying as he did so, "Such-and-such of my ghost ancestors slew you"'.[58]

This annual ritual is notable, because for states, as for individuals, the retention of the head of an implacable enemy could be, if not properly managed, a double-edged sword. Yet the political benefits were clearly worth the spiritual risks. A year after the end of the Gyaman war, Dupuis was present as the

Asantehene reflected on the conflict and on the role of corporeal trophies in the exercise of royal power:

> The wars of the king were ... introduced as a topic of general discussion. That of Gaman [sic] was the favourite subject, and the king occasionally took up the thread of the narrative ... As he caused the linguists to interpret to me the particular feats of himself, the king of Banna and Apoko, his eyes sparkled with fiery animation, and at one period he threw himself into a sort of theatrical attitude, which appeared to be unpremeditated, and unaffected. He then seemed to be wrapped up within himself in delightful cognitions, and at this crisis, some of the auditors like the bards of 'olden times', rose to the hum of the war song, and recited their parts in a pleasing mellifluous strain. The king enjoyed this scene in extacy [sic] and frequently motioned with his body and feet in cadence with the metre of the verse. This reverie and the recitation occupied many minutes, and were ultimately succeeded by irony and satire cast upon the memory of his fallen enemy. 'His scull [sic] was broken,' said the king, 'but I would not lose the trophy, and now I have made a similar scull of gold. This is for my great customs, that all the people know that *I* am the king.[59]

8

Slaves

WITH THE EXPANSION of plantation economies in the Americas in the second half of the seventeenth century, European demand for West African slaves began to rise steadily. By the 1720s, human captives had surpassed gold as the Gold Coast's most valuable export commodity, a Dutch report observing that 'that part of Africa which as of old is known as the "Gold Coast" . . . has now virtually changed into a pure Slave Coast; the great quantity of guns and powder which the Europeans have from time to time brought there has given cause to terrible wars among the Kings, Princes and Caboceers of those lands, who make their prisoners of war slaves'.[1] Gold retained its status as a currency and its symbolic power in mortuary exchange, but throughout the eighteenth century and until the overseas slave trade was terminated in the years after 1807, economic life on the Gold Coast was orientated more towards the acquisition and export of human captives. For those in a position to benefit, the ownership and sale of slaves represented an important road to fulfilment, a route to a rich and successful life.[2] For those who fell victim to slavery, in contrast, it represented less a fruitful way of life than an annihilating 'way of death'.[3]

This chapter considers the entanglement of slavery and death on the Gold Coast. Its focus is two eighteenth-century texts which reflect on life, death and anticipation of the afterlife in the Ga towns on the eastern reaches of the coast. The Ga (or Accra) had a long and intimate relationship with the Akan peoples to their north and west. A powerful kingdom in the mid-seventeenth century, Accra fell to conquest by the expansionist Akwamu in 1677–81, in one of the most destructive of the 'terrible wars' noted by the Dutch report quoted above. The survivors gradually reconstructed the Ga social formation, under Akwamu suzerainty, in a series of seaside towns until, in 1730, Akwamu rule was overthrown and replaced by that of the Akyem and then, from 1742 to the early

1820s, the Asante. Despite this succession of Akan overlords, Ga merchants carved out a lucrative intermediary role and three prosperous towns grew up in association with the European forts in their midst: Kinka (or Dutch Accra), James Town (English Accra) and Osu (Danish Accra). These were complex, hybrid urban centres, in which commercial and political power was contested between shifting alliances of Akan suzerains, European forts and local Ga hierarchies.[4] Their social fabric was further complicated by the emergence of rival town quarters and of Euro-African populations which straddled local communities and the company forts. As in the entrepôt ports all along the Gold Coast, many townsfolk earned their livelihood from fishing and farming, others from salt-making and food production, and a few as goldsmiths and other skilled artisans. Yet prosperity was sustained largely by trade, in particular the exchange of slaves for a range of imported commodities: cloth, liquor, metal goods, firearms, tobacco—all of which we have already seen come to feature in local funerary cultures. This exchange drew a further element into the population mix of the towns and their hinterlands: enslaved captives, both those destined for transportation across the Atlantic and those retained in bondage in local households and as 'castle slaves' by the European forts. If, for the free householder, death represented an ultimate accounting to the ancestors of his or her contribution to collective increase—of people, material goods and wealth—what did death represent to those at the other end of the social spectrum, themselves objects of accumulation? How did slaves die, where and how were their corpses disposed of, and what were their prospects in the afterlife?

The scholarly literature on slavery in Atlantic Africa has touched on these questions only in passing. They must, however, be framed by broader debates on the nature of servitude in the region and how it was transformed by the rise and decline of the overseas slave trade. There are two broad schools of thought on the character of slavery on the Gold Coast and in its forest hinterland. One is that it was essentially paternalistic, domestic and, by any comparative historical standard, relatively benign. In this view, slavery was more an 'institution of marginality' than one geared to the regimented extraction of labour for production, enabling slaves gradually to traverse a continuum from servile outsider to partial membership of local kinship groups. The other is that slavery, as everywhere, was underpinned by coercion and violence and that many slaves, at least, were regarded as chattel. According to this view, both the magnitude and the exploitative character of slavery escalated because of the demand from European slave traders and, further, with the subsequent withdrawal of that demand in the nineteenth century, as labour that hitherto had been exported to the Americas was put to work in the era of so-called legitimate commerce.[5] Besides change over time, this debate is complicated by the fact that slavery, far from being a uniform condition, encompassed a variety of forms, each with distinct roles, obligations and rights. The Akan, the Ga, and the Adanme and Ewe to their east all recognized very different sorts of servitude, extending (to use the Twi terminology) from the status of *akoa* (subject) and *awowa* (a temporary pawn) to *odonko* (a foreign-born slave from the northern savanna) and *akyere* (one destined to be sacrificed).[6] The view of a benign and assimilationist slavery must be tempered by ample evidence of the harsh treatment of the rising numbers of *nnonkofo* (sing. *odonko*), whose perceived identity on the fringe of humanity was stated emphatically by Asantehene Kwaku Dua Panin in 1841: 'The small tribes in the interior fight with each other, take prisoners and sell them for slaves; and as I know nothing of them, I allow my people to buy them as they please: they are of no use for any thing but slaves; they are stupid, and little better than beasts'.[7]

Where historians have begun to address the issue of slavery and death is with respect to the Middle Passage and to enslaved communities in the Americas. Three recent works are relevant for an understanding of slavery on the Gold Coast as part of a broader Atlantic 'way of death'. In *Saltwater Slavery*, Stephanie Smallwood considers the experiences of the approximately three hundred thousand captives transported from the Gold Coast aboard Royal African Company ships bound for the English (and then British) American colonies between 1675 and 1725, focusing on survival and death during the Middle Passage itself and the process of dehumanization by which people were transformed into commodities. Vincent Brown's *The Reaper's Garden* examines in turn how Gold Coast and other African slaves reconstructed mortuary repertoires as a way of reclaiming that humanity on the plantations of Jamaica. Most recently, Walter Rucker analyses the creation by enslaved Africans of a 'Coromantee' identity, a term derived from the Fante port of Kormantse but which in the Americas incorporated a polyglot mix of Akan, Ga, Adanme and other captives. Rucker's *Gold Coast Diasporas* is not specifically about death, although he has much of value to say about it—including on the Gold Coast. While acknowledging the importance of Smallwood's and Brown's work, he is critical of their lack of attention to established African perceptions of mortality and of their tendency to stress the rupture or 'social death' brought about by enslavement rather than the continuity of cultural forms.[8]

In this respect, these works are situated in a historiographical framework that lies beyond the scope of our concerns here: the debate between those scholars who detect African survivals in the New World and those who stress the invention of creolized African American cultural forms. Yet in their insights into the crucibles of the slave ship and the American plantation complex, all suggest productive ways of thinking about the nexus of commodity trade, violence, servitude and death in Atlantic Africa. Indeed, the analysis can be taken beyond the issue of continuity and change in the diaspora: if ideologies and cultures of mortality were crucial to the reconstruction of a Coromantee (or Amina) identity in the New World, then they might be seen to be at the heart of being 'Akan' in the first place. Bryan Edwards's notorious defence of the institution of slavery in the Caribbean need not obviate his observations on these matters:

> The circumstances which distinguish the Koromantyn, or Gold Coast negroes, from all others are firmness both of body and mind; a ferociousness of disposition; but, withal, activity, courage, and a stubbornness, or what an ancient Roman would have deemed an elevation of the soul, which prompts them to enterprises of difficulty and danger; and enables them to meet death, in its most horrible shape, with fortitude or indifference.[9]

That violent nexus is nowhere more profoundly encapsulated than in African attempts to comprehend the motives for the escalating export of slaves. What fuelled the apparently insatiable demand for African bodies and the European willingness to purchase those bodies with valuable and desirable commodities? One interpretation, widely reported along Africa's Atlantic littoral as well as among slaves in the Americas, was that people were being purchased to be eaten.[10] 'All the slaves, like most other blacks, believe that we buy them to eat them', Barbot wrote in the 1680s. 'It is this which makes many slaves die on the passage across, either from sorrow or from despair, there being some who refuse to eat or drink'.[11] Bosman believed that this dread was especially prevalent among those from the deep interior with no knowledge of Europeans and, if instilled into a shipload of captives awaiting departure, was the primary cause of rebellion.[12] A different if equally horrific perception was shaped by the fact that the Ga region represented a frontier between two distinct currency regimes: the gold zone of the Gold Coast and Akan forest, to the west; and the cowrie-shell zone of the Slave Coast, to the east. 'In this respect I have heard of an unpleasant conception the slaves have', Rask wrote of the early eighteenth century, 'that they believed that the *Blanke*, as they usually call the Christians, buy them for one purpose, which is that when they are out to sea they will sink them to the bottom and use them to gather *bossies* [i.e., cowries]'.[13] Such terrors appear to be shaped by idioms of witchcraft as a form of elicit consumption and can be seen metaphorically to distil the implacable economic logic of Atlantic commerce. Metaphor aside, the belief on the part of captives that their bodies were destined to be cannibalized or used as bait to harvest aquatic money represented an extension of the notion of bad death beyond established apprehensions and into the stuff of nightmares.

The entanglement of Atlantic commerce with servitude, violence and death can be approached via two accounts produced in eighteenth-century Osu, the Ga seaside town that grew up around the walls of the Dane's Christiansborg Castle. Both have been analysed with insight by Ray A. Kea, whose interpretations, although somewhat different from my own, I draw on here.[14] The first appeared in the memoirs of the Lutheran pastor Johannes Rask of the four years he spent at Osu in 1709–12. Reflecting on local beliefs concerning death and the afterlife, Rask offered an anecdote concerning one Hans Lykke, who Kea suggests may be identified as an Osu notable remembered in oral histories as Noete Doku:

> A number of Negroes among the Akras, when they have become ill, throw various things out into the paths, as gifts and presents for the devil, so that he will let them live yet a little longer, before he takes them. This is because they believe that the devil rules over illness and death, and that after death they come to the devil, but they do not fear this much, rather they wish for it, when things do not go their way. I have been told by many of a Negro from Ursou, the town that lies under Christiansborg—called Hans Lykke after a [Danish] chief who had formerly been at Christiansborg—that he often wished he was dead, so that he could go to the devil, since the devil, he said, *bringarer*, or refreshes himself daily with brandy, palm wine and other good drinks; he has many women; he owns great cannons and a great deal of gunpowder with which to entertain himself. [Lykke] said he greatly wished to be in that company, and was sure he could deport himself as well as any young devil. The Aqvambus beheaded that same Negro in a battle during the spring of 1709, just before I arrived in this country.[15]

The second is by Ludewig Rømer, the Danish slave factor stationed at Osu in the 1740s. As we have seen, Rømer took a great interest in local spiritual matters and enjoyed discussing them with his friend Okpoti.

> They have many differing opinions on their condition after death. Putti says that God considers the pious worthy to be received to Himself, and especially those who die on their bed (mat) and are given an honourable funeral. But he has a comment on death which is unintelligible. It is this, that the body, when separated from this world, is the greatest obstacle for the soul in the other life, since (he says) it is also separated. Putti become completely unintelligible when, to explain this, he tells of his dreams and revelations. I have heard an old Negro sigh and wish that after death he might become a rich European, and when asked the reason, he answered, 'I would rather be a poor Black than a poor White, since a poor White must have the same superfluous things—shoes, stockings, and clothing—as the rich, and, therefore must at times starve'. It must be noted that this Negro, like others, believed in reincarnation, and was convinced that his soul [would] travel to Europe and he would be born [again] as a European. There are those who believe that their souls travel in animals, birds, or fish.

Both Okpoti and the unnamed elderly interlocutor offer corroborating evidence on a number of key understandings of body, soul and the afterlife that we have already considered. Yet it is the next part of Rømer's text, which records a rare conversation with an enslaved person, which is perhaps the most intriguing:

> Yet another belief is illustrated by the following example. One of our black mason apprentices, the company slave, Qvacu, kept working at 12 o'clock midday, although they were free from 11 o'clock to 2 o'clock. A European walking by said to him, 'Qvacu! Why are you working? It is 12 o'clock.' He answered (quite annoyed), 'Our Master is so mean to me today that he says I have not worked enough and therefore, before I may stop, I must finish this piece. But I know what I shall do.' *Question*. 'What will you do, then?' *Reply*. 'When I die, I shall ask God not to send me back into the world as the slave of the Whites, and if that prayer does not help, I shall discuss it with him.' *Question*. 'What do you want to be, then, when you come into the world again?' *Reply*. 'The slave of Frempung.' (Frempung was a great Akim king.) *Question*. 'Why do you not ask to be Frempung himself?' *Reply*. 'No, that is not possible, for I know that as often as I come back, I

must be a slave.' When I pointed out to Putti that this statement, and other things, showed that his countrymen were of differing opinions, he answered, 'Sir (*Siegnore*)! I have never been dead and come back to life, to enable me to debate with such certainty about the other life, as your holy man did in the time he was here.'[16]

There is a lot to unravel here. Again, both texts need to be situated in the history of military violence and political upheaval which saw suzerainty over the Ga towns pass from Akwamu to the Akyem and finally, in 1742, to Asante. Thus, Hans Lykke (or, if we accept Kea's identification, Noete Doku), who rose to prominence in Osu as a leading *caboceer*, trade broker and *wulomo* (priest, or religious specialist) in the opening years of Akwamu domination in the 1680s, was killed and decapitated while leading Osu forces in an abortive uprising against Akwamuhene Akono in 1709.[17] Three decades later, the enslaved mason Kwaku's reverie on the afterlife was shaped by the overthrow of Akwamu rule by the Akyem and the advent of Akyem Kotokuhene Frimpon Manso as the overlord of Osu. A powerful and wealthy king whose diplomatic skills ensured an amicable relationship between the Akyems and Asantehene Opoku Ware, Frimpon Manso died in 1741—an event precipitating the military campaign which brought the eastern Gold Coast into the southern provinces of the Asante empire.[18] Politically, the Ga were reduced to the status of *nkoa* (subjects) of alien Akan overlords and by the 1730s looked back with nostalgia to the time before the overthrow of Great Accra in the late 1670s. Economically, however, many took advantage of what they saw as their crude and unsophisticated Akwamu overlords, whose militarism ensured that the supply of slaves continued to flow via Ga brokers to the forts and ships of the European companies.

Arising from this era of political turmoil, the two texts offer evocative reflections on the afterlife from two very different figures: Hans Lykke, a wealthy and influential Ga *lumo* (notable) who, before his fatal rebellion, was one of the middleman elite able to take advantage of the opportunities offered by Atlantic commerce, and Kwaku, also associated with the Danish company but in the lowly capacity of a castle slave. Despite this contrast in status, the similarity of what Kea calls the 'death-wish' of the two individuals is striking: both envisage a posthumous future which improves on their life in the present. For Hans Lykke, that existence awaits him in the *gbohiiajen* (or, in a Ga borrowing from Twi, the *sisaman*), the realm of the dead where 'the devil' has on offer a range of desirable commodities: liquor, women, great cannons and gunpowder. For the downtrodden and aggravated Kwaku, the ideal future appears not to be as a *sisa*, or 'spirit', in the *gbohiiajen*—where according to received logic he would continue to be a slave labouring for the Danes—but to return to earth reincarnated at the court of the powerful Akyem Kotokuhene. Kwaku does not mention material improvement but no doubt knew that Frimpon Manso was served by a great retinue of *akrafo*, or 'soul washers', who, as Rømer explained, 'have made an agreement with their king to die when the king dies ... therefore each of the other subjects must show them respect and give them everything they want'.[19]

Speaking in the late 1730s, Kwaku imagined a better posthumous life at the court of Frimpon—but he may well have altered his view when, in 1741, the latter's death was followed by reports reaching Osu of the grisly mass immolation of his wives and *akrafo*. Ironically, the grim realities of military violence may also have thwarted Lykke's death wish: if, as is likely, his decapitated head was retained by his Akwamu killers, then this would have been seen as preventing his entry into the afterworld—which may be why his story as recounted by Rask ends on the abrupt note it does. Indeed, it is the importance of the integrity of the corpse for the fate of the soul which appears to be what Okpoti was struggling to explain to Rømer three decades later: 'the body ... is the greatest obstacle for the soul in the other life'. Lykke, like the decapitated sister of the grief-stricken woman we encountered in the previous chapter, was, to use the vernacular metaphor, 'eaten' (*di*) by Akwamu military power. The same term was used to describe the consumption of commodities, both material and human—including the metaphorical cannibalism of malign 'witches'. After the suppression of the 1709 rebellion, the Akwamu captain Amputi Brafo stood triumphantly outside the gates of Christiansborg Castle with his musketeers and horn-blowers, who performed a song which declared that he 'had "eaten" so many blacks, now he would like to "eat" some of the whites'.[20]

Kea extrapolates from Rask's brief story of Hans Lykke to explore the historical conditions which might have shaped the latter's deferral of life's pleasures to the realm of the dead, *gbohiiajen*. Yet Kea fails to address one crucial question about Lykke's perception of that realm: who, or what, does he mean by 'the devil'? He assumes, perhaps, that the term is simply Rask's imposition—that is, that the Lutheran pastor considered African belief to be essentially diabolical and that the spiritual entity who 'rules over life and death' and who Lykke wished to '*bringer*' with was actually the supreme deity, Nyonmo, the Ga equivalent of the Akan's Onyame. But this seems not to be the case. Rask makes it clear that he does not equate Satan with Nyonmo, and that he has grasped the distinction between the aloof creator deity and the myriad *jemawonjii*, or 'gods of the world': 'the Akras call god *Jungo* [Nyonmo], and the Aqvambus call god *Jankumpung* [Nyankonpon]. They admit, and know that Satan exists, whom they credit as being very powerful, but Satan is considered to be an ill-humoured and stubborn man, and ... that it is necessary to have the devil as a friend.'[21] 'They refuse to believe that the damned are tortured in Hell', he observes elsewhere, 'but do say that *Sasa*, or the Devil, is a very disobedient and contrary man against God.'[22]

Lykke's vision of the devil as a roguish character with a taste for booze, fast women and explosive weaponry, I would argue, suggests a braggadocio reading of Christian eschatology. Africans saw in descriptions of the Christian devil attributes of their own gods, who were neither good nor bad but capricious, troublesome, ill-humoured and stubborn. Strikingly similar tales of bold encounters with Satan ('How Jack Beat the Devil') infuse African American folklore.[23] This opens up a further interpretation, one inspired by Michael Taussig's analysis of the devil and commodity fetishism. Taussig considers the significance of the devil in the folkloric beliefs of proletarianized workers in two regions of capitalist development in South America, the sugar plantations of Colombia and the tin mines of Bolivia, concluding that the Christian figure of evil, as blended with indigenous deities, came to mediate the tensions embodied in capitalism and social change. The aspect of this analysis which most resonates with the accounts above is the notion that the devil presides over 'an economic system which forces men to barter their souls for the destructive powers of commodities'.[24] Hints of an ambivalence towards commodity fetishism can be detected in Lykke's death wish, as well as in Rømer's unnamed interlocutor sighing about the desirable but 'superfluous' things brought by European trade. Yet it emerges most clearly as Rask pursues his theme with yet another version of the myth of the creation of Africans and Europeans offered by a local stonemason:

> Another Negro ... called Pajennen ... believed, due to wondering about the quantity and variety of goods that were brought from Europe, that it was the devil who was the artistic master who made them and, then, gathered them at a certain place where the Europeans weighed as much gold for him as they wished to give him as payment for those goods. They laid the gold there, the devil was satisfied, took the gold, and the Whites ... took the goods. All this amounts to the same idea, that, as they believe, everything that is more artistic than what they can manage is a product of the devil's art.[25]

'Old Negroes on the Gold Coast, when they become confidential with a European, can philosophize quite sensibly over the state of their country', Rømer would later write. '"It is you, you Whites", they say, "who have brought all the evil among us. Indeed, would we have sold one another if you, as purchasers, had not come to us? The desire we have for your fascinating goods and your brandy, bring it to pass that one brother can not trust the other"'.[26]

We know even less about Kwaku than we do about Hans Lykke. A 1736 register of slaves notes that he was aged 30 at the time and was born into servitude; his name appeared again in a register of 1755 and thereafter disappears.[27] He was, therefore, a 'company' or 'castle' slave, one of the retinues of servile men, women and children who laboured to maintain the European forts as tradesmen, servants, soldiers, messengers, cooks and washerwomen.[28] As such, he was enmeshed in the skeins of merchant capital dedicated to exporting so-called chained slaves to the Americas, free from the horrors of the awful dungeons in which they were stored and allowed a certain liberty of movement and social intercourse in the seaside towns but, as the conversation recorded by Rømer indicates, subject to the strict work discipline established by his Danish masters. It is this discipline that Kwaku can be seen to be kicking against in his desire to swap the drudgery of labour at Christiansborg Castle for the allure of the court of the great *omanhene* Frimpon Manso, to whom the Danes themselves owed allegiance; in Kea's words, 'he chafes against history and the social and occupational role he was forced into'.[29]

Kwaku's vision of a posthumous escape from the constraints of that ordained role was shaped by two doctrines of the afterlife. One bore an unmistakable imprint of temporal power: that the realm of the dead was ordered along the same hierarchical lines as the world of the living; it was a realm, to reiterate, in which those with wealth and power would continue to enjoy both, while slaves would remain enslaved. This belief in turn underpinned the most extreme manifestation of violence visited upon the enslaved: their immolation at the funerals of the powerful in order that they would continue to serve them beyond the grave. Kwaku's dismissal of the fantastical idea that he might posthumously 'become' Frimpon Manso reflects this hegemonic view. The other was the notion by which at least one of the spiritual components of a human being might, in particular circumstances, be reborn in an individual of a subsequent generation. In this regard, Kwaku's stated desire to be reborn as an *okra* serving Frimpon Manso seems more of a reverie than a considered pronouncement on Ga understandings of *blamo*, reincarnation. One thing, however, is certain: that a smooth passage to the afterlife, and from there on to potential reincarnation, was understood largely to be dependent upon the nature of the death and a proper funeral. 'God considers the pious worthy to be received to Himself', it will be recalled that Okpoti explained to Rømer, with a twist of Christian eschatology, 'especially those who die on their bed . . . and are given an honourable funeral'. How, then, were slaves buried and mourned? Were they ever granted 'honourable funerals', or was the exploitation and violence visited on them in life continued after death?

For castle slaves like Kwaku, the answers can be only guessed at. Whereas the mortal remains of powerful African trade brokers were sometimes interred within the forts from where in life they had operated and made their fortunes, no records appear to exist of how the corpses of slaves were disposed of. Many were ethnic outsiders: those in the English forts, for example, were often imported from hundreds of miles away on the Gambia River or the Slave Coast. Any funeral celebration would have depended on the degree of social bonding between fellow slaves and whether the various companies allowed them to bury each other. Precisely because slaves were property, however, their demise needed to be accounted for, giving rise to what may be Ghana's earliest recognizable death certificates. A sequence of fragile, mould-damaged slips of paper produced at Cape Coast Castle and its outstations in 1752, these do little more than name the deceased, their occupation, 'tally' number, and the date of and, in some cases, reason for their death—information certified by the company surgeon or other officials: 'August 15th 1752. These are to Certifie the Committee of the Company of Merchants Trading to Africa or whom else it may Concern that this Day Died Effebah Labourer a negro woman Slave belonging to the Said Company at this place Aged 70 years. Her Tally's Lost'. Or, other examples: 'Commenda Fort 23rd February 1752 . . . this day died Aberebah Company's Slave & washer woman of agues of 6 days'; 'this day died Quow a Negro boy belonging to the Royal African company of England aged 2 years'.[30] It is in contrast to the muted voices of these otherwise forgotten slaves that Kwaku's extraordinary testament must be set.

More can be said about those in bondage within indigenous communities. Barbot provides the earliest evidence for the brutal treatment of slaves in death as well as in life. 'They can . . . be recognized by their often having on their backs the marks of their wretchedness, being covered with wounds from blows', he observed in the 1670s–80s. 'They have little care taken of them, most of them even lacking the necessities of life. ... When they die they are thrown in a ditch. I have myself seen instances.'[31] Rask elaborates on the matter three decades later, noting that, in contrast to the interment of the wealthy and powerful within their houses, 'if it is an Akraish child, or an inherited slave, or any unattached and free Negro who dies, they are usually buried at a special place behind the *negeri* [i.e., the 'Blacks' town']'.[32] He does not specify how the corpses of purchased or captured rather than inherited slaves were disposed of, but the implication is that they were cast unburied into the bush. The 'special place behind the town' lay within the liminal zone which in both coastal and forest communities separated the cultural order of human settlement from the realm of nature beyond. Called by the Ga *husunaa* and by the Akan *kurotia*, this was seen as a place of pollution: it contained middens; huts used by menstruating women; and groves (Twi: *asamanpow*) where the bodies of unloved slaves, witches and those deemed to have died a bad death were cast (see further chapter 13). Haunted by the lingering presence of the unhappy dead, its charged supernatural environment was certainly dangerous yet could be harnessed to benefit the living: it is likely to have been where Rask noticed people throwing objects onto the paths so the devil 'will let them live a little longer'. Two centuries later, the anthropologist M. J. Field found 'the rubbish heap at the back of a town always worth a visit', as it was embedded with ritual objects 'connected with the riddance of misfortune'.[33]

Yet Rask goes on to suggest that the stipulation that certain categories of deceased were not to be accorded a proper burial was sometimes circumvented, possibly surreptitiously: 'The closest friends of the deceased carry, weekly, some millie porridge, *ahaj* or beer, or brandy to the grave, and offer it in old pots or broken glass, which are left there for the *fitis*. If the deceased has some close friends who are wealthy, they usually build a roof over the grave . . . covered with palm or coconut leaves.'[34] Similar attention was sometimes given to the corpses of another category of the servile dead: those held in pawnship, usually as security for a debt. Here, mortuary practice was determined by economic factors, as taking charge of someone's burial and funeral entailed responsibility for their debts. Those who held pawns therefore refused to bury them if they died, and in an effort to extract the debt from surviving relatives often left the corpses exposed on elevated platforms until such time as it was paid. By the early nineteenth century, when the expansion of trade led to an increase in pawnship, the outskirts of commercial centres such as Accra were noted to be dotted with such platforms, said to be designed to prevent the putrefying bodies being devoured by hyenas. 'In Accaraish [i.e., Ga] this type of post carrion is called *akba*', Monrad wrote, 'which is one of the terms the Negroes use for Europeans who are particularly hated among them'.[35]

As for the expanding populations of *nnonkofo* slaves, those from the savanna regarded by Kwaku Dua Panin as 'little better than beasts', the best they might hope for, as noted for Cape Coast, was a hasty burial 'along the pathways of the suburbs of the town' or 'in the common near the saltpond'.[36] In Asante, where *nnonkofo* were regularly in mortal danger from immolation at funerals, little or no thought was given to their posthumous welfare. Freeman reported from Kumasi in 1842 that the corpses of all foreign slaves, 'except a few favoured ones', were dumped into the encircling Nsuben River, where they were eaten by great shoals of sacred mudfish.[37] Coming across one elderly slave lying in the Kumasi market in 1873, the missionaries Ramseyer and Kühne record that 'her mistress sent her away sick, with the words, "Go to the bush and die"'.[38]

Yet not all deceased slaves' mortal remains were consigned to the filth or waters on the edge of the town or to a lonely spot on a forest path beyond. Nineteenth-century sources suggest that mortuary customs may have been shaped by the assimilationist model of slavery as much as they were by that stressing exploitation ('go to the bush and die'). Invited to the funeral of 'a domestic slave girl' at Cape Coast while serving there in 1847–8, British army surgeon Charles Gordon was taken aback to find the corpse 'dressed in a rich damask robe; . . . the neck, arms, and toes bearing gold ornaments . . . ; the whole of the upper part of the person further decorated with various designs made by artistically sprinkling gold-dust over adhesive matter . . . while before the deceased was a table well replenished with rum and tobacco'—that is, made ready for the grave as would be any freeborn woman of high status.[39] Further evidence comes from the records of the British courts on the Gold Coast, which from their constitution in the 1840s provided a novel arena for debates over property and custom. In 1847, the creditor of a deceased slave threatened another man with a gun because the slave 'had been buried by the Public', thereby preventing the former from reclaiming his debt.[40]

More nuanced detail is found in a sequence of disputes from Cape Coast in the decade before the British abolished the legal status of slavery in 1874. In 1864, John Dawson brought a case against Aba Ekum, accusing her of 'causing to be removed and disturbed out of its grave in Plaintiff's house the remains of [his] late father'.[41] Aba's son had lived in a room in the house that Dawson had inherited from his father, and when the son died Aba directed that his corpse be interred under the house, leading to the gravediggers inadvertently exhuming the remains of Dawson's father. Testimony revealed that over the generations the bodies of both domestic slaves and their masters were buried side by side under the house. This seemed out of the ordinary: 'It is not usual to bury slaves with their masters', one witness testified, another confirming that 'slaves are generally buried in a place at the Eastern end of the town'. When it did occur, however, the etiquette of interment was precise. 'When bones are found in digging for a grave inquiries are made of the elderly persons and [the] grave is dug in another place—in [the] case of a slave', one William Jones explained. 'But if the person was a blood relation he is buried in the same grave where the bones are found.... It is customary to bury *old* slaves in the house— [but] not in the same room with the family—not in the same graves.'

Yet the distinction between slaves and blood relatives was often far from clear. The complexity of identities within slave-owning families is revealed in a case from 1870, in which Kofi Sackey brought a suit against Sinnay on the grounds that he was entitled to service from her and her twelve descendants.[42] Sinnay was a slave from Lagos who had been purchased and then married by Sackey's ancestor Annan Kuma ('the younger') in the 1810s. But Annan Kuma was himself a slave, owned by one Annan Panin ('the elder'), who, Sinnay claims, had provided the money to buy her. The British judicial assessor and the panel of Cape Coast chiefs presiding over the court had to disentangle three generations' worth of deaths, inheritances, successions and marriages in order to decide who ended up 'owning' the elderly Sinnay and her descendants. It was obligations to the dead which determined rights over the living. Sackey's claim to own Sinnay rested on the fact that he provided money, gunpowder and rum for the funeral of her husband; likewise, Sinnay disavowed her allegiance to the family, but evidence showed that, despite having removed herself to neighbouring Komenda, for every annual custom she sent two flasks of rum for the departed spirit of Annan Kuma. In an emphatic statement of assimilationist ideology, it was stated that 'when a slave dies his master should bury him'.[43] As another case some years later made clear, this was particularly so when slaves had acquired property—in addition to simply *being* property. 'I have owned slaves in my day [and] some ... died in my hands', Chief James Thompson of Cape Coast testified. 'If they had left property I should have taken it—if a woman, no matter who she married, I should bury her and take her property. I should bury her with my own family or any where else where I pleased and go to the same expense as if she were one of my own family.'[44]

Of the approximately thirteen million Africans transported across the Atlantic in the course of the slave trade, one million originated from the Gold Coast and its hinterland. Countless others torn from their communities were condemned to servitude within Africa itself, where, like those who disappeared into the cauldron of the plantation complex, they struggled to maintain their humanity against those who sought to remove it from them. Okpoti's comment to Rømer that the body 'is the greatest obstacle for the soul in the other life' points to the burial of the dead as a key site of that struggle. That the corpses of many slaves were simply tossed into the *asamanpow*, the 'thicket of ghosts', represented a form of eschatological violence as intimidating in its own way as the threat of physical coercion. As we will see in the next chapter, the two would come together in the practice of human sacrifice, in which the enslaved body and soul would join gold and Atlantic commodities as an object of mortuary exchange.

If slavery was a fatal embrace, it was also an intimate one. As Kwaku's preference for an afterlife as a slave of Frimpon Manso suggests, servitude within African society at least held the possibility of acquiring a degree of kinship rights—which might see faithful retainers or slave wives given some form of funeral and their corpses buried alongside those of their owners. Yet even when enslaved captives were able to negotiate a passage into local communities, the lingering animosity of their dead might continue to haunt the generations. In a process best documented among the Anlo-Ewe, anxieties about the injustices of a slave-owning past have led in the late twentieth century to the embrace of a new cultic movement designed to placate the spirits of enslaved ancestors together with the vengeful deities of the communities from which they were torn. 'The slave master's family made a big mistake', one adept explained. They treated an enslaved woman well in life, but 'did not know how to perform her funeral when she died ... so they were not able to please her in death, and she remains an unhappy presence'.[45] 'I recall the behaviour of an elder, important and respected, but of slave birth', Field wrote in the 1930s, who wept bitterly on the death of a migrant labourer from the Northern Territories. 'I inquired whether the weeping elder had been a friend of the dead man. "Oh no", was the answer, "but he always weeps when strangers die because that reminds him that when his own death comes he too will be laid in the strangers' cemetery among people who do not know their origin".'[46]

9

Human Sacrifice

OVER THE COURSE of three days in June 1858, the colonial secretary, R. D. Ross, recorded depositions from six slaves who had fled from Asante and sought refuge in the Assin kingdom, on the northern frontier of the British Gold Coast Protectorate. All were identified as 'Donkoes'—that is, *nnonkofo* (sing. *odonko*)—slaves originating from the savanna country to the north of Asante, and all claimed that they had run away because they feared being sacrificed at a funeral or at other 'customs'. Testifying before a mixed commission of Ross, the king and chiefs of Cape Coast, and an Asante delegation charged with returning them to their owners, the runaways spoke of the nature of their servitude and of living with the gnawing anxiety that they might at any minute be given up for sacrifice.[1] One, Sayeebah, said that he was part of a retinue of about a hundred slaves, three or four of whom had been 'delivered up to the King for Custom making' by his master, who 'was always threatening to kill him'. Moosoo, who was owned by the same man, 'has often heard his master say if you do not do so and so I will cut your head off', and although he clung to the belief that this threat was meant only to frighten him, he had observed that slaves were often specially brought into Kumasi to be killed during 'custom making'. It was the testimony of Kwadwo Tookoo, however, that made a particular impression on the commission: 'the whole of this young and intelligent lad's evidence is worthy of attention', Governor Bird reported, as 'it gives a vivid and harrowing picture of the cruelties practiced at the demoniacal customs of that country'. Kwadwo was owned by the sister of Asantehene Kwaku Dua Panin and despite his Akan day-name was also an *odonko*, from Daboya, in the tributary kingdom of Gonja. His mistress 'often kills her slaves', he said, and when her own daughter died 'no less than 100 people were sacrificed in making custom for the child'. 'He knows how to count 100—ten times ten make 100. He remembers perfectly well ten, ten people being killed one at a time until the whole 100 were sacrificed. He remembers the names of three of his fellow servants who were killed on the occasion, two women and one man: their names were Carawah, Orawahcarrie, and Shim.' When his mistress threatened him too with decapitation, he resolved to flee at the first opportunity to the Gold Coast, where it was known that the British had outlawed human sacrifice. 'He naturally felt alarmed at the threat when he knew that the lives of Princes were often taken; and what was he?—a slave.'

In support of his plea for asylum, Kwadwo Tookoo explained the standard manner of execution in Kumasi:

> When persons are going to be sacrificed the first thing done by the Executioners is to bind their hands behind their back, then stick a knife through... their cheeks so that they cannot cry out: they are then led to the place of execution, made to sit down, and ranged off in a row—they are left there in the sun, for several hours until the custom making begins; when, the executioners walk up to them, oblige them to stand up, then throw them down on the ground and cut their heads off. If a man is very strong and struggles hard two knives are thrust though his cheeks. Their legs and arms are frequently cut off. Their bodies are dragged and thrown into a ditch. When there is a general custom the people assemble to witness the scene, but frequently the king sacrifices people for his own pleasure and his executioner is then sent to the person he has determined to sacrifice.... Whether a slave behaves well or ill his life is not safe—frequently cases are trumped up against him in order to have an excuse to hand him over to be sacrificed.

Neither was it just lowly *nnonkofo* who were in danger. 'It is the custom for a certain number of Prisoners'—Kwadwo seems here to mean prisoners of war—'to be sacrificed in the event of the death of a chief or headman' and 'he has seen Chiefs and Headmen killed'. One such high-status victim he identified as an Akyem chief named Afawpah—whose execution was confirmed by the Asante officials present. In the face of these horrors, he and his fellow refugees were adamant that they would never go back to Asante; 'if the Governor wishes to kill him let him do so', Moosoo was recorded as having declared, 'but he will not return'.

From the missions of the first British and Dutch envoys to visit Kumasi in the 1810s to the termination of Asante sovereignty in 1896, European sources are replete with similar accounts of what most condemned as the moral outrage of human sacrifice. Indeed, Wilks argues that the practice was fundamental in shaping perceptions of the great forest kingdom: 'throughout the nineteenth century', he writes, '"Ashantee" and "human sacrifice" were virtually inseparable terms in the European imagination'.[2] Asante, that is, was portrayed as a land of death, where a cruel ruling elite, as Kwadwo Tookoo testified, would immolate sacrificial victims for some sort of perverse pleasure. Although Kwadwo's testimony is one of only a handful of accounts by a potential victim of ritual immolation, it accords with an extensive corpus of evidence pointing to the prominence of the practice in the Akan kingdoms.[3] The records of the 1858 commission encapsulate a number of contentious issues in the historiographical debate about human sacrifice in Asante and the Akan world more broadly: the predominance of hearsay as opposed to eyewitness accounts; a fixation with the magnitude of killings; the distortion of evidence by the overlay of European moral indignation or by outright fabrication for the purpose of imperial propaganda; the conceptual overlap between human sacrifice and judicial execution. The refugees presented a problem for the British authorities, who by the terms of the 1831 peace treaty with Asante were obliged to repatriate both escaped slaves and fugitives from justice but, unlike the tough-minded George Maclean in the 1830s, were increasingly unwilling to do so. Writing to Kwaku Dua Panin, Bird therefore apologized that he was unable to return them as requested but assured that they would be transported as punishment for the crime of swearing his oath on protectorate soil. The Asantehene acquiesced to this ruling but politely reminded the governor of the precedent in cordial relations between the two powers set by Maclean: 'if you do as he did everything shall be in good order'.[4]

It is the confusion between ritual immolation and judicial punishment that lies at the heart of the scholarly debate. Wilks placed inverted commas around the term 'human sacrifice' in the statement quoted above as he believed that it did not accurately describe the nature of the killings witnessed by or reported to Europeans. He first essayed this argument in *Asante in the Nineteenth Century*, making the case that European observers either mistakenly or wilfully misrepresented what were legally sanctioned capital punishments as ritualistic human sacrifices. While acknowledging that 'there appears to be little doubt that those thus executed were regarded as being despatched to the *Asaman*, where they constituted a servile class', he insisted that the victims were always either convicted criminals or members of a deceased person's household who willingly chose to accompany them to the afterlife.[5] This view was first questioned by Robin Law, who, in a survey of the history of human sacrifice in West Africa, argued that Wilks's agenda systematically 'to describe and interpret

Asante society in terms of categories transferred from the European experience' may well have led him mistakenly 'to assimilate the practice of human sacrifice in Asante to a recognizable European custom'.[6] Subsequent criticism along the same lines was to follow.[7] Wilks responded in a rejoinder in which he reiterated and elaborated his argument. That elaboration rested on an attempt more precisely to define the concept of sacrifice in the Akan context. Sacrifice (Twi: *aforebo*), he argued, is an offering to the gods (*abosom*), whereas the immolation of humans at the funerals of men and women of status was aimed at dispatching them to the *asamando* to serve the deceased or to propitiate ancestors. 'If the slain were human', Wilks wrote, 'the slaughter was not sacrificial. It had to do either with punishment and deterrence, which I shall refer to as "judicial executions", or with maintaining the quality of life of the ancestors, which I shall refer to as "mortuary slayings". These distinctions were not apparent to early nineteenth century visitors to Kumase'.[8]

It is certainly the case that there is sometimes a lack of clarity in our sources about whether an observed or reported immolation was a judicial execution or a mortuary slaying—if for no other reason than that the two were often one and the same. Criminals convicted of capital offences, that is to say, were often killed at funerals: by the mid-nineteenth century, these so-called *nkyere* (sing. *akyere*) were settled in special villages where they awaited their fate.[9] The distinction would often not have been readily apparent to local observers, either. It is also the case that by the end of the century, lurid and often exaggerated descriptions of sacrifices were being used by the Gold Coast administration to press its case for imperial intervention in Asante.[10] Whether Wilks's attempt to assimilate the immolation of humans to the secular realm of judicial punishment or, where a ritual element is grudgingly acknowledged, to impose a narrowly restrictive definition of 'sacrifice' can be sustained, however, is another matter. As is clear from the testimony given by the runaway slaves in 1858, his assertion that those killed either were convicted criminals or willingly went to their deaths does not withstand scrutiny. Neither is it appropriate to deny that symbolic violence had any sacrificial element simply on the grounds that it dispatched those victims to *asamando* or propitiated the ancestors. The majority of slayings were associated with funerals, but they also featured at regular points in the ritual calendar and at other highly charged moments which called for cathartic bloodletting. Indeed, theoretical analyses beginning with Hubert and Mauss's foundational statement, first published in 1898, stress both the multifaceted nature of sacrifice and its capacity to mediate communication with the sacred realm—including, but not exclusively, with hallowed ancestors.[11] With the exception of McCaskie's essay on the bloody aftermath of the death of Kwakua Dua Panin in 1867, however, the Akan literature is both strikingly under-theorized and reticent about engaging with features seen elsewhere to have been key to explaining the dynamics of human sacrifice, including the transgressive, cathartic and performative nature of ritual violence.[12]

Human sacrifice was not peculiar to Asante or the broader Akan world. As established by Law, the practice was widespread in those parts of the West African coastal and forest zones largely untouched by Islam, both in powerful states such Benin, Dahomey and Asante and among non-centralized peoples such as the Igbo in present-day southeastern Nigeria. In the Yoruba city-states of southwestern Nigeria, too, human sacrifice was well attested, although, perhaps owing to the growing influence of Islam, in decline among at least the Oyo and Egba by the mid-nineteenth century.[13] Neither was it that human sacrifice was a residual survival in these societies after declining in savanna regions to the north where Islam became a powerful presence. Evidence suggests that it may well have increased in magnitude in the era of the Atlantic slave trade, as increasing levels of militarization and accumulation generated new forms of violence, predation and consumption.[14] As Law cautions, however, the evidence of European observers does need to be used with care; like Muslims, they found the idea of human sacrifice repugnant and were not above exaggerating its magnitude and brutality in order to make a distinction between Christian European civilization and pagan African barbarity. In the eighteenth century, this supposed barbarity became a trope in polemical justifications of the slave trade: purchasing war captives and transporting them to the Americas, the argument ran, saved them from cruel sacrifice. Even after the abolition of the slave trade, similar arguments were advanced by British officials in defence of what some rationalized as the relatively humane institution of 'domestic slavery' on the Gold Coast. 'If they were not bought by the Fantees, many of them would be sacrificed at the Ashantee customs', Cruickshank wrote of the 'Donkoes', who continued to be in high demand—and, until 1875, quite legally enslaved—in the protectorate. 'By being brought into the countries under our protection, their lives are spared; they receive a more humane treatment; they are shielded from oppression, and are placed within a higher degree of civilization.'[15]

FIGURE 9.1. A brass gold-weight, or *abramo*, depicting an *obrafo* and his bound victim, photographed by R. S. Rattray. The latter has the *sepow* knife thrust through his cheeks and tongue in order to prevent him uttering a curse on those responsible for his impending death, and in his lap is the *gyabon suman*. Pitt Rivers Museum, University of Oxford, 1998.312.227.1.

The earliest evidence for human sacrifice in the region, however, came from the Gold Coast itself, where, as elsewhere in West Africa, it was identified as an integral part of mortuary customs for the wealthy and powerful. Portuguese sources from the early sixteenth century refer to the interment of wives and retainers in the graves of kings in Senegambia and the kingdom of Benin; writing in 1602, de Marees was the first to observe this on the Gold Coast and to explain its cosmological rationale.[16] Some, especially 'loving wives', willingly volunteered their posthumous services to the king. But de

Marees makes it clear, pace Wilks, that others were neither volunteers nor convicted criminals:

> Furthermore, any Nobleman who may have served the King during his lifetime will present him when he has died with a Slave to serve him; other Men also offer one of their Wives to serve him and to cook his food; other bring their Son in order that he may journey to the other World with the King; and all these person are killed and decapitated. But they do not know it, because the people who make these offers to the King do not tell them that they will be killed.... When the time comes for the funeral, they send them somewhere on an errand or to fetch water and follow that person with an Assegai and murder him on the way. Then they take the corpse to the King's Court, so that people may see what faithful service he renders to the King.[17]

The corpses of those killed were smeared with blood and interred in the royal grave, while their decapitated heads, as we have seen, were arranged on top 'as a great ornament in honour of the king'.

Subsequent seventeenth-century accounts suggest that it was slaves who composed the majority of those immolated at royal funerals. Müller makes an important observation that one's (posthumous) reputation among the established ancestors in the *asamando* was considered to be as vital as it had been in the world of the living. After death, he wrote, 'they become much more magnificent and important than they have been during their life here. Thus not only do these blind people, as long as they live, strive after great power, honour and wealth, but also, when they die, many bondsmen and bondswomen are slaughtered, to wait on their master in that kingdom, so that he may be all the more esteemed'.[18] Neither were these victims necessarily established members of the deceased's household, Barbot noting the existence of a market village near Cape Coast 'where the Blacks buy slaves to be kill'd and bury'd, at the funeral of their kings'.[19] Bosman also witnessed the dispatch of slaves, wives and 'principal servants' of the powerful dead. 'But what is most abominable', he thought, 'is that several poor wretched Men, who through Age or Inability are incapable of Labour, are sold on purpose to be made Victims of these accursed Offerings. 'Tis a most deplorable Spectacle to see these miserable Creatures killed in the most barbarous Manner in the World; what with Hacking, Piercing, Tormenting, & they endure a Thousand Deaths'.[20]

On the magnitude of slayings, Müller records more than eighty at the funeral in 1662 of the powerful *dey* of Fetu—Acrosan, or 'Johann Classen'—a few months before his arrival on the coast ('I myself counted eight-five skulls above his grave'); more than thirty at the funeral of the *omanhene* of Fetu's principal councillor; and seven at that of Ando, a captain in the service of the Danes.[21] Bosman notes that he witnessed eleven slaves being killed at a funeral in the manner described above, while when the *omanhene* of Fetu, Panin Ashrive, himself died in late 1687, an English visitor to Cape Coast, J. Hillier, was on hand to record the subsequent immolations: 'how many there was 'tis hard to say, the highest Account gives 90, the lowest 50, the middle 70'. 'They say also', he reported, 'that many more will follow at half a Years distance from his Death'.[22] Higher numbers of dead are given by Villault, who spent forty days at Fetu in 1667 and drew on conversations with Müller and the commander of the Danish fort. Villault did not witness a royal funeral, but his account is important because it provides the earliest evidence for an aspect of mortuary slaying sidestepped by Wilks and which undermines the contention that victims either died voluntarily or were criminals: an outburst of more indiscriminate killing after the death of a powerful *omanhene* conducted by young men of the grief-stricken royal household—as reported in detail by two eyewitnesses in Kumasi in 1867.[23] 'Whilst the Slaves are employ'd in the interrement of the King', the English translation of Villault runs, 'the Inhabitants of the Town run up and down like mad, cutting the throats of man, woman, child and slaves, to make his equipage as they call it, and attend his Majesty into the other world, in so much, that if he be a great Prince, they kill four or five hundred persons sometimes at the day of his funeral'.[24]

Evidence on the early Akan states of the forest interior is mostly embedded within oral traditions. We have already noted a number of these in passing—including the Asante account of the victory over Denkyira in 1701, which identified the flight from the latter of the so-called Bontwumafo, the 'red clay people' destined for sacrifice, as key to Osei Tutu's success. Historical reflection on sacrifice, punishment and power over life and death often focused on the *abrafo* (sing. *obrafo*) or, specifically in Asante, *adumfo*, the office-holders charged with carrying out executions. The importance of the *obrafo* to the exercise of political power is captured by the myth that, at the dawn of time, Odomankoma created in turn a herald (*osene*), a drummer (*okyerema*) and an executioner, 'and the precedence of these officials in an Ashanti Court', Rattray noted, 'is in that order'.[25] That ur-*obrafo* was Obrafo Nyam, whose original victim was said to be 'the first person ever killed, a hermaphrodite called Awo' who 'was sacrificed to "Asase Ya" (Mother Earth) to make her fruitful'.[26] Obrafo Nyam might therefore be seen to have furthered the

FIGURE 9.2. Memory of 'the knife'. An elderly *obrafo* holding the *sepow* in his mouth, photographed by R. S. Rattray during the yearly Apo ceremony at Tekyiman, in the Bono region of northern Asante, in April 1922. Pitt Rivers Museum, University of Oxford, 1998.312.658.1; published as figure 65 of *Religion and Art in Ashanti*, facing 161.

transition from an anarchic world-in-progress to one where the gendered human form took definitive shape; his successors were certainly seen as the implacable defenders of the social and political order that resulted. Yet their intimacy with death meant that executioners, like *akomfo*, were popularly regarded with a deep ambivalence. With their distinctive shaggy hairstyles and headgear, ferocious demeanour and theatrical display of the tools of their trade—most notably the *sepow*, the knife that was thrust through the cheeks of victims in order to pinion the tongue and prevent their uttering a curse on the king—the *abrafo* inspired both awe and fear. One of the three categories of *abosom*, the gods of the sky, or *ewim*, were frequently anthropomorphized as *abrafo* owing to their reputation as being similarly unbending, judgemental and merciless.[27] The *abrafo* themselves, however, faced a dangerous enemy: the *sasa*, or vengeful spirit, of their victims. Their main defence against this was the *gyabom*, a powerful *suman* (amulet) placed in the lap of the victim before decapitation in order to prevent the *sasa* from returning to torment the executioner or the king.[28]

For it was the king who was said ultimately to 'hold the knife'. Other traditions of the emergence of Asante record how the self-sacrifice of certain individuals served to guarantee the victory over Denkyira—while securing an exemption for their descendants from ever being subject to *osekan*, 'the knife', whether for a criminal offence or otherwise. Such an individual, Asare was told in the early twentieth century, was Kumawuhene Tweneboa Kodua, who offered himself up on that condition when Komfo Anokye insisted that a noble warrior must be sacrificed before the battle. Rather than putting Tweneboa Kodua to death, however, 'Anokye cast a spell on him, that made him an expiation for the entire nation.... He informed Osei Tutu and the Asanteman that Tweneboa Kodua should fight at the forefront on the day that they engaged the Denkyirahene in combat. If he died in action... it would symbolize the Asantehene's defeat of Denkyira'.[29] This, of course, came to pass. Whether such sacrifices were voluntary, as in the case of the heroic Tweneboa Kodua, or coerced, as in the case of the Bontwumafo, appears otiose. So too does the distinction between whether ritual killing was designed to propitiate the ancestors or the gods. Either way, it is clear that the ritual preparation for war—as well as its aftermath—was another crucial context for human sacrifice.[30]

It was not until the mid- to late eighteenth century that reports of extravagant human sacrifices in the powerful Akan forest states entered the written record. An early account was that which reached Accra of the aftermath of the death of Akyem Kotokuhene Frimpon Manso in 1741, Rømer reporting that 336 of his wives and 3,000 *akrafo* were buried—alive—with the corpse. Neither the numbers killed nor the manner of their interment seems credible—although the report that the limbs of the victims were first broken does resonate with that in *History of Ashanti Kings* for the *sora* ritual of a deceased Asantehene.[31] Then, in the closing years of the century, a violent and well-documented dynastic dispute in Asante led to the overthrow of Asantehene Osei Kwame (1777–1803) by forces rallied by Asantehemaa Konadu Yaadom; his replacement with Konadu Yaadom's own son, Opoku Fofie (1803–4); and, after Opoku Fofie's premature death, the restoration of order with the accession of Osei Tutu Kwame (1804–23). One aspect of this multifarious crisis appears to have been a contest over the magnitude—and perhaps even the very 'morality' itself—of human sacrifice.

Neither may it have been the first time that debate over the practice emerged: according to Reindorf, the third Asantehene, the elderly Kusi Obodom (1750–64) 'was the most humane of all the monarchs, [who] forbade the human sacrifices, and brought peace among the chiefs. Yet they did not approve of his being so less blood-thirsty, so that many tried to irritate his feelings by committing acts against the law'.[32] There has been some uncertainty over this statement: a more likely cause of chiefly discontent may have been Kusi Obodom's lack of military success—and, after an inconclusive conflict with Dahomey, the concomitant shortage of enemy prisoners to immolate in propitiation of those killed.[33] 'After the defeat of Sai Akwasy [Kusi Obodom]', Dupuis was told in 1820, 'the kingdom was filled with grief and mourning; the provinces were severally beaten up for victims to sacrifice in the capital, in expiation of offences done to the guardian gods, and to appease the shades of the great captains who fell in the war'. 'The streets of Coomassy', Dupuis's indignant Muslim informants related, 'were drenched in human blood and animal gore during the whole of the great Adai custom'.[34] Other sources, however, confirm Reindorf's reading of Kusi Obodom's humane impulses, recording that it was he who introduced the practice of *atitodee*, or 'buying one's head', for offences which hitherto had carried a mandatory death sentence.[35]

Similarly ambiguous evidence for rising discord over the exercise of power over life and death exists for the collapse of Osei Kwame's authority in the 1790s. One element in the opposition to the Asantehene was said to be his 'attachment to the Moslems, and, it is said, his inclination to establish Koranic law for the civil code of the empire'. Again, the source for this was Dupuis's interlocutors among Kumasi's population of Muslim traders, in particular the cleric Muhammad al-Ghamba (the Bashaw).

> Sai Koamina, according to the Bashaw, was a believer at heart; but the safety of his throne would not allow him to avow his sentiments. His name is handed down to posterity as the most merciful of the race of kings. Towards the end of his reign, he prohibited many festivals at which it was usual to spill the blood of victims devoted to the customs; yet he could not be prevailed upon to relinquish the barbarous practice of watering the graves of his ancestors with human gore. These and other innovations were of a tendency to alarm the great captains; they feared, it is said, that the Moslem

religion, which they well know levels all ranks and orders of men, and places them at the arbitrary discretion of the sovereign, might be introduced, whereby they would lose the ascendancy they now enjoy.[36]

A contemporary Danish account, however, explains matters differently: after the death of the heir apparent Opoku Kwame—allegedly poisoned by Osei Kwame and at whose funeral some 1,500 people were said to have been immolated—Konadu Yaadom and her allies withdrew from Kumasi in rebellion, and on regaining the capital determined that the Asantehene 'may no longer kill or sacrifice anyone' or confiscate the property of the dead; rather, malefactors were to be sold into slavery on the coast.[37] Whichever faction was responsible, the attempt to curtail human sacrifices was temporary at best. In 1817, Bowdich was told that the funeral custom for the deposed and executed Osei Kwame was the greatest that was ever known, informants assuring him that it 'was repeated weekly for three months, and that two hundred slaves were sacrificed, and 25 barrels of powder fired, each time'.[38] Its only equal, he reported, was that for Konadu Yaadom herself in 1809, when the ranks of sacrificial victims were swollen by large numbers of prisoners captured in the recent war against the Fante. 'The King himself devoted 3,000 victims (upwards of 2,000 of whom were Fantee prisoners) and 25 barrels of powder', while the *aman* of Dwaben, Kokofu, Bekwai, Nsuta and Mampon 'furnished 100 victims, and 20 barrels of powder, each, and most of the smaller towns 10 victims, and two barrels of powder, each'.[39]

All of this has been subjected to a variety of interpretations. Law attempts to reconcile the contradictory accounts by arguing that Osei Kwame, rather than completely suppressing human sacrifice, might have sought to limit its impact on free subjects or to restrict it to what he calls 'the cult of the royal ancestors'—that is, the cycle of *adae* celebrations and the annual Odwira—and thereby prohibited slaying at funerals. Osei Kwame's opponents, Law suggests, 'in turn sought to impose limits on the ancestral sacrifices', in what was at root a contest between royal and chiefly power.[40] This is certainly possible. There is a problem, however, with Dupuis's account of Osei Kwame's leanings towards Islam, which might be seen as the wishful thinking of his Muslim interlocutors. Bowdich makes no mention of Islam in his account of events, emphasizing instead that it was the Asantehene's refusal to return to Kumasi in order to preside over Odwira which was the proximate cause of his destoolment.[41] In light of this, Muhammad al-Ghamba's statement that 'towards the end of his reign, he prohibited many festivals at which it was usual to spill the blood of victims devoted to the customs' may well be a memory of Osei Kwame's extraordinary refusal to conduct the 1802 Odwira. Neither was Law in a position to take full account of the fraught circumstances of the deaths of the heir apparent Opoku Kwame (allegedly poisoned by his ascribed brother), Osei Kwame (executed at the behest of his ascribed mother), Opoku Fofie (killed by the vengeful ghost of his predecessor) and Konadu Yaadom (also possibly killed by the ghost of Osei Kwame). We will return to the posthumous powers of these ghosts in the next chapter. It can be suggested here, however, that the desire of those responsible to assuage their guilt—that is, to placate the vengeful *sasa* of the deceased—may have motivated this sequence of unusually elaborated and bloody funeral celebrations.

For Wilks, however, Bowdich's and Dupuis's accounts of the bloodletting, together with the former's firsthand reports of the immolations conducted during the Odwira of 1817 and the latter's of the killing of prisoners of war after the Gyaman campaign in 1819, were little more than 'lurid stories' which 'gave spice to the published accounts of their experiences'.[42] Quite aside from the fact that throughout his corpus Wilks was untroubled with mobilizing an extensive range of other evidence from both writers, it is tendentious to accuse either of peddling lurid stories. Certainly, both shared with Kumasi's resident Muslims a repugnance of human sacrifice.[43] Yet both were aware of its cosmological rationale, of the voluntary nature of the death of royal wives and *akrafo*, and of the fact that a considerable proportion of those killed were indeed *nkyere* or condemned criminals reserved for immolation at funerals or other celebrations—just as they also reported the sacrifice of other, ostensibly 'innocent' victims: slaves, war captives and randomly targeted free citizens.[44] Bowdich recorded the details of Osei Kwame's and Konadu Yaadom's funerals as they were remembered by his informants in Kumasi, just as Dupuis reported Asantehene Osei Tutu Kwame's own explanation of the fate of the prisoners he had marched back to Kumasi from the Gyaman campaign just the year before: 'some of these people being bad men, I washed my stool in their blood for the fetische. But then some were good people, and these I sold or gave to my captains ... and what can I do? Unless I kill or sell them, they will grow strong and kill my people'.[45]

Osei Tutu Kwame's statement on the immolation of Gyaman war captives raises two interpretive issues with which to conclude. First, did mortuary slaying also have a parallel instrumental rationale of keeping slaves cowed in subjugation—and might the growth of the servile population in the nineteenth century have led, as Law suggests for West Africa generally, to an increase in the magnitude of human sacrifice? Statistical evidence is too impressionistic to answer that question with any certainty, although Austin has argued for a possible correlation between the fluctuating monetary value of slaves and the number of sacrificial victims, driven by the logic that as prices fell with increased supply, 'mourners would have wished to maintain the overall value of the resources they consumed at funerary rites'.[46] The rising price of slaves from mid-century may have meant that 'the same total cost now represented fewer corpses'—although testimony from the 1858 runaways indicates that that brought little or no comfort to vulnerable and despised *nnonkofo*. The entanglement of cosmological hierarchy with social control was encapsulated in the threatening maxim 'Odonko opo berebe a, ye de no ko ayi' (When a slave gets very familiar, we take him to a funeral custom).[47]

Second, if Dupuis's translator did accurately capture the Asantehene explaining that the victims died in propitiation of 'the fetische' (i.e., the *abosom*), then this points to a greater complexity in what was being transacted than Wilks has allowed. This raises the fundamental problem of making 'human sacrifice' intelligible. Bowdich and Dupuis found it difficult to reconcile the sophistication and civility they encountered in Asante with the grisly violence of ritual killing. So too did subsequent nineteenth-century visitors to Kumasi, notably the Methodist missionary T. B. Freeman—although for Freeman and later churchmen, the problem of human sacrifice did have a readily identifiable cause (and solution): the absence of revealed religion. Neither was Freeman the hysterical tub-thumper that Wilks caricatured him as: while his journals of 1839–41 certainly betray a despair at what he saw as a needless loss of innocent life, his later reminiscences display considerable insight into the dynamics of symbolic violence.[48] It is clear that Wilks himself struggled with this conundrum. His solution was also straightforward, if tendentious: by insisting that victims were either *akyere* or volunteers killed exclusively to be dispatched to the *asamando*, their deaths need therefore not be classified as 'sacrifice' at all. 'It will be apparent', he concluded, 'that, in Asante, the taking of life was regarded with a certain indifference, a certain nonchalance (though no more so than in most societies past and all too many present). . . . Life is Asante was not "cheap", but death was not to be feared'.[49]

From the perspectives of both those doing the killing and those being killed, Wilks, I would argue, is wrong about this. There is ample evidence not only that many victims were neither *akyere* nor died voluntarily but also that the emotionally charged, performative drama of immolation operated at a level of complexity far beyond the 'nonchalant' or functional dispatch of retainers to the afterlife. Life in Asante was very much not cheap: as in much of Africa, Akan state and society can be seen historically to have been single-mindedly fixated on the value of human life, on wellbeing and on demographic increase—including that of enslaved retainers. Elsewhere, Wilks himself notes the importance of *mogya*, 'blood', as a vital life force, the shedding of which 'was therefore seen as fundamentally antithetical to the natural order and was regulated by the Seventy-Seven Laws of Okomfo Anokye'.[50] The sanctioned taking of life was certainly not regarded with indifference; rather, it was perceived as a momentous and essentially transgressive act. It was precisely that which infused it with such numinous and cathartic power.

As for death not being feared, one might as well assert that the doctrinal offer of salvation in Abrahamic religions meant that, historically, the prospect of dying caused no particular apprehension where those faiths held sway. Not so. Certainly, a code of bravery meant that there was an imperative for those facing execution to confront their final moments with a display of defiant stoicism. Bowdich was struck by this during the opulent funeral custom for the mother of Asafohene Kwaakye Kofi on 2 August 1817, when the intensity of the drama was heightened by the presence of the Asantehene himself. On the arrival of Kwaakye Kofi, carried aloft in a palanquin through the surging crowd of mourners, 'the victims, with large knives driven through their cheeks, eyed him with indifference; he them with a savage joy, bordering on phrenzy: insults were aggravated on the one, flattery lavished on the other'. Neither was such stoicism an exclusively masculine attribute: in 1868, Winwood Reade was told of a woman in Akuapem whose slaying at a funeral was botched by the *obrafo*. 'She was only stunned by the blow; awaking, she found herself surrounded by dead bodies. She ran back to the town, where the elders were sitting in council, informed them that she had been into the Land of the Dead, and that the king had sent her back because she had no clothes. The elders must dress her finely and then kill her over again; and this was accordingly done.'[51]

Yet Bowdich had also observed the scene triggered by the discharge of musketry announcing Kwaakye Kofi's mother's death: 'in an instant you see a crowd of slaves burst from the house, and run towards the bush, flattering themselves that the hindmost, or those surprised in the house, will furnish the human victims for sacrifice, if they can secrete themselves until the custom is over'. On the death of an Asantehene, moreover, when 'the brothers, sons, and nephews of the King, affecting temporary insanity, burst forth with their muskets, and fire promiscuously among the crowd', Bowdich was told that 'few persons of rank dare to stir from their houses for the first two or three days, but religiously drive forth all their vassals and slaves, as the most acceptable composition of their own absence'.[52] It was this fate which in 1858 prompted Kwadwo Tookoo and his companions to flee to the Gold Coast. As in early modern Europe, habituation to the recurrent spectacle of death did not breed indifference.[53] A premature and grisly death was an aberration to be avoided—but when one's time came, as we have seen among slaves in the West Indies, it should be faced with defiance. That is why the executed dead were so angry, and why victims died with the *gyabom* placed on their laps to drive away their resentful *sasa*. For those directing proceedings, meanwhile, ontological security in an uncertain world was surely key: if Odomankoma was killed by the figure of death he created, then symbolic violence might be seen as way of 'killing death' itself.

10

Poison

THE DATE IS 20 January 1482: let us return to that first encounter between African and European on the Elmina seashore. 'To impress his dignity', João de Barros wrote of Caramansa, 'he walked with very slow and light steps, never turning his face from side to side'. And then, before any words were exchanged, a further sequence of bodily gestures, beginning with Caramansa taking Azambuja's hand and snapping his fingers as he released the handshake. 'The snapping of the fingers is a sign among them of the greatest courtesy that can be afforded. Then the king stepped aside allowing his men to approach Diogo de Azambuja, to do the same; but the manner in which they snapped their fingers differed from that of the king: wetting their fingers in their mouths and wiping them on their chests, they cracked them from the little finger to the index finger, a kind of salute here given to princes; for they say that the fingers can carry poison if they are not cleaned in this manner.'[1] The deft clicking of fingers when shaking hands remains ubiquitous in Ghana today, five centuries later. Yet the performance of wetting the fingers is equally arresting. Whether its explanation was based on an observation by Azambuja, on Barros's own subsequent experience of the Mina coast or on Portuguese understandings of poisoning from elsewhere in Guinea is unclear.[2] Nonetheless, it is the earliest indication of the existence of a 'poison culture' in West Africa, one which took a variety of forms over time but would continue to prey on the minds of Africans and Europeans alike. 'It is said that every native conceals under his left thumb-nail a toxic substance that possesses almost "the devastating subtlety of prussic acid"', Hertz observed about the western Gold Coast in his 1909 essay on the contrasting symbolism of the left and right hands.[3] By the 1920s, British colonial administrators, realizing how little they knew about indigenous medicine and its shadowy other, 'native poisoning', attempted to initiate a scientific investigation into local pharmacology and toxicology.[4] Little came of this initiative, and talk of the ready recourse to poison remained more a matter of rumour than proven fact. Yet despite—or perhaps because of—this absence of stable representation, poison maintained its menacing character and centrality in African understandings of the mysteries of death.

'Poisons possess an incontestable materiality', David Arnold writes in a recent work on India; 'but poison and poisoning are also extraordinarily rich in their semantic and cultural deployment, as metaphors of malice and emblems of evil'. Exploring the social cognition, scientific understanding and colonial governance of poison, Arnold seeks to establish 'a significant and distinctive poison culture' in India, as established toxic histories took new forms in the age of biomedicine.[5] As Ian Burney has shown for Victorian Britain, poison's metaphorical power was rooted in its impalpable nature: 'Conceived as an act committed in the absence of direct and visible contact between the perpetrator and victim, poisoning appeared as a form of violence that operated beneath the threshold of perception'.[6] Drawing on these insights, this chapter explores the cultural register of poison and poisoning on the Gold Coast and in its forest hinterland. European apprehension about guileful native poisoners is certainly part of this story, but it will be argued that these anxieties, far from simply being febrile orientalist imaginings, were in part derived from African perceptions of the quotidian ubiquity of poison—both medicinal and magical. Its cultural terrain is examined by way of a sequence of episodes beginning at Accra in 1745, moving to the Asante court at Kumasi in the 1790s–1810s, and then back to the Gold Coast in the mid-nineteenth century, when accusations of poisoning began to emerge in British colonial courts.

First let us consider the spectrum of vernacular concepts encapsulated by the term 'poison'. As elsewhere, poison in the Akan world had both a discrete materiality and an extensive and unstable semantic range. The Twi language points to the presence of what Burney and Arnold refer to as a *pharmakon*—that is, the ancient Greek idea of a body of medicinal substances that functioned both as curatives and as poisons. In contrast with an extensive literature on malign 'witchcraft', the ambiguity of the *pharmakon* has been neglected in the historiography of healing and harming in Africa.[7] The generic Twi word for medicine is *aduru* (from the same root as *edua*: plant, tree or wood), while that for poison is *adurubone*, 'bad medicine'. As in other medical cultures, both 'traditional' and biomedical, the distinction between therapeutic medicine and harmful poison was often determined by the method they were administered or by the size of the dose. There was no clear distinction between pharmacological concoctions, the efficacy of which required them to be ingested or applied to the body, and what can be called 'magical' preparations, which might be deployed from a distance and activated by intent or incantation.[8] Both forms of *aduru* were seen to harness spiritual power and to intersect on the cosmological spectrum with *asuman*, more potent agents typically manifested as protective amulets. While the continuum of *abosom–asuman–aduru* served to protect against destructive invisible forces, moreover, so too did *adurubone* intersect with the most fearsome of those forces: *bayi*, or 'witchcraft'. It is here that care is needed in the interpretation of English-language sources, as accusations of poisoning often refer not to the ingestion of a toxic substance—such as a concoction hidden under the fingernail—but to a practice which approximates the notions of sorcery or witchcraft.[9]

This conceptual doubling might be illustrated by two passages from Bosman, the earliest reflections on medicine and poison on the Gold Coast. Bosman, who survived the coast's hostile bacteriological environment for fourteen years, was suitably impressed with local pharmacology and its practitioners (*aduyefo* or *adunsinni*). Extolling the use of 'the Roots, Branches and Gumms of Trees' and 'about thirty several sorts of green Herbs, which are impregnated with an extraordinary Sanative Virtue', he wrote that he had seen 'several of our Country Men cured by them, when our own Physicians were at a loss what to do' and that the herbs 'are of such wonderful Efficacy, that 'tis much to be deplored that no European Physicians has yet applied himself to the discovery of their Nature and Virtue'. It was only when such medicines had no effect in restoring the health of the patient, he observed, that 'they apply their false and superstitious Religious Worship, as more effectual to those Ends: and what contributes to the promotion of this Custom, is, that he who here acts the part of a Doctor, is also a *Feticheer* or Priest'. The herbalist at this point takes on the role of the *akomfo* or the *sumankwafo* (master of the *suman*) to conduct sacrificial offerings or to fabricate appropriate amulets. These methods were also sometimes resorted to by Europeans; in the case of those who fell sick but remained aloof from local practice, their servants or 'mulatto' mistress (and here Bosman was no doubt speaking from personal experience) would secretly conceal in their bedchamber 'some things consecrated or charmed by the Priest, laid there on purpose to defend their Master from Death'.[10]

When it came to harming rather than healing, Bosman also located the practice of poisoning within the realm of the fetish:

> If they are injured by another they make *Fetiche* to destroy him in the following manner: they cause some Victuals and Drink to be Exorcised by their *Feticheer* or Priest, and scatter in some place which their Enemy is accustomed to pass; firmly believing that in that way it can not harm them. Neither can it do any harm to their carriers, because the exorcised matter can only do harm to the person for whom it is intended. So this is really more modest than what I have read about some of the Italians, who are also well versed in the art of poisoning: when they want to get rid of their enemies they do not hesitate to put innocent people into great danger too. Therefore I cannot very much like the *Fetiche* of the Italians, and I would rather walk over all that the *Negroes* can lay for me, than have anything to do with theirs.[11]

Although Bosman doubts the efficacy of these methods compared with those he imagines are employed by the more cynical Italians, he makes an important observation: that 'if any Person is caught strowing [i.e., scattering] this Poison, he is very severely punished, nay, sometimes with Death'. Like the destruction of life by the invisible power of *bayi*, or 'witchcraft', the murderous use of *adurubone* was a criminal offence of the highest order.

Bosman goes on to describe two legitimate uses of poison: in judicial ordeals and in the swearing of an oath (or 'eating fetish'). Ordeals took a variety of forms, but the most common, as elsewhere in Atlantic Africa, was the person under investigation being forced to swallow large quantities of water infused with the red bark of the *odom* tree (*Erythrophleum suaveolens*), a powerful and potentially fatal emetic. Verbal oaths, as we have seen, were also often accompanied by the ingestion of a ritually empowered concoction; 'if you ask what Opinion the Negroes have of those who falsify their Obligations confirmed by the Oath-Drink', Bosman explained, 'they believe the perjured Person shall be swelled by the Liquor till he bursts; or . . . that he shall shortly dye of a Languishing Sickness: The first Punishment they imagine more peculiar to Women, who take the Draught to acquit themselves of an Accusation of Adultery'.[12] Here we see women, as a result of their own supposed immoral actions, as the victims of poison. As in Europe and elsewhere, however, witchcraft and poisoning were often associated with women, both forms of occluded aggression understood to be weapons of the weaker sex.

Poison was often suspected in any startlingly unnatural death. 'When someone has died there is often talk of poisoning', Monrad wrote of Accra in the early nineteenth century, 'and no other cause of death is considered, other than the fetish has killed that person'.[13] In Akuapem in the 1860s, 'when a person dies suddenly poison is immediately talked of'.[14] The deceased's past would be raked over for clues as to potential enemies, investigations made, the corpse interrogated by being carried through the town (*afunsua*)—and if a suspect was identified, judicial inquiry, possibly in the form of *odom* or another ordeal, would ensue. Punishment ranged from the payment of financial satisfaction to the family of the deceased to execution. After the death in 1814 of King Aggery of Cape Coast and the identification of his poisoner as the *opanyin* (or elder) Kwesi Ampon, for example, the African Company was forced to transport the latter to Sierra Leone in order to prevent him from being killed.[15] Five years later, Aggery's successor was himself rumoured to have been implicated in another poison plot, when the sudden death at Cape Coast of an Asante commissioner, 'a young athletic man', was 'not without a strong suspicion of poison, which, it was whispered, had been administrated by a slave of the caboceer'.[16]

A rapid succession of deaths heightened such suspicion to a fever pitch, often giving rise to a fear that a particularly vindictive poisoner was at large. Such an episode occurred at the Danish headquarters of Christiansborg Castle in 1745, when three governors died within a space of six weeks and suspicion fell on a Euro-African woman named Anna Sophia. Anna Sophia was the wife of a Danish sergeant, Cornelius Petersen, incarcerated for his role in a rebellion against company authority, and, according to the Euro-African pastor F. P. Svane, 'was notorious all over the country for her designs on the life of Mr Billson and all his supporters, in order to get her husband out of detention'.[17] Governor Billsen died after a short illness on 11 March 1745, having been attended by a Dutch barber-surgeon said to be in a sexual relationship with Anna Sophia. Twelve days later, his successor Brock also died, along with a number of other guests at the customary feast given by newly appointed governors. The dead, according to Svane, were found to have 'blue on the lips and below the eyes, on the nails, behind the ears, the teeth, and so on, sometimes with foam and much frothing from the mouth', all of which pointed to poison—'which the careful efforts of the Negroes in truth found and proved to be so'.[18] If Anna Sophia was responsible, then she appeared to have employed a more

Italianate method of poisoning than the discriminating method described by Bosman. A month later, it was the turn of interim governor Wilder, who perished in the same circumstances. Wilder was in turn succeeded by the trader A. F. Hachenburg, who, alarmed by the rumour that he too would die if Petersen was not given his freedom, promptly released the mutinous sergeant.[19] The expedient Hachenburg survived, and he went on to become the progenitor of one of Osu's many illustrious 'mulatto' merchant families: his great-grandson was the Basel Mission pastor and pioneer historian Carl Reindorf.

Did Anna Sophia murder the three Danish governors? Svane certainly thought so. So too, on reflection, did Ludewig Rømer, who was also implicated in the mutiny against Billsen and forced to flee to British protection at Cape Coast, from where he wrote an account of events in an effort to exonerate himself.[20] Rømer at first was uncertain: whereas he believed the evidence for the poisoning of Brock to be 'incontrovertible', Danish and Dutch doctors at Accra had agreed that Billsen had actually died owing to complications arising from 'a quicksilver cure he was taking for a venereal disease'; Wilder, meanwhile, was a dissolute drunkard, whose constitution gave out when 'the first thing he did was to take a couple of Negresses in addition to the one he had, and become more of a drunkard than he had been before'.[21] In his later book, however, Rømer was in no doubt that 'a mulatto woman, a Christian, in the course of one year had had several persons at our Fort poisoned'. This had been publicly confirmed in dramatic fashion during the annual Homowo festival, when Anna Sophia had approached the shrine of the Lakpa oracle. 'When she brought forward her sacrifice (which was a bottle of brandy)', Rømer recounted, '*Giemawong* would not accept it, as he did the others. Instead, (it is strange, and I ask to be excused for writing it) he farted, and damned her with these words, "Your memory shall be obliterated". Many Blacks have told me this, and all our servants at the Fort know it, so that the woman ... dared not come to the Fort during an entire year, for fear of being railed at by our soldiers'.[22]

For Rømer, these events, together with a subsequent incident at Accra in 1748, were evidence that 'the Blacks sometimes poison Europeans' and that Europeans were not above poisoning each other. Straddling the two was the Euro-African community, whose cultural hybridity was exemplified by Anna Sophia, who identified as a Christian but also sacrificed to Lakpa.[23] It is tempting to suggest that Euro-African women, given their sexual entanglements with European traders, coupled with the latter's fearful mortality rates, may have been particularly vulnerable to accusations of poisoning. Yet there is little clear evidence for this. Bosman, who had a strange and vehement antipathy for 'mulattos' ('a Bastard Strain . . . made up of a parcel of profligate Villains' and 'publick Whores') and who otherwise discusses poisoning, makes nothing of the matter.[24] What the episode does convey is a sense of the fractious and febrile relations among the small and isolated contingents in the coastal trading forts, where the numbing routines of the slave trade were punctuated 'by sudden fears about fatal illnesses or death at the hands of local people'.[25] Given the ready recourse to poisoning as an explanation for sudden death within local communities, it was hardly surprising that fears of toxic attack would prey on the minds of Europeans. Weighing up the evidence, the well-informed Monrad was 'in no doubt that the Negroes are in possession of both rapidly and slowly working poisons'—the latter a classic cross-cultural trope of occluded criminality, operating beneath the threshold of perception.[26]

Such anxieties resurfaced in 1838, when Letitia Landon died in mysterious circumstances at Cape Coast Castle. A popular London-based writer newly married to the president of the British settlements, George Maclean, Landon appears to have overdosed accidentally on a prussic acid-based medicine—although this likelihood did not quell the local rumour that she had been poisoned by her husband's native mistress. This episode saw West African poison culture intersect with that of the imperial metropolis, not least because Landon had herself been criticized for her melodramatic portrayals of 'poison lore' at a time when a more scientific notion of toxicology was struggling to emerge; in a bitter irony, a case of prussic acid poisoning had featured in her final novel, *Flowers of Loveliness* (1838).[27]

By poisoning, what Rømer and Monrad meant was the ingestion of a toxic substance rather than the magical action of an 'exorcized' object, as described by Bosman. The discoloured condition of the corpses of Anna Sophia's alleged victims also points to an eighteenth-century shift in European perceptions of the action of poison, from 'some Occult or Unknown Principle' to 'the known Laws of Motion'.[28] But what were these poisons? Monrad recounts a number of episodes pointing to a local knowledge and use of deadly botanical substances, including the suicide of a man facing execution and another of an enslaved debtor threatened with the Middle Passage. 'The Negroes even tell of a poison so strong that if one has some of it only under his nail, and dips it into a drink, or food . . . one can thereby poison another.'[29] Twentieth-century botanical research certainly suggests a long-established and sophisticated knowledge of powerful toxins, including those derived from the *odubrafo* (lit. 'executioner tree'; *Maryea micrantha*) and *obua* (*Napoleonaea vogelli*).[30]

Specific information, however, was hard to come by: Monrad writes that one English governor offered a reward to any African who could bring him a deadly poison, but because 'according to the laws of the Negroes, there has been established the death penalty for anyone who owns poison', none was forthcoming. In addition to the use of *odom* for ordeals, one exception to this law was the use in hunting and in warfare of poisoned arrows, the potency of which has been well attested since the sixteenth century.[31] Arrow poison could be made from botanical products (such as *Strophanthus hisbidus*, in the northern savanna) but on the coast the most commonly mentioned ingredient was crocodile gall. It was crocodile gall that Rømer believed to be the substance of choice of murderers like the determined Anna Sophia, and it is likely that its unauthorized possession came within the ambit of the capital offence noted by Monrad. Great sensitivity therefore surrounded the hunting of crocodiles: as late as 1891 and again in 1915, disputes arose in Accra when Muslim migrants were accused of doing so for the suspected purpose of manufacturing poison.[32]

Yet toxins such as crocodile gall were difficult to acquire and, except in cases of domestic intimacy, to administer. In part for this reason, as becomes apparent when more detailed evidence begins to emerge from the mid-nineteenth century, the criminal use of *adurubone* was more likely to have involved the manipulation of non-pharmacological objects. In 1753, another Euro-African at Christiansborg, a soldier named Essau Christensen Quist, was charged with purchasing a 'fetish' with the object of killing the chief Danish factor. Seven years later, one of the Osu notables who gave evidence in that case, the trade broker Sodsha Duomoro, was himself accused by a rival of poisoning the latter's brother.[33] As with the events of 1745, the structural context for the accusation against Sodsha Duomoro was the ferociously competitive, rancorous and sometimes murderous world of Atlantic commerce in the coastal towns. Some scholars have argued that the entangled idioms of witchcraft and poison in Atlantic Africa emerged as a result of the deathly working of the slave trade.[34] The existence of these idioms deep in the Akan forest, however, suggests that this analysis is difficult to sustain. Slave commerce, moreover, was not the only arena in which personal rivalry and ambition could escalate into the homicidal mobilization of noxious objects; the other, of course, was politics. To consider this, we turn to two episodes of alleged poisoning at the highest reaches of Akan political power, the royal court of Asante.

The first of these toxic episodes was entangled with the overthrow of Asantehene Osei Kwame in 1803. As we saw in the last chapter, the mounting hostility to Osei Kwame in the 1790s has been the subject of some historical debate: suffice to say that a combination of dynastic rivalry and alarm about the direction of government policy saw the emergence of the forceful Asantehemaa Konadu Yaadom at the head of a movement of opposition to her adoptive son.[35] Of concern to us here is the event which escalated the simmering power struggle into open hostility: in late 1797, a report reached the Danes at Osu that Osei Kwame had been accused by Konadu Yaadom of poisoning the heir apparent (and her own biological son) Opoku Kwame. It was in the aftermath of this accusation that she withdrew from Kumasi and then, having rallied her forces, reportedly forced a raft of reformist policies on the Asantehene which sought to limit his sovereignty over life and death and his right to death duties and to allow the family of a transported criminal to 'mourn for him as if he were dead'.[36] Osei Kwame in turn withdrew from the capital to Dwaben, from where he seems to have attempted to rule. Such a radical relocation from the sacral geography of Kumasi, however, was untenable: as recounted to Bowdich in 1817, when the Asantehene refused to officiate over the annual Odwira ceremony, possibly in 1802, he was destooled and replaced by another of Konadu Yaadom's sons, Opoku Fofie.[37] Some time later, Osei Kwame either committed suicide or submitted to execution: Bowdich was told that he was dispatched—as befitting a royal, whose blood should never be shed—by being strangled with a rope weighed down by elephant tusks; Reindorf, however, understood that 'residing in Dwabeng, he poisoned himself'.[38]

Yet Opoku Fofie did not survive long on the Golden Stool. Sources differ on the chronology of his abbreviated reign, but it appears that he was enstooled in late 1803 or early 1804, immediately after the death of Osei Kwame. Within a matter of months, if not weeks, however, he was himself dead. This sequence of events is important, because in 1820 Dupuis's informants revealed the cause of Opoku Fofie's demise, after a 'lingering illness': 'This was one of the most promising princes the nation ever had. He was the brother of the deposed Koamina, who (in revenge it is supposed) occasioned his death, it is said, by sorcery.'[39] Dupuis says nothing of the death of Osei Kwame, but the chronology is clear: when he killed his successor by 'sorcery', he was himself already dead. Reindorf, who had access to information from within the royal household, elaborates on what was understood to have transpired: Opoku Fofie 'died suddenly, being, it is said, visited by the apparition of his late brother, when in bed with one of his wives by name Firempoma Tanno.'[40]

Authoritative oral tradition written down in the 1930s–40s offers further explanation. Firempomaa Tanowa had been a favourite consort of Osei Kwame and, as was customary, became the wife of his successor. 'The *osaman* or departed spirit of Osei Kwame appeared in the room, and asked why Opoku Fofie had presumed to marry a royal widow, when he had not yet fully carried out the funeral obsequies due to his predecessor. The embittered *osaman* then threw Opoku Fofie to the ground, where he died.'[41]

The significance of this historical reading, McCaskie argues, lies in the causal connection 'between the uncompleted or otherwise unsatisfactory mortuary rituals of one *Asantehene*, and the disastrously premature death of another'.[42] Given the compressed timeframe, this must certainly have been the case. Yet Bowdich was told that, ultimately, 'they made the greatest custom for [Osei Kwame] which has ever been known'—characterized by the large numbers of sacrificial victims, discussed in the previous chapter.[43] That the disgraced Osei Kwame had died an ignominious death either by his own hand or at those of the royal executioners makes this an intriguing observation. As he was believed posthumously to have killed his successor, was this stupendous funeral a desperate attempt by Konadu Yaadom to placate and banish his murderous *osaman twentwen*, 'evil haunting ghost'? Bowdich's next sentence—surely reflective of the narrative as it was recounted to him in 1817—is telling: 'The sable Cleopatra died soon after him.'[44] Was Konadu Yaadom, too, believed to have been a victim of Osei Kwame's ghost? 'Often there is talk of someone's death as if the fetish, moved by gifts from enemies of the deceased, has killed him', Monrad wrote just a few years later, describing the criminal activation of deadly ritual power that would fall within the ambit of 'poisoning'. 'In general', he added, 'they suppose that the dead haunt them, and exercise great influence over those survivors with whom they had been in close contact; indeed, they are capable of killing them.'[45] The vengeful dead themselves could kill, a belief which serves significantly to expand the semantic penumbra of poisoning and sorcery.

In 1818, Kumasi was again rocked by a conspiracy to overthrow the Asantehene involving accusations of murderous poison. The leading protagonists this time were Opoku Fofie's successor Osei Tutu Kwame (1804–23) and Adoma Akusua, who in 1809 had succeeded Konadu Yaadom as Asantehemaa, and the abortive rebellion occurred during the celebrated war against Gyaman. Less than two years later, Dupuis was given an account of events, which began as Osei Tutu Kwame made the usual elaborate ritual preparations for a military campaign. Some of these preparations were witnessed by the British consul

Hutchinson in January 1818 and suggest that the power of the king's mother, Konadu Yaadom, had not ended with her death: to 'make the war successful', her bones were taken from her coffin, 'bathed in rum and water with great ceremony; after being wiped with silks, they were rolled in gold dust, and wrapped in strings of gold, aggry beads, and other things of the most costly nature'.[46] The priests, Dupuis subsequently recounted, then 'prepared a certain Fetische compound [i.e., *aduru*], which they delivered to the king, with an injunction to burn the composition daily in a consecrated fire pot within the palace; and upon no account to neglect the fire, so as to suffer it to go out; for as long as the sacred flame devoured the powder, he would triumph over his foes'.[47] Adoma Akusua, together with three of the Asantehene's most trusted wives, were put in charge of the powerful *aduru*. Dupuis:

> During the king's absence, this arbitress of his fate formed a connexion with a chief of Bouromy [i.e., Bron], whose ambition suggested a plan to seat himself upon the throne. In this conspiracy, seventeen of the king's wives and their families are said to have joined; the fire-pot was broken to pieces, and the chief commenced arming his party. But the king, added my informer, who had sustained early losses in the early part of the war, *and was unable to account for the audacity of the enemy*, performed an incantation over a certain talisman, which gave an insight into what was transacting in the capital. He therefore dispatched a body of men under Ousu Cudjo, who, after an impotent struggle on behalf of the enemy, effectively crushed the rebellion.[48]

On the Asantehene's return to Kumasi, the inevitable judicial repercussions followed: Adoma Akusua was executed by the same method as reported for Osei Kwame, the rebellious wives decapitated, and the Bron chief and his supporters tortuously dismembered at the grave of Konadu Yaadom.

In contrast with the events of 1797–1804, those of 1818–19 did not arise from an identifiable context of dynastic rivalry. Aside from her liaison with the unidentified Bron chief, Adoma Akusua's motives are obscure and Dupuis's account gives every impression of a futile, even suicidal, conspiracy undertaken by a cabal of deluded women in the royal palace whose sole weapon was the manipulation of toxic ritual power. Indeed, it is the gendered dimensions of the affair which are the most striking, underlined by the only other reference to it in the historical record. The 'History of Ashanti' tells that the conspirators went on to stage a mock funeral for the absent Asantehene: a wooden image of Osei Tutu Kwame was placed in a coffin and followed through the streets of Kumasi by lamenting female mourners, as if he had been killed in battle. Meanwhile, the women potters at Abuakwa were instructed to mould his funerary bust, which was then used to perform the *sora* custom (see chapter 6).[49] In one further turn of events, the Asantehene, on returning to Kumasi and entering the palace as the execution of the plotters was taking place, was embraced by several more wives who appear suddenly to have thrown themselves towards the monarch, compelling the accompanying office-holders—forbidden ever to gaze upon the faces of royal wives—'to cover their faces with both hands, and fly from the spot'. The women, it transpired, were menstruating. Dupuis thought that their 'anxiety to embrace their sovereign lord impelled them thus to overstep the boundary of female decorum'.[50] But in a society in which the segregation of menstruating royal wives was enforced with the utmost rigour, this can not have been the case. Rather, this action must have been a final, desperate attempt by residual conspirators to poison the Asantehene by bringing him into contact with a substance recognized as ferociously toxic to the royal body. The gravity of this heinous crime was duly reflected in its punishment: the women were summarily executed and their corpses dismembered and cast into the forest, 'to be devoured by birds and beast of prey'.[51] If poisoning across cultures was so often a crime of intimacy, then this action might be interpreted as an intimate conjugal betrayal of the highest order.

These tumultuous events demonstrate how the idioms and the praxis of *aduto*, poisoning, featured at the apex of political culture. To consider how apprehensions about poison featured in the life of ordinary folk, however, we can turn to a later corpus of sources: the judicial records of the emergent British colonial project on the Gold Coast. The campaign against the Atlantic slave trade in the early nineteenth century signalled a shift to a more interventionist approach on the part of the European trading outposts to issues of law and order, as officials sought to expropriate from African authorities the right to try criminal offences and to adjudicate civil disputes in the coastal towns and their hinterlands. British efforts began to take definitive legal shape from 1844, when, after a fifteen-year period of merchant rule dominated by the assertive administration of George Maclean, the so-called forts and settlements reverted to crown rule and a judicial assessor (initially the demoted Maclean) was appointed to advise African chiefs on the 'just application' of indigenous law. In 1853, the British created a Supreme Court, in which the judicial assessor simultaneously presided over the exercise of English law as chief justice; local commandants or Euro-African residents (until the 1870s, often one and the same) commissioned as justices of the peace, meanwhile, continued to hold makeshift tribunals in the main coastal towns. This created a complex market in judicial services, with litigants moving between different tribunals to secure a successful outcome to a particular dispute. Between 1844 and the further expansion of British power on the Gold Coast in the mid-1870s, a considerable number of these disputes involved the spectrum of maleficent practices encompassing notions of poison, sorcery and witchcraft. That they emerged from the mechanics of the inchoate colonial legal system adds an additional context to earlier toxic scares: they were, that is, part and parcel of the gradual bureaucratization and secularization of death on the nineteenth-century Gold Coast.

Many of these cases were civil actions for slander in which the plaintiff had been publicly denounced as having caused someone's death by poison, witchcraft or 'fetish', and were sometimes heard as appeals after primary adjudication by African (and occasionally Dutch) tribunals. A number of early poison cases heard at Cape Coast, for example, had initially been tried by the Fante oracle Nananom Mpow at nearby Mankessim.[52] Some are perfunctory; a typical transcript from the 1840s records only that 'Plaintiff complains of Defendant having accused him of having, 'by Fetish' or Witchcraft, caused the death of his (Dfd's) wife. Complaint proved, and Plf's expenses in appearing here, which are assessed at five Ackies of Gold, are ordered to be paid by Dfd, who is further ordered to find security . . . of oz. 10 of Gold that [he] shall not revive the charge against Plf., or, give him further trouble.'[53] The density of narrative in others is overwhelming, revealing a degree of everyday lived experience not hitherto present in the documentary archive. Yet even the abbreviated transcript quoted here points to the beginnings of a historical shift in legal understandings of death: the tendency of colonial courts to rule against established local perceptions of the causes of 'unnatural' or 'bad' deaths. Such decisions did not necessarily involve the imposition of an alternative, biomedical cause of death—yet the implication is there. Three decades later, a British judge, after hearing a case involving the alleged murderous use of *adurubone* in Akyem Abuakwa, dismissed that allegation, ruling that 'the persons who died did so I have no doubt from natural diseases, and if the Fetishmen would give themselves to studying the qualities of diseases and the proper remedies . . . they might be very useful to their countrymen. Two of those whose illness was described . . . appear not to have received any proper treatment. They might have died—No one can say—but they might have lived'.[54]

Let us consider one intriguing case, which touches on three key issues in histories of poison: gender, the ambiguity of the *pharmakon*, and the unstable distinction between toxic substance and magical potion. Heard in 1859 at Cape Coast by the judicial assessor, the case was an action for slander brought by Adwoa Sanewa against her husband, Kwesi Kuma, both of the Fante town of Ajumaku.[55] Adwoa explained to the court that around 1840 she had been pawned to Kwesi Kuma, who subsequently purchased her outright as a slave and then married her. When in 1857 Kwesi Kuma became gravely ill, he and his other wives accused Adwoa of being a 'devil' (i.e., an *obayifo*, or witch) and therefore causing his illness by somehow poisoning him with her toxic blood. She was then informed by the *omanhene* of Ajumaku that if her husband died, 'you will have to carry the body till it rots and then you will be killed'. Before this, she then admitted, 'my husband had treated me very ill in not providing me with food and clothing and I often complained to him but he took no notice', so she had an affair with another man; when this was discovered, he tied her to a tree, flogged her, then told her to 'go wherever you like with your children and kill yourselves'. She then fled to Cape Coast and took out a summons against him.

Taking the stand in his defence, Kwesi Kuma denied that he had called Adwoa an *obayifo* and accused her instead of dealing in poison, *adurubone*. She acquired this 'bad medicine', he claimed, from her lover, another of his own household servants, Asuanghor. When asked to describe this medicine, he testified that 'it was made of many . . . strings and beads. It did not talk. I saw the fetish with her and knew the man had given it [to] her. I am not a fetish man. When a man ties round his waist string with beads . . . how can he . . . know it was fetish . . . [or] it was to make you impotent'. He was then asked why he attributed his sickness to Adwoa. 'What more can I say', he replied, 'when all . . . [my] wives attended me and she did not but went *about cursing me*'.[56] Another of Kwesi Kuma's slaves called in his defence, one John Farmer, testified that Asuanghor had previously been accused of causing death with his 'fetish' and of providing Adwoa with the substance; in that palaver, according to Farmer, Asuanghor had claimed 'that what they called fetish was not so but a medicine which he gave to Plf to make her fruitful'. 'I did nothing to make him ill', Adwoa repeated when recalled to the stand; 'his disorder was one he was frequently subject to, Diarrhoea'. The judicial assessor agreed: 'Judgement for Plf. Damages oz. 3 or Dft to give Plf her Freedom in lieu of the Damages'.

We see here how substances classified as legitimate medicine, *aduru*, might in certain circumstances become poison, *adurubone*. The most obvious circumstance was the death of a sick person undergoing treatment, an event which could leave herbalists, midwives, *akomfo* and spouses dangerously exposed to grief-stricken allegations of homicide.[57] Also apparent is the unstable register of *bayi* and *aduto*—an entanglement which British officials were not unaware of. 'The word which we translate [as] witchcraft has not in the native language precisely the meaning we attach to it', Governor Pine had written in 1857. 'It includes crimes punishable even by our law, among others that of poisoning.' 'Some of the native poisons are of so subtle a character that they cannot be detected by any known tests', Pine continued, pointing out that they were the same toxins revealed at the Old Bailey to have been used by the notorious William Palmer in a sensational poisoning case just two years previously. In the light of this subtlety, he argued, the use of *odom* poison by African jurists was not only legitimate but effective: 'can we wonder then if in cases where they believe death has been caused by poison, they try to supply the want of evidence by a recourse to the ordeal, which, moreover, owing to the affect of conscience, often really detects the guilty?'.[58]

Further instability in the toxic register emerges at the centre of a case in 1877, when one Kweku Essell was accused by Chief Isaac Robertson, an influential office-holder and Christian convert, of the possession and use of deadly poisons in Cape Coast. When Essell was apprehended, Chief Robertson testified, 'certain Medicines and Fetishes had been produced in the Magistrate's Court... but His Worship had directed that the chiefs should enquire into matters... as His Worship could not understand them'.

> The Fetishes were counted to be nothing. We had no faith in them; but the medicines we condemned as noxious and poisonous. We spread all the medicines on a table before us and examined them. We discovered a poisonous medicine which when administered to a person would cause madness, giddiness, insanity... by its action on the brain. We discovered another which would render a man impotent if administered internally. In some cases when introduced under the skin after an incision had been made, it will produce the same effect. The most dreadful medicine discovered... is called 'Addalay' or 'Kakun' which is the *Upas tree*. The medicine is prepared by taking the sap and mixing it with the gall of the Alligator and the juice of the India rubber tree; and also a juice from a plant resembling

indigo which gives a deep red dye to all this is added the marrow of human bones. When a potion of this is administered . . . it produces instant death.[59]

The chiefs believed that Essell's substances may have been the same as those exposed in previous toxic attacks in Cape Coast, recalling an incident in 1841, during the administration of Maclean, when 'a person who was found to be in possession of these medicines was sentenced to a very long term of imprisonment and publicly flogged'. Between then and the death of Maclean in 1847, Robertson stated, 'persons discontinued keeping bad medicines and Fetishes' in the town. Thereafter they began again to be produced, culminating in a notorious episode in 1851, when, in the aftermath of a conflict between local converts of the Methodist mission and the priests of Nananom Mpow, the latter were convicted of attempting to poison prominent local Christians by burying toxins at the gates of their houses (see chapter 11). Such a method, he explained, 'causes a swelling of the feet [and] brings on other diseases, which eventually produces death. In other instances it is given to the servant of the person to introduce into his master's food, the servant being bribed to do so'. As in 1851, however, the poison scare of 1877 appears not to have resulted in any fatalities. The court adopted the recommendation of the six-man jury of native chiefs: that 'gong-gong be beaten and people advised not to put any faith in the efficacy of Fetishes', that the human bones be interred and that Kweku Essell he fined and 'cautioned not to repeat his Fetish practices under heavy punishment'.

Poison would persist as an unstable object of fear and fascination into the late nineteenth and early twentieth centuries. Allegations of its deployment as an impalpable instrument of criminal aggression continued to be debated in colonial courts, while the advent of a local print culture in the form of African-run newspapers served, as in Victorian Britain and India, further to inflame its menace. In the course of 1882, for example, the *Gold Coast Times* reported on the discovery of a 'foul plot' to poison the populace of the coastal town of Anomabo, on another plot in Shama, on an upsurge in 'the numberless, frightful materials (drugs, etc) in use for killing others' and on rising anxieties that 'the fetish priests of Cape Coast have not infrequently recourse to certain poisonous "medicines" for very bad purposes'.[60] As indicated in the Essell case, growing condemnation of the nefarious activities of 'fetish priests' was shaped both by Christian conversion and by the beginning of a separation between occult and natural principles in the toxic register ('the fetishes were counted to be nothing ... but the medicines we condemned as noxious and poisonous'). The *pharmakon* also began to be deployed in new ways to counter toxic attack: by 1885, the *Gold Coast News* was running an advertisement for a local medical practitioner with proven treatments for all manner of ailments and an 'antidote to all poisonings in rum, etc'.[61] *Aduru* and its sinister other, *aduru-bone*, would never entirely shed their magical associations. Yet as a new biomedical interpretation of morbidity and mortality gained a firmer foothold in local society, so too did indigenous doctors seek to legitimize their practice, mobilizing to turn themselves from 'fetish priests' to 'native herbalists'.

11

Christian Encounters

DEATH LOOMED OVER the nineteenth-century encounter between Christianity and the peoples of the Gold Coast. This is not to suggest that Victorian-era missionaries faced an existential threat from opponents of their evangelical project: those who died in the 'field' succumbed to tropical diseases rather than perishing as martyrs at the hands of pagan enemies. Neither, with the exception of potential converts in Asante, did their African acolytes place themselves in a life-threatening position by declaring fellowship with the new faith. Rather, evangelists sought to overturn established values and ways of life in order to challenge the very idea of mortality itself: by abandoning idolatry and embracing the salvation offered by Christ, converts were offered a new vision of everlasting life after death. If African religious practice was resolutely this-worldly, aimed at maintaining the beneficence of deities and ancestors in order to defer death, Christianity was distinctly otherworldly, seeking to wash away sin so that the repentant might enjoy a blissful life beyond the grave. As elsewhere in Africa, the Akan and their neighbours regarded death as an implacable enemy, to be stoutly fought off if possible but to be interrogated only when its dread appearance demanded explanation or the emotional closure offered by mortuary ritual. The centrality of the doctrine of eschatology to the Christian message, in contrast, meant that the nature of death would emerge as a key component of debates between missionaries and African communities. As the mission frontier expanded from its coastal footholds in the 1830s into the forest interior, this dialogue became increasingly complex and, at times, fraught. By the end of the century, small but significant Christian minorities had emerged, laying the foundation for the further expansion of the faith into Asante and the acceleration of conversion in the era of colonial rule. New perceptions of life after death, new funerary customs and new ways of dying were crucial components of this religious transformation.

'The large-scale adoption of Christianity', J.D.Y. Peel writes, 'has been one of the master themes of modern African history'.[1] The nature of that process, however, has been the subject of much debate. Focusing on conversion among the Yoruba peoples of southwestern Nigeria, Peel has stressed the ways in which Africans actively appropriated the message of both Christianity and Islam by reshaping them according to their needs and making them their own. Others, in contrast, have argued that the Christian message represented a key ingredient in the imposition of a hegemonic European order.[2] There is no doubt that in the Akan region, most notably among the Fante of the central Gold Coast, Christianity was part and parcel of a broader package of Victorian civilization that included the adoption of European names, dress, manners, tastes, education and funerary culture. That the rise of an anglophone, Christianized commercial elite on the coast of West Africa stretching from Freetown to the Bight of Biafra was the result of an insidious evangelism working in concert with colonial power, however, is difficult to sustain. As early as the 1850s, members of that elite on the Gold Coast were expressing criticism of aspects of British policy, and by the end of the following decade the literate leadership of the proto-nationalist Fanti Confederation would be dominated by products of Methodist rectitude. Neither were members of the indigenous elite above casting a critical eye on the evangelical endeavour. 'As for a material hell, the scarecrow of the missionaries, he merely smiles at such a suggestion', J. E. Casely Hayford—son of Rev. Joseph de Graft Hayford—wrote of the typical African's response to eschatological doctrine. 'Is there not enough trouble in this world? God knows there is. Why should God add trouble to trouble? Thus he reasons with philosophy.'[3]

Protestant chaplains were dispatched irregularly to the European forts on the Gold Coast from the mid-seventeenth century to cater to the pastoral needs of traders and their Euro-African progeny. While some of these pastors demonstrated a willingness to debate matters of faith with local interlocutors, none were charged with attracting converts; their main tasks, according to the first historian of Christianity in Ghana, were to bury the dead and to console the dying.[4] Despite indications that elements of Christian doctrine were absorbed into local cosmologies at points of sustained encounter, the general response appears to have been the polite but puzzled consideration described by Casely Hayford. The principal achievement of these churchmen was to begin to forge the connection between Christianity and literate education. When, in 1751–6, Rev. Thomas Thompson served at Cape Coast as a dedicated missionary for the Church of England's Society for the Propagation of the Gospel, he admitted to attracting only four potential converts. Thompson did, however, dispatch three young men to London for education, one of whom, Philip Quaque, returned in 1766 as an ordained minister in the service of the society. Between that date and his death in 1816, Quaque ran the 'castle school' at Cape Coast, which, together with Danish and Dutch equivalents at Accra and Elmina, would produce small but significant groups of literate, mostly Euro-African and at least nominally Christian scholars.[5] Literacy in the coastal towns would acquire an almost magical power, Monrad reporting from Accra the belief that the dead 'become as wise ... as the Whites, and as a symbol of this they sometimes stand at funerals with open books in their hands'.[6]

Sustained missionary enterprise got underway in the 1840s, with the advent of the Wesleyan Methodist Missionary Society and Basel Evangelical Mission Society. Founded in 1813 and 1815, respectively, these missions had their roots in the late eighteenth-century Evangelical Revival in Protestant northwest Europe, a movement emerging in dissenting churches and characterized by an ethos of emotional, charismatic evangelism. The methods of the nondenominational Basel Mission were also shaped by the stern doctrines of Württemburg Pietism, with its emphasis on spiritual rebirth, individual asceticism and social conservatism. Suspicious of the unsettling social changes generated by the industrial revolution, pietism stressed the ideal of self-contained rural communities of farmers and artisans—a goal which would be manifested on the Gold Coast in the segregated Christian village, or 'Salem'. Because it was believed that such communities should possess a strong sense of their own history and culture—albeit in a redeemed, Christianized form—the Basel Mission was also distinguished by a sustained programme of research into local African languages in order that they might form the basis of vernacular education and biblical translation.

The first party of (four) Basel missionaries arrived at Christiansborg in 1828. In common with the Moravians who had ephemerally attempted to establish a mission within the Danish sphere of influence on the eastern Gold Coast in the 1770s, the Basel missionaries were appalled by the dissolute lifestyle of the Euro-African community at Accra and attempted to relocate beyond the town. In less than a year, however, all four were dead; a second party (of three) followed in 1832, of whom only one, Andreas Riis, survived the 'seasoning fever'—that is, their first bout of malaria. Riis put his survival down to the care he was given by a local herbalist, and in 1836 was granted permission by the Danish governor and African authorities to relocate to Akuropon, the main town of the Akan kingdom of Akuapem, located on a range of hills to the northwest of the Accra plains. It was here that Riis was able to establish a permanent station and to initiate linguistic research; in 1843 the fledgling community was bolstered by the arrival of a party of twenty-four liberated slaves recruited from Moravian congregations in Jamaica. Over the following two years, hymns began to be sung and sermons preached in Twi, a Twi-language school was opened (the West Indian children were taught in English), and the first vernacular primers were printed; meanwhile, the mission re-established its presence at Osu and began a parallel programme of scholarship in the Ga language. Conversions were few, however. 'Some have raised doubts whether the African will ever be converted and whether the European will ever penetrate into this land of death', the director of the mission wrote in 1850. 'This harvest of death is yet a blessing to the Mission's existence. It is the most serious defect in the Mission, if no one is in a position to face death for the sake of Africa.'[7]

The spectre of death also haunted Methodist beginnings. While the Basel Mission had been invited to the eastern Gold Coast by the Danish authorities, the Wesleyan Methodist Mission was contacted by a group of young Euro-Fante men, literate products of Cape Coast's castle school, who, in 1831, under the leadership of William de Graft, formed the Society for Promoting Christian Knowledge. The Methodists responded to the appeal for a missionary and bibles and, in 1834, Joseph Dunwell was dispatched to establish a mission at Cape Coast. Dead within six months, Dunwell was replaced by two more missionaries, who, along with their wives, were also carried away by malarial fever. As with Andreas Riis, it would take the survival of a single dynamic individual to consolidate the Methodist presence: that individual was Thomas Birch Freeman, a gardener of mixed English and African Caribbean parentage, who arrived with his wife at Cape Coast in January 1838. Under Freeman's leadership, the mission would create a network of stations in the Fante region, establish outposts at Accra and further east among the Yoruba, and lead the attempt to implant Christianity in what was regarded as the ultimate evangelical goal: Asante. By mid-century, when the use of quinine began to improve survival rates, the geography of the Christian encounter had taken shape: the Basel Mission, divided into Twi and Ga districts headquartered at Akuropon and Chistiansborg, respectively, located on the eastern Gold Coast and its hinterland; and the Wesleyan Methodists, concentrated among the Fante of the central coast but with more expansive ambitions to the east and in Asante. In 1847, the North German (or Bremen) Mission Society also began to work across the River Volta among the Ewe-speaking peoples on the eastern frontier of the Gold Coast, but the position of the two pioneering missions would remain unchallenged until the belated arrival of the Roman Catholics at Elmina in 1881.[8]

The 'harvest of death' tested the missionary resolve to extend the gift of everlasting life in Christ to what were regarded as benighted heathens. Quite how those 'heathens' viewed the mortality rate among evangelists whose message was based on the claim of superior spiritual knowledge is unclear. While such a claim would have been recognizable as that used by local purveyors of innovative ritual resources, its veracity was similarly dependent upon concrete evidence of keeping death and other misfortune in abeyance. The accompanying denouncement of local deities as worthless—the notion, that is, of complete 'conversion'—in contrast, must often have perplexed local observers. In the opening decades of the encounter, before the withdrawal of zealous converts from established obligations reached a level that threw up tensions within communities, there is every indication that the missions were regarded as another intriguing new cultic formation—with potentially useful access to the world of European knowledge and material goods, but vulnerable owing to their single-mindedly exclusive approach to spiritual protection. This is captured in an incident recorded by Freeman, as he reflected on the death of his wife in February 1838. 'A few days after our arrival at Cape Coast we were walking out to enjoy the cool air of the morning when we passed several of the native heathen', he recalled. 'One of them, an elderly female, looked very earnestly on us and said something in the native language and on enquiring of the person . . . accompanying us what the woman said he answered, "She is expressing a wish that you may both continue to live"'.[9]

Such expressions of tenderness did not prevent Freeman from denouncing Fante society in the same breath as 'presenting an unbroken scene of moral desolation'. For missionaries, the regular eruption of exuberant mortuary customs was one of the most salient features of this dismal scene. As early as 1837, Rev. George Wrigley was insisting that Fante converts exclude themselves from all participation in heathen funerals, including the obligation to contribute to the cost of those for deceased relatives. Given the moral imperative to take part in funeral customs, this ruling presented potential converts with a serious dilemma, but Wrigley used his Sunday evening 'exhortation meeting' to attack these and other 'vain and foolish customs'. 'With the institution of this meeting', the historian of Ghana Methodism, Rev. F. L. Bartels writes, 'the separation between Church and community had started'.[10]

Rev. Robert Brooking expressed similar outrage on witnessing the elaborate funeral for a Ga chief at Accra in 1840. 'I could not help weeping to see the Lord's Day so violated', Brooking noted in his diary on Sunday 29 March, subsequently expressing astonishment that three weeks later the celebrations— 'during which time all kinds of wickedness prevailed'—were still going on. Despair, however, was mixed with a grudging admiration for the martial vigour of the assembled Ga military companies (or *asafo*) and, more surprisingly, for the attendant 'fetish priests'. 'The fetish men [Ga: *wulomei*] appeared very conspicuous in their long white robes, gliding in and out among the people that by their presence they might prevent any danger', he observed. 'The fetish women [*woyei*], too, were seen in great numbers, bearing large calabashes of water on their heads, and carrying in their hands bunches of green herbs, which they would dip into the water and sprinkle among the throng to prevent accidents.'[11] In his diary of a journey to Asante the following year, Brooking would pen a more standard denunciation of mortuary customs: that not only were they spiritually futile, but their exorbitant cost was the cause of untold misery for the living:

> These poor deluded, benighted, heathens think it quite indispensable, that this custom should be made to quiet the spirits of the departed, and hence they will *pawn* their children, that is in reality, sell them as slaves, in order to procure money to defray the expenses. It is from this course alone, that two thirds of the slavery of this part of Africa exists, for, after their children are so pawned it is a thousand to one if ever the parents can raise money enough to redeem them again. They are always obliged to pay 50 per cent on the money that is advanced. Ah! When shall a better state of things prevail here? Not until the gospel shall be embraced.[12]

If the Gold Coast was a 'land of death' crying out for salvation by the gospel, then Asante was the dark heart of that forbidding landscape. A year after his arrival, Freeman undertook his first journey to Asante; Riis followed later that year, but his visit was less of a success and thereafter the Basel Mission left Kumasi to their Methodist rivals until the end of the century. Freeman and Brooking returned in 1841, accompanied by the two *aheneba* (princes) Owusu Ansa and Owusu Nkwantabisa, surrendered to George Maclean as security for the peace treaty ten years earlier and who had been educated and had converted to Christianity in London. Freeman established a good rapport with

Kwaku Dua Panin, who permitted Brooking to remain behind in the capital, where the Methodists maintained a regular presence into the early 1850s. They were subjected, however, to close surveillance and control: movement beyond Kumasi was restricted and repeated requests to open a school were politely but firmly refused. The implied egalitarianism of their doctrine of personal salvation challenged the ideological hegemony of the Asante state. 'Do you mean to say that we are to escape the everlasting fire you speak of and enter heaven only for forsaking our sins and receiving the death of Jesus as our sacrifice?', Rev. Thomas Picot was asked by a village chief as he approached Kumasi during a renewed Methodist approach in 1876. 'I answered "Yes, that is just it". "Well", said he, "I do hope that you will succeed in obtaining from the King permission for us to become Christians, for it is a good religion, and I wish to be happy after death, and I shall be the first to be a Christian in this place; but it cannot be now, for the King would kill me"'. On reaching the capital, Asantehene Mensa Bonsu explained the matter from his perspective: 'It is a tradition among us that Ashantis are made to know they are subjects, altogether under the power of their King, and they can never be allowed liberty of conscience. The Bible is not a book for us. God at the beginning gave the Bible to the white people, another book to the Cramos and the fetish to us. Our fetishes are God's interpreters to us. If God requires a human sacrifice or a sheep, He tells our fetishes, and they tell us, and we give them'.[13]

If by mid-century Freeman and other astute observers such as the Basel Mission's linguistic scholars J. G. Christaller and Johannes Zimmermann came to comprehend the cosmological rationale for human sacrifice—deluded and horrific, perhaps, but pointing at least to a belief in the immortality of the soul—there was little sympathy for what was perceived as the nefarious activities of so-called fetish priests. Brooking's remarks quoted above are uncharacteristically generous: the Akan *akomfo* and Ga *wulomei*—together with their female equivalents, who were often spirit mediums—were generally condemned as the avowed enemies of Christianity, duping credulous victims and plotting to thwart the evangelical endeavour at every turn. The principal motif of the Basel Mission yearly reports from 1850, Smith notes, 'is an implacable antagonism to "fetishes" and "fetish priests" who were regarded as agents of the devil and the main obstacles to the spread of the Gospel'.[14] Describing Akuropon in 1851, Paul Steiner wrote how 'the tribal chiefs still ruled with the old despotism over their subjects, oppressing them as slaves without rights. This oppression was increased by the fetish-priest [*Teufelspriester*: devil priest] and sorcerer, who, by the use of poison and magic incantations exploited the people and made them the slaves of fear'. In contrast to this heathen world was the perceived haven of the Salem. 'Lying on the outskirts of the town', Steiner continued, 'it was exposed day and night to all the heathen commotion, whether from the salvoes of flintlock guns, from the raucous yells during the gruesome ceremonies for the dead, political quarrels which led to bloody street fights, from the frantic deceptions of the fetish priest, or from the wild dancing and drumming during festivals'.[15] East of the Volta, too, the Bremen Mission deplored the sonic onslaught of 'heathen lamentations'.[16] Despite the scholarly advances of Christaller and Zimmermann in the 1850s, Noel Smith writes, the approach of many Basel missionaries 'continued to be determined by the attitudes engendered by human sacrifice, cruel customs, the "tyranny" of chiefs and the deceit of "fetish" priests'.[17]

The stereotypical missionary loathing of fetish priests as, at best, tricksters or, at worst, death-dealing poisoners returns us to the *pharmakon* and the equivocal identity of its practitioners. Riis credited an African healer with saving his life; so too did Zimmermann, whose cure from a life-threatening illness on his arrival on the coast in 1850 appears to have been the catalyst for a particularly profound and sympathetic engagement with African society, including, shortly after, marriage to Catherine Mulgrave, one of the African Caribbean repatriates.[18] More commonly, however, the missions latched on to the wariness, apprehension and sometimes outright hostility which formed part of the local attitude towards those figures seen to straddle the registers of healing and harming. Their suspicions were only confirmed by the occasional conversion of religious and medical practitioners, most notably that of the Ga *wulomo* Owu, a priest at the Lakpa shrine who was baptized in 1857 as Paulo Mohenu. The subject of popular vernacular pamphlets, Mohenu's conversion was considered a spectacular evangelistic breakthrough and he became an energetic lay preacher in Krobo and the Accra plains.[19] He revealed, Smith writes, 'that the entire craft, apart from the use of healing medicines, was a deceptive fraud'.[20] Such revelations fuelled the more confrontational approach of missionaries such as J. A. Mader, whose reputation at Akuropon for physically attacking fetish priests earned him the nickname Kwadwo Okoto, 'Kwadwo the Stick'. Mader's zeal extended to ordering his seminary students to fetch soil from a sacred grove for the mission gardens, a provocation which may have resulted in a curse being placed upon his head. 'Many people', Debrunner notes, 'were converted when Mader did not die as had been expected'.[21] Conversely, another dramatic 'conversion event' was reported from the Akuropon town of Larteh, where the native catechist Edward Samson was said to have restored a dead child to life by prayer.[22]

The Methodist attitude towards the Fante *akomfo* was also one of general hostility leavened with a grudging acknowledgement of the skill that some demonstrated as healers. Freeman is our best guide to this ambivalence. 'Some who are possessed of a great many medicines and are inflated with flattery, when they fail in restoring the health of the sick after having given many vain promises to the contrary, confess their inability by saying "Death worked faster and harder than the fetishman"', he wrote. 'This confession does away with the vain power with which they pretend to combat with death, and leaves the simple inference that when God grants health, the fetishman claim the praise for their idols'. Yet Freeman also noted the existence of 'aged and good minded fetishmen-doctors', who, like Paulo Mohenu, 'tell you plainly that the possessing of medicines is the only thing really true among fetishmen, and that all they do beside administering and selling medicines consists of tricks of sleight of hand, and falsehoods, by which they obtain their living'.[23] That said, when in 1842 Freeman purchased a plantation near Cape Coast in an effort to create, along Basel Mission lines, a segregated Christian village, the community, which he named Beulah, became popularly known as *Kyirakomfo*, 'hater of *akomfo*'. 'Up to the time of writing', Bartels observed in 1965, visitors to Beulah 'would be told that no fetish priest had ever stepped into the village and that fetishism had always been anathema'.[24]

Reflecting in 1853 on the transformations wrought by the combined impact of legitimate commerce, British protection and Methodism, Brodie Cruickshank took a typically balanced view of the encounter between Fante society and Christianity. Acknowledging the many 'advantages arising from intercourse with the missionaries' and their contribution to the progress of the country, Cruickshank also cautioned against the 'indiscreet zeal' that had at times characterized evangelism. 'The first missionaries, appalled at the moral waste which the degraded state of the African population presented to their view, and believing it impossible that any race of people, living in such a state of spiritual desolation, would close their ears against a knowledge of the truth, burned with an intemperate enthusiasm approaching to fanaticism to communicate the glad tiding of salvation.'[25] Freeman's more judicious and gradualist approach, Cruickshank thought, provided a model for the way forward, but he was still concerned that a headlong assault on native customs, 'conveyed in such loud and objurgatory language' would serve only to generate a 'spirit of opposition'.[26] Cruickshank and his friend Freeman were in a position to appreciate this. Just two years before, in 1851, both had been involved in what to that point represented the most serious collision between Christianity and the African spiritual realm on the nineteenth-century Gold Coast. The confrontation occurred at Mankessim, the historical epicentre of Fante culture, and it took the shape of an assault on the renowned oracular shrine of the *obosom* Nananom Mpow.

We have encountered Nananom Mpow before. Rømer's informant Okpoti, it will be remembered, lamented in the 1740s that the *obosom* had done a better job protecting the Fante in war than Lakpa had done protecting the Ga, and the Dane's description of the sacred grove, based on eyewitness information from one Bassi, a son of the Anomabo *caboceer* John Currantee, is the most vivid account of the working of the oracle.[27] By the early nineteenth century, however, that situation had been reversed: whereas the Ga had enjoyed a stunning military victory over the Asante at the battle of Katamanso in 1826, Fante country had been devastated by a sequence of Asante military campaigns. The shrine of Nananom Mpow survived this catastrophe; but as Fante society began to recover, its oracular authority—together with the judicial clout of its presiding *akomfo* and *abrafo* (the Braffoes)—was in decline.[28] Sources hint at popular disquiet with the increasing venality of these servitors, and in 1836 it was reported that the *obosom*, 'offended with the caboceers in the bush, for allowing their people to renounce the gods of their fathers', had declared against Christianity and threatened to withhold the rains 'if they did not immediately renounce the new religion'.[29] By 1843, the *ohene* of Mankessim, Edu Kuma, informed the Methodists at Anomabo that despite the opposition of the *akomfo* he favoured the extension of the mission and its educational project to the town: 'I look upon Cape Coast, and upon Annamaboe . . . where they have teachers, and no evil consequences ensue: on the contrary those places are better, and more prosperous than formerly'.[30] Eight years later, in 1851, Christians from Anomabo established a community provocatively close to the sacred grove at Assafa, converting an *okomfo* and, after a series of confrontations, cutting wood within its precincts. An infuriated Edu Kuma now turned against the Christians, uniting with the *akomfo* in burning down their village and driving them out.

As anti-Christian sentiment spread throughout the region, the British authorities sought to arbitrate and to re-establish law and order. The narrative of the ensuing palavers and judicial proceedings needs not detain us here. Two aspects of the episode, however, are relevant to our central concerns. First, the authority of Nananom Mpow, literally the 'grove (*mpow*) of the ancestors (*nananom*)', was rooted in the belief that the site was the burial ground of the three remembered leaders of the ancient Fante migration to Mankessim. It was therefore in some ways an 'ancestor cult', which, as Okpoti explained to Rømer, protected the Fante and served as a mnemonic for the foundation of their identity. The *obosom* was also, according to Bassi, 'very bloodthirsty', demanding the regular immolation of slaves and providing ritual sanction for its *abrafo* to exercise the power of capital punishment.[31]

Second, what became a stand-off between traditionalist defenders of Nananom Mpow, on the one hand, and the British authorities, the Christian community and their indigenous allies, on the other, was complicated by the allegation of poisoning being levelled at the former. By the early nineteenth century, the Braffoes and *akomfo* had, in the face of British pressure, surrendered their sovereignty over life and death. Yet when, during the initial attempt at arbitration, the *ohene* of Abora, Otu Kwasi, collapsed in the palaver hall of Anomabo fort and died two months later, this was taken as a 'signal mark of the vengeance of the Fetish, as he was a firm supporter of English authority'. 'We are not altogether without suspicions', Cruickshank added, 'that his death ought to be attributed to the agency of the Fetishmen'. These suspicions were compounded when one of the *abrafo* broke ranks and informed Cruickshank of a plot to poison four prominent Fante Methodists, revealing also that the oracular pronouncements of Nananom Mpow were a sham, cunningly staged by the *akomfo*. 'The Fetishmen believed, if they could manage to cut these men off, that it would not be difficult to persuade their superstitious dupes that the great Fetish had killed them.'[32] Nineteen men and women were duly convicted in the judicial assessor's court, the men sentenced to be flogged in the marketplace at Cape Coast before serving five years' hard labour and the women to two years' imprisonment.

Cruickshank portrayed the exposure of the *akomfo*'s deceptions as a blow against fetishism by the forces of rationalism and progress. Yet his account of the ensuing popular bewilderment displays some sympathy with those whose faith in Nananom Mpow was so suddenly undermined. 'It was impossible to see their only stay and support, thus rudely shattered to pieces, without a feeling of pity for their desolate condition, bereft of every spiritual trust. Many of them left the castle sorrowful and downcast, and were heard repeating to each other, "What can we do now in sickness and distress?" "Whither can we fly for succour?" "Our gods have been proved to be no gods!" "Our priests have deceived us!"'³³ The following year, Freeman wrote to Cruickshank that the 'practical results of the destruction of the Grand Fetish are now being clearly developed': the local church had a congregation of eighty; new mission stations were being opened; and, at Mankessim, Edu Kuma had placed fifteen children from his household in the new school which had been built atop the ruins of the grove.³⁴ The reconstruction of Fante society appeared to be taking a new turn. Looking on from Kumasi, the Asante ruling elite was singularly unimpressed. 'It is your religion that has ruined the Fanti country, weakened their power and brought down the high man on a level with the low man', Asantehene Mensa Bonsu told Picot in 1876. 'The God of the white man and of the Fantis is different from the God of the Ashantis and we cannot do without our fetishes.'³⁵

By the 1850s, the Basel Mission was also growing in confidence. At Akuropon, the first baptisms of young men had taken place in 1847 and those of young women in 1853; three years later, the station chronicle recorded the baptism of two elderly women, both of whom had royal connections and explained that they wished to die as Christians. Whether or not they did so is unclear, but in 1859 the town witnessed the first funeral of a local convert, a schoolgirl named Lydia, whose body, despite opposition from her family, was interred in the new Christian cemetery.³⁶ Like the Methodists, the mission was also beginning to recruit African catechists from the ranks of its young scholars: one, David Asante, a scion of the ruling lineage of Akuapem, was sent in 1857 for training to Basel; twelve years later, he would be ordained as its first native minister. As evangelical and educational endeavour began to bear fruit, the mission looked to extend its outreach deeper into the forest hinterland. In 1852, missionary Simon Süss undertook a journey northwest to the Akyem kingdoms, visiting the Akyem Kotokuhene at Gyadam and the Akyem Abuakwahene (or Okyenhene) at Kyebi, both of whom expressed an interest in literacy. Inquiring of Süss what motivated his journey, the Okyenhene received the following answer: 'Because I love you black people, and I heard in my country that you were an unhappy people, with no peace, and knowing nothing about eternal life, and then I thought I would come to tell you about eternal life so that you may receive it and become holy in time and eternity.'³⁷ The goal of reconfiguring African society by inserting it into a new, redemptive temporal framework could not be more clearly stated. It points to why death—as the gateway to that eternal life—would emerge as a key battleground on the expanding missionary frontier.

In 1853, Süss established a station at Gyadam. Despite debilitating bouts of fever and misunderstandings with his hosts, reports were optimistic: his Sunday preaching and hymn-singing classes were well attended and disputations with local elders rewarding. 'The white man is right ... the priests are swindlers', he began to overhear people say, while others admitted during debates that 'you speak the truth, and we are all terribly afraid of death'.[38] The challenge was to convince people that their determination to defer death by maintaining the goodwill of the *abosom* and the ancestors was sinful and must be replaced with an embrace of everlasting life in Christ. Missionary Baum, who joined Süss in 1856 and the following year began to preach in Twi, reported that a crucial element in this process was to inculcate among prospective converts the correct nature of prayer. Even those who seemed pious, he feared, were actually praying to God not for redemption but for health—or, worse, for gold.[39] On Christmas day 1857 the two missionaries made their first four baptisms; nine more would follow in 1859.[40] Despite the typically marginal identities of many of these converts and the propensity for backsliding, the mission had begun to put down its first local roots. In 1860, however, war broke out between the two Akyem kingdoms, which resulted in the evacuation of Gyadam. Abandoning its outpost in the depopulated town, the mission relocated to Kyebi, capital of the victorious Okyenhene. It was Akyem Abuakwa which would remain the focus of evangelism on the forest frontier for the coming decades.

In contrast to the position of the Methodists in the coastal Fante region, the Basel Mission's expansion into the forest hinterland took it beyond the reach of effective British jurisdiction. Like Asante, Akyem Abuakwa was a warrior state whose rulers also sought to assert ideological control over belief and knowledge. Despite having been drawn into the vague ambit of British 'protection', it remained a sovereign kingdom. This would present the missionaries with a challenging environment, which they often put down to the hostility of Okyenhene Amoako Atta (1866–87) and his strong-willed and staunchly traditionalist queen mother. Reflecting on the death of the king's predecessor in 1866, Christaller took a more nuanced view, noting how the increasing recourse to British colonial courts had served to undermine African law and to 'damage the actual conduct of private and public affairs'.[41] Private and public affairs would further be disrupted, moreover, by the mission itself, as its growing communities of converts (in German, *Gemeinde*) were spatially segregated into Christian Salems or, as they were locally known, *oburoni kurom*, 'the white man's village'. 'We don't have much communication with the Christians', one Akyem explained to a British court in 1877. 'We go to our farms. They go to their books.'[42]

The escalating conflict between Amoako Atta and his traditionalist subjects, on the one hand, and the Basel Mission and its *Gemeinde*, on the other, is well documented from both sides.[43] After cordial beginnings, shifts in the political and socio-economic landscape drew the two parties into a headlong collision. In 1874, Akyem Abuakwa became an integral part of the new crown colony of the Gold Coast and the following year the administration enacted legislation to outlaw slave-dealing and emancipate slaves. The impact of emancipation has been debated, but historians agree that it was most profoundly felt in Akyem Abuakwa, where large numbers of recent captives took the initiative to abandon their masters. Many sought refuge in the mission Salems.[44] The situation was given added piquancy by the fact that David Asante, who headed the mission's Kyebi station and loudly proclaimed emancipation as a triumph over heathenism, was a kinsman of Amoako Atta. Amid rising tensions, both would fall foul of the colonial government: in 1878 it insisted that the mission transfer the overzealous evangelist and in 1880, after reports of human sacrifice at funerals, it deported Amoako Atta to Lagos.[45]

If the Basel Mission and local communities engaged in what Peter Haenger has called a 'cultural battle' over the control of Christian slaves, then entangled with that was another battle over death and the dead.[46] This was fought in a variety of ways. One was ongoing doctrinal debate about the nature of the afterlife and, for Christians, how best to get to heaven. This entailed not only new ways of living and dying, but the obligation at baptism 'to renounce the devil and all his works'—including the stricture on participation in heathen obsequies (*Todten-costüme*). The demand that converts remove themselves from obligations towards the living and dead was a struggle for many, resulting in backsliding, punitive exclusions from the *Gemeinde* and, when it was grudgingly adhered to, resentment and aggravation. The fervent rejection of established mortuary custom by others is captured by a report on the death at Kyebi in 1870 of a slave named Abraham Boama, who, with the permission of his pagan master, was in his dying days moved to the Salem. 'You must bury me and pray over my grave', Abraham insisted on his deathbed. 'I don't want to be buried by the heathen, nor placed in their cemetery. I don't want to be buried like the heathen. You must make me a coffin, and when you put me in it you must not smear me with white earth like the heathen do for purification, nor must you wrap my body in a cloth, but in a shroud.'⁴⁷ As a slave, Abraham would have been lucky to receive the 'heathen' send-off he described, but, be that as it may, it was those in servitude and other marginalized individuals for whom the new faith often had the most to offer.

Given the antipathy on the part of many slave-owners towards their slaves dying within the house, perhaps Abraham's master was more than happy for him to be removed to the *oburoni kurom*.⁴⁸ In other cases, the Christian death-bed became the scene for determined domestic struggles, involving the dying themselves and those attending them. Consider this episode reported by the African catechist Kwabi from the Akyem town of Kukurantumi, as abstracted by Paul Jenkins:

> During the year an excluded Christian, Paul Teaseye, died. Three days before his death he was persuaded—partly because a fetish priest would do nothing for him unless he renounced Christianity—to die as a Christian, signifying this by laying a hand on his forehead and a hand on his breast. Near his death a 'crown prince' of Kukurantumi, Atta Kwaku, tied a fetish round his neck by force, though the man himself later tried to get rid of it when [*sic*: but?] he was too weak. At his death he asked to be taken out into the open air, in order to die looking at God, and Kwabi took this as enough evidence of his dying a Christian to bury him in the Christian cemetery.⁴⁹

A further aspect of the cultural battle was the readiness by non-Christians and Christians alike to regard morbidity and mortality as observable evidence of their conflicting religious claims. Death, particularly when it occurred in a situation of existing social discord or struck in rapid succession, had long provoked alarm and judicial intervention. As tensions mounted, it is therefore unsurprising that the death of Christian converts would be mobilized as evidence for the folly of spurning the time-honoured succour provided by *abosom* and ancestors. Basel reports are replete with such incidents, which are also recorded in those of the Bremen Mission among the Ewe to the east.⁵⁰ The imperative to claim the living and the dead is underlined by the precise enumeration of their fledgling communities so typical of nineteenth-century mission records: ledgers of souls saved and souls lost, with little crosses penned in to designate those who died in Christ.

A sequence of reports from the outstation at Begoro captures something of the atmosphere of swirling rumour and mutual recrimination. The situation at Begoro from 1876 was complicated by recurring outbreaks of typhus, which resulted in many deaths in the town and which presented problems for Rev. Adolph Mohr's efforts to relocate Christians in the Salem. One convert had elderly parents who refused to budge because of a fear that if they moved into the *oburoni kurom*, 'the fetish would kill them'.[51] When two recently baptized Christians did die, it was clear to the townspeople that 'the school kills'; the African catechist Obeng countered by demanding 'why then are so many people dying in Begoro town?'.[52] Despite reporting on the virulence of typhus, neither did Mohr take an entirely disenchanted view of mortality. When the relative of two converts died, the deceased man's grandmother, described as 'an old fetish priestess', claimed that her *obosom* had killed him and therefore that his body must be thrown away in the bush. Mohr, however, took possession of the corpse and buried it in the Salem, 'to the joy of the family'. Five more family members, all in their prime, then died in quick succession, which convinced Mohr that the grandmother was indeed responsible: 'she is old and lame, and since she can no longer take attendants with her by having them killed at her funeral, she is poisoning them beforehand'.[53] As the wave of deaths continued into 1878, the townspeople identified the proximate cause as the Christians having cut down sacred *odum* trees. There were more accusations of poisoning. By April 1878, 170 people had died of typhus, and there was talk of driving Mohr and the Christians out of Begoro 'just as Asante had been driven out of Kibi'. Reflecting on the situation, Mohr cited Amos 3:6 as evidence that the deaths were the result of God trying to lead the people to faith: 'Shall a trumpet be blown in the city, and shall the people not be afraid? Shall there be evil in a city and the Lord hath not done it?'.[54]

Let us end with the story of one more death, that of Amoako Atta. The death of an Akan *omanhene*, as we have seen, represented a moment of extreme rupture, triggering an eruption of intense collective grief and cathartic disorder which was in turn quelled by highly elaborated and protracted mortuary ritual. The events following the death of the Okyenhene on 2 February 1887 continued this normative pattern. Yet they were also shaped by the novel circumstances pertaining in the 1880s, when Akyem was convulsed by a renewed round of sectarian tension as it was struggling to come to terms with incorporation into the framework of British rule. The embattled Okyenhene died, that is, in a rapidly changing world, one in which ideas of Christian salvation and of colonial modernity were beginning to play a prominent part.

Returning from exile in 1885, Amoako Atta found that the Basel Mission's congregations had continued to expand. Whether he set out deliberately to uproot Christianity from his kingdom is unclear; there can be little doubt that he at least sought to reimpose royal authority over converts—who by then included members of his own family. While the missionaries portrayed this as simple persecution, colonial administrators took a more circumspect view. Christian converts 'considered themselves no longer bound by native laws', one wrote. 'They refused to attend native tribunals by which [the Okyenhene's] revenue had become greatly diminished . . . [and] openly ridicule their Fetish customs and disturbances ensue.'[55] Matters came to a head in December 1886, when leading Christians associated with the royal court were accused of stealing an amount of gold dust from the treasury. Amid mounting disturbances, the administration ordered both Amoako Atta and Christian representatives to Accra. Yet shortly after arriving, accompanied by 2,300 armed followers, he fell gravely ill, news of which prompted another 4,500 subjects to march down to the colonial capital.[56]

Amoaka Atta died in the morning of 2 February 1887. Chief medical officer John Farrell Easmon, in whose care he had been placed, reported the cause of death to be double pneumonia with high fever and, ultimately, heart failure. The disease took fatal hold when the Okyenhene arrived at Accra during what was an especially debilitating *harmattan* season, when the cool, dry wind blowing south from the Sahara caused an increase in pulmonary diseases. The Sierra Leonian Easmon, who did not mince his words when it came to denouncing what he regarded as pernicious native customs, elaborated further: 'I attribute the death of this patient to the ignorance and neglect of his people'. He had engaged in a running battle with Amoako Atta's own doctor, both of whom insisted that the ailing king desist from taking the other's medicines. Whether Easmon's prescriptions—'Brand's Essences, Valentines Meat Juice, etc, from the Hospital'—would have had any more impact than those provided by the Akyem *oduyefo* is questionable. So too is the rumour that, as the end approached, Amoaka Atta told his sister Okyerewa that he wished to be baptized.[57] For the colonial government, anxious about the presence of thousands of armed warriors in Accra, his demise served to inflame an already volatile situation. 'It puts a stop to the inquiry intended', Governor Brandford Griffith wrote to London, 'and the natives, always suspicious, will be inclined to attribute his death to any, but no real causes.'[58]

Brandford Griffith was partially right: for the Akyems, both Christian and non-Christian, Easmon's certification of death, based on a biomedical understanding of mortality, would have meant little. Far from attributing the death of their *omanhene* to 'any' cause, however, they readily pinpointed its proximate catalyst. On leaving Kyebi for Accra, the already ailing Amoako Atta had been seen off by Mohr with a sinister threat: that, this time, he would never live to return to his homeland.[59] The missionary had committed a heinous transgression of the rules of Akan orality by directly referring to the death of an office-holder in such a way that could only be perceived as invoking a maleficent curse. Mohr's attempts to deny the incident were undermined by the production of a letter he wrote to the late Amoaka Atta's clerks, ridiculing the claims about the stolen gold dust. 'But you . . . neglected to tell him that God Almighty taketh revenge of those who persecute his people? And because Ata . . . took every bad and devilish means to carry out his plan, the Lord has called him before His throne that he might answer for this wicked deed. And in fact, Kyebi town is cursed by God for this evil done against his people.'[60] 'Who among the mission's friends did not believe that Ata's death was a judgement?' he later wrote.[61] The late Okyenhene's people, led in the interregnum by the forthright *ohemaa* Amma Ampofoaa, were incensed: on arriving back in Akyem with the body of their dead king, they set about destroying mission property and driving Christian communities from their Salems. So too were colonial officials, who had considerable sympathy with efforts by the ruling elite at Kyebi to manage relations with the Swiss missionaries. 'I thought they came here to bring us into light because they brought a bible but after all I found that they came for nothing but political affairs', Amma Ampofoaa wrote; 'myself and my people will not stop with them, because two kings will not live [in] one town together'.[62]

Amma Ampofoaa was wrong: in time, African rulers and Christian converts would learn to live and to die together in reasonable harmony. The tumultuous episodes surrounding the destruction of Nananom Mpow in 1851 and the death of Amoako Atta in 1887 demonstrate how contests over death and the dead played a crucial role in shaping the nineteenth-century missionary frontier. Yet Christian encounter was also characterized by quiet negotiation, experimentation and accommodation, much of it occurring within the domestic realm and largely beneath the radar of the historical record. Christians and non-Christians were not two undifferentiated interest groups; neither did conversion—the Twi term adopted for the process was *anibue*, 'the opening of the eyes'—necessarily entail a clear-cut set of choices about how to live and how to die. In 1894, the Basel Mission gave its total church membership as 12,074 (of whom 5,198 were full communicants), while in 1890, Methodist congregations numbered 18,290 (5,812 as full members).[63] Some of these churchgoers had no doubt embraced with fervour the Christian message and its associated values, but for many others the process of working out an acceptable balance between the promise of personal salvation and the modernity of the new faith, on the one hand, and established beliefs, rights and obligations, on the other, would be prolonged, tentative and contingent. Contests over death and burial, as we will see in the next chapter, would continue. When in 1885 the Basel missionary Huppenbauer met a drunken dancer at a funeral, he noted the incident as an example of the twin evils of drink and fetish belief. Yet his report seems perfectly to capture the opening stages of the Christian encounter in all its discordant ambiguity and syncopated possibility: the dancer, he wrote, 'believed that his left foot belonged to the devil, his right foot to God'.[64]

12

From House Burial to Cemeteries

IN MARCH 1888, the Legislative Council of the Gold Coast Colony passed a law designed to replace the practice of burying the dead within their houses with that of burying them in modern, Western-style cemeteries. 'An Ordinance to provide for interments in cemeteries and to prohibit intramural sepulture', referred to as the Cemeteries Ordinance, represented a major intervention into the necrogeography of the coastal towns. Aware that the legislation was of a sensitive nature and fearing resistance from the inhabitants of Accra, to where in the first instance it was to be applied, the administration proceeded with caution. By April a new public cemetery designed to accommodate 1,283 graves had been laid out in Osu (the old Danish Accra, or Christiansborg), one half of which was consecrated for Christian burial. In August, Governor William Brandford Griffith convened a meeting of Ga chiefs, European and African churchmen, and members of Accra's merchant elite in order to explain the advantages of cemetery burial. 'I pointed out that the matter . . . was a very delicate subject to touch upon in any part of the world', Griffith reported to the Colonial Office, 'but that Her Majesty's Government were anxious to do all in their power to make the towns on the Gold Coast healthier than they had been, so as to prolong the lives of the people and to attract capital to the country'.[1] Turning to the unofficial African member of the Legislative Council, the Fante merchant John Sarbah, the governor asked him whether it remained the custom at the old colonial headquarters, Cape Coast, to inter the dead in their houses, 'and he said it had been given up long ago and most wisely too'. Scientific backing for the ordinance was then voiced by the Sierra Leonian medical officer John Farrell Easmon, who insisted that it was essential in order to eliminate the mortal threat from 'noxious emanations' arising from the mass of tombs crammed under people's living quarters. Having secured what he believed to be the support of the assembled dignitaries, Griffith proceeded with the laying out of a second cemetery, with another 1,871 plots, in Accra proper and to make provisions for the appointment of a registrar of deaths, a sexton and five gravediggers. On 1 September, with these appointments in place, the ordinance was activated and applied to the colonial capital.[2]

The anticipated popular resistance duly materialized. Yet despite this resistance and the limited initial reach of the law, the 1888 Cemeteries Ordinance was a landmark in the bureaucratization of death on the Gold Coast, marking the beginning of a fundamental shift in the dominion of the dead. The outlawing of intramural burial and the establishment of regulated public cemeteries can be seen to represent (in the coastal urban centres of the colony, at least) the same transition that scholars have identified in the history of death in the West: the moment when the dead's long-established cohabitation with the living in the space of human culture was ended by their forcible relocation to the edge of town. The nature of this transition has been the subject of considerable debate. Philippe Ariès, in particular, established a clear watershed between the thousand-year epoch in Western history characterized by easy promiscuity between the living and the dead and the shattering of that intimacy, from the late eighteenth century, with the displacement of the dead and their segregation in cemeteries. Subsequent historians, most recently Thomas W. Laqueur, have sought to qualify this narrative by adding lines of continuity to Ariès's emphasis on dramatic rupture.[3] Here we consider how this development played out on the late nineteenth-century Gold Coast with respect to a crucial element in Ariès's notion of 'modern' death and Laqueur's of a 'new regime' of the dead: the legally enforced disposal of mortal remains in ordered, purpose-built and communal cemeteries.

We have seen how house burial emerged as a distinctive feature of mortuary culture in coastal towns in the age of Atlantic commerce. By the end of the eighteenth century, it was reported that, in Accra at least, 'every single Black is buried in the room in his house where he died'.[4] The reasons for this custom were said to be varied, although the emphasis put by most observers on the secrecy with which corpses were interred points to an imperative to guard against grave robbery or desecration in an era of growing insecurity, uneven accumulation and an increase in the use of gold as a grave good. Whatever the precise motive, the inhabitants of dwellings under which reposed the mortal remains of revered ancestors were reluctant ever to abandon them. This became apparent to African Company officials in the early 1790s, when in the course of a conflict with the inhabitants of Anomabo, a company of soldiers, reinforced by sailors from a slave ship, dug up and looted a number of graves in the town. The action was condemned as 'horrid and dreadful' by the local council and the commander of Anomabo fort was removed from his post, but the outraged townspeople demanded hefty compensation and the dispute lingered on.[5] When the British attempted to clear an esplanade around the fort, the move was resisted by local inhabitants, led by a prominent trader known as Yellow Joe. 'I apprehend much difficulty', Governor Dalzel wrote, 'for the habitations of the Natives serve them also for Tombs. Yellow Joe . . . has not yet attempted to [re]build, [but] when he does, I purpose to allow him a consideration to induce him to remove the Dead Bodies, and the treasure which may have been deposited with them'.[6] The fierce attachment to ancestral houses, however, was stronger than Dalzel's financial inducements and threats of force: 'after a variety of messages and several meetings, it was found that they would not relinquish a single inch of the ground'.[7] 'They bury the dead in their houses', company officer Henry Meredith confirmed two decades later, 'and will not move from the spot, if they can possibly help it'.[8]

Another innovation which emerged during the eighteenth century was the use of wooden coffins. The coffin, as the immediate 'house' within which a corpse was laid to rest, was entangled in a variety of ways with the transition from intramural to cemetery burial. Yet the British were never required to enact legislation to enforce burial in coffins, as their widespread use in the coastal towns predated the Cemeteries Ordinance and continued to diffuse independently of colonial diktat. When, during a visit to Kumasi in 1842, Robert Brooking constructed a handsome coffin for the body of a Methodist colleague, it became an object of great interest, including on the part of a princess of the royal household: 'Ah!', she exclaimed, 'If I were sure of being buried in such a beautiful box I would consent to die tomorrow!'.[9] By 1875, the demand was such that John Sarbah opened what seems to have been the Gold Coast's first undertakers and coffin emporium on Jackson Street in Cape Coast, advertising in the *Gold Coast Times* that 'orders will be executed to the entire satisfaction of the parties, and those so desiring can have Funerals conducted for them on the most approved and economical style'.[10] Indeed, coffins were not mentioned in colonial law until the ordinance was amended in 1891 in order to clamp down on surreptitious dual burials—a subterfuge for which a coffin was essential.

Most corpses were traditionally buried either wrapped in a mat or encased in a wicker basket. They were then placed in the horizontal niche of an L-shaped grave and the niche was walled off with sticks or mats—'so as the Earth came not near it', Villault observed in the 1660s.[11] By then—at the same time that the use of coffins was becoming more widespread in western Europe—the bodies of certain prominent individuals were being buried in wooden coffins.[12] These were often recycled European gun or cloth chests (*ndaka*, sing. *adaka*), which gave rise to the Twi word for coffin, *funnaka* (*efunu*, corpse, and *adaka*). 'The Europeans, too, use gun chests', Monrad wrote in the early nineteenth century, 'and there is an expression among the English on the Coast when someone is very ill, "He only wants a gun chest"'.[13] The use of coffins, however, was not without controversy, emerging as matter of violent dispute on the death of the powerful Ga *caboceer* Okaija in 1770. 'It was a custom among the Akras, never to coffin a deceased king who had been a priest to their national fetish', Reindorf recorded.

> Chief Okaidsha had died and the educated princes among his sons proposed to coffin their venerable father; but the other members of the royal family objected to this. His remains were nevertheless coffined. This led to a contest between the people and the educated princes who were (as [Dutch] government officials) backed by the soldiers in the Dutch Fort. His remains were honourably interred in the fort. This originated the oath of Gbese: 'Okaidsha adeka' i.e. Okaidsha's coffin, because several lives were lost when the people were fighting to gain the remains of the chief.[14]

Whereas on the coast the spread of wooden coffins appears to have been derived from a European model, references to their use as receptacles first for the corpses and then for the rearticulated skeletons of the rulers of the Akan forest kingdoms point to a parallel indigenous origin. It will be recalled how the coffin containing the body of Asantehene Osei Tutu became embedded with Akyem bullets, which gave rise to the mnemonic praise 'the coffin that receives bullets, he is the dead one whose corpse still fights'. A second account relates to Osei Tutu's successor, Opoku Ware (c. 1720–1750). According to Rømer, when the great warrior king fell gravely ill, 'the Assiante fetish reminded him that he (this is, the fetish) had often warned him not to spill the blood of so many people'. 'Now all the blood was transformed into fire in his body. It would burn him and within a few years he would die.' Faced with this grim prognosis, Opoku Ware 'asked the Dutch general to send him a coffin of glass and a throne, and after a short time these arrived at Elmina from Holland'.[15]

Dutch documentation confirms this request, recording that in 1744–5 an Asante envoy travelled to Holland in order to bring back a coffin fitted with a glass-windowed head end.[16] In the second half of the 1740s, however, the Fante blocked the trade route from Elmina to Kumasi and it seems unlikely that the coffin was ever delivered. Yet Opoku Ware's motives are intriguing. In line with the original purpose of such a coffin, did he wish others to be able to look in to see his mortal remains? Or did he wish his remains to be able to look out?

———

The intervention by the colonial administration into the established necro-geography of the Gold Coast followed on the heels of the great metropolitan campaigns of sanitation and burial reform that by the 1850s had resulted in the crumbling of what Laqueur calls the old regime of the dead. The desire on the part of reformers and visionaries in France and in Britain to close what they perceived as increasingly congested and noxious inner-city churchyards and replace them with spacious, ordered garden cemeteries on the model of an ancient Elysium extended back a century or more, to the early decades of the Enlightenment, but took definitive shape with the opening in 1804 of the Cimetière du Père-Lachaise in Paris. By the 1830s, amid mounting alarm over the supposed threat that the dead posed to the health of the living, calls for reform gathered pace, culminating in Britain in Edwin Chadwick's *Supplementary Report on the Results of a Special Inquiry into the Practice of Interment in Towns* of 1842. Not everybody, including Anglican clergy with a stake in the old regime, was convinced of the mortal danger of dead bodies, but by mid-century the demand for a radical transformation of burial practice was unstoppable and 'the dead had moved into a new universe with new people in charge'.[17] That universe was cosmopolitan, secular and, in line with Foucault's notion of 'biopower', governed by the bureaucratic state that exercised sovereignty through its control over bodies, both dead and alive.[18] The 1880 Burial Act and the 1882 Burial Reform Act dealt a final blow to the parish churchyard as an ancient community of the dead, representing, for Laqueur, 'the definitive end of the old regime'.[19] The disposal of mortal remains had become primarily a civic rather than a religious or community responsibility, and, as a new imperial age dawned, the Victorian imperative to reorder the dead was set to extend from the metropole to the colonial periphery.

While this transformation in the regime of Western burial is beyond dispute, the precise motives for it have been the subject of debate. For Ariès, it was a consequence of the emergence of a new and, in his view, unwholesome set of attitudes towards death itself, characterized by the ostentatious displays of bourgeois grief and sentiment typical of the Victorian age and then by the 'hushing up' and segregation of the very idea of death itself in the twentieth century. An alternative explanation emphasizes the growing scientific evidence for the danger posed to public health by the accumulation of dead bodies at the heart of the rapidly expanding nineteenth-century city. Then there is the whole issue of Foucauldian biopower, which disenchanted the dead body 'as it became just one more locus for the scientific study of life'.[20] Laqueur takes issue with aspects of all these approaches, insofar as none can fully explain either the timing of the rise of the cemetery or the new forms of enchanted work that the dead would take on in the modern world. Thus, while the miasmic theory of disease causation held that ancient churchyards overflowing with rotting corpses gave off a deadly effluvia, the empirical evidence as presented by Chadwick and other reformers that such noxious emanations actually resulted in a crisis of public health was always less than convincing. Debates about disease were crucial, Laqueur argues, but burial reform must also be seen in terms of wider political and cultural changes, including opposition in both Britain and France to the control over burial exercised by established churches as well as new bourgeois conceptions of bodily, social and moral hygiene which viewed the corrupted corpse as dirt, 'matter out of place'.

It is here that an analysis of how this transformation unfolded in the small West African colonial outpost of the Gold Coast can usefully be brought into play. The departure of the Dutch in 1872 and the military defeat of Asante in 1873–4 were twin catalysts for the consolidation of British sovereignty throughout the Gold Coast littoral, which was declared a formal crown colony in July 1874. The first legislative action of the new regime was to abolish the legal status of slavery, and in 1877 the colonial headquarters was transferred from Cape Coast to Accra. 'By the late 1870s', I argued in an earlier work, 'issues of disease and medicine began to join those of law and order in official efforts to reshape the cultural space of Accra. Indeed, "sanitation" and "order" became linked in an emerging imperial ideology in which the new concern with tropical medicine contained a variety of encoded messages about wider social control'.[21] The drive to cleanse and to control the new colonial capital extended from enforced street sweeping and the removal of livestock to attempts to rid the town of African customs deemed to be unsuitable for the envisaged showcase of expatriate commerce and ordered modernity. Restrictions were placed on the celebration of the yearly Homowo festival, which, like the Akan Odwira, was in essence a prolonged and intense conversation with departed ancestors. 'Indecent dancing', the discharge of firearms, the recreational and ritual beating of drums, and the activities of fetish priests were also the targets of restrictive legislation. All of these played a role in mortuary customs, but to this list of practices which attracted the ire of colonial officialdom can specifically be added the celebration of funeral customs and the disposal of the dead.

As in Europe, the transition from the old to the new burial regime on the Gold Coast was a contested process. Imperial ideology linking hygiene and social control was one thing, but the willingness and ability of the fledgling colonial state to enforce measures in the face of stubborn local resistance was another. Neither was the contest over the control of urban space simply between the colonial state and the collective upholders of African tradition: many members of the literate African elite were robust proponents of the Victorian civilizing mission. It also had roots in earlier innovations: while the European trading companies interred their superior dead as well as favoured African intermediaries within the coastal forts, the bodies of the subaltern dead, European, Euro-African and African alike, were laid to rest in burial grounds in the surrounding countryside. By the early nineteenth century, these began to be designed according to emerging European notions of sepulchral order. In 1804 the Dutch laid out a new walled graveyard at Elmina and in 1816 the British did the same at Cape Coast, the latter being described as having 'a very respectable appearance; several head stones have lately been erected with the names of the deceased cut on them'.[22] Danish Accra also had a new, garden-like, cemetery outside the town. 'It is well enclosed with the so-called "prikkelthorn" [i.e., cactus] ... which forms an excellent hedge', Monrad noted approvingly. 'The entrance to it is through a black iron-barred gate which hangs on two large brick posts. Inside the cemetery there are beautiful palm and coconut trees. Before the cemetery was so arranged the bodies there were, as in the open fields, dug up and devoured by jackals and other wild animals'.[23]

Monrad was disappointed, however, with the reluctance of Euro-Africans to abandon house burial, noting a variation on the subterfuge of the double burial:

> Despite the fact that they now rest securely, we can hardly persuade the Christian Mulattoes to bury their dead there. It is said that, earlier, they had disappointed the chaplain by letting him cast earth in the cemetery on an

empty coffin, while the body was buried at home. To prevent this, in my time, the body had to be shown in the morgue. The natives' tender love for their dead, mixed with fear of them doing harm, and that they might be restless in the cemetery, makes it highly probable—as I have often been told by reliable people—that even Mulatto corpses that had been buried there in the daytime were dug up at night by the family and brought to the houses in the village.[24]

Neither was it just the so-called mulattos who persisted with intramural burial. In 1842, Wulff Joseph Wulff, a Danish Jew serving at Christiansborg, stipulated in his will that he wished his body to be buried not in the Christian cemetery but beneath the house in which he lived with his Euro-African wife, or 'Mulatinde', Sara Malm and their children. Wulff was insistent that other key elements of local funerary practice, however, were to be avoided: 'I wish that no cross be placed on my coffin, nor do I wish that anyone hold a wake over my deathbed, nor perform my "custom" . . . I wish, therefore, that no resources from my fortune be used for this. I most prefer that my Mulatinde and children mourn in silence in their home, without drinking any brandy'.[25] Similar instructions were left the following decade by James Bannerman, who stipulated that his remains be buried in native fashion beneath the house in James Town owned by his wife Yaa Hom and that his funeral ceremony be 'most private and above all no custom to be made'.[26]

Bannerman died in 1858, his corpse duly interred according to his wishes. That same year, African funerary practices began to attract the ire of colonial administrators. As in the metropole, mounting concern about the danger of the dead was characterized by an entanglement of moral indignation and medical disquiet, both of which were refracted on the imperial frontier through the prism of mid-Victorian racial thought. The dead body was dangerous, it was now widely accepted, but the African body particularly so. Just seven years after Bannerman, a 'gentleman of colour', had headed the Gold Coast government, the emergence of a more strident, racialized discourse is apparent in an angry tirade by the recently arrived Governor Pine. 'As a further illustration of the barbarous state of these settlements', Pine wrote to the Colonial Office, 'I cannot forbear describing a scene which I witnessed a short time ago in James Town, Accra'.

> I observed a crowd in the Street making Custom, as it is called, for a man just dead, by shouting, firing off muskets, and drinking rum. Presently a Coffin containing the . . . body of the man was brought out of a house on

the shoulders of men reeling with drink, and danced up and down among the mob amidst brutal songs and drunken revelry. . . . No words can convey the . . . Ghastliness of this scene; the Dance of Death, this hideous sport between sin and its avenger. I cannot tell you . . . the shame and indignation with which I saw such a scene (I am told a very common one) enacted in a Town close to a British Fort over which the British flag had floated for 200 years. This affair leads me to mention that in all the Coast Towns . . . it is the practice to bury the dead in private houses underneath the floors of the rooms in which people live. This most disgusting practice is not the least among the many means by which the brutality of man has added to the unhealthiness of this pestilential climate. In fact the Towns in which we live are at once dunghills and Grave Yards. There seems no chance of putting an end to this practice by any means short of main force.[27]

As in the debates over metropolitan burial reform, British officialdom did not yet speak with the same voice. Turning to Cruickshank's *Eighteen Years on the Gold Coast of Africa* (1853), a Colonial Office civil servant minuted in response that intramural interment was treated very differently 'by writers with a different *animus*'; indeed, Cruickshank—who, with an African wife and family, must have taken part in countless funerals—describes Fante mortuary rites with characteristic insight and even tenderness.[28] "The contrast is a curious one", observed the secretary of state. When, the following month, Pine issued a proclamation setting out sumptuary regulations for funeral customs, a ban on house burial was not among them. The emphasis was instead on maintaining law and order for their duration and limiting their ruinous expense, which was believed often to lead to the pawning of children or other family members. The custom 'for the death of a King, or great Chief' was accordingly limited to three days, for an 'inferior Chief' to two days and for 'a private person' to one day—'and no more.'[29]

In the first extensive medical report produced for the Gold Coast the same year, the colonial surgeon Dr Clarke condemned intramural burial from a more dispassionate, scientific perspective, urging that 'this hurtful custom cannot be too soon discontinued'. 'I may mention', Clarke wrote, 'that several persons have been buried in the floor of the Medical Store of the Colonial Hospital, in the Surgery, and in the kitchen used by the female prisoners.'[30] That five years after Clarke's report no action had been taken was a matter of dismay to a European resident of Cape Coast, whose letter to the chairman of the London-based African Aid Society was published in the society's journal, the *African Times*. 'You may imagine what a nice place the centre of a cemetery must be to live in a hot climate like this', the correspondent wrote, reporting that the government graveyard 'is at present so full that they are burying persons only three feet deep'.[31] This prompted a scathing response from an African resident, who shifted the blame away from the failings of local society and towards those of the British administration. 'If the state of filth, squalor and positive barbarism in which people of the town are immersed calls forth such loud expressions of disgust', he wrote, 'how much ought it to come from us, who pay more than *half our income* in the shape of a 2 per cent duty on all imports, for the ostensible purpose of rectifying the very grievances complained of'. In support of his assertions, the writer quoted an extract from an 1858 issue of the *West African Herald*: 'Horrible stenches arise from the burial-ground, spreading disease among the tenants of the houses in the neighbourhood. A merchant, whose house is situated close to the cemetery, informs us that there is almost always sickness among his family, which he attributed to the ... frightful and pestilential odours ... wafted to his dwelling'.[32] The robust tone and style of the letter, signed 'Quamina', leave little doubt that its author was Charles Bannerman, eldest son of the late James and editor of the *Herald*.

Some relief came in 1865 with the arrival of an energetic new administrator, Colonel Conran. As reported in the *African Times* (again, Bannerman was the likely correspondent), Conran was horrified by the range of 'nuisances and abuses which preceding Governments had tolerated': 'The streets impassable, because so encumbered with putrefying animal filth and decomposing vegetable matter!—every house a graveyard!—no proper supply of water!—no observance of the Christian Sabbath!'. The solution, Conran proposed to an assembly of townspeople, was 'a large and convenient graveyard that will be set apart for your special use—your religious ideas and professions being respected'. The principal religious idea that needed to be accommodated, he recognized, was the imperative on the part of families to maintain intimate and exclusive contact with the remains of their ancestors. 'Each family will have their own portion of this cemetery set apart for their own use', he suggested, 'on which they can erect tombs according to pleasure, and I shall have it well enclosed all round'.[33] Two months later, Bannerman (as 'Spero Meliora': 'I hope for better things') reported progress on the new graveyard—although whether it was made up of discrete family plots is unclear.[34] Certainly, the fear that the ancestral dead would be removed from symbolic circulation to undifferentiated public space would continue to generate resistance to efforts at reform.

We see here the continuing sway of the ancient theory of deadly miasma, together with the rise of what Laqueur calls a new age of 'olfactory vigilance', when, 'for the bourgeoisie, certain street smells and the bodily smells of the poor became troublesome and quite possibly dangerous'.[35] These entangled notions were mapped onto the particular medical and social topography of the coast of Guinea, long regarded by Western observers as the most pestilent of all tropical environments. Vague eighteenth-century fears of 'the white man's grave' were given the sanction of Victorian medical science by the Sierra Leonian army surgeon James Africanus Horton, whose *Physical and Medical Climate and Meteorology of the West Coast of Africa* (1867) made much of the morbid threat posed to Africans and Europeans alike by noisome vapours emanating from human waste and from the fetid earth itself.[36]

Certainly, the odour of corruption was bad, as acknowledged in his diary by Wulff, six years before he left instructions for his own intramural burial: 'the dead are buried in the houses, producing a terrible stench, but we cannot dissuade them from this practice, even if we threatened to set the entire town afire by shooting from the Fort'.[37] The question, Laqueur writes, is 'why the ancient smell of hidden corrupting flesh became pollution, why a commonplace odor became a threat not just to health but to the social and moral order'?[38] A simple answer, if we pose the question for the mid-nineteenth-century Gold Coast, would be that that moral order was a specifically imperial order and that Victorian bourgeois sensibilities were further shaped—and magnified—by emerging notions of race. That interpretation is accurate to a point, but fails to take account of the more complex intersection between race and class in the coastal trading towns. Men such as Charles Bannerman and James Africanus Horton, long considered to have been pioneering figures in the emergence of West African nationalism, were acutely conscious by the 1860s of the rising tide of European racialism. But they were also resolutely and self-consciously middle-class, Victorian gentlemen, whose stout defence of local society was tempered by a progressive urge to purge it of 'backward' traits.

That debates over moral hygiene transcended the racial divide is further apparent from events in Cape Coast in 1872, when the issues of funeral customs and house burial again emerged at the forefront of town affairs. The catalyst was the funeral on 8 October of the wife of a leading Cape Coast officeholder, Chief Attah, into which was incorporated a girls' nubility rite called

Akwo. The following month, the Colonial Office received a letter from agents of the expatriate trading firm of Messrs Foster and Smith, complaining about the ceremonies and alleging that they were the result of the liberal governor Pope Hennessy having deliberately 'encouraged bad native Customs on the Gold Coast'. Pope Hennessy denied this, informing London that far from condoning such customs, the local administrator had successfully concluded a protracted negotiation with African office-holders to end house burial and henceforth to inter all the town's dead in a new, native cemetery. 'I am disposed to regard it, in a sanitary and moral point of view', he wrote, 'as one of the most important reforms effected on the Gold Coast since the active days of Governor Maclean'.[39] The new administrator, Colonel Harley, concurred, expressing satisfaction that the local chiefs had finally consented 'to relinquish the ancient but very deadly custom . . . which has made Cape Coast a vast graveyard for so long a time'.[40]

In a further effort to defend himself, Pope Hennessy instructed Harley to gather evidence from representatives of local society on the nature of the combined funeral and nubility custom. Harley did so, writing 'to certain Gentlemen, European, and Native, who represent the several professions and classes of this community, from whom it is reasonable to assume, I would receive an impartial opinion as to the revival of the barbarous processions and ceremonies known as "Customs" at Cape Coast referred to by Messrs Foster and Smith'.[41] Opinions were mixed: whereas some local worthies supported Pope Hennessy's position that there had been no revival of unseemly native customs, others begged to differ. The most strident criticism came from African members of the Methodist Church; the Rev. Timothy Laing; and three catechist schoolteachers, A. W. Parker, R. J. Hayfron and J. P. Brown. 'It is quite correct that old Customs of a vile nature have recently been revived with a vigour which has caused the enlightened portion of the Community to shudder', Brown wrote, while Parker declared that he had 'turned away with disgust, lamenting the revival of such barbarous custom, mentally praying for the speedy arrival of the time when all these debasing and demoralizing practices shall be swept away before the soul-elevating and nation-exalting rays of the sun of Righteousness'.[42] It was left to the ex-administrator C. S. Salmon to defend the record of the administration by lauding the agreed end of house burial and contrasting the limited ability of the Methodist mission 'to make any universal and permanent impression on the body of the people' with that of 'the secular power of the Government . . . to improve the manners of the people, induce orderly behaviour, and general decency'.[43] 'Mr Salmon leaves me but little to add', Harley wrote, 'except that I concur with him in thinking that "in a Town the population of which is unfortunately pagan, there is a case required in drawing a line where *forcible* authority ... shall not interfere, especially in a Country, where the powers of the Government are so doubtful when dealing with social questions".[44]

The impact of the 1872 declaration by which the chiefs of Cape Coast agreed to end intramural burial in the town is unclear. War with Asante the next year, followed by the declaration of the crown colony and the abolition of slavery, directed the attention of officials elsewhere, and it would be another fifteen years before the administration was willing and able to exercise its 'forcible authority' in the matter. Mortuary entrepreneur John Sarbah, as we have seen, claimed that by then house burial in Cape Coast was a thing of the past. This is doubtful, and evidence suggests otherwise.[45] Yet at least some of the town's middle-class Christians had developed the same desire for their dead to repose in a tranquil garden setting that had characterized the transition to the Victorian cemetery in Britain. This yearning was articulated in Cape Coast's *Western Echo* newspaper in 1885:

> It is impossible to count them, for all our cemeteries are not walled or railed, not laid out in straight and sinuous walks, not planted with ... flowers and avenued with trees, not adorned with the deft chisellings of the sculptor and the stately erections of the stone-mason, and are not set off with pretty little mortuary chapels within which the services for the dead may be read. And this is because they are found in all sorts of places. Sometimes by the roadside, for some towns have a custom of burying there those who die on the road either by a falling tree or by a gun accident or by their own suicidal hand. Sometimes the place of sepulture is beneath that quiet spot where you would eat your breakfast, write your letters or take your siesta. You may not know it, but beneath many an African mat there sleeps the skeleton of some departed worthy.[46]

Officials may indeed not have known of the extent to which house burial continued in Cape Coast. By the 1880s, however, the focus of cemetery reform had switched to the new colonial capital of Accra, whose Ga inhabitants had long been seen to be especially devoted to keeping their 'worthy' dead as close as possible. The reformist impulse was further reactivated by the creation of a Medical Department in 1885 and then a separate Sanitary Department in 1888, whose officials drew on the scientific legitimacy offered by the emerging field of tropical medicine to create for themselves an influential role in the colonial bureaucracy.

A key figure advocating legislative intervention was John Farrell Easmon, who was appointed as an assistant colonial surgeon in 1880 and four years later made a notable contribution to medical research when he identified the aetiology of hemoglobinuric or, in his coinage, 'blackwater' fever.[47] In April 1887, shortly after the death of his erstwhile patient Amoako Atta, Easmon wrote another paper which combined pathological and meteorological data in order to account for an apparent increase in mortality among the inhabitants of Accra during the season when the cool *harmattan* wind blew south from the Sahara. He faced an obstacle, however, from what he described as 'the disinclination, arising from ethical considerations, which the natives have for any one connected with the Government to know anything about the deaths of their relatives or friends, lest they should be compelled to inter the corpse in properly appointed cemeteries, instead of in their private houses as at present obtains'.[48] This disinclination, Easmon believed, was in part due to the abhorrence with which Africans regarded post-mortem examinations: 'if its probability is once suspected, not the slightest demonstration of grief would be evinced until the corpse had been, according to their ideas, satisfactorily disposed of, or some plan or falsehood to deceive the authorities, agreed upon'. The damaging impact of local mortuary practice, moreover, did not end with issues of data collection. 'The pernicious system of "customs" for the dead, the annual "customs" for the "fetish of the home" and other customs—orgies of drink and vice—have decimated and impoverished the older families in Accra', Easmon continued. 'Finally, all those who died during this period were with a very few exceptions . . . buried in their own houses. . . . Science teaches that the habitual breathing of foul air lowers the standard of normal vitality'.

The development of germ theory in the subsequent decade would undermine the established orthodoxy on pestilent miasma and effluvia. It would take somewhat longer until notions of medical wellbeing became detached from those of moral wellbeing, a connection further developed in a sanitary report the following year. Despite Easmon's own African heritage, he did not mince his words:

> Of the moral and social condition of the native population much of interest, ethnological and sociological, may be noted; regarding, however, purely from the health point of view, the system of overcrowding of individuals

and 'compounds' of huts which . . . obtain as direct result of their social system is deserving of serious consideration: for the great part played in the evolution of moral progress by the physical surroundings of a people is nowadays generally admitted. . . . A barbarous community, the individual units of which are swayed by various . . . tribal and religious feelings, here pagan, there Mohammedan, elsewhere so-called Christians, yet all pervaded by the common vices of barbarism: low cunning, artifice, deceit, with a few semi-educated persons know vulgarly as 'Scholars' characterised by great ambition and little attainment—such is the mosaic constituting the Accra community.[49]

For Easmon, cemetery reform would not simply clear the atmosphere of poisonous emanations—it was a crucial step in curing the 'moral turpitude' of native society.

Three weeks after the Cemeteries Ordinance was applied to Accra on 1 September 1888, Brandford Griffith reported to the Colonial Office on its impact. House burial, he was disappointed to say, was continuing unabated.[50] Despite the assurances of town dignitaries and the threat of steep penalties—fines of up to £20 or three month's imprisonment, plus the possible prohibition of the use of houses under which burials occurred—there had been only ten interments in the new public cemeteries. The dramatic adaptation to funerary practice as a response to the threat of post-mortems that had earlier been noted by Easmon became widespread, as the bereaved attempted quietly to inter their dead without alerting the sanitary authorities. Demonstrative displays of female grief, the firing of guns, drumming and the tumultuous processions which conveyed the corpse around the town quarters suddenly disappeared. Although these customs had long been the target of official chagrin, the governor now expressed shock that the townspeople should hide 'the expression of natural regret at the loss of those dear to them'. Ordering that public notices be posted around the town offering a reward for information leading to the conviction of those breaking the new law, he also directed, in an effort to underline government resolve, that six graves ominously be kept open in each cemetery to receive the newly dead.

Within a few weeks, the first prosecutions began to be heard in Accra's district court. The records of some of these make for poignant reading. 'Yesterday about 10 a.m., I was on duty in James Town Street [and] I passed round to prisoner Odadaye's quarters', testified Constable Moshi. 'I found her crying. I asked why she cried and she said nothing and I looked into the room and discovered a man had been buried. Prisoner Odadaye told me it was her son. Prisoner begged me to let it be, saying she had done wrong. She also brought a flask of rum. She said "My son is dead and I have business inside".[51] So soon after the enactment of the law, however, it proved impossible to be sure how long ago the burial had taken place and the grieving Odadaye was acquitted. Another unsuccessful prosecution the following month demonstrated that burials were now taking place in the dead of night, with lookouts posted on street corners and with family members ready to take evasive action: on the appearance of a police patrol, the offending body, lying on display in a courtyard, wrapped in a mat, was passed out a window and hurried away.[52] Yet another, this time resulting in a conviction, is notable on account of the energetic role played by Easmon himself and of an early documented appearance of the 'fake burial' ploy. Acting on a tip-off that an empty coffin had been interred in the cemetery, the police exhumed the coffin and indeed found that it contained only stones. Easmon then applied for a warrant to excavate the floor of the deceased's house, discovering a newly buried corpse—and in its mouth the damning evidence of 'a pipe with fresh tobacco'.[53]

Rising tensions in Accra boiled over in February 1889, after the compulsory demolition of a number of dwellings in the densely populated Asere quarter of Kinka, or old Dutch Accra. The Asere people resolved to resist any further incursions by sanitary inspectors, leading to a confrontation with the colonial constabulary which left several people wounded and thirty arrested.[54] The administration was divided on this course of action, which arose from complaints of offensive smells emanating from the vicinity of the king of Accra (or Ga *mantse*) Taki Tawia's quarters. When the long-serving chief medical officer, Dr McCarthy, was sent to investigate, however, he reported that he 'perambulated the narrow alleys which intersect that human "rookery", but failed to find a single spot which in any way agreed with the Inspector General's description'. McCarthy's sarcastic rebuff of a fellow official—for which he was censured by the governor—demonstrates that the new age of 'olfactory vigilance' identified by Laqueur to be so central to the new burial regime was not without its dissenters. 'I am glad to be able to state . . . that the whole place is exceptionally clean', McCarthy continued, 'and free from any deposits which could give rise to unpleasant odours which so offended the hypersensitive olfactory sense of a gentleman whose only experience of odour is happily derived from the fragrant essence of Rimenal and Atkinson'.[55]

The longer-term popular response to the legislation was characterized by evasion and innovation rather than by overt resistance. The disappearance of prosecutions from the criminal record books by early 1889 suggests either that Accra's townspeople had became adept at secretly interring their dead in the old manner or that they had accommodated rapidly to the new regime. Colonial officials believed, cautiously, the latter to be the case: when in late 1891 the administration amended the ordinance, the queen's advocate reported that 'cemeteries have been established in a number of places and many others are in contemplation and the people are getting more accustomed and inclined to bury in them'.[56] One problem, however, was apprehension about the looting of buried wealth from exposed graves, a concern which the government attempted to allay by imposing a stiff penalty of up to seven years' imprisonment for grave robbery. That the amended ordinance was also designed to crack down on dual burial points to an awareness that the ploy was being practised: any person 'who shall knowingly bury . . . any coffin in which there is no corpse shall incur a penalty of £20 or 3 months imprisonment'.[57] Yet it is unlikely that the government was ever able to exert the degree of surveillance in the old downtown quarters of Accra necessary to eliminate house burial. 'Even if the zealous sanitary authorities were to challenge the coffin [en route to the cemetery] and find that it duly contained the corpse', the anthropologist M. J. Field wrote in the 1930s, 'it is doubtful where the remains would finally come to rest'.[58] According to popular rumour, the subterfuge of the fake burial remains commonplace in Ghana today.

Beyond outright evasion, one form of spiritual innovation which allowed people to accommodate to the new regime was a greater willingness by some to embrace, or to re-embrace, Christianity. 'This law has . . . placed our work in Christiansborg in a most hopeful position', native pastor and historian Carl Reindorf wrote in January 1889.[59] Fear of being consigned to the new public cemetery rather than the more sanctified Basel Mission cemetery was encouraging the return to the fold of elderly backsliders, who, as they felt the approach of death, had abandoned the church in order specifically to be laid to rest in their own homes. Reindorf cited the case of Mrs Sarah Wulff (née Malm), who, forty-six years after the death of her husband, had wished to be laid beside him in the house they lived in together—and, it might be said, continued to occupy together since. Others 'now prefer to become Christians and be buried as such, than to die as a Heathen and be thrown away—They mean by throwing away, the burial in the Government Cemetery'.[60] The desire to at least be buried in one's own town, if not one's own house, would, however, emerge as a countervailing force against church expansion. 'Cemetery case is another impediment in winning more Accras to our society here', catechist Isaac Odoi Philipps reported in 1897 from the stubbornly 'pagan' town of Kinka. 'Some unconverted ... friends ... say [to] ... those coming to us that if you join the Basel Mission here and die you will be buried at Christiansborg and not in your own town Accra and will not get more mourners to follow and attend your funeral. Many were offended by these sayings and consequently shrink back.'[61]

By the mid-1890s, other mortuary innovations began to emerge in Accra. Rather than being buried underneath their houses or in the new public cemeteries, some Ga office-holders chose to have their remains interred in monumental, Akan-style mausoleums on the outskirts of the city. That this liminal zone between culture and nature had long been the place where vile bodies were 'thrown away' underlines what a fundamental reimagination of the town's necrogeography this represented. The first recorded mausoleum was built in 1895, but the most dramatic signal of this shift occurred with the death of Ga *mantse* Taki Tawia in 1902. The funeral custom for the old and influential king was attended by a huge crowd of townspeople, who witnessed his interment in a royal mausoleum, *manprobi*, located on a rise to the north of Korle lagoon.[62] Aside from the difficulty of concealing the house burial of leading office-holders from the colonial authorities, the adoption of mausoleums appears to have arisen from a desire on the part of the chiefly elite to preserve the established hierarchy of the dead. 'Kings and ... important members of the ruling houses were buried in the clan or family houses, and not in the public cemetery where the "common" stock of humanity were buried', the Ga scholar and, later, nationalist politician Ako Adjei wrote of the new burial regime in 1943. With the advent of mausoleums, however, 'a new institution has developed out of the ruins of the old'.[63] The common townspeople, meanwhile, began to inter in their houses a miniature coffin of relics—hair, fingernail and toenail clippings, and the sacred sponge used to wash the corpse—as a substitute for the entire body. 'Where these are buried is the place which the dead man will always regard as his own home, and to which he will always return.'[64]

The seaside towns of the eastern Gold Coast did not therefore cease to be cities of the dead. When during the annual Homowo festival the Ga sprinkle *kpekpei* (a mixture of new-season corn and palm oil) for the ancestors to eat, they continue to this day to do so on the floors of the old family houses, 'to which they will always return'. Yet the events of 1888–91 marked the point at which the colonial state began to impose itself on the established dominion of the dead. By 1893, at least six further public cemeteries had been created in coastal towns, while existing Christian mission graveyards as well as the private burial grounds of Akan office-holders had begun to be brought under the remit of the ordinance.[65] The extension of the bureaucratic regime of biopower into the interior of the colony and the full registration of births and deaths would unfold over many decades. In its wake would come an era of exhumation, as mortal remains were again on the move in order to fit into the reordered necrogeographies of town and country. One relocation in Accra had particular resonance: in 1912, fifty-four years after his death—and a decade after that of Taki Tawia had signalled a radical shift in the burial of chiefs—the bones of James Bannerman were exhumed from their resting place under the late Yaa Hom's residence, placed in a miniature coffin draped with a Union Jack and solemnly reinterred in the Wesleyan cemetery.[66]

Despite the imposition of colonial biopower, we have also seen how the transition from the old to the new burial regime was shaped by changing sentiments and debates within coastal society. The emergence of a literate Christian elite gave rise to an improving Victorian reformism which viewed extravagant funeral customs and intramural sepulture as best consigned to a pagan past. As the *Western Echo*'s eulogy for the restful repose on offer in ordered garden cemeteries indicates, neither was this reformist imperative limited to ethnic outsiders such as the controversial campaigning physician J. F. Easmon. Let us end with a reflection by the lawyer and pioneering nationalist J. E. Casely Hayford, which further underlines the ways in which the Victorian cemetery became, to borrow Laqueur's term, a 'new place of sentiment'. 'I shall not soon forget a scene I witnessed in a grave-yard on the Gold Coast not so long ago', Casely Hayford wrote.

> A widow had lost her only son, whom I knew. He had belonged to a friendly society, and at his burial the 'brethren' had brought flowers for the bier. A few days afterwards I noticed this woman come to the grave of her son, who had belonged to the Church, with the usual food and drink for the dead. But she had brought something else—a bunch of flowers. Surely her son would want flowers—would like them. I saw her—a simple native woman, who, probably, in all her life had never loitered by the wayside to wonder at God's simply daisy—amidst her tears, gently place the flowers upon her son's grave.[67]

13

Ghosts and Vile Bodies

IN JANUARY 1896, a British expeditionary force marched unopposed from the Gold Coast Colony to Kumasi, arrested Asantehene Agyeman Prempeh and brought Asante under British 'protection'. Empowered to exercise civil and criminal jurisdiction but wishing to interfere as little as possible in the day-to-day affairs of Asante's constituent kingdoms, the British Resident Captain Stewart hurriedly constructed a rudimentary administration, appointing a three-man Native Committee to assist in the governance of Kumasi and directing that, with the exception of cases of murder, the regional *amanhene* were to continue to dispense justice via their established tribunals. By the start of 1897, two colonial courts had been established, one presided over by the Resident himself and the other by Kumasi's cantonment magistrate. It is the inaugural session of the latter that concerns us here, as the opening case involved the suspected murder of a pregnant woman, named Abena Baidu, and the brutal treatment of her corpse. For, as we have seen, death during pregnancy or in childbirth was categorized by the Akan as *atofowu*, a transgressive or blasphemous death. In such an event, the corpse was 'thrown away' without a funeral; not to do so was deemed a taboo (*akyiwadie*) of the worst kind, a so-called red taboo (*yekyi kokokoko*), violation of which defiled the entire nation.[1] Like the putrefying remains of unburied slaves, criminals and debtors, it became a vile body: *ebin*, filth. The spirit of the deceased, meanwhile, was also destined to become something nasty: an *otofo* (pl. *atofo*), an unworthy, restless ghost, cast out from the cosmic community of the living, the dead and the unborn. At the very moment that colonial law first began to take shape in Asante, it sought to intervene in fundamental understandings of the dominion of the dead.

Abena Baidu was a wife of Pong Yaw, noted in the court record as 'King of Wam' but actually the *omanhene* of Domaa, a state on the northwestern frontier of Asante of which the town of Wam was part.² Pong Yaw and his fellow defendants testified that Abena had died two years before from a chest infection; according to a deposition made by her brother on which the prosecution was based, however, she had been executed after a charge of adultery just three months earlier—subsequent, that is, to the imposition of British rule. Pong Yaw and his notables were therefore on trial for murder. One thing on which both parties did agree was that, because Abena was pregnant at the time of her death, her body had been cut open and the unborn foetus removed. Prosecution witnesses further testified—although this was denied by the defendants—that the foetus was then burnt. 'The native custom is that when any woman dies in pregnancy the Child is taken from the abdomen and buried separately', one of Pong Yaw's representatives explained. 'They made funeral custom all over the town and the king went in mourning', he continued, striving to demonstrate that Abena, as a royal wife, was still accorded some form of funeral rite. Two of her fellow wives, however, refuted this. Like Abena, they were slaves originating from nearby Berekum who as children had been captured during secessionist fighting in the region in the 1870s. They testified that they had been made to witness Abena's execution 'as a warning' and that her body was indeed disposed of without interment.

Unable to arrive at any definitive account of what transpired, the magistrate returned a verdict of not guilty—although Pong Yaw was back in court the following year, charged this time with permitting human sacrifices after the imposition of British rule. Both prosecutions demonstrate the way in which the expanding colonial state moved swiftly to confiscate from African officeholders their sovereignty over life and death, a process which had been underway on the Gold Coast for a good part of the nineteenth century. The focus of the chapter, however, is less on the colonial appropriation of capital punishment than on understandings of *atofowu*, and on the result of such blasphemous death: the lingering presence of *atofo*, or 'ghosts'. If, as Clive Seale has argued, revenants are manifestations of a social presence outlasting the body and their propensity to haunt the living 'a good indicator of the degree to which death is disruptive of the social order', then histories of haunting and of spectrality in the Akan world need to be taken seriously.³

In terms of physical space, we return to the *kurotia* (or, for the Ga, *husunaa*), the melancholy liminal zone on the outskirts of settlements which was a dumping-ground for vile bodies: the corpses of unloved slaves, executed criminals and those deviants, like the unfortunate Abena Baidu, whose lives were terminated by various forms of *atofowu*, or 'bad death'. Writing in the 1930s of the Ga seaside town of Labadi, Field made vivid the fearful aspect of these zones:

> The accursed grove, the burial place of these dead women, is on the north side of the town and is a much dreaded spot. A waterhole not far away is believed to be haunted by these restless and wretched dead. These ghosts may be seen, I am told, in broad daylight looking just like living people, washing their clothes and the small clothes of their dead infants. The mere sight of them in the distance brings on a severe headache and fever; to meet them at close quarters is to be belaboured with blows by them and nearly thrashed to death.[4]

This identifies a key attribute of the ghostly dead: their sheer ordinariness. Like the *dybbuk* of Jewish folklore, it was the *atofo*'s likeness to the living that made them so unsettling; one way of identifying them, Field noted, was the shrill, nasal speech with which they communicated with each other.[5] A typical encounter, from the 1750s, involved a Cape Coast *caboceer* passing and waving to an acquaintance on the seashore, only to find when he arrived in town that the man had recently been decapitated.[6]

We need too to recall the fundamental distinction between a good death (Twi: *owu pa*) and a bad death (*owu bone*), as well as the traumatic impact that the latter could have on the living. Eva Meyerowitz's inquiries into these matters in the Bono kingdom of Takyiman in the 1940s are revealing. Death during pregnancy or childbirth, Meyerowitz was told, was one of the five categories of death that in Takyiman had been allotted particular funeral rites by the ancient queen mother Kurono Kese. Those who died from *abodwewu*, 'natural' death, or from *nsramuwu*, death in battle, were accorded full funeral customs. The three other categories were all *owu bone*:

> *Anwobawu*—death of a childless woman or man. Anyone who dies without issue had failed his or her life on earth: 'the barren have no face in the Other World (*asaman*)'. The corpse was therefore washed outside the house, and a ball of pepper pushed into the corpse's rectum. In the case of a woman, the husband paid for the funeral expenses.
> *Atofowu*—the death of a transgressor, which included suicide, death by leprosy and accidental deaths by lightening, earthquake, drowning,

and so forth, which were regarded as a punishment for sin. The body was not to be brought home; and had to be buried unwashed, and without any rites—unless the deceased held an important position.
Amumuwu—a woman's death during pregnancy or childbirth, or in consequence of an abortion or still birth. The corpse was buried unwashed and sitting on a chair (*akentendwa*). Nobody might weep for her, because this sort of death was also regarded as a punishment for sin. The dead child or foetus had to be buried, unwashed, in an old cooking pot.[7]

One aspect of this list of accursed deaths is its extensive character—although it can be taken neither as definitive in its classification nor as comprehensive. Meyerowitz's informants, headed by Takyimanhemaa Nana Afua Abrafi, allotted death during pregnancy or childbirth its own category: *amumuwu* (from *omumo*: bad, evil or ugly), although other sources tend to associate it with the concept of *atofowu*, with which it clearly overlapped. To the list of 'accidental' deaths classed as *atofowu* can be added those caused by wild animals, particularly snake-bite, and by falling trees.[8] There was also a temporal dimension to transgressive death, in that anyone who died, for any reason, during the great yearly festivals such as Odwira or the Ga Homowo were denied—at least temporarily—burial and funeral rites. Neither does the Takyiman list mention witchcraft (*bayi*), although the bodies of those identified as *abayifo* would also invariably be cast away. A posthumous conviction of witchcraft could also lead to a corpse being disinterred and punished. 'Natives who have been prematurely cut off, either from the inroads of some occasional epidemic, or the ordinary maladies of the season, are frequently supposed to become endowed with the potent prerogative of generating disease and destroying life', Daniell observed in Accra in the 1840s. When two or three family members died in quick succession, it was common 'to attribute their departure to the agency of the first . . . the corpses of which . . . are summarily removed from their houses . . . ignominiously burned on the outskirts of town, and their ashes scattered to the winds, amid the mingled groans and execrations of the populace'.[9] Even the bodies of those who were themselves believed to have been the innocent *victims* of witchcraft, sorcery or curses might be treated in the same fashion. This is evident from an episode in the Asante village of Adeebeba in 1875, when a young woman named Yaa Kuruboaa was said to have died as a result of an evil curse (*nnome*) laid upon her. 'Custom in such a case ordained that the body should be "thrown away somewhere" (*too gu*) without any funeral rites being performed', writes McCaskie. Yaa's mother Adwowaa Bemba pleaded for her body to be buried properly, 'but the community had already disposed of the corpse so as to protect the village'.[10]

The imperative to protect human culture was the overriding concern of the living at such moments of acute spiritual vulnerability. With the exception of elderly, contented individuals whose tranquil demise accorded clearly with the notion of *owu pa*, the recently dead were always angry—particularly when their allotted time on earth was cut short by sudden or violent misfortune. Why, then, risk making the hostile dead even more angry by denying their bodies proper interment and therefore preventing their departure from the known world? One reason was that the corpses of transgressors presented a more immediate and life-threatening danger if they were not summarily disposed of. This danger was discussed in the judicial assessor's court in 1858, when a group of men from Winneba were charged with dismembering and burning the corpse of a woman named Ambah Edusurabah, who had been suffering from leprosy.[11] The episode took place on the seashore, a ritually charged space which in coastal towns represented an extension of the *kurotia* and where the bodies of slaves and the accursed dead were also disposed of. 'The country people entertain the belief that in the event of a person dying of a malignant and incurable disease the complaint of which the party dies will be communicated to the relatives unless the body is dismembered and destroyed by fire', it was explained to the court. If the corpse was buried, 'the disease would rise from the ground'. The judicial assessor recommended no action, on the grounds that the barbarity of the custom was mitigated by the family's 'kindness to their relative while labouring for years under a loathsome disease . . . and their attempts to relieve and cure her of the complaint was highly commendable'. Two generations later, by which time the colonial state had outlawed such dismemberment of corpses, leprosy was still regarded as the most fearsome of all maladies, 'so dreaded', T. E. Kyei recalled from his Asante childhood, 'that its name, *kwata*, was not to be mentioned to the hearing of anybody'. It was 'talked of as a "bad" disease (*yare bone*) and so its victim was not given the normal funeral, but was buried in an anthill to prevent his/her reincarnation into the *abusua* (lineage)'.[12]

Kyei identifies here a second reason for the denial of proper burial and funeral rites to the transgressive dead: it barred them from being reincarnated either in a later generation or, in the case of infants or children, as the next born. While it was desirable for the spirit of a revered predecessor to be reborn in a new generation, it was imperative to prevent that possibility in the case of an individual whose life was deemed to have been less than a success. Weakness and misfortune, that is to say, would be replicated, as explained bluntly by Field with respect to suicides: 'the reincarnation of a suicide is not desired, for it will again end in suicide. The suicide is therefore not mourned'.[13] The result, however, was that a suicide might return as a particularly fearsome revenant, an *osaman twentwen*, in Kyei's translation an 'evil haunting ghost', or, according to Rattray—perhaps because in Asante suicides were often posthumously tried and decapitated—'a ghost wandering about in search of its head'.[14]

The same held for deceased infants and young children, who it was believed would be encouraged by ostentatious mourning to reappear as the next born—only to die once again prematurely.[15] It is with regard to the death of the newborn that we can perhaps best observe the ways in which reflexive human grief was shaped by culture. As was common in many societies before the advent of twentieth-century biomedicine and midwifery practices reduced historically high levels of infant mortality, the newborn were regarded not as humans but as sprites only partly removed from the spirit world. 'When a child is born in this world, a ghost-mother mourns the loss of her child in the *samandow*', Rattray explained—and that grieving ghost-mother was believed to want her child back.[16] Elaborate lengths were therefore gone to in the first week of an infant's life to fool the ghost-mother into thinking that the living family could not care less about its survival: 'it is given any kind of old mat or old rag to lie upon; it is not addressed in any endearing terms; water or pap, if given to it, is administered out of an old banana skin or ground-nut husk'. 'Should the infant die before the eighth day', Rattray continues, 'the attitude of suspicion and distrust, which one notes struggling with maternal love, turns to genuine anger. The little body is whipped (sometimes mutilated by having a finger cut off); it is wrapped in sharp cutting spear-grass . . . ; is placed in a pot and buried in the village midden heap, which was formerly also the women's latrine'.[17] Such sprites who returned from whence they came were therefore known as *nkuku mma* (sing. *nkuku ba*), 'pot children'. More ritual action followed, as the family attempted further 'to disgrace the "ghost child" and thus to deter its "ghost mother" from sending it down [again] to earth where she had no intention it should remain'.[18]

The attempt to deceive death was even more prolonged when two or more infants died in succession. In such instances, an elaborate subterfuge was mounted in an attempt to convince the denizens of the spirit realm that the next born was of no worth whatsoever. Among both the Akan and the Ga, the infant was given a 'horrible name': the most common was *donko* (a slave from the north), but other examples were *asaseasa* ('there is no ground left [to bury you in]'), *yempew* ('we don't want you'), *sumina* (midden, or rubbish heap) or, as reported in 1823, 'that of some ferocious animal'.[19] In time, scarification resembling that of *nnonkofo* slaves was cut into the child's face and their hair was left to grow into shaggy dreadlocks, hung with protective amulets. These children were known by the Akan as *begyina mma* ('come-and-stay children') and by the Ga as *gbobalo*; their high visibility in communities into the early twentieth century was evidence of the persistence of high levels of infant mortality. 'I saw one little girl *Gbobalo* wearing a necklace of fishes' vertebrae instead of beads, "because they are ugly"', Field observed in the 1930s.[20] As for deceased older children, Rattray thought that in precolonial Asante they too were classified as *nkuku mma* and disposed of on the village midden. Evidence for this, however, is sketchy: it seems not to have been the case by the time he was writing in the 1920s, while nineteenth-century sources indicate that clan burial grounds might include a corner reserved for the bodies of prepubescent children. When in 1869 the Basel missionary Friedrich Ramseyer and his wife lost their own infant child—an event which caused considerable consternation on the part of their Asante captors—they interred the body in a shady grove of banana trees, noting that this was 'the usual burying-place for children'.[21]

From a structural perspective, death in childbirth was seen as a horrific conflation of birth and death, *awo* and *owu*. But as the categories of bad death recorded in Takyiman indicate, such a demise was more readily explained by some sinful action on the part of the deceased. In the case of pregnant women, in particular, the ideology of human increase can be seen to have overwhelmed 'natural' grief. Maternal mortality levels, like those for infants, were also historically high. 'Not a few Negresses die in childbirth', Monrad observed. 'If this happens before the birth is completed, they are . . . thrown out into the bush, to be devoured by wild animals. They have not, according to the Negroes' concepts, fulfilled their true purpose, to give birth to children . . . It even brings disgrace upon the family . . . and, if one does not wish to insult them, one never mentions that fact in their presence.'[22] 'When a pregnant woman dies she is considered the virtual murderer of her child', Field confirmed, a century later.[23] Likewise, when a woman who died in childbirth was shown to have committed adultery during her pregnancy, the man involved was regarded as having murdered the child. The *ntoro* of the adulterer and that of the husband were believed to meet in the body of the woman, Meyerowitz was told, causing 'a miscarriage, a still-birth, or her own death in childbirth'.[24] Such

FIGURE 13.1. Fooling death. A *begyina ba*, or 'come-and-stay child', photographed by R. S. Rattray in Agona, in Asante. Pitt Rivers Museum, University of Oxford, 1998.312.459.1.

an incident resulted in a conflict between two towns in 1913, when the alleged adulterer was told by his accusers that 'if we [still] had the power in Ashanti, we would kill you'.[25] Consider too this evocative description by Rattray from the 1920s:

> It is considered a great disgrace for a woman to die in childbirth. All pregnant women in the particular village go and cut a budding plantain leaf, entering the compound where the body is lying, point the shoot at the corpse, saying: '*Poom! fa wo musuo ko, wantumi anwo, wantumi anko, wa ko ato.*' 'Bang! (imitating a gun) begone with your evil, you have been unable to bring forth, you have been unable to fight, you have fought only to die.' The woman who told me the above spoke in a whisper, at the same time snapping her fingers about her ears 'lest any pregnant woman should hear her words'.[26]

Childbirth, that is, was equated with warfare—albeit with attrition rates far in excess of any but the worst battlefield.

Abuse of the corpses of those who died a childless death, *anwobawu*, was dictated by the same fierce ideology. The placing of a ball of hot pepper into the rectum in Takyiman can be seen as the antithesis of the insertion of 'cool' silver dust into the orifices of queen mothers, although Rattray records that the more common practice was to drive large thorns called *pammewuo* (lit. 'link me with death') into the soles of the feet. Again, the motive was to prevent the reincarnation of the infertile: 'at the same time the corpse was addressed with these words, "*Wonwo, 'ba, mma sa bio*" ("You have not begotten . . . a child; do not return again like that")'.[27]

These ethnographic insights are crucial to an understanding of why certain forms of death were transgressive and how they were dealt with. But let us turn to the historical record to get a sense of what happened after such abominations, when the living had to contend with the angry dead. A number of early accounts of the Gold Coast note widespread apprehension about malevolent ghosts, although references are too fragmented to enable any clear sense of historical change in the nature of haunting. Only in the late nineteenth century did members of the literate African elite begin to reflect on an issue that from the eighteenth century had marked a turning point in the cultural history of ghosts in western Europe—that is, whether such spectres were physical apparitions or phantasmic imaginings of the mind's eye.[28] Before that point, there can be little doubt that ghosts were regarded as 'real', revenants from the supernatural realm. 'In their imagination the Africans see spirits, ghosts and supernatural beings everywhere at night', Monrad typically commented—although his description of vampiric shape-shifters which 'in fiery forms . . . suck blood from people, make them ill, and bring about an early death' is identifiably that of *abayifo*, or 'witches'.[29] Bosman is more specific in identifying the spirits of the dead among the host of nocturnal spectres: 'They steadfastly believe the Apparition of Spirits and Ghosts, and that they frequently disturb and terrifie some People: So that when any, but more especially any considerable Person dyes, they perplex one another with horrid Fears, proceeding from an Opinion that he appears for several nights successively near his late Dwelling.'[30]

Given the generalized trauma occasioned by the demise of powerful officeholders, it is unsurprising to see in Bosman's description the imprint of political power on levels of anxiety about the lingering dead. Observing the full sequence of funeral rites was, under normal circumstances, regarded as sufficient to remove these fearsome spirits to *asamando*. When such rites were either neglected or deliberately denied, however, their presence continued to be felt, as Bowdich made clear: 'Those whose enormities nullify the mediation of the funeral custom, or, whom neglect or circumstances might have deprived of it, are doomed, in the imagination of others, to haunt the gloom of the forest, stealing occasionally to their former abodes in rare but lingering visits. Those who have neglected the custom, or funeral rites of their family, are thought to be accursed and troubled by their spirits'.[31] Bowdich's wife, Sarah, reported such a visitation from the spirit of a deceased Cape Coast trader whose family had skimped on his funeral custom. 'I had not a servant that would venture a dozen yards from the door after dark for fear of meeting the indignant ghost', Sarah wrote, and such was the public disquiet that the family was forced to disinter the corpse and conduct the funeral over again in order 'to pay proper respect to his remains'.[32] Monrad recorded a similar haunting a decade earlier in the town of Ningo, to the east of Accra, involving the spirit of a rich man who in life 'never treated others but brooded over his own wealth'. After this man's death—the implication being that his passing was not greatly mourned—'he appeared every night in the cottage of his surviving brother, complaining that he was not comfortable enough where he was, and asked that [the brother] hold a more costly ceremony for his funeral'. This demand was acceded to, 'and the deceased found peace'.[33]

It was not simply that the powerful possessed the most fearsome aspect when dead, but also that those in positions of authority were regarded as being particularly vulnerable to attack from hostile ghosts. That haunting element was identified, in the broadest terms, as *sasa*. 'The remorse that might drive the murderer in this country [i.e., Britain] to confession or to suicide', Rattray explained, 'the Ashanti would explain at once as the operation of the *sasa* of the murdered man upon his murderer'.[34] Chiefs and their executioners, therefore, went to elaborate lengths to protect themselves from the *sasa* of those whose deaths they were responsible for: their most formidable prophylactic in Asante was the *gyabom*, the *suman* produced during executions and at key points of the ritual calendar in order to drive away 'evilly disposed disembodied human spirits'.[35] It was the action of such a vengeful spirit that forced

Dwabenhemaa Sewaa to seek medical help from the visiting Methodist missionaries Freeman and Brooking in 1842. The old queen mother, Brooking was told, had 'once killed a woman with her own hands with whom her husband had committed adultery' and 'it is said that almost at the same instant the pain in her little finger was felt occasioned by the spirit of the departed woman which has never ceased to trouble her'.[36]

Monrad's anecdote from Ningo provides a glimpse of the ways in which kinship and personality shaped collisions between the living and the dead. Yet it is only in the rare instances when the historical record is rich enough to yield the inner workings of families that ghostly encounter can be subjected to a degree of interpretation beyond generic reportage of visitations by the troublesome dead. One such family is the Oyoko Kokoo *abusua*, the ruling dynasty of Asante. We have already seen how in 1804 Asantehene Opoku Fofie was believed to have died at the hands of his deceased predecessor Osei Kwame, an event followed by a concerted effort to banish the latter's vengeful *sasa* or *osaman twentwen*. Half a century later, the Oyoko dynasty would again be convulsed by fratricidal psychic drama and spectral visitation, this time involving Asantehene Kwaku Dua Panin and the ghost of his uterine sister, Asantehemaa Afua Sapon. In common with domestic disputes at all levels of the social strata, the matter was regarded as *afisem* (lit. a 'household matter', a family secret), but such was its gravity that it came to be known, and alluded to in the most circumspect terms, by the strict avoidance metaphor of *konnurokusem* (a vile or despicable matter). As *afisem*, the events of 1859 are virtually invisible in Asante oral histories. Two fugitive written sources, however, provide crucial evidence for what could not openly be spoken of: one an account in Charles Bannerman's *West African Herald* and another by the Basel Mission agent Rev. N. V. Asare, who was stationed in Kumasi throughout the first decade of the twentieth century.[37]

The dynastic genealogies, relationships and tensions leading to the *konnurokusem* of 1859 are of great complexity.[38] In short, Afua Sapon and her son and heir apparent to the Golden Stool, Osei Kwadwo, were suspected by Kwaku Dua of plotting to overthrow him. Their plot uncovered, the two were stripped of office, banished and, amid a large-scale slaughter of suspected accomplices, were themselves executed. Of concern to us is what happened eight years later, as the Asantehene lay on his deathbed. 'King Kwaku Dua lived to a great old age before passing away', Asare wrote. 'Allegedly, during his final illness, he was haunted by the ghosts of those relatives he had eliminated as a result of spurious litigation. Consequently, several sheep were slaughtered in propitiation. But as a result, he did not die peacefully.'[39]

In itself, the description of the dying Kwaku Dua Panin being tormented by the ghosts of his sister and nephew is as bald as that by Monrad of the haunting at Ningo. In both cases, propitiation was attempted: successfully in Ningo ('the deceased found peace'), unsuccessfully in Kumasi ('he did not die peacefully'). Thanks in part to Asare, however, we know something of the back story to this deathbed visitation. The *konnurokusem*, his Asante informants told him, was cunningly engineered by Afua Sapon's own daughter Afua Kobi, who, in shocking contravention of kinship norms, drove a wedge between Kwaku Dua and his sister in order to have one of her own sons replace Osei Kwadwo as the heir apparent. Kwaku Dua and Afua Sapon had been very close: they were each other's only surviving sibling and the latter had cared for her younger brother in trying political circumstances after the death of their mother. On the death of Asantehene Osei Yaw in 1834, moreover, Afua Sapon, as Asantehemaa, had supported Kwaku Dua's elevation to the Golden Stool, despite concerns that his father was of relatively modest birth. Kwaku Dua, the *West African Herald* reported, 'felt all through life that his birth was the subject of uncomplimentary remark' by his opponents—including, at times, his own sister, whose father was of the highest rank and 'was also accustomed to indulge in sarcastic remarks in reference to the low birth of Quaku Duah's father'.[40] These insinuations, McCaskie postulates, shaped Kwaku Dua's personhood as well as the autocratic and often ruthless nature of his regime. They may also have made him susceptible to the machinations of Afua Kobi. 'Afua Kobi decided to alienate Kwaku Dua and the Kumasi elders from her mother Afua Sapon and her brother Osei Kwadwo by accusing them of attempting to bewitch the king', Asare recounted. 'She further supported her allegation by adding that the queenmother was in the habit of speaking against the king and cursing him because she claimed that although she had been instrumental in his appointment to the stool he was not providing for her. Therefore she [Afua Sapon] wished he were dead so that her own son could ascend the stool. Afua Kobi claimed to be very disturbed by all this.'[41]

In the face of mounting evidence, Kwaku Dua was persuaded to have his sister and her son tried in open court, where they were found guilty of conspiring against him through the use of witchcraft (*bayi*) and curses (*nnome*). Both were exiled from Kumasi to the village of Aboboaso, where they remained until Kwaku Dua acted decisively to remove them as a threat. Asare reports the matter with economy: 'While residing there, they were eliminated one night'. A fuller account of their end, and one which confirms the subsequent anguish felt by Kwaku Dua, came to the ears of the captive missionaries

Ramseyer and Kühne in the early 1870s: 'It is said that in a moment of excitement, Kwakoo Dooah once sent to his sister a silken band, with a message to the effect, that the best thing she could do was to hang herself. She accepted the brotherly suggestion, and committed suicide. . . . It is said that in his last days Kwakoo deeply regretted his conduct towards her'.[42] Kwaku Dua Panin came to realize that he may have made a ghastly miscalculation. He grew to loathe Afua Kobi and set about eliminating those who had played a key role in the case. When asked to exercise clemency in legal matters, he was given to retort: 'Kumasi elders, if you understand the subject under consideration why then didn't you plead for mitigation when I had a dispute within my own family, and thereby lost my relatives'.[43]

In March 1867, approaching the age of 70, Kwaku Dua suddenly took ill, reportedly fainting in his palanquin after a visit to the *asamanpow* (grove of the dead) to attend to his departed predecessors. He rallied sufficiently to be able to resume some official duties, on 26 April presiding over the one-year funeral celebration of a late royal and the following morning paying a visit—quite possibly to offer a final valediction to his ancestors—to the Bantama mausoleum. His condition again deteriorated and he died around midnight on 27 April.[44] What form did the ghosts of his departed sister and nephew take? Did they manifest as spectral visitations, or haunt his mind's eye as he entered the murky borderland between life and death? Our sources do not elaborate further; neither can we be certain how they might have been categorized by the dying Asantehene and those tending him. McCaskie suggests that they were *asamanfoo*, but as the spirits of a suicide and an executed criminal, might they not have been something more vindictive and more terrifying: *sasa*, *atofo* or *asamanfoo twentwen*, 'evil haunting ghosts'? Were Afua Sapon and Osei Kwadwo accorded proper funeral rites in order to neutralize their potentially hostile posthumous presence? As royals, quite possibly: the categories of death from Takyiman indicate that *atofowu* demanded the summary disposal of the corpse—unless, that is, 'the deceased held an important position'. One thing does seem clear: that after thirty-three years on the Golden Stool, dying at an advanced age in his own bed and leaving behind an enormous progeny and a kingdom in sound financial and political order, Kwaku Dua can be seen to have died an exemplary death, *owu pa*. Yet as a person rather than as a king, haunted as the darkness drew in by the psychic legacy of his own fratricidal violence, he signally failed to achieve the ideal of *abodwewu*, a death characterized by inner tranquillity and contentedness at a life well lived.

Let us return to the late nineteenth century, when the Victorian civilizing mission confronted African practices governing the mortal remains of the transgressive dead. In Asante from the late 1890s, that encounter was largely one between the colonial state and the collective upholders of custom. As we have seen in the previous chapter, however, the demand for intervention into mortuary affairs in the towns of the Gold Coast also came from a reformist African elite. In 1877, the *African Times* published a series of letters from Accra revealing the horrors occasioned by death during pregnancy and insisting on stern action against the corrupt 'fetish priests' seen to benefit from it.[45] These were the *wulomo* (male ritual specialist) and *woyo* (female spirit medium) of the Ga goddess of childbirth, Naa Dede Oyeadu, whose task it was to conduct the purification rites after the disposal of the corpse in the bush on the edge of town. Aside from the treatment of dead bodies, what aroused the ire of the correspondents was that the entire household of the deceased was deemed to be unclean for a period of twenty-four days and prevented by public derision from venturing outdoors. The deceased's property, moreover, was confiscated by the *wulomo* in order to pay for the purification. Both the local African elite itself and the British administration were deemed to be culpable. 'This evil custom is but too well known of by the educated natives of Accra, men who think themselves better than the other classes', one letter ran. 'Do these scholars patronize civilization and colonization as Lagos and Sierra Leone did? I answer they do not.'[46]

Like intramural sepulture, deviant burial (and the punishment of corpses) was seen to have no place in the envisaged ordered modernity of the colonial city. 'Now that Accra has become the chief seat of British government', the *African Times* railed, 'this, and kindred fetish abominations ... can no longer be overlooked and winked at ... We call upon the Executive to cleanse this fetish Augean stable without further delay.'[47] The British administration, however, was generally reluctant to intervene in matters of African religious faith, and it was not until 1905 that it moved finally to suppress the Naa Dede Oyeadu cult in Accra. Such caution was even more pronounced in the rural hinterland, where the inchoate ideology of indirect rule held that collaborating chiefs were to remain responsible for native custom—as long as that custom was deemed not to be repugnant to 'civilized values'. These debates re-emerged in the early 1890s, as the colonial state gradually extended its authority in the forest kingdoms on the frontiers of the Gold Coast Colony. Again, the issue at hand was the disposal of the corpses of *atofo* and, again, the protagonists represented a complex array of interest groups: chiefs, priests, colonial officials, literate African elites and Christian missionaries.[48]

The setting was the western reaches of the Akyem region, where in the course of the previous generation two heterodox religious movements had made their presence felt. One was the Basel Mission church and the other the cult of the indigenous *obosom* Katawere. The origins of Katawere are obscure, but the deity seems to have been gaining adherents on the grounds that it protected against the existential threat posed by *bayi*, 'witchcraft'. In a pattern which would recur in subsequent healing movements, individuals who had not joined the cult in communities where it became established and who then died were identified as *abayifo* killed by Katawere. Such a death was regarded as *atofowu*. 'Kotoku is a stronghold of fetishism where all the crimes of heathenism are committed without restraint', the Basel missionary Wilhelm Rottman alerted the British government in 1891. 'Now and then it happens that when a person dies the priest of Katawere [says] . . . openly "the man has been killed by the fetish Katawere". In such a case the corpse is . . . wrapped into leaves of plantains and thrown into the forest.'[49] At one Akyem Kotoku town, Rottman added, the presiding *okomfo* 'threatened the people saying that everyone becoming a Christian will be killed by Katawere'. In an accusation which would come to characterize opposition to later anti-witchcraft cults, he also suspected the priests of themselves poisoning victims, motivated by the custom that they had the right—as in the case of Naa Dede Oyeadu—to confiscate the deceased's property. British officials who investigated the matter thought this not to be the case, but, finding that corpses were indeed thrown into the bush, asked Akyem Kotokuhene Ata Fua and Akyem Bosomehene Kofi Ahinkora to ensure that all their deceased subjects were decently interred.

Two years later, Katawere continued to flourish. In 1893, Commissioner H. M. Hull was dispatched to Akyem to determine whether the cult possessed the power of life and death; if so, it was deemed imperative 'to break the power of the Fetish and disperse the Priests'.[50] On the outskirts of Swedru, the capital of Akyem Bosome, Hull was taken to a 'fetish grove' (i.e., *asamanpow*) containing some two hundred human skulls and other remains: it looked, he wrote, 'like one of Gustave Doré's ghastly illustrations not a living fact'.[51] Believing the deceased to have been murdered, he ordered that the remains be buried and recommended that Katawere be proscribed. In January 1894 the cult was banned under the provisions of the 1892 Native Customs Ordinance and the following year a military detachment under Captain Stewart—soon to be appointed as Resident in Kumasi—completed its suppression with the destruction of various sacred groves and the arrest of the chief *okomfo*, Kwamin Asare. Despite Stewart's assertion that 'there is no doubt that plenty of poisoning went on', the attorney-general found that there was no evidence to bring criminal proceedings against Asare, who therefore could be detained as a political prisoner only. The episode took a further turn when Asare sought legal representation from the Accra advocate Edmund Bannerman (the late Charles's younger brother) and his son the barrister C. J. Bannerman, who in May 1896 applied for a writ of habeas corpus on behalf of the *okomfo*. In June, Asare stood trial on the vague charge of 'practising witchcraft'; after his acquittal, the Bannermans lodged a claim for £500 in damages for false imprisonment and petitioned the secretary of state for the colonies on the matter.[52]

The rise and fall of Katawere was the precursor for a wave of healing movements which between 1900 and 1950 would sweep through the Akan forest and the Gold Coast. Responding to a popular perception that escalating levels of mortality were the result of new, virulent forms of *bayi*, these cults fought back by mobilizing exotic ritual powers either to cure or to eliminate witches. The posthumous punishment meted out to the mortal remains of those believed to have been killed by these protective deities would remain a concern for the colonial administration. The debate over Katawere, moreover, complicates the antipathy that members of Accra's literate elite expressed towards the non-burial of corpses two decades earlier. It was not that figures like Edmund and C. J. Bannerman had much sympathy for such ritual practices—but they were concerned that any British action against African custom should proceed within the rule of colonial law.[53] Neither can we assume a unity of thought on these matters between the Christian missions and the colonial regime. Woven through the controversy over Katawere in Akyem Kotoku was a dispute between the kingdom's powerful *omanhene* Ata Fua and local agents of the Basel Mission, who, as in neighbouring Akyem Abuakwa, were encouraging local converts to remove themselves from the legal jurisdiction of the former on the grounds that any action would involve them swearing a 'fetish oath'. More concerned with maintaining law and order than promoting conversion, the administration supported Ata Fua, firmly reminding the mission that 'the adoption of the Christian religion does not free [converts] from the operation of the Native laws'.[54] Dependent on the active collaboration of African rulers, the government was neither willing nor able to monitor, let alone to transform, the local ritual realm. Two generations later, Field reported that foetuses continued to be removed from the bodies of women who died in childbirth. If Christian, the two bodies were interred in the mission cemetery, 'but there was no mourning or crying'; if not, they were still cast into the forest 'or—a more modern custom—buried in a special cemetery for "bad deaths"... called the *atofodai*'.[55]

If among the Akan and their neighbours the dominion of the dead weighed heavily on that of the living, then the burden was most onerous when the frontier between the two realms was traversed by revenants. Even consecrated ancestors, comfortably ensconced in the afterlife, were capricious and moody, requiring careful propitiation and regarded with a mixture of affection and wariness. *Atofo*, lost souls excluded for their sins and failures from the ongoing project of humanity, were regarded more unambiguously as vindictive and dangerous. Carrying into the afterlife the strong impulse among the living to secure vengeance when wronged by enemies, they sought to harm those who had rejected them by casting their mortal remains away. *Atofo*, that is, were the stereotypical vengeful ghosts. As in other societies where the intimate engagement of hallowed ancestors with the affairs of the living gave rise to highly elaborated mortuary cultures and respect for mortal remains, those deemed to have transgressed fundamental norms were treated with violence and disdain. Like intramural burial, this profane treatment of the corpses of the transgressive dead offended the Victorian sensibilities of the colonial civilizing mission, which sought, in fits and starts, to reform what were deemed to be such barbaric practices. The extent to which these efforts modified local understandings of ghosts, however, is unclear. Colonial-era ethnography indicates that the fear of spectral visitations continued to be widespread and that changes in custom, such as the creation of *atofodai* noted by Field, were ones of degree rather than of kind. Despite colonial legislation, modern rationalism and the spread of Christianity, the world remained far from disenchanted and the living continued to be haunted by the presence of the dead.[56]

Yet there are hints too of a reluctance to abandon the evil dead to their prescribed fate. Whether owing to reflexive human grief or to fears about the capacity of *atofo* to secure post-mortem vengeance, the bereaved sometimes sought to circumvent customary procedure with regard to the expulsion of vile bodies and souls from the realm of culture. We see these counter-currents in a number of episodes considered here: the claim that Abena Baidu was actually granted a funeral; Adwowaa Bemba's desperate pleas for her daughter's body to be buried properly; the interment of dead infants in a banana grove rather than in the filth of the village midden; the mingling of both 'groans and execrations' noted by Daniell on the disinterment of the corpse of an individual posthumously accused of witchcraft. In the 1880s, Ellis described a moving ceremony for *atofo*, those 'lost' by violent death or by drowning: 'a miniature coffin is made . . . and, in the latter case, is carried to the sea-shore. Rum is scattered on the waves, and the name of the deceased is called aloud three times, the mourners crying at the same time in a harmonious but melancholy chant: "We have sought you but cannot find you"'. If this was not done, Ellis explained, it was feared that 'the *sisa* will come into the dwellings of the neglectful relatives, cause sickness, and disturb them by night'.[57] In his excavations of the middens surrounding Twifo Heman, Bellis unearthed the remains of a woman who died in her thirties, possibly having been executed—but was buried nonetheless with accompanying grave goods: eleven ivory bangles and three pieces of gold jewellery carefully placed in a copper dish at her side.[58] It is notable too that accursed corpses, even when not buried, were often reported to be left propped against termite mounds—which were considered to be gateways into the afterworld. Might such placement be seen as an attempt to afford an otherwise vengeful spirit a back door to posthumous peace? Like *asamanfo*, the legions of *atofo* were all around, lost to the world but still a distinct if flickering cosmic presence, like the Milky Way—in Twi, *atofokwan*, 'the way of ghosts'.[59]

14

Writing and Reading about Death

FOUNDED IN 1874 by James Hutton Brew, the *Gold Coast Times* was the Gold Coast's second African-owned newspaper. Appearing two years after the death of Charles Bannerman and the consequent demise of his pioneering *West African Herald*, the *Times* was published fortnightly at Cape Coast and under Brew's editorship inherited its predecessor's reputation as a champion of African rights, unafraid when necessary to hold the colonial administration to task. We have already seen how the London-based *African Times* emerged in the 1860s as a vehicle for the modernizing aspirations of the anglophone commercial elites of West Africa's trading towns, its letter columns, correspondent reports and editorials demanding cemetery reform and denouncing what were perceived to be obnoxious native mortuary customs. The content of this new print culture, moreover, extended beyond Victorian moralizing to the reportage of everyday matters of life and death. Consider the following items as they appeared in the 'General News' column of just one issue of the *Gold Coast Times* in February 1882:

> A gentleman in Winnebah was a day or two ago very suddenly bereft of two children—a boy and a girl. Both died from unknown causes and apparently on the same day.
> The heathens of Ahkrah recently tried 'to bring to life' a friend who had died in that locality. They surrounded the corpse and performed many curious ceremonies over it.
> In Winnebah, not long since, a woman was severely beaten for failing to cry at a funeral.
> On or about the 11th instant a foul plot was discovered in Annamaboe. A number of people had collected together a quantity of poisonous herbs for the purpose of killing certain residents of the town. Had it not been for the

timely information which fortunately reached the King, who ... ordered the herbs to be thrown away, the object of the plot might have been achieved.

The Government showed its liberality on the death of the King of Acconfie by sending a sum of £10 to his relatives to assist in the defrayal of his funeral expenses. The custom was very grand. All the principal chiefs and their followers, living in the vicinity and adjacent towns took part in the funeral obsequies. The grave of the King was dug in a little plot of ground outside the town of Ebrim, where he died. His remains were not interred until fourteen days after his death; they were placed in an ordinary wooden coffin, which was laid over the grave, but over which no earth was thrown till the expiration of the fourteen days. Around were placed the late monarch's banners, cutlasses, swords, arms, stools and umbrellas; and over the spot was a canopy of red silk—all of which were kept there throughout the whole of the fourteen days; during the period guns were fired frequently and more than 100 small kegs of powder must have been used.

Nearly all the members of the local Temperance Society attended the funeral of the late Miss Adaboo. Each wore a regalia.[1]

These snippets of news are all of historical interest. Some allude to abiding themes in local deathways: the unsettling impact of sudden death; the desperate trauma of grief; the gendered dynamics of mourning; the ubiquitous fear of poison. Others point to innovation: an emerging distinction between 'heathen' and 'modern' practice; the rise of the temperance movement and other new associations in funerary display. Yet what concerns us here is less the content of these nuggets than their collective nature as written texts. Literacy began gradually to expand on the Gold Coast in the mid-nineteenth century: from beginnings in the eighteenth-century 'castle schools' and the households of Euro-African commercial brokers, it received a boost with the consolidation of the Basel and Methodist missions and the establishment of primary schools in their respective zones of influence. While the commercial elite continued to send their favoured sons—and occasionally daughters—to schools in Britain or Sierra Leone, the more grassroots educational programmes of the two missions, together with that of the Bremen Mission in the Ewe-speaking region across the Volta River to the east, began to expand the practice of reading and writing beyond the parlours of European-style 'storey houses' in the principal coastal towns. The result, as on other missionary frontiers in Africa, was the emergence of a local print culture and a fledgling literate public sphere.

The looming presence of death and the dynamics of mortuary cultures were core concerns of this sphere. Oral discourses about death were 'entextualized': detached from their immediate spatial and temporal contexts by being written down and circulated among a reading public.[2] In seeking out news of the dead and dying, those readers opening their copy of the *Gold Coast Times* on 18 February 1882 were engaging in an age-old practice, but in a radical and potentially transformative new way.

This chapter considers the transformation from a culture of speaking about death to one which included writing and reading about death. Its focus is the final quarter of the nineteenth century, from the creation of the British Crown Colony of the Gold Coast in 1874 to its expansion with the formal incorporation of Asante and the savanna hinterland to the north in 1901–2. Our concern is therefore with literacy and print culture as they developed on the Gold Coast littoral, a process which would extend into Asante and beyond only in the twentieth century. The indigenous uses of literacy in the region that would become Ghana were not, however, born of that place and time: written texts in Arabic had long been produced in the kingdoms of the middle Volta savanna, and by the early nineteenth century the Asante government was drawing on the services of clerks able to write in Arabic and in European languages in order to communicate with its neighbours and, as Wilks has argued, to develop a bureaucratic component to the state.[3] On the Gold Coast, too, limited use of the written word had begun to diffuse from the European forts to surrounding communities: the writing of wills by African traders can be dated to the early 1700s, while by the end of that century a handful of indigenous pastors associated with the Danish, Dutch and British forts were producing a variety of written texts which have left a residue in the documentary archive. Yet it was not until the advent of mission education and print technology broadened the reach of the written word that a fledgling reading community along the lines of Habermas's late eighteenth-century European public sphere can be seen on the Gold Coast.[4] This print culture comprised both vernacular African languages and, with the departure of the Dutch in 1872, the language of the remaining colonizing power: English. The former was particularly associated with the Basel Mission, whose European and African agents pioneered the transcription of Ga and Twi as written languages and produced the first vernacular printed texts: prayer books, primers, dictionaries, the gospels and, by the 1860s–70s, compete translations of the Bible.

The Bible, of course, has a great deal to say about mortality and the ends of life. But I wish to concentrate here on a different, secular medium of entextualized discourses about death: newspapers, which, as in Europe, 'accorded mortality new openings'.[5] With the exception of Governor McCarthy's *Gold Coast Gazette* (1822–3) and the Basel Mission's *Christian Messenger*, published from 1883 in various combinations of Twi, Ga and English and still going a century later, the early Gold Coast press was in English only and was mostly owned, edited and written for by scions of the African and Euro-African commercial elite. From the appearance of the *West African Herald* in 1857, it was associated with the aspirations and identities of that class of so-called Victorian gentlemen of colour; Charles Bannerman's father, James, served as lieutenant-governor of the British Gold Coast Protectorate in 1850–51, and Charles and his brothers served as commandants at various British forts and as attorneys in the fledgling colonial courts. From the 1870s, however, a hardening of racial divisions saw the exclusion of Africans from the upper echelons of the colonial administration and, as a more aggressive European imperialism escalated into the Scramble for Africa, the demotion of 'coloured gentlemen' to the hold-all category of 'natives'. It was at this historical moment that the local press began to flourish: first in Cape Coast in the 1880s and then in Accra in the 1890s. It never completely shed its patrician tone—at least, not until the rise of more populist papers in the 1930s—or its disdain for the worst excesses of paganism. Neither, in turn, did the traditional realm of orality abandon a lingering distrust of the written word: at the end of the twentieth century, Kwesi Yankah reports, the Akan still referred to the press as *koowaa krataa*, 'loose-tongued paper'.[6] But in a period when an increasingly racialized European colonialism intersected with the termination of the age-old threat posed by Asante militarism, the coastal press became an important vehicle for an emergent cultural nationalism: an embrace of the idea of 'Africa' and of a modernized African identity.[7] Reportage of and reflection on African deathways, old and new, would be shaped by the nuances of this cultural project.

The beginnings of Gold Coast print culture have been obscured by the survival of only a few issues of the *West African Herald*, produced by Charles Bannerman over sixteen years in Accra, Freetown and Cape Coast.[8] Bannerman's grit is exemplified by the fact that he began to issue his paper before having obtained a printing press, laboriously writing out copies in longhand. The *Herald* can therefore be seen to straddle the age of coterie manuscript culture and that of commercial print; by 1859 he had informed the Colonial Office that his enterprise was firmly established, with 310 subscribers.⁹ A key issue in the study of textual production is the nature of the transition from an oral culture, via coterie manuscripts, to the more widely disseminated print culture of the modern public sphere. What happened to discursive strategies when, in Karin Barber's words, 'fledgling vernacular print cultures were overlaid upon vital, flourishing oral cultures'?[10] The weight of evidence, Barber argues, suggests not only that oral cultures in West Africa and beyond remained resilient but also that the advent of reading and writing was characterized by a high degree of continuity from established forms of verbal discourse. Discursive strategies concerning death among the Akan are central to Barber's analysis: the *apaee*, the praise poems often delivered as funeral dirges, are cited as an exemplary form of African oral text, one in which the recitation of 'name, memory and reputation' represented 'the strongest affirmation of personal distinctiveness and individual agency'.[11] How, then, did this dramatically performative culture of speaking about the individual dead—combined with circumlocutions of speaking generally about death—feed into new strategies of writing about them?

The opening phase of literary production and consumption on the Gold Coast was restricted to a small urban elite whose ways of life and of death were by the mid-nineteenth century already diverging from those of surrounding communities. This process was shaped by the emergence of a distinct Euro-African identity in the main coastal towns, by the advent of Christianity, and by secular Enlightenment notions of intellectual and moral uplift—a combination manifested in the creation by African Company officers in 1789 of a literary and philosophical society at Cape Coast Castle, the Torridzonians. Aside from meeting to debate the issues of the day—including, it must be assumed, abolitionism—the Torridzonians set about 'educating twelve coloured Children of this Country, principally the Offspring of distressed and deceased parents', placing the scholars under the care of the Fante pastor Philip Quaque.[12] Later products of Quaque's castle school would come together in 1831 under the leadership of William de Graft to form the Bible group which invited the Methodist mission to Cape Coast. A generation later, by which time the Methodists' and Charles Bannerman's printing presses were in operation, the town's first secular literary clubs began to appear, beginning with J. P. Brown's Try Company in 1859 and The Reading Room a year later. Around the same time, two other forms of modern association were established: in 1858 a multiracial Masonic lodge (the Torridzonian Society appears to have formed the basis of an ephemeral lodge in 1810) and in 1862, ten miles down the coast, the Anomabo Temperance Society, whose leading light was the progressive

African trader and Christian convert R. J. Ghartey.[13] Both of these organizations would influence mortuary culture and its reportage: the freemasons, because of their elaborate and esoteric burial ceremonies; the temperance movement, because of its condemnation of the tradition of extravagant funerals lubricated by the copious consumption of alcohol.

A complication in analysing emergent print culture is that most writing in newspapers was anonymous or pseudonymous. Focusing on the early twentieth-century press, Stephanie Newell has explored the ways that Gold Coast writers used anonymity as a tool with which to confront colonial power and to manipulate ideas of African identity.[14] These strategies are apparent from the 1860s, although in this period the matter often played out somewhat differently: it speaks volumes about the complex identity of the mid-Victorian coastal elite that it is sometimes difficult to determine whether anonymous articles were written by Africans or Europeans. Any number of examples might be cited, but let us take one letter written to the *African Times* in 1863 on that aspect of mortuary custom perceived by many, both Black and White, to encapsulate an Africa in urgent need of redemption: human sacrifice. In this case the correspondent, who signs his name as 'Tom Coffee' (that is, the Akan day-name Kofi), is responding to a letter published by the London *Times* and signed 'An African'. 'The writer . . . is no more an African than you are, Mr. Editor', Tom Coffee writes, although 'no-one out here . . . is likely to be bamboozled . . . [by] one who disguises himself in our much-despised skin in order to obtain currency for his spurious statements relative to the customs of the country'.[15] What is striking about this debate is that Tom Coffee accuses the 'impostor' of *defending* human sacrifices in Asante and Dahomey by arguing that 'they are not committed out of sheer addiction to the shedding of a man's blood for pleasure's sake, but they are committed in obedience to a sense of religious duty'. Tom Coffee regarded this as a racial slur against Akan religion, citing a recent incident observed during a visit to Kumasi by the Methodist missionary Rev. William West, the Asante convert and newly ordained Rev. John Owusu Ansah and R. J. Ghartey in which Asantehene Kwaku Dua Panin, in retaliation for a woman falsely swearing the great oath, ordered his executioners to proceed to her village and 'to slay every man, woman, child, sheep, goat, dog, fowl, and living creature therein . . . *These orders were executed literally.* This is only one instance out of one hundred . . . to prove that the King of Ashantee always has the power, and much too frequently the inclination also, to shed blood for amusement, mere show, or to gratify his vindictive feelings or his avarice'.[16]

Fear and loathing of Asante became an established trope of the early Gold Coast press, which tended to portray the great forest kingdom as a barbaric threat to the project of a modernized coastal nationhood based on legitimate commerce and Victorian civilization. Championed by the *African Times* and in the writings of the Sierra Leonian physician James Africanus Horton, this project took ephemeral political shape in the Fanti Confederation, which between 1868 and its demise in 1873 sought to unite the Fante states under a combined leadership of established office-holders and literate elites.[17] Beyond blood-curdling denunciations of human sacrifice and other customs such as the post-mortem interrogation of corpses, reformist aspirations would shape much early writing about death and the dead.[18] This took a variety of forms, from accounts of the death and burial of prominent individuals to reportage of fatal outbreaks of smallpox, of sensational death by murder, accident or suicide and on to coverage of court cases arising from disputed wills.

Print also provided a platform for the discussion of new ideas about the nature of the human body and soul, informed both by modern medicine and by Victorian morality. In 1864, for example, the *African Times* carried a report of an address given to Ghartey's Anomabo Temperance Society on the topic of 'The House I Live In, or, the Human Body; What to Eat, Drink, and Avoid'.[19] Indeed, it was radical ideas about the body, worthy of Diogenes, which caused the society temporarily to split from the Methodist Church. 'The soul is everything, the body nothing', it was reported as believing, 'and therefore when the body is dead and the soul departed, the corpse is merely carrion, and should be thrown into the bush'.[20] Such behaviour was anathema both to local society and to the Methodists. 'Those who are acquainted with the feelings of the negroes in respect to the treatment of the body—the Egyptian reverence they bestow upon the corpse', Winwood Reade observed, 'must confess that the Christian religion is becoming a force in this country'.[21]

Reports on the death of prominent individuals appearing in the *African Times* in the 1860s and 1870s are revealing of the complex sensibilities of the literate elite. While accounts of the demise and funeral customs of unreformed Akan potentates such as Asantehene Kwaku Dua Panin, the *omanhene* of Akuapem Kwaw Dade and the *omanhene* of Wassa Kwabena Enimil invariably focus on the bloodletting of human sacrifice, those of coastal merchants emphasize the restrained, sombre and therefore more 'genuine' grief of the ideal Victorian funeral.[22] Take the report of the funeral in 1869 of the wealthy and influential Thomas Hughes of Cape Coast: 'Thousands, we are told, gathered around his grave on 12 July, and their evidently real sorrow testified that *he was a good* man! ... He had great knowledge of native medicines and many lives were saved by him, particularly of those affected with dysentery'.[23] Hughes was, in fact, a controversial character, whose knowledge of the local pharmacopoeia extended to abortifacients, the illegal use of which he had been convicted of in the colonial courts.[24] Another of Hughes's roles had been as political advisor to the *omanhene* of Cape Coast, the Methodist convert John Aggery, who in the atmosphere of rising proto-nationalist sentiment had fallen foul of the British and was exiled to Sierra Leone in 1866. Anxious that Aggery not die in exile, however, the British allowed him to return to Cape Coast on the condition that he renounced his claim to the stool. There he died, in late 1869. 'Poor Aggery ... is no more', the *African Times* reported. 'He died ... really of a broken heart, through degradation and misery to which he had been subjected.' Aggery's status as a martyr to the cause of African self-government was underlined by his peaceful, Christian end, which was contrasted with the turbulent demise of his adversaries: 'Only one European attended his funeral but ... every native was there in tears and the Wesleyan school children strewed flowers on his coffin as he was lowered into his body's resting place. ... A correspondent ... adds: "Blackall (the curse of Africa) is in a far-off land, Conran died a fearful death, poor Aggery fell asleep in Jesus on the morning of 5 Nov. 1869, and we are here to tell the tale"'.[25]

A similar Africanist interpretation was developed in accounts of the deaths of two members of the merchant community, John Bruce of Accra, also in 1869, and Joseph Smith of Cape Coast, in 1870. The self-identity of the coastal elite may well have rested upon its embrace of the civilizing capacity of legitimate commerce, but these texts also reveal an awareness of the potentially destructive side of merchant capital. John Bruce, a scion of one of Accra's trading dynasties, committed suicide by swallowing poison, after misunderstanding a credit note and falling into debt.[26] 'The poor young man ... became so terrified that his senses ... left him', Edmund Bannerman wrote, 'and in order to avoid the miseries of an indefinite incarceration in one of the subterranean dens of James Fort, put an end to his existence which, up to that date, had been a happy one'. Entry into world of literacy and commerce, he warned, was fraught with danger: 'the deceased had received a fair education in the Accra Mission School, but his knowledge of the English language was by no means sufficient to enable him to comprehend to its full extent the nature of the responsibilities he was incurring by attaching his name to the document'.

The death in similar circumstances of Joseph Smith, not by his own hand but, like King Aggery, 'of a broken heart', also produced an epistolary denunciation of the ruthless side of the trading economy. In this case, the anonymous correspondent provided a clear rationale for putting pen to paper, one which can be seen as a continuity from oral funerary culture: 'As much misapprehension has arisen relative to the unfortunate position in which the family of the late Joseph Smith is left, it is necessary that a clear and comprehensive statement should be made public, in order that his memory may receive that respect and his family that sympathy which they deserve after the ruthless persecution to which they have been subjected'.[27] Unlike the callow Bruce, Smith was a prominent man of affairs in Cape Coast: a product of Quaque's school, he had travelled to England in 1831 as tutor to the Asante prince Owusu Ansah (later Rev. John Owusu Ansah) and, after his return, held the posts of government schoolmaster, private secretary to Maclean, justice of the peace and member in 1858 of Cape Coast's first municipal council. Smith was also an agent for the trading company of Messrs Forster & Smith, and when in 1858 he suspected that he was being overcharged, he took them to court. He lost and was declared a bankrupt and imprisoned. The final indignity, which supposedly triggered his death, came with the seizure of his residence and, with it, the very bones of his antecedents: 'his family house, where lie now the mortal remains of his mother and other members of his family ... was wrested from him by the avaricious agent ... of that wealthy firm'. 'Thus ended the history of an intelligent native', Smith's eulogist concluded, 'who commenced life most prosperously, did extensive business transactions, but died a ruined man, and left his bereaved family to the charity of friends'.

The establishment at Cape Coast of J. H. Brew's *Gold Coast Times* in 1874, and of its successors in the 1880s, extended the range of written reflection on death and the dead. As indicated by the news items quoted above, the local press now reported on everyday matters of life and death, interspersed with funeral announcements, obituaries and notices of the granting of letters of administration. Politically, the turbulent era of the 1860s and early 1870s was succeeded by one of formalized British rule, the agitation for African self-government giving way to a resigned acceptance that modernization would take place within the new colonial dispensation. It was in this context that the Gold Coast's expanding print culture became a vehicle for 'cultural nationalism': a re-embrace of aspects of African culture and a recovery of the past in the service of a progressive future. As elsewhere in West Africa, most prominently the Yoruba-speaking region of present-day Nigeria, mission Christianity was a key component of this renovation, and it is no accident that the pioneering histories of both regions, Rev. Samuel Johnson's *History of the Yorubas* (1921, but completed 1897) and Rev. Carl Christian Reindorf's *History of the Gold Coast and Asante* (1895), were written by indigenous churchmen. Given the prominence of funerary culture, it is also unsurprising that it would emerge as a subject of heated discussion in the emergent public sphere. Local gossip about who was dead, how and why they had died and what happened at the funeral began to be translated into print. Entangled with this quotidian reportage were questions about the very nature of mortuary culture: which aspects should be discarded, which modified and which retained in the modern world?

As we have seen with the treatment of corpses of women who died in childbirth and with the campaign against house burial, elite voices continued to inveigh against degrading or unhealthy mortuary practices. 'What we call "Funeral Customs" in this country are something positively outrageous to civilized people', an article in the *Gold Coast News* declared in 1885. 'What are our people in many instances? . . . Do they not sometimes compel the traducers of our race to stick to their views that the Negro is no better than the savage and can not be dissociated from the latter?'[28] For this writer, the most unsavoury aspect of funeral customs was the exuberant participation of those who were not truly grieving, a practice which extended to 'some of our very best people' (see chapter 4). 'Let any one just die on your premises and in no time you will have the whole house full of "mourning friends". But the great trouble is to tell . . . whether the crying, the deep sighing, or loud lamentations, are the outcome of real sympathy'. Perhaps to avoid the fate of the woman from Winneba who three years earlier was reported to have been beaten for failing to cry at a funeral, 'some will attend . . . with small packets . . . of onions. These are rubbed in the eyes till tears run down'. All of this went against the Victorian ideal of deep, contemplative mourning: 'when a person loses a friend or relative, it is natural to suppose that he would like to enjoy as much peace and quietness as possible'. In Cape Coast, however, 'it is "high treason" not to attend a funeral. If you see a funeral procession passing through the street whether you knew the deceased or not you are supposed to fall in. . . . As to the great noise and crying . . . , this is what is termed African etiquette'. The writer's Victorian sensibilities were also offended by the absence of black crape and the wearing, instead, of 'half yellow and half black, or half red and half blue'—an early reference to the emerging fashion for the wearing of a uniform cloth by mourners. 'A few ... will ... be seen clad totally in black. But unfortunately this mark of decency and good sense does not find favour among the masses.'

Yet not all aspects of 'modern' deathways were necessarily applauded. Three years before, the *Gold Coast Times* reported on the funeral of one Charles Mensah, who, as a Freemason and a member of the rival Oddfellows, was accompanied to his grave by processions of both fraternities. 'About a funeral there is something generally inexpressibly impressive', the *Times* wrote, 'but the various features assumed by the ceremonies at his grave took away greatly from the solemnity of the occasion'.[29] This writer took also issue with the garish colours of the fraternities' regalia, as well as with the esoteric ceremonies on display. 'But why all that, useless, gay and pompous pageantry? ... Black mourning crape was all that was required at that moment. In future when a gentleman dies pray let us be plain. . . . We must have no more coloured bows and ribbons in our cemeteries. Alas! Vanity and its caprices!'[30] Neither were traditional customs universally condemned. This damning report can be contrasted with another the following year of the traditional funeral for a local centenarian, Madame Agribah. 'Guns were fired and drums were beaten. . . . During the wake a dance was introduced. The deceased was buried with a large quantity of trinkets. A drink of rum was consumed by the mourners.'[31] Despite all of these elements being at one time or another the target of elite censure, the custom was described in glowing terms as having 'a most imposing character'. Even a mock funeral staged in Cape Coast in 1885 was described as proceeding with great dignity—this despite the fact, unreported in the press, that such ceremonies were often designed to hasten the death of a living enemy. 'The parties, including women and children, daubed their bodies with red and white clay, and holding sticks in their hands they went about the quarter of the town . . . chanting a well-known dirge befitting the occasion, while rum was generously passed around . . . and consumed with all the solemnity peculiar only to funerals.'[32]

With the demise of the *Gold Coast Times* in 1885, Brew launched a new title, the *Western Echo*. Perhaps because of the editorial assistance of his nephew, the lawyer and pioneering nationalist J. E. Casely Hayford, it was more radical than its predecessor, unapologetic about voicing grievances against the British administration. This muscular approach, together with the cryptic and satirical column by 'The Owl' (certainly written by Casely Hayford), made the *Echo* at once notorious and popular. The first of its many campaigns was for a more bureaucratic approach to the governance of life and death. 'There is not one single Registrar of Births or Deaths in any town in this Settlement', it fulminated in its opening number. 'It is obvious that it is neglect of a pitiable nature which involves a disregard by a government of the means . . . of ascertaining the increase of the population over whom they are placed.'[33] 'Has any body in this settlement ever heard of the *census returns* of the Gold Coast Colony?' it continued in the second issue, ten days later. 'As a matter of fact, the Government have never troubled themselves about the number of people under their administration.'[34] And in the next, the argument was advanced with a report of a suspicious death—reflective too of the deep-seated anxiety about poisoning: 'The person is of course buried; but nevertheless . . . it would be better for the protection of life if in such cases of sudden or suspicious death the Government made it a rule for a Coroner's inquest and a post mortem to be held, notwithstanding the objections of the family of the deceased to such inquiry. There are more deaths caused by foul play than is credited.'[35]

The *Western Echo*'s call for the creation of a modern bureaucratic structure entailing the registration of births and deaths, a census, inquests, post-mortem examinations, and modern cemeteries represents a significant shift in the discussion of death in the new public sphere. In common with other campaigns championed by the paper, it is indicative of the changed political climate in the coastal towns of the mid-1880s: if British colonial rule was a reality, then it must be held to account and made to work in the interests of progress and modernity. Rather than resisting a regime of biopower, then, the literate elite sought in some ways to extend its remit. Yet these demands also reflected an older, deeply engrained strain of thought: the obsessive care with which the Akan and their neighbours enumerated births and deaths. Such precise recording had long underpinned oral discourses—most pronounced at Odwira, Homowo and other yearly festivals—of the incremental progress of families, states and all humankind. These declamatory public pronouncements of human increase in the face of adversity and implacable death would also emerge in more introspective form in private diaries kept by mission catechists and other literate 'scholars', which often carefully tabulated yearly numbers of births and deaths.[36]

Older concerns with issues of human wellbeing also took new textual shape in written debates about sanitation, morbidity and mortality. An early example arose in 1886 after the death of one John Ogoo, who was serving a fourteen-year term of imprisonment for slave-dealing in Elmina prison. 'It is an undoubted fact', the *Echo* reported, 'that poor Ogoo succumbed from a broken heart'—the cause of death often cited in the press, as we have seen, for an individual suffering persecution from the colonial authorities.[37] In this case, however, the standard line was challenged by a letter from 'Philo Medicus'— likely to be J. F. Easmon—who cautioned against wild and unscientific accusations concerning the cause of death.[38] The intervention from Philo Medicus was in turn challenged by further correspondents, who insisted on the culpability of the prison and medical authorities for the death of a man suffering not so much from a 'broken heart' but from diagnosed heart *disease*, and for whom the belated application of 'a kenkey poultice to his chest' came too late to save.[39] Picking up on the *Echo*'s earlier concerns, the matter was exacerbated by the haphazard nature of the inquest, from which the medical officer was said to have been absent.

Take too this item from 1887 reporting an alarming rise in death rates in Cape Coast: 'In one week lately upwards of 13 souls passed away—some said 15.... the rate has not been known to be so great... since the Small Pox epidemic of 1873. Local philosophers have no doubt been racking their brains as to the probable causes of the mortality. But of course the only solution of the problem lies in atmospheric influences'.[40] This alarming spike in death rates prompted an intervention from The Owl a few weeks later. 'Approachist thou the dread presence of The Owl', the column opened in its customary, mock-Gothic manner.

> Speak, then, and explain, I conjure ye, how it cometh about that the dead roam the fields of reality and make their weird appearance unto sober men, frightening them out of their senses. Explain unto me the dark and hidden things of nature; how cometh it that spirits are permitted to send messages from beyond the grave. It hath been urged that once dead a human being is dead; but if dead how cometh he to be able to speak unto the living? How cometh he to trouble men in their dreams, old women in their dotage?[41]

As likely to have been influenced by the recent rise of spiritism in the West as by Akan understandings of ghosts—the Society for Psychical Research had been founded in London in 1882—The Owl's inquiries prompted considerable debate in the columns of the *Echo* and, it must be assumed, beyond.[42] 'Death is a subject which should engage the attention of all persons living in this sublunary globe', the paper proclaimed, and the topic was taken up under the heading 'Is There a World of Spirits?'.[43] One correspondent answered in the affirmative, explaining 'what has gained currency in town as regards the appearance of a certain gentleman recently deceased'. The dead man was said to have appeared repeatedly to the living: 'parties have dreamed the same story of him the same night and . . . he has exhibited himself to others who did not know him when living, and given them messages on subjects of which they could have had no previous cognisance'. Either an anomalous burial or a curse was rumoured to have caused his restless state: 'ministers who died before him are said to have refused to permit him to be interred in peace in the ground in which he was buried; finally he is said to have been carrying his coffin on his head'. Another reported case, with added sexual frisson, points to the unsettlingly lifelike appearance of revenants discussed in the preceding chapter. A man 'had followed a body to whom he was making love before he had left town to her house as she was walking a few yards in front of him in the broad daylight . . . to find, on his entering the house and asking the mother for her daughter, that the daughter had departed this life only a few weeks before. . . . How do you account for this, Mr Editor?'.[44] How indeed?

Perhaps the most important new mode of writing about the dead, however, was the newspaper obituary. As a formalized genre which sought publicly to record and to celebrate the achievements of individuals seen to have made a mark on the world, the obituary represented a written reformulation of the conventions of the *apaee* (praise poem) or funeral dirge. Like biographical profiles of historical figures and later memorial poems, obituaries, in Newell's words, gave 'thickness and textual form to the names of the dead'.[45] The written naming of the dead evolved from the first brief death notices of the early 1870s, via accounts of funerals, to, by the mid-1880s, narratives of the life of the deceased.[46] These accounts varied in length and tone, many condensing the extensive oral elaborations of the *apaee* to pithy summaries of the deceased's outstanding achievements, with extreme old age, martial endeavour and large numbers of progeny, as in the past, drawing inevitable praise.

Consider this lapidary obituary of 97-year-old Affo Daday of Accra:

> We . . . announce the death of Madam Affo Daday the mother of Chief Antonio Ankrah . . . The deceased was born in 1800. She was present at the battle of Dodowah with her husband Old Chief Ankrah and received a wound in her right thigh. The bullet has never been extracted up to the time of her death. She was buried in the Government Cemetery.[47]

Less than two months later, Antonio Ankrah himself died. His obituary, like that of his mother, stressed his participation in Accra's various military conflicts, but added another standard formulation: his status as the progenitor of an extensive family and as possessing a reputation that transcended the different classes of the town:

> The death is announced of Chief Antonio Ankrah of Otoo Street... The deceased is one of the sons of King Ankrah of Otoo Street. At the time of his death, he was acting head Chief of Otoo Street. During the Awuna war of 1871 and also the Ashanti campaign of 1873–4 he went as commander of the Otoo Street people, he is highly respected by all classes in town, he left many sons and daughters and a very large relatives [sic] and friends to mourn his death.[48]

When a reputation was marred by political or social discord, however, the written obituary employed similar strategies of circumlocution and glancing allusion as the *apaee*, as can be seen in a more extensive obituary of John Aggery's successor as Oguaahene, or King of Cape Coast, Kwasi Atta, in 1887. 'While living the unfortunate potentate was a much-abused ... character', the *Western Echo* reflected—including, it might have added, by the town's educated elite which composed its main readership. But 'this is not the proper time nor place to endeavour to clear his character', the paper added. 'While in reality he acted as but the tool of unscrupulous Governors who deceived him.... In happier circumstances ... a better King could not have been had; and we feel confident that notwithstanding his shortcomings, it will be long ere his memory will be forgotten among his people.'[49]

A final example can be cited. On 30 July 1897, R. J. Ghartey died at the age of 75. Ghartey, whom we met above, had been a leading figure in Gold Coast affairs throughout the second half of the nineteenth century: a wealthy trader, early Methodist convert and pioneer of temperance, in 1869 he was appointed president of the Fanti Confederation and in 1872, after its demise, as King Ghartey IV, *omanhene* of Winneba. Although he had never attended school and was therefore not literate, Ghartey's credentials as a progressive modernizer were impeccable—he was even credited with the invention of the *kabasrotu* (a corruption of 'cover shoulder'), a women's blouse which, in line with Methodist rectitude, he designed in the 1860s for the women of his household and which remains ubiquitous throughout Ghana today.[50] It is fitting, therefore, that his life, death and burial received extensive coverage in the *Gold Coast Methodist Times*, by the late 1890s Cape Coast's leading newspaper. Alongside a detailed account of his funeral and an obituary, the *Methodist Times* printed two letters dictated by Ghartey to his son Joseph two days before his death, one addressed to J. P. Brown, vice-president of the newly formed

Aborigines' Rights Protection Society, and the other to the native Methodist ministers A. W. Parker and J. A. Solomon. These letters appear to be the earliest extant examples from the Gold Coast of a traditional deathbed valediction being written down.

In the first, the dying Ghartey reflects upon the political struggles of the past and those about to be joined by the ARPS:

> God has so willed it that I must now resign my charge, and by His grace I do so fearlessly. Now is the big struggle before us *re* the Land Bill etc the history past, present and future call with the Lord voice [*sic*] for Loyalty, Unity of purpose, and perseverance in actions.... Hopefully therefore I fall in this Battle field with many wounds fresh and old and deep scars of the defunct Fanti Confederation. Kindly convey my last farewell to all true patriotic native Kings and friends of the Country's cause here and elsewhere and to the Aborigines Society in England. Be constitutional. GOD bless you, our country and the Queen.[51]

Ghartey uses the second letter to reflect upon his personal faith, employing the standard martial imagery of dissenting Protestantism.

> My master hath need for me elsewhere, and I must sooner or later disappear from among you to join the great Army of the redeemed above. As my last Christian Experience I wish to say that I enlisted under the Banner of Christ at an early age and that in all the vicissitudes of life private and public which were often sore and trying my God never forsook me.... I die a Soldier of Christ, Victorious in his arms. May the cause of the Temperance Society ... ever and ever flourish for the glory of God—Amen.[52]

In life, and in death, Ghartey's identity—his 'self-fashioning'—was complex. As a Christian progressive and proto-nationalist activist who in later life was enstooled as an *omanhene*, he straddled the realm of traditional kingship and the milieu of the literate urban elite. It is telling, too, that he produced a third valedictory letter, which has not survived, addressed to the governor of the Gold Coast, who paid him the honour of visiting him on his deathbed on the same day that he dictated the two printed in the *Methodist Times*.[53] That letter must also have spoken of constitutionalism and loyalty—although no doubt with the emphasis more on queen and empire than on the political aspirations expressed in that to J. P. Brown. There was no letter, however, to the dignitaries of his own *oman* of Winneba: that farewell would have been oral, in the vernacular—and not for public consumption.

Ghartey's elaborate funeral further reflected his multiple identities. His body was laid in state for three days in an imported glass-headed coffin valued at 500 US dollars, during which time 'corpse and casket were photographed by Mr. J. E. Yemoah and sketched by R. Seibelist Esquire'.[54] After a funeral service at Winneba's Methodist chapel, the body was carried through the town, accompanied by a procession including members of the Ancient Order of Foresters, local schoolchildren, the Methodist 'singing band' and traditional office-holders, which periodically paused as members of the town's *asafo* military companies unleashed the traditional volleys of musket fire. Although Ghartey's final journey began in his beloved Methodist chapel, it ended not at the church's cemetery but at Winneba's royal burial ground. As his final valediction stressed, he died a Methodist—but was interred as an *omanhene*. After rehearsing his many achievements, adventures and talents—which extended to being a renowned healer, 'especially in Midwifery'—Ghartey's obituary ended on a traditional note, the precise tabulation of his progeny: 'By King Ghartey's first wife Mary, he has 3 sons and 7 daughters; of whom 2 sons and 3 daughters survive. The eldest son Johannes died in England while a student in college. By his second wife, Sarah, 4 sons and 2 daughters of whom 1 son and 1 daughter have died, i.e., 5 sons and 4 daughters, in all 9 surviving'.[55]

15

The Colony of Medicine

BY THE MIDDLE of the twentieth century, death and dying in what in 1957 became independent Ghana had in one crucial respect undergone significant change. It was a change, moreover, which affected the whole of Africa: the continent's population had begun to increase dramatically. From an estimated 142 million in 1920, it had risen to some 200 million by the late 1940s and to nearly 300 million by 1960. By 2020, that figure was 1.3 billion. Demographic historians have been divided over the reason for this, some pointing to rising birth rates and others to falling death rates. Despite the widespread paucity of reliable data, an emerging consensus points to the latter as the key factor: while available evidence suggests that in most regions women's fertility levels remained broadly the same over the first half of the century, there are indications of an accelerating decline in mortality rates, particularly among infants and young children. The precise reasons for this in turn are multiple and contested. Yet the overall impact is clear: Africans were, on average, living longer and dying older. If, as has been suggested, the life expectancy at birth in precolonial tropical West Africa was in the vicinity of 20 years, the figure for the Gold Coast by 1921 has been estimated to have reached 28 years; by 1948, 39.5 years; by 1960, 45.5 years; by 1970, 50.5 years; and by 2020, 64 years. For a historically underpopulated continent, demographic increase, John Iliffe argues, was the single most important consequence of colonial occupation.[1]

'There is no automatic or mechanistic relationship between demography and attitudes towards death', Rebekah Lee and Megan Vaughan point out in the introduction to their recent collection of essays on the history of death in Africa. 'Yet it is also unlikely that the religious, cultural and social practices which surround death in any society are completely free-floating, and unconnected to changing demographies.'[2] Indeed, it was this issue which lay at the heart of the first attempts by historians to reconstruct changing attitudes towards death, Chaunu arguing for 'a more or less direct correlation between rising life expectancy and the increasing denial of death' in eighteenth-century France.[3] Chaunu's fellow Annalistes, Lebrun and Vovelle, suspected otherwise, stressing ideological rather than demographic reasons for the emergence of a distinctively modern *mentalité* towards death and dying.[4] Be that is it may, by the time we reach the twentieth century a crucial factor in the increasing denial of death, first in industrialized societies and subsequently in the global South, was its 'colonization', not just by the modern state but by modern medicine. Twentieth-century death, that is, was 'brought under the sway of biology, and biology of the service of the administrative state'.[5] To what extent can this be said for West Africa in the era of colonial rule? Individual life expectancy and the overall population in the Gold Coast may have begun to increase dramatically, but how did these changes impact upon attitudes towards death and upon the experience of dying?

Consideration of these questions is circumscribed by the almost total absence of demographic data for the precolonial period, together with limitations to the data for the eras of colonial and even of postcolonial rule. Registration of vital statistics in the Gold Coast began only in 1912, with the Births, Deaths and Burials Ordinance, which was applied at first to sixteen urban centres, most of them coastal towns. It was not until 1929 that the ordinance was applied to any part of the Northern Territories or to the mandated area of Togoland acquired from Germany after the First World War, and as late as 1940 only 9 per cent of the total Gold Coast population lived in the thirty-five towns where registration was legally required (rising to 12 per cent by 1960). Yet relative to much of the African continent, mortality statistics for at least parts of the colonial Gold Coast are reasonably good: by 1925, 88 per cent of deaths in Accra were medically certified and by 1929 some two-thirds of deaths across all the registration areas.[6] In 1931, the fourth decennial edition of the *Manual of the International List of Causes of Death* (*ICD*) was sent by the Colonial Office in London to the Gold Coast for use in registration.[7] Additional data on morbidity and mortality are also available from hospital records and from the censuses of 1931 and 1948. Like vital registration, these too suffer from a heavy urban bias. By the middle decades of the twentieth century, however, enough is known about the changing epidemiological situation of the Gold Coast to make some tentative conclusions about the nature of the dying experience: where people died, at what age and for what reasons.

In common with the broader West African forest zone, the southern Gold Coast did not suffer from the increase in mortality and ensuing demographic decline experienced elsewhere in the continent as a result of colonial conquest in the late nineteenth and early twentieth centuries.[8] Prolonged exposure to European-borne diseases may have given populations in the region greater immunity, while the Akan forest managed to escape the devastating violence, dislocation, famines and epidemics of sleeping sickness which characterized the early colonial crisis throughout much of central and eastern Africa. Rather, a combination of rising living standards and biomedical intervention began to improve the epidemiological environment. This impact, it must be stressed, was uneven in spread and uncertain in nature—and remains so today. Sustained access to preventative and therapeutic biomedicine was limited to only a few favoured urban centres throughout the colonial period, and it is likely that most people continued to die of the same infectious diseases as they had done in the past. While these diseases were mainly chronic and endemic—notably, malaria, pneumonia, dysentery and measles—significant numbers of victims continued to be carried off by outbreaks of epidemic disease: smallpox, yellow fever, plague, and, in the northern savanna region, cerebro-spinal meningitis and trypanosomiasis (sleeping sickness).[9] The global influenza pandemic of 1918–19 accounted for between eighty thousand and one hundred thousand deaths, or some 4 per cent of the population. As elsewhere in Africa, tuberculosis and sexually transmitted diseases also emerged as the emblematic maladies of colonial modernity. The fatal impact of so-called killing diseases, moreover, was often exacerbated by the presence of debilitating chronic conditions such as yaws, guinea worm and other parasitic infestations, and malnutrition. Owing perhaps to the high incidence of existing chronic conditions, the Northern Territories were especially badly hit by the influenza pandemic; indeed, that, combined with the large number of deaths from repeated outbreaks of meningitis from 1906 and cyclical food insecurity, meant that the savanna region may have experienced an early colonial demographic crisis more typical of other parts of the continent.[10]

That said, the population of the Gold Coast expanded over the first half of the twentieth century at a rate significantly higher than in the continent as a whole. Given that fertility rates appear to have remained broadly static—and factoring in the considerable level of in-migration from neighbouring colonies and improved enumeration in the colony's censuses—this demographic expansion was driven largely by declining death rates, particularly among infants and children. We have seen how punishing levels of infant and child mortality shaped a powerful ideology of human increase as well as attitudes towards its hateful enemy, death. Babies and toddlers, K. David Patterson writes, were 'exposed to the entire spectrum of infectious diseases, with malaria, diarrheal diseases, respiratory tract infections, measles, and whooping cough being important causes of death'.[11] When in 1915 an African medical practitioner, F. V. Nanka-Bruce, alerted Governor Clifford to the devastating levels of infant and maternal mortality in Accra—between 1910 and 1915 an average of 31 per cent of deaths in the city were of infants under one year—a committee was appointed to inquire into the matter.[12] Its recommendations for the establishment of a maternity hospital and the training of local midwives took some time to implement, but by the mid-1920s infant welfare was one area of public health where the colonial state was making a concerted effort, with clinics run by women medical officers opening in Accra, the coastal towns of Sekondi, Shama and Cape Coast, and the inland centres of Kumasi and Koforidua.[13]

The decline in Accra's infant mortality was striking: from a staggering 483 per 1,000 in 1918, the rate dropped to 405 per 1,000 in 1920, 259 per 1,000 in 1926–7 and 113 per 1,000 in 1930. Some of this improvement may well have been due to more complete registration, Patterson cautions, while in rural areas, especially in the Northern Territories, it is unlikely that any change in the first half of the century was more than marginal.[14] Entrenched cultural attitudes towards the dead, such as those complained about by Easmon in the 1880s, mean that such statistics must, moreover, be taken with caution. In the fertility survey undertaken as part of the 1948 census, Caldwell notes, 'enumerators must have omitted over a quarter of all births. The explanation lies almost certainly in the reluctance of mothers to remember or to admit to interviewers the birth of many babies who subsequently died.... Some associated the reluctance with the feeling that it was unlucky to recall the dead, especially dead infants'.[15]

Yet shifts in the religious landscape point to a sense that increasing numbers of children were indeed surviving. Although the statistical data may suggest otherwise, there is ample evidence for the widespread perception of a crisis in fertility and wellbeing unleashed by colonial conquest. In line with established explanations of such crises, this was invariably understood to be due to a rising tide of witchcraft and poisoning, in turn giving rise to wave after wave of popular healing movements which swept through the Akan forest from the 1900s.

'The Creator had from the commencement of creation fixed the fate of every creature that all may depart from this world in their old ages [sic] with gray hairs to heaven', the personified 'medicine' of the first of these heterodox movements, Aberewa, was reported in 1907 to have announced; 'but now [a] lot of the creatures had come to us in the heaven without [having] been called and we learnt from them they were sent out from this world so prematurely by witches and poisoners'.[16] People's *nkrabea*, or 'destiny', that is, was being subverted by maleficent invisible forces. Originating mostly from shrines located in the northern savannas, Aberewa and subsequent anti-witchcraft cults formed part of an increasingly diverse therapeutic register, purporting to combat the enemies of human wellbeing in rural areas largely beyond the reach of colonial biomedicine. Yet by the 1950s they were in sharp decline.[17] Anxieties about occluded maleficence did not disappear, but there was a sense that the crisis years had passed. By then, fertility rates too were beginning to rise, combining with an accelerating decline in mortality rates to propel the explosive demographic growth of the postcolonial era.

A second factor in explaining the decline in death rates was the prevention of crisis mortality. In this respect the experience of the Gold Coast was typical of that of much of the continent, as colonial states targeted epidemic diseases and as the expansion of market economies and transport infrastructure lessened the threat of famine. Perhaps most importantly, smallpox ceased to be a major killer by the 1930s. A longstanding and dreaded scourge, smallpox had been reported throughout the era of the slave trade and into the nineteenth and early twentieth centuries: epidemics broke out in Accra in 1864, along much of the coast between 1871 and 1874, at Cape Coast in 1889, along the coast again in 1899–1902, in northwest Asante in 1908–9, at Accra in 1920, and in the Northern Territories in 1924–6.[18] Many communities had long practised variolation and there was some early resistance to colonial vaccinators, but the success of an immunization campaign at Accra in 1920 encouraged large-scale efforts throughout the colony to counter the epidemic of 1924–6; thereafter, despite isolated outbreaks in the Northern Territories into the 1940s, the mortal threat from smallpox was largely over. So too was that from famine, which had long stalked not only the northern savannas but also the relatively dry coastal littoral, where drought, locust plagues and military violence had in the past often created food shortages and hunger that killed.[19] Nutritional deficiencies were not eliminated but, here too, progress was made: in the early 1930s, the Accra-based medical officer Cecily Williams identified the aetiology of the childhood condition known to the Ga as *kwashiorkor*, caused by severe protein deprivation and characterized by the distended stomach so typical of young victims of famine.

The broad trend, then, is unmistakable: by the mid-twentieth century, Ghana stood on the cusp of the 'mortality revolution' which had gathered pace in industrialized societies in the nineteenth century, its relative prosperity putting it somewhat ahead of the average curve for sub-Saharan Africa. According to one theory of epidemiological history, it can be seen to have entered the transitional period of 'receding pandemics', between the so-called age of pestilence and famine and that of degenerative disease. As Allan Kellehear and others have pointed out, however, this theory, while useful, tends to obscure the variety of dying experiences in all three historical periods.[20] The figures for average life expectancy at birth can be misleading, as the extreme level of infant and child mortality meant that a considerable proportion of people did survive into old age, when no doubt many succumbed to cancer, heart disease, dementia and other degenerative conditions associated with the modern world. As Patterson points out, the contribution of such non-infectious diseases to morbidity and mortality was obscured by 'the tremendous burden of microbial and helminthic [i.e., intestinal worm] infections'.[21] Some evidence does point to this—or, perhaps, to the beginning of the era of transition. In his 1887 report on the causes of mortality in Accra, Easmon reckoned that heart disease, along with pneumonia and dysentery, was a significant cause of death among adults, while records of 3,645 autopsies conducted in the colonial capital between 1921 and 1953 revealed evidence of cardiovascular disease in 12.8 per cent of cases.[22] Conversely, the partial and aggregated nature of the statistical data, even in the late twentieth century, fails to capture the complex mix of wealth and poverty, the sharply uneven access to modern biomedicine, and the consequent variation in life expectancies typical of developing nations. The likelihood is that in deep rural areas beyond the reach of the Births, Deaths and Burials Ordinance, particularly those in the impoverished northern savanna, the majority of deaths continued to be due to contagious disease.

Neither can demographic statistics, on their own, tell us much about changing perceptions of morbidity and mortality. This has been recognized in the scholarly literature on disease and medicine in Africa, which in recent decades has shifted away from its early focus on historical epidemiology—typified by Patterson's pioneering work on Ghana—and towards vernacular concepts of health and healing and the political economy of medical provision.[23] The continent's twentieth-century medical history is now less a narrative of the gradual success of modern medicine in ameliorating a debilitating disease burden, and thereby increasing life expectancy, than one which emphasizes the limitations and coercive nature of biomedical interventions, the ongoing importance of therapeutic pluralism, and recent setbacks resulting from state contraction and the devastating impact of the HIV/AIDS pandemic. An important strand in this more nuanced story is the notion that African bodies, in sickness and in health, and both living and dead, were colonized by the regime of biopower. 'Biomedicine in colonial Africa', the editors of a recent volume on contemporary public health argue, 'was intimately tied to a repressive, coercive, and violent system of power and knowledge, which reached deep into African lives and identities'.[24] It was not just colonial biomedicine, moreover, which was regarded with ambivalence: as we have seen with discourses of poison, vernacular therapeutic technologies were also entangled with what Nancy Rose Hunt has described as a 'harming register'.[25]

Let us return to the attempt by the colonial state to impose a degree of surveillance and management of human life and death. We left this process in the 1890s, with the inhabitants of Accra struggling to come to terms with the new regime of burial imposed by the Cemeteries Ordinance. In an 1892 report on the progress of the Medical Department, Easmon recorded with satisfaction that responsibility for the sanitation of the colony was now firmly in the hands of trained medical officers. The outstanding achievement of the new dispensation, he believed, was 'the abolition of intra-mural sepulture of the dead, the provision of public cemeteries and the organization of burials of the dead by the appointment of Registers of Deaths, Sextons, etc.'.[26] By 1892, however, the ordinance had been applied beyond the capital to only the small seaside towns of Labadi, Teshi, Nungua and Ada to the east. A survey of burial arrangements elsewhere on the coast and in the southeastern regions of Akuapem, Krobo and Peki compiled to facilitate the further extension of its provisions revealed the challenges ahead. The necrogeography of many regions was highly elaborated: the Fante town of Saltpond, for example, had three different 'public' burial grounds, two others for the families of individual chiefs, two Methodist graveyards and one Roman Catholic graveyard, a burial ground on the beach (presumably for slaves), another for 'persons dying violent death', and yet another for those dying of smallpox.[27] Here, and elsewhere, these various sites would have to be either closed or redeveloped and brought under the provisions of the ordinance, with the inhabitants instructed in the new laws and encouraged to abandon deeply engrained methods of disposing of different classes of the dead.

The extension of the bureaucratized burial regime would proceed in fits and starts throughout the period of colonial rule. In 1911, in an effort further to medicalize mortality, it was ruled that medical officers be appointed deputy registrars of death in place of district commissioners. This created considerable confusion among colonial officials. Instructing his officers to hand over all existing registration documentation so it might be passed on to the Medical Department, the commissioner of the Eastern Province (CEP) was taken aback to learn that in Akyem Abuakwa, one of the most important and populous native states in the colony, 'there are no public Cemeteries ... and no book in this office in connection with the registration of deaths'.[28] In response, the CEP drew the attention of district commissioners (DCs) to section 17 of the 1891 Cemeteries Ordinance, which required chiefs, if instructed, to create their own demarcated graveyards. It was the turn of the DCs to be surprised. 'With the exception of the Christian Cemeteries, there are no proper burial grounds in the district', the DC at Kyebi explained. 'The people have not become sufficiently enlightened to have a portion of land fenced and assigned as a burial place for their dead; and as a consequence one finds graves scattered here and there in the bush around the town. I visited the place at Abetifi [in neighbouring Kwawu], which was said to be the burial ground of the heathens, and found numerous graves some distance apart and occupying some eight or ten acres of dense forest'.[29] District commissioners were not especially bothered by this, expressing a reluctance to support the extension of the ordinance to their districts and suggesting instead that chiefs should simply take it upon themselves, if they considered it necessary, to reconfigure established burial practices. 'The hardship upon the Chief laid down by this Ordinance', the DC at Akuse, on the Volta River, insisted, 'seems to me to be out of keeping with British Justice'.[30] Not for the first or the last time, commissioners citing political expediency resisted the increasingly autonomous clout and scientific authority of the colonial medical establishment.

These divisions explain the promulgation in 1912 of the Births, Deaths and Burials Ordinance, which, by subsuming the provisions of the 1891 Cemeteries Ordinance and extending its remit to the registration of vital statistics, created a stronger legal framework for regulating death and burial. Thus, the very mechanism which demographic historians rely on in order to reconstruct changing mortality rates can be interpreted as a key element in the attempt to colonize the African body, alive and dead. Both aspects of the bureaucratization of dying are apparent in contemporary African perceptions. The statistical confirmation of the perception of alarmingly high infant and child mortality rates in Accra, for example, played a role in mobilizing Dr Nanka-Bruce and other elite figures in order to improve maternal and infant welfare in the capital. At the same time, popular resistance continued. When not a single birth was registered in Cape Coast for the month of November 1915, the provincial commissioner was forced to ask Chief Kofi Sackey to 'beat gong-gong' throughout the town to remind the populace of the legal requirement of registration.[31] Such requests needed periodically to be reiterated. 'In the case of births it is very difficult to get them registered with the 14 days allowed', the medical officer at Cape Coast wrote in 1921. 'The Sanitary Inspectors do their best . . . but fail to find out births before the 14 days have elapsed. The women hide the fact that a birth has occurred in the house.'[32]

In part this resistance was due to antipathy towards the intrusive regime of sanitary inspection. By the interwar period, Patterson notes, it was 'one of the most frequent contacts between ruler and ruled', the assiduous targeting of those careless enough to allow mosquitoes to breed in standing water in the vicinity of their houses leading the Police Magistrate's Court to become 'known as the *Loloi* (larva) Court among the women of Accra'.[33] It also reflected the deep-seated sensitivity about dealing with death and the dead—which also impacted upon the registration of births. This is revealed in a 1931 report on the reaction to the regime of registration in colonial Ashanti, where the Births, Deaths and Burials Ordinance was belatedly promulgated in 1925 after an outbreak of plague. The Asante, the senior health officer wrote, 'are easily disquieted and deterred by the mere appearance of "Castle" weight and police powers in matters which to them have a certain traditional religious significance. For instance, since the [1931] Census, it has happened that a Village Overseer has been accused of responsibility for the death of an infant, because he enumerated it among the rest of the family'. People were actually less reluctant to register a death than a birth, the officer explained, 'the deceased being now less exposed to unlucky consequences'.[34] The fourteen-day period within which registration was required, that is, largely coincided with the period before a child's 'outdooring'—during which it was not considered a fully formed human being and any explicit acknowledgement of its existence was enough to risk it being claimed back by its 'ghost-mother'.

Yet all of this was a factor only in the urban locations where the Births, Deaths and Burials Ordinance was applied. By 1919, this amounted to sixteen towns: ten along the coast, from Keta in the east to Axim in the west, and six inland, including the gold-mining centre of Tarkwa.[35] In 1925 the ordinance was applied to the four Ashanti administrative centres of Kumasi, Obuasi (the other main mining town), Kintampo and Sunyani, and in 1928 to Tamale and Salaga, in the Northern Territories.[36] By 1940, there were thirty-five registration districts, including the northern centres of Bawku, Lawra and Wa, where 'a considerable number of labourers in the gold, diamond and manganese mines return to their homes in the Protectorate'. 'Many of them carry with them the seeds of disease (eg. tuberculosis) contracted whilst working in the mines. Without a knowledge of vital factors, it is quite clear that preventative measures cannot be devised in such districts.'[37] The registration regime, that is, followed the skeins of the colonial migrant labour economy into the savanna hinterland. Yet all these districts still represented a mere 9 per cent of the total population. In the countryside beyond, despite ad hoc efforts by indirect-rule chiefs to regulate burial customs and funeral expenditure by way of local bye-laws, established necrogeographies were characterized more by continuity than by change. Even into the era of decolonization in the 1950s, efforts were still being made by central government to foist the registration of vital statistics onto the native authorities.[38] As Ghana stood on the cusp of independence in 1957, it is hard to make a convincing argument for the effective colonization of the dead African body.

At best, a patchwork of contested jurisdictions might be said to have haphazardly been imposed over the dominion of the dead—bearing in mind that, as far as the dead themselves were concerned, the real authority moved in the other direction. In a process which would come to define funerary cultures across modern Africa, mortal remains began to move back and forth across emerging lines of demarcation, as corpses were carried from town to country and from country to town. In cases where remains were reinterred in or exhumed from public cemeteries in the urban registration zones, the colonial state was able to impose some degree of bureaucratic control over their movement: each removal required a separate 'exhumation order', gazetted by the government, to ensure the maintenance of hygiene standards and oversight by a medical officer.[39] Movement of mortal remains, however, often happened either beyond or beneath the radar of the state: in 1934, for example, the Registrar of Births, Deaths and Burials in Kumasi was informed that the corpses of many people who died in the city were being 'taken surreptitiously by the relatives for burial in neighbouring villages'. 'You will realize', he wrote to the Kumasi DC, 'that this practice may result in missing cases of deaths from infectious diseases and I should be grateful if you would instruct the Chiefs that this must cease.'[40] Given ongoing rumours of house burial, double interments and decoy empty coffins, there is every likelihood that it did not do so.[41]

Neither were necrogeographical contests waged simply between the colonial state and its African subjects. For families and communities increasingly differentiated by uneven patterns of Christian conversion, wealth creation and social change, where and how bodies were buried or reburied often became matters of dispute. Given the ongoing role of the dead in the world of the living and the state of heightened emotions generated by bereavement, it is unsurprising that attempts by some to modify customary practice were resisted by others, causing heated stand-offs at funerals, struggles over the possession of bodies and the staging of rival ceremonies. As we will see in the next chapter, growing numbers of the dying sought to use written wills in order to impose their own wishes for a particular form of burial or to forestall anticipated domestic conflict. While the written word served to strengthen the ability of the dead to shape events after their departure, older forms of posthumous agency continued to make themselves known. After Essie Yiakwa died in Saltpond in 1905, for example, it was clear to those attending her funeral that she was not happy with the town's regime of modern cemetery burial. 'There was a remarkable scene in the street before Miller's Factory on Monday', the *Gold Coast Leader* reported, 'when a dead body (according to native custom) would not go to the Cemetery and all of a sudden the coffin fell down, the top opened and the dead rolled off some 13 feet from the coffin'. 'The followers were sadly moved', the report continued, but 'they got it nailed up again' and went on their way.'[42]

The regularization of coroners' inquests and of post-mortem examinations was another aspect of the bureaucratization of modern death and dying. Employed in cases of violent or unexplained death in the main coastal towns by the mid-nineteenth century, inquests were extended to the forest interior in the early twentieth century and to the Northern Territories by the 1930s.[43] Like volumes of wills and probates, inquest records represent an intriguing but methodologically challenging historical source. How to read the dizzying number of individual cases, each a fleeting glimpse into a life and its often tragic end? One line of interpretation is to consider the role of the inquest and the autopsy in advancing alternative, medicalized explanations of the causes of death, as set down by the *ICD* manual. We have seen how the Akan and their neighbours, like other African peoples, historically invested a great deal of time and effort into determining the cause of unexplained death. With the consolidation of colonial rule, the British sought to suppress established methods such as *afunsua* and the *odom* poison ordeal and, by doing so, to relocate death from its social context to one located within the individual body and governed by the state.

If the certification of death, the inquest ruling and the autopsy represented key moments in a new, legally documented regime of dying, it is to the Gold Coast press that we can again turn to consider how the African public might have perceived the changing order of things. While generally embracing the scientific modernity of biomedicine, literate commentators continued to use the language of public health to criticize the failings of the colonial regime. 'The unpleasant odour that many times fouls the air in the vicinity of the mortuary from the decomposition of a dead body awaiting examination, warns the public to the danger to their health', a report from the coastal town of Axim ran in 1915. 'We hope the sanitary officer would recommend its entire removal in the interest of public health.' The same article took up the matter of the disposal of unclaimed bodies by the authorities: 'the dead of whatever rank, since it demonstrates to us the end even of Royalty, should be respected and not treated in a manner that wounds human feelings. For the dead to be placed on a dust-bin truck bare and buried without leaves (coffin being too much to mention) is revolting in the extreme. Everyone complains against this unnatural procedure. Cannot something to be done to remedy matters?'.[44] That dead bodies of all ranks should be treated with equal dignity represents a real shift in attitudes. It in fact took decades before these matters were remedied. It would not be until after the Second World War that Accra and Kumasi received their first 'air conditioned' (i.e., refrigerated) mortuaries—a technological advance which would come to have a great impact on postcolonial funerary culture, allowing corpses to be preserved for extended periods before burial.[45] Meanwhile, demands continued for the provision by local authorities of suitably dignified pauper funerals.[46]

By the interwar period, the press also provided a forum for reflection on old and new meanings of death—and on how potentially to reconcile the two. In 1920, the *Leader* published a three-part essay titled 'Why I Am Not Afraid to Die'. In a striking commentary on the shift from a long-established intimacy with death to its sequestration in the modern age, as later established by Ariès, the anonymous local writer traced his own passage from being terrified as a young man of the prospect of death to a calm acceptance in old age of his own mortality. 'To most ancient peoples death was a circumstance so gruesome, so appalling that a lifetime of philosophizing was not considered too long a preparation to meet it nobly', he wrote, drawing, in a fashion typical of the educated elite, a parallel between classical and traditional African civilizations. Yet, 'we moderns do the thing better, it seems to me. We think the problem once through to the end, and then ... resolutely turn our attention to something else'.[47] It might be argued that keeping death in abeyance by confronting it head-on when necessary but then resolutely turning one's attention to the things of life was one of the strengths of older African attitudes to mortality. But for this commentator, at least, 'we moderns do the thing better', and his thoughtful essay points to the fact that for the first generation of colonized Africans, an individual's journey of self-discovery from anxious youth to resigned maturity intersected with the shift from tradition to modernity.

At a medical rather than philosophical level, extensive coverage was also given to the publication of the annual reports of the Registrar of Births, Deaths and Burials, which by the 1930s were scrutinized for indications of the failure to improve mortality rates. Despite the much lauded opening of the Korle Bu teaching hospital at Accra in 1923, the government was reminded by a vigilant press that medical provision remained limited. 'Considerable Wastage in Childbirth. Deadly Diseases Take a Heavy Toll', ran the headline over coverage in J. B. Danquah's *Times of West Africa* of the registrar's report for 1932–3, for example.[48] 'Are People Perishing from Poverty?' the *Times* asked a year later, suggesting that the deepening economic depression was taking a toll on the health of Accra's inhabitants. 'What is the Government doing to safeguard the population?'[49] Even within the colonial capital, moreover, few patients actually died in hospital. Growing numbers of people willingly sought treatment for a variety of ailments at Korle Bu and other colonial hospitals, but if death appeared to be looming, the imperative remained to die at home.

It was in the interwar period, too, that a sustained case began to be presented for the efficacy of indigenous therapeutic resources and their recognition within a pluralist healing register. This campaign was influenced by the outlawing of successive anti-witchcraft movements, which led growing numbers of *aduyefo* and *sumankwafo* to seek legitimacy by repositioning themselves as 'native herbalists' rather than 'fetish priests'. The most prominent innovator in this respect was J. A. Kwesi-Aaba, owner of a herbal medicine outlet in Sekondi called Sunwunku Industries, who in 1931 founded the Society of African Herbalists.[50] By 1934, the society was offering training and diplomas in African herbal medicine; the following year, Kwesi-Aaba explained its activities in a series of public lectures, each focused on a different aspect of disease and medicine—'the digestive organs', 'the respiratory organs', et cetera.[51]

When the *Africa Morning Post* criticized Kwesi-Aaba and argued for the greater efficacy of Western biomedicine, the *Gold Coast Times* in turn published a stout defence of African herbalism by J. W. Quartey-Papafio, who noted that his late kinsman Dr B. W. Quartey-Papafio and other pioneering physicians had successfully combined the use of local medicines 'in addition to their professional remedies'. '*There is no guarantee against death*', Quartey-Papafio reminded his readers, 'and there are a number of cases treated by European Doctors or African Doctors which have proved fatal. *Does this show that this class of Physicians are quacks?*'.[52]

———

As in nineteenth-century Russia or India, death in colonial Africa was not yet fully the 'colony of medicine'.[53] Building on the 1888 Cemeteries Ordinance, the 1912 Births, Deaths and Burials Ordinance sought further to shift the management of the dead on the Gold Coast from the realm of family and community to that of the state. The certification of death, in particular, located its causes within the individual body, as the coroner's inquest and the autopsy began to replace older, proscribed methods of post-mortem interrogation. The fledgling regime of surveillance, management and medicine, however, had a limited impact on established discourses of morbidity and mortality; indeed, the dislocations and dissonances of the opening phase of colonial conquest appear to have given rise to widespread anxiety that those implacable enemies of human wellbeing, witches and poisoners, were once again abroad. Yet, by the middle decades of the twentieth century, as colonial rule gave way to the era of renewed African sovereignty, a combination of biomedical intervention and rising living standards reduced death rates and triggered a fundamental transition in the region's demographic history. As infant and child mortality decreased and life expectancy increased, death became increasingly associated with ageing rather than with random or malevolent forces: more and more people, in the words of the Aberewa medicine, were once again able 'to depart from this world in their old ages with gray hairs'.

16

Wills and Dying Wishes

BORN AROUND THE YEAR 1860, Joseph Sackey was a Ga fisherman of Kinka, the old Dutch section of Accra. Netting from the great wooden canoes in the rolling Atlantic waters off the Gold Coast was a hard existence, and the fishing communities which crowded into the dilapidated downtown quarters of the colonial capital were far from wealthy. Yet the tough nature of work on the sea gave local fishermen a powerful sense of masculine honour and corporate identity; after a lifetime of labour, Sackey had the satisfaction of reaching the pinnacle of his profession when he was appointed to the office of Kinka's 'chief fisherman'. In 1944, he hurt himself in a fall and, unable thereafter to walk properly, decided to put his house in order and prepare for death by drawing up a will. This was an unusual move for a labouring man: in the mid-twentieth century, the making of written wills was still largely the preserve of the literate, propertied classes. Yet despite having little or nothing in the way of formal education, Sackey was no stranger to the world of letters: he had carefully kept records of the expenses incurred in paying for the funerals of various members of his family, while his role as chief fisherman also entailed written communication with the municipal authorities. His name suggests too that he was a Christian—although the fact that he made no stipulation for Christian burial in the will indicates that any link with the church may have been a tenuous one.

'My name is Joseph Sackey. I am Chief Fisherman of Ussher Town, Accra', his will opens, in a declamatory manner. 'I am about 85 years of age. I fell down in my house about a year ago . . . but my mind is very sound. I know everything and I can remember everything. I had always worked with my own money. I never dealt with family properties or moneys.'[1] Here we have a clue to Sackey's motivation, for the desire to circumvent customary laws of inheritance in order to dispose of self-acquired wealth and property as one saw fit was a principal factor in the emergence of wills on the Gold Coast and, later, in Asante. So too was the ability to use the written word to record a desired vision of the future. 'Within a week after my death, i.e., at the family meeting which will be held to examine the funeral expenses, this will should be read in the presence of the family', he continues. 'I appoint Messrs James Addy of Adabraka and Fixon Owoo of Accra . . . my executors and they should always try and see that peace and harmony prevail among my family, my children and grandchildren.' He then gave instructions for the disposal of his house, half of which he left to his late grand-niece Korkor's children and grandchildren and half to another grand-niece, Dadaye Arkanuah, whom he requested to arrange his funeral. Finally, he asked that after his obsequies, eight named male friends—a fishing crew, perhaps—were each to be presented with a cloth. The document is brief, occupying less than a page of the record book into which it was copied after Joseph Sackey died, eleven months later, on 29 May 1946. Without it, the old man would still have lived on in the memory of family and friends, one of the departed ancestors for whom *kpekpei* was sprinkled on the floors of houses throughout the Ga townships each year at the Homowo festival. Yet his last will and testament—with its self-conscious sense of summation, of looking back over a life and forward to an unknown future—fixes in history an otherwise unremarkable old fisherman.

Written wills have been recognized as a crucial source for reconstructing attitudes towards death and dying ever since historians of the Annales school began research into the topic. In 1500, only some 5 per cent of Parisians made a will, but by 1700 that figure had risen to 18 per cent and it continued to expand, both in Paris and beyond, throughout the eighteenth century. Two pioneering works, Pierre Chaunu's *La mort à Paris* and Michel Vovelle's *Piété baroque et déchristianisation en Provence*, drew on this increasingly abundant documentary resource to come to different conclusions about changing eighteenth-century *mentalités*: whereas Chaunu identified a correlation between rising life expectancy and the 'denial of death', Vovelle argued that the Enlightenment obsession with life rather than with death was due to ideological and social rather than material transformations.[2] Although the Gold Coast literate elite was responsible for producing some of the first written wills in Africa south of the Sahara, the numbers who did so relative even to the total urban population by the early twentieth century remained tiny—perhaps around the 5 per cent figure estimated for early sixteenth-century Paris. The quantitative methods employed by the Annalistes are therefore not appropriate for the smaller Gold Coast colonial archive, which consists of ten volumes recording the granting of probate (including a copy of the will) and of letters of administration (for intestate deaths) for Accra (1887–1959), six volumes for Cape Coast (1906–55) and three volumes for Kumasi (1946–59). More recent textual analysis of native wills from the early modern Americas, however, points to the ways in which individual testaments can be revealing of changing notions of personhood, collective identity and mortuary exchange in a context of cultural encounter, Christian conversion and colonial jurisdiction.[3] As in the colonial Americas, the emergence of wills on the Gold Coast reminds us too that mortuary practices often began long before death, and after that moment proceeded in the form of a dialogue between the living and the dead which was mediated in part by the written word.

In its focus on wills, this chapter seeks to extend the discussion of writing and reading about death in the Gold Coast's late nineteenth-century print media. There is, however, a crucial difference in these two uses of literacy: whereas newspapers were the principal medium of an emergent public sphere, wills—like Christianity—can be seen to represent a shift towards a greater individualization of death, removing matters of inheritance from custom and community to the private, 'bourgeois' realm. Yet here, too, established oral culture did not steadily give way to the modernity of the written word. Written wills may have been an innovation that spread from the European outposts on the Gold Coast, but African societies already possessed a testamentary tradition in the form of a nuncupative (i.e., oral) will which could legally override custom: the deathbed deposition known as *samansie* (variously *samansew* or, for the Ga, *shamansho*), usually translated as 'that left aside by a ghost'. In this respect, the chapter also develops the themes examined in that on gold, wealth and burial. As social change generated by the expansion of the cocoa-based cash economy generated debates over self-acquired wealth, inheritance and the very future of the Akan matrilineage, *samansie* emerged by the 1940s as a matter of considerable attention. Orality, that is to say, remained entangled with the written word, as did older concerns with the sanctity of the deathbed and with the lingering power of ancestral *asamanfo*, 'ghosts'.

Given the fearsome levels of mortality among the officers of the European companies in the era of the gold and slave trades, it is unsurprising that many sought to determine the disposal of their wealth and property in the event of death. Such wills not only provided a model for their African collaborators but also involved local communities, as European men sought to varying degrees to provide for the women with whom they had cohabited and produced children.[4] In the course of the eighteenth century, the use of written wills as legal instruments began to be adopted by local brokers for whom European merchant capital offered opportunities to accumulate personal wealth. A pioneering figure was the literate Euro-African Edward Barter, who, in the 1690s, controlled much of the trade at Cape Coast. In 1703, a year before his death, Barter fell out with the English and moved his operations to nearby Komenda, where he made the Dutch commander the executor of his will and the king of Komenda his legatee.[5] Dutch records from mid-century indicate that both 'mulatto' and African traders sought to circumvent Akan matrilineal inheritance by designating in writing their own children as heirs.[6] Among the predominantly patrilineal Ga of Accra, too, prominent figures began to use wills to break free of local custom. One example was Wetse Kojo, who had risen from humble beginnings as a castle slave, imported from the Slave Coast, to a position of authority as the caboceer of British Accra. 'Cudjoe tho' he is not a very old man, yet he is infirm, and his constitution is much broke', the governor of the African Company wrote in 1764. 'For these reasons, and because he is a Company's slave, and consequently may dispose of his effects in what manner he thinks proper, He has made a will, appointing the Governor and Council here for the time being his Executors'. Despite—or perhaps because of—Kojo's lack of kinship at Accra, however, it was feared that his attempt to determine the disposal of his wealth would be resisted: 'if you do not give orders to the Governor and Council to take Cudjoe's Heir into their protection and at all events to see justice done him, your town at Accra after Cudjoe's decease will be ruined, for those who have effects in this country, but want family and friends to protect 'em, assuredly become prey to their greedy neighbours'.[7] Despite ill health, Kojo lived for another twelve years, dying in 1776, when his inheritance and succession appears to have passed off without the anticipated predation from 'greedy neighbours' or breakdown of British authority.[8] Yet, the stereotypical European portrayal of native lawlessness aside, the case of Wetse Kojo points to two key factors in the early history of will writing on the Gold Coast: that its pioneering practitioners tended to be wealthy accumulators who stood, in various ways, outside of the structures of local society, and that a written will was only as effective as far as it was generally recognized as a legitimate legal instrument.

In common with these eighteenth-century precursors, wills written by Africans in the first half of the nineteenth century seem not to have survived. The earliest I have discovered, that of the Anomabo Euro-African merchant James Francis Parker, dates to 1847; in it, he directs that his estate should be managed by his wife, Fassuah, until his son and heir James Swanzy Parker comes of age—'so long', that is, 'that he conducts himself, to stop at my House, and do everything that is proper and right in the Eye of all'.[9] Like many later testators, Parker was most anxious to preserve his good name: should his young son 'turn out to be bad and misconduct himself, in the Eye of all, so as to bring disgrace upon my House and family, then I wish that Fassuah, my wife, and Elizabeth Swanzy, my sister, take away the property ... and divide [it] amongst themselves as their own for ever'. Another early example, dated 1857, is that of James Bannerman, who bequeathed his property to his Asante wife, Yaa Hom, and, as we have seen, left instructions for his body to be interred within their house, without native custom. By the early 1860s, we see the first wills made by women: Chocho (i.e., Korkor) Badoo, a literate woman of James Town, Accra, and Barbara Mayer, a so-called Christiansborg mulatto who, signing her name with a mark, left to her daughter Matilda Wulff her entire estate, 'including lands, houses, furnitures, slaves, monies and all debts owing to me'.[10] Other early testators from Accra include members of the so-called Tabon community of ex-slave returnees from Brazil: again, ethnic outsiders who wished to avoid the customary laws of inheritance of their Ga hosts.

By the 1840s, however, debates over inheritance generated by contested written testaments as well as by oral deathbed dispositions, *samansie*, began to be heard in British courts. The prominence of women and of domestic slaves in these disputes points to the importance of both in the post-mortem settlement of property. In a case heard at Cape Coast in 1850, for example, a Mrs Kwaku claimed 'under her lawful husband's will the right to enjoy the property bequeathed to her', while the defendant, Kofi Fynn, maintained 'that he married Plaintiff after his brother's death (country fashion to entitle him to the property)'.[11] Although the role of the judicial assessor was to oversee the just application of African law, the decision was in favour of Mrs Kwaku: the production of the will was enough to override the customary matrilineal inheritance underpinned by the law of levirate (Twi: *kuna awadie*, 'widow marriage'). The previous year, the same court had judged a contested oral disposition that had been heard in the first instance by King Aggery's tribunal. In this case, Kwabena Incoom and other plaintiffs were slaves owned by one Kweku Tawiah, deceased. Tawiah, they testified, declared just before his death that his brother, who resided in Sierra Leone, was to be his sole heir and that until the latter's return, his estate—which included the plaintiffs themselves—was to be managed by his friend Kwabena Attopee. By paying Tawiah's funeral expenses, Attopee by custom sealed his role as executor, but 'the day after the funeral, defendant who is a nephew of deceased, came to the house, and called all the slaves together to give them blue baft, which the slaves refused to take as they said he would by and by take possession of the property'.[12] According to the defendant Amshia, Aggery's court had already ruled that no proof could be produced for the *samansie* and that as a nephew of the deceased he, by Akan law, was the rightful heir. The judicial assessor ruled inconclusively that no decision could be made until the return of the deceased's brother, ordering the estate to be managed in the interim by a third party. Both cases, then, turned on a fundamental point of law, one which would continue to feature in countless contests down the generations: in what circumstances might an individual's last will and testament—whether in the form of a written or an oral disposition—override normative laws of inheritance and succession?

One further mid-century legal contest can be cited, a case brought in 1860 by Afosua Attah, widow of the late John Hayfron, against Kwabena Adoo, who may or may not have been Hayfron's uterine brother.[13] Afosua was a slave wife, first purchased and then married by Hayfron at Anomabo. Like Mrs Kwaku a decade earlier, Mrs Hayfron based her claim to inherit from her husband on the fact that they had operated as a joint economic unit. 'I was first married to him Country fashion when very young', she testified. 'I worked . . . with him . . . when the world was very hard . . . to obtain what property he had [so] I consider myself entitled to some of it.' Then, their lives were transformed when both converted to Methodism in 1835. One Kwabena Incoom—a friend of the late John Hayfron and quite possibly the same man who had featured as plaintiff in the case examined above, now going by the Christian name of Josh Martin—elaborated on the events following the Hayfons' conversion. Hayfron had had other wives and children, but in accordance with church rules he was forced to disavow them, retaining only Afosua, who was childless. Why her? Because, Incoom testified, 'she belonged to his house and because in case of his death Plaintiff might keep any property he has in his house'—a common motivation for a man to purchase a slave to marry, and yet another method of avoiding matrilineal inheritance rules. By the mid-1850s, however, Hayfron was having second thoughts about monogamy and asked Afosua to consent to him taking other lovers. When she refused, their relationship came under strain and she applied successfully to the British court to redeem herself for seven ounces of gold, on the grounds that her husband still considered her his slave. The defendant used this narrative in an attempt to show that Afosua was estranged from Hayfron and therefore did not attend him on his deathbed; according to Afosua, she had been absent only because she was ill and had left Anomabo to recover in the bush, returning immediately when she heard he had died. This undermined her case, as an ability to prove attendance on the dying was considered crucial in any anomalous inheritance claim. More problematic was the simple fact that Hayfron died intestate. In contrast with the earlier suit brought by Mrs Kwaku, the judicial assessor ruled against Afosua Hayfron. In this case the court was unwilling, despite Afosua's Christian marriage, to overturn Akan custom in the absence of documentary evidence of her late husband's dying wishes.

Was the writing of wills simply a modernized form of an older nuncupative practice, or did both emerge in parallel as a result of the increasing accumulation of mercantile wealth? The leading Fante jurist John Mensah Sarbah suggested the latter, arguing that *samansie* 'seem to be recognized not so much because of any assumed right to make such a disposition, as because, from feelings of affection, respect, or even superstition, the last wishes of the deceased are considered to be entitled to weight, among the members of his family'. The transaction, however, 'is really opposed to the fundamental principles of the ties binding the members of the family'—and by 'family', Sarbah meant the Akan *abusua*, or matrilineage.[14] The dubious legitimacy of *samansie* also emerges from its use in Asante, where, as we have seen, the transfer of self-acquired wealth to a man's children was perceived historically to be a method of avoiding death duties. Rattray agreed with Sarbah that it fell short of a full testamentary disposition because it was valid only with the consent of the *abusua*, which, he was told, would firmly remind a dying man that it was they who were responsible for his funeral custom and the settlement of his debts.[15] On the matter of its antiquity, however, Rattray thought that, as its clout 'rested entirely in the sanctity placed upon the words of one who had become a spirit ancestor when his wishes came into force, the custom carries us back to times antecedent to the advent of Europeans'.[16] 'A dead man might own property just as a living one', was how one of his informants explained the ongoing vigilance of the deceased testator. 'This property may be handed over to the heir, but if he (the heir) does not look after it well, the *saman* (ghost) will quickly make him sick.'[17] Yet even dangerous ghosts might be challenged. 'The testator's wishes were generally (but not always) carried out', Rattray writes, citing as evidence the Asante maxim *osaman kye adie a, na wanhu kye a, na oteasefo kye bio*—'when a ghost has made an improper distribution of his (private) property, the living will make a new one'.[18]

Cruickshank's mid-nineteenth-century description of a typical oral deposition captures something of the gravitas of the deathbed scene:

> the head of a family summons around his death-bed his relations. He instructs them about the state of his affairs, and how his property was acquired, and how to be disposed of. He is most particular to furnish them with proofs respecting the acquisition of slaves, mentions the names of the witnesses to the transactions, the circumstances under which they took place, and the sums paid for them, in order that his successor may be enabled to defend his rights, in the event of their attempting to obtain their liberty or redemption at the death of their master. He also recounts the names of his debtors, with the sums which he owes to others. His death-bed declarations, made in the presence of reliable witnesses, are always received as evidence in the event of litigation afterwards. Having made these arrangements, he calmly resigns himself to death, apparently unconcerned about a future state.[19]

With the exception of instructions for the disposal of slaves, whose legal status was ended by the British emancipation ordinance of 1874, the tenor of these last words reappear in written form in many wills from the 1880s. So too do another set of directions overlooked by Cruickshank but noted by Rattray in Asante: those concerning the preparation of the body and its burial, especially the interment of grave goods. 'Any reasonable request to bury the owner's private property with him when he died was obeyed', Rattray was informed. 'Most persons, when very ill and about to die, will point out what they wished to be buried with them, saying, *Adie yi, me wu a, now nfa m'adie me nko. Now nnfa ma me a, me ko a, me de now nsamantoa* (This thing which is my own property you must let me take with me. If you do not permit me to do so, when I go I shall report you to the spirits).'[20] The distinction between items buried with the body and those handed down as heirlooms has much to tell us about both individual personhood and collective bonds across the generations.

The military defeat of Asante and the creation of a formal crown colony on the Gold Coast in 1874 marked the triumph of a particular vision of Victorian laissez-faire merchant capitalism, one long championed by the commercial elites of the coastal towns and which provided a model too for those in Asante who aspired to individual accumulation free from state exactions. At the core of this vision were property rights, including the desire to control the terms of inheritance. Testamentary disposition was regularized with the reorganization of the Supreme Court on the Gold Coast in 1876, which brought into force the 1837 English Wills Act governing the issue of probate (i.e., the official verification of a will) to named executors, and of letters of administration for the estates of those who died intestate.[21] Another piece of colonial legislation impacting on the dynamics of inheritance was the Marriage Ordinance of 1884. Advocated by the Christian missions as a weapon again polygamy and designed to resolve the sort of confusion around the civil status of converts apparent in the case of Afosua Attah, the ordinance distinguished between monogamous 'contract' or 'church' marriage, on the one hand, and 'native' or 'customary' marriage, on the other. The devolution of property of those married under the former was henceforth to be governed by English common law and of those married under the latter by African law; in a key ruling in 1894, moreover, the Supreme Court determined that those married by contract could not make a valid *samansie* and if not having made a written will would therefore die intestate.[22] Despite some antipathy on the part of the Christianized commercial elite towards customary inheritance, however, 'ordinance marriage' was unpopular and few married under its provisions. This was in part due to the near impossibility of securing a divorce—but also to the rise of the countervailing ideology of cultural nationalism, which held the Marriage Ordinance, in the words of Mensah Sarbah, to be destructive of 'family confidence, sympathy and natural support'.[23]

Ranging from documents of just a few lines in length, hurriedly dictated in the vernacular in the last days of life, to highly elaborated inventories and pronouncements, often couched in legal or in sacred literary conventions and sometimes revised in multiple codicils, the corpus of testaments from the colonial Gold Coast is, as elsewhere, resistant to concise interpretation. We will therefore focus on three fundamental questions. First, what sorts of property and wealth were being bequeathed, and to whom? Second, what sorts of instructions did testators provide for their burial and funerals? Third, what sorts of advice did testators leave for the living in order to influence a world they would no longer bodily be part of?

As the majority of early testators were members of the propertied commercial classes of the coastal towns, it is unsurprising that houses feature prominently in bequeaths. Successful businessmen and women invested heavily in urban real estate, and large, European-style 'storey houses' became important monuments to accumulative prowess and new, modern lifestyles. The same holds true in Ghana today. By the late nineteenth century, real estate had replaced slaves and gold as the principal store of wealth, and houses were typically bequeathed with the same precision as Cruickshank had earlier observed for slaveholdings. Bequeaths often captured the complex domestic arrangements of a society in transition, reflecting an imperative to accommodate the needs of matrilineal or patrilineal family, of wives and children, and, in many cases, of ex-slaves and retainers. The instructions left in 1894 by Samuel Bannerman, grandson of James, for the disposal of his residence at Winneba is a good example: the house was in the first instance to be left to his wife Hannah 'for the term of her natural life', after which it was to pass to the five children he had with two other women, Daday and Adacoo, and after their decease was then 'to revert to the children of my sister Ambah Koontuah known as Mrs Lecour by Mr Lecour (and not to her black children lately begotten)'.[24]

Such temporal precision was often matched with spatial exactitude, as in the case of the trader Samuel Yawson of the coastal town of Saltpond:

> I direct that ... my son T. A. Yawson should enjoy my own bedroom in No. 2 house until his death and should take part in settling disputes ... in the house and see that no member of the house is wronged, as I would do when I was alive, and nephew Josiah Samuel Andrews to occupy the hall attached to the same bedroom, floors of both places having tiles; also the remaining rooms in No. 2 house should be used by my niece Mary Comfort Assam and children any time they happen to be at Saltpond; and I further direct that my daughter Abba Sarbah should occupy one room downstairs of the No. 2 house and Kwesie Awisa also remain in one room.[25]

Directions were often accompanied by an exhortation that a residence must under no circumstances be sold. William Quartey of Accra, for example, directed his wife and their nine children to pay off a mortgage held by a kinsman as 'it is my sincere wish that [they] ... shall endeavour to redeem that house and keep it as a family house'.[26] Officer Ali, a renowned soldier of the Hausa Constabulary and leader of Accra's Muslim community, was more emphatic: leaving his residence to his wife Madame Amina and their children Mariam and Mama (plus £20 each to seven other named wives), he stated simply that 'the house is never to be sold'.[27] It stands in downtown Accra to this day, emblazoned with a name typical of many ancestral residences in the city's old quarters: Officer Ali Memorial House.

Family houses, then, retained the great symbolic power of the past as well as a new monetary value. Even modern residences built by those whose mortal remains now lay in ordered cemeteries rather than beneath the floorboards were seen as monuments to past generations. The spirit of the dead also adhered to smaller, more intimate possessions—both those which had long constituted individual personhood and those symbolic of new forms of modernity. Items of clothing and jewellery—perceived, as in many cultures, to be an extension of the individual body itself—were prominent among the former and often handed down across the generations, their status shifting from that of self-acquired property to that of family heirlooms or, in Twi, *agyapadie* ('things of the ancestors'). As elsewhere, *agyapadie* 'constructed family memory and kept the self alive for future generations'.[28] Joseph Sackey's bequest of a cover cloth to eight friends indicates the social importance of textiles, as is that by Moses Dadzie of Saltpond, who left to his son 'my double barrelled gun and four silk Ashanti Kente cloths valued at £15, £12, £10.10/- and £6.15/- respectively for his own use absolutely, directing that such cloths *should be worn* by him each annual commemoration of my obsequies after my death'.[29]

John Hammond, also of Saltpond, included a detailed inventory of a typical mix of the traditional and modern consumer goods which filled storey houses, including:

> a bookcase with books therein, my old piano ... silk kente cloth and one tin trunk ... clothes, shoes, hats, underwears, sandals, hosiery and ties ... my meat safe ... my lamps and H.M.V. Gramophone with records ... crockery, beddings, one large Nelson's Bible ... the large framed photograph of my late father. ... All photographs will be at the disposal of my wife Isabella Hammond except that she must hand over one framed group wedding photograph to my sister for the nephews.[30]

Like clothing and jewellery, photographs were powerful mnemonics imbued with the spirit of the dead and were disposed of with great care. The two intersect in the will of Samuel Watson, who left to one of his sons 'all photographs of my good self especially that which was taken dressed in native garb on board the "Balmoral Castle" in mid ocean between Cape Town and Southampton'.[31] Ajitey, meanwhile, a non-literate testatrix from Osu, insisted that because her son Adjei Ansah had been disrespectful and had deserted her, 'I give him nothing'. She directed, moreover, that 'my four Enlargement Photographs [sic] taken from my custody by this wicked son of mine ... be recovered from him by my ... Executors, and have the same displayed on the Walls of my Hall in [my] House and that should he refuse to give up the said... Photographs to exercise extreme legal force... to compel him to return them forthwith.'[32]

The tension between tradition and modernity emerges too when we consider the directions testators left for their burial. Like James Bannerman in 1857, many members of the reformist commercial class insisted on a simple funeral, shorn of elaborate public mourning rituals. Indeed, given the importance of these customs to local societies, it might be argued that their rejection represented the clearest possible statement of a distinct elite identity. In some cases, this rejection was reinforced by an embrace of Christianity, in others by a more secular belief in the progressiveness of a modest send-off. 'I request... my Executors not to hold any country custom or native funeral rites at the time of my death but I desire my funeral to be conducted according to the Christian form and in the plainest manner', the Accra merchant George Cleland testified in 1885, warning that anyone disregarding this would thereby forfeit any interest in his estate.[33] By the interwar period, the growing desire for a modest, Christian funeral was often expressed in the conventional legalese that it must be 'without the least admixing of heathen ceremonies'. Such admixing extended from the drinking of alcohol to the interment of grave goods and on to ostentatious grieving at what one testator described in 1939 as 'the most idolatrous lengthy wakes now shamefully in vogue'.[34]

Wills became increasingly explicit in their demands that old mortuary practices be abandoned. Samuel Sago wished his body 'to be taken up to Anomaboe Cemetery if I decease at Egyaa', where his wife Elizabeth was 'to furnish me a coffin, shroud, and all necessary dressings and on no account... to render herself to undergo any other expenses neither to pay money... as is ordinary done [sic] in native custom'.[35] The Akan custom Sago referred to was the payment by a deceased's spouse and children to his or her *abusua* of a 'funeral donation', or *asiedie* (in Fanti-Twi, *esiadze*). By the interwar period, many testators specifically denounced *asiedie*, which had become a touchstone in broader debates about the escalating cost of funerals and the merits and demerits of matrilineal inheritance. 'I desire that my mortal remains be accorded a Simple Christian burial', John Koomson of Elmina testified in 1931, 'and that my... children... be not requested by my family according to Native Customary Law to pay any Asiadze to the Ntwa Family, of which I am a member or any other family, tribe or clan.'[36] A desire for one's own children to inherit also began to be underwritten by instructions as to the location of burial. Joseph Molenaar, who was from Elmina but lived with his wife and children at Cape

Coast, directed that 'all my children lawful or otherwise are to unite together with my lawful wife' in order to take charge of his burial, which, he insisted, must under no circumstances take place at Elmina, but at Cape Coast.[37] A final, emphatic, example might be cited, from the will of Joseph Amuah, 'of Anomabo and Mankessim': 'I surrender my body to my children . . . *my remains should be buried at Anomabo or Cape Coast* but never at *Mankessim*, as the family there are my *Enemies*'.[38]

Along the central, Fante-dominated reaches of the coast, a number of male testators were specifically concerned to curtail the customary participation of the traditional town militias, or *asafo* companies, in their obsequies. The propensity of the *asafo*s for excessive drinking and rowdy behaviour at funerals may well have been the motive, but a more specific issue was their role in the *kunayo*, the sequence of ceremonies by which widows defiled by the death of their husbands were ritually cleansed. Godfrey Sam, originally from Anomabo but resident at Cape Coast, instructed his executors to prevent the Anomabo No. 4 Company from attending and playing their drums at his funeral, 'but should only be allowed to claim their usual Customary money from my wife quietly and peaceably'.[39] 'I desire Christian burial and custom without any admixture of tribal or martial heathen rites', Kofi Baffoe of Elmina stipulated. 'My No. 1 Military Company to be therefore formally warded off, after the Ceremony of spreading the Company's flag behind my mortal bed'.[40] Even James Jackson, himself a *supi*, or commander, of Cape Coast's No. 3 Company, sought to prevent the tradition by which the widow of a member would be paraded around the *asafo*'s ritual headquarters or *posuban*: 'my wife Ablah Gyaki shall not be taken to the Company post . . . but my Company shall deal with her in my house privately'.[41] Likewise, Kwesi Gyafu left instructions on how to prevent a clash at his funeral between the two *asafo*s of the Oguaa state of which at different times he had been a member, setting out an elaborate ploy by which two wives should be dealt with separately by one company and 'the rest of my wives' by another.[42]

If wills became a vehicle for expressing a new kind of modern selfhood, then they could also serve as one in which tradition might be defended. Adherence to rather than rejection of custom emerges most strikingly with regard to instructions for the preparation of the corpse and the interment of grave goods—as Rattray observed, traditionally a crucial part of the final deathbed testament. The most elaborate directions for dressing the body for burial and for the next life tended to be made by women. Consider this example from Ambah Fynnebah of Cape Coast: 'I direct that Mrs J. E. Halm . . . open my box... and take from it the following silver jewels viz: one necklace, a pair of ear-rings, three hair pins and a pair of bracelets these with other few silver jewels... Mrs Halm may think fit to lend from friends to dress my body with; but when I am about to be placed in the coffin to remove those jewels but my own... to remain on me to the grave. And I earnestly desire and strictly protest that 'No Gold' of whatever nature be used at this occasion'.[43] Silver ornaments, it will be recalled, were customarily interred by the Akan on the body of an *ahemaa* (queen mother) only, so Ambah's forceful instructions in this regard may well indicate that she held such an office. She was not, however, a complete traditionalist, directing that 'the customary hair-shaving of members of my house at such occasion be dispensed with'.

A generation later, in 1946, Essie Yennebah of Elmina set down the most detailed set of instructions yielded by the archive on the preparation of her body and the conduct of her funeral. There is in Essie's will a sense of a reaction on the part of traditionalists towards the agitation for modesty, economy and sobriety—a reaction that is likely to have been expressed in oral testaments but rarely would have found its way into writing. Essie, a non-literate trader who had made good, insisted on the full bash, not just detailing the enormous array of gold jewellery she wished her body, from head to toe, to be laden with ('all these to be buried with me i.e. not to be removed before placing my body in the coffin') but also calling for the addition of cloths and silk headkerchiefs and—'this must be carefully observed'—instructing that 'the sum of one guinea... being my working amount should be tied in a handkerchief and another one guinea being my family amount being tied in another handkerchief and four shillings to be separately tied in another handkerchief to be buried with me'.[44] Essie was taking no chances as she mounted the ladder of death. She then detailed the type of music she wished to be played at the various stages of the funeral and, in contrast to those who sought to curtail the role of the *asafo*s, insisted that Elmina's 'Company No. 4 should accompany my body to the cemetery together with Adenkum players'. There was, however, one strikingly modernist element of Essie's testament: her instructions for the participation of local mutual societies, or *kuw*. She appears to have been a member of at least five of them and, true to character, directed her executors to ensure that all donations from them to the funeral be in hard cash.

Finally, let us consider testamentary advice to the living. Joseph Sackey's desire to ensure peace and harmony among his survivors was quite typical, although such pronouncements varied from the cursory to the highly elaborated. The degree to which they were consistent with deathbed declarations is unclear: while it is hard to believe that a dying paterfamilias or materfamilias would not have set out a vision of the future, the emphasis on maintaining domestic harmony or reconciling differences may have emerged as a result of the growing propensity from the nineteenth century to use both *samansie* and written testaments to accommodate spouses and children at the expense of the 'family'. Not all testators, however, displayed even-handed magnanimity: as we have seen with Joseph Amuah, many remained intransigent towards those they regarded as enemies. A recurring sentiment in such cases was a desire that certain individuals or even entire branches of a family must be prevented from gazing upon their dead body. Joseph Mensah, for example, was adamant that 'my late father's niece Ekua Mannan and all other domestics under her must on no account and under no circumstances or consideration whatsoever be allowed to see my body'.[45] Amba Sackah of Elmina, who wrote her will in 1935 and died a year later, desired a simple, Christian burial with no alcoholic drinks. Her testament, however, might be seen as less than fully Christian in spirit: 'I emphatically direct that none of my late Sister Pusroom's children and grandchildren . . . be allowed to view my face or body or take part in my funeral custom. . . . They cannot be reconciled to me when I am dead'.[46] A variation on this theme is the punitive bequest of one penny or of a Bible, accompanied by a stern admonition, designed to shame the recipient. Comfort Amegatcher, lying dying in Korle Bu hospital in Accra in 1946, for example, bequeathed to her husband 'the sum of Ten-shillings with which to buy a Bible from which to learn to be kinder to his next wife'.[47] Likewise, James Glover devoted most of his testament to detailing the various grievances he had against family members, ending with a warning to his executors to be on the lookout for any signs of false mourning on the part of one ingrate, 'as it would be a vain "crocodile tears" that he may attempt to shed for me'.[48]

One moving example was left by Adwoa Awotwi in 1949. Originally from Elmina but residing in Asante, Adwoa was concerned to set the record of her life straight. Her will is worth quoting at some length, as it serves further to illustrate a theme we have already touched on: the treatment of women, both in life and in death, who either had lost or were unable to bear children:

> My life time made me understand that when any woman in this world had no children from her womb . . . Woe betide her, because one day she would be disgraced in public from [i.e., by] her family. Though . . . I had two children from own womb with Mr J. W. Derby of Cape Coast who was my first husband, but as God pleased all died, thence I had not born again.

Though while I was living very lonesome, in fact, my sisters ... gave me some of their children for training of which Akura Mensah was one and when he came to the age ... I put him into school. ... [she later set Mensah up in business, but he cheated her and she took out a complaint against him before one Chief Gyase]. The family put my complaint to him to answer ... he opened his mouth ... and said in the presence of the family '*Sadwi besa yi*' that is 'The barren woman' brought me before you ... and I must go back to Kumasi to get a child from [my] own womb ... [I]f not [for] Sanka Abba and her daughter Essie Esiam who comforted encouraged and helped me I would have committed suicide, I thank God that through their comfort and help I was able to bear the disgrace and worriness in this world up to my proper death.[49]

It was to Sanka Abba and Essie Esiam that Adwoa, whose 'proper death' came two years later, in 1951, bequeathed her treasured United Africa Company trade passbook.

The entanglement of established perceptions of mortality with the modernity of written testaments is nowhere more intriguing than in the invocation of the ongoing vigilance of the dead. Albert Bainn of Cape Coast made no bones about what he would visit upon his children from beyond the grave if they failed to fulfil his last wishes: 'Albert and Otoo after my death you must take great care in supporting your mother and sisters, without, my soul will vex you too much'.[50] Another vehement example is that by Kwaku Manukure, an Akuapem cocoa farmer: 'on no account on earth, whatsoever, must my own nephew Kwame Yirenchie be allowed to inherit my properties and any person who will dare to determine the case or grievances existed between myself and him, and to offer to pacify my dead ghost or spirit in the grave will suffer and does so at his or her own risk'.[51] Yaw Krah, an early testator from the Asante region, also warned that as a departed *saman* he will enforce his will: 'He who quarrels, abuses or *litigates* with Kwame Ntow about my seat [i.e., stool?] ... given to him, is with case or matter with [i.e., will be in dispute with] my Ghost'.[52] Some wills explicitly reiterate what had previously been declared orally by a deceased antecedent. In dividing his property between his family and his wife and children, storekeeper William Sey directed that 'my wife is to live happily with my brother as my father told me when he was dying'.[53] Seeking to prevent anything of his family estate passing to his sister, William Quaye testified that 'the ghost of our mother had forbidden her *not* to stay in the House according to her own prophecy in the presence of all our relatives.

These conditions apply to her children as well because they follow the example of their mother'.⁵⁴

Our focus here has been the textual nature of wills rather than their contested legal aftermath or broader debates about inheritance. The shift in the testamentary tradition from oral deathbed disposition to written wills occurred within the context of the changing dynamics of wealth accumulation and the expansion of the judicial machinery of the colonial state, and was in part an attempt by African property owners to mobilize the latter in order better to manage the former. If, however, the documentation of dying wishes was a strategy designed to privilege one's chosen heirs by avoiding the reversals to oral *samansie* described by Rattray ('when a ghost has made an improper distribution, the living will make a new one'), then it was only partially successful. By the 1940s, as McCaskie writes with respect to Asante, the 'courts were deluged with contested last wills and testaments, and Kumase lawyers were taking up the lucrative business of representing the parties in dispute'.⁵⁵ Indeed, by mid-century the entire system of inheritance on the Gold Coast and in Asante was characterized by widespread contest. The heavy use of conjugal labour in the cocoa economy from the 1890s had accelerated the propensity of men to privilege inheritance by their wives and children, while increasing numbers of women themselves were making the same argument that Mrs Kwaku and Afosua Attah had made in the mid-nineteenth century: that they had a moral right to inherit at least some of the estate that they had worked so hard with their husbands to build. The result was growing uncertainty over the future of the Akan *abusua* itself: by the 1930s, sections of the Gold Coast intelligentsia regularly railed in the press against the 'backwardness' of the matrilineal system, while others sought to uphold the integrity of native law and custom. Precisely what that 'custom' was, moreover, came under intense scrutiny—in the papers, in the courts, in chiefly councils and, it can be surmised, in the minds of those anticipating the end and attempting to formulate their dying wishes.⁵⁶ By 1937, the assiduous James Glover, whom we have already encountered, was citing Danquah's *Akan Law and Customs* (1928) in his will—'see in my book library'—as evidence for the legitimacy of his bequest; as written wills became more common in Asante, meanwhile, many included detailed genealogical tables in order to support the decisions of the testator.

Yet it should be remembered that by the mid-twentieth century only a small minority of those dying had made a will. Although the expansion of the colonial economy had increased the capacity of individuals to accumulate self-acquired wealth and property, most continued to be disposed of without recourse to a written testament. It is in this context that *samansie* re-emerged at the centre of the deepening debate over inheritance. Emerging from disputes heard in both native tribunals and colonial courts, the question of what constituted a legitimate *samansie* moved up the hierarchy of indirect rule to the chiefs' councils of the Gold Coast and of Asante.[57] Must a *samansie* properly be made on a deathbed in contemplation of immanent demise, or might it be made before that, in full health? If the latter, might it be revoked? What witnesses were required to be present and must a 'thanksgiving drink', or *aseda*, be consumed to seal the transaction? Must it then be publicly announced at the funeral to be valid? After much scrutiny of case law and consideration of opinion, African and European legislators, led by the progressive *omanhene* of Akyem Abuakwa, Nana Sir Ofori Atta, attempted to resolve these questions by making a clear legal declaration in 1943 of what an oral deathbed disposition entailed. But the truth was that opinions continued to differ—one reason being that the 'custom' of *samansie* was itself changing. To underpin its authority, some oral testators in Asante had begun to swear the great oath; others began to write down the declaration as it was made—thereby blurring the line between oral and written testaments. Debates over *samansie* therefore continued into the second half of the century and, no doubt, continue today.[58] What was transacted on the deathbed remained a matter of the gravest importance. The wishes of those hovering on the brink of eternity must be respected, Fortes was told in the 1940s, 'since one cannot dispute with a ghost'.[59]

17

Northern Frontiers

GANDAH, *naa*, or 'chief', of Birifu, a dispersed settlement of traditional mud-walled compounds located near the bank of the Black Volta River in the north-western corner of the Northern Territories of the Gold Coast, died on 8 February 1950. Since the British began to consolidate their rule on the remote frontiers of the protectorate in the opening decades of the twentieth century, commissioners had made a point of noting the demise of the chiefs they had appointed to oversee local communities in the relevant district record book. Such entries are typically perfunctory—so-and-so chief of such-and-such a locality died yesterday—and include a comment on the deceased's efficacy as a functionary of colonial rule. As far as the documentary record is concerned, such intermediary figures remain, in death as in life, little more than cardboard cut-outs, fading names on worm-eaten pages. Gandah is an exception. He was born in the 1870s, a decade before agents of the European Scramble for Africa first traversed the savannas of the middle Volta basin, and had been chief of Birifu since 1917, establishing a reputation with British officers as a tough, dependable operator and with Africans—those of his own community and far beyond—as a formidable figure whose wealth and good fortune were underpinned by his accumulation of an extraordinary array of ritual powers. As an 'improving' chief, Gandah also had the foresight to send some of his more than one hundred children to the local school run by the Catholic White Fathers mission. One of his educated sons, Kumbonoh Gandah, took it upon himself to write a biography of his father, recently published as *Gandah-Yir: The House of the Brave*.[1] Just six months after the old chief's death, moreover, the anthropologist Jack Goody arrived in Birifu in order to study the religious life of the people he called the LoWilli and LoDagaa (now Dagara), forging a lifelong relationship with the late chief's family. Goody's fieldwork resulted in *Death, Property and the Ancestors* (1962), the first book-length ethnographic treatment of mortuary custom in Africa and a key contribution to the emerging cross-disciplinary literature on death.[2] Goody never knew Gandah, but the departed chief's powerful presence hung over Birifu during his year of residence there—posthumously shaping the terms of the ethnographic encounter.[3]

If any long life might be seen as a protracted struggle against mortality, then Gandah's was visibly so. As Kum Gandah's biography underlines, his father was born in a place and time where disease, hardship, violence and the precariousness of human existence conspired to give death the upper hand from the outset. Mortal threat, both visible and invisible, came from every quarter and reminders of its presence lay all around—from the family graves marked by overturned pots that formed a penumbra around each fortified homestead to the bleaching human bones that lay strewn over a hillside on the outskirts of Birifu, the result of an old blood feud between two neighbouring settlements.[4] Even achievement was fraught with danger: the young Gandah acquired a reputation as a fine xylophonist and a dead shot with bow and arrow, 'hence a good defender of his family home, the patriclan and the village at large against outside invaders'. 'However, his father was dead against his talents on the xylophone for fear that he might be poisoned or shot dead while he was still at a tender age by his enemies or rivals', and, indeed, 'many times Gandah's life was physically threatened when he went across the river to play at *bagre* festivals or at funerals'.[5] It was in fighting off such attacks that Gandah became a *ziesob*, a 'homicide', an ambivalent identity that aroused a mixture of horror and awe—and which would shape the nature of his burial customs in February 1950.[6] The concept of 'homicide', however, took on a different complexion after the imposition of British rule in the 1900s, when Gandah's stout defence of self and family put him on the wrong side of colonial law. In 1912, one of his wives, Manduor, died after giving birth, along with her newborn child. As was customary after any unnatural death, soothsayers were consulted and it was revealed that mother and child had been killed by a witch. Identifying the culprit, a known practitioner of witchcraft named Deri, who appeared to confirm his guilt by refusing to attend Mandour's funeral, Gandah swore to avenge the deaths. In this instance, his prowess as a bowman let him down: attacking Deri but failing to kill him, Gandah was arrested, convicted of attempted murder and imprisoned at the Northern Territories headquarters at Tamale.

This episode marked a turning point in Gandah's life. Rather than let it alienate him from colonial power, he made a strategic decision to engage with it, and in 1917, following his early release, was appointed the second *naa* of Birifu. According to Kum Gandah, he immediately laid down a set of new regulations for the community, including the insistence that all illnesses ('epidemic or not'), all inward and outward migration, and all births and deaths be reported to him. Had his father had the services of a literate clerk, Kum reflects, these rules 'would have provided the basis of the first recorded demographic and medical statistics for the village'.[7] Neither these regulations nor Gandah's growing prowess as a healer, however, was enough to keep death from his door. By 1932, his household numbered some 120 people, but in the years that followed its strength was eroded by an alarming sequence of fatalities. 'All through 1933 we continually buried the dead', Kum remembers, 'and it made one to wonder whether the gods were not actually angry with us. My father tried in vain to seek for the cause. He sent people outside Birifu to look for diviners and soothsayers who prescribed remedies in the form of sacrifices to the various gods. Sacrifice upon sacrifice was made to these gods but it seemed they were never appeased, for we still mourned and buried the dead until the beginning of 1934 when there was a short lull'.[8] Then, Wule, Gandah's chief wife (*poona*) and Kum's mother, died of blood poisoning, having trodden on a vicious thorn. When in a paroxysm of grief Gandah attempted to stab himself to death he was saved by his protective ritual powers, which turned away the blade of his sword. As with the death of Mandour, witchcraft was identified as being behind Wule's death and, again, Gandah went after the suspected culprits. Rather than hunting them down, however, in a sign of the times he brought charges against them in the district commissioner's court and secured their imprisonment. Shortly after, all three culprits died, one after the other: victims, Kum hints, of mystical retribution by Gandah's ritual powers.

It was Gandah's renown as a healer and accumulator of ritual 'medicines' which characterized the final stages of his life. In a pattern which was emerging at other shrine centres in the Northern Territories, when in the late 1920s he granted two Asante travellers access to one of his medicine deities, Kukpenibie (lit. 'I will not live with evil-doers'), it was transformed into a trans-regional healing cult known in the south as Kankamia.[9] In the early 1930s, after the protective powers of Kankamia had reportedly impressed Asantehene Agyeman Prempeh, Gandah himself travelled to Kumasi in order to oversee the installation of an ancillary shrine in the nearby village of Kwapra.[10] Throughout the 1930s and into the 1940s, Kankamia's renown drew an influx of Asante pilgrims to Birifu, adding more wealth to Gandah's burgeoning household.

In 1948, Gandah's health deteriorated and his eyesight began to fade. Two years later, he died. Kum's biography of his father concludes with an account of his burial and funeral, which were also recounted to Goody. One of the first things done after the death of any Dagara, both sources stress, is that soothsayers must determine whether the deceased can actually be mourned in public. The list of bad deaths (*ku faa*) which would prevent this was a long one, and included those killed by infectious disease, by arrow, by poison or by lightning; those identified as witches, suicides or slaves; and those—like Gandah—who were *ziesob*, who had themselves killed others. In the last case, the corpse was regarded as particularly dangerous and had to undergo a sequence of purificatory rites: it was rolled over three times with ebony poles by other *ziesob*, one of whom then chewed a certain medicinal root and spat the red juice on the corpse's left arm—the one that held the bow—after which the *ziesob* performed a mimed dance which enacted the deceased's feats in battle.[11] Aware he was dying, Gandah sent one of his sons to fetch a renowned 'homicide medicine' for his corpse from a distant settlement; in order to do so, the son also had symbolically to become a *ziesob* by shooting a dog as a substitute for a person (in earlier times, a human corpse encased in clay was set up to be shot with arrows for the same purpose).[12] Only then could drums, xylophones and gunshots be unleashed to announce the death. After seven days of rites, Gandah's coffined body was buried in front of his house amid great lamentation. An even greater funeral custom was held, as among the Akan, one year later, an announcement of which, Kum notes with pride, was made over Radio ZOY, the Gold Coast's national radio network. Kwame Nti, one of the two men to whom Gandah had given Kukpenibie in the 1920s, arrived from Kumasi with a large entourage of adepts and a brass band. Events culminated on 8 February 1951 at Birifu's ancestral shrine (*kpiin par*), where a wooden statue representing Gandah was placed among those of the other ancestors. 'For that was the day that his soul is supposed to have left this earth of ours to the land of the ghosts or the spiritual land (*kpiime teu*). From then on his soul has been blessed to join the kingdom of the dead and he has since become one of the ancestors of the Gandah house.'[13]

Gandah's story encapsulates key themes in the history of death and the dead in the Northern Territories in the first half of the twentieth century. This was a region that was in many ways quite distinct from the Akan forest and Gold Coast to the south. Historically, connections between the Akan world and the peoples of the middle Volta savannas did exist: Asante armies extended imperial overrule deep into the savanna zone in the eighteenth century, facilitating the supply of northern captives—*nnonkofo*—to the forest kingdoms and on to European slave traders on the coast. Yet in terms of ecology, culture and political structure, the savanna, as the Akan perceived it, was another realm: remote, alien, primitive and, especially with regard to the decentralized peoples who lived beyond the reach of the so-called Mossi-Dagomba kingdoms, on the fringe of humanity itself. 'I know nothing about them', Asantehene Kwaku Dua Panin told Freeman in 1841. 'I allow my people to buy them as they please: they are no use for any thing but slaves; they are stupid, and little better than beasts.'[14] This notion of the otherness of the savanna region was to some extent inherited by the British colonial state. The Northern Territories, that is to say, was regarded as a remote and essentially 'tribal' periphery of the Akan-dominated core of the Gold Coast to the south, a subordinate relationship neatly captured by the title of Rattray's landmark ethnographic survey of the region: *The Tribes of the Ashanti Hinterland* (1932).[15]

Historians have been able to reconstruct in broad outline the emergence of a complex of kingdoms forged by horse-riding migrants who from the fifteenth century entered the savannas of the Volta basin straddling present-day Burkina Faso and northern Ghana. What little is known about the precolonial past of the region tends to be focused on these conquest states, whose courtly and commercial elites came to profess, to varying degrees, an adherence to Islam and where royal lineages were preserved by oral traditions and a scattering of written Arabic chronicles. It is only with the advent of European conquest at the turn of the twentieth century, however, that the social life of the non-centralized peoples who lived beyond these zones of state-building can begin to be discerned. Sometimes falling under the nominal overrule of states but more often inhabiting the interstices between them, these peoples formed a patchwork of dozens of small ethnic and linguistic groups: often not coherent 'tribes' at all, but congeries of fiercely independent households, clans and communities bound together by overlapping ties of kinship and ritual affiliation. Underlying this fragmented ethnic landscape, however, was a significant degree of cultural unity, nowhere more so than in the ubiquitous distinction in the realm of religious belief and practice between the cult of the earth (*teng*) and the cult of the ancestors (variously *bo'ar, boyar, bagre*). These two parallel cults, in turn, shaped mortuary culture and the ongoing relationship with the dead. The latter was, if anything, even more intimate than among the Akan: the ferocious patriarchy of these small-scale agriculturalist societies carried over into the realm of the ancestors, whose stern denizens stood watchfully over each and every aspect of the social life of the living.

The savanna peoples incorporated into what in 1902 became the Northern Territories of the Gold Coast needed all the help they could get from both earth and ancestors. The process of colonial conquest tended to be more violent and destabilizing than in the south, as a period of insecurity and rising mortality caused by renewed slave raiding, drought and rival European military campaigns in the 1880s–90s extended in many frontier regions into the 1910s in the form of predation by colonial auxiliaries and punitive expeditions against supposedly recalcitrant tribes. The eventual imposition of 'colonial peace' did serve to reduce high levels of interpersonal violence—as illustrated by the transformation of the bow-and-arrow-wielding Gandah into a law-abiding functionary of the new regime. Yet blood feuds and other 'bow and arrow palavers' continued to claim many deaths, particularly those of young men, in frontier regions. Gandah himself lost members of his family to homicidal feuds with the 'French Lobi' across the Black Volta frontier into the 1920s, and chafed under the terms of the *pax Britannica*: 'If the Commissioner was not here I would cross [the river] the same day with the whole of my young men, and pay my debt', he declared. 'Our enemies on the French side are laughing at us. They say I am a coward because I dare not avenge my relations. Now we are as women. I am ashamed.'[16]

Under British rule, moreover, the protectorate remained a marginal, underdeveloped zone where life for many was a constant struggle against a harsh and unforgiving environment. Food shortages were common, both during the cyclical 'hungry season' (the months before the annual harvest) and as a result of outright crop failure due to drought or locust plague. As we have seen, biomedical infrastructure barely existed and infectious disease, compounded by poor nutrition and debilitating chronic conditions, remained a major killer. Among the Dagara and their neighbours in the northwest, recurring epidemics of cerebro-spinal meningitis took an especially heavy toll in lives. The result, as far as can be told from the rudimentary statistical record, was a discrepancy in death rates and life expectancy between the more prosperous southern Gold Coast and its impoverished northern hinterland.[17]

Like Kwaku Dua Panin, British officers knew little or nothing of the northern peoples they were sent to rule in the opening years of the twentieth century. This lack of knowledge began in many regions with the question of who exactly those peoples were, as administrators struggled to make sense of a social landscape in which identities were fluid and where a community's own 'ethnic' name for itself was often quite different from that given by its neighbours and different again from that given by more distant outsiders.[18] As elsewhere in colonial Africa, repeated attempts would be made to impose order upon these seemingly disordered landscapes. The imposition of chiefs where none had hitherto existed—like Gandah in Birifu—was the preferred initial method. By the interwar period, however, ethnographic research had revealed the underlying importance of the earth priests, or *tengdana*, in local 'constitutions', a number of which were resurrected and codified in the 1930s in an effort to facilitate a shift towards indirect rule. It also paid considerable attention to how people buried their dead. Research into mortuary customs and the realm of the ancestors became increasingly sophisticated, moving from the first rudimentary compilation of 'native law and customs', in 1908, to the work by Rattray in the 1920s, Meyer Fortes in the 1930s and Goody in the 1950s. Indeed, mortuary custom and belief were identified as an important way by which the different 'tribes' of the Northern Territories might be identified, ruled and, in time, understood.[19]

The earliest accounts of mortuary customs in the region underlined the received bifurcation in the political landscape between the centres of Mossi-Dagomba state-building, on the one hand, and the surrounding 'pagan tribes'—the term itself borrowed from Muslim interlocutors—on the other. It was in the former that Islam had had some impact and where funerals conformed to a varying extent with the Muslim norm: overseen by a *liman* (or *malam*) and expedited with a minimum of ceremony and ostentation. Certain aspects typical of Islamic practice throughout Sudanic West Africa were observed, notably the writing of Quranic verses on a wooden tablet which were then removed with water used subsequently to wash the face of the corpse, as well as the ongoing use of local grave architecture—that is, an L-shaped grave, with the corpse placed in the horizontal part of the L and then sealed off to prevent it coming into direct contact with the earth.[20]

In contrast, 'pagans' were revealed to indulge in complex and protracted rites—unless, that is, a death was identified as a bad one, in which case the corpse was summarily disposed of in the bush. Great attention was therefore given to determining whether a death was 'natural' (that is, determined by the ancestors) or the result of mystical retribution by spiritual agents or by maleficent human witches. 'A knowledge of the actual cause of death is of great importance to those who remain behind', Goody would later write of the Dagara.[21] If witchcraft was detected, severe retribution would often be sought.[22] This raised issues for a colonial regime which sought to stem interpersonal violence and monopolize capital punishment. As we have seen with Gandah, however, officials in the north did make allowances for the established recourse to the *lex talionis*, the law of an eye for an eye, and for the regular flaring up of 'bow and arrow palavers'. Burial customs were also the cause of official disquiet: not only the widespread practice of interring certain corpses within rooms or in the courtyard of walled compounds, as in the south, but the use by a number of peoples of large family tombs, accessed by a vertical shaft, which would regularly be reopened to accommodate new bodies. Just when the 1912 Births, Deaths and Burial Ordinance was seen to have provided an instrument for the imposition of order over African mortuary practices on the Gold Coast, an alarming vista of necrogeographical disorder suddenly opened in the Northern Territories.

By 1914, the medical establishment was urging legislation to lessen the threat of contagion by bringing the protectorate in line with the Gold Coast Colony.[23] In regions where 'settled rule' had only recently been imposed, however, administrators were concerned about the impact of intervening in the spiritual realm. A set of draft rules governing the laying out of modern cemeteries was drawn up, but Chief Commissioner Armitage was reluctant to enact it either in the centralized kingdoms or on the stateless frontiers. 'The burial of Chiefs and their relations apart from the "common herd" is an old established custom in the protectorate, and one, in my opinion, not to be discouraged', Armitage wrote, later adding that 'I do not think it would be wise to bring into operation suddenly a prohibition against the burial of relatives in the compounds of houses, as it is an almost universal custom'.[24] Governor Clifford in Accra accepted the case for political expediency, but requested more information. In July 1914, the acting chief commissioner accordingly instructed his officers to furnish him with a report 'on the Custom of burials in houses practiced among the Tribes in your Province', including 'whether the grave is inside a house, compound or just outside the compound', 'what attitudes the Chiefs would adopt were restrictions placed on this Custom' and 'whether (as in Dagarti) a grave will be opened irrespective of the length of time elapsed since the last body was put in'.[25]

The findings only reinforced the reluctance of the protectorate administration to interfere with the dominion of the dead. 'With few exceptions it is the universal custom for natives of the tribes inhabiting this Dependency to bury their dead either in a room, in the compound or just outside the compound', Moutray-Read summed up. Support from the chiefs for any attempt to prohibit those customs, he believed, would not readily be obtained. 'The reason among a Pagan population (with great and firm conviction in the existence of spirits and the necessity of propitiating them) for this custom is obviously to safeguard the spirits of the departed and in my opinion if the proposed rules were applied to all stations it would cause much uneasiness and unrest among the people who would rather desert their compounds and go and live elsewhere where they would not be interfered with than submit to them.'[26] Political expediency, perhaps, but, for 1915, this was an enlightened and accurate assessment. Local informants in various regions had suggested a range of other explanations for intramural burial, including the fear of desecration by enemies and the danger of fresh graves being dug up and the corpses eaten by marauding hyenas. But subsequent anthropological inquiry would confirm the imperative to keep the spirits of the ancestors in intimate quotidian contact with the living. 'The duty of burying a parent and celebrating his or her funeral is the first step in the most exacting of all filial duties, the cult of the dead parents', Fortes would write. 'A man can not rest secure until he has assimilated his father's or mother's spirit into the framework of his life, domesticated it, so to speak... For that reason Tallensi want to have the graves of their parents near their dwellings. True, a man's ancestor spirits accompany him wherever he goes, but they are most tangibly present in his house, where he sacrifices to them.'[27]

Another key aspect of mortuary practice which emerged from the 1915 inquiry, one which was distinct from that of the Akan world, was the widespread existence of specialist gravediggers. Among the Mamprussi, Talensi and other peoples in the northeast of the protectorate, these sextons were called *bayaase*, but they appear to have been most prominent among the Dagara and Sisala in the northwest, where the grisly task of reopening collective chamber vaults required special training and protection in order to withstand the mystical contagion understood to emanate from decomposing corpses.[28] 'Induction into the grave-diggers' fraternity involves the consumption of a special powder known as *bo tii* or *tii tuo*, which ... may be called "grave medicine"', Goody explained. Training also involved being forced down into the chambers; in Gonja, it was reported that the apprentice was 'buried with the corpse for at least an hour', during which time 'the grave is closed on him'.[29] Neither was the *bayaase*'s role limited to grave construction and interment: crucially, their mystical training gave them the ability to detect when the soul of a grief-stricken mourner attending a burial slipped its bodily moorings and was drawn into the open grave by the corpse. They then could entice the soul back out, thereby averting the death of its owner.[30]

After considering the findings of the mortuary survey, the chief commissioner informed Accra that he did not think it advisable to apply the draft regulations prohibiting burial within or adjacent to native compounds. It would be another twelve years until there was any further attempt at legislation, when in 1927 the Births, Deaths and Burials Ordinance was extended to the Northern Territories. Proceeding cautiously, the administration applied the ordinance in the first instance to only two localities: the headquarters of the protectorate, Tamale, and that of its Eastern Province, Salaga.[31]

New cemeteries comprising separate 'pagan', Muslim and Christian sections were laid out in both, gravediggers appointed, and provisions made for the issuing of death certificates. Yet even in these urban centres problems arose in enforcing the new regime. The paucity of medical staff meant that it often proved impossible to determine the cause of death and therefore to issue a death certificate, without which an 'ordinance burial' could not proceed. There were ongoing concerns that hyenas would disinter and eat newly buried bodies.[32] More serious in the longer term, however, was the profound attachment of local communities to customary rites—including the imperative, for both Muslims and non-Muslims, that corpses be interred by their own specialist gravediggers. In 1935, a delegation of Gonja dignitaries approached the district commissioner at Salaga to protest at 'the whole system of the working of the cemetery', from the exorbitant fees—the charge of four shillings per adult body was said to represent eight days work for one man—to 'the old strong objections on the part of the Moslem to the graves for their dead being dug by pagans'.[33] When four years later the Medical Department urged that the ordinance be extended, district commissioners cited the importance of the *bayaase* in pagan communities as the main stumbling block. 'There is a well-organized system running throughout this Division', the DC of Mamprussi explained, and 'it is important for Medical Officers to realise that none but the properly appointed persons may bury a dead body'.[34] Other political officers concurred. 'This move would be quite useless as far as the registration of deaths was concerned', wrote the DC of Dagomba. 'It would mean that the great majority of deaths would be kept secret in order that the corpses be buried outside the cemetery'.[35] The perception remained that cemetery burial was no different to the body being thrown into the bush, as explained from Tumu a generation before: 'they say the Dead spirits would come and accuse them of having buried them outside the walls of the Compound, when they were not suffering from an infectious disease, and would then kill them'.[36]

The enduring perception of the Northern Territories as a remote tribal hinterland locked in the grip of tradition meant that its mortuary cultures would be subjected to a degree of anthropological inquiry which in many ways went beyond that in the Akan world to the south. In the space of two decades, Rattray, Fortes and Goody were all drawn to the zone of statelessness straddling the frontier between the British protectorate and French-ruled Upper Volta (now Burkina Faso) in search of small-scale communities untainted by the forces of colonial modernity. In that time, too, the discipline of anthropology in Africa itself changed, as the era of the colonial officer turned self-taught ethnographer—Rattray—was supplanted by the first generation of professionally trained scholars, many of whom, such as Fortes, were associated with the new functionalist approach pioneered by Bronislaw Malinowski. The result is an extensive body of work which contains a wealth of insights into how the Nankani (or Gurense), the Talensi and the LoDagaa (or Dagara) understood death and the dead. Fortes's two famous monographs on the Talensi, together with subsequent theoretical extrapolations, were fundamental in establishing the ubiquity of the ancestors in African cosmological thought as well as the final fashioning of an individual's social personality by their death. Goody extended these findings, exploring in more detail the elaborate sequence of mortuary rites deemed necessary to close the rupture in the social fabric and to ensure the domestication of the unruly dead as benevolent ancestors. Scholarly awareness of the ancestral dead in sub-Saharan Africa, mediated by this corpus, emerged in large part from the stateless communities of the Gold Coast's northern savannas.[37]

The challenge for the historian is to insert these accumulated insights into processes of change.[38] All three anthropologists approached the societies they studied as if they existed in a pristine precolonial time warp. Yet how might established perceptions of death and the dead have been reshaped by the impact of colonial conquest over the first half of the twentieth century? Here, Gandah's biography provides some insight. Far from being rooted in the world of tradition described by Goody in 1950–51, Gandah's long life was plainly fashioned by a range of historical forces swirling through Birifu and beyond, from the violence and depredations of the late nineteenth century to his accommodation with colonial power after 1917 and on to his role as renowned ritual entrepreneur mediating access to the protective and life-living powers of Kukpenibie. As Jean Allman and I have argued with regard to the Talensi's Tongnaab cult, the colonial-era transformation of savanna shrines into dynamic trans-regional healing movements represented one of the principal ways in which the history of the stateless societies on the remote frontiers of the Northern Territories became entangled with that of the Akan world to the south. Knowledge of Kukpenibie, Tongnaab and other healing powers was generated by colonial mobility: by the large-scale movement of migrant workers to the south in order to escape the hardships of life in the impoverished north, and by the movement of pilgrims to the north in search of ritual solutions to the increasing anxieties and mortal dangers of life in the south.

Labour migration can be seen as a twentieth-century transformation of an older movement across the savanna–forest divide: the way of death that was the precolonial slave trade. That the former dovetailed into the latter can be seen in the person of Victor Aboya, Rattray's principal informant during the first phase of his ethnographic research in 1928. Born around 1888, Aboya fell victim to the devastating famine that coincided with the era of colonial conquest in the mid-1890s, when he was exchanged by his uncle for a few baskets of grain in order that the rest of his family might survive. Sold into slavery in Kumasi, he was released into the care of the Basel Mission, attending school, converting to Christianity and, ultimately, returning home to Winkogo on the frontier between the Nankani and Talensi countrysides.[39] Aboya's contribution to Rattray's work was enormous: he wrote an extensive treatise in the vernacular on Nankani social life, which in his own English translation was incorporated verbatim into *Tribes of the Ashanti Hinterland*. This included a detailed account of different sorts of funeral rites, including those for a man who possesses *tobega*, or a homicide ('*tobega* means that you have gone down into the valley with arrows and killed a man'), and the evocatively worded 'funeral custom of a child who is really a fairy'.[40] Yet Aboya must have been painfully aware that as someone who himself had been sold into slavery, he too was fated to die a bad death. Divination might determine matters otherwise, but like 'a child who is really a fairy'—that is, a *kolkpaareg*, a capricious 'bush sprite'—having been enslaved endangered an individual's ability to attain the status of a full social being in death. 'The physical cause of the death makes no difference to the issue', Fortes later explained. 'He was a disguised bush sprite. He is not given human burial, he does not join his forefathers, he does not become an ancestor spirit.'[41] That is established mortuary belief and practice: the 'custom' which first colonial officers and then anthropologists sought to record and codify. But the misfortune that befell Victor Aboya in the era of conquest, his enslavement as an *odonko*, the return home to his family and emergence as a pioneering mediator of his people's culture—that is history, in all its contingency and disorder.

Fortes was surely right in arguing that the intricate bonds of Talensi kinship, clanship and ritual belonging represented a reassuringly rock-solid 'social structure' in an otherwise uncertain world plagued by insecurity, hardship and the threat of sudden death. At the heart of that structure stood the notion of filial piety, which in turn was translated into a profound reverence for the ancestors. 'Tallensi say that one must respect one's living parents; but to one's dead parents one owes reverence and submission in surpassing degree', Fortes wrote. 'That is what the proverb "Fear the dead and do not fear the living" means to them. One can defy a living parent sometimes and rely on being forgiven; one cannot defy a dead parent. . . . In the religious practice of the Tallensi the ancestors exercise their powers without compunction. They punish and slay as arbitrarily as they bless.'[42] As elsewhere, therefore, filial piety was marked by a deep ambivalence. Young men in small-scale savanna societies chafed under the stern patriarchal control of their fathers, and in the aftermath of colonial conquest great numbers took advantage of the opening of new horizons to escape that control by migrating to the mines, cocoa farms and booming towns of the south. Indeed, it was a constant refrain of chiefs and elders like Gandah that their sons—and sometimes even their daughters—were abandoning them and 'running way' to Dagbon and, beyond, to Asante. The continuing precariousness of existence for many in the Northern Territories also propelled this movement: like the 1890s, the 1930s was a time of widespread drought, locust plagues, hunger, and heightened morbidity and mortality. 'Sickness, food shortage, and lack of medical and hygienic knowledge conduced to a chronically high death-rate, especially among infants and the aged', Fortes recalled of the 1930s, when he was conducting his fieldwork. 'The complex of divination, sacrifice, and prayer among the Tallensi cannot properly be understood without taking into account their experience of living under what had for generations been to them the shadow of perennial and inescapable uncertainty, unpredictability, and threat.' [43]

The injunction to 'fear the dead' served to draw bereaved migrants back to their communities in order to lay their mothers and fathers to rest. 'Nowadays the death of a parent is one of the strongest sanctions that induce the men who go to work abroad to return home', Fortes noted.[44] He cited the examples of two Talensi men, Pal of Zubiung and Dema of Tengzugu, both ex-soldiers in the colonial army who after their discharge had migrated 'abroad'.

They told the same story. Wives and children had died; there had been repeated bouts of sickness in the family; other misfortunes had piled up over the years; and all, as the diviners declared, because they had "rejected (*zayah*) their fathers (*banam*)" by remaining in foreign parts. It did not matter much while there were older brothers at home to "give water (*zan kuom ti*)", that is, make sacrifices, to the ancestral shrines. But when they were left as heads of their lineage segments they had to come home. Their fathers' spirits would have killed them if they had not done so.... Pal... feels that he had no option, and there is even an element of pride in his submission to the *force majeure* of his dead father.[45]

The inability or unwillingness of the colonial state to extend the regime of modern cemetery burial to the protectorate meant that, unlike the Gold Coast Colony and Ashanti to the south, it did not become a zone of exhumation and reinterment, in which dead bodies were increasingly on the move. Yet neither did it remain a zone of static 'tradition'. Rather, it was the bereaved who did the moving, covering long distances and expending hard-earned resources to attend to the demands of the deceased. As Pal's testimony indicates, the ancestral dead were hard taskmasters, their stern presence embodied in the ubiquitous conical ancestor shrines which continue today to stud the finely constructed compound houses of the northern grasslands. Here surely is evidence not just for the continuity of structures of kinship into the afterlife, but for the notion that 'with disembodiment, presence expands'.[46] Indeed, the implacable authority of northern ancestors meant they themselves were soon on the move, drawn across the savanna–forest divide as the animating powers of the waves of protean healing movements which sought to keep mortality and misfortune in abeyance in the Akan world to the south.

18

Reordering the Royal Dead

IN 1924, Agyeman Prempeh was granted permission to return to Asante from exile in the Seychelles. Much had changed since 1896, when the 23-year-old monarch and other members of the royal court were marched off to captivity as political prisoners. Asante had effectively been dismantled by the British, its constituent kingdoms governed as separate 'native states' by *amanhene* who answered to the colonial administration. Meanwhile, the expansion of cocoa farming represented a lucrative new avenue for wealth creation, underpinning a booming colonial economy which had begun to alter the fabric of local society. Nowhere were these changes more apparent than in Kumasi. Not only had the capital lost its king; it was being transformed into a bustling commercial centre and a showcase of colonial modernity. 'Kumasi has big mansions, Banks [and] Churches', a group of local businessmen hoping to prevent a return to the precolonial order wrote to the chief commissioner in 1930. 'Lights have defeated Darkness, wills making [sic] and letters of administration have sunk capricious freebootering [of] deceased's estate and we are tax-payers to the British Government to help make the Electric Lights, Water Works, Schools, Churches, Roads and other comfortable things.'[1]

Agyeman Prempeh too had changed in the course of his twenty-eight years in detention. Together with his late mother Yaa Kyaa, he had converted to Christianity and become a communicant of the Anglican Church. He had learned to read and write in English and from 1907, drawing on the knowledge of Yaa Kyaa and the assistance of his son Frederick, had authored *The History of Ashanti Kings and the Whole Country Itself*. As far as it is possible to tell, he had reconciled himself to the loss of sovereignty and had determined to work for the modernization of Asante within the new colonial dispensation. It was on these conditions, at least, that in 1924 he was repatriated as a private citizen, Mr Edward Prempeh. Two years later, having cemented a reputation among

British officials as a progressive figure, he was appointed 'Kumasihene', head of the reconstituted Kumasi division of colonial Ashanti. That said, in his own mind and in those of his people, Agyeman Prempeh remained Asantehene. Despite agreeing not to meddle in political affairs or, in his capacity as Kumasihene, to concern himself with those beyond his own circumscribed division, it is clear that he sought to reconstitute what he could of the prerogatives of Asante kingship. Underpinning these prerogatives was the role of Asantehene as the fulcrum between the living, the dead and the yet to be born—the obligation to ensure the welfare of the entire cosmic community. Despite his embrace of Anglicanism and colonial modernity, Prempeh was acutely conscious of this historical role and worked assiduously until his death, in 1931, to heal the wounds of the past and to ensure a reinvigorated future by attending to the dignity of the royal dead. This chapter examines his project, which took the form of three interconnected campaigns: to reorder the dominion of the dead in Kumasi; to rebuild the destroyed mausoleum at Bantama; and to repatriate the remains of those who died in the Seychelles and elsewhere. Together, they constitute a key episode in the political life of dead bodies in colonial West Africa. Shortly after presiding over the last of these tasks, Prempeh himself died, his funeral rites encapsulating the tensions between tradition and modernity in his own personhood and in a changing Akan world.

Agyeman Prempeh's return from exile was a significant event in Ghana's twentieth-century history.[2] After a long sea voyage via Liverpool, he arrived at the port of Sekondi on 11 November 1924, boarding an overnight train to Kumasi and alighting the following morning to an emotional welcome. 'The scene presented by the huge assembly of Ashantis with their white head bands signifying rejoicing or victory, some laughing and cheering, while others wept with emotion, was a most moving and never-to-be-forgotten scene.'[3] Prempeh was accompanied by a party of three other chiefs and forty-five dependents, including the nonagenarian Akwamuhene Asafo Boakye, who had reputedly sworn that he would survive exile and return home—and did so with just months to spare, dying in April 1925. Twenty-four other office-holders, including Prempeh's father Kwasi Gyambibi (d. 1903), his mother Yaa Kyaa (d. 1917), his brother Agyeman Badu (d. 1917) and the famous warrior queen of Edweso, Yaa Asantewaa (d. 1921), had died in exile.

These numbers mattered a great deal. In April 1925, Chief Commissioner Maxwell received a request from Akyeamehene Kwasi Nuama that the Kumasi chiefs and provincial *amanhene* be permitted to proceed in full regalia and accompanied by drummers from the town centre to Agyeman Prempeh's temporary residence in order that they might 'tell the news here to him and in return to tell us his'.[4] Maxwell was concerned about the drumming—a permit for which was required within Kumasi—but allowed the event to proceed. Accordingly, on 13 April Prempeh was formally welcomed home and updated on the state of the nation. In return, he distributed typed copies of a document titled 'A History of Nana Prempeh's Adventure during His 30 Years Captivity, Namely, Elmina, Sierra Leone and Seychelles'.[5] This history comprised a precise record of the fate of all those who had accompanied the Asantehene into the successive stages of his detention and an enumeration of those born in exile. It was, that is, a written version of the custom publicly to account for losses and gains to the kingdom's human stock: three decades' accumulated equivalent of the yearly pronouncements of fecundity and wellbeing made at the Odwira festival. That the dead must properly be accounted for appears also to have been the imperative in writing down the Oyoko dynasty's oral traditions as the *History of Ashanti Kings*. The impetus for this came from Yaa Kyaa, who was said to have been concerned that as successive members of her family died in the Seychelles, 'all their names would be lost'.[6]

'I am pleased to tell you that omitting those who are dead, both young and old, I have returned to Kumasi the amount of people taken and I have got 64 persons in surplus', Agyeman Prempeh reported in the history of his 'adventure'. Despite the calamity of conquest and the despair of exile, he had fulfilled his historic role by presiding over human increase. But let us focus on the dead. Of the fifty-five individuals 'interred or buried in foreign countries, that is one at Elmina, 5 at Sierra Leone and 49 at Seychelles', pride of place was given to a table of the twenty-four office-holders who died in the Seychelles. Beginning with Chief Kweku Fokuo, 'died 17/9/1900 that is 24 yrs 3 ms ago' and ending with Chief Kwami Gyansah, 'died 4/5/1923 that is 2 yrs 7 ms ago' and Chief Kofi Fofea, 'died on the sea when voyaging back to Kumasi', each is listed according to the date of their death and to how long ago that was from January 1925. In 1921, Agyeman Prempeh records, 'we all subscribed and purchased a large plot of ground where a vault was built. In the vault we placed the remainings [sic] of all our deceased, that is those bodies which have got five years and upwards and not below five years'. The bodies of ten individuals, that is, awaited exhumation and removal to the vault. 'But before my leaving Seychelles I took all necessary precautions in order that the graves will never get lost till one day you will give me assistance . . . to exhume them and place them in the vault.' It would be another three years before Agyeman Prempeh formulated a more ambitious plan: to repatriate all of the remains for reburial in Asante.

The urge to ensure that the mortal remains of kin who died far from home were returned for burial in their native soil was an abiding one. Because it was feared that the spirit of those not retrieved might forever be 'lost', the preservation, exhumation, movement and reinterment of copses and body parts were long-established practices. Bodies humanized the land, their material presence mediating the relationship between the living and the dead. As had earlier been the case in Accra, however, the built environment of colonial Kumasi was beginning to overlay its older sacred geography. In common with expanding urban centres in many part of the world, the result was a reconfiguration of the city's dominion of the dead, as established burial sites were replaced by new ones and mortal remains were on the move.[7] This reconfiguration was part of the changing fabric of Asante into which Agyeman Prempeh began to reinsert himself in 1924.

Kumasi's necrogeography was also reshaped by colonial epidemiology. Just eight months before Prempeh had travelled by train from Sekondi on the final leg of his journey home, bubonic plague had made its way up the same railway line to Kumasi, where it infected 156 people, of whom 146 died.[8] The aftermath of the outbreak saw the Births, Deaths and Burials Ordinance extended to Ashanti and the formation of the Kumasi Public Health Board, whose three African members were Akyeamehene Kwasi Nuama; Malah Sallo Katsina; the Serikin Zongo, or headman of the northern 'stranger's quarter'; and Edward Prempeh. Prempeh's engaged membership of what served as an embryonic town council was a stepping-stone in his recognition the following year as Kumasihene. 'Prempeh takes a keen interest in all matters appertaining to the progress and civilization of his country, and is very modern and up to date in his ideas', Maxwell noted. 'He is an earnest Christian, a member of the Church of England, and has the real interests of his country at heart.'[9]

There is no doubt that this was so. But it was also the case that Agyeman Prempeh, like his predecessors as Asantehene, would have regarded the interests of his country and those of his own Oyoko dynasty as one and the same thing. Many in the past had seen things differently, and many would continue to do so under colonial rule. Prempeh had come to power in 1888, at the end of a five-year civil war which had convulsed much of Asante and alienated many ordinary people from what they saw as a self-serving and predatory ruling elite. Indeed, the resulting social dislocation meant that mortal remains may have been even more mobile than ever in the opening years of British rule, as refugee populations sought to reclaim ancestral property rights by rehumanizing the land with the displaced dead.[10] Divisions within Asante were encapsulated in the most notable reinterment of the opening years of colonial rule: that of Agyeman Prempeh's predecessor, Asantehene Mensa Bonsu (1874–83), whose destoolment was the catalyst for civil war. Mensa Bonsu died in British captivity in April 1896 at Praso, on the frontier of Asante and the Gold Coast Colony.[11] In 1909, the chief commissioner was petitioned by Kwasi Nuama to allow the removal of his remains to Kumasi, a request repeated the following year by Mensa Bonsu's sister Akua Afriyie.[12] This was agreed to, on condition that the exhumation was supervised by a medical officer under the terms of the Cemeteries Ordinance. Accordingly, Akua Afriyie was able belatedly to conduct a full funeral ceremony for the deceased Asantehene. The popular reaction, however, was decidedly mixed. 'The King was the most cruel amongst all the Asante sovereigns', Rev. Asare observed. 'He was not only cruel, but very wicked and avaricious. . . . The chiefs in Kumase did not mingle themselves much in the funeral as it was expected. The chiefs still have ill feelings against the King because some of them suffered much in his reigning time.' In contrast, Asare added, those 'who saw the golden time of Asante Kingdom mourned greatly and [were] very much cast down'.[13]

Despite the outpouring of emotion that greeted Agyeman Prempeh in November 1924, Asante was far from united in its response to his return. Many looked to Prempeh to restore 'the golden time of Asante'; others—like the businessmen who lauded the modernization of colonial Kumasi, quoted above—had no desire to rehabilitate the old order or the death duties which underpinned it. These tensions had erupted three years earlier, when the Golden Stool, which had been hidden as the British approached Kumasi in 1896, was discovered and desecrated by a group of 'youngmen'. Soon after his return, Agyeman Prempeh was handed what remained of the stool, which, unbeknown to British officials, he directed to be restored. Constrained in the public arena by the conditions of his return, Prempeh began to work behind the scenes to revive the key symbolic embodiments of kingship. Emboldened by his appointment as Kumasihene, in late 1926 he revealed the Golden Stool to Chief Commissioner Duncan-Johnstone. On moving into his new palace at Manhyia, he also abandoned monogamy, restoring the royal harem and thereby foregoing his status as a full communicant of the Anglican Church. By early 1927, Agyeman Prempeh was able to turn to other pressing matters: 'to restore appropriate respect and dignity to his own and the nation's royal ancestors'.[14] It was a task which would occupy him for the remaining four years of his life.

Kumasi's royal necrogeography had been dominated by two hallowed locations: the *barim kese*, or 'great burial ground', at Bampenase, and the *baamu*, or mausoleum, at Bantama. The *barim kese*, it will be recalled, was known as *asonyeso*, 'the place of drippings', where the corpse of deceased Asantehenes was deposited to allow its corrupted flesh to fall away and the cleaned skeleton to be rearticulated and coffined. On the anniversary of the death, during the great *afehyia*, the remains were removed to their final resting place in the *baamu* at Bantama. Only those Asantehenes who died in office, however, were accorded the privilege of joining Osei Tutu at Bantama. Those who had been destooled—Kusi Obodom (1750–64), Osei Kwame (1777–1803) and Kofi Kakari (1867–74)—were interred at another *barim*, most likely at Breman, three miles north of Kumasi, where they were joined in 1910 by the remains of Mensa Bonsu. The city had four other major royal burial grounds, all located on the eastern fringe of the precolonial city: Akyeremade, Heman (or Ahemaho, the resting place of *ahemaa*, 'queen mothers'), Adum and Adwama.[15] Noble lineages not part of the Oyoko dynasty maintained their own burial grounds, numbers of which continued to dot the early colonial city.

That geography was profoundly disrupted in 1896, when the British blew up the Bantama *baamu*. Ever since Bowdich wrote of the human sacrifices 'to water the graves of the Kings' during the celebration of Odwira, Bantama had occupied a fearful place in the European imagination.[16] During his one-day occupation of Kumasi in 1874, Sir Garnet Wolseley had—to the chagrin of some observers—declined to destroy the mausoleum.[17] Twenty-two years later, Governor Maxwell exhibited less restraint and ordered it to be razed, a task carried out with gusto by Major Baden-Powell, the future founder of the Boy Scouts.[18] Fearing the worst, the mausoleum guardians, or *barimfo*, had removed to safety the eight brass coffins housing the royal remains, together with their associated regalia, including the *kuduo* containing the gold belonging to the royal *asamanfo* and the crania of their defeated enemies. Where all of these hallowed objects were hidden remains unclear—but it was likely to have been Breman. Rattray wrote a circumspect account of a visit there ('the

FIGURE 18.1. The *baamu*, or royal mausoleum, at Bantama, with the *aya kese* in the foreground, photographed in the 1880s or 1890s.

village of B–') in 1923, where he admitted to having only viewed the coffins of Kofi Kakari and his brother Mensa Bonsu but noted that he 'had repeatedly heard the Ashanti, anticipating the destruction of Bantama in 1895 [*sic*], had removed the skeletons of their kings to this place'.[19] Like the desecration in Sudan of the tomb and mortal remains of the Mahdi after the battle of Omdurman two years later, the razing of the *baamu* was a calculated act of imperial erasure, designed to punish the Asante for the moral transgression of human sacrifice. To that end, the most notable sacred item that the *barimfo* were unable to remove to safety, the *aya kese*, or 'great brass basin', which lay between two sacred trees at the entrance to the mausoleum enclosure, was carried away as a trophy of war. Believed by the British to be associated with ritual immolations, the basin was taken to London, where, together with 'part of Fetish Tree at Coomassie, under which 80 slaves were annually sacrificed', it was displayed in the Royal United Service Museum in Whitehall.[20]

The exile of the Asantehene, the destruction of his ancestors' resting place at Bantama and the disappearance of the Golden Stool in effect ended the tabulation of calendrical time based on the forty-two-day *adaduanan* cycle in the Asante capital. In contrast to the constituent *aman* of the empire and to the Akan kingdoms beyond it, the marking of time with the celebration of the *awukudae*, the *akwasidae* and the annual Odwira festivals went into abeyance, replaced by the linear time of colonial modernity. It is notable, then, that upon his return in 1924, Agyeman Prempeh was reported to have begun quietly to celebrate the two *adae* festivals.[21] Focused on the propitiation of the ancestors—'really in a sense funeral customs', as Rattray described them—these had culminated in the visit of the Asantehene to the *baamu* in order to commune with his forebears.[22] Whether or not Prempeh surreptitiously visited the hidden remains of his ancestors at Breman or elsewhere is not known; it is clear, nonetheless, that he had begun to reinstate both the *adaduanan* cycle and the ritual communication between the living and the dead which propelled it.

By the 1920s, the remains of Kumasi's old necrogeography was in danger of joining the *baamu* in being erased by the forces of colonial progress. A good sense of this is provided by Rattray's description of a tour he made around what had been key locations in the celebration of Odwira, guided by an elderly executioner, or *adumfo*. The Ahemaho burial ground, for example, now stood at one of the city's busiest thoroughfares, near the junction of Adum Street and Kingsway; next to it was *nkram*, 'in the midst of blood', one of the sites where sacrificial victims had been executed.[23] In 1922, after an incident where Kwadwo Akoto of the Adenkyemenaso quarter was charged by his fellow Kumasi chiefs with digging around in Ahemaho, the colonial administration moved to peg out the royal burial grounds. Besides agreeing to construct walls round them, the chiefs expressed a desire to build a new 'burial house' at Bantama.[24] In early 1924, however, the administration's building inspector reported that the royal cemeteries remained 'in a very derelict condition' and suggested that 'special precautions should be taken to preserve these features as National Monuments'.[25] Meanwhile, there was also the pressing issue of finding room for the ordinary dead of the rapidly growing city. In a sign of the times, Bantamahene Kwame Kyem and other chiefs asked the chief commissioner in July 1924 to assist them in developing a new public cemetery; 'we beg to mention', the chiefs wrote, 'that it is not right nowadays to bury dead bodies in the middle of the town'.[26]

The Births, Deaths and Burials Ordinance came into force in Kumasi on 1 June 1926. Included in its provisions were the compulsory registration of vital statistics and the regulation of all public cemeteries and private burial grounds.

By the end of the year, Agyeman Prempeh had begun to formulate plans for a new royal cemetery which would replace the old burial grounds now hemmed in by Kumasi's commercial district. The location was a piece of land adjoining the existing public cemetery on the Mampong Road; there, he explained to the DC, 'the Royals, Princes, big Chiefs and the important people of the town' could be laid to rest.[27] Colonial officials had no problem with the cemetery's exclusive nature but pointed out that it must come under the terms of the new ordinance. Prempeh objected, arguing that 'he alone has the right to nominate those persons who may be buried there' and that he must maintain his own staff of sextons and gravediggers.[28] The first of these demands was agreed to, but Senior Sanitary Officer Dr Selwyn-Clarke insisted that the site be gazetted as an extension of the public cemetery and placed under government control. Agyeman Prempeh acquiesced. In November 1927, he sent to the chief commissioner a list of named individuals whose remains he wished to be exhumed from the Ahemaho and Adwama burial grounds. 'When I was taken away along with my Brother nobody was left to look after the same', he wrote. 'I find now . . . that cemeteries at Hemanho and Adjwama burial grove are unsuitable by reason of long years [of] neglect. The Hemanho in particular is encroached by the Court Building and is not suitable at all. It is a shaming thing to see that our Hallowed Dead are overlooked. We CANNOT FORGET them. They are our HEROES and HEROINES of Ashanti.'[29]

Encoded within these emphatic statements was a great deal of complex and sensitive dynastic history. Agyeman Prempeh identified two sets of remains for exhumation. The first named ten individuals interred at Ahemaho, most of whom were the daughters and sons of various Asantehemaas whose remains were to be reburied at the new royal cemetery. The second named 'Yitaa (queen mother Dako tribe)' and seven others interred at Adwama, whose remains were destined not for the new Kumasi cemetery but for another royal cemetery in the *oman* of Nsuta.[30] The 'Dako tribe' refers to a suppressed segment of the Oyoko dynasty, two scions of which—twin brothers known as *Dako ne Dako*—had contested for the Golden Stool on the death of Asantehene Opoku Ware around 1750. *Dako ne Dako* were defeated and killed, and their lineage segment officially erased from historical memory—'completely annihilated', Asare reported, on the death of its last surviving member in 1908.[31] Agyeman Prempeh's lauding of the hallowed dead, that is, was only half true and, in its overstatement, revealing: the Dako were indeed 'forgotten'. His motives for removing the Dako dead from Adwama can be only guessed at. What is known is that the remains were so ancient that they were reported to have entirely disintegrated; 'all that is required', the chief commissioner noted, 'is the removal of some soil from the Royal Burial Grove at Adwama to the Nsuta Cemetery in order to satisfy Native Custom'.[32]

On *akwasidae* 17 June 1928, the refurbished Golden Stool was paraded through the streets of Kumasi for the first time since 1896. It was a triumphant moment in Agyeman Prempeh's efforts to rehabilitate the symbolic power of Asante kingship. In the months that followed, he began to envisage what was to be the final phase of this project: the repatriation of the mortal remains of those who died in the Seychelles and the rebuilding of the Bantama *baamu*. Prempeh explained his motives for the former as he anxiously awaited news of the arrival of the bones in 1929: 'in the Ashanti Native Custom, if the head of the family, or any of the important family dies, and the Funeral Custom is not made, two cases arise: 1. That a party of the family is always in bad terms with the other party; 2. That if the funeral custom is not made in time, the remaining family dies one by one'.[33] He therefore planned to hold a 'Great Funeral Custom' for the deceased exiles and for other leading royals such as his grandmother Asantehemaa Afua Kobi (d. 1900) and his aunt Akua Afriyie (d. 1921), as well for a number of the latter's daughters, whose remains were scattered in various locations.[34] The desire to exhume the remains of these women and provide them with proper obsequies suggests that the great funeral was far from being simply a matter of sentiment. Shortly before requesting that Mensa Bonsu's remains be returned to Kumasi in 1908, Akua Afriyie herself had expressed alarm at the death in rapid succession of no fewer than eight royal women, blaming, for some obscure reason, the neglect of the soul-cult of a brother of Asantehene Kusi Obodom.[35] There was a serious shortage, that is, of Oyoko women, who, according to the rules of matrilineal succession, were essential for the survival of the dynasty. By the end of 1929, Agyeman Prempeh had exhibited the Golden Stool once again, this time at a thanksgiving service at St Cyprian's Anglican church, where he offered prayers in thanks for his return from exile. Yet this in no way precluded the pressing need to settle accounts with his disturbed royal ancestors. Leaving aside any speculation on the precise content of Prempeh's personal beliefs, once again we see the deep-seated fear that the neglect of the dead endangered the lives of the living.

In January 1930, two sealed cases arrived in Kumasi. One contained the remains of twenty persons recovered from the vault constructed in 1921 and the other those of nine persons exhumed from graves in the government cemetery in Victoria, Seychelles. Officials were concerned that the deterioration of the receptacles holding the former would prevent identification, but the identity of each was able to be determined by the enclosed grave goods. The remains of Yaa Kyaa, Kwasi Gyambibi and Agyeman Badu were interred at Breman, while those of the other exiles were collected by their families to be interred in lineage burial grounds in Kumasi and beyond.[36]

The great funeral custom was scheduled to be held one year later, in March 1931. Agyeman Prempeh, meanwhile, proceeded with his plan to rebuild the Bantama *baamu* and to refurbish and relocate the Bampenase *barim kese*. The administration, eager to erase the vestiges of Kumasi's precolonial necrogeography from the commercial centre, looked on the scheme favourably and the town engineer drew up a blueprint for a new mausoleum. There were, however, two problems. One was money. The estimated cost of the building was £3,000, which Prempeh hoped would be raised with a contribution of £100 each from twenty-one *amanhene* and eight leading Kumasi chiefs.[37] In September 1929, he wrote to the *amanhene* and set out his objectives:

> The Ashantiman has, as you know, two National Monuments which embody for us all that is most sacred in our lives, and all that we revere most deeply. These monuments known as BAMPANASI-EBAM and BANTAMA-DAN-KESE are the burial places of our Ashanti Kings and have for us a meaning which is the basis of our religion and our reverence for our dead. In the olden days these Monuments were carefully tended and were guarded and venerated as the holy places of Ashanti. To-day although our own dwelling places have improved with the times, the sacred resting places of our Kings have fallen into decay and ruin and are no longer an honour to us but a source of shame. In these days elaborate tombstones for deceased relatives are rising up all over the country-side. Not a village but has some precious reminder of its dead. Our dead Kings deserve no less of us.[38]

Not all the *amanhene* shared the depths of Agyeman Prempeh's concern for 'our dead kings'. Some refused outright to contribute, while others were either unwilling or unable to raise £100.[39] With contributions still trickling in, in early 1930 the administration abandoned the demand that it be paid upfront and proceeded with the building works, in the hope that the Kumasihene would somehow raise the required cash.

The other problem concerned the *aya kese*. Despite money concerns, the new Bantama mausoleum was completed in July 1930. Agyeman Prempeh then asked Chief Commissioner H. S. Newlands to arrange for the return of the looted brass basin, which he described as 'a very important Vessel in the eyes of the Ashantis' that 'would enhance the historical character of the Mausoleum'.[40] Concerned that the basin had been used as a receptacle for the blood of sacrificial victims, Newlands requested further information. This was received in the form of a five-page account, in which Prempeh drew on the *odomankomasem*, or creation myth, which comprised the opening of the *History of Ashanti Kings*.[41] It tells of how, at the dawn of time, a gold chain descended from the sky, down which came attendants carrying a bell, a stool and the *aya kese*; the stool was placed inside the pan ready to receive the apical ancestress of the Oyoko, Ankyewa Nyame, who in turn climbed down the chain and sat upon it. Not liking the look of that place—it was in Akyem Abuakwa!—Ankyewa Nyame reappeared at Asantemanso with the pan, which was carried by the Oyokos as they moved through the forest in search of living space to Kokofu and then to Kumasi. On becoming the first Asantehene, Osei Tutu declared that the pan was so great that it 'should be placed where he was to be buried ... i.e. Bantama ... and it remained there till 1896 when it was removed to England'. 'The Brass pan had always remained unchanged since it came to the Earth, and all the Asantimans' souls are within it', Agyeman Prempeh concluded, insisting that 'the allegation that human beings were killed in the Brass Pan is not a fact at all and therefore it is not correct'.

Newlands was inclined to accept this assertion, which was also the considered opinion of Rattray. Officials in Accra, however, were not, and after some deliberation Governor Slater declined Agyeman Prempeh's request.[42] The great funeral custom and opening of the new mausoleum at Bantama proceeded in March 1931 without the *aya kese*.[43] It was, nonetheless, another moment of triumph for Prempeh. Accra's *West Africa Times* published a vivid account of proceedings, which opened on *akwasidae* Sunday 22 March with the Kumasihene and his sister, *ohemaa* Konadu Yaadom, receiving the *amanhene* and their retinues into the city.[44] As in the great Odwira celebrations of the past, Kumasi's population was reckoned to have swollen from 28,500 to 200,000, as crowds wearing 'Manchester prints died in deep or light red or black', their 'faces and hands ... bedaubed with red clay', surged through the streets. Monday witnessed the ceremonial firing of guns by the retinues of each *oman* in turn, of particular note because 'for many years, the people had been forbidden to fire guns at funeral celebrations in Kumasi'. One stirring moment occurred when the *ohemaa* of Edweso appeared wearing full battle-dress in memory of her predecessor, Yaa Asantewaa, whose remains were among those returned from the Seychelles. 'Dancing to the tune of her State singers chanting the memorable war song "Yaa Asantewaa obaa basia a oko aprem" ("Yaa Asantewaa a mere woman who fought before cannons") ... she fired out two shots.' Another was the appearance of Agyeman Prempeh himself. Nana Prempeh, the *Times* reported, had recently been unwell, so his approach caused a sensation among the crowd. What only palace insiders and his doctors knew was that Prempeh, who a year before had been diagnosed with pernicious anaemia, was terminally ill. Wearing the *batakari kese* battle smock and weighed down with masses of gold regalia, Prempeh took two hours to be carried in the state palanquin from Manhyia palace to Maxwell Park, where 'with tears in his eyes [he] followed his gunners in firing to the honour of his late good parents, members of his immediate relation [*sic*] and those Ashanti Chiefs and people who in the service of their Oman died many miles away from their homes'.

The celebrations culminated on 30 March with the official opening of the mausoleum. Then came an intriguing turn of events: Agyeman Prempeh decided not to relocate the remains of his predecessors to the handsomely domed new building. The hallowed coffins and associated regalia were instead installed in the new *barim kese* out at Breman, which, according to oral testimony recorded in the 1960s, appears to have been spatially configured in the same way as the *baamu* destroyed in 1896.[45] The Bantama mausoleum remained empty, and remains empty today. There is no known record of Prempeh's motives for this decision, but there is every indication that it was due to the absence of the *aya kese*. In a final plea for the return of the basin, he made it clear that he fully intended to house the royal remains, as planned, at Bantama. 'The spiritual fact is the Brass Pan is needful to those who dwell forever in the Mausoleum and if not they will keenly feel its loss to them. I know well that you have our best interest at heart so I send you this to answer my prayers to return the Brass Pan to stop the plans becoming spoiled.'[46] The *aya kese*, Prempeh had made plain, was Asante's most ancient sacred relic, appearing at the very moment of the creation of human order; Osei Tutu himself, whose powerful presence dominated that of all the dead Asantehenes, had wished to be buried in its presence. Obsessed with the old spectre of human sacrifice, the government in Accra demurred. The brass pan was retained as a mnemonic of imperial conquest in London, where it remains, now in the National Army Museum.[47]

Agyeman Prempeh died on Tuesday 12 May 1931, aged 59. Whether he died as Asantehene or as Nana Edward Prempeh, *omanhene* of the Kumasi division and a 'loyal and valuable servant' of the British Empire is a matter of interpretation.[48] There can be no doubt, however, that he died a Christian. Prempeh's preoccupation in the final year of his life with restoring the dignity of his ancestors must have been entangled with anticipation of his own death, and behind the scenes he worked to ensure that his obsequies would incorporate both Asante rites and those of the Anglican Church.[49] To this end, he carefully planned his funeral in liaison with the clergy of St Cyprian's, Kumasi, securing the agreement of his family for what he wished to be a largely Christian event. 'It was his dying wish', one insider wrote, 'that his people should not prevent a church burial'.[50] With some modification, this was what transpired; certainly, the apprehension that Kumasi might witness a return to the disorder and even the bloodletting of the past did not eventuate. There was much self-congratulation in official correspondence on the successful negotiation of the funeral—a reflection, acting Chief Commissioner Taylor reported to Accra, of 'the mutual confidence which happily exists between the native Ashanti authorities and the officers of Government'. 'The death of an Ashanti king, and to the public the deceased was still an Ashanti king', Taylor wrote, 'had not occurred for nearly forty years and the rapid transition from savagery to civilization which has taken place meantime seems to have been forgotten in the memory of ancient cruelties'.[51] In fact, it had been sixty-five years since the last full-scale funeral of a reigning Asantehene—that in 1867 of Kwaku Dua Panin, which had indeed been characterized by an unprecedented degree of violence. Yet it was not simply the memory of 'ancient cruelties' which welled to the surface, but the cathartic explosion of emotion and weight of accumulated tradition unleashed by the death of a king.

The morning of Agyeman Prempeh's death, the chief commissioner received a telephone call from the vicar of St Cyprian's, informing him that he wished to preside over a Christian burial 'with the full rites of the Church, and for a lying-in-state all the preceding night in the Church building'.[52] Taylor replied that he regarded the funeral arrangements to be the personal affair of the family of the deceased, an opinion he repeated to a deputation from Manhyia palace which arrived to announce formally the grievous news. In fact, Prempeh's body lay in state not in church but in a richly decorated apartment in the palace, closely attended, according to custom, by *ohemaa* Konadu Yaadom and other women, with retinues of royal *nhenkwaa* crowded into adjacent rooms. That night, Rev. H. St John Evans led a procession consisting of St Cyprian's choir, priests and other church members to Manhyia to sing hymns. Entering the apartment where the body was laid out, St John Evans was perturbed by the presence of the royal *adumfo*, who 'looked especially terrifying in their leopard-skin hats, with a pouch containing three knives slung around their heads'.

> After a few minutes we started a hymn. Africans can at least sing loudly, and we completely drowned out all the other noises. After two or three more hymns we stopped for a rest. An executioner then came forward with a dagger in his outstretched hand and delivered a panegyric before his dead master, recounting many of his former exploits and glories, to the accompaniment of the shouts and cries of all the mourners. When we felt things were getting a little too excited and hysterical, we started another hymn. And so it went on till 5 o'clock in the morning.[53]

On the afternoon of Thursday 14 May, a procession bearing Agyeman Prempeh's body, together with the Golden Stool, left Manhyia for St Cyprian's church. Aside from the visual spectacle, it is notable that St John Evans' allusions to the tension between customary and Christian practice should continue to focus on the matter of noise. 'Amidst terrific shouting and a crowd of dancing and gesticulating attendants the Golden Stool arrived. . . . They readily accepted our invitation to bring the Stool into the church, and it was placed near the place where the coffin was to lie. . . . The huge brass coffin, covered with green silk, was borne by more than a dozen men, while on all sides of it were heathen thurifers. The noise at this moment was indescribable.'[54] Leading the sonic onslaught were the *asakwafo*, the royal horn-blowers, who, as the Asantehene's sextons, were responsible for the body. After the service the coffin was then carried, in a steady rain and as darkness fell, to the Bantama mausoleum, where St John Evans and the other priests read the committal. 'We all then fell on our knees in silent prayer, and to our amazement everyone in the room, executioners and all, did the same. For a full minute there was dead silence.'[55] After saying goodbye to Nana Konadu Yaadom, the Christian contingent then departed the scene, marching home to the tune of 'O Valiant Hearts'. Later that night, the royal corpse was conveyed to Breman for initial interment.[56]

The obsequies for Agyeman Prempeh were concluded a year later with the *afehyia*, conducted over two weeks, from 21 May to 2 June 1932. In contrast to the initial funeral, the *afehyia* was almost entirely a customary affair. Comprising an elaborate sequence of public celebrations and sequestered ritual enactments, it culminated in the final transfer of authority from the now fully 'departed' Asantehene to his successor. This sequence is set out in an account of the funeral custom commissioned by Agyeman Prempeh's successor, Osei Agyeman Prempeh II (1931–70) and written by his secretary, J.W.K. Appiah.[57] For Chief Commissioner Newlands, the value of this document lay in the fact that it described a celebration that was, 'in effect, that appropriate to an Asantehene', and he used his own report to Accra on the custom to make a case for abandoning the invented colonial title of Kumasihene and replacing it with Asantehene.[58] Three year later, that would happen, when in 1935 the colonial government reinstated Osei Agyeman Prempeh II as Asantehene and 'restored' the Asante Confederacy.

Let us conclude, however, by considering one aspect of Appiah's account of Agyeman Prempeh's *afehyia*, which returns to the topic of the sculpted faces of the dead: the *sora*. As noted in chapter 6, the *sora* represented the climactic moment of the mortuary rituals conducted for ordinary folk and great *ahene* alike: the point of cathartic release at which 'the ghost departs for the land of the spirits'. In 1932, preparation began on the afternoon of the seventh day of the *afehyia*, 27 May, when the royal family gathered at Bogyawe and 'basked ("Hata") themselves under the scorching sun signifying that they were drying the "Eyitam" (mourning cloths)'. While *ohemaa* Konadu Yaadom constructed a small shelter called a *pata*, Gyaasewahene Kwadwo Poku departed for Abuakwa to fetch the *abusua kuruwa*, the 'lineage pot' topped with the terracotta likeness of the deceased, which was brought to Kumasi in the dead of night, filled with the shaved hair and the fingernail and toenail clippings of the royal family, and placed in the *pata*. Meanwhile, the *werempefo* carried the Golden Stool and other regalia to a location beyond the city. There, a new stool was carved to perpetuate the memory of the deceased, who until that point was understood still to be in possession of the royal regalia; the new and old stools were then carried back to the *pata*.

The *sora* day, 28 May, began with the symbolic clearing of the road to Breman, down which that night the *abusua kuruwa* would be carried. As Prempeh himself had recorded twenty-five years before in the *History of Ashanti Kings*, in the precolonial era that path ran to Kumasi's royal *asensie*, 'the place of pots', in the ward of Daaboase, and was lined by royal servants awaiting execution and dismemberment. In 1932, Nana Ama Akyia, a niece of Agyeman Prempeh, carried the terracotta pot topped by his likeness to the new Banpanasi in

Breman and placed it 'alongside the other Abusua Nkruwa of the past Asante Ahene'. 'The procession to Banpanasi was accompanied by all kinds of African music', Appiah wrote. 'Until one o'clock the following morning, the *kete* ensembles played sentimental songs narrating the great deeds of the past Ashanti kings.' After a life of trial and tribulation, of defeat, exile and partial redemption, Agyeman Prempeh had joined the reordered ranks of his ancestors, his deeds becoming one with the great deeds of them all.

19

Making Modern Deathways

IN 1953, the novelist Richard Wright, author of the best-selling *Native Son*, travelled to the Gold Coast to observe at first hand the rising tide of anti-colonial nationalism beginning to sweep across the African continent. Two years earlier, Kwame Nkrumah's Convention People's Party had won a landslide victory in the Gold Coast's first elections and Nkrumah, as 'Leader of Government Business', was working in tandem with the British governor to move the colony towards full independence. An African American born and raised in the segregated South who in the 1930s worked on the Federal Writers' Project and identified with the socialist left, Wright was a sympathetic observer of the emergent African revolution. Yet his account of the journey, published the following year as *Black Power*, betrays a deep ambivalence about African society. Wright clearly struggled to come to terms with the heady mix of tradition and modernity that characterized everyday life in the Gold Coast, tending to regard the former at best as colourfully exotic and at worst as atavistic or unfathomable. As for many sojourners on the coast over the centuries, Wright's discomfort seemed most pronounced when he was confronted with one highly visible aspect of local culture: mortuary rites. These emerge as something of a leitmotif in *Black Power*, which contains repeated descriptions of exuberant funeral ceremonies and of popular beliefs concerning the afterlife.[1]

Take just one example from Accra, the colonial capital and one of West Africa's most vibrant and progressive urban centres. Being shown around the downtown Ga quarters of the city, Wright was alerted by the sound of drumming, lamentations and gunfire to a passing funeral procession:

> a wave of flowing robes, red, yellow, scarlet, and russet was rolling down the street. Huge drums were being pounded by men who sweated and whose

faces were tense. Men bearing vast umbrellas marched and behind them came men holding red flags aloft ... Men and women came rushing madly from all directions.... The men, dressed in red, formed a huge circle in a vacant lot and began firing the muskets they held. A funeral? How was that possible? It seemed more like an advertisement for a circus.... My mouth dropped open. A group of men bore aloft on their shoulders a brass coffin, gleaming and polished until it glittered in the sun.... I was afraid that the coffin would fall and smash against the concrete pavement, but, evidently, the men had long experience bearing whirling coffins on their heads and the coffin spun slowly, the men rushing with it seemingly at random from spot to spot.... I found myself standing next to an African dressed in Western clothes.... 'But who's dead?' I asked. 'It's a chief,' he told me.... 'But the dead man, won't he fall out of that coffin?' 'There's no dead man in the coffin,' he said. 'What? It's *empty?*' I asked, dumbfounded. 'Then why are they rushing about with it like that?' 'The coffin has the dead man's hair and fingernails in it,' he explained. 'The body is buried somewhere in secret, that is, after the brain has been taken out—'.... 'It's a kind of farewell that they're giving to the dead man, you see. But they are trying to fool the spirit away at the same time. Now, they take the coffin, running with it, back to all the places in the city where the dead man had enjoyed himself.... So, when they rush up like that, spin the coffin, and then rush off, going from left to right, the spirit becomes confused. You understand?'[2]

Wright's astonishment might be dismissed as that of yet another bemused outsider, his naivety and exotic colourings representing little advance in insight from those reaching back to the seventeenth century. Yet the fact that the streets of downtown Accra remained the setting for dramatic mortuary display and subterfuge is revealing of the limited success on the part of the colonial state and its African intermediaries to reform and regulate death. Mortuary cultures had evolved, but not necessarily in the direction of the twentieth-century death identified by Ariès and others: a 'forbidden' death displaced from public space and removed from the control of family and community. Doctors, lawyers, clergy and the state had certainly all begun to play some role in the management of mortality. Yet as the British prepared to relinquish power to African nationalists, death remained far from being effectively colonized. Indeed, new forms of enchantment continued to emerge, as captured on the streets and hinterland of Accra by documentary filmmaker Jean Rouch in *Les maîtres fous* (1954) and *Jaguar* (1957). It was in the 1950s, too, that carpenters' workshops in the seaside towns to the east of Accra began to produce fabulous figurative coffins, said to assist the deceased in continuing to practise their profession or follow their passions in *gbohiiajen*, the Ga afterworld.[3] There, as in the Akan *asamando* and in the Christian heaven, the dead still had important work to do.

We return in this final chapter to that most emblematic aspect of the African encounter with death: the funeral. As historians of death in many cultures have observed, the weight of tradition borne by funeral rites means that they are often stubbornly resistant to innovation. *Mentalités* appear static and cultural practices conservative, Ariès argued, yet at certain moments change becomes perceptible.[4] Such a juncture has been identified in contemporary sub-Saharan Africa, where anthropological research has shown funerary cultures to be undergoing rapid and often dramatic elaboration. In postcolonial Ghana this transformation has been characterized above all by the increasing ostentation of funerals, which are seen by many observers as more about the status of the living than the honouring of the dead. *Abusua do funu* is the Twi maxim often cited in this regard: 'the family loves a dead body'.[5] At the same time, more and more of the responsibility for negotiating death is passing from the family into the hands of professional specialists. Ghanaian society, in other words, can be seen to be following others down the well-trodden path towards the 'modern way of death', where much of the old intimacy with the dead has begun to fade.

As with much of modernity, however, the destination of that path is difficult to discern. Neither have recent transformations in Ghanaian funerary culture been quite as pronounced or uncontested as anthropological studies appear to suggest. Biomedicine, Christianity, the cash nexus and the modern state have certainly conspired to reshape death and burial—yet that process, as we have seen, has been going on for well over a century. Whether the commercialization of funerals has reached a point where they have become more about the living than the dead is also questionable. A deeper historical perspective suggests that the needs of the living and those of the dead have long jostled for space in the complex sequence of enactments which make up African obsequies. Demands that their excesses and exorbitant costs be curtailed, moreover, are far from new. We have considered the ways in which colonial biopower sought to regulate and to secularize death. Our focus here turns to ongoing debates over the funeral, that key moment when normal time seems suspended and the world of the living and the dominion of the dead enter into an intense and intimate dialogue.

Moral outrage at ostentatious funerals in Ghana did not arise as a result of postcolonial commercialization. Condemnation of what was perceived by reformist African elites and British colonial officials alike as an unrestrained and unseemly culture of mourning is apparent from the mid-nineteenth century, first taking legislative form in Governor Pine's 1858 sumptuary regulations limiting the custom for a deceased king to three days, for a chief to two days and for a 'private person' to one day. There is no indication, however, that Pine's proclamation had any impact even within the coastal towns, let alone beyond them. Four decades later, an inquiry into the economic prospects of the colony reported that funerals remained ruinously expensive and detrimental to the regular supply of labour. '"Customs" are probably responsible for seven-eighths of the debts in the country, and weigh like an incubus on its prosperity by causing a vast amount of useless expenditure and implanting in the people a love of drink and idleness', the report ran. 'The observance is enforced by . . . fear of the anger of the dead . . . and fear of public opinion, which applauds the man who makes a "big custom" and stigmatizes as "stingy" the man who spares on such an occasion with all the power which a small community can bring to bear on any member of it.'[6]

By the turn of the twentieth century, calls for reform came from a spectrum of overlapping interest groups: colonial officials, expatriate and African businessmen, the Christian churches, and the progressive coastal elite, whose main concerns, respectively, were law and order, the local economy, 'heathenism', and moral uplift. Like the demand for modern cemeteries, this reformist impulse was not simply a manifestation of a coercive colonial mission to civilize unruly natives. Neither was it limited to the racialized peripheries of empire: growing disquiet about the wastefulness of funerals in the metropole itself led in 1875 to the formation of the National Funeral and Mourning Reform Association, whose paternalistic campaign for moderation among the working class—'they would starve to pay the undertaker', it was noted in 1843—was not dissimilar in tone to that on the Gold Coast.[7]

As in the metropole, there was a strong evangelical strain to such anxieties. For the Christian missions, funerals continued to represent the most visible and defiant manifestation of heathenism, which they sought to combat by enforcing an austere culture of death among their congregations—one in which libation to the ancestors, burial goods, and rites involving widows, fasting, drumming, dancing or firing would not be tolerated. In doctrinal terms, the main transformation brought by Christianity was that neither the manner of death nor the conduct of a funeral played a role in determining the destiny of the deceased. The Christian dead no longer became ancestors but atomized individual souls, whose relationship with their maker was the only one that was supposed to matter. The established domain of the ancestors, meanwhile, was recast as the Christian hell, which remained the destination of those who rejected the evangelical message.

Not that the boundary between pagan and Christian practice was necessarily self-evident. Take one key issue, raised by a resident of Cape Coast in a letter to the *Gold Coast Leader* in 1903: the desire for the dead to be laid to rest in their native soil. 'I write this only to know ... if the Christian body in this town too recognized this kind of custom of exhuming old bones of a human being as being religious and not superstitious as in several cases when the heathens indulged in making this kind of custom of a relative who had gone abroad and died the Christians speak very ill of it as utterly superstitious.'[8] Having observed a reburial in a Christian cemetery, however, the correspondent was perplexed. 'As the Christian body has plainly seen that it is not superstitious and have started it themselves it will leave room for other to follow', he wrote, suggesting that Rev. T. B. Freeman, who had died at Accra in 1890, might be reburied in Cape Coast. 'All round I have experienced the moneyed people are better treated in every society than the poor', the writer added, arguing that this was due to the belief that 'because of their money there is some hope of them of doing some good after their death'. Whether he believed that the agency of the dead had survived the transition to Christianity is not clear: 'I leave it to the public to comment'.

And comment the reading public did. Opinion, unsurprisingly, was divided. 'There has been constant and serious complaints made almost everywhere against the practice of our people indulging in the heavy expense at funerals which particularly demand the consideration of our Kings and Chiefs as well as the educated community as to the best method of suppressing, or utterly uprooting such practice', one correspondent wrote.[9] At the heart of the matter was the customary exchange between the bereaved family and the community—that is, the funeral expenses (*ka*), including those for hospitality laid on for mourners, on the one hand, and donations 'in cash and drinkables' (*nsa*), on the other. Notionally, the *nsa* was designed to offset the *ka*. The increasing elaboration of funeral accoutrements ('coffins, rings, dresses, etc') together with the substitution of locally produced palm wine with imported liquor, however, was pushing up costs. The deficit incurred by one funeral might be manageable, but if a family experienced a sudden sequence of bereavements, the financial impact could be devastating—'leading to a few', the writer lamented, 'to put an end to their misery through broken-heartedness or suicide'.

Yet others warned against colonial intervention. In response to a heavy-handed attempt at Axim to use the law requiring a permit for assemblies with music and dance to close down the obsequies of a 'respectable gentleman', the *Leader* mobilized the language of cultural nationalism to mount a stout defence of the therapeutic value of African obsequies. The article might be seen as representing an early, impassioned counter-critique of the twentieth-century 'denial of death':

> We know what it is to be in the presence of the dead. . . . To congregate at a house where the dead lies, to sing songs, dirges, to comfort the bereaved, instruct the reckless as to the uncertainty of life and to the vanity of the things of the world, etc, and to encourage those who may be denying themselves for the good of others . . . cannot be found fault with. As blacks, we are not so phlegmatic, mercurial in fact, as the English—nor as savages are we so reserved as our enlightened, civilized and 'society' masters. . . . We may be 'noisy' but we can't help it, nature must have her course. And to find fault with us, to impose fines, inflict blows, and use dirty and abusive language to us, because, we do not, cannot, put our dead in one room of the house, and go about if nothing extraordinary has happened to us, till it is coffined and taken to be buried, is we say, *not civilization among the blacks*.[10]

As for the prolonged nature of the ceremonies, the *Leader* explained that the culmination of the custom on the eighth day, when the spirit of the deceased departs for the afterlife, represented an essential moment of closure, allowing the bereaved family to 'perform with impunity (with the superstitious, without incurring the anger of the deceased's ghost) their ordinary evocations'. 'These customs cannot be done away with—if ever at all—high handedly or contemptuously. The educated native will fight for them, *en masse* for . . . there is in them to us an inexplicable blend of the past, the present and the future, of the immediate dead one, and through him of his ancestors, which every attendant applies to himself and his, and which 'touch', so to speak, makes all, present at such occasions—rich and poor high and low, educate and illiterate, one.'

The debate re-emerged in 1909, when the secretary for native affairs (SNA) suggested that the time had come for regulation. As in the past, the soaring cost of funerals was one concern, the SNA citing anecdotal evidence ranging from the £400 said to have been spent on the recent obsequies of the sister of the *omanhene* of Sefwi, to the plight of his own cook, who was obliged 'to withdraw from the bank all the savings of several years in order to pay his contribution towards the funeral custom of an Aunt'.[11] More debilitating, however, was the rising consumption of alcohol: a factor which would remain at the centre of debates throughout the colonial period and beyond. This was especially noticeable, the SNA thought, in districts such as Akyem Abuakwa, where the development of the cocoa industry had resulted in a sudden diffusion of wealth and where funerals, previously 'regulated and orderly', were now 'more or less extended in proportion to the condition of the family'. Still, he advised that government would need to proceed with caution: 'practices of this nature cannot easily be altered, but if a strong opinion were expressed by the educated and influential natives of the Colony, it should be possible to induce the various chiefs to take concerted action'. With this in mind, the government sought advice from the two African representatives on the Legislative Council, the barristers John Mensah Sarbah and Thomas Hutton Mills.

It will be recalled that in 1888 the government had relied on the Fante merchant and mortuary entrepreneur John Sarbah to support the enactment of the Cemeteries Ordinance. Twenty years later, his son John Mensah Sarbah judged further intervention into funerary culture to be ill-advised. Hutton Mills, from Accra, was in favour of legislation, but it was the opinion of Sarbah which stayed the hand of government. Setting out his argument in a letter of June 1910, he downplayed the problem of drunkenness, explaining that alcohol consumption remained a feature only at particular moments in the sequence of obsequies. 'Reforms in this matter can be by influencing public opinion', he thought, noting wryly that 'I see no reason why the chiefs and their elders should not help except the chiefs are not noted for their sobriety'.[12] Five months later, Sarbah died suddenly, aged 46. The premature loss of the Gold Coast's most articulate and respected defender of native rights was widely mourned—it is tempting to imagine, by many a raised glass. His replacement on the Legislative Council was Emmanuel Mate Kole, the Basel Mission–educated paramount chief of Manya Krobo, who, as a devout Christian, was noted for his sobriety and who also favoured sumptuary regulation. But Governor Rodger was firm: 'I don't believe in sobriety by legislation'.[13]

The concern with alcohol abuse at funerals also had a broader imperial context. Alarm at the deleterious impact of the global trade in European spirits had led temperance activists in 1888 to form the United Committee for the Prevention of the Demoralization of the Native Races by the Liquor Traffic, whose warnings became part of the ideological justification for the Scramble for Africa. In the aftermath of conquest, the committee continued to press colonial administrations to prohibit imports, arguing that liquor was undermining the fabric of societies and condemning large numbers to an early grave. The superintendent of the Methodist mission on the Gold Coast, Rev. W. R. Griffin, for one, was having none of it. Questioned on the issue in 1911, Griffith—although himself a teetotaller—refuted the committee's propaganda, explaining that his refusal when in England to endorse its view 'that the natives of West Africa were gin soaked' led to him being denounced as favouring strong drink.[14] 'I must emphatically state that I do not see anything of the demoralization spoken of', he wrote. 'I have never seen a drunken black woman in my life though I have lived among the black people for 22 years, and I have very seldom seen a drunken black man.'[15] The consumption of imported spirits had certainly begun to replace that of palm wine, Griffin conceded, but like Mensah Sarbah, he rejected the allegation that funeral celebrations were becoming dominated by drunken carousing.

Colonial officials did share the worry expressed by some literate African commentators about the extravagant cost of funerals. In line with the emerging ideology of indirect rule, however, the administration was prepared to intervene only if the initiative came from the local rulers. The tone of much correspondence, moreover, betrays considerable empathy with the deeply professed traditional reverence for the dead. 'It must be remembered', one official cautioned, 'that the natives use a funeral custom as one of the few occasions when they give themselves up completely to a short period of thorough enjoyment, in which a certain amount of drinking takes place among a certain number; very similar to assemblages of human beings in other parts of the world.'[16] Another agreed: 'drinking and gun firing are and have been for generations the principal features of funeral customs and until Christianity has obtained a much firmer hold . . . they will continue to be so, and it will be impossible to abolish them.'[17] Moral influence only, it was resolved, might be brought to bear on local communities, who 'with the advancement of civilization will gradually themselves curtail the expenditure and the objectionable drinking bouts will no doubt to a large extent cease.'[18]

This was not to be the case. The 'advancement of civilization'—that is to say, social change generated by capitalism, literacy and Christian conversion—did not curtail the heavy investment of time, money and emotional engagement in seeing off the dead. To the imperative to provide mourners with imported liquor was added a whole range of innovations which increased rather than decreased the costs of celebrations. Apparent first in the colony's burgeoning urban centres, innovations quickly spread into the rural hinterland, in particular to those regions where cocoa farming had raised levels of disposable wealth. Neither were the Gold Coast's growing Christian communities insulated from change: the stern Victorian moralizing of the original missions was not entirely a thing of the past, but by the interwar period it began to be tempered by an increase in African clergy and the emergence of independent African churches.[19] Even among Muslim communities—for whom a swift and plain burial was the doctrinal norm—there was concern on the part of reformers about over-elaborate funerals marked by the pervasive influence of customary pagan practice.[20]

The look and the sound of funeral customs in the coastal towns were undergoing change by the early twentieth century. Despite calls by sober-minded reformists for women mourners to replace the dizzying array of fashions with the wearing of sombre black crape, *ayitam* (funeral cloth) evolved in other directions. The result was uniformity—but not in Victorian black; rather, it became the height of fashion for mourners to be fitted out in matching outfits of multiple colours specially made for the funeral. Advances in printing technology also gave rise in the interwar period to 'commemorative cloth' bearing a photographic portrait of the bereaved: an early example was that produced in 1936 for the funeral of Agonahene Nene Nyaarku Eku V, pictured with the Twi expression of mourning, *damarifa due*.[21] Sonic innovation, meanwhile, proceeded from a combination of the emergence of new hybrid forms of music and restrictions on musketry and drumming within town limits. As early as 1909, Cape Coast alone had five brass bands, whose most regular source of income was from playing at funerals. After a confrontation when Coker's Brass Band and the reputedly 'rowdy' Lion Soldier's Band crossed paths, officials moved to regulate their performances: 4 p.m. to 9 p.m. on Monday to Friday and 1 p.m. to 9 p.m. on Saturday—already emerging as 'funeral day'—and no playing on Sundays.[22] Included in the performance permit, moreover, was an undertaking that the band desist from playing 'native songs'—a reference to the tradition, now being reinvented with brass, concertina, tin whistle and guitar accompaniment, of the singing of salacious and provocative songs at funerals and at yearly festivals.[23]

The emergence of professional undertakers on the Gold Coast can be dated to at least the 1870s, when John Sarbah began advertising coffins and the organization of funerals in 'the most approved and economical style'. Yet for those who could afford them—and, it seems, for many who could not—elaborate coffins became important status symbols. Local carpenters may well have been able to turn out economical wooden coffins, but many people wanted imported brass coffins, costing hundreds of pounds.[24] By mid-century, these could be hired from Accra for the duration of the funeral, the corpse being discreetly transferred to a simple wooden coffin for interment.[25] With the move to modern cemeteries, too, came the advent of headstones. In a significant departure from the past, graves became sites of demarcated memory and the names of the dead moved from being memorialized in oral dirges to being inscribed in stone. A survey conducted in 1929 of the old government cemetery at Kumasi indicates that headstones, originally limited to the graves of Europeans and of Syrian traders, had begun by the 1910s to mark those of the African dead.[26] It was the same year that Agyeman Prempeh justified his plans for reordering the city's royal necrogeography on the grounds that elaborate tombstones for deceased commoners were appearing 'all over the countryside'. And it was not just European-style tombstones: a photograph taken before 1911 shows that graves were beginning to be adorned by life-size concrete statues of the deceased, which appear stylistically to combine elements of photographic portraiture and the terracotta *nsanie*.[27] When in 1935 such a monument was discovered to have been erected to the late chief Anamua in Cape Coast's Methodist cemetery, outraged church officials ordered it to be removed forthwith.[28]

The extent to which the Victorian vogue for photographing the dead caught on among the urban elites of West Africa is unclear. We have seen how, in 1897, R. J. Ghartey's body was photographed and sketched, while a reference in 1905 to a laid-out and bejewelled corpse being photographed in a rural town near Accra suggests that, like tombstones, the practice was established enough to be spreading into the hinterland.[29] That the photograph was produced in court as evidence for the alleged robbery of the jewellery from the grave is itself interesting; three decades later in Asante, a group of terracotta *nsanie* were also produced in court as proof of the existence of an ancient burial ground in a dispute over ancestral land.[30] There was not a linear progression from sculpted faces of the dead to the preservation of their physical form by photography: as we have seen, both media were used in 1944 to portray the deceased *omanhene* of Akyem Abuakwa, while grave sculptures and painted portraits often appear to have been copied from photographic originals. By mid-century, however, the photographic image had joined the writing down of the names of the dead

FIGURE 19.1. A modern funerary sculpture of Christiana A. Ansa, photographed by Rudolf Fisch between 1885 and 1911 and captioned 'Memorial on the grave of a deceased native'. Although the details are obscured, the headstone indicates Christiana's dates of birth, baptism and death, together with a reference to the Book of Philippians (probably Phil. 1:21): 'For me to live is Christ, and to die is gain'. Basel Mission Archives QD-32.008.9190.

as a key technology of modern memorialization—the two coming together in commemorative cloth and in the printed obituary notice.

When, in the late 1920s, the demand for regulation was once again renewed, the contribution of all these modern innovations to the soaring cost of obsequies was cited as the ostensible reason. So too was the fear that alcohol was threatening the wellbeing of society. 'The people have been and are being ruined physically, morally and financially by strong drink', Agyeman Prempeh lamented in 1928. 'It has been the contributory cause of the barrenness that is rampant today, amongst the womenfolk . . . [and] the cause of many a sudden and untimely death.'[31] Underlying such expressions of pathological social ruin was a quite different anxiety: that the ostentatious display of new-found commercial wealth at funerals was undermining the distinction between chiefs and commoners—both alive and dead. For the remainder of the colonial period, attempts at sumptuary regulation were invariably initiated by indirect-rule chiefs rather than by European officials, who, after toying with the idea in 1909–12, took a back seat on the matter. In 1928, a number of constituent divisions of Asante framed bye-laws under the 1924 Native Jurisdiction Ordinance which sought to set limits on expenditure according to the status of the deceased. Those submitted by Agonahene Kwadwo Apaw, for example, established six classes of dead: 'The Head Chief: £250; Stool Royals: £160; A Chief and members of his family (i.e. his Stool Royals) [and] the Councillor of the Head Chief: £150; Royals of Chiefs: £100; Any other person of rank: £80; Young men: £40.'[32] A key term here was 'young men', which referred not necessarily to age but to an absence of rank—that is, 'commoners', including those from the entrepreneurial class of so-called *akonkofo* for whom colonial capitalism represented an avenue to enhanced social status.[33] 'Any dispute as to the class to which any deceased person rightly belongs shall be brought before the Head Chief in Council whose decision shall be final', the draft bye-law ran. 'A written account and record shall be kept of the expenditure of any funeral custom, and such person who is performing (that is to say paying for) such funeral custom (eg. the heir of the deceased) shall on demand from his head of Chief produce such account for his inspection.'[34]

Once again, funerary reform became entangled with temperance. After criticism in 1928 by Legislative Council members J. E. Casely Hayford and Nana Ofori Atta of the colonial state's fiscal dependence on liquor revenues, Governor Slater set up a committee to consider the import of spirits.[35] The proposed bye-laws were referred to the six-man committee (which included Ofori Atta and the lawyer John Glover Addo), where it was decided that they could not practicably be enforced.[36] The Asante *amanhene*, too, were divided on the matter: while some were in favour of regulation, others, such as the Bekwaihene, were firmly opposed; 'any endeavour to regulate funeral customs in Ashanti', he was reported as saying, 'would do more harm than good and would rouse the resentment of the people'.[37] British officials tended to agree: despite reports that £700 had recently been spent on one royal funeral in his region, the commissioner of the Western Province of Ashanti also warned against government intervention. 'To spend less . . . would be to insult the dead', he wrote, 'a point which must not be forgotten when legislation is undertaken for a people where the worship of ancestors is a great part of the religion.'[38] Not wishing to alienate their indirect-rule partners, the government allowed native authorities to pass the bye-laws if they so chose, the Asante divisions of Agona and Offinso being the first to do so, in 1929. In both kingdoms, the sumptuary limits at the lower end of the social scale were drastically reduced from those originally suggested: paramount chiefs: £150–£200; divisional chiefs: £25; other persons: £5–£10; labourers £2.10–£6. In death, as in life, the chiefs sought to reinforce established hierarchy in the face of social change.

The following year, similar bye-laws were enacted in various states of the old Gold Coast Colony.[39] Yet there is little indication that in either region did these succeed in curtailing increasing ostentation and cost. In 1935, the issue was the first item on the agenda of the inaugural meeting of the Ashanti Confederacy Council under the leadership of the reinstated Asantehene Osei Agyeman Prempeh II. Prompted by Chief Commissioner Jackson, who reminded the council that, as the colony struggled to cope with the impact of the global depression, 'civilization did not require useless expenditure', the chiefs launched into a debate on the matter.[40] Opinion remained divided—in particular on the thorny issue of the imperative to maintain the distinction between royal office-holders and *arriviste* commoners. The Oyokohene, for one, argued 'that the rules should be made to apply only to the youngmen and not to the Chief'.[41] The reformist Agonahene and Adontenhene, in contrast, argued that all burials should take place the day after death and that funerals should last no longer than four days—'this suggestion, they added, applied equally to stool-holders'.[42] In the end, the Asantehene steered the council towards a compromise: it was resolved that the funeral of a 'youngman' should last no longer than three days and that of a chief nine days, while upper limits were set for individual donations. The council declined, however, to limit expenditure, the Asantehene agreeing with an intervention from the Tafohene, who argued that 'everybody was at liberty to put his money to whatever use he chose'. It was just five years before that Agyeman Prempeh had made an abortive attempt to revive death duties—but there could not be clearer admission by his successor that the reconfigured Asante Confederacy now operated according to the laissez-faire rules of colonial capitalism.

———

There is every indication that in society at large the attitude expressed by Tafohene saw off the lingering reformist impulse. Further attempts to regulate funerals by native authorities followed in the 1940s–50s and, after the end of colonial rule, by what were then reformulated as traditional councils in the 1960s and beyond.[43] Some elements in these campaigns remained constant, notably the anxieties about conspicuous consumption and the blurring of hierarchies among both the living and the dead. By mid-century, however, new elements began to enter the debate. First, mortuary culture continued to be elaborated by the accoutrements of modernity. The advent of commercial printing further shifted the imperative to name the dead with the written word, as public obituary notices, initially the preserve of chiefs and wealthy commoners, became *de rigueur* for all but the poorest deceased.[44] Motor vehicles were increasingly used to transport mourners over long distances and to convey bodies to cemeteries. Perhaps the most profound technological shift, however, was the advent of refrigerated morgues by the 1940s. As anthropologists of contemporary Ghanaian mortuary practices have observed, the increasing availability of what became known as 'the fridge' in the second half of the twentieth century allowed—for a cost—corpses to be stored until such a time as dispersed family members could congregate or sufficient funds be accumulated to hold a lavish send-off.[45] Gradually, the distinction between burial and the subsequent funerary rites began to fade, as refrigeration allowed the latter to take place in the physical presence of the dead body. By the early 1960s, Nketia observed, the customary eight-, fifteen-, forty-, eighty- and one-year rites were no longer strictly observed, it being 'the practice nowadays for one of these days to be selected for the subsequent funeral celebration.'[46] In an era when the institution of chieftaincy was under threat from Nkrumah's nationalist project, old hierarchies in the domain of the dead as well as in that of the living were further eroded.

Second, the emergence of a commercialized funeral business combined with broader patterns of social change to generate new strategies on the part of those anticipating death. We have seen how written wills were increasingly used to stamp one's authority on the future, including by those determined to avoid 'native customs' or ostentation. The late nineteenth century also saw the advent among the urban propertied classes of life insurance policies—the disbursement of which began to feature in wills. For the less well-off, burying the dead also became a central concern of new voluntary associations. Emerging from the 1920s and catering in particular to the welfare needs of newly arrived urban migrants cut off from their communities of origin, the associations functioned in part as thrift societies, members paying a small monthly contribution and in return being eligible to draw on funds in the case of a death in the family or on their own demise.⁴⁷ In the late 1940s, members of the Oguaa Korye Kuw (Cape Coast Union) in the port town of Sekondi-Takoradi, for example, paid a monthly contribution of 9 pence; if a family member died, they received a funeral benefit of £2.4s, and if they died, their family received £7.4s—and, importantly, 'the Society turns out for the funeral'.⁴⁸ Many associations were organized along 'tribal' lines but others according to profession: 'there is a strong comradeship among prostitutes', K. A. Busia noted, 'and their "Union" provides the security of a befitting funeral celebration and burial'.⁴⁹

Third, the degree to which evolving obsequies were compatible with modernity in the era of renewed African sovereignty became entangled with debates over socially corrosive costs and conspicuous consumption. In so far as modernity came with a distinctive Christian cast, communities on the mission frontier had been wrestling with these issues from the nineteenth century. By the mid-twentieth century, as it became apparent that a great many funerals were neither distinctively 'traditional' nor 'Christian' but instead a mixture of the two, the hybridity of mortuary culture became a topic of public debate. On the one hand were those, such as the author of a sequence of tub-thumping articles in the *Gold Coast Nation* in 1918, who denounced the lingering paganism apparent in 'native Christian Customs'. When 'Christian burial has been incautiously associated, and unnecessarily prolonged with the *idolatrous, sinful* and *barbarous* customary rites of the heathen, that the Church . . . succumbs in shameful defeat, to the fiery darts of the devil and his Agents', he thundered, 'it is then that the Christian is said . . . to have made shipwreck'.⁵⁰ On the other hand were more secular voices who applauded the 'beautiful blend of healthy native customs and Christian rites which we would like to see perpetuated'.⁵¹ The funeral being described in this case was that in 1930 of 90-year-old Araba Esibu, a female office-holder of the Intin (No. 3) *asafo* company of Cape Coast, whose coffin was borne three times at running pace around the company's *posuban* or monumental post before being conveyed to the Wesleyan chapel amidst a crowd of townspeople accompanied by the Oguaahene's drummers. 'At the Chapel Square as the coffin was being received by the minister and choir the *Bombaa* ceased beating and the Christian rites began', the *Gold Coast Times* reported. It was one of the biggest funerals Cape Coast had seen in many years—just the sort of exuberant hybrid display that aroused the ire of those dreading the 'fiery darts of the devil'.

As Rev. S. Gyasi Nimako recognized in a study of mortuary culture in a Gold Coast on the cusp on independence, old beliefs and practices remained widespread, surviving often in modified form in the Christian funeral.⁵² The result of an inquiry set up by the Methodist Church after tension in Winneba between its local congregation and a burial association called the Hope Society, Nimako's report mobilized scripture to explain why modern Christians no longer had a 'need for prolonged unmitigated sorrowing and mourning when death occurs' or to perform complicated rites 'calculated to sever connection between the living and the dead, nor to take medicine to drive away the spirit of the dead from the abode of the living'.[53] The intimate relationship between the living and the dead, he lamented, remained deeply rooted in local society. After a century of Christian influence, Fante churchgoers still performed the final libation during the *sora* to sever the deceased from the living—a rite even 'known to have been done in the case of the death of ministers of the gospel!'[54] So too did the treatment of widows continue to be marked by ritualized abhorrence, particularly those whose husbands had been members of the staunchly traditionalist *asafo* military companies. Grieving Fante *akunafo* were still dragged to the company *posuban*, where they were 'mocked, scolded and buffeted' and hung with 'empty tins and filthy rags'.[55] Such rites persisted: in Asante they were high on the agenda when in 1953 the Kumasi State Council created a standing Anti-Funeral Campaign Committee and again, in 1974, when the council once more drew up a list of sumptuary regulations. 'The old custom of "Kunaye" should be modified to the holding of a corn-cob, mint and "Prekese"', the proposals stated. 'The custom of decorating the widow or widower with snail shells, raffia and other articles should be abolished'.[56] Holding a corn-cob and a sprig of pungent *emme* ('mint') might be an improvement on being hung with old snail shells, but it was clear that the unsettled and sexually ravenous ghosts of deceased husbands, far from disappearing, continued to linger.

'Most of us who were raised during and for some time after the colonial era are sharply aware of the ways in which the colonizers were never as fully in control as our elders allowed them to appear', the Ghanaian philosopher Kwame Anthony Appiah wrote in *In My Father's House*. 'We all experienced the persistent power of our own cognitive and moral traditions: in religion, in such social occasions as the funeral, in our experience of music, in our practice of the dance, and, of course, in the intimacy of family life.'[57] Appiah's identification of the funeral as a key site of resistance is one that has been made in many historical contexts, perhaps most movingly in the plantation colonies of the

Americas, where enslaved Africans struggled to affirm their humanity by burying their dead in their own way. Entangled with these struggles in colonial-era Ghana was a more complex story in which mortuary cultures not only persisted but changed. Ensuing transactions and contests over the shifting terrain of death and burial, moreover, were not just between colonizer and colonized but within African society itself. Neither was this a linear process of progressive disenchantment, characterized simply by the sloughing off of outmoded custom. Tradition informed colonial modernity, and vice versa, in a complex variety of ways. One example of many can be considered with which to conclude. On 2 March 1936, the Asante Confederacy began to celebrate the *adaduanan*, or forty-day funeral custom for a dead king—not an Asante king, but the late imperial overlord, George V. On a poster displayed around Kumasi produced by the director of funeral ceremonies, W.J.K. Appiah—Kwame Anthony Appiah's grandfather—it was announced that the occasion would be observed 'in a customary manner . . . ; There will be firing of guns, commencing at 7 am; All are expected to appear in mourning dress'.[58] As many studies of twentieth-century Africa and of mortuary cultures beyond have demonstrated, modern deathways were characterized by new and diverse forms of vernacular re-enchantment.[59]

And one other: half a century later, W.J.K. Appiah's son, Joe—the father of Kwame Anthony Appiah's *In My Father's House*—wrote his autobiography. Tracing his life from a childhood in the Adum ward of early colonial Kumasi to a career as a prominent lawyer and political opponent of Kwame Nkrumah and on to recognition as a sage elder of the nationalist era, the book is in some respects an account of a trajectory from a world of tradition to one of postcolonial modernity. Yet it is also saturated with ongoing encounters with threatening forces issuing forth from an older, mystical realm: ghosts; Mami Wata, the mermaid-like temptress of coastal waters; *mmoatia*, the little tricksters of the deep forest; and, from the beginning of its story to its end, the looming spectre of death itself. In a final embrace of modern deathways, Joe Appiah closes with a reflection on his approaching demise, setting out instructions for his funeral akin to those we have seen gracing many last wills and testaments. 'The exhibition of dead bodies to all and sundry prior to burial and subsequent unnecessary and elaborate funeral celebrations have always distressed me', he wrote; 'therefore, I solemnly request that these abominable trappings be avoided at my passing away'. Unlike his father, he had no truck with sombre funeral cloth: 'I wish my family and friends to remember me as I was before my demise and to clothe themselves in white instead of the traditional black and dark browns that portray man's inevitable transition as a gloomy spectre. And may I be cremated and portions of my ashes scattered at Adum, my garden and over the grave of my grandmother if decent cremation has become possible in Ghana'. Finally, Appiah insisted that a week later 'a service without tributes be held at which the "Hallelujah Chorus" and the hymn "For All the Saints" of my beloved Mfantsipim School shall be sung—and no more! I do not wish to give opportunity for hypocritical eulogies to be paid under the admonition of *de mortuis nihil nisi bonum* (concerning the dead, nothing but good)'.[60]

Joe Appiah died in 1990, soon after completing the autobiography. An account of his funeral in turn forms the epilogue to *In My Father's House*. It was 'an occasion for strengthening and reaffirming the ties that bind me to Ghana', Kwame Anthony Appiah writes; owing to his effort to comply with his father's unorthodox final wishes, however, it was also a tumultuous affair which strained 'my allegiances to my king and my father's matriclan' and seemed to carry him back into 'an almost fairytale world of witchcraft and wicked aunts and wise old women and men'. 'In the midst of it—when partisans of our side were beaten up in my father's church, when sheep were slaughtered to cast powerful spells against us, when our household was convinced that the food my aunt sent me was poisoned—it seemed that every attempt to understand what was happening took me further back into family history and the history of Asante.'[61] *Abusua do funu*, Appiah came to learn: 'the matriclan loves a corpse'. Cognitive and moral traditions may well have persisted—but so too was death and burial a rupture, a suspension of normal time in which mourners ruminated on the past and all too often contested its meanings.

Conclusion

THOMAS KYEI (1908–1999) grew up in the Asante town of Agogo as the child of a Christian mother and a non-Christian father. Ensconced in the segregated Salem, Kyei's mother expressly forbade him to approach either the town's *akom-ase*, the 'fetish dance place', or anywhere that a visitation from death had turned into *ayie-ase*, the place of a funeral. 'Taking advantage of my dual residency', however, he managed one day 'to sneak out to the funeral in a house where a prominent dead person was lying in state. And, Oh! What I saw frightened me terribly'. The corpse was laid out on layer upon layer of costly blankets and covered with rich *kente* cloths, its face decorated with intricate designs fashioned from gold dust and its hands adorned with heavy gold jewellery. A platform at the foot of the bed was groaning with dishes of cooked food to sustain the deceased on his journey to the afterworld. Like Charles Bannerman in 1841, the young Kyei stood transfixed. We are repelled by death, but inexorably drawn to it. When the time came for the body to be coffined, 'the senior relatives of the deceased politely asked to be excused and to be left alone to swear to him and bid him good-bye in secret'.

> I left the house. All the way to my father's house . . . I kept musing: 'And so when a person dies, he goes to live in another place called *"Asamando"*, taking with him some of all the food we eat here, to eat there; the best and the nicest cloths that we wear Here, to wear There. He left bidding all good-bye, and was gone never to return, never to be seen by the living but he was about all the place and saw the doings of the living!' I must confess that I was bewildered for a long, long time by my boyhood experiences of religious incompatibilities and mysteries that could not readily be understood or rationally explained. All these imponderables weighed unbearably on me. They were compounded by the wise drummer in the language we heard

transmitted on the *atumpan* drums on sacred days (*da-bone*), on *akwasidee* and *awukudee*, saying *Odomankama, a / Oboo Adee / Borebore a / Oboo Adee / Oboo Owuo / Ma Owuo kom no* (The Great Mighty who created the 'Thing' / The Creative Creator who created the 'Thing' / He created Death and Death killed Him).[1]

And so we conclude by returning to where we started, to the beginning of time, when Odomankoma fashioned something unspeakable: *adee*, the 'Thing'. The Thing, as recounted by the *ntumpane*, was death, and its first victim was Odomankoma himself. Undone by his own creation, he became the first of countless others to mount the proverbial ladder of death, dead yet somehow not dead, leaving humankind to fend for itself in a threatening and mysterious world. It was then that men and women themselves took up the work of creation, fashioning cultures which served as a defence against the ontological insecurities of the world, the 'imponderables' of being, as Tom Kyei would have it, and the implacable enemy that for each individual would bring their earthly existence to an end. What I hope this book has demonstrated is that death and the dead stood at the very heart of those cultures and that they materialized in myriad ways as historical action. There is nothing especially original about this observation, which has been made in a number of recent histories of death in different parts of the world. For Assmann, 'death is the origin and centre of culture', his analysis of ancient Egyptian mortuary belief and practice demonstrating that 'knowledge of our own mortality... is a first-rate cultural generator'.[2] Focusing on the dead as material remains, Verdery concurs: 'burials and reburials serve both to create and to reorder community', while for Laqueur, 'the dead make social worlds'.[3] And where those worlds collide, as Seeman writes in the case of colonial North America, death is 'virtually unmatched' for understanding the cross-cultural encounter.[4] Life, in short, is pervaded by death, and the dead, 'whatever their manner of death, stand in as pretexts to talk about the living'.[5]

How does our history of death and the dead in one well-documented part of West Africa advance these understandings? To return to the issue raised in the introduction, to what extent can death be seen even to *have* an identifiable history among the diverse peoples of the Gold Coast and the forest and savanna beyond? Certainly, mortuary cultures in what by the end of our story had become independent Ghana appear to have been characterized by a considerable degree of continuity over the four centuries considered here. It is not easy to discern a fundamental narrative of the sort first proposed by Ariès for the West, in which an easy familiarity with what he called a 'tamed death' was supplanted from the later Middle Ages by a growing anxiety about one's own death; in the Enlightenment with an exaltation of the death of the other; and in the modern era with a 'forbidden death' managed no longer by communities but by doctors, lawyers, undertakers and the state. In common with premodern or 'traditional' societies elsewhere, including western Europe, the Akan and their neighbours lived in intimate proximity to death and the dead. But I am not sure that either was ever regarded fully as tamed. In West Africa's unforgiving epidemiological environment, death was all around and could swoop down without warning, snatching people away 'with no more force than the wind stirred by a fan'. Yet we have seen ample evidence to suggest that familiarity did not breed habituation: as in eighteenth-century Paris, people were 'horrified and scandalised by sudden and unexpected death'.[6] Far from being regarded as a natural occurrence, it was as often as not understood to be the result of intervention by malign mystical forces or earthly 'poisoners'. As elsewhere, too, death had a highly public character: from the display of corpses to exuberant funeral celebrations and on to choreographed post-mortem inquisitions and ritual killings, people were drawn to the recurring spectacle of its performance. This visibility did not, however, equate to the racialized trope of a 'land of death', one where mortality was regarded with indifference. Staring death squarely in the face was more an elaborate subterfuge: a stand-off by which the living, struggling not to blink, might at least keep their implacable enemy in abeyance.

Neither was the dominion of the dead necessarily in easy and comforting dialogue with that of the living. Despite highly elaborated funerary rites designed to ease the departure of the deceased into the afterlife and to perform the healing work of mourning, even hallowed ancestors could prove troublesome, requiring dedicated management and careful ongoing propitiation. Then there were the spectres of the unsettled and unhappy dead, the legions of the lost, whose bad deaths and lingering animosity weighed heavily on the living. If local cosmologies sought to salve the trauma of loss and the dread of one's own obliteration by envisaging death as a transition or 'rebirth' to a new existence beyond the grave, one governed by the same notions of kinship and hierarchy as the world of the living, then the trade-off was that the tensions and anxieties which were the stuff of human life also characterized the broader cosmic community. The goal may have been to tame death—but it was at best a work in progress.

Yet we have seen too how social and political change from the nineteenth century led to a reconfiguration in the management of death and care of the dead. A number of key transformations are certainly recognizable from the portrayal by Ariès and others of the sequestered and increasingly individuated death typical of the modern West: the regime of cemetery burial; the surveillance and regulation of death by the colonial state; the rise of the written word as a new vehicle for naming and memorializing the dead. The advent of mission Christianity not only offered an alternative conceptual reading of the cosmos but added the clergy, first European and then African, to the ranks of those agents of modernity who sought to appropriate from local communities the care of the dead. In the twentieth century, those ranks were expanded further by the doctors serving the colony of medicine. By the end of our period, in the 1950s, still only a very few Ghanaians were dying in hospitals. Yet the gradual spread of biomedicine combined with improvements in general living standards to bring about a significant increase in life expectancy and in demographic growth. Just as Christianity offered a new mystical interpretation of death focused on the fate of the individual soul, so biomedicine sought to locate morbidity and mortality within the individual body. As more children survived into adulthood and people were on average living longer, the numbers of those struck down by the scandal of premature death began to decline.

As is becoming increasingly apparent for other parts of the world, however, the terrain of this historical transformation was uneven and contested. In much of colonial and postcolonial Ghana, particularly in the deep rural communities of the northern savannas, the old ways of caring for the dead continued to hold sway and are only now, in the twenty-first century, beginning to change. As noted in the final chapter, anthropological accounts of contemporary Ghanaian deathways, focused mostly on the urban centres of the south, have identified the emergence of increasingly commercialized and ostentatious funeral celebrations in which the secular status of the living is now seen to be more important than the ritual care of the dead. This may well be the case. Yet locating these observations in a deeper historical context suggests a slightly different interpretation. It is not just that debates over sumptuary regulation have been going on for well over a century, but that the elaboration of funerals points to the ongoing importance of the dominion of the dead. Rather than a progressive disenchantment of the dead, that is, their social presence continues to be profound, outliving the existence of the body.

Thomas Kyei died in December 1999, aged 91. I had been introduced to him some years before by my friend Jean Allman, and used to visit him whenever I was in Kumasi. Mr Kyei was frail then, hard of hearing and moved with increasing difficulty around the family residence which sat atop the stationery shop he had run for many decades. Almost to the end, however, he continued to work on his memoirs, the first part of which was published two years after his death as *Our Days Dwindle: Memories of My Childhood Days in Asante*. Despite the childhood urge to escape his mother's leash into the world of tradition and mystery, he had remained faithful to his Presbyterian upbringing, drawing on Psalm 90 for the title of his book: 'Our days dwindle under your wrath / Our lives are in a breath . . . and then we are gone'. Death was on Mr Kyei's mind as the end approached, yet he was able to look back with satisfaction at a life well lived. 'The proverbial life span of three score years and ten has been reached and passed', he wrote. 'The divine injunction on procreation has been fully and faithfully discharged. I have played my part in the perpetuation of the human species. To my children and all who come into being through my genes I leave in the pages that follow a sketchy account of my life.'[7] Much had changed in the course of that long life, but still, in Mr Kyei's time of dying, the ancestors and the yet to be born took shape before him, stretching away into the past and forward into the future.

GLOSSARY

Twi (or Akan) Words

Note: *a-, o-, e-* and sometimes *n-* at the beginning of Twi nouns are prefixes, so words are listed according to their initial consonant.

baamu (or *banmu*). royal mausoleum
barim. royal burial ground or mausoleum
begyina mma. 'come-and-stay children' whose names and unkempt appearance were designed to fool death
obirempon (pl. *abirempon*). a 'big man'; one rewarded for his success at wealth creation
abodwe (pl. *mmodwe*). jawbone
oburoni kurom. segregated Christian settlement, lit. 'white man's village'
abusua (pl. *mmusua*). matrilineage
abusua kuruwa. the family or lineage funerary pot
bayi. witchcraft
obayifo (pl. *abayifo*). witch
obosom (pl. *abosom*). tutelary deity or 'god'
obrafo (pl. *abrafo*). executioner
caboceer. headman
adae. ceremonial days during which offerings were made to the ancestors, differentiated between the *akwasidae* (Sunday or 'great' *adae*) and *awukuadae* (Wednesday or 'lesser' *adae*), each occurring once in every forty-two-day *adaduanan* cycle of time
damarifa. alas, condolences
adinkra. patterned mourning cloth
odom. poisonous bark used in ordeals
odomankomasem. traditions of origin centred on the creator god Odomankoma
odonko (pl. *nnonkofo*). slave of northern origin
aduru. medicine
adurubone. 'bad medicine' or poison
aduto. poisoning
oduyefo (pl. *aduyefo*). herbalist
afehyia. the anniversary celebration of a death
efunu. corpse
funnaka. coffin

afunsoa. 'carrying the corpse' to determine cause of death
agyapadie. family heirlooms
ohemaa (**pl.** *ahemaa*). queen mother
hyire. white clay, as smeared on the human body
okomfo (**pl.** *akomfo*). ritual specialist or 'priest'
konnurokusem. a vile or despicable matter
akonnwa (**pl.** *nkonnwa*). a wooden stool
nkonnwa tuntum. blackened ancestral stools
kra. a component of a human being; the 'soul'
nkrabea. fate or destiny
okrafo. a courtly functionary who embodies the *kra* of an *omanhene*
nkuku ba (**pl.** *nkuku mma*). 'pot child' who died prematurely
kurotia. ritually charged liminal zone dividing zones of culture and nature
akyere (**pl.** *nkyere*). condemned prisoner destined for ritual sacrifice
akyiwadie. a taboo
okyeame (**pl.** *akyeame*). spokesperson or 'linguist' of an office-holder
oman (**pl.** *aman*). kingdom or state
omanhene (**pl.** *amanhene*). ruler of an *oman*
mogya. blood; component of a human being associated with matrilineal descent
amusie. burial, interment; *amusiei*: burial ground, esp. modern cemetery
nananom (**or** *nananom asamanfo*). hallowed ancestors
onipadua. the human body
apaee. praise poems
asafo. military company
osaman (**pl.** *asamanfo*). spirit of a dead person, which could take three forms: *osaman-pa* (a good-natured spirit of one who died a good death); *osaman atofo* (a restless or 'lost' spirit of one who died in battle or an accident); *osaman twentwen* (a malign, lingering ghost)
asamando. the afterworld or abode of the dead
asamanpow. the 'accursed grove', where dead bodies are disposed of
samansie. deathbed nuncupative will
sanie (**pl.** *nsanie*). funerary sculptures
sasa. a dangerous and vengeful mystical element released by death
asensie. the 'place of pots' or location of *nsanie*
sika. gold or money
sora. the ceremony, usually on the sixth day of the funeral, when the soul departs
suman (**pl.** *asuman*). lesser 'god' or protective talisman
sunsum. a component of a human being
ntam. an oath; *ntam kese*: the great oath
ti or *tiri.* the human head
tikoraa (**pl.** *ntikoraa*). skull
atofowu. transgressive or bad death
ntoro. a component of a human being associated with patrilineal descent
atumpan (**pl.** *ntumpan*). talking drum
ntwuma. red clay, as smeared on the human body

werempefo. 'official' mourners, especially at a royal funeral, who have particular responsibilities for the management of the deceased's stool
wiase. the known world of the living
awo. birth
owu. death
awude. things pertaining to death
owufo. a dead person
owu pa. a good death
awunnyadie. death duties
ayi. funeral
ayibuadie. death duties
ayitam. mourning cloth

Ga words

gbohiiajen. the afterworld
jemawon. tutelary deity
kpekpei. new-season corn offered to the ancestors at Homowo
manprobi. mausoleum
mantse. ruler of a town or kingdom (*man*)
nshonaman (pl. *nshonamajii*). seaside town
nyon (pl. *nyojii*). slave
woyo (pl. *woyei*). female ritual specialist or spirit medium
wulomo (pl. *wulomei*). ritual specialist or 'priest'

Words in the Gur family of languages of the northern savanna

bagre, boyar or *bo'ar.* cult of the ancestors
kpeem or *kpiim.* ancestors
naa. a secular office-holder or 'chief'
togbega (**Talen**). a homicide
ziesob (**Dagari**). a homicide

NOTES

Abbreviations

BMA   Basel Mission Archives
CCA   Chief Commissioner of Ashanti
CCNT Chief Commissioner of the Northern Territories
CCP   Commissioner of the Central Province of the Gold Coast
CEP   Commissioner of the Eastern Province of the Gold Coast
CWP   Commissioner of the Western Province of the Gold Coast
DC   District Commissioner
MRO   Manhyia Records Office, Kumasi
PP   Great Britain Parliamentary Papers
PRAAD Public Records and Archives Administration Department, Ghana
SNA   Secretary for Native Affairs
TNA   The National Archives, London
WMMS Wesleyan Methodist Missionary Archive, SOAS University of London

Introduction

1. John Parker, 'The Cultural Politics of Death and Burial in Early Colonial Accra', in David M. Anderson and Richard Rathbone, eds, *Africa's Urban Past* (Oxford, 2000); Jean Allman and John Parker, *Tongnaab: The History of a West African God* (Bloomington, 2005).

2. Columbia 14276D and reissued on Blind Willie Johnson, *Praise God I'm Satisfied* (Yazoo Records, 1989); other recorded versions include Charlie Patton's 1929 'Jesus Is a Dying Bed-Maker' and, more recently, Bob Dylan's 'In My Time of Dyin'' on *Bob Dylan* (Columbia Records, 1962) and Led Zeppelin's 'In My Time of Dying' on *Physical Graffiti* (Swan Song, 1975). The original inspiration is Psalms 41:3: 'The Lord will strengthen him upon the bed of languishing, thou wilt make all his bed in his sickness'.

3. Greil Marcus, *Invisible Republic: Bob Dylan's Basement Tapes* (New York, 1997); Sean Wilentz and Greil Marcus, eds, *The Rose and the Briar: Death, Love and Liberty in the American Ballad* (New York, 2005).

4. J. H. Nketia, *Funeral Dirges of the Akan People* (Achimota, 1955); on the funerary music of the Ewe peoples, see A. M. Jones, *Studies in African Music* (London, 1959), vol. 1, 72–94; see too Sjaak van der Geest, 'The Image of Death in Akan Highlife Songs of Ghana', *Research in African Literatures* 11 (1980).

5. See *Guardian*, 3 Feb. 2013, 'A four-day week please—we're dead tired'.

6. Robert Pogue Harrison, *The Dominion of the Dead* (Chicago, 2003).

7. Thomas W. Laqueur, *The Work of the Dead: A Cultural History of Mortal Remains* (Princeton, 2015).

8. See Joachim Whaley, ed., *Mirrors of Mortality: Studies in the Social History of Death* (London, 1981), 'Introduction', and ch. 5 by John McManners, 'Death and the French Historians'.

9. Philippe Ariès, *Western Attitudes toward Death: From the Middle Ages to the Present*, translated by Patricia M. Ranum (London, 1981), and *The Hour of Our Death*, translated by Helen Weaver (Harmondsworth, 1981).

10. See, e.g., Whaley, *Mirrors of Mortality*; Jonathan Dollimore, *Death, Desire and Loss in Western Culture* (New York, 2001); Allan Kellehear, *A Social History of Dying* (Cambridge, 2007); Julie-Marie Strange, *Death, Grief and Poverty in Britain, 1870–1914* (Cambridge, 2005); Laqueur, *Work of the Dead*.

11. Jan Assmann, *Death and Salvation in Ancient Egypt*, translated by David Lorton (Ithaca, 2005).

12. See, e.g., Allan Kellehear, ed., *The Study of Dying: From Autonomy to Transformation* (Cambridge, 2009); Atul Gawande, *Being Mortal: Illness, Medicine and What Matters in the End* (New York, 2014); Julie-Marie Strange, 'Grave Expectations', *Times Literary Supplement*, 8 June 2018.

13. Timothy Taylor, *The Buried Soul: How Humans Invented Death* (London, 2002); W. M. Spellman, *A Brief History of Death* (London, 2014); Carl Watkins, *The Undiscovered Country: Journeys among the Dead* (New York, 2014); Nigel Barley, *Dancing on the Grave: Encounters with Death* (London, 1995).

14. James L. Watson and Evelyn S. Rawski, eds, *Death Ritual in Late Imperial and Modern China* (Berkeley, 1988); Gary Ebersole, *Ritual Poetry and the Politics of Death in Early Japan* (Princeton, 1989); Catherine Merridale, *Night of Stone: Death and Memory in Russia* (London, 2000); Leor Halevi, *Muhammad's Grave: Death Rites and the Making of Islamic Society* (New York, 2007); Claudio Lomnitz, *Death and the Idea of Mexico* (New York, 2008).

15. Vincent Brown, *The Reaper's Garden: Death and Power in the World of Atlantic Slavery* (Cambridge, Mass., 2008); Erik R. Seeman, *Death in the New World: Cross-Cultural Encounters, 1492–1800* (Philadelphia, 2010); João José Reis, *Death Is a Festival: Funeral Rites and Rebellion in Nineteenth-Century Brazil*, translated by H. Sabrina Gledhill (Chapel Hill, 2003).

16. See the essays collected in *African Studies Review* 48 (2005), 'Mourning and the Imagination of Political Time in Contemporary Central Africa', edited by Bogumil Jewsiewicki and Bob W. White; in *African Studies* 68 (2009), 'The Life of the Corpse', edited by Deborah Posel and Pamila Gupta; in *African Studies* 71 (2012), 'Death and Loss in Africa', edited by Rebekah Lee and Megan Vaughan; and in Michael Jindra and Joël Noret, eds, *Funerals in Africa: Explorations of a Social Phenomenon* (New York, 2011).

17. Katherine Verdery, *The Political Lives of Dead Bodies: Reburial and Postsocialist Change* (New York, 1999); Achille Mbembe, *On the Postcolony* (Berkeley, 2001), and 'Necropolitics', *Public Culture* 15 (2003).

18. For exceptions, see the essays in *Journal of African History* 49 (2008), 'Death and Dying in the History of Africa', edited by Rebekah Lee and Megan Vaughan; Walima Kalusa and Megan Vaughan, *Death, Belief and Politics in Central African History* (Lusaka, 2013); Florence

Bernault, *Colonial Transactions: Imaginaries, Bodies, and Histories in Gabon* (Durham, NC, 2019).

19. Jack Goody, *Death, Property and the Ancestors: A Study of the Mortuary Customs of the LoDagaa of West Africa* (London, 1962); this work has been synthesized in Louis-Vincent Thomas, *Anthropologie de la mort* (Paris, 1975), and *La mort africaine: Idéologie funéraire en Afrique noire* (Paris, 1982); see too Igor Kopytoff, 'Ancestors as Elders in Africa', *Africa* 41 (1971).

20. See, representatively, Michelle Gilbert, 'The Sudden Death of a Millionaire: Conversion and Consensus in a Ghanaian Kingdom', *Africa* 58 (1988); Kwame Arhin, 'The Economic Implications of Transformations in Akan Funeral Rites', *Africa* 64 (1994); Takyiwaa Manuh, 'Changes in Marriage and Funeral Exchanges in Asante: A Case Study from Kona, Afigya-Kwabre', in Jane Guyer, ed., *Money Matters: Instability, Values and Social Payments in the Modern History of West African Communities* (Portsmouth, NH, 1995); Sjaak van der Geest, 'Funerals for the Living: Conversations with Elderly People in Kwahu, Ghana', *African Studies Review* 43 (2000); Marleen de Witte, *Long Live the Dead!: Changing Funeral Celebrations in Asante, Ghana* (Amsterdam, 2001).

21. One exception is Sandra E. Greene, *Sacred Sites and the Colonial Encounter: A History of Meaning and Memory in Ghana* (Bloomington, 2002), which includes discussion of colonial-era burial practices among the Anlo-Ewe people of southeastern Ghana.

22. Mantse Aryeequaye and Sionne Neely, in Programme for Chale Wote 2014 Street Arts Festival.

23. For a recent statement of the former interpretation, see Anthony Ephirim-Donkor, *African Religion Defined: A Systematic Study of Ancestor Worship among the Akan* (Lanham, 2013); for a more ambivalent reading, see Zoë Crossland, *Ancestral Encounters in Highland Madagascar: Material Signs and Traces of the Dead* (Cambridge, 2014).

24. *Guardian*, 26 April 2014, 'Journey's End', a review of Spellman, *Brief History of Death*.

25. Verdery, *Political Lives of Dead Bodies*, 34.

26. Peter Brown, *The Cult of the Saints: Its Rise and Function in Latin Christianity* (2nd ed. Chicago, 2015), 24.

27. Peter Brown, *The Ransom of the Soul: Afterlife and Wealth in Early Modern Christianity* (Cambridge, Mass., 2015), 62.

28. To take one theme, ghosts, across time: Seamus Heaney, trans., *Aeneid, Book VI* (London, 2016), and George Saunders, *Lincoln in the Bardo* (London, 2017); and another: Aeschylus, *The Oresteia*, translated by Ted Hughes (London, 1999), and Max Porter, *Grief Is the Thing with Feathers* (London, 2015).

29. Kwasi Konadu, *Our Own Way in This Part of the World: Biography of an African Community, Culture and Nation* (Durham, NC, 2019).

30. See Enid Schildkrout, ed., *The Golden Stool: Studies of the Asante Centre and Periphery* (New York, 1987); Pierluigi Valsecchi and Fabio Viti, eds, *Mondes Akan: Identité et pouvoir en Afrique occidentale / Akan Worlds: Identity and Power in West Africa* (Paris, 1999); Carola Lentz and Paul Nugent, eds, *Ethnicity in Ghana: The Limits of Invention* (Basingstoke, 2000); *Journal des africanistes* 75/2 (2005), 'Approches croisées des mondes akan II'; and compare, with regard to the historical complexities of Yoruba identity, Andrew Apter, *Oduduwa's Chain: Locations of Culture in the Yoruba-Atlantic* (Chicago, 2018), vii–ix and 8–9.

Chapter 1. Cultural Encounter

1. William Bosman, *A New and Accurate Description of the Coast of Guinea* (London, 1705, 4th ed. 1967), 145–61 and 218–33.

2. Stuart B. Schwartz, ed., *Implicit Understandings: Observing, Reporting, and Reflecting on the Encounters between Europeans and Other Peoples in the Early Modern Era* (Cambridge, 1994); see too Seeman, *Death in the New World*; Eduardo Viveiros de Castro, *The Inconstancy of the Indian Soul: The Encounter of Catholics and Cannibals in 16th-Century Brazil*, translated by Gregory Duff Morton (Chicago, 2011).

3. T. C. McCaskie, 'Cultural Encounters: Britain and Africa in the Nineteenth Century', in Andrew Porter, ed., *The Oxford History of the British Empire. Vol. 3: The Nineteenth Century* (Oxford, 1999), 665.

4. Bosman, *New and Accurate Description*, 146–7; translation amended by Albert van Dantzig, 'English Bosman and Dutch Bosman: A Comparison of the Texts—III', *History in Africa* 4 (1977).

5. On the acculturation of European ideas into African traditions, see David Henige, 'Truths Yet Unborn? Oral Traditions as a Casualty of Culture Contact', *Journal of African History* 23 (1982).

6. William Pietz, 'The Problem of the Fetish, I', *RES: Anthropology and Aesthetics* 9 (1985), 5; see too idem, 'The Problem of the Fetish, II: The Origin of the Fetish', *RES* 13 (1987) and 'The Problem of the Fetish, IIIa: Bosman's Guinea and the Enlightenment Theory of Fetishism', *RES* 16 (1988).

7. Roger Sansi-Roca, 'The Fetish in the Lusophone Atlantic', in Nancy Naro, Roger Sansi-Roca and David Treece, eds, *Cultures of the Lusophone Black Atlantic* (Basingstoke, 2007), 35–6.

8. Christiane Owusu-Sarpong, *La mort akan: Étude ethno-sémiotique des textes funéraires akan* (Paris, 2000), 30.

9. Ivor Wilks, *Forests of Gold: Essays on the Akan and the Kingdom of Asante* (Athens, Ohio, 1993); John Vogt, *Portuguese Rule on the Gold Coast, 1469–1682* (Athens, Ga., 1979).

10. See John William Blake, trans. and ed., *Europeans in West Africa, 1450–1560* (London, 1942), vol. 1, ix–x; A. Teixeira da Mota and P.E.H. Hair, *East of Mina: Afro-European Relations on the Gold Coast in the 1550s and 1560s* (Madison, 1988), 9; P.E.H. Hair, *Africa Encountered: European Contacts and Evidence 1450–1700* (Aldershot, 1997).

11. For English translations, see Blake, *Europeans*, 70–78 (Rui de Pina); G. R. Crone, trans. and ed., *The Voyages of Cadamosto* (London, 1937), 114–22 (João de Barros); for the original Portuguese texts, revised translations and analysis, see P.E.H. Hair, *The Founding of the Castelo de São Jorge da Mina: An Analysis of the Sources* (Madison, 1994).

12. Ibid., 8.

13. See ibid., 3, 55–6 and 85, and Denis Escudier, ed., *Voyage d'Eustache Delafosse sur la côte de Guinée, au Portugal et en Espagne (1479–1481)* (Paris, 1992). That both titles accord with the Malinke term for ruler, *mansa*, also suggests the presence of Mande gold traders on the Mina coast.

14. Crone, *Voyages*, 118; cf. Hair, *Founding*, 22.

15. Crone, *Voyages*, 120–22.

16. Ivor Wilks, 'The Forest and the Twis', *Transactions of the Historical Society of Ghana*, new series, 8 (2004).

17. See R. S. Rattray, *Ashanti* (Oxford, 1923), ch. 22 'The Drum Language'.
18. Hair, *Founding*, 25.
19. Ibid., 27.
20. Cf. Greg Dening, 'The Theatricality of Observing and Being Observed: Eighteenth-Century Europe "Discovers" the ? Century "Pacific"', in Schwartz, *Implicit Understandings*; idem, *Beach Crossings: Voyaging across Times, Cultures, and Self* (Melbourne, 2004).
21. Margaret Makepeace, ed., *Trade on the Guinea Coast 1657–1666: The Correspondence of the English East India Company* (Madison, 1991), James Conget to East India Company, 20 June 1659, 50–53.
22. Crone, *Voyages*, 122.
23. Hair, *Founding*, 40.
24. Ibid., 92; Ralph M. Wiltgen, *Gold Coast Mission History 1471–1880* (Techny, Ill., 1956), 8–9.
25. Blake, *Europeans*, Diogo d'Alvarenga to King Manuel, 18 Aug. 1503, 94–6, and Affonsa Caldeira to King Manuel, 2 Jan. 1513.
26. Wiltgen, *Gold Coast Mission History*, 23; see too Teixeira da Mota and Hair, *East of Mina*, Afonso Gonçalves de Botafogo to the Queen, 18 Apr. 1557, 64.
27. For the 'big bang' thesis of the emergence of the Akan forest kingdoms, see Wilks, *Forests of Gold*, chs 1–3; and for a representative critique, Gérard Chouin and Christopher DeCorse, 'Prelude to the Atlantic Trade: New Perspectives on Southern Ghana's Pre-Atlantic History (800–1500)', *Journal of African History* 51 (2010). On the Atlantic littoral, see Christopher De-Corse, *An Archaeology of Elmina: Africans and Europeans on the Gold Coast, 1400–1900* (Washington, DC, 2001).
28. Wilks, 'Forest and the Twis', 16.
29. See R. S. Rattray, *Ashanti Proverbs: The Primitive Ethics of a Savage People* (Oxford, 1916), 28; J. B. Danquah, *The Akan Doctrine of God: A Fragment of Gold Coast Ethics and Religion* (London, 1944), 56–77; Eva L. R. Meyerowitz, *The Akan of Ghana: Their Ancient Beliefs* (London, 1958), 82.
30. Danquah, *Akan Doctrine*, 57.
31. T. C. McCaskie, *State and Society in Pre-colonial Asante* (Cambridge, 1995), 102–35, quote from 105.
32. Edmond Perregaux, 'Chez les Achanti', *Bulletin de la Société Neuchateloise de Géographie* 17 (1906), cited in Hans Abrahamsson, *The Origin of Death: Studies in African Mythology* (Uppsala, 1951), 5.
33. Ibid.
34. Ibid.
35. J.D.Y. Peel, *Religious Encounter and the Making of the Yoruba* (Bloomington, 2000), 177; see too Viveiros de Castro, *Inconstancy of the Indian Soul*, 25–36.
36. See R. S. Rattray, *Akan-Ashanti Folk-Tales* (Oxford, 1930); Christiane Owusu-Sarpong, *Anthologie critique du conte akan: Histoire d'Ananse l'Araignée* (Paris, 2015).
37. Pieter de Marees, *Description and Historical Account of the Gold Kingdom of Guinea (1602)*, translated and edited by Albert van Dantzig and Adam Jones (Oxford, 1987), 68, 71 and 72.
38. Ibid., 72.
39. On these understandings, see too Adam Jones, trans. and ed., *German Sources for West African History 1699–1669* (Wiesbaden, 1983), Wilhelm Johann Müller's Description of the Fetu

Country, 1662–9, 176–8; Nicolas Villault, *Relation des Costes d'Afrique, appellées Guinée* (Paris, 1669), 261; Jean Barbot, *Barbot on Guinea: The Writings of Jean Barbot on West Africa 1678–1712*, translated and edited by P.E.H. Hair, Adam Jones and Robin Law (London, 1992), vol. 2, 578.

40. Teixeira de Mota and Hair, *East of Mina*, An Anonymous Report on Mina, 29 Sep. 1572, 80.

41. Ibid., 77.

42. Jones, *German Sources*, Andreas Josua Ulsheimer's Voyage of 1603–4, 31.

43. Ibid., Michael Hemmersam's Description of the Gold Coast, 1639–45, 104.

44. Ibid., 122–3.

45. Bosman, *New and Accurate Description*, 156.

46. De Marees, *Description*, 74; letter dd. 23 Oct. 1632, cited in Wiltgen, *Gold Coast Mission History*, 29.

47. Ibid., 48. For the survival of fragments of the statues and residual traces in Dutch-era Elmina of a cult of St Antony ('Ntona') and of Santa Maria, see J. Sylvanus Wartemberg, *Sao Jorge D'El Mina: Premier West African European Settlement* (Ilfracombe, n.d. [c. 1950]), 152–3.

48. T. Edward Bowdich, *Mission from Cape Coast Castle to Ashantee* (London, 1819, 3rd ed. 1966), 261–2. For another nineteenth-century account from Asante, see WMMS MS 380587 'Diary of Robert Brooking, 1839–59', 8 May 1842; and from the Gold Coast, A.J.N. Tremearne, 'Extracts from Diary of the Late Rev. John Martin, Wesleyan-Methodist Missionary in West Africa, 1843–48', *Man* 12 (1912), 10 Dec. 1844, 141. For the survival of key elements of these creation myths in African American folklore, see Zora Neale Hurston, *Mules and Men* (New York, 2008 [orig. 1935]), 74–5.

49. Bowdich, *Mission*, 262.

50. Ibid.

Chapter 2. Body, Soul and Person

1. Roy Porter, *Flesh in the Age of Reason: How the Enlightenment Transformed the Way We See Our Bodies and Souls* (London, 2003), 3.

2. Ibid., 27.

3. Ibid., 3.

4. Michael Carrithers, Steven Collins and Steven Lukes, eds, *The Category of the Person: Anthropology, Philosophy, History* (Cambridge, 1985); Paul Riesman, 'The Person and the Life Cycle in African Social Life and Thought', *African Studies Review* 29 (1986); Michael Jackson and Ivan Karp, eds, *Personhood and Agency: The Experience of Self and Other in African Cultures* (Uppsala, 1990); Michael Lambek and Andrew Strathern, eds, *Bodies and Persons: Comparative Perspectives from Africa and Melanesia* (Cambridge, 1998).

5. See, e.g., Linda Kalof and William Bynum, eds, *A Cultural History of the Human Body*, 6 vols (London, 2010).

6. Porter, *Flesh in the Age of Reason*, 14–15.

7. Clive Seale, *Constructing Death: The Sociology of Dying and Bereavement* (Cambridge, 1998), 1–2; Lambek and Strathern, *Bodies and Persons*, 'Introduction'.

8. Crone, *Voyages*, 117.

9. See Kwesi Yankah, *Speaking for the Chief: Okyeame and the Politics of Akan Royal Oratory* (Bloomington, 1995), ix and 28–9; McCaskie, *State and Society*, 261.

10. Blake, *Europeans*, vol. 2, 378.
11. Porter, *Flesh in the Age of Reason*, xiii.
12. De Marees, *Description*, 28.
13. Ibid., 31.
14. Ibid., 37-8.
15. Ibid., 34.
16. Johannes Rask, *A Brief and Truthful Description of a Journey to and from Guinea*, translated by Selena Axelrod Winsnes (Accra, 2009), 77.
17. Ibid., 111.
18. On the disposal of infants with 'monstrous' deformities, see PRAAD Accra SCT 5/4/14 Civil Record Book, Cape Coast, *Quacoe Buafoo v. King Enimil Quow of Wassaw*, 31 July 1874, 456–502; TNA CO 96/45, Bird to Bulwer Lytton, 11 July 1859, enclosed: Medical Report for the Year 1858; McCaskie, *State and Society*, 436–7.
19. Rask, *Brief and Truthful Description*, 111.
20. See Ray A. Kea, *A Cultural and Social History of Ghana from the Seventeenth to the Nineteenth Century: The Gold Coast in the Age of the Trans-Atlantic Slave Trade* (Lewiston, 2012), vol. 1, 116–17.
21. Ibid., 298–9; Ga *odehe*: a free, noble person; *nyonji* (or *nyojii*): enslaved people.
22. Florence Bernault, 'Body, Power and Sacrifice in Equatorial Africa', *Journal of African History* 47 (2006), and *Colonial Transactions*.
23. Porter, *Flesh in the Age of Reason*, xiv.
24. See esp. Rattray, *Ashanti*; idem, *Religion and Art in Ashanti* (Oxford, 1927); Danquah, *Akan Doctrine*; Eva L. R. Meyerowitz, *The Sacred State of the Akan* (London, 1951) and *Akan of Ghana*; Meyer Fortes, *Kinship and the Social Order: The Legacy of Lewis Henry Morgan* (London, 1969); Kwame Gyekye, *An Essay on African Philosophical Thought: The Akan Conceptual Scheme* (Cambridge, 1987); McCaskie, *State and Society*, 166–80 and 243–67.
25. Rattray, *Religion and Art*, 152; Gyekye, *Essay*, 86.
26. McCaskie, *State and Society*, 407–8, emphasis in original.
27. Villault, *Relation*, 260.
28. Ludewig Ferdinand Rømer, *A Reliable Account of the Coast of Guinea (1760)*, translated and edited by Selena Axelrod Winsnes (Oxford, 2000), 107.
29. Rattray, *Religion and Art*, 6.
30. R. S. Rattray, *Ashanti Law and Constitution* (Oxford, 1929), 214; see too Meyerowitz, *Akan of Ghana*, 26–7; and for the portentous collapse of the *gyadua* in the Kumasi market on 6 January 1874, F. Ramseyer and J. Kühne, *Four Years in Ashantee* (London, 1875), 267 and 292. *Damarifa*: 'alas' or 'condolences'.
31. Meyerowitz, *Akan of Ghana*, 37. An art teacher at Accra's Achimota school, Eva Meyerowitz collected oral histories in the Akan and Bono regions in the 1940s–50s, with a focus on the Bono kingdom of Takyiman and assisted by the artist Kofi Antubam. Her attempts to synthesise these traditions into historical chronologies are idiosyncratic and flawed, although many of her observations on mortuary culture and the ritual realm more broadly are of considerable interest. For comment, see Konadu, *Our Own Way*, 132–6.
32. T. C. McCaskie, 'People and Animals: Constru(ct)ing the Asante Experience', *Africa* 62 (1992), 227; for comparative insights, see Robert Pogue Harrison, *Forests: The Shadow of Civilization* (Chicago, 1992).

33. For the Ga and Ewe to the east of the Akan, see Rev. A. Jehle, 'Soul, Spirit, Fate: According to the Notions of the Tshi and Ehwe Tribes (Gold Coast and Togo, W. Africa)', *Journal of the African Society* 7 (1907); M. J. Field, *Religion and Medicine of the Gã People* (London, 1937); Birgit Meyer, *Translating the Devil: Religion and Modernity among the Ewe in Ghana* (Edinburgh, 1999), 63–5; on savanna peoples, Meyer Fortes, *Religion, Morality and the Person: Essays on Tallensi Religion* (Cambridge, 1987); Goody, *Death*.

34. Meyerowitz, *Sacred State*, 86; see too J. G. Christaller, *Dictionary of the Asante and Fante Language Called Tshi (Twi)* (Basel, 1881, 2nd ed. 1933), 262.

35. Rattray, *Religion and Art*, 154.

36. Meyerowitz, *Sacred State*, 86.

37. Rattray, *Religion and Art*, 319.

38. Ibid.

39. Ibid., 318.

40. Ibid., 319.

41. Meyerowitz, *Sacred State*, 117.

42. Rask, *Brief and Truthful Description*, 133–4; Rømer, *Reliable Account*, 184–5; Bowdich, *Mission*, 291.

43. Cited in Michelle Gilbert and Paul Jenkins, 'The King, His Soul and the Pastor: Three Views of a Conflict in Akropong 1906–7', *Journal of Religion in Africa* 38 (2008), 377.

44. Rattray, *Religion and Art*, 153.

45. Jones, *German Sources*, 271.

46. A. B. Ellis, *The Tshi-Speaking Peoples of the Gold Coast of West Africa* (London, 1887), 149; see too Christaller, *Dictionary*, 262 and 446.

47. See, however, McCaskie, 'People and Animals', 230, which notes that *sasa* was 'a component absent from people'. This seems mistaken: cf. Rattray, *Ashanti*, 59, 99–100, and *Ashanti Law and Constitution*, 295–6 and 299; Christaller, *Dictionary*, 429 and 446.

48. Ellis, *Tshi-Speaking Peoples*, 150.

49. Rattray, *Religion and Art*, 153, and see too ch. 19 'Funerals for Certain Animals and Trees', 182–6; McCaskie, 'People and Animals'.

50. De Marees, *Description*, 72.

51. Jones, *German Sources*, 179–80. *Caboceer*: from Portuguese *cabeçeiro* (headman or chief).

52. Barbot, *Barbot on Guinea*, vol. 2, 580.

53. Bosman, *New and Accurate Description*, 156; see too Villault, *Relation*, 260–61.

54. Sir Thomas Browne, *Hydriotaphia, or Urne-Buriall* (London, 1658), republished in *Religio Medici and Urne-Buriall*, edited by Stephan Greenblatt and Ramie Targoff (New York, 2012), 129.

55. Rattray, *Ashanti Proverbs*, 44.

56. Ellis, *Tshi-Speaking Peoples*, 157.

57. Müller, *German Sources*, 179.

58. Wilks, *Forests of Gold* 107.

59. Bosman, *New and Accurate Description*, 156.

60. Johannes Monrad, *A Description of the Guinea Coast and Its Inhabitants*, translated by Selena Alexrod Winsnes (Accra, 2009), 41; Barbot, *Barbot on Guinea*, vol. 2, 580 and 588–9; Parker, 'Cultural Politics of Death and Burial'.

61. Christaller, *Dictionary*, 423; for analysis, see Wilks, *Forests of Gold*, 232–3.

62. Gyekye, *Essay*, 166–8.

Chapter 3. Speaking of Death

1. Something of the nature of this history from the Akyem perspective can be gleaned from a collection of oral histories compiled in the 1960s: Kumi Attobrah, *The Kings of Akyem Abuakwa and the Ninety Nine Wars against Asante* (Tema, 1976).

2. Yankah, *Speaking for the Chief*, 49–51 and 103–6; T. C. McCaskie, 'Death and the *Asantehene*: A Historical Meditation', *Journal of African History* 30 (1989); and see, more broadly, Giorgio Agamben, *The Sacrament of Language: An Archaeology of the Oath (Homo Sacer II, 3)*, translated by Adam Kotsko (Cambridge, 2010).

3. De Marees, *Description*, 20.

4. TNA T70/30 Inward Letter Book 1753–62, Melvil to Committee, dd. Cape Coast Castle, 11 Mar. 1753, 7–8.

5. Melissa Mohr, *Holy Shit: A Brief History of Swearing* (Oxford, 2013), 168–9; Rattray, *Religion and Art*, 205–15.

6. Joseph Dupuis, *Journal of a Residence in Ashantee* (London, 1824, 2nd ed. 1966), 232–3.

7. N. V. Asare, 'Asante Abasem: Twi Kasamu', 1915, translated by Wilhelmina Joseline Donkoh, 'Rev. N. V. Asare's A History of Asante in Tshi', unpublished master's dissertation, University of Birmingham (1990), 31; see too PRAAD Kumasi ARG 1/2/1/173 The Great Oath of Ashanti.

8. Kwame Arhin, 'The Asante Praise Poems: The Ideology of Patrimonialism', *Paiduma* 32 (1986); Nketia, *Funeral Dirges*.

9. Assmann, *Death and Salvation*, 39.

10. T. E. Kyei, *Our Days Dwindle: Memories of My Childhood Days in Asante*, edited by Jean Allman (Portsmouth, NH, 2001), 192–3.

11. A. Adu Boahen, Emmanuel Akyeampong, Nancy Lawler, T. C. McCaskie and Ivor Wilks, eds, *'The History of Ashanti Kings and the Whole Country Itself' and Other Writings by Otumfuo, Nana Agyeman Prempeh I* (Oxford, 2003). Elements of these traditions were compiled from the 1860s by the Ga pastor Carl Christian Reindorf and appeared in his *History of the Gold Coast and Asante* (Basel, 1895), 43–58.

12. Wilks, *Forests of Gold*, 64.

13. Boahen et al., *History of Ashanti Kings*, 86.

14. Ibid., 90 and 188; see too Reindorf, *History*, 47.

15. Wilks, *Forests of Gold*, 66.

16. Ibid., 66–72.

17. Boahen et al., *History of Ashanti Kings*, 88.

18. See Wilks, *Forests of Gold*, 100–105; T. C. McCaskie, 'Denkyira in the Making of Asante c. 1660–1720', *Journal of African History* 48 (2007).

19. Boahen et al., *History of Ashanti Kings*, 93–6; Reindorf, *History*, 48–9.

20. Ibid.; Boahen et al., *History of Ashanti Kings*, 98; Asare, 'Asante Abasem', 33–6, also has Komfo Anokye in Denkyira.

21. Bosman, *New and Accurate Description*, 75 and 226–7.

22. Reindorf, *History*, 49; see too McCaskie, 'Denkyira', 10.

23. See Rattray, *Ashanti Law and Constitution*, 270–84.

24. T. C. McCaskie, 'Komfo Anokye of Asante: Meaning, History and Philosophy in an African Society', *Journal of African History* 27 (1986), 320.

25. Wilks, *Forests of Gold*, 124.
26. Bosman, *New and Accurate Description*, 156–7; translation amended by van Dantzig, 'English Bosman III'.
27. Wilks, *Forests of Gold*, 109.
28. Thomas, *La mort africaine*, 125–9.
29. McCaskie, 'Komfo Anokye', 321.
30. Ibid., 333–4; idem, *State and Society*, 129–35.
31. Boahen et al., *History of Ashanti Kings*, 104.
32. Bosman, *New and Accurate Description*, 225–6, emphasis in original.
33. Ibid., 226–7.
34. Wilks, *Forests of Gold*, 109–12.
35. Boahen et al., *History of Ashanti Kings*, 108–9.
36. McCaskie, 'Denkyira', 12–13.
37. Reindorf, *History*, 57; Boahen et al., *History of Ashanti Kings*, 107; McCaskie, 'Denkyira', 13–16.
38. Reindorf, *History*, 57–8.
39. Wilks, *Forests of Gold*, 111, quoting Director-General van Sevenhuysen, dd. Elmina, 16 Nov. 1701.
40. Bosman, *New and Accurate Description*, 76–7.
41. Boahen et al., *History of Ashanti Kings*, 109.
42. Asare, 'Asante Abasem', 48.
43. Bowdich, *Mission*, 233; Dupuis, *Journal*, 231–3.
44. Reindorf, *History*, 68–9.
45. Asere, 'Asante Abasem', 32. *Kotoko* (lit. 'porcupine'): an appellation for Asante warriors and, by extension, the entire kingdom.
46. 'History of Ashanti', manuscript prepared by a Committee of Traditional Authorities under the Chairmanship of Otumfuo, Asantehene Osei Agyeman Prempeh II, n.d. [1937–1942], cited in Wilks, *Forests of Gold*, 254; on Komfo Anokye's prophesy, see too Asare, 'Asante Abasem', 48.
47. See Meyerowitz, *Sacred State*, 55, who observes that the ancient 'death taboo was partly abolished when the Asante kingdom was founded, and the first Asantehene preferred to remain a warrior chief'.
48. Margaret Priestley and Ivor Wilks, 'The Ashanti Kings in the Eighteenth Century: A Revised Chronology', *Journal of African History* 1 (1960).
49. Ibid., 89–90.
50. Wilks, *Forests of Gold*, 101; see too J. K. Fynn, *Asante and its Neighbours, 1700–1807* (Evanston, 1971), 48–50; A. Adu Boahen, 'When Did Osei Tutu Die?', *Transactions of the Historical Society of Ghana* 16 (1975).
51. Wilks, *Forests of Gold*, 249–51.
52. See *Ashanti Stool Histories*, recorded by J. Agyeman-Duah and compiled by K. Ampon Darkwa and B. C. Obeka (Institute of African Studies, University of Ghana, Legon, 1976), AS.54 Bantama-Baamu.
53. Reindorf, *History*, 69.
54. Asare, 'Asante Abasem', 32–3; McCaskie, *State and Society*, 313.

55. Wilks, *Forests of Gold*, 255; Rattray, *Religion and Art*, 214.

56. The principal sources for this are Rattray, *Ashanti Law and Constitution*, 279, and 'History of Ashanti' [1937–42] as cited in McCaskie, *State and Society*, 130–31.

57. Rattray, *Ashanti Law and Constitution*, 279; 'History of Ashanti' has this time as just seven days.

58. Ibid.

Chapter 4. Grief and Mourning

1. *West African Herald*, 13 July 1859, 'The Recollections of an Old Sinner'. On the custom of children being taken to see the dead, see F. L. Bartels, *The Roots of Ghana Methodism* (Cambridge, 1965), 230–31.

2. See Osei-Mensah Aborampah, 'Women's Roles in the Mourning Rituals of the Akan of Ghana', *Ethnology* 38 (1999); Kofi Antubam, *Ghana's Heritage of Culture* (Leipzig, 1963), 62–9; Goody, *Death*.

3. Paul C. Rosenblatt, R. Patricia Walsh and Douglas A. Jackson, *Grief and Mourning in Cross-Cultural Perspective* (Washington, DC, 1976); Colin Murray Parkes, Pittu Laungani and Bill Young, eds, *Death and Bereavement Across Cultures* (London, 1997); Reis, *Death Is a Festival*.

4. Robert Hertz, 'A Contribution to the Study of the Collective Representation of Death', in *Death and the Right Hand*, translated by Rodney and Claudia Needham (London, 1960).

5. Peter Metcalf and Richard Huntingdon, *Celebrations of Death: The Anthropology of Mortuary Ritual* (Cambridge, 1979, 2nd ed. 1991).

6. Maurice Bloch and Jonathan Parry, eds, *Death and the Regeneration of Life* (Cambridge, 1982).

7. Metcalf and Huntingdon, *Celebrations of Death*, 4.

8. McCaskie 'Death and the *Asantehene*', 429–30, emphasis in original.

9. See, e.g., Renato Rosaldo, 'Grief and the Headhunter's Rage: On the Cultural Force of Emotion', in E. Brunen, ed., *Text, Play and Story: The Construction and Reconstruction of Self and Society* (Washington, DC, 1986); Sarah Tarlow, *Bereavement and Commemoration: An Archaeology of Mortality* (Oxford, 1999), 28.

10. Richard J. Evans, 'Your Soft German Heart', *London Review of Books*, 14 July 2016.

11. Bosman, *New and Accurate Description*, 228–9.

12. Hertz, *Death and the Right Hand*, 78. Hertz includes Bosman in his citations on this point.

13. Rattray, *Religion and Art*, 149.

14. M. J. Field, *Akim-Kotoku: An Oman of the Gold Coast* (London, 1948), 139.

15. De Marees, *Description*, 180; Rask, *Brief and Truthful Description*, 142; and cf. Reis, *Death Is a Festival*, 90.

16. Mrs R. Lee [Sarah Bowdich], *Stories of Strange Lands* (London, 1835), 18.

17. Brodie Cruickshank, *Eighteen Years on the Gold Coast of Africa* (London, 1853, 2nd ed. 1966), vol. 2, 214–15.

18. Monrad, *Description*, 40.

19. Rattray, *Ashanti Law and Constitution*, 250–51; see too Monrad, *Description*, 39; for a general statement, Rodney Needham, 'Percussion and Transition', *Man*, new series 2 (1967).

20. Joseph S. Kaminski, *Asante Ntahera Trumpets in Ghana: Culture, Tradition, and Sound Barrage* (Farnham, 2012), 69.

21. Monrad, *Description*, 40.

22. De Marees, *Description*, 180.

23. Rattray, *Religion and Art*, 151.

24. Bosman, *New and Accurate Description*, 229; translation adjusted by van Dantzig, 'English Bosman IV', *History in Africa* 5 (1978).

25. De Marees, *Description*, 180–81. 'Anzy' is likely to have been the Twi mourning phrase *ahia me*, 'I am impoverished [by this death]'.

26. Rattray, *Religion and Art*, 151.

27. Henry Meredith, *An Account of the Gold Coast of Africa* (London, 1812, 2nd ed. 1967), 31.

28. Bosman, *New and Accurate Description*, 229; van Dantzig, 'English Bosman IV'.

29. Monrad, *Description*, 40–41.

30. Perregaux, 'Chez les Achanti', 126–7.

31. TNA CO 96/245, Brandford Griffith to Ripon, 7 May 1894, enclosed: H. Vroom to Brandford Griffith, 24 Apr. 1894.

32. Cruickshank, *Eighteen Years*, vol. 2, 218 and 265–9.

33. Nketia, *Funeral Dirges*, 8–9.

34. Ibid., 8.

35. Monrad, *Description*, 41.

36. Ramseyer and Kühne, *Four Years*, 254.

37. Ibid., 255.

38. Antubam, *Ghana's Heritage*, 79; see too George P. Hagan, 'A Note on Akan Colour Symbolism', *Research Review* (Institute of African Studies, University of Ghana, Legon) 7 (1970).

39. De Marees, *Description*, 180; Rattray, *Religion and Art*, 150.

40. T. Edward Bowdich, *An Essay on the Superstitions, Customs, and Arts, Common to the Ancient Egyptians, Abyssinians, and Ashantees* (Paris, 1821), 50.

41. Paul Erdmann Isert, *Letters on West Africa and the Slave Trade: Paul Erdmann Isert's Journey to Guinea and the Caribbean Islands in Columbia (1788)*, translated and edited by Selena Axelrod Winsnes (Oxford, 1992), 133.

42. Antubam, *Ghana's Heritage*, 84; Daniel Mato, 'Clothed in Symbol: Wearing Proverbs', *Passages* 7 (1994).

43. De Marees, *Description*, 180.

44. Meyerowitz, *Sacred State*, 71.

45. Bosman, *New and Accurate Description*, 229; van Dantzig, 'English Bosman IV'.

46. Danquah, *Akan Doctrine*, 156.

47. Ibid.

48. Ibid., 97.

49. McCaskie, *State and Society*, 221–4, quote from 222.

50. Harrison, *Dominion of the Dead*, 154.

51. Meyerowitz, *Sacred State*, 77.

52. Monrad, *Description*, 39, 44 and 48.

53. Field, *Akim-Kotoku*, 140.

54. Aborampah, 'Women's Roles', 258.

55. PRAAD Accra ADM 1/2/418 Letter Book Anomabo Fort, Bayley to White, 31 Aug. 1813.
56. Ibid., Bayley to White, 10 Sep. 1813.
57. Ibid., Bayley to White, 13 Sep. 1813.
58. Aborampah, 'Women's Roles', 260.

Chapter 5. Gold, Wealth and Burial

1. T. C. McCaskie, 'Accumulation, Wealth and Belief in Asante History: I. To the Close of the Nineteenth Century', *Africa* 53 (1983), 26.
2. Rattray, *Ashanti Proverbs*, 163.
3. Wilks, *Forests of Gold*; Timothy F. Garrard, *Akan Weights and the Gold Trade* (London, 1980); M. D. McLeod, *The Asante* (London, 1981); Suzanne Preston Blier, *Royal Arts of Africa: The Majesty of Form* (London, 1998), ch. 3; McCaskie, 'Accumulation I', 'Accumulation, Wealth and Belief in Asante History: II. The Twentieth Century', *Africa* 56 (1986), and *State and Society*, 37–73; Suzanne Gott, 'Native Gold, Precious Beads and the Dynamics of Concealed Power in Akan Beliefs and Practices', *Ethnofoor* 25 (2013).
4. Kwame Arhin, 'Some Asante Views of Colonial Rule: As Seen in the Controversy Relating to Death Duties', *Transactions of the Historical Society of Ghana* 15 (1974).
5. Rattray, *Ashanti Law and Constitution*, 44.
6. McCaskie, 'Accumulation I', 34.
7. Rømer, *Reliable Account*, 156.
8. Meyerowitz, *Sacred State*, 62.
9. Wilks, *Forests of Gold*, 144.
10. PRAAD Accra ADM 11/1/1338, Enquiry into the Tribal Organization of the Adonten Abrempon of Kumasi, 24 March 1925, Notes of Evidence [hereafter Adonten Enquiry, 1925], evidence of Akyeamehene Kwasi Nuama, 77–8; for analysis, see Wilks, *Forests of Gold*, 139–44, and McCaskie, *State and Society*, 42–9. Dapper describes the ceremonies surrounding the installation of wealthy men as so-called *fidalgos* (Portuguese: 'noblemen') on the seventeenth-century Gold Coast: see, translated from the original Dutch edition of 1668, Olfert Dapper, *Description de l'Afrique* (Amsterdam, 1685), 302–3.
11. McCaskie, 'Accumulation I', 34.
12. Wilks, *Forests of Gold*, 144.
13. McCaskie, 'Accumulation I', 31, an analysis reiterated in *State and Society*, 44 and 358, but rejected by Wilks: *Forests of Gold*, 160.
14. Arhin, 'Some Asante Views', 63; Reindorf, *History*, 75.
15. Arhin, 'Some Asante Views', 63–4; Rattray, *Ashanti Law and Constitution*, 107–9; Gareth Austin, '"No Elders Were Present": Commoners and Private Ownership in Asante, 1807–96', *Journal of African History* 37 (1996), 20–22.
16. Adonten Enquiry, 1925, 80.
17. Bowdich, *Mission*, 254, and see 319. *Mperedwan* (sing. *peredwan*): equivalent to 2.25 ounces of gold or £8; 'fetish gold': jewellery and other worked-gold ornaments, rather than ritualized substance.
18. Wilks, *Forests of Gold*, 148.
19. McCaskie, *State and Society*, 48–9.

20. Austin, 'No Elders Were Present', 21–2.

21. Adonten Enquiry, 1925, 61.

22. Bowdich, *Essay*, 25.

23. J. B. Danquah, *Gold Coast: Akan Law and Customs, and the Akim Abuakwa Constitution* (London, 1928), 138.

24. See TNA C113/274, Letter from James Phipps, 2 July 1722, 241, on the funeral of John Kabes of Komenda.

25. Adonten Enquiry, 1925, 62; Rattray, *Ashanti Law and Constitution*, 108; Christaller, *Dictionary*, 322.

26. Adonten Enquiry, 1925, 61–2.

27. Rattray, *Ashanti Law and Constitution*, 108.

28. Ibid., 109.

29. Ramseyer and Kühne, *Four Years*, 174–5; see too Bowdich, *Mission*, 283, for a tabulation of *nsa* given at the funeral of the mother of Asafohene Kwaakye Kofi in Kumasi in 1817.

30. Adonten Enquiry, 1925, 63.

31. Ivor Wilks, *Asante in the Nineteenth Century: The Structure and Evolution of a Political Order* (Cambridge, 1975), 693–5, and *Forests of Gold*, 136–7; McCaskie, *State and Society*, 58–65.

32. Wilks, *Forests of Gold*, 139.

33. Bowdich, *Mission*, 319; for the computation, see Wilks, *Asante*, 693, and McCaskie, *State and Society*, 63 and 364–5.

34. Ibid., 61.

35. TNA CO 96/58, Pine to Newcastle, 10 Dec. 1862.

36. PRAAD Kumasi ARG 6/2/7 Complaints against Kumasihene, Kofi Sraha et al to CCA, 11 Oct. 1930.

37. Garrard, *Akan Weights*, 4, quoting J. K. Fynn, *Oral Traditions of Fante States: No. 2 Eguafo* (Institute of African Studies, University of Ghana, Legon, 1974).

38. Meyerowitz, *Sacred State*, 62; see too Rattray, *Religion and Art*, 150.

39. Raymond A. Silverman, 'Akan Kuduo: Form and Function', in Doran H. Ross and Timothy F. Garrard, eds, *Akan Transformations: Problems in Ghanaian Art History* (Los Angeles, 1983), 20–22.

40. De Marees, *Description*, 188 and 191.

41. From the English translation by John Ogilby, *Africa* (London, 1670), 457; cf. Dapper, *Description*, 299.

42. Bosman, *New and Accurate Description*, 230; translation adjusted by van Dantzig, 'English Bosman IV'. For *conti di terra* (*akori* or *aggrey* beads) as grave goods, see Gott, 'Native Gold, Precious Beads'.

43. Robin Law, ed., *The English in West Africa 1685–1688: The Local Correspondence of the Royal African Company of England, 1681–1699. Part 2* (Oxford, 2001), doc. 31, dd. 31 May 1686, 19; see too TNA T70/31, William Mutter to Committee, 10 Feb. 1764, 71–4.

44. Rask, *Brief and Truthful Description*, 115.

45. Albert van Dantzig, trans. and ed., *The Dutch and the Guinea Coast 1674–1742: A Collection of Documents from the General State Archive at The Hague* (Accra, 1978), Elmina Journal, 21 Mar. 1718, 188.

46. DeCorse, *Archaeology of Elmina*, ch. 6; Sam Spiers, 'The Eguafo Kingdom: Investigating Complexity in Southern Ghana', unpublished PhD thesis, Syracuse University (2007), 94–5

NOTES TO CHAPTER 6   349

and 266–70, and 'The Eguafo Polity: Between the Traders and Raiders', in J. Cameron Monroe and Akinwumi Ogundiran, eds, *Power and Landscape in Atlantic West Africa: Archaeological Perspectives* (Cambridge, 2012).

47. Bosman, *New and Accurate Description*, 231; van Dantzig, 'English Bosman IV'.

48. Rømer, *Reliable Account*, 184; Isert, *Letters*, 132. See too DeCorse, *Archaeology of Elmina*, 100–101 and 187–8 on Elmina, and 248 on the Gold Coast generally; and for house burials in enslaved African communities in Barbados and Jamaica, Seeman, *Death in the New World*, 189.

49. Monrad, *Description*, 43. One *alen* = 63 centimetres, or a cubit.

50. PRAAD Kumasi ARG 1/27/21 Notes of an Inquisition into the death of two Kumawu men, evidence of Kobina Nkam, 22 Jan. 1920.

51. DeCorse, *Archaeology of Elmina*, 189.

52. See, e.g., William F. Daniell, 'On the Ethnography of Akkrah and Adampé, Gold Coast, Western Africa', *Journal of the Ethnological Society* 4 (1856), 16.

53. Meyerowitz, *Sacred State*, 37; Bowdich, *Essay*, 5.

54. Bowdich, *Mission*, 254–5.

55. See PRAAD Kumasi ARG 1/27/21, detailing a case where three ceramic jars containing an estimated £11,000 worth of gold dust were unearthed and allegedly stolen in Kumawu in 1919.

56. TNA T70/4 Extracts of Letters, 1720–42, letter from Cope et al., 8 Mar. 1738, 122–3.

57. Charles Alexander Gordon, *Life on the Gold Coast* (London, 1874), 47; see too John Duncan, *Travels in Western Africa in 1845 and 1846* (London, 1847), 27.

58. George Macdonald, *The Gold Coast Past and Present* (London, 1898), 60.

59. Asare, 'Asante Abasem', 70; *osape*: a spendthrift; see too Sir Francis Fuller, *A Vanished Dynasty: Ashanti* (London, 1921), 145–6.

60. Asare, 'Asante Abasem', 70.

61. Ramseyer and Kühne, *Four Years*, 165.

62. McCaskie, *State and Society*, 160 and 402.

63. Wilks, *Asante*, 512–13.

64. PP 1884 LVI [C. 4052] *Further Correspondence regarding the Affairs of the Gold Coast*, no. 17: Rowe to Derby, 21 Aug. 1883, enclosed: Knapp Barrow's report on his visit to Kumasi, dd. Accra, 5 July 1883, 56.

65. Kellehear, *Social History of Dying*, 89.

Chapter 6. Faces of the Dead

1. Sarah Tarlow and Liv Nilsson Stutz, eds, *The Oxford Handbook of the Archaeology of Death and Burial* (Oxford, 2013); Timothy Insoll, *Material Explorations in African Archaeology* (Oxford, 2015); for a pioneering inquiry from 1658, see Browne, *Hydriotaphia*.

2. To the northwest, cf. Anita J. Glaze, *Art and Death in a Senufo Village* (Bloomington, 1981).

3. Timothy F. Garrard, 'Figurine Cults of the Southern Akan', in Christopher Roy, ed., *Iowa Studies in African Art, Vol. 1* (Iowa City, 1984).

4. For early investigations, see R. P. Wild, 'Baked Clay Heads from Graves near Fomena, Ashanti', *Man* 34 (1934), and 'Funerary Equipment from Agona-Swedru, Winnebah District; Gold Coast', *Journal of the Royal Anthropological Institute* 67 (1937).

5. See Brian C. Vivian, 'Sacred to Secular: Transitions in Akan Funerary Customs', in Judy Sterner and Nicholas David, eds, *An African Commitment: Papers in Honour of Peter Lewis*

Shinnie (Calgary, 1992), which synthesizes many archaeological reports; for Twifo Heman, see James Oren Bellis, 'Archeology and Culture History of the Akan of Ghana: A Case Study', unpublished PhD thesis, Indiana University (1972), and *The 'Place of Pots' in Akan Funerary Custom* (Bloomington, 1982); for the Adansemanso radiocarbon dates, see Wilks, 'Forest and the Twis', 46–7; also Roy Sieber, 'Art and History in Ghana', in Antony Forge, ed., *Primitive Art and Society* (London, 1973); Patricia Crane Coronel, 'Aowin Terracotta Sculpture', *African Arts* 13 (1979); Michelle Gilbert, 'Akan Terracotta Heads: Gods or Ancestors?', *African Arts* 22 (1989).

6. For useful overviews, see Tom Phillips, ed., *Africa: The Art of a Continent* (Munich, 1999), 438–9 (by Doran Ross); Nii Otokunor Quarcoopome, 'Les portraits funéraires akan', in Chrstiane Falgayrettes-Leveau and Christiane Owusu-Sarpong, eds, *Ghana: hier et aujourd'hui* (Paris, 2003).

7. De Marees, *Description*, 179–85, quote from 182.

8. Ibid., 184–5.

9. Barbot, *Barbot on Guinea*, vol. 2, 387.

10. Ibid., 595–6, and 601–2. Brafo: *obrafo*—strictly speaking, an executioner, but among the Fante of the central Gold Coast the term had come to refer to a leading office-holder.

11. Jones, *German Sources*, 258; Bosman, *New and Accurate Description*, 232.

12. Cruickshank, *Eighteen Years*, vol. 2, 270–71.

13. WMMS MS 380587 Diary of Robert Brooking, 22 Apr. 1840.

14. Bellis, 'Archeology', 145–6.

15. Monica Blackmun Visonà et al., eds, *A History of Art in Africa* (New York, 2001), 'The Western Congo Basin', 373–4 (by Robin Poyner).

16. Reindorf, *History*, 64–7.

17. Ibid., 67; see too E.J.P. Brown, *Gold Coast and Asianti Reader* (London, 1929), 144–5.

18. Rattray, *Religion and Art*, 147–66.

19. Bellis, 'Archeology', 89–90 and 113.

20. Field, *Akim-Kotoku*, 39–46.

21. Ibid., 44–6.

22. Kwame Frimpong, 'The Final Obsequies of the Late Nana Sir Ofori Atta, K.B.E. Abuakwahene', *Africa* 15 (1945), 83.

23. Richard Rathbone, *Murder and Politics in Colonial Ghana* (New Haven, 1993).

24. Rattray, *Religion and Art*, 104; see too Field, *Akim-Kotoku*, 45.

25. Boahen et al., *History of Ashanti Kings*, 123–4.

26. Ibid., 124.

27. Ibid., 123.

28. PRAAD Accra ADM 11/1/1342, Report on the Great Funeral Custom of the Late Nana Edward Agyeman Prempeh I, Kumasihene, prepared by J.W.K. Appiah, 11 June 1932.

29. Garrard, 'Figurine Cults', 181. Garrard's hypothesis is followed by Nolwenn L'Haridon and Jean Polet, 'Les statuettes funéraires en terre cuite de la Côte de l'Or témoignent-elles d'une première christianisation?', *Journal de africanistes* 75-2 (2005).

30. Phillips, *Africa*, 438–9 and 449–50; Herbert M. Cole, 'Akan Worlds', in Visonà et al., *History of Art*, 208–9; see too Quarcoopome, 'Les portraits funéraires akan', 129–32, and the cautious comments by DeCorse, *Archaeology of Elmina*, 189–90 and 250–51, and Gilbert, 'Akan Terracotta Heads'.

31. Meyerowitz, *Akan of Ghana*, 109.

32. Wild, 'Funerary Equipment', 71; see too idem, 'Baked Clay Heads', 1.

33. Antubam, *Ghana's Heritage*, 128.

34. On this point, see Blier, *Royal Arts*, ch. 3.

35. Bellis, 'Archeology', 111–12.

36. Vivian, 'Sacred to Secular', 166.

37. Quarcoopome, 'Les portraits funéraires akan', 132.

38. Roland Barthes, *Camera Lucida: Reflections on Photography*, translated by Richard Howard (London, 2000), 9; see too Marleen de Witte, 'Of Corpses, Clay, and Photographs: Body Imagery and Changing Technologies of Remembrance in Asante Funeral Culture', in Jindra and Noret, *Funerals in Africa*.

Chapter 7. The Severed Head

1. Kwame Yeboa Daaku, *Trade and Politics on the Gold Coast, 1600–1720* (Oxford, 1970), chs 5–6; Adam Jones, trans. and ed., *Brandenburg Sources for West African History, 1680–1700* (Wiesbaden, 1985), 2–6.

2. Van Dantzig, *The Dutch and the Guinea Coast*, 'Story of What Has Happened during the Expedition against Great Frederieksburg', 13 June 1718, 204.

3. John Atkins, *A Voyage to Guinea, Brasil, and the West Indies* (London, 1735), 75.

4. Ibid., 77.

5. Ibid., 80.

6. A. B. Ellis, *A History of the Gold Coast of West Africa* (London, 1893), 91; see too C. W. Welman, *The Native States of the Gold Coast: History and Constitution. II: Ahanta* (Accra, 1930), 33–49.

7. Daaku, *Trade and Politics*, 142.

8. Julia Kristeva, *The Severed Head: Capital Visions*, translated by Jody Gladding (New York, 2012).

9. See too Assmann, *Death and Salvation*, ch. 1 'Death as Dismemberment'; Michelle Bonogofsky, ed., *Skull Collection, Modification and Decoration* (Oxford, 2006); Regina James, *Losing Our Head: Beheading in Literature and Culture* (2005); Frances Larson, *Severed: A History of Heads Lost and Found* (London, 2014).

10. De Marees, *Description*, 91. For evidence that this royal burial ground later became a sacred grove, see Gérard Chouin, 'Archaeological Perspectives on Sacred Groves in Ghana', in Michael J. Sheridan and Celia Nyamweru, eds, *African Sacred Groves: Ecological Dynamics and Social Change* (Oxford, 2008), 190–92.

11. Quoted in Wiltgen, *Gold Coast Mission History*, 34; for this account, see António Brásio, ed., *Mounumenta Missionaria Africana* (Lisbon, 1952–81), 1st series, vol. 8, Carta de Colombino de Nantes a Peiresc, 20 June 1634, 278–88. See too Jones, *German Sources*, Hemmersam's Description, 117.

12. Ibid., 'Müller's Description', 199.

13. Ibid., 'Brun's Voyages', 93.

14. Barbot, *Barbot on Guinea*, vol. 2, 566; see too Villault, *Relation*, 316; Thomas Phillips, 'A Journal of a Voyage made in the Hannibal of London, Ann. 1693, 1694', in A. & J. Churchill, *A Collection of Voyages and Travels*, vol. 6 (London, 1732), 201.

15. Captain Charles Johnson [i.e., Daniel Defoe], *A General History of the Pyrates* (London, 1725), 281–329.

16. Robin Law, '"My Head Belongs to the King": On the Political and Ritual Significance of Decapitation in Pre-colonial Dahomey', *Journal of African History* 30 (1989); Insoll, *Material Explorations*, 105–11.

17. Rømer, *Reliable Account*, 79.

18. Bosman, *New and Accurate Description*, 232.

19. Monrad, *Description*, 107.

20. Brown, *The Reaper's Garden*, 133–7; Douglas R. Egerton, 'A Peculiar Mark of Infamy: Dismemberment, Burial, and Rebelliousness in Slave Societies', in Nancy Isenberg and Andrew Burstein, eds, *Mortal Remains: Death in Early America* (Philadelphia, 2003).

21. William Snelgrave, *A New Account of Some Parts of Guinea and the Slave Trade* (London, 1734; 2nd ed. 1971), 183–4. Cormantee (variously Coromantee, Kormantyn, etc.): a term used for slaves from the Gold Coast, derived from the Fante port of Kormantse, near Cape Coast, where first the Dutch and then the English established an early base for the purchase of captives.

22. Rømer, *Reliable Account*, 125; see too Monrad, *Description*, 106.

23. Bowdich, *Essay*, 29–30.

24. Bowdich, *Mission*, 300.

25. Kaminski, *Asante* Ntahera *Trumpets*, 48–50.

26. J. H. Nketia, *Drumming in Akan Communities of Ghana* (Accra, 1963), 128; see too idem, 'Asante Court Music', in Schildkrout, *The Golden Stool*.

27. Rømer, *Reliable Account*, 126–7.

28. Rask, *Brief and Truthful Description*, 123.

29. See Rosaldo, 'Grief and the Headhunter's Rage'.

30. Jones, *German Sources*, 200; Villault, *Relation*, 314.

31. Rømer, *Reliable Account*, 129.

32. Rattray, *Ashanti Law and Constitution*, 310.

33. TNA T70/4 Extracts of Letters 1720–42, letter dd. Cape Coast Castle, 30 June 1729, 42–4.

34. Ole Justesen, trans. and ed., *Danish Sources for the History of Ghana, 1657-1754* (Copenhagen, 2005), vol. 2, Sekret Council resolution re relations with the Dutch, Dutch Accra and Fante, 1748, 707–13.

35. Major Ricketts, *Narrative of the Ashantee War* (London, 1831), 38.

36. On the tormented and malign spirit of a beheaded man, see PRAAD Accra SCT 17/4/2 District Commissioner's Court Book, Accra, 1875–6, *Quaku Blay and Quarmin Darku v. Yaw Ofaye*, 13 Sep. 1875, 149–51.

37. Rømer, *Reliable Account*, 181.

38. Ibid., 125–6.

39. Wilks, *Asante*, 271–3; Emmanuel Terray, *Une histoire du royaume abron du Gyaman: Des origines à la conquête coloniale* (Paris, 1995), 601–30; Tom McCaskie, 'Telling the Tale of Osei Bonsu: An Essay on the Making of Asante History', *Africa* 84 (2014).

40. Reindorf, *History*, 173.

41. D. M. Warrren and K. O. Brempong, eds, *Techiman Traditional State. Part 2: Histories of the Deities* (Techiman, Ghana, 1971), History of the God Taa Kora, by Nana Kwabena Dwuomo, 134–5.

42. Reindorf, *History*, 173–4; Asare, 'Asante Abasem', 53–63; Rattray, *Ashanti Law and Constitution*, 201; 'History of Ashanti' [1937–1942], cited in McCaskie, 'Telling the Tale', 364; Warren and Brempong, *Techiman*, 134–5.

43. Reindorf, *History*, 174; see too McCaskie, 'Telling the Tale', 364–5, for further detail drawn from 'History of Ashanti'.

44. 'History of Ashanti', cited in ibid., 366.

45. Thomas Birch Freeman, *Journal of Various Visits to the Kingdom of Ashanti, Aku, and Dahomi* (London, 1844, 3rd ed. 1966), 148–9.

46. *Ashanti Stool Histories*, vol. 1, AS.86 Ofiri and Manso Stool History; Warren and Brempong, *Techiman*, 134–5; McCaskie, 'Telling the Tale', 365.

47. Rattray, *Ashanti*, 178.

48. Bowdich, *Mission*, 237–8.

49. Dupuis, *Journal*, 244.

50. Ibid., 79–81.

51. Wilks, *Asante*, 670–71.

52. Reindorf, *History*, 138–9; and see *Ashanti Stool Histories*, vol. 1, AS.28 Oyoko Stool History.

53. Ann Brower Stahl, *Making History in Banda: Anthropological Visions of Africa's Past* (Cambridge, 2001), 73, 155–8 and 227.

54. Bowdich, *Mission*, 245. Bowdich subsequently quoted Tamia's speech, discreetly translated into Latin, in which she graphically described the exchange of sex organs: *Essay on the Superstitions*, 31.

55. Asare, 'Asante Abasem', 55.

56. Kwame Arhin, 'The Asante Praise Poems: The Ideology of Patrimonialism', *Paiduma* 32 (1986), 177 and 191; McCaskie, 'Telling the Tale', 363–4.

57. Ibid., 363.

58. Rattray, *Religion and Art*, 132.

59. Dupuis, *Journal*, 164–5. 'Apoku': Gyaasewahene Opoku Frefre, an influential military commander.

Chapter 8. Slaves

1. Van Dantzig, *The Dutch and the Guinea Coast*, Extract from the Minutes of the Meeting of the Directors of the Chamber of Zeeland, 7 Feb. 1730, 240–1.

2. Cf. Keith Thomas, *The Ends of Life: Roads to Fulfilment in Early Modern England* (Oxford, 2009).

3. Joseph C. Miller, *Way of Death: Merchant Capitalism and the Angolan Slave Trade, 1730–1830* (Madison, 1988).

4. John Parker, *Making the Town: Ga State and Society in Early Colonial Accra* (Portsmouth, NH, 2000).

5. For the first of these views, see Akosua Adoma Perbi, *A History of Indigenous Slavery in Ghana: From the 15th to the 19th Centuries* (Accra, 2004); for the second, Paul E. Lovejoy, *Transformations in Slavery: A History of Slavery in Africa* (3rd ed. Cambridge, 2011); for balanced overviews, Rebecca Shumway and Trevor Getz, eds, *Slavery and Its Legacy in Ghana and the Diaspora*

(London, 2017), and, on the nineteenth century, Peter Haenger, *Slaves and Slave Holders on the Gold Coast: Towards an Understanding of Social Bondage in West Africa* (Basel, 2000).

6. For Asante, see Rattray, *Ashanti Law and Constitution*, 33–46, and McCaskie, *State and Society*, 95–101; for the Ga, Parker, *Making the Town*, 87–97; and the Ewe, Sandra E. Greene, *West African Narratives of Slavery: Texts from Late-Nineteenth and Early-Twentieth Century Ghana* (Bloomington, 2011).

7. Freeman, *Journal*, 132.

8. Stephanie E. Smallwood, *Saltwater Slavery: A Middle Passage from Africa to American Diaspora* (Cambridge, Mass., 2007); Brown, *The Reaper's Garden*; Walter C. Rucker, *Gold Coast Diasporas: Identity, Culture, and Power* (Bloomington, 2015), esp. 9–17; and see too Rucker, '"Earth from a Dead Negro's Grave": Ritual Technologies and Mortuary Realms in the Eighteenth-Century Gold Coast Diaspora', in Shumway and Getz, *Slavery*.

9. Bryan Edwards, *The History, Civil and Commercial, of the British Colonies in the West Indies* (London, 1783), vol. 2, 70–74, quoted in Rucker, *Gold Coast Diasporas*, 131.

10. See John Thornton, 'Cannibals, Witches, and Slave Traders in the Atlantic World', *William and Mary Quarterly* 60 (2003).

11. Barbot, *Barbot on Guinea*, vol. 2, 550.

12. Bosman, *New and Accurate Description*, 365. Asantehene Kwaku Dua Panin reported in 1848 that the belief was current in Asante when he was a child: see PP 1849 XXXIV [C.399] *Missions to the King of Ashantee and Dohomey*, Journal of Lieutenant-Governor Winniett's Visit to the King of Ashantee.

13. Rask, *Brief and Truthful Description*, 51.

14. Ray Kea, '"But I Know What I Shall Do": Agency, Belief and the Social Imaginary in Eighteenth-Century Gold Coast Towns', in Anderson and Rathbone, *Africa's Urban Past*, and Kea, *Cultural and Social History*, vol. 1, 21–114 and 144–65.

15. Rask, *Brief and Truthful Description*, 153–4. I have amended the translation according to that in Kea, *Cultural and Social History*, vol. 1, 21. *Bringarer*: from the Portuguese *brincar*, to play or caper.

16. Rømer, *Reliable Account*, 107–8. Cf. Kea, *Cultural and Social History*, 144–5: rather than 'if that prayer does not help, I shall discuss it with [God]', Kea has 'if my prayer is not answered I shall *beat* God'.

17. Kea, 'But I Know What I Shall Do', 164–8, and *Cultural and Social History*, 42.

18. See Rømer, *Reliable Account*, 139–44.

19. Ibid., 185.

20. Kea, *Cultural and Social History*, 88, quoting a Danish letter dd. 9 Oct. 1711.

21. Rask, *Brief and Truthful Description*, 77–8.

22. Ibid., 143.

23. Hurston, *Mules and Men*; for an analysis of such entanglements as a result of nineteenth-century missionary activity in the Ewe-speaking region, see Meyer, *Translating the Devil*.

24. Michael T. Taussig, *The Devil and Commodity Fetishism in South America* (Chapel Hill, 1980), xii.

25. Rask, *Brief and Truthful Description*, 154.

26. Rømer, *Reliable Account*, 35; for discussion, see Kea, 'But I Know What I Shall Do', 173–7, esp. 174, where, rather than 'your fascinating goods', Kea has 'your enchanting merchandise'.

27. Justesen, *Danish Sources*, vol. 2, 'Specifications of the Company's Slaves and Receivables', 15 Apr. 1736, 514.

28. See Rebecca Shumway, 'Castle Slaves of the Eighteenth-Century Gold Coast (Ghana)', *Slavery and Abolition* 35 (2014).

29. Kea, *Cultural and Social History*, 146.

30. TNA T70/1519 Detached Papers, 1752–3. 'Ague': malarial fever.

31. Barbot, *Barbot on Guinea*, vol. 2, 549.

32. Rask, *Brief and Truthful Description*, 155.

33. Field, *Religion and Medicine*, 161–2.

34. Rask, *Brief and Truthful Description*, 155.

35. Monrad, *Description*, 94; see too Daniell, 'Ethnography of Akkrah', 18. By way of comparison, it was only in 1804 that the practice in Britain of holding up the burial of debtors until their debts were paid was definitively ruled against as 'revolting to humanity': Laqueur, *Work of the Dead*, 150–51.

36. TNA CO 96/45, Bird to Bulwer Lytton, 11 July 1859, enclosed: Medical Report for the Year 1858.

37. Freeman, *Journal*, 135–6; WMMS, 'Reminiscences and Incidents of Travel and Historical and Political Sketches', by T. B. Freeman, n.d. [but 1859–60], 110–11.

38. Ramseyer and Kühne, *Four Years*, 142; see too Perregaux, 'Chez les Achanti', 130.

39. Gordon, *Life on the Gold Coast*, 46–7; see too A. Ffoulks, 'Funeral Customs of the Gold Coast Colony', *Journal of the African Society* 8 (1908–9), 154.

40. PRAAD Accra SCT 5/4/3 Civil and Criminal Record Book, Cape Coast, 1847–8, *Quamino Ahwill v. Quabina Abbacan*, 16 July 1847, 168.

41. PRAAD Accra SCT 5/4/8 Civil and Criminal Record Book, Cape Coast, 1864–5, *John Dawson v. Abbah Eccoom*, 9 Jan. 1865, 69–75.

42. PRAAD Accra SCT 5/4/93 Civil Record Book, Cape Coast, 1870–71, *Coffee Sackee v. Sinnay*, 23 Nov. 1870, 103–12.

43. Ibid., evidence of Quamina Day; an obligation confirmed in TNA CO 96/41, Pine to Labouchere, 1 Oct. 1857.

44. PRAAD Accra SCT 5/4/19 Civil Record Book, Cape Coast, 1876–7, *Abinabah Mansah v. Samuel Watts*, 25 Jan. 1877, 305–17 and 331.

45. Quoted in Meera Venkatachalam, *Slavery, Memory, and Religion in Southeastern Ghana, c. 1850-Present* (Cambridge, 2015).

46. Field, *Akim-Kotoku*, 21.

Chapter 9. Human Sacrifice

1. TNA CO 96/43, Bird to Bulwer Lytton, 11 Aug. 1858, enclosed: Depositions of Refugees, 25–28 June 1858.

2. Wilks, *Forests of Gold*, ch. 7, 'Space, Time and "Human Sacrifice"', 215.

3. See too Sandra E. Greene, 'Experiencing Fear and Despair: The Enslaved and Human Sacrifice in Nineteenth-Century Southern Ghana', in Alice Bellagamba, Sandra E. Greene and Martin A. Klein, eds, *African Voices on Slavery and the Slave Trade* (Cambridge, 2013).

4. TNA CO 96/43, Bird to Bulwer Lytton, 27 Aug. 1858, enclosed: Quacoo Duah to Bird, dd. 16 June [but July] 1858.

5. Wilks, *Asante*, 589–95, quote from 593.

6. Robin Law, 'Human Sacrifice in Pre-colonial West Africa', *African Affairs* 84 (1985), 55.

7. Clifford Williams, 'Asante: Human Sacrifice or Capital Punishment? An Assessment of the Period 1807–1874', *International Journal of African Historical Studies* 21 (1988), plus Wilks's response in ibid., 'Asante: Human Sacrifice or Capital Punishment? A Rejoinder'; McCaskie, 'Death and the *Asantehene*', 417–18, and *State and Society*, 17 and 102; on Akuapem, see Michelle Gilbert, 'The Christian Executioner: Christianity and Chieftaincy as Rivals', *Journal of Religion in Africa* 25 (1995).

8. Wilks, *Forests of Gold*, 217.

9. Rattray, *Religion and Art*, 106, and *Ashanti Law and Constitution*, 42–3; McCaskie, *State and Society*, 98–9.

10. See Kwabena O. Akurang-Parry, 'The Rumor of the Human Sacrifice of Two Hundred Girls by *Asantehene* (King) Mensa Bonsu in 1881–2 and its Consequent Policy Implications and African Responses', in Toyin Falola and Matt D. Childs, eds, *The Changing Worlds of Atlantic Africa: Essays in Honor of Robin Law* (Durham, NC, 2009).

11. Henri Hubert and Marcel Mauss, *Sacrifice: Its Nature and Function*, translated by W. D. Halls (London, 1964); M.C.F. Bourdillon and Meyer Fortes, eds, *Sacrifice* (London, 1980); Luc de Heusch, *Sacrifice in Africa*, translated by Linda O'Brien and Alice Morton (Manchester, 1985); Robert G. Hamerton-Kelly, ed., *Violent Origins: Walter Burkert, René Girard, and Jonathan Z. Smith on Ritual Killing and Cultural Formation* (Stanford, 1987); Kathryn McClymond, 'The Nature and Elements of Sacrificial Ritual', *Method and Theory in the Study of Religion* 16 (2004).

12. Compare Inga Clendinnen, *Aztecs: An Interpretation* (Cambridge, 1991); Davíd Carrasco, *City of Sacrifice: The Aztec Empire and the Role of the Violence in Civilization* (Boston, 1999).

13. See Peel, *Religious Encounter*, 69–71; Olatunji Ojo, 'Slavery and Human Sacrifice in Yorubaland: Ondo, c. 1870–94', *Journal of African History* 46 (2005).

14. Law, 'Human Sacrifice', 61–3.

15. Cruickshank, *Eighteen Years*, vol. 2, 246.

16. De Marees, *Description*, 184; for the Portuguese sources, see Law, 'Human Sacrifice', 61–2.

17. De Marees, *Description*, 184. Wilks quotes this passage, but only up to 'these people are killed and decapitated', thereby removing evidence of involuntary killings, and commenting only that 'there is nothing in De Marees, it will be noted, about "sacrifice"': *Forests of Gold*, 236.

18. Jones, *German Sources*, 179; see too TNA C113/274 Letters and Reports from Cape Coast Castle to the Royal African Company in London, 1721–2, 'The Coast Management' n.d. [but 1722], 266.

19. Barbot, *Barbot on Guinea*, vol. 2, 396.

20. Bosman, *New and Accurate Description*, 231. Again, Wilks quotes this passage but excludes the final sentence detailing the prolonged corporal violence inflicted upon those killed: *Forests of Gold*, 236.

21. Jones, *German Sources*, 179.

22. 'Part of Two Letters from Mr. J. Hillier, dated Cape Corse, Jan. 3 1687/8 and Apr. 25 1688', *Philosophical Transactions of the Royal Society* 232 (1697), 688.

23. See McCaskie, 'Death and the *Asantehene*'.

24. Villault, *Relation*, 346; translation from Sieur Villault, *A Relation of the Coasts of Africk called Guinee* (London, 1670), 246–7.
25. Rattray, *Ashanti*, 263.
26. Rattray, *Religion and Art*, 135 and 280.
27. McCaskie, *State and Society*, 109, 277 and 280.
28. Rattray, *Ashanti*, 100. Rattray also noted that the *gyabom* was re-empowered with a human sacrifice, 'one of the very few exceptions to the rule that human sacrifices were only made with the idea that the spirit so released might be set free to serve another human spirit', his informant describing such a sacrifice which occurred around 1900.
29. Asare, 'Asante Abasem', 47; see too Rattray, *Ashanti Law and Constitution*, 219; Reindorf, *History*, 54.
30. See too Jones, *German Sources*; 169; Law, 'Human Sacrifice', 70.
31. Such numbers should be seen as figurative indications of a large amount: compare the normative 3,333 wives of the Asantehene and note the recurrence of the number 3 in such calculations.
32. Reindorf, *History*, 137–8.
33. Fynn, *Asante*, 84–98, followed by Law, 'Human Sacrifice', 82.
34. Dupuis, *Journal*, 239–40; for an account of the campaign and a list of the leading office-holders killed—minus any mention of the immolations which followed—see Wilks, *Asante*, 320–21.
35. See McCaskie, *State and Society*, 41 and 356.
36. Dupuis, *Journal*, 245.
37. Fynn, *Asante*, 137, quoting a report by Johan P. Wriesberg, dd. Accra, 6 Nov. 1797.
38. Bowdich, *Mission*, 239 and 289.
39. Ibid., 289.
40. Law, 'Human Sacrifice', 82.
41. See McCaskie, *State and Society*, 389.
42. Wilks, *Forests of Gold*, 215.
43. For Muhammad al-Ghamba's balanced reflections, see Dupuis, *Journal*, 97–8 and 128.
44. Bowdich, *Mission*, 262, 279, 291; Dupuis, *Journal*, 240.
45. Ibid., 164, and see 117.
46. Gareth Austin, 'Between Abolition and *Jihad*: The Asante Response to the Ending of the Atlantic Slave Trade, 1807–1896', in Robin Law, ed., *From Slave Trade to 'Legitimate' Commerce: The Commercial Transition in Nineteenth-Century West Africa* (Cambridge, 1995), 103.
47. Rattray, *Ashanti Law and Constitution*, 43.
48. Freeman, *Journals*, and WMMS 'Reminiscences'.
49. Wilks, *Forests of Gold*, 230.
50. Ibid., 335.
51. Winwood Reade, *The African Sketch-Book* (London, 1873), vol. 2, 130; for commentary, see Rattray, *Religion and Art*, 106–7; Thomas, *La mort africaine*, 111.
52. Bowdich, *Mission*, 285, 282 and 288; see too Dupuis, *Journal*, 140–41, on the deserted aspect of Kumasi during the celebration of the *adae*.
53. See Arlette Farge, *Fragile Lives: Violence, Power and Solidarity in Eighteenth-Century Paris*, translated by Carol Shelton (Cambridge, Mass., 1993, 185).

Chapter 10. Poison

1. Crone, *Voyages*, 118.

2. Hair, *Founding*, 21–2; on the carrying of poison under the thumbnail in the Senegambia region, see André Álvares de Almada, *Tratado breve dos Rios de Guiné (c. 1594)*, translated by P.E.H. Hair (Liverpool, 1984), 68–9.

3. Robert Hertz, 'The Pre-eminence of the Right Hand: A Study in Religious Polarity', in *Death and the Right Hand*, 105, citing Lartigue, 'Rapport sur les comptoirs de Grande-Bassam et d'Assinie', *Revue Coloniale*, 2e série, 7 (1851).

4. PRAAD Accra ADM 11/1/1060 West African Materia Medica and Toxicology, 1930.

5. David Arnold, *Toxic Histories: Poison and Pollution in Modern India* (Cambridge, 2016), 1, 3 and 10.

6. Ian Burney, *Poison, Detection and the Victorian Imagination* (Manchester, 2006), 5.

7. But see Abena Dove Osseo-Asare, *Bitter Roots: The Search for Healing Plants in Africa* (Chicago, 2014); Daniel K. Abbiw, *Useful Plants of Ghana* (London, 1990), 206–31.

8. The term 'magic' became freighted in the imperial age with European theories of 'primitive thought', but the association of poison with the occult was historically also a feature of European registers: Burney, *Poison*, 46–7.

9. For the Twi lexicon, see Christaller, *Dictionary*, 98–101; for the 'magical' element in curative practices, Rattray, *Religion and Art*, 38–47, and Field, *Religion and Medicine*, 110–34; for botanical pharmacopoeia, D. Maier, 'Nineteenth-Century Asante Medical Practices', *Comparative Studies in Society and History* 21 (1979); and for the cosmological spectrum and witchcraft, Allman and Parker, *Tongnaab*, 121–5.

10. Bosman, *New and Accurate Description*, 221–5.

11. Ibid., 148; translation amended by van Dantzig, 'English Bosman III'. On poisoning as an Italian art, see Burney, *Poison*, 13.

12. Bosman, *New and Accurate Description*, 149–50; see too Jones, *German Sources*, 161 and 174–5.

13. Monrad, *Description*, 47.

14. *African Times*, 23 Jan. 1864, 'Necromancy: Consulting the Dead'.

15. TNA T70/36 Inward Letter Book, 1813–18, White and Hope Smith to Committee, 10 Mar. 1814, 34–6.

16. Dupuis, *Journal*, xiii–xiv.

17. Justesen, *Danish Sources*, Declaration by Frederich Pedersen Svane, 1 June 1748, 746.

18. Ibid., 747.

19. Ibid., 448, and Diary Kept at Christiansborg, 1744–5, 663.

20. Ibid., Rømer to the Directors of the West India and Guinea Company, 28 Feb. 1745, 635–50.

21. Ibid., 649.

22. Rømer, *Reliable Account*, 86–7. 'Giemawong': Ga jemawon, tutelary deity.

23. Bosman, *New and Accurate Description*, 224.

24. Ibid., 141. Monrad notes one case of a European revealing to him on his deathbed 'that he had certainly been poisoned by his Mulatto woman's family': *Description*, 163.

25. T. C. McCaskie, 'On Mouri Beach in 1821: The British and Empire in the Gold Coast', in Toyin Falola and Emily Brownell, eds, *Africa, Empire and Globalization: Essays in Honor of A. G. Hopkins* (Durham, NC, 2011), 264.

26. Monrad, *Description*, 163.

27. Burney, *Poison*, 55.

28. Richard Mead, *Mechanical Account of Poisons in Several Essays* (London, 1702), quoted in Burney, *Poison*, 47.

29. Monrad, *Description*, 162, and see 161–4.

30. Abbiw, *Useful Plants*, 206 and 210.

31. De Marees, *Description*, 90; Jones, *German Sources*, 92, 112, 116 and 194.

32. Parker, *Making the Town*, 164–5.

33. Kea, *Cultural and Social History*, vol. 1, 313–8, and vol. 2, 574.

34. Rosalind Shaw, *Memories of the Slave Trade: Ritual and the Historical Imagination in Sierra Leone* (Chicago, 2002).

35. Fynn, *Asante*, 137–8; Wilks, *Asante*, 251–4 and 342–4; McCaskie, *State and Society*, 136, 180–84 and 389.

36. Fynn, *Asante*, 137, quoting a report by Johan P. Wriesberg, dd. Accra, 6 Nov. 1797.

37. Bowdich, *Mission*, 238–9; cf. Dupuis, *Journal*, 244–5.

38. Bowdich, *Mission*, 239–40; Reindorf, *History*, 142.

39. Dupuis, *Journal*, 245 and 247.

40. Reindorf, *History*, 142.

41. McCaskie, 'Death and the *Asantehene*', 429, paraphrasing 'History of Ashanti' [1937–42].

42. McCaskie, 'Death and the *Asantehene*', 429; for a similar sequence culminating in the death of the nineteenth-century Mamponhene Kwame Gyima, see Rattray, *Ashanti Law and Constitution*, 240.

43. Bowdich, *Mission*, 239 and 289.

44. Ibid. Konadu Yaadom actually died five years later, in 1809, reportedly in childbirth.

45. Monrad, *Description*, 47.

46. Bowdich, *Mission*, 420.

47. Dupuis, *Journal*, 115.

48. Ibid. Emphasis in original.

49. T. C. McCaskie, 'Anti-witchcraft Cults in Asante: An Essay in the Social History of an African People', *History in Africa* 8 (1981), 128, citing 'History of Ashanti'. On the staging of mock funerals as a type of 'bad medicine' to induce death, see *Gold Coast News*, 27 June 1885; Field, *Religion and Medicine*, 128.

50. Dupuis, *Journal*, 116.

51. Ibid.

52. PRAAD Accra SCT 5/4/20 Judicial Assessor's Note Book, 1849–51, *Quansah v. Fetish Priests of Braff[o] Country*, 20 July 1849, 37–8; SCT 5/4/5 High Court Cape Coast, Civil and Criminal Record Book, 1852–3, *Quacoo Adoo v. Coffee Ampeow*, 14 July 1852, 142–3.

53. PRAAD Accra SCT 5/4/3 Cape Coast Civil and Criminal Record Book (Judicial Assessor), 1847–8, *Quaye Abomine v. Coffee Aquah*, 28 Dec. 1846, 62–3.

54. PRAAD Accra SCT 2/4/12 Divisional Court, Accra, Civil Record Book, 1877–9, *Accosuah Entolwah v. Yowah Assemamah*, 19 Nov. 1877, 317–35.

55. PRAAD Accra SCT 5/4/25 Judicial Assessor's Note Book No. 5, *Adjuah Sanewah v. Quashi Coomah*, 8 Apr. 1859, 14–25.

56. Ibid., emphasis in original.

57. For one case, in which an elderly midwife was denounced as a poisoner, see PRAAD Accra SCT 2/4/2 Civil Record Book, Accra, Vol. 1A, 1861–4, *Adooquaye v. Molie*, 31 Mar. 1862, 322–5.

58. TNA CO 96/41, Pine to Labouchere, 2 Dec. 1857; on the Palmer case, see Burney, *Poison*, ch. 4.

59. PRAAD Accra SCT 5/4/102 Civil Record Book, Cape Coast, 1877–9, *Chief Isaac Robertson v. Quarcoe Essell*, 24 Apr. 1877, 56–67.

60. *Gold Coast Times*, 18 Feb., 4 Mar., 9 Sep. and 14 Dec. 1882.

61. *Gold Coast News*, 21 Mar. 1885.

Chapter 11. Christian Encounters

1. Peel, *Religious Encounter*, 1.

2. Jean Comaroff and John Comaroff, *Of Revelation and Revolution: Christianity, Colonialism, and Consciousness in South Africa*, vol. 1 (Chicago, 1991).

3. J. E. Casely Hayford, *Gold Coast Native Institutions* (London, 1903), 102.

4. Hans W. Debrunner, *A History of Christianity in Ghana* (Accra, 1967), 36 and 52–3.

5. Thomas Thompson, *An Account of Two Missionary Voyages* (London, 1758); Vincent Carretta and Ty M. Reese, eds, *The Life and Letters of Philip Quaque: The First African Anglican Missionary* (Athens, Ga., 2010).

6. Monrad, *Description*, 33.

7. Quoted in Noel Smith, *The Presbyterian Church of Ghana, 1835–1960* (Accra, 1966), 43.

8. On Methodism, see Arthur E. Southon, *Gold Coast Methodism: The First Hundred Years 1835–1935* (Cape Coast, 1935), and Bartels, *Roots*; on the Bremen Mission, Meyer, *Translating the Devil*.

9. WMMS Box 587A, 'History of the Rise and Progress of Wesleyan Missions on the Gold Coast', by T. B. Freeman, 1838.

10. Bartels, *Roots*, 26.

11. WMMS MS 380587 Diary of Robert Brooking, 29 Mar. and 22 Apr. 1840.

12. Ibid., 7 Nov. 1841.

13. WMMS Gold Coast Correspondence [GCC], T. B. Picot to Rev. W. B. Boyce, 3 May 1876. 'Cramos': *nkramo*, Muslims. See too McCaskie, *State and Society*, 136–43.

14. Smith, *Presbyterian Church*, 88–9.

15. Ibid., 88, quoting P. Steiner, *Auf Einsamen Pfaden* (Basel, 1906).

16. Meyer, *Translating the Devil*, 10.

17. Smith, *Presbyterian Church*, 87–8.

18. Ulrike Sill, *Encounters in Quest of Christian Womanhood: The Basel Mission in Pre- and Early Colonial Ghana* (Leiden, 2010), 125, and on Mulgrave, who was enslaved as a child in Angola, 110–32.

19. Debrunner, *History*, 169.

20. Smith, *Presbyterian Church*, 90.

21. Debrunner, *History*, 161; see too Smith, *Presbyterian Church*, 90–91.

22. Ibid., 51.

23. WMMS, Freeman, 'Reminiscences', 185–6.

24. Bartels, *Roots*, 70.

25. Cruickshank, *Eighteen Years*, vol. 2, 115, and 95–123 passim.

26. Ibid., 116.

27. Rømer, *Reliable Account*, 95–8; see too John Beecham, *Ashantee and the Gold Coast* (London, 1841, 2nd ed. 1968), 201–3.

28. T. C. McCaskie, 'Nananom Mpow of Mankessim: An Essay in Fante History', in D. Henige and T. C. McCaskie, eds, *West African Economic and Social History: Studies in Memory of Marion Johnson* (Madison, 1990); Rebecca Shumway, 'The Fante Shrine of Nananom Mpow and the Atlantic Slave Trade in Southern Ghana', *International Journal of African Historical Studies* 44 (2011).

29. Beecham, *Ashantee*, 279.

30. McCaskie, 'Nananom Mpow', 145, quoting the diary of Rev. G. Chapman, 10 June 1843.

31. Rømer, *Reliable Account*, 95 and 97–8.

32. Cruickshank, *Eighteen Years*, vol. 2, 324.

33. Ibid., 331.

34. Ibid., 333–5.

35. WMMS GCC, Picot to Boyce, 3 May 1876.

36. Sill, *Encounters*, 233–5.

37. Basel Mission Archive D-12 Paul Jenkins' Abstracts from the Gold Coast Correspondence of the Basel Mission [hereafter BM Abstracts], Süss to Basel, 3 Feb. 1852, 3–4.

38. BM Abstracts, Süss to Basel, 25 Oct. 1854, 24.

39. BM Abstracts, Baum to Basel, 14 July 1857, 34.

40. BM Abstracts, Süss to Basel, 28 Dec. 1857, 37; Haas to Basel, 29 Aug. 1859, 41–2.

41. BM Abstracts, Christaller's report, 1 Oct. 1866, 529.

42. PRAAD Accra SCT 2/4/13 Divisional Court Civil Record Book, 1877–9, *The Queen v. Quaco Botchey*, 3 Dec. 1877, 342; for reflections on this separation in his own childhood, see Kyei, *Our Days Dwindle*, ch. 12 'Where I Belonged'.

43. Debrunner, *History*, 190–98; Rathbone, *Murder and Politics*, 21–31; Robert Addo-Fening, *Akyem Abuakwa, 1700–1943: From Ofori Panin to Sir Ofori Atta* (Trondheim, 1997); Sonia Abun-Nasr, *Afrikaner und Missionar: Die Lebensgeschichte von David Asante* (Basel, 2003), 192–212.

44. Raymond Dumett and Marion Johnson, 'Britain and the Suppression of Slavery in the Gold Coast, Ashanti and the Northern Territories', in Suzanne Miers and Richard Roberts, eds, *The End of Slavery in Africa* (Madison, 1988); Haenger, *Slaves and Slave Holders*.

45. For the latter, see PRAAD Accra ADM 11/1/1094 Akim Abuakwa Native Affairs, 1883–93, Report on the cases of Chief Amoo, Quamin Teah, Quasie Ainsah and Appeah Quosan condemned to death on May 10, 1880 on charges of murder, by J. Marshall, Chief Justice, 11 May 1880.

46. Haenger, *Slaves and Slave Holders*, 45.

47. BM Abstracts, Lodholtz to Basel, 5 Jan. 1871, 561.

48. See BM Abstracts, Eisenschmid to Basel, 5 May 1862, 509.

49. BM Abstracts, Kwabi's Jahresbericht for 1871, 21 Dec. 1871, 566.

50. On the Bremen Mission, see Sandra E. Greene, *Slave Owners of West Africa: Decision Making in the Age of Abolition* (Bloomington, 2017), 65–6 and 73–4.

51. BM Abstracts, Mohr's Jahresbericht for 1877, 15 Jan. 1878, 71.

52. BM Abstracts, Glatzle's report, 26 Dec. 1877, 75.

53. BM Abstracts, Mohr's report, 28 May 1877, 72.

54. BM Abstracts, Mohr to Basel, 10 Apr. 1878, 104.

55. TNA CO 96/184, White to Holland, 31 Oct. 1887, enclosure 11: Report of the Mission to Eastern Akim, by B. Lethbridge, 14 Sep. 1887; cf. enclosure 2: Paul Steiner and others to Brandford Griffith, 9 Feb. 1887.

56. TNA CO 96/179, Brandford Griffith to Stanhope, 28 Jan. 1887; CO 96/180, Brandford Griffith to Stanhope, 2 Feb. 1887.

57. BM Abstracts, Mohr to Basel, 2 May 1887, 686; Debrunner, *History*, 197.

58. TNA CO 96/180, Brandford Griffith to Stanhope, 2 Feb. 1887.

59. Ibid., enclosure 9: Report of the Mission to Eastern Akim, 8 Apr. 1887; CO 96/184, Report . . . by Lethbridge, 14 Sep. 1884.

60. Ibid., enclosure 6: Mohr to Hudson and Oforidee, 7 Feb. 1887.

61. BM Abstracts, Mohr to Basel, 10 Aug. 1887, 690–92.

62. TNA CO 96/180, enclosure 12: Queen Ambah Amporfua to Lethbridge, 29 May 1887.

63. Reindorf, *History*, 232 and 246.

64. BM Abstracts, Huppenbauer's report, 20 Aug. 1885, 660.

Chapter 12. From House Burial to Cemeteries

1. TNA CO 96/194, Brandford Griffith to Knutsford, 19 Sep. 1888.

2. Ibid.; TNA CO 97/3, 'Cemeteries Ordinance, 1888'; Parker, 'Cultural Politics of Death and Burial'.

3. Ariès, *Western Attitudes toward Death* and *The Hour of Our Death*; Laqueur, *Work of the Dead*; see too Peter C. Jupp and Glennys Howarth, eds, *The Changing Face of Death: Historical Accounts of Death and Disposal* (New York, 1997); Lomnitz, *Death and the Idea of Mexico*.

4. Isert, *Letters*, 132; see too William Hutton, *A Voyage to Africa* (London, 1821), 85; *Royal Gold Coast Gazette*, 25 Feb. 1823.

5. TNA T70/153 Acts of Council, 1782–99, 11 May 1791; Randy J. Sparks, *Where the Negroes Are Masters: An African Port in the Era of the Slave Trade* (Cambridge, Mass., 2014), 215–20.

6. TNA T70/33 Inward Letter Book, 1781–99, Dalzel to Committee, 27 Sep. 1792, 344–7.

7. Ibid., Dalzel to Committee, 20 Jan. 1793, 361–4.

8. Meredith, *Account*, 106.

9. WMMS MS 380587 Diary of Robert Brooking, 3 June 1842.

10. *Gold Coast Times*, 23 Feb. 1875.

11. Villault, *Coasts of Africk*, 202; see too Rattray, *Religion and Art*, 162.

12. Dapper, *Description*, 299; Barbot, *Barbot on Guinea*, 591; cf. Laqueur, *Work of the Dead*, 141 and 226.

13. Monrad, *Description*, 42.

14. Reindorf, *History*, 99.

15. Rømer, *Reliable Account*, 172.

16. Fynn, *Asante*, 79; Wilks, *Asante*, 202.

17. Laqueur, *Work of the Dead*, 229, and ch. 5 'The Cemetery and the New Regime', passim.

18. Ibid., 184–5; Michel Foucault, *The Birth of the Clinic: An Archaeology of Medical Perception*, translated by A. M. Sheridan (London, 1973).

19. Laqueur, *Work of the Dead*, 533, and see 298.

20. Ibid., 184.

21. Parker, *Making the Town*, 99–100.

22. TNA T70/36 Inward Letter Book, 1813–18, Dawson to Committee, 5 Nov. 1816, 191–4; *Gold Coast Leader*, 23 Jan. 1904, 'Elmina. The Governor and the Old Dutch Cemetery'.

23. Monrad, *Description*, 44.

24. Ibid.

25. Selena Alexrod Winsnes, trans. and ed., *A Danish Jew in West Africa. Wulff Joseph Wulff: Biography and Letters, 1836–1842* (Trondheim, 2004), 47–9 and 205–6.

26. Land Title Registry, Accra, 1845–1866 Vol. 2, Will of James Samuel Bannerman, 23 Dec. 1857.

27. TNA CO 96/43, Pine to Labouchere, 2 Feb. 1858.

28. Cruickshank, *Eighteen Years*, vol. 2, 213–21.

29. TNA CO 96/43, Bird to Stanley, 10 June 1858, enclosed: Proclamation by Sir Benjamin Pine.

30. TNA CO 96/45, Bird to Bulwer Lytton, 11 July 1859, enclosed: Medical Report for the Year 1858, by Robert Clarke.

31. *African Times*, 23 June 1864, Letter to Alfred S. Churchill, 14 May 1864.

32. *African Times*, 23 Sep. 1864, Quamina to editor, 13 Aug. 1864.

33. *African Times*, 23 Oct. 1865, 'Sanitary and other Important Reforms at Cape Coast'.

34. *African Times*, 23 Nov. 1865, Spero Meliora to editor, dd. 12 Oct. 1865.

35. Laqueur, *Work of the Dead*, 222.

36. James Africanus B. Horton, *Physical and Medical Climate and Meteorology of the West Coast of Africa* (London, 1867); for these discourses in South Asia, see David Arnold, *The Tropics and the Travelling Gaze: India, Landscape, and Science, 1800–1856* (Delhi, 2005), ch. 2 'In a Land of Death'.

37. Winsnes, *A Danish Jew*, diary entry dd. 19 Dec. 1836, 74.

38. Laqueur, *Work of the Dead*, 222.

39. TNA CO 96/94, Pope Hennessy to Kimberley, 27 Nov. 1872.

40. Ibid., Pope Hennessy to Kimberley, 10 Dec. 1872, enclosed: Harley to Pope Hennessy, 26 Nov. 1872.

41. Ibid., Pope Hennessy to Kimberley, 28 Dec. 1872, enclosed: Harley to Pope Hennessy, 10 Dec. 1872.

42. Ibid., enclosed: Brown to Harley, 6 Dec. 1872, and Parker to Harley, 6 Dec. 1872. Brown would go on to head the proto-nationalist Aborigines' Rights Protection Society, founded in 1897.

43. Ibid., Salmon to Harley, 7 Dec. 1872.

44. Ibid., Harley to Pope Hennessy, 10 Dec. 1872, emphasis in original.

45. *Gold Coast Times*, 22 Aug. 1884.

46. *Western Echo*, 9 Dec. 1885, 'West African Cemeteries'.

47. Adell Patton, Jr., 'Dr. John Farrell Easmon: Medical Professionalism and Colonial Racism in the Gold Coast, 1856–1900', *International Journal of African Historical Studies* 22 (1989), 609.

48. TNA CO 96/180, Griffith to Holland, 5 Apr. 1887, enclosed: Report on the increased mortality among Natives of Accra and Christiansborg during the Harmattan Season 1886–7, by J. F. Easmon.

49. PP 1889 LXXVI [C.5897] *Gold Coast Sanitary and Medical Reports for 1887 and 1888*, Sanitary Report for the Accra Station for the Quarter and Year ended 31 December 1888, by J. F. Easmon.

50. TNA CO 96/194, Griffith to Knutsford, 19 Sep. 1888.

51. PRAAD Accra SCT 17/5/8 District Court, Accra, Criminal Record Book, 1888–1889, *Moshi v. Aryaryee and Odadaye*, 5 Oct. 1888, 141–2 and 146–8, emphasis in original.

52. Ibid., *Quabina Donkor v. Allotey* et al., 15 Nov. 1888, 165–7.

53. Ibid., *J. F. Easmon v. Tetteh Davies* et al., 28 Mar. 1889, 451–5.

54. Parker, 'Cultural Politics of Death and Burial', 214.

55. PRAAD Accra ADM 11/1/1087 Accra Native Affairs, McCarthy to Colonial Secretary, 15 Jan. 1889.

56. TNA CO 96/218, Hodgson to Knutsford, 9 Sep. 1891, enclosed: Bruce Hindle to Hodgson, 8 Sep. 1891; see too Macdonald, *Gold Coast*, 60–61 and 226–8.

57. TNA CO 97/3, Ordinance No. 9, 1891, sec. 23.

58. Field, *Religion and Medicine*, 199; on the Anlo-Ewe region, see too Greene, *Sacred Sites*, 72.

59. BMA D-1, 48/62, Reindorf to Committee, 16 Jan. 1889.

60. Ibid.

61. BMA D-1, 66/145, I. Odoi Philipps to Committee, 31 Dec. 1897.

62. Parker, 'Cultural Politics of Death and Burial', 214–5.

63. Ako Adjei, 'Mortuary Usages of the Ga People of the Gold Coast', *American Anthroplogist* 45 (1943), 92.

64. Field, *Religion and Medicine*, 198.

65. TNA CO 96/234, Griffith to Ripon, 12 June 1893, enclosed: List of existing Cemeteries in the various districts of the Colony, n.d.

66. *Gold Coast Nation*, 4 July 1912; on exhumation, cf. Laqueur, *Work of the Dead*, 336–61.

67. Casely Hayford, *Gold Coast Native Institutions*, 103–4.

Chapter 13. Ghosts and Vile Bodies

1. Rattray, *Religion and Art*, 58; K. A. Busia, *The Position of the Chief in the Modern Political System of Ashanti* (London, 1951), 74.

2. PRAAD Kumasi ARG 19/2/1 Cantonment Magistrate Court, Kumasi, 1897, *Regina v. Apon Yow and others*, 15 Feb. 1897, 1–5 and 58–61.

3. Seale, *Constructing Death*, 52.

4. Field, *Religion and Medicine*, 59.

5. Ibid., 202–3.

6. Thompson, *Account*, 46–7; see too Winwood Reade, *African Sketch-Book*, vol. 2, 128–31.

7. Meyerowitz, *Akan of Ghana*, 112; for Ewe categorization, see Jakob Spieth, *The Ewe People: A Study of the Ewe People in German Togo*, translated by Emmanuel F. Tsaku et al (Accra, 2011 [orig. 1906]), 307–44; compare R. C. Finucane, 'Sacred Corpse, Profane Carrion: Social Ideals and Death Rituals in the Later Middle Ages', in Whaley, *Mirrors of Mortality*, 54–5.

8. McLeod, *The Asante*, 36–7; see too, also with a focus on perceptions from Takyiman, Konadu, *Our Own Way*, 22.

9. Daniell, 'Ethnography of Akkrah', 19; for similar beliefs and practices in eastern Europe, compare Paul Barber, *Vampires, Burial and Death* (New Haven, 2010); Verdery, *Political Lives of Dead Bodies*, 42–5.

10. T. C. McCaskie, *Asante Identities: History and Modernity in an African Village 1850–1950* (Edinburgh, 2000), 65.

11. PRAAD Accra SCT 5/4/7 Judicial Assessor's Court Record Book, Cape Coast, Vol. 1, Deposition relative to the death of Edusurabah, 29 Jan. 1858, 61–7.

12. Kyei, *Our Days Dwindle*, 99.

13. Field, *Akim-Kotoku*, 148.

14. Kyei, *Our Days Dwindle*, 103; Rattray, *Ashanti Law and Constitution*, 299.

15. Monrad, *Description*, 65.

16. Rattray, *Religion and Art*, 59; see too idem, *Akan-Ashanti Folk-Tales*, 26–31.

17. Rattray, *Religion and Art*, 59–60.

18. Idid., 60; see too Field, *Akim-Kotoku*, 149–50; and for material evidence of *nkuku mma*, Kwaku Effah-Gyamfi, *Bono Manso: An Archaeological Investigation into Early Akan Urbanism* (Calgary, 1985), 66–7. On recent advances in the understanding of how emotion was 'performed' by grieving parents, see Katie Barclay and Kimberley Reynolds, with Ciara Rawnsley, eds, *Death, Emotion and Childhood in Premodern Europe* (London, 2016), 3–5.

19. *Royal Gold Coast Gazette*, 18 Feb. 1823; Florence Abena Dolphyne, *A Comprehensive Course in Twi (Asante)* (Accra, 1996), 125–6.

20. Field, *Religion and Medicine*, 177–8; see too Rattray, *Religion and Art*, 65.

21. Ramseyer and Kühne, *Four Years*, 46.

22. Monrad, *Description*, 64.

23. Field, *Religion and Medicine*, 169.

24. Meyerowitz, *Akan of Ghana*, 118–19.

25. PRAAD Kumasi ARG 6/29/2/3 DC Kumasi's Palaver Book (Civil Cases) 1910–13, Enquiry held in the palaver between Bompata and Agogo, 13 May 1913, 369–83.

26. Rattray, *Religion and Art*, 58.

27. Ibid., 67.

28. *Western Echo*, 16–30 Sep. 1887, 'Is There a World of Spirits?'. For comparative insights, see R. C. Finucane, *Appearances of the Dead: A Cultural History of Ghosts* (London, 1982); Terry Castle, *The Female Thermometer:18th-Century Culture and the Invention of the Uncanny* (New York, 1995); Marina Warner, *Phantasmagoria: Spirit Visions, Metaphors, and Media into the Twenty-first Century* (Oxford, 2006).

29. Monrad, *Description*, 95.

30. Bosman, *New and Accurate Description*, 159.

31. Bowdich, *Mission*, 262–3; see too Dupuis, *Journal*, 239–40.

32. Lee, *Stories of Strange Lands*, 32.

33. Monrad, *Description*, 38.
34. Rattray, *Religion and Art*, 153.
35. Rattray, *Ashanti*, 99–100; see too Antubam, *Ghana's Heritage*, 98–9, on the role of *aperahofo*, tailswitch bearers, in physically sweeping *atofo* away from chiefs.
36. WMMS MS 380587 Diary of Robert Brooking, 6 May 1842, 26.
37. *West African Herald*, 13 June 1871; Asare, 'Asante Abasem', 63–9.
38. For the full background, see T. C. McCaskie, '*Konnurokusem*: Kinship and Family in the History of the *Oyoko Kokoo* Dynasty of Kumase', *Journal of African History* 36 (1995), and *State and Society*, 180–99.
39. Asare, 'Asante Abasem', 69.
40. *West African Herald*, 13 June 1871.
41. Asare, 'Asante Abasem', 65.
42. Ramseyer and Kühne, *Four Years*, 309.
43. Asare, 'Asante Abasem', 66.
44. McCaskie, 'Death and the *Asantehene*', 431–2.
45. *African Times*, 1 Aug. 1877, 'Heathenism at Accra' and 'Abominable Fetish Custom at Accra', and 1 Nov. 1877, 'A Native' to editor, 17 Sep. 1877.
46. *African Times*, 1 Aug. 1877. 'One of Them' to editor.
47. *African Times*, 1 Aug. 1877.
48. PRAAD Accra ADM 11/1/1298 Katawere Fetish, 1891–1906.
49. Ibid., Rottman to Colonial Secretary, 25 Feb. 1891.
50. Ibid., Hodgson to Hull, 19 Aug. 1893.
51. Ibid., Hull to Acting Governor, 6 Oct. 1893.
52. Ibid., C. J. Bannerman to Joseph Chamberlain, 21 April 1897.
53. Ibid., E. Bannerman to Hodgson, 9 Sep. 1895.
54. PRAAD ADM 11/1/1126 Oda Native Affairs, 1875–1910, Hodgson to Rev. J. Jaeger, 24 Oct. 1893.
55. Field, *Akim-Kotoku*, 147. For an archaeological investigation of such a cemetery on the outskirts of Eguago, called Atofosie, see Spiers, 'The Eguafo Kingdom', 117–22.
56. On the recycling of revenant lore into contemporary Ghanaian cinema, see Birgit Meyer, *Sensational Movies: Video, Vision and Christianity in Ghana* (Oakland, 2015), 199–204.
57. Ellis, *Tshi-Speaking Peoples*, 222–3.
58. Bellis, 'Archeology', 58–64.
59. Christaller, *Dictionary*, 525; Jehle, 'Soul, Spirit, Fate', 412.

Chapter 14. Writing and Reading about Death

1. *Gold Coast Times*, 18 Feb. 1882.
2. See Karin Barber, *The Anthropology of Texts, Persons and Publics: Oral and Written Culture in Africa and Beyond* (Cambridge, 2007).
3. Ivor Wilks, Nehemia Levtzion and Bruce Haight, *Chronicles from Gonja: A Tradition of West African Muslim Historiography* (Cambridge, 1986).
4. Jürgen Habermas, *The Structural Transformation of the Public Sphere*, translated by Thomas Burger (Cambridge, Mass., 1992 [orig. 1962]); Benedict Anderson, *Imagined Communities: Reflections on the Origin and Spread of Nationalism* (London, 1983).

5. Porter, *Flesh in the Age of Reason*, 211; see too Seale, *Constructing Death*, ch. 6 'Reporting Death'.

6. Kwesi Yankah, *Free Press in Traditional Society: The Cultural Foundations of Contemporary Ghana* (Accra, 1998), 5.

7. See David Kimble, *A Political History of Ghana: The Rise of Gold Coast Nationalism, 1850–1928* (Oxford, 1963); P. F. de Moraes Farias and Karin Barber, eds, *Self-Assertion and Brokerage: Early Cultural Nationalism in West Africa* (Birmingham, 1990).

8. Ten issues are reproduced on microfilm in the British Library; another six, the location of which is uncertain, are noted in K.A.B. Jones-Quartey, *History, Politics and Early Press in Ghana* (Accra, 1975).

9. Bannerman to Secretary of State for the Colonies, 11 July 1859, reproduced in ibid., facing 62.

10. Barber, *Anthropology of Texts*, 143.

11. Ibid., 112.

12. Carretta and Reese, *Philip Quaque*, Quaque to Rev. William Morice, 28 Jan. 1789.

13. Kimble, *Political History*, 63 and 146–7; Augustus Casely-Hayford and Richard Rathbone, 'Politics, Families and Freemasons in the Colonial Gold Coast', in J. F. Ade Ajayi and J.D.Y. Peel, eds, *People and Empires in African History: Essays in Memory of Michael Crowder* (Harlow, 1992).

14. Stephanie Newell, *The Power to Name: A History of Anonymity in Colonial West Africa* (Athens, Ohio, 2013).

15. *African Times*, 23 Nov. 1863, Tom Coffee to editor, 14 Oct. 1863.

16. Ibid., emphasis in original; the incident is reported in *Wesleyan Methodist Magazine* 8 (Sep. 1862), 'Visit of the Rev. W. West and the Rev. John Ossu Ansah to Kumasi', 858–62.

17. James Africanus B. Horton, *West African Countries and Peoples* (London, 1868, 2nd ed. Edinburgh, 1969); Kimble, *Political History*, 222–63.

18. See, e.g., *African Times*, 23 June 1864, 'Necromancy: Consulting the Dead'.

19. *African Times*, 23 Jan. 1864, 'Anamaboe Temperance Society'.

20. Winwood Reade, *African Sketch-Book*, vol. 2, 135.

21. Ibid, 135–6; on the Anomabo 'heresy', which was reincorporated into the Methodist Church in 1870, see too Debrunner, *History*, 158–9; Bartels, *Roots*, 82.

22. For the former, see *African Times*, 23 Jan. 1867, 'The Late Quao Dade, King of Aquapim'; 23 Nov. 1867, 'Death of King of Ashantee—Dreadful Slaughter'; 23 Jan. 1872, 'Human Sacrifices—Efforts by the Agent of the Fanti Confederation to Prevent Them'.

23. *African Times*, 23 Sep. 1869, emphasis in original.

24. TNA CO 96/16, Fitzpatrick to Grey, 4 July 1849.

25. *African Times*, 23 Dec. 1869, 'Death of John Aggery, Late King of Cape Coast'.

26. *African Times*, 23 Mar. 1869, 'Accra—Painful and Distressing Suicide'.

27. *African Times*, 24 Oct. 1870, 'The Late Joseph Smith of Cape Coast. A Mournful Case'.

28. *Gold Coast News*, 30 May 1885.

29. *Gold Coast Times*, 28 Oct. 1882. The Good Templars joined the Freemasons in establishing a lodge at Cape Coast in 1877, the Oddfellows in 1880, and the Grand Ancient Order of Foresters in 1882: Kimble, *Political History*, 147.

30. Compare the *Gold Coast News*, 13 June 1885, for a glowing report of the Masonic funeral of Chief Isaac Robertson of Cape Coast.

31. *Gold Coast Times*, 16 Nov. 1883, 'News of the Week'.

32. *Gold Coast News*, 27 June 1885.

33. *Western Echo*, 18 Nov. 1885, 'What Society Says'.

34. *Western Echo*, 28 Nov. 1885, emphasis in original. The colony's first census would be conducted in 1891.

35. *Western Echo*, 9 Dec. 1885.

36. See, e.g., Marion Kilson, ed., *Excerpts from the Diary of Kwaku Niri (alias J. Q. Hammond) 1884–1918* (Institute of African Studies, University of Ghana, Legon, 1967) and John E. Ocansey, *An African Trading; or, The Trials of William Narh Ocansey of Addah, West Coast of Africa, River Volta*, edited by Kwame Arhin (Institute of African Studies, University of Ghana, Legon, 1989 [orig. 1881]).

37. *Western Echo*, 17 Mar. 1886.

38. *Western Echo*, 24 Apr. 1886, 'The Late John Ogoo'.

39. *Western Echo*, 8 May 1886, 'The Late John Ogoo' and 'Philo-Medicus Answered'; *kenkey*: steamed soured cornbread, a staple of the coastal diet.

40. *Western Echo*, 16–30 July 1887.

41. *Western Echo*, 17–31 Aug. 1887.

42. See John Gray, *The Immortalization Commission: The Strange Quest to Cheat Death* (London, 2011).

43. *Western Echo*, 17–31 Aug. 1887, 'Death', and 16–30 Sep. 1887, 'Death, Cont.' and 'Is There a World of Spirits?'.

44. Ibid.

45. Newell, *Power to Name*, 20; see too Harrison, *Dominion of the Dead*, 124–41.

46. See, on the *omanhene* of Winneba, the *West African Herald*, 31 Mar. 1871, 'Deaths'; *Western Echo*, 6 Mar. 1886, 'Obituary. The Late James Robert Thompson'.

47. *Gold Coast Chronicle*, 17 May 1897. Dodowa: i.e., the 1826 battle of Katamanso.

48. *Gold Coast Chronicle*, 6 July 1897.

49. *Western Echo*, 10–27 Jan. 1887, 'Obituaries. King Attah of Cape Coast'.

50. Brown, *Gold Coast and Asianti Reader*, vol. 1, 165–6.

51. *Gold Coast Methodist Times*, 15 Sep. 1897, Ghartey to J. P. Brown, 28 July 1897.

52. Ibid., Ghartey to Revds J. A. Solomon and A. W. Parker, 28 July 1897. Solomon's son, Rev. S.R.B. Solomon (who later changed his name to S.R.B. Attoh-Ahuma) was editor of the *Methodist Times*.

53. Ibid., 'The Late King Ghartey IV'; see too *Gold Coast Leader*, 5 Sep. 1903 and 12 Sep. 1903, 'Glimpses of the Past', a profile of Ghartey's eldest daughter, Elizabeth, to whom he was especially close and who 'was the first called in council beside the dying bed' when the three letters were produced.

54. *Gold Coast Methodist Times*, 15 Sep. 1897, 'The Late King Ghartey IV'.

55. Ibid., 'Brief Sketch of the Life of the Late King Ghartey IV of Winnebah'.

Chapter 15. The Colony of Medicine

1. John Iliffe, *Africans: The History of a Continent* (3rd ed. Cambridge, 2017), 253; Shane Doyle, 'Demography and Disease', in John Parker and Richard Reid, eds, *The Oxford Handbook of Modern African History* (Oxford, 2013); J. C. Caldwell, 'Population Change', in Walter

Birmingham, I. Neustadt and E. N. Omaboe, eds, *A Study of Contemporary Ghana, Vol. 2: Some Aspects of Social Structure* (London, 1967); K. David Patterson, *Health in Colonial Ghana: Disease, Medicine, and Socio-Economic Change, 1900–1955* (Waltham, 1981); Étienne van de Walle, Gilles Pison and Mpembele Sala-Diakanda, *Mortality and Society in Sub-Saharan Africa* (Oxford, 1992).

2. Lee and Vaughan, 'Death and Dying', 347.

3. Whaley, *Mirrors of Mortality*, 11, citing Pierre Chaunu, *La mort à Paris: 16e, 17e, 18e siècles* (Paris, 1978).

4. John McManners, 'Death and the French Historians'.

5. Laqueur, *Work of the Dead*, 309; see too Merridale, *Night of Stone*.

6. Patterson, *Health in Colonial Ghana*, 85–6 and 90; see further K. David Patterson, 'Health in Urban Africa: The Case of Accra 1900–1940', *Social Science and Medicine* 13 B (1979).

7. *Manual of the International List of Causes of Death* (4th ed. Paris, 1931), retitled from its sixth edition in 1948 as the *Manual of the International Statistical Classification of Diseases, Injuries and Causes of Death* and known as the *ICD*. On the ICD's global use, see Glennys Howarth, 'The Demography of Dying', in Kellehear, *Study of Dying*.

8. Patterson, *Health in Colonial Ghana*, 96; Iliffe, *Africans*, 223–7.

9. J.W.S. Macfie, 'The Prevalent Diseases of the Gold Coast', *Transactions of the Royal Society of Tropical Medicine and Hygiene* 16 (1922).

10. K. David Patterson, 'The Influenza Epidemic of 1918–19 in the Gold Coast', *Journal of African History* 24 (1983), and *Health in Colonial Ghana*, 97; James W. Brown, 'Increased Intercommunication and Epidemic Disease in Early Colonial Ashanti', in Gerald W. Hartwig and K. David Patterson, eds, *Disease in African History: An Introductory Survey and Case Studies* (Durham, NC, 1978).

11. Patterson, *Health in Colonial Ghana*, 92.

12. TNA CO 96/598, Clifford to Milner, 17 Mar. 1919.

13. Stephen Addae, *History of Western Medicine in Ghana, 1880–1960* (Edinburgh, 1997), 148–58.

14. Patterson, *Health in Colonial Ghana*, 23–4 and 91–3.

15. Caldwell, 'Population Change', 88.

16. PRAAD Kumasi ARG 1/30/1/6 Chief Fetish Priest 'Abirewa', Ben Ampofo to DC, Kumasi, 'Some details about fitish [sic] Aberewa', n.d. [1907]; see Allman and Parker, *Tongnaab*, 125–41.

17. For the continent more widely, see Iliffe, *Africans*, 253.

18. Patterson, *Health in Colonial Ghana*, 69–71 and 133; *African Times*, 23 Dec. 1864, 24 Apr. 1871 and 23 Sep. 1871; *West African Herald*, 26 July 1871; TNA CO 96/205, Hodgson to Knutsford, 1 Oct 1889; PRAAD Kumasi ARG 13/2/1 Refusal of Chief of Ofinsu to vaccinate his people against Small Pox.

19. See J. D. La Fleur, *Fusion Foodways of Africa's Gold Coast in the Atlantic Era* (Leiden, 2012), 136–44.

20. Kellehear, *Social History of Dying*; Howarth, 'Demography of Dying', and Julie-Marie Strange, 'Historical Approaches to Dying', both in Kellehear, *Study of Dying*.

21. Patterson, *Health in Colonial Ghana*, 80.

22. TNA CO 96/180 Brandford Griffith to Holland, 5 Apr. 1887, enclosed: Report on the increased mortality among the Natives of Accra; Patterson, *Health in Colonial Ghana*, 81.

23. See Nancy Rose Hunt, 'Health and Healing', in Parker and Reid, *Oxford Handbook*.

24. Ruth J. Prince, 'Situating Health and the Public in Africa', in Ruth J. Prince and Rebecca Marsland, eds, *Making and Unmaking Public Health in Africa: Ethnographic and Historical Perspectives* (Athens, Ohio, 2016), 6; see too Megan Vaughan, *Curing their Ills: Colonial Power and African Illness* (London, 1991); David Arnold, ed, *Imperial Medicine and Indigenous Societies* (Manchester, 1988); cf. David Arnold, *Colonizing the Body: State Medicine and Epidemic Disease in Nineteenth-Century India* (Berkeley, 1993).

25. Hunt, 'Health and Healing', 384–6.

26. TNA CO 96/234, Brandford Griffith to Ripon, 12 June 1893, enclosure 15: Report on the Progress of the Medical Department from 1885 to 1892, by J. F. Easmon, 19 Dec. 1892.

27. Ibid, enclosure 19: List of Existing Cemeteries in the various districts of the Colony, n.d.

28. PRAAD Accra ADM 39/1/144 Cemeteries Quittah, 1911–43, DC Kibbi to CEP, 15 Feb. 1911.

29. Ibid., DC Kibbi to CEP, 1 Mar. 1911.

30. Ibid., DC Akuse to CEP, 1 Apr. 1911; see too DC Quittah to CEP, 28 June 1911.

31. PRAAD Cape Coast ADM 23/1/664 Births, Deaths and Burials, 1912–48, CCP to Chief Kofi Sackey, 8 Dec. 1915.

32. Ibid., MOH Cape Coast to CCP, 8 Apr. 1921.

33. Patterson, 'Health in Urban Accra', 356, citing *Gold Coast Independent*, n.d. [1928].

34. PRAAD Kumasi ARG 1/35/8 Births, Deaths and Burials, Senior Health Officer to CCA, 26 May 1931. 'Castle' weight: a reference to Christiansborg Castle in Osu, which became the seat of the colonial government.

35. TNA CO 96/602 Slater to Milner, 18 July 1919, enclosed: Report of the Committee ... Appointed to Consider the Births, Deaths and Burials Ordinance of 1912, n.d., and J. B. Alexander, acting Registrar of Births, Deaths and Burials, to Principal Medical Officer, 31 Mar. 1919.

36. PRAAD Kumasi ARG 1/1/121 Plague—Legislation concerning (Births, Deaths and Burials), 1924–6; PRAAD Accra ADM 56/1/167, Principal Registrar of Births, Deaths and Burials to CCNT, 8 June 1928.

37. TNA CO 96/724/2, Annual Summary and Report of the Principal Registrar of Births, Deaths and Burials, 1935.

38. PRAAD Kumasi ARG 6/1/15 Births, Deaths and Burials, 1934–49; ARG 6/1/78 Births, Deaths and Burials, 1949–53.

39. See PRAAD Accra CSO 11/16/83 Dead Bodies Removed from Chief's Cemetery, 1934; CSO 11/14/131 Orders for Exhumations of Bodies, 1930–35; CSO 11/14/333 Fees for Supervision of Exhumation of Bodies, 1941–5; CSO 11/14/334 Exhumation of Bodies, 1942; CSO 11/14/332 Orders for the Exhumation of Bodies, 1949.

40. PRAAD Kumasi ARG 6/1/15 Births, Deaths and Burials, 1934–49, S. R. Baxter to DC Kumasi, 25 Aug. 1934.

41. See, e.g., ibid., Kofi Donkor to Medical Officer of Health, Kumasi, 16 Oct. 1939.

42. *Gold Coast Leader*, 21 Oct. 1905.

43. See, e.g., PRAAD Accra SCT 22/10/3 Inquest Record Book, Sekondi, 1923–36; ADM 28/4/197 Inquest Record Book, Winneba, 1935–43; SCT 17/10/12 Inquest Record Book, Accra, 1942–3; PRAAD Kumasi ARG 1/27/24 Inquisitions, 1923–6; ARG 1/27/26 Inquests, 1926–37.

44. *Gold Coast Nation*, 11 Mar. 1915; see too *Gold Coast Leader*, 15 Apr. 1911, 'Burying a Pauper without Coffin'.

45. PRAAD Accra CSO 11/11/170 Air Conditioned Mortuaries, 1943; De Witte, *Long Live the Dead!*.

46. *West Africa Times*, 17 June 1931; PRAAD Accra CSO 11/1/141 Pauper Funerals, 1933–9; PRAAD Kumasi ARG 1/35/16 Burial and Cemeteries—Administration of by Kumasi Town Council, 1948.

47. *Gold Coast Leader*, 23 Oct. 1920, 'Why I Am Not Afraid to Die'.

48. *Times of West Africa*, 10 June 1933.

49. *Times of West Africa*, 14 Apr. 1934; see too ibid., 29 May 1934; *Gold Coast Times*, 2 June, 16 June and 23 June 1934.

50. *Gold Coast Times*, 13 Sep. 1930, 'African Roots, Barks and Leaves. Sunwunku Improved Native Medicine'; 27 June 1931, 'West African Herbalism'; 14 Jan. 1933, 'Secret Practices of Evil Disposed Persons. Poisoning', by J. A. Kwesi Aba; Allman and Parker, *Tongnaab*, 170–80.

51. *Gold Coast Times*, 6–13 Jan. 1934, 19 Jan. 1935, 18 May 1935 and 1 June 1935.

52. *Gold Coast Times*, 15 June 1935, 'In Defense of African Herbalists', emphasis in original; see too 28 Dec. 1935, 'Mr Kwesi Aaba and African Herbalism'.

53. Merridale, *Night of Stone*, 29–30; see too Arnold, *Colonizing the Body*.

Chapter 16. Wills and Dying Wishes

1. PRAAD Accra SCT 2/4/352, Will of Joseph Sackey, 12 June 1945, 40.

2. Chaunu, *La mort à Paris*; Michel Vovelle, *Piété baroque et déchristianisation en Provence au XVIIIe siècle* (Paris, 1973); see McManners, 'Death and the French Historians'.

3. Susan Kellogg and Matthew Restall, eds, *Dead Giveaways: Indigenous Testaments of Colonial Mesoamerica and the Andes* (Salt Lake City, 1998); Mark Christensen and Jonathan Truitt, eds, *Native Wills from the Colonial Americas: Dead Giveaways in a New World* (Salt Lake City, 2016).

4. PRAAD Accra ADM 1/2/421 Copies of Wills, Committee of Merchants Trading to Africa, 1792–1829.

5. Daaku, *Trade and Politics*, 98–9.

6. Harvey M. Feinberg, 'Africans and Europeans in West Africa: Elminas and Dutchmen on the Gold Coast during the Eighteenth Century', *Transactions of the American Philosophical Society* 79 (1989), 116–17.

7. TNA T70/31 Letter Book, 1762–73, Mutter to Committee, 20 July 1764, 96–102.

8. TNA T70/32 Letter Book, 1773–81, Mill to Committee, 7 May 1776, 32–5.

9. PRAAD Accra SCT 5/4/3 Civil and Record Book, Cape Coast, 1847–8, Will of James Francis Parker, 13 Feb. 1847, 93–4.

10. PRAAD Accra 2/4/3 Civil Record Book, Accra, 1865–7, Will of Barbara Meyer, 9 Feb. 1865, and Will of Chocho Baddoo, 17 June 1863.

11. PRAAD Accra SCT 5/4/20 Judicial Assessor's Note Book, 1849–50, *Mrs Quacoe v. Coffee Fynn*, 3 Jan. 1850, 72–3.

12. Ibid., *Incoom and others v. Amshia and others*, 9 Apr. 1849, n.p.

13. PRAAD Accra SCT 5/4/28 Judicial Assessor's Note Book, 1860–61, *Mrs John Hayfron v. Quamina Adoo*, 8 Oct. 1860, 106–11.

14. John Mensah Sarbah, *Fanti Customary Laws* (London, 1897, 3rd ed. 1968), 96–7. For subsequent opinions, see N. A. Ollennu, *The Law of Testate and Intestate Succession in Ghana* (London, 1966), 270–84, and Samuel Azu Crabbe, *Law of Wills in Ghana* (Accra, 1998), 1–51.

15. Rattray, *Ashanti Law and Constitution*, 338–9.

16. Rattray, *Ashanti*, 239.

17. Rattray, *Ashanti Law and Constitution*, 333; see too Wilks, *Forests of Gold*, 149–50.

18. Rattray, *Ashanti Law and Constitution*, 339; on this, see Bosman, *New and Accurate Description*, 202–3.

19. Cruickshank, *Eighteen Years*, vol. 2, 213–14.

20. Rattray, *Ashanti Law and Constitution*, 332.

21. Crabbe, *Law of Wills*, 52–73.

22. On this landmark case, *In re: Isaac Anaman, deceased*, see Sarbah, *Fanti Customary Laws*, 221–7.

23. Cited in Roger Gocking, 'Competing Systems of Inheritance before the British Courts of the Gold Coast Colony', *International Journal of African Historical Studies* 23 (1990), 611–12; see too PRAAD Accra ADM 11/1/1457 Marriage, 1905–22.

24. PRAAD Accra SCT 2/4/349, Will of Samuel Bannerman, 20 Feb. 1894, 22–5. All subsequent citations from the SCT 2/4 (Accra) and 5/4 (Cape Coast) volumes in this sequence are from PRAAD Accra.

25. SCT 5/4/264, Will of Samuel Hagan Yawson, 13 June 1927, 200–203.

26. SCT 2/4/349, Will of William Quartey, 4 Apr. 1894, 91–2.

27. Ibid., Will of Ali, 12 Dec. 1901, 316–17.

28. Frank Trentmann, *Empire of Things: How We Became a World of Consumers, from the Fifteenth Century to the Twenty-First* (New York, 2016), 104.

29. SCT 5/4/264, Will of Moses Koom Dadzie, 26 May 1935, 398–400, this and following emphases in original.

30. SCT 5/4/264, Will of John Hammond, 13 Nov. 1934, 393–5.

31. SCT 2/4/357, Will of Samuel George Watson, 3 Apr. 1957, 43–7.

32. SCT 2/4/354, Will of Adjieter, 26 Sep. 1947, 196–8.

33. SCT 2/4/349, Will of George Frank Cleland, 17 Feb. 1885, 1–7.

34. SCT 5/4/265, Will of Edward Peter Dontoh, 13 Dec. 1939, 242.

35. SCT 5/4/262, Will of Samuel Edward Sago, 18 Mar. 1911, 111–12.

36. SCT 5/4/264, Will of John Gershom Koomson, 4 Feb. 1931, 336–8.

37. Ibid., Will of Joseph Simons Peter Molenaar, 31 Aug. 1931, 304–5.

38. SCT 5/4/265, Will of Joseph Christophorus Amuah Senior alias Kwamin Amua, 20 Jan. 1941, 207.

39. Ibid., Will of Godfrey Sam, 29 July 1937, 151–6.

40. SCT 5/4/264, Will of Kofi Baffoe, 26 Mar. 1917, 194–5.

41. SCT 5/4/265, Will of James Jackson Kuofi, 14 Mar. 1936, 6.

42. SCT 5/4/266, Will of Kwesi Gyafu, 2 Dec. 1946, 153.

43. SCT 5/4/263, Will of Ambah Fynnebah, dd. June 1914, n.p.

44. SCT 5/4/266, Will of Essie Yennebah, 29 Apr. 1946, 69.

45. SCT 5/4/263, Will of Joseph Mensah, 13 May 1916, 104–6.

46. SCT 5/4/265, Will of Ambah Sackah, 6 Oct. 1935, 17–19.

47. SCT 2/4/354, Will of Comfort Amegatcher aka Mrs Comfort Carbutey, 3 Apr. 1946, 132–3.

48. SCT 2/4/351, Will of James Captain Glover, 20 Sep. 1937, 239–44.

49. PRAAD Kumasi ARG 18/1/7, Will of Adjuah Awotwi, 15 July 1949, 237.

50. SCT 5/4/264, Will of Albert Augustus Bainn, 1 July 1929, 339–40.

51. SCT 2/4/352, Will of Kwaku Manukure, 14 Aug. 1945, 130–33.

52. PRAAD Kumasi ARG 18/1/7, Will of Yaw Krah, 17 Feb. 1951, 204.

53. PRAAD Kumasi ARG 1/23/5 Albert William Sey, 1917.

54. SCT 2/4/354, Will of William Nee Ademah Quaye, 19 Oct. 1948, 152–8.

55. T. C. McCaskie, 'The Last Will and Testament of Kofi Sraha: A Note on Accumulation and Inheritance in Colonial Asante', *Ghana Studies* 2 (1999), 181.

56. Jean Allman and Victoria Tashjian, *'I Will Not Eat Stone': A Women's History of Colonial Asante* (Portsmouth, NH, 2000), 105–22; Gocking, 'Competing Systems'.

57. PRAAD Accra CSO 21/1/180 Oral Death-Bed Disposition of Property (Samansew), 1940–43; PRAAD Kumasi ARG 2/2/46 Akan Customary Law of Succession—Inquiry, 1947–61.

58. SCT 5/4/182 Divisional Court Civil Record Book, Cape Coast, Vol. 79, *William Richardson v. Kwesi Mensah*, 27 June 1940, 1–14; Ollennu, *Law of Testate*; Crabbe, *Law of Wills*.

59. Fortes, *Kinship*, 164.

Chapter 17. Northern Frontiers

1. S.W.D.K. Gandah, *Gandah-Yir: The House of the Brave. The Biography of a Northern Ghanaian Chief (ca. 1872–1950)*, edited by Carola Lentz (Legon, 2009); see too S.W.D.K. (Kum) Gandah's autobiography, *The Silent Rebel*, edited by Jack Goody (Accra, 2004).

2. Goody, *Death*; see too idem, *The Social Organization of the LoWilli* (London, 1957, 2nd ed. Oxford, 1967), and *The Expansive Moment: The Rise of Social Anthropology in Britain and Africa, 1918–1970* (Cambridge, 1995), 124.

3. Goody, *Death*, 331.

4. Gandah, *Gandah-Yir*, 10.

5. Ibid., 12 and 18. *Bagre*: the ancestor cult.

6. Goody, *Death*, 115.

7. Gandah, *Gandah-Yir*, 30.

8. Ibid., 57.

9. Ibid., 50–54; H. Debrunner, *Witchcraft in Ghana: A Study on the Belief in Destructive Witches and Its Effect on the Akan Tribes* (Accra, 1959), 108; Allman and Parker, *Tongnaab*, 136–41.

10. Gandah, *Gandah-Yir*, 52–3.

11. Goody, *Death*, 51–2 and 62–3; Gandah, *Gandah-Yir*, 106.

12. Goody, *Death*, 115.

13. Gandah, *Gandah-Yir*, 115; see too Goody, *Death*, 224 and 238–40.

14. Freeman, *Journal*, 132.

15. R. S. Rattray, *The Tribes of the Ashanti Hinterland* (Oxford, 1932); see Allman and Parker, *Tongnaab*, 25–37.

16. PRAAD Accra ADM 56/1/200 Wa District Native Affairs, 1914–26, St. John Eyre-Smith to Provincial Commissioner, Northern Province, 15 Aug. 1921, enclosed: Report by Chief of Burifo; see too ADM 61/5/8 Lorha Informal Diary, 1917–21, 9 Aug. 1920, Burifo Intelligence, 401.

17. A. W. Cardinall, *The Gold Coast, 1931* (Accra, 1931), 219; Patterson, *Health in Colonial Ghana*, 91.

18. For the northwest, see Goody, *Social Organization*, and Carola Lentz, *Ethnicity and the Making of History in Northern Ghana* (Edinburgh, 2006); for the northeast, Allman and Parker, *Tongnaab*.

19. TNA CO 96/493, Robertson to Crewe, 19 Jan. 1910, Native Law and Customs; Meyer Fortes, *The Dynamics of Clanship among the Tallensi* (London, 1945), *The Web of Kinship among the Tallensi* (London, 1949), and *Religion, Morality and the Person: Essays on Tallensi Religion*, edited by Jack Goody (Cambridge, 1987); on Fortes's research, see Allman and Parker, *Tongnaab*, 182–216.

20. See TNA CO 96/493, Robertson to Crewe, 19 Jan 1910, enclosed: 'Mamprussi', by E. A. Irvine, 28 Dec. 1908; see too 'Wa or Wala', by B. Moutray-Read, 22 Nov. 1908.

21. Goody, *Death*, 213; see too Fortes, *Web of Kinship*, 233–5.

22. See, e.g., PRAAD Accra ADM 56/5/13 Lawra-Tumu District Informal Diary, 1923–30, 1 Mar., 3 Mar., 23 Apr. and 20 May 1924.

23. PRAAD Accra ADM 56/1/167 Cemeteries, Northern Territories, 1913–46, F. Harper, Principal Medical Officer, to CCNT, 5 Sep. 1914.

24. Ibid., Armitage to Colonial Secretary, 9 Oct. 1914 and 3 May 1915.

25. Ibid., B. Moutray-Read, acting CCNT, to Provincial Commissioners, 16 July 1915.

26. Ibid., Acting CCNT to Colonial Secretary, 6 Oct. 1915.

27. Fortes, *Web of Kinship*, 178.

28. PRAAD Accra ADM 56/1/167, Provincial Commissioner, North Western Province to CCNT, 19 Aug. 1915; PRAAD Tamale NRG 3/2/1, History and Custom of the Mamprussi Tribe, 1922.

29. PRAAD Tamale NRG 8/2/34, Commissioner of the Southern Province to Assistant Director of Medical Service, 16 June 1930.

30. Rattray, *Tribes*, 184–6; Fortes, *Religion*, 266–7.

31. PRAAD Accra ADM 56/1/167, J. Byrne, Medical Officer, Salaga, to DC Salaga, 18 Oct 1927; Principal Registrar of Births, Deaths and Burials to CCNT, 8 June 1928.

32. Ibid., CCNT to Registrar of Births, Deaths and Burials, 6 Nov. 1928. For the consequent association of hyenas with the supernatural realm, see John Parker, 'Northern Gothic: Witches, Ghosts and Werewolves in the Savanna Hinterland of the Gold Coast, 1900s–1950s', *Africa* 76 (2006).

33. PRAAD Accra ADM 56/1/167, DC Gonja to CCNT, 21 Oct. 1935.

34. Ibid., DC Mamprussi to CCNT, 10 Jan. 1939.

35. Ibid., DC Dagomba to CCNT, 11 Feb. 1939.

36. Ibid., DC Tumu to Provinical Commissioner, North Western Province, 5 Aug. 1915.

37. See Igor Kopytoff, 'Ancestors as Elders in Africa', *Africa* 41 (1971).

38. See Allman and Parker, *Tongnaab*; John Parker, 'The Dynamics of Fieldwork among the Talensi: Meyer Fortes in Northern Ghana, 1934–7', *Africa* 83 (2013).

39. See Allman and Parker, *Tongnaab*, 107–14.

40. Rattray, *Tribes*, 184–214 passim, esp. 203–7.
41. Fortes, *Web of Kinship*, 229–30.
42. Ibid., 173, and see 171–86 passim.
43. Fortes, *Religion*, 36; see too Allman and Parker, *Tongnaab*, 185–7.
44. Fortes, *Web of Kinship*, 179.
45. Ibid., 173–4.
46. Michael Taussig, *The Magic of the State* (New York, 1997), 3.

Chapter 18. Reordering the Royal Dead

1. PRAAD Kumasi ARG 6/2/7 Complaints against Kumasihene, Kofi Sraha and others to CCA, 11 Oct. 1930.

2. See William Tordoff, *Ashanti under the Prempehs, 1888–1935* (London, 1965); Emmanuel Akyeampong, 'Christianity, Modernity and the Weight of Tradition in the Life of *Asantehene* Agyeman Prempeh I, c. 1888–1931', *Africa* 69 (1999); Boahen et al., *History of Ashanti Kings*; T. C. McCaskie, 'Anglicanism and Asantehene Agyeman Prempeh', in Toyin Falola, ed., *Christianity and Social Change in Africa: Essays in Honor of J.D.Y. Peel* (Durham, NC, 2005).

3. Annual Report on Ashanti, 1924–5, quoted in Tordoff, *Ashanti*, 186.
4. Akyeamehene to CCA, 8 Apr. 1925, quoted in ibid., 206.
5. Boahen et al., *History of Ashanti Kings*, 175–82.
6. Ivor Wilks, 'Agyeman Prempeh as Author: Textual History', in ibid., 60.
7. See, e.g., PRAAD Kumasi ARG 1/2/1/68 Chief Kwesi Busumprah—Asking Permission to remove remains of his Fore-fathers, 1910.
8. Patterson, *Health in Colonial Ghana*, 49.
9. Annual Report on Ashanti, 1924–5, quoted in Tordoff, *Ashanti*, 217.
10. See, e.g., PRAAD Kumasi ARG 1/2/1/49 Mankessim Stool, 1907.
11. TNA CO 96/273, Hodgson to Chamberlain, 8 May 1896.
12. PRAAD Kumasi ARG 1/2/25/1, Chief Akwesie Induama to CCA, 24 June 1909, and Eccuah Effrieyi to CCA, 31 Aug. 1910.
13. BMA D-1/95, Annual Report on Kumase, by N. V. Asare, quoted in McCaskie, *State and Society*, 70.
14. Boahen et al., *History of Ashanti Kings*, 182.
15. PRAAD Kumasi ARG 1/2/25/5 Kumasi Sacred Burial Places, and ARG 1/35/5 Native Princes Cemeteries; Rattray, *Religion and Art*, 144–6; Boahen et al., *History of Ashanti Kings*, 182; McCaskie, *State and Society*, 148–50, which offers a different etymology for *(a)hemanho*: 'do not give offence to the king'.
16. Bowdich, *Mission*, 289.
17. Winwood Reade, *The Story of the Ashantee Campaign* (London, 1874), 353–4; *African Times*, 1 Sep. 1876, 'Journey to Kumasi, the Capital of Ashanti. Human Sacrifices'.
18. R. S. S. Baden-Powell, *The Downfall of Prempeh: A Diary of Life with the Native Levy in Ashanti 1895–96* (London, 1896), 130–31.
19. Rattray, *Religion and Art*, 144–6.
20. *Official Catalogue of the Royal United Service Museum*, complied by Lieut.-Colonel Sir Arthur Leetham (London, 1908), 160.

21. Tordoff, *Ashanti*, 205–6.
22. Rattray, *Religion and Art*, 186.
23. Ibid., 112–14.
24. PRAAD Kumasi ARG 1/2/25/5, Chief Osei Tutu and others to Provincial Commissioner, 23 Oct. 1922, and Provincial Commissioner to Building Inspector, n.d. [Dec. 1922].
25. PRAAD Kumasi ARG 1/35/5, European Building Inspector to Police Magistrate, 7 Jan. 1924.
26. Ibid., Head Chief Kwame Kyim and others to CCA, 16 July 1924.
27. PRAAD Kumasi ARG 3/1/25 Cemeteries at Obuasi, 1926–32, E. Prempeh to DC, 11 Jan. 1927; see too ARG 1/35/6 Chiefs Cemeteries, P. S. Selwyn-Clarke, Senior Sanitary Officer, to CCA, 6 Jan. 1927.
28. PRAAD Kumasi ARG 3/1/25, F. Jackson, acting CCA, to Senior Sanitary Officer, 28 June 1927.
29. Kumasihene to DC Kumasi, 27 Nov. 1927, quoted in Boahen et al., *History of Ashanti Kings*, 182–3.
30. Ibid; see too PRAAD Kumasi ARG 1/2/25/8 Kumasihene's Cemetery / Asantehene's Cemetery, 1927–1940, Kumasihene to DC, 9 Jan. 1928.
31. Asare, 'Asante Abasem', 51–2; McCaskie, *State and Society*, 78, 175–7 and 370.
32. PRAAD Kumasi ARG 1/2/25/8, CCA to Colonial Secretary, 31 Mar. 1928.
33. PRAAD Kumasi ARG 6/2/8 Kumasihene's Affairs, 1929–33, Kumasihene to DC, 11 Nov. 1929.
34. PRAAD Kumasi ARG 1/2/24/20 Bodies of Ashanti Notables, 1930–37, Kumasihene to DC, 6 Feb. 1931.
35. Wilks, *Asante*, 369, citing Akua Afriyie to CCA, 14 May 1908.
36. PRAAD Kumasi ARG 6/2/8, Superintendent of Public Works, Seychelles, to CCA, 9 Oct. 1929, and Kumasihene to DC, 7 Feb. 1930; ARG 3/2/73 Remains of Ashanti Royal Personages; Boahen et al., *History of Ashanti Kings*, 183–4.
37. PRAAD Kumasi ARG 1/2/25/8, Kumasihene to CCA, 12 July 1929, and CCA to Colonial Secretary, 2 Aug. 1929.
38. Ibid., Kumasihene to Amanhene, n.d., in CCA to Commissioner of the Western Province, 12 Sep. 1929.
39. PRAAD Kumasi ARG 6/1/11 Kumasi Mausoleum, Ejisuhene to DC Kumasi, 9 Dec. 1929.
40. PRAAD Accra ADM 11/1/1370 Brass Basin removed from the Burial place of Ashanti Kings, E. Prempeh to CCA, 17 July 1930.
41. Ibid., 'History of the Bantama Brass Pan', by Edward Prempeh, 29 August 1930, which is reproduced in Boahen et al., *History of Ashanti Kings*, 185–9.
42. PRAAD Accra ADM 11/1/1370, CCA to Colonial Secretary, 14 Nov. 1930, and Governor to Colonial Secretary, 27 Dec. 1930; Rattray, *Religion and Art*, 113–14.
43. PRAAD Kumasi ARG 1/2/24/23 The Great Funeral Custom—Kumasi.
44. *West Africa Times*, 30 Mar. 1931, 'Great Ashanti State Funeral'.
45. *Ashanti Stool Histories*, AS.54 Bantama-Baamu, and AS.91 Baamu.
46. Agyeman Prempeh to DC, 22 Feb. 1931, cited in Boahan et al., *History of Ashanti Kings*, 190.
47. There are alternative accounts of the origins of the *aya kese*. Rattray, *Religion and Art*, 114, noted that it was, 'according to a tradition, captured from the Sefwi'. Akyeampong, 'Christianity',

302–3, and *History of Ashanti Kings*, 53–4, speculates that it might have been the 'huge copper dish' which 'History of Ashanti Kings' records was sent by Denkyirahene Ntim Gyakari to Osei Tutu with the demand that it be filled with gold—the rejection of which triggered the war culminating in Asante independence. The four brass lions on its rim are not in Akan figurative style, suggesting that they, at least, may be of foreign—possibly North African—manufacture.

48. PRAAD Accra ADM 11/1/1342 Edward Prempeh—Omanhene of Kumasi, 'Obituary', published in *Gold Coast Government Gazette* no. 32 of 1931. In contrast to reportage in the Gold Coast press, this official obituary makes no mention of his life before 1926: see *West Africa Times*, 13 May and 15 May 1931.

49. McCaskie, 'Anglicanism', 509–10.

50. *Gold Coast Times*, 11 July 1931, 'In Memoriam. Nana Edward Fredua-Agyeman Prempeh, Kumasihene (by an Ashanti)'.

51. PRAAD Accra ADM 11/1/1342, Taylor to Colonial Secretary, 31 May 1931.

52. Ibid.

53. St John Evans's account was published in *Golden Shore* 6 (1931), the journal of the Anglican Diocesan Association of Accra, and is reproduced in McCaskie, 'Anglicanism', 511–14.

54. Ibid.; see too *West Africa Times*, 18 May 1931, '20,000 Persons Witness Prempeh's Official Burial. Blood-Curdling Contortions with Swords and Guns. Song that Chilled the Atmosphere. Where is Prempeh's Body?'.

55. St John Evans, in McCaskie, 'Anglicanism', 514; see too *Gold Coast Times*, 11 July 1931.

56. *West Africa Times*, 15 May 1931, 'The Burial of Prempeh', explained to its readers the double interment, first of the body and then of its 'uncorrupted part' at what was still assumed to be Bantama. MAG 1/3/3A, Kumasihene Agyeman Prempeh II to DC, 1 Aug. 1931, notes the eightieth-day custom, but there is no explicit record of the re-articulation of the royal bones.

57. PRAAD Accra ADM 11/1/1342, Report on the Great Funeral Custom of the Late Nana Edward Agyeman Prempeh I, Kumasihene, by J.W.K. Appiah, 11 June 1932, published by the Gold Coast government as *Report on the Observance of the Funeral Custom of the Late Kumasihene* (Accra, 1933).

58. PRAAD Accra ADM 11/1/1342, Newlands to Colonial Secretary, 30 June 1932.

Chapter 19. Making Modern Deathways

1. Richard Wright, *Black Power* (London, 1954); see too Kevin K. Gaines, *American Africans in Ghana: Black Expatriates and the Civil Rights Era* (Chapel Hill, 2006), ch. 2 'Richard Wright in Ghana'.

2. Wright, *Black Power*, 128–32; on these parades, see too *Times of West Africa*, 2 Nov. 1933, 'Our Custom of Burying the Dead: Some Dangerous, Meaningless and Unchangeable Aspects'.

3. Regula Tschumi, *The Buried Treasures of the Ga: Coffin Art in Ghana* (Berne, 2008), 56; Thierry Secretan, *Going into Darkness: Fantastic Coffins from Africa* (London, 1995).

4. Ariès, *Western Attitudes towards Death*, 1.

5. Van der Geest, 'Funerals for the Living', 119; De Witte, *Long Live the Dead!*, 78.

6. PP 1890 XLVIII [C.5897–40] *Economic Agriculture on the Gold Coast, 1899*, 10–11; the commission which drew up the report included the Euro-African businessmen W. F. Hutchinson and J. P. Brown.

7. Quoted in David Cannadine, 'War and Death, Grief and Mourning in Modern Britian', in Whaley, *Mirrors of Mortality*, 189–92; see too Strange, *Death, Grief and Poverty*.

8. *Gold Coast Leader*, 25 Apr. 1903.

9. *Gold Coast Leader*, 4 July 1903.

10. *Gold Coast Leader*, 19 Sep. 1903, 'A "Carousing" or Custom'.

11. PRAAD Accra ADM 11/1/43 Funeral Customs, minute by W. Robertson, SNA, 28 Jan. 1909.

12. Ibid., Sarbah to Robertson, 15 June 1910.

13. Ibid., minute by Rodger, n.d. [but 1 Feb. 1911].

14. Ibid., Griffin to Lamond, 6 Oct. 1911.

15. Ibid. Griffin to SNA, 5 Oct. 1911.

16. Ibid., CWP to SNA, 3 Apr. 1912.

17. Ibid., J. T. Furley, CCP, to SNA, 5 June 1912; see too PRAAD Cape Coast ADM 23/1/197 Native Customs, 1911–1950.

18. PRAAD Accra ADM 11/1/43, Extract from letter from Provincial Commissioners, 11 July 1912.

19. The Basel Mission was expelled during the First World War and its congregations taken over by the Presbyterian Church, under whose auspices the clergy underwent rapid Africanization.

20. John M. Hanson, *The Ahmadiyya in the Gold Coast: Muslim Cosmopolitans in the British Empire* (Bloomington, 2017), 185–6; on the period from the 1950s, see Ousman Murzik Kobo, *Unveiling Modernity: Twentieth-Century West African Islamic Reforms* (Leiden, 2012).

21. Erin Haney, *Photography and Africa* (London, 2010), 142.

22. PRAAD Cape Coast ADM 23/1/134 Cape Coast Native Affairs, 1907–16, letter from DC, 4 Feb. 1909.

23. See PRAAD Kumasi ARG 19/2/4 Cantonment Magistrate's Court, Kumasi, Civil Record Book, 1906–8, *Chief Akwasi Adidai v. Kobina Owusu*, 21 Jan. 1907, 132–7, and ARG 1/1/15 Enquiry on certain alleged indecent dances, 1907.

24. See *Gold Coast Times*, 2 Apr. 1932, 'Brass Coffin for West African Chief'.

25. David W. Brokensha, *Social Change at Larteh, Ghana* (Oxford, 1966), 196.

26. PRAAD Kumasi ARG 1/35/6, Medical Officer of Health to CCA, 12 Aug. 1929.

27. Haney, *Photography*, 145–6.

28. *Gold Coast Times*, 2–9 Feb. 1935, 'Effigy of late "Chief" Anamua'.

29. PRAAD Accra SCT 2/5/6 Divisional Court, Accra, Criminal Record Book Vol. 12, 1905–1907, *Rex v. Adeshina*, 11 July 1905.

30. Wild, 'Baked Clay Heads', 3.

31. PRAAD Kumasi ARG 1/26/3/12 Consumption of Liquor at Funeral Customs, Kumasihene E. Prempeh, Queen Mother Quardo Yeadom and others to DC Kumasi, 1 June 1928.

32. Ibid., Kwadjo Apaw, Omanhene of Agona, to DC Kumasi, 20 Apr. 1928.

33. Kwame Arhin, 'A Note on the Asante *Akonkofo*: A Non-literate Sub-elite, 1900–1930', *Africa* 56 (1986).

34. PRAAD Kumasi ARG 1/26/3/12, 'Regulation of Funeral Customs ... Division Bye-Laws', n.d.

35. Emmanuel Akyeampong, *Drink, Power and Cultural Change: A Social History of Alcohol in Ghana, c. 1800 to Recent Times* (Portsmouth, NH, 1996), 90–92.

36. PRAAD Kumasi ARG 1/26/3/12, Colonial Secretary to CCA, 8 Sep. 1928.

37. Ibid., Commissioner of Eastern Province to CCA, 9 May 1928.

38. Ibid., Commissioner of Western Province to CCA, 21 Nov. 1928.

39. PRAAD Accra ADM 11/1/1039 Regulation of Funeral Customs Byelaws.

40. PRAAD Kumasi ARG 1/2/26/4, Minutes of the First Session of the Ashanti Confederacy Council, 6 June–17 June 1935, 4–5.

41. Ibid., 15.

42. Ibid., 16.

43. PRAAD Accra CSO 21/6/84 Funeral Customs, 1943; PRAAD Kumasi ARG 2/1/3 Funeral, 1961–2; MRO Kumasi MAG 1/1/245 Funeral Celebration, 1953–78 and MAG 1/2/367 Native Custom; for a further attempt in Asante in 1998, see De Witte, *Long Live the Dead!*, 160–61.

44. On Asante, where the programme of the one-year funeral celebration for Agyeman Prempeh in 1932 was remembered as the catalyst for this fashion, see McCaskie, 'Writing, Reading, and Printing Death'.

45. De Witte, *Long Live the Dead!*; Sjaak van der Geest, 'Between Death and Funeral: Mortuaries and the Exploitation of Liminality in Kwahu, Ghana', *Africa* 76 (2006).

46. Nketia, *Drumming*, 58–9.

47. PRAAD Accra ADM 11/1/1436 Cooperative Societies in the Gold Coast.

48. K. A. Busia, *Report on a Social Survey of Sekondi-Takoradi* (London. 1950), 74–9.

49. Ibid., 108.

50. *Gold Coast Nation*, 4 May 1918, 'Native Christian Customs for the Dead', by K. Tarpim.

51. *Gold Coast Times*, 18 Jan. 1930, 'The Passing of a Chieftainess'.

52. S. Gyasi Nimako, *The Christian and Funerals* (Cape Coast, 1954); see too *Times of West Africa*, 12 Oct. 1933, 'Memorial Services. The Heathen and Christian Forms'.

53. Nimako, *The Christian*, 9 and 41.

54. Ibid., 78.

55. Ibid., 70; see too *Gold Coast Nation*, 4 May 1918; *Gold Coast Times*, 23 May 1931, 'Funeral Custom'.

56. MRO Kumasi MAG 1/1/274, Proposals on Funeral Customs by the Standing Committee of the Kumasi Traditional Council, n.d. [1974–5]; on the ongoing importance of *kuna* rites in postcolonial Akuapem, see Michelle Gilbert, 'Vengeance as Illusion and Reality: The Case of the Battered Wife', *Man*, new series 29 (1994).

57. Kwame Anthony Appiah, *In My Father's House: Africa in the Philosophy of Culture* (New York, 1992), 7–8.

58. MRO MAG 1/3/8 Members of Royal Family—death of.

59. See, e.g., Meyer, *Translating the Devil*; Bernault, *Colonial Transactions*; Paul Gifford, *Christianity, Development and Modernity in Africa* (London, 2015).

60. Joseph Appiah, *Joe Appiah: The Autobiography of an African Patriot* (New York, 1990), 368.

61. Appiah, *In My Father's House*, 181.

Conclusion

1. Kyei, *Our Days Dwindle*, 60–61.
2. Assmann, *Death and Salvation*, 1 and 9.
3. Verdery, *Political Lives of Dead Bodies*, 108; Laqueur, *Work of the Dead*, 1.
4. Seeman, *Death in the New World*, 4.
5. Richard Cobb, *Death in Paris, 1795–1801* (Oxford, 1978).
6. Farge, *Fragile Lives*, 187; see too Cobb, *Death in Paris*, 90; Harrison, *Dominion of the Dead*, 130.
7. Kyei, *Our Days Dwindle*, xix.

INDEX

Abena Baidu, 210–12, 226–27
Aberewa cult, 249, 258
Abetifi, *114*, 252
abirempon, 76, 78, 79, 82–83
Aborigines' Rights Protection Society, 242–43
abosom, 19, 20, 22, 40, 44, 114, 118, 119, 142, 147, 149, 152, 157, 178, 181–83, 184, 186
Aboya, Victor, 288–89
abrafo. See executioners
abusua, 34, 46, 214, 261; funerals and, 61, 66, 270, 325; inheritance and, 265, 275–76
abusua kuruwa (lineage funerary pot), 98–100, 306–7
Accra, 2, 3, 5, 17, 86, 88, 117, 174; cemeteries in, 191, 203–9; certification of death in, 246; climate of, 188, 204; as colonial capital, 196, 203–9, 253; funerals and mortuary customs at, 63, 67, 69, 73, 97, 115, 135–36, 177, 194, 213, 223–24, 308–9; house burial in, 191–92, 203–9, 223; maternal health in, 248, 252; merchant elite of, 58, 59, 130, 235, 270; poison and, 156, 159–62; the press in, 231–32; smallpox and, 249; wills and, 261, 268, 273–74. See also Ga peoples
Ada, 251
adae ceremonies, 29, 149–50, 298, 300, 302, 326–27
Adanme peoples, 126
Adanse, 46, 93, 103
Adoma Akosua (Asantehemaa 1809–19), 164–66

Adoui, 32–34
adultery, 44, 158, 168, 210–11, 216–17, 220
adumfo. See executioners
aduru. See medicine
Adwoa Awotwi, 273–74
Adwowaa Bemba, 214, 227
Afo Daday, 241
Afosuah Attah, 264–65, 267
African American mortuary cultures, 59, 111, 126–27, 132, 323–24
African nationalism, 201, 235, 236, 238, 243, 308–9; culture and, 231, 236–37, 313, 323–24
afterlife, 13, 22, 34–41, 73, 128, 129–30, 326
afterworld, 35, 37, 81, 212, 219, 310; decapitation and, 111; location of, 39–40, 50–51
Afua Kobi (Asantehemaa c.1859–83), 89, 221–22, 300
Afua Sapon (Asantehemaa c.1826–59), 90, 220–22
Aggery (*omanhene* of Cape Coast d. 1814), 159
Aggery, Joe (*omanhene* of Cape Coast d. 1851), 263–64
Aggery, John (*omanhene* of Cape Coast d. 1869), 234, 242
Agogo, 326
Agona, 97–98, 104, 112, 316
Agona Akyempim, 57
Agribah, Madame, 238
agriculture, 42, 46, 76, 125. See also cocoa economy
Agyeman Badu, 292, 301

Agyeman Prempeh (Asantehene 1888–1931), 46, 47, 210, 279, 291–307, 317–19, 320; death and funeral of, 101, 304–7; 'The History of Ashanti Kings' and, 46–48, 101–2, 103, 104, 291, 302, 306
Ahanta, 107–8
ahemaa, 68, 88, 89–90, 104, 272, 296, 299, 304–5
Ajitey, 269
Ajumaku, 96, 115, 168
Akan kingdoms, 1, 23, 42; formation of, 42–57; funerary cultures of, 86–87, 194, 291–307; human sacrifice and, 139–54; tabulation of time in, 297–98. *See also individual kingdoms*
Akan language. *See* Twi language
Akan peoples: identity of, 7–8, 126; curation of relics and, 103–23; funerary cultures of, 60–75, 92–106, 291–307, 308–30; personhood and, 26–41; religious belief and practices of, 9, 17, 32; savanna zone and, 279–81; state-building by, 1, 17–18, 42–57, 76; trade and, 12–16, 42, 76; wealth and, 76–91
akomfo, 42–43, 49–51, 57, 157, 167–68, 169, 170, 180–83, 184, 224–25. *See also* Komfo Anokye
akrafo, 37, 100, 114, 131, 148
Akron, 112, 116
Akua Afriyie, 295, 300
Akuapem kingdom, 37, 159, 174–75, 178–79, 183, 234, 251, 274
Akuropon, 174–75, 178–79, 180, 183
Akwamu kingdom, 23, 42, 48–49, 86, 112, 113–14, 117, 124, 128, 130
akyeame, 44, 80, 123
Akyem kingdoms, 43, 53, 86, 112, 115, 117, 122, 124, 130, 140. *See also individual kingdoms*
Akyem Abuakwa, 81, 100–101, 167, 183–89, 225, 252, 276, 302, 314
Akyem Bosome, 224
Akyem Kotoku, 61, 99–101, 129–30, 183–84, 224
alcohol: afterlife and, 130; imports of, 32–33, 51, 106, 110, 125, 316; mortuary customs and, 58, 59, 63, 66, 81, 97, 108, 114, 116, 118, 135, 136, 190, 209, 238, 271; opposition to use of, 198–99, 204, 232–33, 270, 273, 314–15, 318–19 (*see also* temperance movement); palm wine, 21, 71, 312; poison and, 171; ritual use of, 160, 276
Allman, Jean, 288, 330
amanhene: death of, 33–34, 43, 44, 68, 187–89, 242–43, 293, 304–7; funerals and, 83; funeral celebrations of, 60, 99–102, 229, 295, 304–7; indirect rule and, 210, 276, 291, 301, 304, 319–20; souls of, 37
Amankwatia, 43, 48–49, 55, 57
Ambah Fynnebah, 271–72
Ambah Sacka, 273
Amegatcher, Comfort, 273
Amma Ampofoaa (Akyem Abuakwa *ohemaa*), 189
Amoako Atta (Okyenhene 1866–87), 184–88, 187–89, 204
Amuah, Joseph, 271, 273
amulets. *See asuman*
Ananse, 10, 20, 43
ancestors, 18, 25, 34, 35, 41, 280, 283, 289, 312, 320: in Africa, 5, 287; accounting to, 77, 78, 125; adulation of, 29, 45, 122, 208–9; colour symbolism of, 70; communication with, 46, 60, 184, 196–97, 200; cursing of, 115; domestication of, 280, 285, 287; filial piety and, 289; mobility of, 290; mortal remains of, 192–93, 200; obligations to, 78, 90, 265, 296, 304; ownership of gold by, 89–90; presence at funerals of, 63, 313; propitiation of, 141, 172, 226, 290, 298, 328; punishment by, 289–90; of slaves, 138
Anglican Church, 100, 291, 294, 295–96, 300, 304
Anglo-Asante wars, 70, 89, 196, 203, 242, 266, 296
Angola, 11, 17
animals, 38, 39, 46, 57, 79, 129, 162, 213; consumption of corpses by, 118, 135–36, 197, 216, 285–86

Ankrah, Antonio, 241–42
Ankyewa Nyame, 46, 302
Annales school, 3, 6, 245–46
Anomabo, 170, 181–82, 193, 228–29, 232–33, 263, 264, 270, 271
Ansa, Christiana A., *318*
anthropology, 3, 5, 6, 310; in the colonial era, 27, 32, 283, 287–88; of mortuary ritual, 59–60, 277–78, 285, 329; of personhood, 26, 32
Antubam, Kofi, 70, 104, 341n31
apaee, 45, 117, 118, 122, 232, 241–42. *See also* names of the dead
Appiah, J.W.K., 306, 324
Appiah, Joe, 324–25
Appiah, Kwame Anthony, 323–25
Araba Esibu, 322
archaeology: 87, 92–106
Ariès, Philippe, 3, 192, 195–96, 256, 309–10, 327–28, 329
Armitage, C. H., 284
art: of coffins, 3, 309–10; portrayal of death in, 4, 5, 92; of terracotta funerary sculptures, 92–106
Asaase, 73, 146
Asafo Boakye (Asante Akwamuhene d. 1925), 292
asafo military companies, 177, 244, 271, 272, 322–23
asamando. *See* afterworld
Asante, David, 183, 185, 187
Asante kingdom, 1, 7, 35, 230, 279, 291–307; accumulation and, 77–84, 266–67; civil war in, 78, 84, 294–95; colonial conquest of, 46, 210–11, 291–93; emergence of, 23, 42–57, 77, 344n47; gold and, 76–84; human sacrifice and, 139–43, 146–54, 233–34; military campaigns of, 114, 117–23, 124–25, 130, 231, 266, 280–81; poison and, 163–66, political power in, 18, 60, 146, 300
Asantemanso, 46–47, 302
Asare, Rev. N. V., 53–54, 89–90, 122, 148, 220–21, 295, 299
Assin kingdom, 51, 139

asuman, 21, 46–47, 56, 144, 157; *sumankwafo* and, 157, 257–58
Assmann, Jan, 3–4, 327
Ata Fua (Akyem Kotokuhene), 224–25
Atkins, John, 107–8, 109–10, 116
Atlantic world, 4, 126; commerce of, 9, 11, 12, 16–17, 23, 90–91, 106, 128, 162. *See also* Atlantic slave trade
Atlantic slave trade, 2, 106, 124, 126, 138, 143, 161; abolition of, 117, 124, 125–26, 143, 166, 232; African perceptions of, 127; poison and, 162
autopsies, 204, 239, 250, 255–56, 258
Axim, 17, 23, 253–54, 256, 313
aya kese ('great brass basin'), 297, 301–2, 376–77n47
Azambuja, Diogo de, 13–16, 28, 85, 155

Baffoe, Kofi, 271
Bainn, Albert, 274
Bampenase burial ground, 296, 301
Banda, 119–20, 123
Bannerman, Charles, 58–59, 71, 200–201, 220, 225, 228, 231–32, 326
Bannerman, C. J., 225
Bannerman, Edmund, 225, 235
Bannerman, James, 58, 198, 200, 209, 231, 263, 270
Bannerman, Samuel, 268
Bantama, 56, 57, 298
Bantama royal mausoleum, 43, 88, 89–90, 101, 117, 122, 222, 292, 296, 297, 298, 300–303, 305
Barber, Karin, 232
Barbot, Jean, 39, 95–96, 106, 109, 127, 132–35, 145
Barros, João de, 13, 155
Barter, Edward, 107, 262
Barthes, Roland, 27, 101
Basel Mission, 37, 89, 160, 174–75, 178–80, 183–90, 207–8, 216, 224–23, 229–31, 288, 314, 378n19
Bawku, 254
beaches, 15–16, 214, 251
beads, 86, 90, 97, 165, 168

Begoro, 186–87
Bekwai, 150
Bellis, James, 97, 98, 104, 105, 227
Benin kingdom, 143, 145
bereavement, 59–60; of spouses, 64–65. *See also* widows
biomedicine, 4, 156, 245–58, 310; colonial rule and, 199, 203–4, 209, 282; social control and, 196; understandings of death and, 171, 188–89, 234, 239–40, 255–56, 329
Birempomaa Piese, 47
Birifu, 277–78, 283, 287
birth, 20, 36, 46, 72, 122; of ancestral dead, 73, 104, 328; and death, 69, 72, 88, 119–20, 216, 223; enumeration of, 239, 244, 248, 279, 293; fertility rates and, 247; human increase and, 239, 244, 293
Births, Deaths and Burial Ordinance, 252–55, 257, 258, 284, 286, 294, 298
blood: as component of personhood, 35; menstruation and, 135, 166; shedding of, 37, 149, 153, 163, 194, 233, 298; stools and, 29; as toxic substance, 168, 194
Boakye Yam, 80, 83.
Boamponsem, 48, 51–52
bones, 36–37, 115, 137, 165, 169–70, 236, 278; jawbones, 31, 108–9, 112–13, 114, 115, 116
Bono peoples, 8, 12, 18, 65, 68, 103–4, 147, 212; gold and, 76, 85; kingdoms of, 8; religious belief and practice of, 118
Bontwumafo ('red clay people'), 52–53, 146, 148
Bosman, Willem, 9–10; on the afterlife, 39, 40–41, 49–50; on Denkyira, 48–49; on ghosts, 218–19; on myths of creation, 10–11, 19–20, 21, 24; on healing and poison, 157–58, 160; on Komfo Anokye and Asante, 49–51; on mortuary customs, 61, 66–67, 71, 87, 96, 98, 111, 145; on the slave trade, 127
Bowdich, T. E.: on the afterlife, 24–25; on Banda war, 119; on death duties, 79–81; 83; on decapitation, 112–13, 119; on funerary customs, 71, 88, 150–51, 153–54, 296; on Gyaman war, 117, 121–22; on myths of creation, 24; on Osei Kwame, 163; on Osei Tutu, 53
Brandenburgers: on the Gold Coast, 23, 51, 106
brass bands, 280, 316
brass pots (*kuduo*), 85, 87–89, 296
Brazil, 12; Tabon community and, 263
Breman, 296–97, 298, 301, 303, 305, 306
Bremen Mission, 176, 179, 186, 229
Brew, James Hutton, 228, 236, 238
British colonial rule, 1–2, 6, 78, 214, 275, 309, 329; African perceptions of, 84, 253, 256, 323; in Asante (or Ashanti), 210–11, 216–17, 223, 230, 253, 290, 291, 304, 306; economic change and, 276; in the Gold Coast Colony, 185, 191, 196–97, 203, 223–26, 230–31, 236, 238–39, 266, 290; indirect rule and, 210, 254, 315, 319–20; mobility and, 288, 289–90; in the Northern Territories, 230, 246, 277–78, 288, 290; poison and, 155–56; public health and, 248–49; in the Togoland mandate, 246
British courts, 137, 156, 166–70, 182, 184, 205–7, 210–11, 231, 235, 253, 267, 279; African law and, 166–67, 169–70, 184, 210, 214, 263, 267, 276; inheritance and, 263–66, 275
Bron peoples. *See* Bono peoples
Brooking, Rev. Robert, 97, 177, 193, 220
Brown, J. P., 202, 232, 242–43, 399n6
Browne, Sir Thomas, 92
Bruce, John, 235
burial: of Akan office-holders, 209; of children, 135, 216; in groves, 40; in home soil, 69, 111, 207, 294–95; to humanize the earth, 47, 73, 294–95; origins of, 20; secondary burial and, 60, 96; secrecy surrounding, 87, 193, 204, 206, 286, 309; of slaves, 134–37; of trade brokers, 134; wills and, 267; of warriors, 109. *See also* graves; house burial

INDEX 385

Cape Coast, 61, 88, 96, 109–10, 115, 134, 136–37, 145–46, 193. 197, 212, 219, 262; Christianity and, 176, 180, 232; funeral reform and, 201–3, 312; funerals at, 235, 237, 238, 316, 322; house burial in, 136, 191, 199–200, 203, 236; literate elite of, 232, 236, 242; maternal health at, 248; poisoning at, 159, 167–70; the press in, 228, 231–32; vital registration at, 253; wills and, 261, 270–72, 274.

capital punishment, 71, 83, 84, 89, 109–10, 116, 118, 162, 182, 210–11; by the colonial state, 101; human sacrifice and, 141, 149, 151; poison and, 158, 159, 166, 168

Caramansa, 13–16, 28, 85, 155

Casely-Hayford, J. E., 173, 209, 238, 319

Catholic missions, 17, 109, 176, 277

cemeteries, 138, 183, 191–209, 329; of religious denominations, 209, 251–52, 317; in Europe, 195

Cemeteries Ordinance, 191–92, 193, 205, 207, 251–52, 258, 295, 314

certification of death, 134, 246, 258

chests, 82, 85, 89, 115, 194

chiefs. See *amanhene*

childlessness, 48, 74, 273–74, 318–19

children, 74–75, 98, 105, 139, 214–15, 232, 329; burial of, 135, 213, 216; death of, 215–17, 228, 248, 288; of European traders, 262; ghost-mothers of, 214, 253; inheritance and, 262, 268, 275; pawning of, 199

Christaller, Rev. J. G., 40–41, 178–79, 184

Christianity, 4, 13, 18, 23, 103, 160, 172–90, 226, 260, 310, 326, 329; African clergy and, 17, 174, 183, 191, 202, 230, 236–37, 243, 316, 322–23; Asante and, 172, 175, 177–78; the Bible and, 174, 175, 178, 183, 230, 232, 269, 273, 330; burial and, 191, 270, 273; conversion to, 13, 27–28, 169, 176, 179–80, 183, 188, 288; doctrine of eschatology and, 13, 28, 50, 132, 134, 153, 172 (*see also* heaven; hell); European clergy and, 30, 173–74; 'fetish priests' and, 177, 178–80; funerary customs and, 172, 183, 185, 187, 207, 270 311–12, 315, 322–23; literacy and, 173–74, 175, 177, 181, 230; marriage and, 264–65, 267. *See also individual missions*

Christiansborg (Danish Accra), 30–31, 110, 113–14, 174, 198, 208, 263. *See also* Osu

Cleland, George, 270, 289

Clifford, Sir Hugh, 248, 284

cloth, 17, 21, 28, 125, 269; mortuary exchange and, 79, 81, 82, 86, 260, 264, 272, 326. *See also* funeral cloth

clothes, 30, 173, 242; of the deceased, 73, 81, 153, 269; personhood and, 269

cocoa economy, 275, 291, 314, 316

coffins, 54, 73, 85, 87, 185–86, 193–95, 198, 229, 244, 255, 256, 270, 272, 280, 312, 316–17; in Asante, 122, 165, 193, 194–95, 296, 305, 326; dual burial and, 207, 255, 309; figurative shapes of, 3, 309–10; ghosts and, 241; miniature simulacra of, 208, 227; parading of, 198–99, 205, 309, 322

colour symbolism, 70, 96, 100, 292; of black crape, 237–38, 316; of the dead, 22, 40, 324–25; of red clay (*ntwoma*), 33, 53–54, 57, 70–71, 122, 146, 238, 302; of white clay (*hyire*), 22, 65, 70–71, 122, 185, 238

commodity imports, 17, 20–22, 23, 24, 125; the devil and, 131–33. *See also* alcohol; cloth; firearms; tobacco

Conran, Edward, 200

coroner's inquests, 239, 240, 255–56, 258

corpses: absence of, 69–70, 72, 227; as actors in funerals, 59–60, 255; adornment of, 22, 71, 77, 85–88, 271–72, 326; anthills and, 214, 227; burning of, 213–14; of the childless, 218; dangers to health from, 195–96, 204, 298; decomposition of, 79, 101, 106, 285, 296; dishonourable disposal of, 135–36, 166, 187, 207, 210–27, 234, 237, 256, 283, 286; fear of, 6, 326; of infants, 69; interrogation of, 22, 63, 69, 159, 228, 234, 255–56, 258; of kings, 53, 55; looking at, 48, 58, 273, 324, 326, 328; maltreatment of, 87, 113, 118, 135–36, 210–27; mobility of, 254, 294–95, 321; preparation of, 61,

386 INDEX

corpses (*continued*)
66, 280, 283; preservation of, 55, 111, 256, 294; of queen mothers, 88; racial thought and, 198, 201; reinterment of, 295; reverence for, 87, 226, 234; of slaves, 134–37; smell of, 200–201, 256; of witches, 135, 213
cosmology, 20–21, 25
Côte d'Ivoire, 93
creation myths, 10, 18–20
Cruickshank, Brodie, 63, 96, 104, 143, 180, 182–83, 199, 266, 268
cultural encounter, 9–10, 28
curses, 115, 147, 168, 189, 213–14, 221, 241, 325

Dadzie, Moses, 269
Dagara peoples, 32, 277–78, 283, 284, 285, 287
Dagbon kingdom, 286, 289
Dahomey kingdom, 110, 143, 149, 233
dancing, 66, 67, 118, 179, 190, 197, 238, 310, 323, 326; by ghosts, 113
Danes: on the Gold Coast, 23, 30, 38, 86, 110, 112, 115, 128–34, 146, 159–61, 163, 174–75, 197, 198, 230. *See also* Christiansborg
Danquah, J. B., 18, 27, 72–73, 81, 257, 275
Dapper, Olfert, 85
dead bodies. *See* corpses
dead people: danger from, 64, 73, 286, 300; hostility of, 69, 73, 122, 213–14; memory of, 236, 242, 248, 260; racial transformation of, 22; sensory perception of, 63, 113; sound of, 113; Western ideas of, 3
death: *amanhene* and, 83, 222; bad death, 3, 7, 35, 40, 60, 69, 74, 128, 135, 164, 187, 203, 210–27, 280, 283, 288, 304, 328; bravery in the face of, 153, 154; bureaucratic regulation of, 245–58; causes of, 51, 235; in childbirth, 69, 278; good death, 3, 25, 40, 90, 129, 212, 214, 222; of infants, 68–69, 215–17, 253; legal understandings of, 167; myths of origins of, 9, 11, 18–20, 46–47; of pregnant women, 210–11, 223; reporting of, 80–81; scandal of, 328–39; scholarship on, 3–6

deathbeds, 186, 222, 242–43, 261, 264–65, 266, 271, 272–73, 274, 276, 368n53
death duties, 76–84, 163, 295, 320; avoidance of, 80, 83, 265
decapitation, 31, 43, 74, 107–23, 128, 131, 139–40, 212. *See also* human sacrifice; skulls
debt, 79–80, 87, 135–36, 177, 263, 265, 266, 310
De Graft, William, 175, 232
De la Fosse, Eustache, 13
De Marees, Pieter, 20–23, 29–30, 38, 44, 61, 62, 63, 65, 71, 85, 93, 95–96, 104, 108–9, 144–45
demographic growth, 245–46, 249, 279; life expectancy and, 245, 329
Denkyira kingdom, 23, 42, 48–49, 51–53, 82, 146, 148
destiny (*nkrabea*), 32–3, 34, 249
devils, 14, 21, 70, 128, 131–33, 135, 178–80, 185, 190, 322. *See too* hell
dirt, 135, 136, 200, 215, 227; corpses seen as, 196, 210; defilement and, 210, 223; smell and, 201, 206; widows and, 323
disease, 245–58, 278, 282; blackwater fever, 204; cerebro-spinal meningitis, 247; dysentery, 235, 247, 248, 250; heart disease, 230, 250; influenza, 247; leprosy, 212–13, 214; malaria, 174, 247, 248; measles, 247, 248; parasitic infestation and, 247, 250; plague, 247, 294; pneumonia, 188, 247, 250; sexually-transmitted disease, 247; sleeping sickness, 247; smallpox, 234, 247, 249, 251; tuberculosis, 247, 254; typhus, 186–87; whooping cough, 248; yellow fever, 247
Dixcove, 74
doctors, 75, 188–89, 199, 201, 204–5, 248, 249–50, 251–52, 256
Domaa, 48, 122
dreams, 35, 129, 240–41
drowning, 69, 212–13, 227
drums, 19, 35, 146, 293, 326–37; colonial legislation and, 197, 293; curation of bones on, 109, 15, 112–13, 114, 119; playing

of at funerals, 59, 100, 179, 205, 238, 271, 272, 280, 308–9, 310, 322
Dupuis, Joseph, 45, 53, 117, 119, 122–23, 149–52, 163, 164–66
Dutch: Asante and, 53, 194–95; on the Gold Coast, 9, 20, 22, 48–49, 106, 124, 167, 174, 194, 196, 197, 230, 262
Dwaben, 150, 163

Easmon, John Farrell, 188–89, 191, 204–6, 209, 240, 248, 250, 251
Eguafo kingdom, 13, 85, 109
Egypt, 3, 45–46, 234
Ellis, A. B., 38, 108, 227
Elmina: in British colonial era, 239, 270, 271, 273–74, 293–94; burials in, 87, 95–96, 272, 273; Christianity in, 176; Dutch and, 23, 174, 197; Portuguese and, 9, 12, 16–17, 23, 103, 155
emme leaves, 64, 65, 122, 323
emotions, 59–60, 61, 66, 72–73, 100, 113–14. *See also* grief
English: on the Gold Coast, 23, 39, 74, 115, 126, 161, 197, 262; Royal African Company (later Company of Merchants Trading to Africa) and, 66, 126, 134, 193, 232, 262
Enlightenment thought, 3, 26, 27, 28, 39, 195, 232, 260, 328
enslaved people. *See* slaves
Euro-Africans, 17, 58, 59, 125, 157, 159–61, 162, 166, 173–74, 175, 229, 263; funerary practices of, 197–98; the press and, 58, 231–32
European sources, 1, 9, 43; problems of interpretation of, 9–10, 27, 28
European trading companies, 1, 9–11, 43, 76, 81, 261; brokers of, 107, 262; burial in coastal forts of, 86, 194, 197; graveyards of, 197. *See also* Brandenburgers; Danes; Dutch; English
Ewe peoples, 34, 39, 71, 126, 138, 176, 186, 229
executioners, 38, 102, 114, 122, 140, *144*, 146–48, *147*, 164, 219, 233, 298, 305
exhumation, 88, 193, 209, 213, 219, 227, 254, 290, 293–95, 300, 312

famine, 246, 249–50, 282, 288
Fante peoples, 44, 55, 63, 85, 110, 115, 117, 150, 194, 199, 271; Christianity and, 173, 176, 180–83, 323
Fanti Confederation, 173, 234, 242–43
'fetish', 10, 19, 75, 96, 110, 159, 167, 170–71, 187, 326; 'eating' of, 44; and 'fetish priests', 177–80, 223, 257; origins of concept of, 11, 20–21. *See also abosom*; *asuman*
Fetu kingdom, 13, 16, 17, 38, 39, 96, 109 114–15, 145–46
Field, M. J., 61, 73, 99–101, 103, 104, 135, 138, 207, 212, 214–16, 225–26
firearms, 23, 48–49, 52, 111, 269; banana-leaf simulacra of, 217–18; colonial legislation and, 197, 302; the devil and, 128, 130; use at funerals of, 57, 59, 61, 64, 66, 125, 150, 153–54, 179, 198–99, 205, 229, 238, 244, 280, 302, 308–9, 310, 315, 324. *See also* warfare
food, 19, 21, 125; for the dead, 63–64, 95–96, 97, 98, 135, 145, 209, 326; shortages of, 249, 282
forest environment, 46, 52; colour symbolism of, 70; location of graves in, 86–87, 95, 252; *mmoatia* and, 324; perceptions of, 33–34; settlement of, 12; state-building in, 42. *See also* trees
Fortes, Meyer, 5, 27, 32, 36, 276, 282, 285, 287, 288–89
Foucault, Michel, 27, 195
Freeman, Rev. T. B., 118, 152, 175–76, 177–78, 180–81, 183, 220, 312
freemasonry, 232–33, 238, 244
Frimpon Manso (Akyem Kotokuhene), 129–30, 133–34, 138, 148
funerals: 4, 61–75, 308–25; of *amanhene*, 100–101, 150–51, 164; *asafo* companies and, 271; attendance at, 53, 66, 237; of children, 288; colonial regulation of, 199; commercialization of, 310, 321; in contemporary Ghana, 2, 5, 207, 310; contests over, 255, 312–13; costs of, 219, 254, 260, 264, 270, 310, 312–13, 318–20;

funerals (*continued*)
cross-dressing at, 71; donations for, 81, 229, 270, 272, 314; economics of, 5, 152, 193, 212; emotional complexity of, 59, 66, 73; mock staging of, 165–66, 238; neglect of, 219; noise of, 2, 59, 61, 62, 63, 66, 179, 198–99, 237, 305, 311, 316; in oral traditions of origin, 47, 57; of paupers, 256; radio and, 280; reform of, 66, 270, 310, 318–20; reportage of, 229, 234–35, 238; terracotta sculptures and, 92, 94–102; wills and, 267, 270; written announcements of, 236
funeral cloth (*ayitam*), 2, 33, 35, 65, 71, 117, 237–38, 302, 306, 312, 316, 318, 324–25
funeral dirges, 45, 67, 241. *See also* names of the dead

Ga kingdom (Great Accra), 42, 112, 124–25, 130
Ga peoples, 3, 7, 17, 30, 34, 110–12, 127–28, 181; funerary customs of, 71, 73, 97, 177; house burial and, 86–87; language of, 175, 230–31; religious belief and practice of, 32, 34, 39, 110–11, 116, 131, 177, 215–16, 223, 260; seaside towns of, 124–25, 128–34, 135, 162, 208–209. *See also* Accra; Homowo festival
Gandah, 277–80, 282–83, 284, 287
Gandah, Kum, 277–80
Garrard, Timothy F., 103–4
gender, 18–19, 36, 120–22; 146–47, 165, 167–68; funeral celebrations and, 58–75, 104, 229; grief and, 58–75, 113–14
Ghartey, R. J., 232–33, 234, 242–44, 317
ghosts, 22–23, 32, 35, 36, 41, 63, 113, 210–27, 275, 276, 313, 324; appearance of, 71, 212; homicide by, 151, 163–64; inheritance and, 261; sexual desire of, 64, 163–64, 323; sound of, 212; spiritism and, 240–41; vengeance of, 226, 265, 274
Glover, James, 273, 275
Glover Addo, John, 319
gold, 1, 10, 53, 76–91, 184, 188, 268, 303; on corpses, 58, 85–88, 326; as currency, 127–28, 167; as demiurgic substance, 76; and the devil, 132; as a grave good, 85, 192, 207, 272; as jewellery, 13–14, 21, 37; royal relics and, 165; in traditions of origin, 46, 47, 302; trade in, 17, 21–22, 42, 124; trophy heads made of, 120, 121, 122, 123; trans-Saharan trade in, 12, 76
Gold Coast Forts and Settlements/Protectorate, 84, 89, 122, 139, 166–67, 181–83, 184–89; funeral reform and, 198–200, 202–3; slavery in, 143
Golden Elephant Tail, 78–79
Golden Stool (*sika dwa kofi*), 35, 51, 76, 77, 78, 89–90, 102, 121, 122, 163, 295, 297–98, 299–300, 305, 306
gold-weights, 35, 144
Gonja kingdom, 83, 139, 285, 286
Goody, Jack, 5, 32, 277–78, 280, 283, 285, 287
graves, 34, 62, 73, 283; desecration of, 285; flowers and, 209; opening of, 88, 284, 285; ornamentation of, 95; robbery of, 85–87, 192, 193, 207, 317; terracotta sculptures and, 92–106. *See also* burial; house burial
gravediggers, 136–37, 192, 285, 286, 299
grave goods, 62, 87, 91, 92, 95, 301, 310
gravestones, 197, 301, 317
grief, 4, 58–75, 81, 113–17, 149, 187, 195–96 205, 215–17, 229; Victorian ideal of, 234, 237–38. *See also* mourning; weeping
Griffin, Rev. W. R., 315
Griffith, Sir W. Brandford, 188, 191–92, 205
Gyaman kingdom, 117–23, 151–52, 164–65

hair, 29, 93–94, 94, 98, 147, 208, 216, 217, 272, 306, 309
Hammond, John, 269
Hayfron, John, 264–65
Hayfron, R. J., 202
health and healing, 9, 50, 156–57, 179–80, 257–58, 279, 287–88; popular movements for, 2, 224–25, 249, 257, 279–80, 288, 290. *See also* medicine
heaven, 21, 178, 185
heirlooms, 269

hell, 14, 178
Hennessy, J. Pope, 201
herbalists, 157, 169, 171, 174–75, 257–58
Hertz, Robert, 59–60, 61, 155
HIV/AIDS, 4, 251
Homowo festival, 60, 160, 196–97, 208–209, 213, 239, 260
Horton, James Africanus, 201, 234
hospitals, 199, 246, 248, 257, 273, 329
house burial, 34, 86–87, 136, 191–209, 237, 251, 255, 263, 284–85; toxic emanations from, 191, 199, 201, 204
houses: of merchant elite, 58, 229, 291; in the savanna, 278, 290; wills and, 263, 267–69
Hughes, Thomas, 234–35
human body, 26–41, 45, 112, 234; adornment of, 13–14, 28, 71, 105, 216. 269 (*see also* cloth; clothes; hair; jewellery); dismemberment of, 31, 102, 107–23, 140, 306 (*see also* decapitation); enslavement and, 31, 127; European view of, 28, 30, 127; metaphysical elements of, 32–41, 129; poison and, 157, 159, 161, 169–70
human sacrifice, 22, 31, 33, 68, 69, 100–101, 133, 138, 139–54, 178, 187; of *akyere*, 53, 126, 142, 151, 152–53; of *akrafo*, 37, 100, 131, 148, 151; in Asante, 24, 70, 82, 102, 146–48, 148–51, 164, 178, 211, 296–98, 302; of bereaved wives, 95, 131, 144, 151; debates over, 148–51, 233–34; on the Gold Coast, 95, 96, 115, 144–46, 181–82; of *nnonkofo* slaves, 136, 139–40, 152; of prisoners of war, 140, 149–51
Hutton Mills, Thomas, 314

infanticide, 30
inheritance, 76–77, 261–62, 267, 270, 274–75
intramural sepulture. *See* house burial
Isert, Paul Erdmann, 87
Islam, 4, 56, 149–50, 173, 281, 283

Jackson, James, 271
James Town (English Accra), 125, 198, 205–6, 262, 263

Jesus Christ, 7, 23, 172, 178, 184, 186, 235, 243
jewellery, 13–14, 269; as grave good, 227, 238, 271–72
Johnson, Blind Willie, 2
Johnson, Rev. Samuel, 237

Katawere cult, 224–25
Kea, Ray A., 128, 130, 131, 133
Keta, 253–54
kinship, 27, 34, 36, 220–21, 268, 270; as 'freedom', 31, 125, 138
Kintampo, 254
Kabes, John, 107
Kankamia (or Kukpenibie) cult, 279–80, 287–88
Kinka (Dutch Accra), 125, 194, 206, 207–8, 259
Kofi Fofea, 293
Kofi Kakari (Asantehene 1867–74), 70, 82, 84, 89–90, 296–97
Koforidua, 64, 248
Kokofu, 33, 47, 48, 150, 302
Komenda, 109, 262
Komfo Anokye, 42–43, 48–53, 57, 148, 153
Konadu Yaadom (Asantehemaa d. 1809), 148–51, 163–64
Konadu Yaadom (Asantehemaa d. 1945), 302, 304–5, 306
Kongo kingdom, 11, 17
Konny, John, 107–8, 109, 115, 116
Koomson, John, 270
Korkor Badoo, 263
Kormantse (Kormantin), 55, 126, 352n21
kra, 15, 34–36, 72, 100, 104, 112
Krobo, 179, 251, 314
Kumasi, 24, 42, 45, 55, 70, 86, 88, 118–19, 120, 178, 330; British occupation of, 89, 210–211; in colonial period, 79, 348, 261, 275, 279–80, 288, 291–307, 324; founding of, 47, 48, 101, 302; human sacrifice in, 139–40, 146, 148–51; necrogeography of, 101–2, 136, 254–55, 292, 294–303; poison and, 156, 163–66; runaway slaves from, 139–40

Kusi Obodom (Asantehene 1750–64), 149, 296, 300
Kwabena Encoom (a.k.a. Josh Martin), 263–64
Kwabena Fori (Adansehene), 94
Kwabena Wiredu, 97, 104, 105
Kwabia Anwanfi, 47
Kwadwo Adinkra, 117–23
Kwadwo Apaw (Asante Agonahene), 319–20
Kwadwo Gyamfi, 84
Kwadwo Tookoo, 139–40, 154
Kwaku (Osu 'castle slave'), 129–30, 131, 133, 134, 138
Kwaku Dua Panin (Asantehene 1834–67), 78, 82, 84, 89, 118, 126, 136, 139, 141, 177–78, 233, 281, 282; death and funeral of, 101, 143, 146, 220–22; 234, 304
Kwaku ('Kweku') Fokuo, 293
Kwaku Manukure, 274
Kwakye Kofi (Asafohene), 153
Kwaman, 42, 47, 48, 51, 52
Kwame Frimpon (Asante Adontenhene), 79, 80–82
Kwame ('Kwami') Gyansah, 293
Kwasi Atta (*omanhene* of Cape Coast d. 1887), 242
Kwasi Gyambibi, 292, 301
Kwasi Gyani, 84
Kwasi Nuama (Asante Akyeamehene), 79, 293–95
Kwawu, 114, 252
Kwesi-Aaba, J. A., 257–58
Kwesi Gyafu, 271
Kyei, Thomas E., 46, 214–15, 326–27, 330

Labadi, 110, 112, 212, 251; and Lakpa oracle, 110, 160, 179, 181
Lagos, 137, 185, 223
Laing, Rev. Timothy, 202
Lake Bosomtwi, 40, 50
lamentation, 73–74
Landon, Letitia, 161
Laqueur, Thomas W., 3, 6, 192, 195–96, 201, 206, 209, 327

law: in African states and societies, 27; in Asante, 49, 84; post–mortem trials and, 50. *See also* British courts
Law, Robin, 141–43, 151–52
Lawra, 254
lawyers, 225, 275, 309, 314, 319, 32
legitimate commerce, 126, 180; dangers of, 235–36
libation, 97, 114, 310, 323
life insurance, 321
literacy, 10, 22, 24, 185, 229, 263; in Arabic, 230, 281; in Asante, 230; the Bible and, 230; dangers of, 231, 235
literate African elite, 27, 173, 197, 234, 243, 259; funeral reform and, 198–200, 203, 209, 223; literary clubs and, 232; the press and, 228–31
literate education, 58, 173–74, 181, 183, 187, 229, 235, 277, 288, 325
Lykke, Hans (a.k.a. Noete Doku), 128, 130–33

Maclean, George, 141, 161, 166, 170, 177, 202, 236
Mali kingdom, 12
Mampon, 19, 29, 150
Mamprussi peoples, 285, 286
Mankessim, 167, 181–83, 271
Manu, 47
marriage, 36–37, 275; Marriage Ordinance and, 267
Mate Kole, Emmanuel, 314
matrilineages. *See abusua*
mausoleums, 95, 100–101, 208
Maxwell, Sir John, 293, 294
McCarthy, Sir Charles, 115, 122, 231
McCaskie, T. C., 18, 32, 34, 49–50, 60, 73, 77–78, 80, 143, 164, 213–14, 221, 275
medicine, 9, 46–47, 57, 156–57, 161, 165, 168–69, 179–80, 234–35, 249, 279, 285, 323. *See also* biomedicine; health and healing
Melvil, Thomas, 44
Mensa Bonsu (Asantehene 1874–83), 84, 178, 183, 295–97, 300
Mensah, Charles, 238

Mensah, Joseph, 273
Meredith, Henry, 66, 74, 193
Methodist mission, 151, 170, 173, 174, 175–76, 180–83, 190, 193, 202, 232, 234, 235, 243–44, 264, 315, 322–23
Meyerowitz, Eva, 34–37, 72, 85, 88, 212–13, 216, 341n31
midwifery, 215, 244, 248
modernity, 7, 187, 192, 226, 256–57, 270, 271, 274, 308, 310, 328–29; colonial rule and, 196–97, 236–38, 287, 291–92, 294, 295, 298, 321, 324
Mohenu, Paulo, 179–80
Mohr, Rev. Adolph, 187–89
Molenaar, Joseph, 270–71
Monrad, Johannes, 63, 67, 69, 73, 87, 135–36, 159, 161–62, 164, 174, 194, 197–98, 216, 218–19, 221
monuments, 95–98, 100, 107–8, 117, 122, 197, 208–9, 297, 298, 301–3, 317, 318, 322
mortality rates: of Africans, 204, 245–46, 250, 257, 289; of children, 247–48, 250, 252; of Europeans, 160, 172, 174–75, 176, 201, 261; of infants, 215–16, 247–48, 250, 252, 289; of women in childbirth, 216
mortal remains. *See* corpses; skeletons; skulls
mortuaries, 198, 256, 321
mortuary slaying. *See* human sacrifice
mourning, 68–75, 215, 280. *See also* grief
mourning cloth. *See* funeral cloth
Muhammad al-Ghamba, 149–51
mulattos. *See* Euro-Africans
Müller, Wilhelm, 38, 39, 96, 109, 114–15, 145–46
murder, 74–75, 97, 100–101, 116, 210–11, 219, 278, 280; poison and, 155–71; reportage of, 234
music, 2, 33, 109, 113, 114, 131, 272, 278, 280, 307, 316, 323. *See also* drums; funeral dirges
Muslims: in Accra, 205, 268; in Asante, 53, 118, 119, 149, 151, 162, 178, 294; funeral reform and, 316; human sacrifice and, 143, 149, 151; in the savanna north, 281, 283, 286
mutual societies, 272, 221–23, 323

Naa Dede Oyeadu, 233
names of the dead, 19, 45, 46, 186, 241, 321, 329; on gravestones, 197, 317; spoken at funerals, 65, 232. *See also apaee;* funeral dirges; obituaries
Nananom Mpow, 110–11, 115, 167, 170, 181–83, 189
Nanka-Bruce, F. V., 248, 252
Nankani peoples, 287, 288
Nene Nyaarko Eku V (Agonahene), 316
Newell, Stephanie, 233, 241
Newlands, H. S., 302, 306
newspapers, 58, 199–200, 203, 228–44, 256–58; literate African elite and, 228, 275
Nimako, Rev. S. Gyasi, 322–23
Ningo, 219–20, 221
Nketia, J. H., 67–68, 113
Nkrumah, Kwame, 308, 321, 324
Northern Territories, 138, 255, 277–90; disease and demography in, 246–47, 248–49, 250, 254. *See also* savanna peoples
Nsoko, 68
Nsuta, 150, 299–300
ntoro, 36, 216–17
Ntim Gyakari, 43, 52, 376–77n47
nuncupative (oral) wills. See *samansie*
Nungua, 251
Nyako Kwaku, 97–98
Nyankonpon, 132

oaths, 43–45, 158; great oath (*ntam kese*) and, 45, 54, 233, 276
Obiri Yeboa, 47–48
obituaries, 236, 241–43
obituary notices, 3, 5, 317, 321
Obuasi, 254
Odomankoma, 14–15, 17–19, 25, 72, 146, 154, 327; *odomankomasem* and, 14–15, 19, 43, 302

Odwira festival, 37, 60, 73, 89–90, 122–23, 150–51, 163–64, 196–97, 213, 239, 293, 296, 298, 302
Offinso, 320
Ofori Atta, Nana Sir, 100–101, 276, 319
Okaija, 194
Okpoti, 110–11, 129–30, 138, 181–82
Officer Ali, 268
old age, 70, 187, 214, 241, 256–57, 258, 259–60
Onyame, 15, 34–35, 40
Opoku Fofie (Asantehene 1803–4), 148, 163–64, 194–95, 220
Opoku Kwame, 150–51, 163
Opoku, Rev. Theophilus, 37
Opoku Ware (Asantehene c.1720–50), 53, 57, 77, 79, 88, 130, 299
orality, 30, 43–4, 189, 230–31, 261; oral histories and, 5, 6, 281. *See too* speaking about death
Osei Agyeman Prempeh II (Asantehene 1931–70), 55, 306, 320
Osei Bonsu (Bantamahene 1901–16), 56
Osei Kwadwo (Asantehene 1764–77), 82, 120
Osei Kwadwo (drummer), 19
Osei Kwadwo (Asante heir apparent d. 1859), 220, 222
Osei Kwame (Asantehene 1777–1803), 83, 119, 148–51, 163–64, 220, 296
Osei Tutu (Asantehene c.1701–17), 42–43, 47; death of, 53–56, 86, 111, 146, 296, 302, 303, 376–77n47
Osei Tutu Kwame (a.k.a. Osei Bonsu; Asantehene 1804–23), 55, 117–23, 148, 151, 164–66, 194
Osei Yaw Akoto (Asantehene 1823–34), 58, 84, 90, 221
Osu (Danish Accra), 31, 110, 125, 128, 175, 191, 269
Oti Akenten, 47–48, 101
Owusu Ansah, John, 177, 233, 236
Oyoko dynasty, 46–48, 52, 102, 220, 293, 294, 296, 299, 300, 302

Pal (of Zubiung), 289–90
palm oil, 48, 104, 208–9
Paris, 195, 260, 328
Parker, Rev. A. W., 202, 242–43
Parker, James Francis, 263
Patterson, K. David, 248, 250, 253
pawnship, 126, 135–36, 177, 199
Peel, J.D.Y., 20, 172
Peki, 251
personhood, 26–41, 269, 271
Phipps, James, 88
photography, 100, 106, 244, 269–70, 316, 317–18
Pietz, William, 11, 44–45
Pina, Rui de, 13
Pine, Sir Benjamin, 198–99, 311
poison, 51–52, 69, 150, 155–71, 179, 182–83, 187, 224–25, 228–29, 239, 248–49, 251, 258, 278, 279, 325, 328; toxic emanations and, 205; *odom* ordeals and, 158, 159, 162, 169, 255–56; suicide and, 235
Pong Yaw (Domaahene), 210–11
Porter, Roy, 26–27
Portuguese: on the Gold Coast, 12–17, 21–22, 28, 92, 103, 109; language, 11, 15, 12
post–mortem examinations. *See* autopsies
post-mortem trials, 50, 84, 118, 213
pottery, 98–99, 99, 101–2, 215, 278, 306
praise poems. See *apaee*
Pra River, 12, 42, 43, 93
print culture, 27, 229–32, 236–37. *See also* newspapers
proverbs, 43–44, 68, 76, 152, 265, 289, 310

Quaque, Philip, 174, 232, 236
Quartey, William, 268
Quartey-Papafio, B. W., 258
Quartey-Papafio, J. W., 258
Quaye, William, 274–75
queen mothers. See *ahemaa*

Ramseyer, Friedrich, and J. Kühne, 70, 82, 99, 114, 136, 216, 221–22
Rask, Johannes, 30, 61, 86, 113–14, 128, 135
Rattray, R. S.: on Asante history, 57, 119, 146, 302; on death duties, 80–81, 82; on infant and maternal mortality, 215–18; on

mortuary customs, 63–64, 66, 71, 77, 98–99, 102, 122, 298; on savanna peoples, 281, 283, 287, 288; on personhood and the soul, 33, 35, 36, 38, 219; photography by, 19, 29, 56, 65, 68, 147, 217; on *samansie*, 265, 271, 275

registration of deaths, 192, 209, 238–39, 246, 251, 252, 286

reincarnation, 35, 36, 74, 129, 133–34; prevention of, 214, 218

Reindorf, Rev. Carl Christian, 48–49, 53–54, 55, 79, 118, 120, 149, 160, 163, 194, 207, 237

revenants. *See* ghosts

Riis, Rev. Andreas, 174–75, 177, 179

Robertson, Chief Isaac, 169–70

Rømer, Ludewig, 32–33, 87, 115, 116, 117, 129–31, 138, 148, 160–61, 181–82, 194

Rouch, Jean, 309

Sackey, Joseph, 259–60, 269, 272

Saltpond, 251, 255, 268, 269

São Jorge da Mina, 12, 17. *See also* Elmina

Sago, Samuel, 270

Salaga, 254, 286

Sam, Godfrey, 271

samansie, 261, 263–66, 267, 273, 275–76

Sarbah, John, 191, 193, 203, 314, 316

Sarbah, John Mensah, 265, 267, 314

sasa, 38, 65, 113, 116, 122, 147–48, 151, 219; and the *gyabon suman*, 144, 147–48, 154, 219, 367n28

savanna peoples: Akan perceptions of, 105, 216, 281, 287, 290; ancestors and, 280, 281–82, 283, 287; arrow poison and, 162; blood feuds and, 278, 282, 284; colonial rule and, 277–90; enslavement of, 126, 139–40; Gur languages of, 7; homicide and, 278, 280, 282, 288; identities of, 281, 282–83; kinship of, 37, 281, 289, 290; mortuary customs of, 278, 283–86, 329; religious belief and practice of, 277, 279, 281

schools. *See* literate education

seascapes, 15–16, 34, 324

Sefwi, 314, 376n47

Sekondi–Takoradi, 74–75, 86, 248, 257, 292, 293, 322

Senegambia, 11, 12, 134, 145

Sewaa (Dwabenhemaa), 219–20

sexuality, 30, 33, 48–49, 60, 70, 120–22, 160–61, 241

Sey, William, 274

Seychelles, 46, 291, 293–94, 300

Shama, 12, 17, 28, 170, 248

Sierra Leone, 12, 46, 159, 173, 188, 201, 223, 229, 231, 234, 235, 263, 293–94

Sisala peoples, 285

skeletons, 55, 89, 203, 297

skulls, 43, 54, 107–23, 114, 224, 296

Slave Coast, 128, 134, 262

slaves, 1, 55, 61, 124–38; ancestors of, 138; assimilation of, 136; afterlife and, 37, 129–30, 131, 133–34; death of, 74–75, 185–86, 280; disposal of corpses of, 69, 251; of European companies, 75, 125, 129–30, 134, 262; inheritance of, 79, 81, 263–66; marriage and, 264; ownership of, 31, 124; human sacrifice of, 22, 95, 139–54; from savanna north, 126, 139–40; subjugation of, 31, 151–52; violence inflicted upon, 111; wills and, 263, 268

slavery, 124–38, 143, 168, 177, 280; British abolition of, 136, 185, 196, 203, 239

slave trade, 17, 23, 30–31, 42, 150, 280–81, 288; violence and, 112, 124, 130. *See too* Atlantic slave trade

Smith, Joseph, 235–36

social hierarchy, 16, 22, 28, 71; of the dead, 24–25, 37, 40–41, 81, 83, 85, 133, 145, 208, 284, 299, 319–21 (*see also* afterlife; afterworld)

Solomon, Rev. J. A., 242–43

sora ceremony, 98–99, 101–2, 148, 306–7, 323,

soul, 26–41, 50, 59–60, 274, 285; Christian idea of, 14, 50, 312, 329; metempsychosis of, 38, 39, 129. See also *kra*; *sunsum*

speaking about death, 15, 32, 33–34, 42–57, 120, 189, 216, 230. *See too* orality

Stewart, Capt (later Sir) Donald, 210, 225

stools (*nkonnwa*), 28, 29, 46, *68*, 274, 306; blackening of, 28, 29, 70; stool-carriers and, 29, 48, 55. *See also* Golden Stool
suicide, 61, 111, 118, 119, 161, 163, 165, 203, 212–13, 219, 222, 234, 235, 274, 279, 280, 313
sunsum, 35, 51, 76, 104
Sunyani, 254
Svane, Rev. F. P., 159–60

Taa Kora, 118, 119
Taki Tawia (Ga *mantse* 1862–1902), 206, 208, 209
Takyiman kingdom, 104, 118, 122, *147*, 212, 216, 218, 222
Talensi peoples, 32, 285, 287, 288–89
Tamale, 254, 278, 286
Tano River, 119
Tarkwa, 253–54
temperance movement, 229, 232–33, 234, 243, 314–15
terracotta funerary sculptures, 92–106, 306, 317
Teshi, 251
tobacco smoking, 58, 71, 87, 97, 107, 116, 125, 136, 205; portrayal in sculpture of, *96*, *97*
Tongnaab cult, 288
Torridzonians, 232
Towerson, William, 28
trees, 38, 47, 98; cemeteries and, 197; accidental death caused by, 213; funerals for, 33; human bodies and, 30, 33–34; medical properties of, 156, 157; as metaphors for death, 44, 54; poison and, 158, 161, 169; ritual use of, 96, 187
Tumu, 286
Tweneboa Kodua (Kumawuhene), 148
Twi language, 12, 18, 41, 43–44, 72, 115, 156, 174–75, 189–90, 194, 230–31
Twifo Heman, 93, 97, 98, 105, 227

undertakers, 193, 316–17
urban culture, 2, 7, 125, 232; necrogeography and, 191, 199–200

vengeance, 113, 226; of ghosts, 226
Verdery, Katherine, 4, 6, 7, 327
violence, 74–5, 108, 143, 152, 249, 278; colonial conquest and, 247, 282, 283–84, 287; poison and, 156; slavery and, 112, 125–26, 127–28, 130–31, 282
Villault, Nicolas, 32, 115, 146, 194
Volta River, 40, 176, 179, 229, 252

Wa, 254
wakes, 65–66, 198, 238, 270, 277
warfare, 33, 42–3, 45, 48, 52, 70, 89, 107, 115, 181; childbirth and, 216–17; desecration of graves during, 86, 87; enslaved captives and, 117, 120; obituaries and, 241; ritual preparation for, 48, 56, 164–65. *See also* firearms
Wassa kingdom, 97, 104, 234
Watson, Samuel, 269
weeping, 57, 66, 67, 114, 138, 213, 228, 237, 273, 303
werempefo, *68*, 306
Wesleyan Methodist Missionary Society. *See* Methodist mission
Wetse Kojo, 262
widows, 63–65, *65*, 71, 72, 98, 271, 310; inheritance of, 81; law of levirate and, 263
Wild, R. P., 94, 104
Wilks, Ivor, 14, 17–18, 46, 47, 49–50, 54–55, 77, 79, 80, 83, 119–20, 230, 323; on human sacrifice, 140–42, 145, 146, 151, 152–53
wills, 198, 230, 234, 255, 259–76, 291, 321, 324; letters of administration and, 236, 261, 267; testamentary advice and, 272–75; women and, 263, 271–72
Winneba, 214, 228, 242–44, 268, 323
witchcraft, 35, 69, 128, 131, 156, 157, 158, 167, 168, 169, 218, 221, 225, 248–49, 258, 278–79, 280, 283, 325; corpses of those accused of, 213; ritual protection against, 224–25, 249
women, 19; funerals and, 58–75, *62*, 304–305, 325; grief and, 58–75, 114; lamentation by,

61; poison and, 158; terracotta funerary sculpture and, 94, 94–95, 96, 99–100, 104; wills and, 263, 271–72, 274–75
Worosa (Bannahene), 119–20, 121, 122
Wright, Richard, 308
Wulff, Sara (née Malm), 198, 207
Wulff, W. J., 198, 201, 207

Yaa Asantewaa, 292, 302–3
Yaa Hom, 58, 198, 209, 263
Yaa Kuruboaa, 213–14, 227

Yaa Kyaa (Asantehemaa 1883–1917), 46, 291, 292, 293, 301
Yamoa Ponko, 82–83, 84
Yaw Boakye, 82
Yaw Krah, 274
Yawson, Samuel, 268
Yennebah, Essie, 272
Yiakwa, Essie, 255
Yoruba peoples, 8, 20, 143, 173, 175, 237

Zimmermann, Rev. Johannes, 178–79

A NOTE ON THE TYPE

This book has been composed in Arno, an Old-style serif typeface in the classic Venetian tradition, designed by Robert Slimbach at Adobe.

GPSR Authorized Representative: Easy Access System Europe - Mustamäe tee
50, 10621 Tallinn, Estonia, gpsr.requests@easproject.com

www.ingramcontent.com/pod-product-compliance
Lightning Source LLC
Chambersburg PA
CBHW031425160426
43195CB00010BB/619